THE REGULATORY ENVIRONMENT OF BUSINESS

Business Law Textbooks from John Wiley and Sons

THE REGULATORY ENVIRONMENT OF BUSINESS

James E. Inman
The University of Akron
College of Business Administration

John Wiley & Sons
New York/Chichester/Brisbane/Toronto/Singapore

Library of Congress Cataloging in Publication Data:

Inman, James E.
   The regulatory environment of business.

   Bibliography: p.
   Includes index.
   1. Industrial laws and legislation—United States.
2. Trade regulation—United States. I. Title.
KF1600.I55 1984   343.73′07   83-21845
ISBN 0-471-87707-7   347.3037

Printed in the United States of America

10 9 8 7 6 5 4 3 2 1

To my parents

preface

A major trend in management education during the last two decades has been an increased emphasis on nontraditional areas of study. The traditional business school curriculum has been expanded beyond the "functional fields" of accounting, finance, economics, marketing, production, personnel, etc., to include quantitative methods, organizational theory and behavior, strategic management, international business, computer applications, and—the focus of this text—the business firm and its environment. Business executives and management educators agree that a solid understanding of the complex interactions and reciprocal impacts between business organizations and other social institutions, particularly government, are essential intellectual equipment for well-prepared, successful managers. Consequently, modern collegiate business education, as mandated by the American Assembly of Collegiate Schools of Business (AACSB), requires business students to study the "economic and legal environment . . . (of business organizations) along with ethical considerations and social and political influences (on) . . . such organizations." Since business students normally complete a separate course in economics, the other changing environmental forces that have an impact on managerial policies and practices are often relegated to a legal environment of business course. Typically, such courses stress public laws that regulate business behavior and organizational structure.

In designing this text for a legal environment course, several basic principles provided guidance. First, I have emphasized public laws and thereby relegated coverage of private laws to advanced, and probably elective, courses in the business curriculum. Second, I have expanded the topical coverage beyond the usual subject matter contained in a traditional legal environment course. This expanded coverage allows the course to conform more closely to the curriculum standards of the AACSB by including more discussion of the social, political, and ethical aspects of the environment of business. Third, I have attempted to stress a managerial perspective, emphasizing both the necessity and means of managerial compliance with laws and the opportunities available for managerial participation in the formulation and modification of laws.

Essentially, the text provides a description of the environment of business by analyzing selected public policy issues and reviewing the processes of social and legal change in the environment in which business operates. Executive leadership qualities are fostered through analytical and conceptual study of legal and social processes and trends, especially when coupled with the development of a value preference for sane and deliberate resolution of public policy in a free atmosphere of public debate of the issues.

The text is largely composed of narrative and case excerpts of legal opinions written by judges. Questions immediately following the cases challenge the student to recall and analyze legal concepts discussed in the case. Discussion questions and case problems at the end of the chapters require the student to evaluate public policy issues or to apply legal principles to alternate factual situations.

The Suggested Readings at the end of the chapters provide the student with references for in-depth study of particular legal or social issues. Collectively, the chapter materials are sufficient for student learning and adaptable to a variety of instructional methods. A glossary of legal terms is included at the end of the book to help the student understand the material.

In Part I, the developments in society that cause business and government to become involved with each other are explored. The process of social change is discussed in the context of the historical evolution of the capitalistic system, the expanse of governmental controls, and the development of social responsibilities of business. In Part II, the legal process is discussed in materials on the nature and sources of law, the judicial and administrative processes, and the interaction of law and social change. In Part III, the government's efforts to preserve the competitive market system through the adoption of antitrust laws is explored. In Part IV, government regulations affecting electrical utilities, labor-management relations, safe employment practices, equal employment opportunities, securities distribution, consumer protection, and ecological protection are reviewed. Finally, Part V concludes the text with discussions about the limitations of the legal process necessitating further development of ethical managerial behavior, including the necessity for business participation in the development of public policy.

In preparation of this text, I have received generous support from Dean James W. Dunlap and The University of Akron. Many valuable suggestions were obtained from reviewers: Jan Henkel, University of Georgia; Harold Hotelling, University of Kentucky; Michael Litka, The University of Akron; Arthur Marinelli, Ohio University; George Spiro, University of Massachusetts-Amherst; and Robert Wagley, Wright State University. Research assistance from my colleague, David Redle, and my graduate assistants, Patricia Ritzert and David Simmons, have been most helpful. My administrative assistant, Charlene Cook, and student typists, Chris Esterle and Debbie Brinker, have been cheerful and effective throughout this project. The text is better because of the contributions of all of these, but none of the text limitations is attributable to them. I alone am responsible for its shortcomings.

J. E. INMAN

contents

part II THE LEGAL PROCESS   57

chapter 4
THE NATURE AND SOURCES OF LAW   59

chapter 5
THE ADJUDICATORY PROCESS   84

chapter 6
THE ADMINISTRATIVE PROCESS   103

chapter 11
HORIZONTAL COMBINATIONS 230

chapter 12
VERTICAL COMBINATIONS 253

chapter 13
PRICE DISCRIMINATION 279

list of cases

part I
THE PROCESS OF
SOCIAL CHANGE

Often it is difficult to keep the ideals in which one believes in harmony with the action one takes. Business firms often praise the principles of free competition while lobbying in Washington for restrictions on competing imports. Sometimes business firms advocate the philosophical principle of equality of opportunity while practicing racial or sexual discrimination in employment and promotion opportunities. Examples of hypocritical behavior could easily be illustrated for doctors, lawyers, ministers, and even professors. However, the gaps that often occur between ideals and behavior are less hypocritical than they are merely the result of the rapid social change that causes philosophical ideals to become outmoded or obsolete.

Part I discusses the evolution of social and economic ideals concerning the proper role and functions of business and government institutions. What was deemed proper governmental policy in one era was judged detrimental to society in another. Those adhering to an outdated ideology in the changed social conditions found their ideology suggesting inappropriate action in the new era. In a similar manner, the ideological beliefs of businessmen concerning their role in society change. The chapters in this part illustrate how business philosophy has changed in recent years and focuses attention on the ideological dilemmas likely to be faced in the future. One can be sure that as long as the philosophies of business direct business practices to contribute positively to social goals, society will accept and support contemporary business practices. On the other hand, if business ideology gives rise to business practices that society believes are contrary to the common good, society will utilize government institutions to legislate restrictions against those policies.

chapter 1

THE EVOLVING RELATIONSHIP OF BUSINESS AND SOCIETY

Business management has entered the age in which it must be concerned with much more than its economic performance. The success of business is dependent on managers' being able to adapt to the surrounding social and legal environment. The social and legal environment is demanding changes in business philosophy, attitudes, social relationships, and techniques used by managers to deal with external forces of the environment.

The rapidly changing social and legal environment challenges managers at all levels of the business organization to respond to rising social expectations in more effective ways. Meeting these challenges requires that training of prospective managers begin with the development of an appreciation of the changing nature of the environment.

Society is a complex system whereby a variety of elements influence social change. Some of these elements are (1) the social structure, (2) the ideologies of the society, and (3) the society's historical experiences. These elements are difficult to define conceptually or to measure with precision. Similarly, it is difficult to fit all these elements together into a generalized model of social change. The models explaining why and how change takes place have varying explanatory power, perhaps even less predictive value in anticipating future social change. Nevertheless, a limited discussion of some elements involved in social change is a prerequisite for understanding the changing role of business in American society.

THE SOCIAL STRUCTURE

The social structure of society involves the means by which society identifies problems and develops policies of solution. The structure of the social-political process influences the kinds of problems that get attention in society and the public policies it eventually adopts to deal with those problems. Consequently, two fundamental ways of looking at the structure of society are reviewed next.

THE POWER ELITE MODEL

According to the power elite model there are three major classes in society: the ruling elite, the middle class, and the lower class.

The ruling elite or the "establishment" is a class small in number, but great in wealth. It is a homogeneous class whose members share similar attitudes and goals for themselves and the country as a whole.

The middle class is large and controls a substantial portion of the wealth. However, this class is a heterogeneous group composed of many different kinds of people. Since they do not share similar attitudes and goals, they are often in conflict with one another over public issues. Given its diversity, the middle class can never organize itself as a force to control society. Therefore, its influence in making public policy for society is limited.

The lower class is large in numbers, but has little in wealth. The members of the lower class spend such energies in maintaining their existence that they are not very influential in formulating public policy.

These definitions of the various classes point out the major contention of the power elite model: that the establishment largely "runs" society. The elite identifies social problems and shapes society's formulation of a policy solution. The elite "runs" society by controlling the public policy response process. They hold high positions in social institutions and exercise a broad scope of decision-making power. They also control the various reward and punishment systems of society to shape individual and group behavior.

A good deal of literature has maintained that the power elite social structure exists in a variety of cultures. This literature has also suggested that in the past and in the present, a ruling elite exists within American society.[1]

THE PLURALIST MODEL

In the pluralist model there are no reasonably well-defined classes. Instead, there are a number of organizations or groups with varying degress of influence on the public policy process. Since power is diffused among society's many organizations, no single class or group (such as business, government, or labor) has concentrated power. In effect, the pluralistic system prevents power from being concentrated in the hands of a few.

In the pluralistic model, social problems are identified and public policy is developed in a "bottom up" manner. Grass roots organizations express social discontent and use the media to attract attention to their problems and proposed solutions. Sometimes these issues grow into major public issues and the formulation of a new public policy.

An effective pluralistic society must maximize freedom of expression and action by striking a balance between the extremes of monism (a single social organization) and anarchy (an indefinite number of social organizations). Since individuals profess allegiance to many differing groups, pluralism minimizes the danger that a leader in any one organization will be able to dominate society. Consequently, pluralism possesses an inherent set of checks and balances with the ability of group interaction without the probability of any one organization becoming dominant. On the other hand, a pluralistic system may result in no central direction for unified efforts. In addition, the "conflict" between pluralistic groups may eliminate the attainment of effective and efficient social responses to social problems.

A MIXTURE OF MODELS

Societies are often a mixture of both the elite and pluralistic models. Both the establishment and the interest groups identify problems and participate in the development of public policies to deal with social problems. At any point in time, however, one of these models more correctly describes reality. Both the establishment and pluralistic groups have been instrumental in the development and modification of the political-economic system of the United States. It is helpful to be aware of the historical patterns of elitism and pluralism and their role in the development of the capitalistic system. But first, a discussion of ideological change and its role in the process of social change is appropriate.

SOCIAL IDEOLOGIES

In trying to understand the process of social change, it is important to recognize the role of values and beliefs, otherwise called ideology. Ideology is a set of beliefs and ideas concerning what is and what should be. Without an ideology, there can be no coherent choice or purposeful action. Ideology provides an individual with a judgmental process or a choice-making, problem-solving capability that guides the individual's selection of behavioral practices.

A consensus of individual beliefs forms a "prevailing ideology" for society. Similarly, the prevailing ideology suggests social policies and guides institutional behavior. It conveys legitimacy and status to those in power and supports social institutions. If ideology provides the blueprint for institutional organization and for social policy, it follows that a change in the prevailing ideology will bring about a change in all that constitutes the social system.

Some thinkers have argued that ideological creation is an individual act. New ideologies are created by individuals who grapple with the dilemmas of their age and who ask questions and seek answers to the uncertainties of their generation. Martin Luther or Karl Marx may be identified as individuals who created new ideologies. New ideologies are usually the creations of those who dwell off the mainstream of contemporary life. They live a contemplative life and are far removed from the treadmills of power and action. As one commentator has declared, the task of ideological creation has historically fallen to the "rabbis, the monks, the scholars, the jobless intelligentsia, and the leisured aristocrats."[2]

While ideological creation is the result of an individual act, most individuals do not create ideologies. Normally, individuals learn ideologies through education and indoctrination. And, since individuals learn, the common lessons of social experience allow societies to learn also. Social learning can change social values and deflate ideological commitments and social arrangements. The path of society's transformation will often depend on the quality of the ideologies that capture the seats of power and the energy and commitment of those who adhere to the new ideology. In this manner, an ideology can become the initiator of social change. Such was the argument of Max Weber in his contention that the Protestant Ethic (ideology) gave rise to and spearheaded the development of the economic system of "private capitalism."[3]

On the other hand, social change may occur without the impetus of ideological change. Exogenous forces, such as war, natural calamity, or technological advancement, may precipitate social change without ideological intent. Thus, situations may be created that are inexplicable in the framework of the prevailing ideology. To deal with a wartime situation, a natural calamity, or a new technology may require social choice that is outside the scope of prevailing ideological commitments. Social policy, therefore, may just emerge or happen without expressing an ideological intent. This drift of social event and redirection of social policy can produce problems of ideological crisis; for when ideological change is not the producer of social change, surely ideological change must follow that social change. When ideology lags behind the changes in the social system, then the widened gap between ideology and social experience must erode society's faith in the prevailing ideology. The inoperability of social policy as dictated by the prevailing ideology causes a search for another outlook, another ideology that can give purposeful direction to the social change.

THE HISTORY OF CAPITALISM

The history of the capitalistic system reveals the evolution of social ideologies concerning the proper role and functions of both business and government institutions. The study of business history provides a perspective for understanding, comparing, and judging present trends and events. The focus of the following review of business history is on the development of business as a *social*

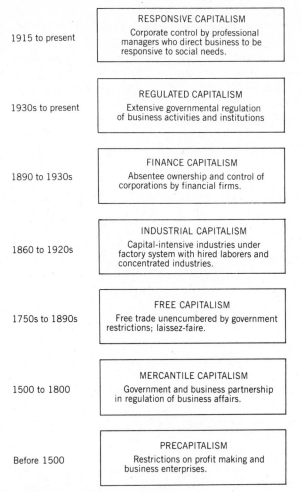

Figure 1-1.   Stages of capitalism.

institution. Change in social values and social systems usually is a continuous process with one stage's development building on that of previous stages. Each successive step of social change usually retains portions of the older social values and adds new ones. (See Figure 1-1.)

PRE CAPITALISM

Following the fall of the Roman Empire in the fifth century, the feudal system of the Middle Ages produced a stable social system that was not favorable to market activities. Feudalism solved the problem of lawlessness caused by the fall of the central governing body of Rome by protecting individuals on a tightly knit local basis. The feudal system was premised on the stratification of social classes. Rights and obligations of each class were clearly defined and every person knew his or her position. The economic system was agriculturally based and centered on the self-sufficient manor. The population was largely immobile and "tied to the soil." Agricultural workers, or serfs, paid rent or service to the nobleman or lord of the manor in return for political stability and military protection.

Besides the usual allegiences owed the lord of the manor, the serfs were also instructed by church doctrine to obey the manorial lord. The church taught that God chose to have individuals born into a specific social strata, which was where God intended that individual to remain. The serf was taught not to worry about material possessions on earth, but to concentrate on his heavenly rewards. Moreover, the church condemned commercial activity in which merchants attempted to improve their status in life. The church believed that commercial activity turned men from the search for God and fostered self-interest in the pursuit of gains. Therefore, the church opposed trade, as it opposed all sin.

Without a centralized governing body, each manor became a self-governing unit that passed its own laws and controlled its own activities. This patchwork of political authorities operated as a deterrent to the development of widespread business activities. The traveling merchant found himself subjected to numerous tolls and taxes by various landlords as he crossed the country. Even towns discriminated against "outside" traders. In short, market activities were burdened by regulations imposed by local landlords, were frustrated by the desire of manors to obtain self-sufficiency, and were evaluated as immoral by the prevailing Catholic Ethic.

The decline of the medieval world was hastened by changes in ideology and by independent events. First, the Black Plague (1348–1349) swept across Europe taking the lives of about one third of the population. From an economic perspective, the shortage of labor weakened the control of manorial lords over the serfs. Serfs sought better bargaining terms from their landlords and often bargained to become free men after a period of service. Thereafter, they sought to work for themselves. As free workers they could seek even higher wages or initiate business activities. Second, the Crusades stimulated economic demand for ships, food, and armaments. New trade routes to the East were developed and commerce in general was enlarged. Third, the rebirth of intellectual freedom in the Renaissance stimulated new ideas concerning individual political and religious freedoms.

Part of the movement for religious freedoms was the Protestant Reformation. The beginning of this revolution is usually attributed to Martin Luther, who rejected the Catholic ideals of asceticism and the monastic life as the way to salvation. He argued that morality could be achieved in a secular life, depending on a man's faith, not his self-denying life-style. Calvin transformed Luther's passive reform of Catholic teaching into an aggressive attack against the Catholic Ethic. To Calvin, it was man's duty to glorify God, which duty could be accomplished by fulfilling God's work on earth in a temporal calling. The Puritans added the notion that salvation rested in the hard, constant, and continuous work in one's calling. The wealth accumulated was a mark of faithfulness in regard to one's duty to God. The evolving Protestant Ethic approved of social mobility and the seeking of wealth. It approved of workers seeking higher wages and of merchants seeking market prices for their goods. The Protestant Ethic emphasized the virtue of work, the evil of idleness, the dignity of the individual, the virtue of thrift, and the justification for the accumulation of wealth. Max Weber believed that the very theory of capitalism came as a by-product of the religious ethic of Protestantism. Others have challenged Weber's views, but it is surely true that the new theology nurtured the evolving capitalistic system just as the Catholic Ethic had fostered the stability of the feudalistic system.

Finally, the force of the ideology of nationalism eroded the political power base of the feudal lords. A nation is a large community of individuals who identify with each other because of a sense of sameness or because of the sharing of culture accomplished through common history. They often share the same language, beliefs, and traditions. Many times the sense of nationhood has been stirred through defeat by an opposing community whose nationhood has flowered to a more efficient military and political system. Sensing similarities that differentiated them from the alien conqueror, the conquered have sought to emulate their conqueror by realizing their own nationhood and giving it political embodiment. Machiavelli was one of those who sought to awaken a sense of nationhood among his own people, the Italians.[4] His strategy, which was to be followed by new nationalists everywhere, was to oppose the existing, entrenched, decentralized power of feudal authority. Instead, absolute support was given to the greatest of the feudal lords so that "the prince" could subjugate the lesser lords and thereby develop a national domain. Businessmen of that age who rode this tide of nationalism were called mercantilists. They sought to maximize the flow of treasure into the king's coffers so that he could build fleets and hire infantry to crush his enemies. In return, the king could eliminate the myriad regulations and taxes that had been imposed on the business community by feudal lords. Nationalism was viewed by the merchants as a systematic approach to centralize political authority and thereby avoid local political interference with business affairs.

In summary, the social events of the Black Plague and the Crusades provided economic and social opportunities for the development of new thoughts. The evolving patterns of the ideas of the Renaissance, the Protestant Reformation, and the nationalistic movements collectively formulated formidable ideological changes and social transformations that the feudal ideological commitments could not arrest.

MERCANTILE CAPITALISM

The disintegration of the feudal system was accompanied by (or separated by) the changing social values and ideologies. The new ideals of materialism and profit making approved by Protestantism joined with national patriotism in the formation of a new economic and political system called mercantilism. This system can be generally characterized as the concentration of political power in the hands of the king who sought to control the economic life of the country. In short, mercantilism was devoted to building strong nations with economic superiority.

Merchant capitalists found it in their best interest to join with rising central monarchies to enhance their power in the struggle with feudal lords and the authoritarian power of the church. The merchant class, through alliances with the central political authority, formulated policies to advance mutual interests. Mercantilists easily convinced kings that their power could be enhanced by increasing their accumulation of treasure in the form of precious metals. Sufficient hordes of precious metals gave power to the king to command resources and field military ventures. Mercantilists were also able to convince the king that they were best suited to aid him in the accumulation of national treasure. Besides reducing the burdens of local government regulation, the centralizing of political authority brought several benefits to business, including the widening of domestic markets, the development of uniform sets of laws and currency, and the establishment of monopolies for privileged merchants.

The centralizing of political authority, however, merely replaced the legal rigidities of feudalism with the legal rigidities of a national authority. Since theoretically the king controlled all businesses, he could select particular economic activities to be under the control of certain privileged merchants. Accordingly, international trading companies, such as the East India Company or the Hudson Bay Company, were established with exclusive trading rights in certain foreign trading markets. The king, of course, shared in these adventures by extracting royalties. To protect the grant of a monopoly, the king promulgated governmental controls that prohibited other merchants from performing similar business ventures.

Mercantilists believed the nation must maintain self-sufficiency, just as the feudal manor attempted self-sufficiency in order to repel invasion and to avoid starvation. The nation should produce its own foodstuffs and manufacture its own articles. Mercantilists advocated that the nation must maintain its own merchant shipping fleet and establish colonies. The colonial system enabled the nation to secure necessary raw materials without relying on rival nations as a source of supply. Moreover, the colonies could absorb surpluses of manufactured goods produced by the mother country. Of course, the government was required to exercise regulatory control to achieve self-sufficiency. It supported appropriate industries in the mother country and suppressed colonial aspirations. Governmental controls were extensive and included regulations on labor, finance, agriculture, and manufacturing. Governmental controls also regulated consumption. For example, laws were enacted that required people to wear woolen caps on certain days as a technique to stimulate wool manufacturing.

The king was obliged to supply sufficient military power to sustain and hold foreign markets, including the colonies. Military power also protected merchant shipping. In turn, centralized national power depended on economic activities as directed by the mercantilists to provide sufficient money to finance this international protection. Mercantilist policies designed to achieve national treasure included the directive that exports were to exceed imports; the balance of trade would amount to an inflow of money (precious metals). Mercantilists also utilized tariffs and other import restrictions to discourage undesirable imports. On the other hand, exporting industries received governmental support.

FREE CAPITALISM

Like feudalism, the merchantilist nations underwent gradual change and were replaced by a system of free capitalism. Unlike feudalism, mercantilism sowed the seeds for its own destruction. It had emphasized the value of materialism to be obtained through wider trade opportunities. Subsequently, the question arose as to whether greater wealth and broadened trade opportunities could be better achieved by a state- (king-) directed economy or by free merchants unencumbered by state direction. Increasingly, the methods of state control seemed less acceptable to society. Moreover, the basic foundations of the evolving free capitalistic system were being developed during the mercantilistic age. The right of the individual to own and use property in business opportunities was increasingly favored by society. The laws also upheld the sanctity of contracts, and a larger body of free workers was available to take advantage of the contractual work relationship. Mercantilism had developed a system of money and credit. It had provided for greater accumulation of capital and the development of an entreprenuerial class. Finally, it had conditioned society to competitive market prices, in which the work of the businessman and his inherent right to profit from business activity were becoming increasingly acceptable to society.

Mercantilism, like feudalism, had left little room for individual freedom. The feudal system emphasized the responsibilities of each social class owed to other classes; individual social mobility and privileges were constrained within the class. Mercantilism, on the other hand, tended to sacrifice the individual for the greater glory of the state. The state directed economic activities in conformity with the interests of the centralized authority. However, new ideas began to develop questioning the view that it was desirable for the government to regulate economic and social life. As one example, John Locke philosophized that men in their original state in nature were free and equal, not subject to subordination or subjection.[5] He argued, instead, that there were natural laws governing the relationships between men; that men possess inalienable rights of life, liberty, and property. To avoid interference with these rights, governments were created by the consent of the governed. This theory of "natural law" enhanced society's belief in individualism. The notion that a "natural," orderly economic system could operate on the basis of individual self-interest, rather than on governmental control, was being born.

In his book *An Inquiry Into the Nature and Causes of the Wealth of Nations,* Adam Smith questioned the appropriateness of mercantilistic policy.[6] He argued that the wealth of a nation was not in its hoard of precious metals, but its cumulative increases in productivity. The real wealth of the nation lay in its power to produce the substance of welfare, not in the accumulation of royal treasure. Hence, governmental policy should be directed toward the improvement of productivity. Smith emphasized the advantages of specialization for workers, regions, and even nations. Through specialization, workers and nations could increase their productivity. The increased surpluses could be exchanged for the betterment of both parties. Smith also argued that maximum motivation of workers is achieved through society's utilization of an individual's self-interest. Maximum production is achieved through the energetic self-interest of workers and capitalists who work together for mutual betterment. Smith borrowed the French phrase *laissez-faire* (let us alone) from the physiocrats in France to express the notion that government should not dictate the terms of trade. The welfare of the individual and society would be best served by individual initiative, rather than state dictation.

Laissez-faire liberalists argued that the way to raise the level of production was to eliminate the complex of regulations and restraints imposed by traditional mercantilistic policy. Instead, the natural force of self-interest was to be relied on to motivate and organize economic activity. Liberalists proposed to eliminate the state-chartered monopolies that had been created through the royal grants of political favors. They argued that such monopolies restrained the natural forces of the market and thereby reduced output and the full utilization of resources. Liberalists argued that political restraints on international trade likewise frustrated productivity. They sought to eliminate the mercantilistic limitations on imports, since such limitations would correspondingly reduce the level of international exchange to purchase exports.

To enhance their cause for freedom, liberalists, in agreement with the philosophical teachings of Locke, argued that free markets were "natural." Correspondingly, mercantilism was perceived as unnatural or a political contrivance. Liberalists argued that property, competition, and individuals working on the basis of self-initiative were natural. Regulations imposed by the mercantilists were argued to be artificial; hindering the free flow of individual effort and ingenuity. The function of government is not to check private greed or to further privileges of special groups, said the liberalists, but rather to protect private property, contractual liberty, and the freedom to compete. Let men be given free and full range to pursue their personal ambition and private greed. As each seeks more for himself, all will work harder, avoid waste, and organize economic resources efficiently. In short, the new ideology of liberalism pleaded with the public authority to give free rein to the natural force of self-interest and private initiative. Liberalists relied on the competitive market to channel private initiative into productivity and to protect public interest from overreaching private greed.

The American colonies were a direct result of the English mercantile policy. However, British mercantilism did not work well in America. The desire of the colonies to operate as a separate economic unit, instead of as extensions of British mercantilistic design, led to the breakdown of mercantilism. In the beginning, the colonies had been founded on the opportunity for private gain. Large tracts of land had been transferred to private ownership, and the individual farmer started out as a capitalistic farmer. He owned his own land and tools and produced surplus for the market. American craftsmen were free to operate outside the guild systems of England that controlled production, wages, and the system for worker advancement. In contrast, the American craftsman enjoyed the freedom to engage in local markets unencumbered by mercantilistic control over the craft. In addition, many settlers had abandoned their home country to escape governmental control in their business, political, and religious affairs. Any regulation imposed by the absentee government of England was viewed as contrary to the best interests of the evolving concepts of American nationalism. The following War of Independence was not only a national uprising, but also a rebellion of liberalism against mercantilistic powers. When the founding fathers set about to write the Constitution, they were most cognizant of their own experiences with economic tyranny from England and of the laissez-faire ideology advocated by Adam Smith.

While Smith advocated a quite limited sphere of governmental interference in economic affairs, he also provided one exception after another to this basic principle. He advocated extending some governmental regulations over business, such as the curbing of monopolies, the public ownership and management of highways and toll bridges, and the progressive taxation of users of toll bridges, which were to impose a greater tax burden on the rich. Because Smith's works gyrated from one viewpoint to another, it is possible that Smith's views could be used to expound a laissez-faire doctrine and at the same time support a thesis of major governmental interference in economic affairs. Nevertheless, the mainstream of economic thought in America interpreted Smith as expounding a limited government, laissez-faire doctrine. However, in spite of the popularity of the laissez-faire doctrine, operational governmental policy often favored the mercantilist's tradition of supporting agriculture and commercial activities. On the other hand, manufacturing was largely ignored by the new government. The southern agrarian aristocracy retained control of the federal government in its early years and opposed governmental programs urged by the growing manufacturing community in the North. Manufacturing firms called for protective tariffs, a sound banking system, a cheap labor supply, and federal support of railroads and canals. Nevertheless, the government, dominated by the South, opposed protective tariffs, favored state control of banking with its "cheap" money, refused to support a favorable immigration plan, and was against federal support of railroads or canals.

INDUSTRIAL CAPITALISM

Prior to the Civil War, the United States was largely a nation of small businesses and farms. During the first half century there was no ideological pressure for governmental intervention in economic affairs. While life was hard, it was simple and full of opportunity. Most people lived on farms and produced what they needed for their living. Moreover, the frontier offered new land to satisfy individual ambition and hope. Hard work set a minimum condition of life for the enterprising individual. But as the century progressed, America was changing.

There was a fundamental economic transformation occurring. While industrialization began before the Civil War, it was during and after the war that the economy industrialized with growing momentum.

During the Civil War northern business firms began to prosper from the stimulus of increased governmental expenditures for armaments and goods necessary to support the army. The control of Congress by the North led to the establishment of public policies favorable to the rising industrial interests. Protection of industries through tariffs were granted by Congress. Wartime requirements also lead to the use of production methods (interchangeable parts) that expanded the opportunities for large-scale mass production.

The impetus toward industrial development created by the Civil War continued unabated during the rest of the century. The opening of the West stimulated the development of the transcontinental railroads and agricultural machinery, which enabled large-scale farming. The western railroad industry was further spurred by the cattle and mining industries, which demanded increasing railroad services. The United States also was the recipient of large capital investment expenditures from foreign investors who recognized profitable opportunities in the developing U.S. industries. Finally, millions of immigrants (new laborers) were allowed to come to the United States during this period of industrial development.

Gradually the right of incorporation became available to all businessmen, and the corporate form became commonplace. Corporations soon rose to a position of dominance because the corporate form was so successful in raising risk capital and because larger enterprises could take advantage of large-scale production techniques. As the technologically optimum size of the firm grew larger, other firms went under. Also, corporations became dominant because of the development of business combinations. These combinations, often in the form of a trust, were established to eliminate competition and regulate the marketplace. In the absence of laws requiring competitive market practices, business firms found it easy to combine into cartels restricting production and increasing prices. The result was the concentration and centralization of economic power, not in governmental agencies as in mercantilism, but in autonomous private corporations.

The modern factory system with its automatic machinery, standardized products, rationalized operations, and wage labor had replaced the individual worker on the farm or in the shop. Men were discovering they could no longer make it on their own. They became submerged in organizations; they depended on organizations. Other laborers waited on the outside of the factory gate for a chance to work in the factory. What happened to workers depended on what happened within the organization and what happened to the organization itself. Fate of the organizations depended on the shifting winds of world demand and on the onslaught of new technology. Periods of boom and bust became more frequent as the market system attempted to balance increasing productive supply with the weak demand resulting from low-paid workers and hard-pressed farmers. During business depressions, competition for survival had always led to falling prices. Business firms soon learned that reductions in the price of goods they offered for sale often gave little encouragement to consumers to buy more of them. Instead, large corporations developed the strategy of laying off workers. Because of these increased gyrations in the business cycle, businesses were further encouraged to combine and form monopolies over output so as to control production excesses and stabilize prices.

The dominant ideology of free capitalism remained a comfort for those who could afford it. However, there was a growing number of other individuals who were victims of the system. While not shouting for an elimination of private liberties protected by private property and expressed in the free market system, they nevertheless cried out for reforms. While possessing no countervailing ideology, they exerted pressure in the political processes to ameliorate the miseries of an industrialized society. They sought the substitution of political authority for the market system in isolated instances. They pressured for laws to protect against the horrors of child labor, the overextension of working hours for men and women in factories, the excessive fees charged by middlemen and railroads who exploited the urgent needs of others. These and other causes that came before the political authority were argued to be exceptions to the general rule of laissez-faire capitalism. Governmental interference and control of economic activity was still to be limited. "Meddling" in the market system was piecemeal and only in those instances when the market's result was less than satisfactory to society. Eventually, given the growing distance between the ideals supposed to be obtained from the laissez-faire ideology and the existing reality, the pressures for reform would cause the laissez-faire ideology itself to burst asunder.

FINANCE CAPITALISM

Capital goods, such as machines, must be financed; that is, someone must wait to receive the benefits that capital goods create. Someone must save to create capital goods. The savings must be channeled to those who put the capital goods to use. Therefore, there is a need for an intermediary to bring the saver and the user together. This function is performed by investment bankers, who secure long-term capital funds by selling corporate securities.

Investment banking largely developed during the Civil War when the federal government borrowed over $2.5 billion to aid the war effort. Thereafter, investment bankers raised long-term capital for the emerging corporate enterprises. Subsequently, a few groups or syndicates of investment bankers gained dominance over the marketing of large issues of corporate securities. As a condition to underwriting the securities of corporations, investment bankers usually demanded representatives on the board of directors of issuing corporations. Investment bankers also extended their control over the agencies that gathered savings, such as insurance and trust companies and savings banks. The investment bankers also affiliated with commercial banks and thereby gained control over both long-term and short-term funds.

Financial capitalists were able to manipulate credit to gain control over manufacturing enterprises. To ensure profits from the productive enterprises they controlled, financial capitalists utilized their interlocking directorates and other techniques to stifle competition. They were able to limit production, fix prices, rig security markets, and often pervert the judicial and legislative processes. The power of the financial capitalist is perhaps best illustrated by "The House of Morgan." J. P. Morgan and his allies held directorships in corporations that at that time held about one fourth of the total American corporate assets. Moreover, the financial capitalists were able to take control of Carnegie Steel Company from Andrew Carnegie himself. Financial capitalists wanted the Carnegie Steel Company to assimilate into their own United States Steel Corporation, which was a combination of 12 large firms that had previously been formed from earlier combinations of 180 separate companies.

The formulation of these combinations was an enormous source of profit for the investment bankers. For example, in the formation of the National Tube Company, one quarter of the $80 million worth of stock issued was retained by the investment bankers. In the formation of the American Sheet Steel Company, $33 million in stock was issued and $5 million of that accrued to the investment bankers. In the process of forming United States Steel Corporation, the underwriting syndicate made a profit of nearly $63 million. The new company controlled three-fifths of the steel business of the country, and after the merger of the new supertrust, prices were raised. As a result of their control over financial markets and their seemingly insatiable greed for profits, the financial capitalists with interlocking directorates were often more effective in stifling competition that the industrial capitalists had been with their efforts to establish outright cartels.

REGULATED CAPITALISM

The economic abuses and social transformation of the era of industrial and finance capitalism ushered in the modern era of regulated capitalism. The victims of the industrial and financial empires sought relief from their economic woes. The farmers sought legislation that would regulate the rates charged by railroads and grain elevators. Populous movements for antimonopoly laws were formed. Others lobbied for laws against abusive child labor practices. Laborers sought legislative solutions for low wages and burdensome working conditions. Political intervention was perceived to be the only countervailing power available to employ against the large business corporations and "interlocks" that had eroded, if not completely eliminated, the power of competition.

The state governments were the first to respond to the rising political pressures of the populous movements. Various states enacted laws that regulated railroads, grain elevators, child labor practices, and labor working hours and conditions.

The federal government followed the states in legislating the Interstate Commerce Act, which was to regulate the railroads. The 1890 Sherman Act outlawed monopolistic combinations of businesses and contractual restraints on competition and trade. The first piece of consumer regulation, the Pure Food and Drug Act of 1906, was passed as a result of the public outcry against the meat-packing industry following Upton Sinclair's vivid description of the horrors of meat packing in *The Jungle*.[7] Regulatory controls over public utilities were enacted. Further antimonopoly attitudes were expressed in the Clayton Act and the Federal Trade Commission Act of 1914.

The depression in the Thirties brought in a new wave of legislation regulating business affairs. The National Labor Relations Act in 1935 required corporations not to interfere with unionizing activities and to bargain with certified unions. The Fair Labor Standards Act established minimum wages and maximum hours for laborers. The Social Security Act provided for industrial funding of pensions for retired workers or assistance for workers' widows and orphans. Small businessmen received protection in the Robinson-Pattman Act of 1936 from unfair competitive tactics used by large firms. The Securities Act of 1933 and Securities and Exchange Act of 1934 attempted to eliminate abuses by the finance capitalists who manipulated securities' prices to the disadvantage of public investors. The Glass-Steagall Act of 1933 required separation of the commercial and investment banking businesses. The Public Utility Holding Act of 1935 attempted to lessen the concentration of control in the electric and gas industries. Other legislation of the New Deal involved extensions of the federal regulatory power over trucking, airlines, communications, and electric utilites.

During the Depression, the federal government attempted to revive the economy with legislative programs. After the Second World War, the government expressed in the Employment Act of 1946 the notion that the federal government should seek to maintain economic stability and avoid the gross gyrations of the business cycle that the industrial age had aggravated. The Depression had proved that the economy, with its complex interdependencies of technologies, was vulnerable to collapse. It lacked the regenerative power of ages past. What was to be done about this problem was not clear, then or now. But few could doubt that the problem had to be dealt with by the political authorities. The ideology of laissez-faire was impotent in dealing with the social calamity of the Depression. Faith in laissez-faire, consequently, was shattered by the experience. Political authority became indispensable, the only potent force for dealing with the problems of the industrial age.

By the late 1930s John Maurice Clark, in his widely read *Social Control of Business*, was articulating basic criteria for permissible economic controls by the political authorities.[8] He argued that public action may be needed to protect individuals in situations where their problems lie beyond their capabilities to solve them. He argued that public interest may require public intervention into the internal affairs of corporations or unions. Clark felt the political authority should uphold "social minimums" for individual welfare and ensure "equality of opportunity." Among other suggestions, he felt that the public authority should remedy the failure of the industrial system to utilize its capacity during depressions. But with all these new expansions of responsibilities for the political authority, Clark and other economists of liberalism shared a general antagonism against political intervention. Clark wrote:

No large state yet seen on earth has given evidence of sufficient collective wisdom to devise a system which would work . . . as effectively as the competitive struggle does . . . . In spite of its limitations, a state may command enough wisdom . . . to see where [the market system's] worse wastes and perversions lie, and to modify it here and there . . . . [However], no power of control should ever be presumed to exist unless there is a specific need for the exercise of that power.[9]

The consequences of the industrialization process and the countervailing pressures of interest groups had caused the government to rationally and pragmatically grope for new solutions in spite of the opposition of laissez-faire ideology. The result has been the emergence of a mixed or regulated capitalistic system. The ideology of free capitalism remained preeminent, but its imperfections were to be corrected by the "inferior" system of government.

RESPONSIVE CAPITALISM

Throughout history, philosophers and theologians have advocated that the responsibilities of businesspeople extend beyond operational efficiency and profit-making. However, the proponents of Adam Smith's theory of self-interest have successfully convinced business practioners and classical economic theorists that the main activity of business is the pursuit of strictly economic goals. Business provided paternalistic social services only when practical business considerations prompted concern for social conditions. For example, company housing and stores or other participation in employee welfare helped attract and retain employees, besides providing social services.

Later, when businessmen like Andrew Carnegie believed it their moral duty to amass a fortune to be used in the public interest, philanthropy became the main emphasis of business involvement in social welfare. However, as the power of public opinion found expression in numerous legislative enactments in the period immediately preceding and following the turn of the century, businessmen learned their responsibilities to society could not be so narrow. In 1912, Arthur Hadley wrote: "Industrial corporations grew up into power because they met the needs of the past. To stay in power, they must meet the needs of the present and arrange their ethics accordingly."[10] Hadley and others advocated the philosophy of "corporate trusteeship" wherein businessmen are to be not only trustees for the stockholders of their corporations, but also trustees on behalf of the public.

One effort of business to overcome its unfavorable public image was massive public relations programs. However, preoccupation with public image and corporate contributions often led business interest away from other key issues of public concern, such as industrial relations and social security. The resulting events of the Depression reemphasized the requirement that business concern for social issues could not be limited to public relations and philanthropy.

Following the Second World War, the public's confidence in business grew as a result of the production successes of the war effort. The idea of increased social responsibilities by business also grew. In 1953, Howard Bowen in the *Social Responsibilities of the Businessman* argued that general social and economic benefits might accrue from the recognition of social goals in business decision making.[11] Others argued that the production of goods and services was no longer the only requirement of business. New social needs required new social responsibilities by business in order for it to be accepted and successful. Many urged businesses to be socially responsive so as to reduce the need for additional governmental regulations. The socially responsive corporation was not only to obey the laws involving social concerns, but also was to make every effort to go beyond the legal requirements if necessary to serve social expectations. Through the following decades, one large corporation after another embraced this new social responsibility ethic.

Assuming that business corporations continue to move in a socially responsive direction, the United States will be entering a new stage of capitalism involving creative attempts by business to respond to new social challenges and serve human needs in better ways. The new stage is called *responsive capitalism* because of business' response to the social needs of a society. A system of socially responsive corporations would take advantage of decentralization in decision making and of private initiative to solve social dilemmas without governmental interference. Pluralistic decision making by a host of socially mindful corporations would thereby be enriched at the sacrifice of the possibility of a monolithic governmental authority.

CONCLUSION

Social change normally operates through the existing social structure, but the balance of power between the establishment and pluralistic groups changes. Social change also occurs through intentional directives of ideological commitments, or from autonomous forces like technological adaptations or social unrest with prevailing conditions. In the latter situations, new ideological contours are formed so that subsequent social changes can be goal directed. The capitalistic system of the United States has evolved from both autonomous forces and ideological directives. A first step in understanding its further evolution involves a clear understanding of its prior development.

Historically, business activities have not been accorded high social status. Social, religious, and political restrictions on business activities have flourished for centuries, not only in the feudal and mercantilistic eras but in numerous other societies.

In America, business has been accorded a more receptive hospitality by the societal adoption of laissez-faire ideology. The retreat from the limited role of government in the economic affairs became inevitable when the fruits of laissez-faire in the industrial age included the concentration of economic power and the outcries of victims. Pragmatic experimentation with the powers of the political authority reformed the free capitalistic system into the modern age of regulated capitalism.

Partly as a result of enlightened self-interest and partly as a result of good faith efforts to comply with societal expectations, modern business corporations seem to be developing socially responsive attitudes and practices that may evolve into a *responsive capitalism* to forestall the ever increasing regulatory force of government in economic affairs.

DISCUSSION QUESTIONS

1. Contrast the power elite and pluralist models of social structure.

2. What are the advantages and disadvantages of pluralism?

3. Which is first, a new ideology that creates a new society, or a new society that creates a new ideology?

4. Identify key elements of the feudalistic system that restricted business activities.

5. Explain the essential attributes of the Catholic Ethic. How did the Protestant Ethic challenge its basic doctrines?

6. Identify similarities between the mercantilistic policies and present-day government policies concerning business.

7. How did the merchant class strategically utilize the social ideology of "nationalism" to reduce government regulation of market activities?

8. How did the merchant class strategically utilize the social ideology of "liberalism" to reduce government regulation of market activities?

9. What is the "wealth of a nation" according to mercantilism? According to Adam Smith?

10. Identify some basic duties of government according to Adam Smith.

11. What social conditions changed during the industrialization process that modified the capitalistic system?

12. How was finance capitalism more restrictive of competition than industrial capitalism?

13. Explain the reasons for America's movement from free capitalism to regulated capitalism.

14. What is your understanding of responsive capitalism? Is it a real movement or the public relations ploy of large corporations?

15. "Adam Smith's analysis doesn't mean anything anymore. One of the things that bothers me is that a lot of people still quote Adam Smith as an important rationale for the existence of the capitalist system. That is nonsense.

Adam Smith's Wealth of Nations dealt with an entrepreneurial situation where you had 10 employees at the most and if the owner/manager worked like hell and used his mind well, he succeeded. Today, as Berle and Means pointed out in 1932, the owners don't manage and the managers don't own. It is an entirely different kind of system." Comment.

SUGGESTED READINGS

Collings, John W., "Law in the Business Curriculum," *American Business Law Journal,* Vol. 15, No. 1, Spring 1977, pp. 46–51.

Davis, Keith, William C. Frederick, and Robert L. Blomstrom, *Business and Society: Concepts and Policy Issues,* 4th ed. (New York: McGraw-Hill Book Co., 1980), Chaps. 4 and 9.

Solo, Robert A., *The Political Authority and the Market System* (Cincinnati, Ohio: South-Western Publishing Co., 1974), Chaps. 1, 3, and 4.

Steiner, George A., *Business and Society* (New York: Random House, Inc., 1975), Chaps, 2, 3, and 4.

ENDNOTES

1. See, for example, Edward D. Baltzell, *The Protestant Establishment* (New York: Random House, 1964); William G. Domhoff, *Who Rules America?* (Englewood Cliffs, N.J.: Prentice-Hall, 1967); Morton Mintz and Jerry S. Cohen, *America, Inc.: Who Owns and Operates the United States?* (New York: Dial Press, 1971).

2. Robert A. Solo, *The Political Authority and The Market System* (Cincinnati, Ohio: South-Western Publishing Co., 1974) p. 17.

3. Max Weber, *The Protestant Ethic and The Spirit of Capitalism* (New York: Schribner, 1952).

4. Niccolo Machiavelli, *The Prince* (1513) (Oxford: Clarendon Press, 1909).

5. John Locke, *Treatise in Civil Government* (1691).

6. Adam Smith, *An Inquiry into the Nature and Causes of the Wealth of Nations* (2 vols.; London: printed for W. Strahan and T. Cadell in *The Strand,* 1776).

7. Upton Sinclair, *The Jungle* (New York: Doubleday & Page, 1906).

8. John Maurice Clark, *Social Control of Business* (2d ed.; New York: McGraw-Hill Book Co., 1939).

9. *Ibid.* pp. 160, 163.

10. Arthur T. Hadley, *Standards of Public Morality* (New York: Macmillan, 1912) p. 96.

11. Howard R. Bowen, *Social Responsibilities of the Businessman* (New York: Harper, 1953).

chapter 2

THE ISSUE OF GOVERNMENT OR MARKET SYSTEMS

Chapter 1 emphasized the expanding role of the institutions of business and government in American society. This chapter further discusses the era of "regulated capitalism" with its expanding role for government in economic affairs. The next chapter contains more discussion of "responsive capitalism" with its emphasis on the expanding social role of business.

The public sector of the U.S. economy has grown rapidly in this century. Various groups have asked government to assume a proliferation of new social responsibilities. Consequently, government at the federal and state level has expanded its activities because business did not respond to public demands. On other occasions, business contributed to government expansions into the economic system when it sought subsidies or regulations for its own development. Whatever the instigation for increased governmental activity, its cumulative impact on all participants in the economy is now pervasive.

MARKET OR GOVERNMENT SYSTEMS

FUNDAMENTAL ECONOMIC QUESTIONS

The economic problem of society is scarcity. Faced with the problem of scarcity of economic resources, society must make certain fundamental economic decisions. First, *what goods should be produced?* Society must choose which goods are to be produced and in what quantities. Second, *how should these goods be produced?* A variety of methods for combining the scarce resources could conceivably be utilized to produce the goods. Society must choose which production techniques or combination of resources it is going to utilize. Third, *who should receive the goods that society produces?* The methods that could be followed in allocating the production among members of society must be chosen. Goods could be distributed according to individual need, according to the contributions made to the production effort, or on some other basis formulated in the political area. Fourth, *how shall society maintain flexibility for changes over time?* Because advances in technology continually expand our productive capabilities and because consumers alter their tastes and preferences, society is confronted with questions of change. Decisions of acceptance or rejection of change must continuously be made. These changes may be adopted voluntarily or coerced through economic pressures or political action.

MARKET SYSTEM

The *market system* is one way of organizing the economy to answer the fundamental questions derived from the economic problem of scarcity. The distinguishing feature of the market system is its reliance on decentralized markets. There is no central authority guiding the economy. Instead, each member of society independently pursues his or her self-interest through private market transactions. Consequently, these impersonal market transactions resolve the economy's problems of resource allocation, production techniques, distribution of goods and services, and economic change.

First, the consumers' purchases of goods determine where resources will be allocated in the future. Lack of consumer demand for particular products will cause producers to shift resources away from production of those products. Second, firms use production techniques that maximize their self-interest or profits. A profit-seeking firm attempting to minimize costs makes greater utilization of abundant resources because they have the lowest relative cost. Scarce resources, with higher prices, are conserved, and allocative efficiency is thereby achieved. Third, the goods produced under a market system are distributed among individuals through market transactions. Only those individuals who have income as a result of their contribution to the production process will be able to select and enjoy their portion of society's production. Fourth, business firms must utilize the latest technology in order to offer competitively priced goods to the public. Likewise, changes in consumer taste are reflected in purchasing decisions, which will cause redirection of business production efforts. In short, the market relies on the price mechanism, without central direction, for unconscious coordination of the actions of millions of diverse individuals. The system of rewards and penalities within the market economy endows it with vital self-correcting forces that continually answer society's fundamental economic questions.

GOVERNMENT SYSTEM

A government system, or command system, is also a decision-making process that answers the fundamental economic questions. Unlike the market system where consumer preferences are articulated and communicated through the pricing mechanism, the command system utilizes the political and governmental systems. Social preferences are articulated by a variety of citizens' petitions to candidates for governmental offices. Social preferences are then aggregated in party platforms and coalitions. Political communication is achieved through social events and organizations that broadcast their views and opinions through the news media. Ultimately, government decisions on the fundamental economic questions are implemented through rule-making, rule application, and rule ajudication. In short, government utilizes collective, official decision-making to develop answers to the economic questions of what, how, who, and what's to be changed.

HISTORICAL PREFERENCE FOR MARKET SYSTEM

The birth of the United States and laissez-faire economics occurred in the same era as a reaction against British mercantilism and its government-dictated economic policies. Because of this heritage of a limited role of government, Americans have tended to overlook the fact that governmental domination over economic affairs has been the norm in history and a relatively free market economy the exception. Instead, Americans have viewed their short history, with its reliance on the market mechanism and on relative freedom from governmental restraint, as the natural state of the national economy. Consequently, the subsequent development of government regulations of business resulted only when the populace perceived failures of the market system.

Adam Smith popularized the "invisible hand" concept; the idea that an individual who "intends only his own gain," is, nevertheless, "led by an invisible hand to promote . . . the public interest." There seems to have been ever since a dominant tendency of thought that decisions reached individually will, in fact, be the best decisions for the entire society. Similarly, since a market economy makes the fundamental economic decisions automatically, the government's role has been seen to be limited.

In 1776, Adam Smith also postulated that the market system left the government with three duties: (1) providing for national defense, (2) administering justice, and (3) engaging in certain public works that were unprofitable to private enterprise, yet valuable to society.[1] Part of the process of "administering justice" is the governmental role of establishing an environment that facilitates market transactions. In support of the market system, government must (1) preserve property rights, (2) ensure the voluntary nature of the markets, and (3) enforce contracts as established by the parties in their market transactions. These limited roles for government have historically been referred to as laissez-faire economic policy—a policy of minimal governmental interference in the economy so that economic decisions could be made by private individuals in a marketplace unencumbered by governmental restrictions. In short, the government merely enforces the basic "rules" of property and contract laws to enhance the competitive process of the market system that will best promote society's welfare through pursuit of self-interest. Besides the enhancement of economic well-being, this philosophy also fits well with democratic institutions and the preservation of individual freedoms. The market system relieves society from the necessity of a strong centralized "command economy" with coercive rules.

JUSTIFICATIONS FOR GOVERNMENT INTERVENTIONS

Historical experiences have revealed that a laissez-faire economic policy has not always maximized society's welfare. The maximization of individual self-interest sometimes fails to bring about an enlargement of public interest as well. Sometimes, market forces have failed to optimize the allocation of society's resources. Consider Garrett Hardin's "Tragedy of the Commons"

The tragedy of the commons develops in this way. Picture a pasture open to all. It is to be expected that each herdsman will try to keep as many cattle as possible on the commons. Such an arrangement may work reasonably satisfactorily for centuries because tribal wars, poaching, and disease keep the number of both man and beast well below the carrying capacity of the land. Finally, however, . . . the inherent logic of the commons remorselessly generates tragedy.

As a rational being, each herdsman seeks to maximize his gain. Explicitly or implicitly, more or less consciously, he asks, 'What is the utility to me of adding one more animal to my herd?' . . . Since the herdsman receives all the proceeds from the sale of the additional animal, the positive utility is nearly +1. . . . Since, however, the effects of overgrazing are shared by all the herdsmen, the negative utility for any particular decision-making herdsman is only a fraction of −1.

Adding together the component partial utilities, the rational herdsman concludes that the only sensible course for him to pursue is to add another animal to his herd. And another; and another . . . But this is the conclusion reached by each and every rational herdsman sharing a commons. Therein is the tragedy. Each man is locking into a system that compels him to increase his herd without limit—in a world that is limited. Ruin is the destination toward which all men rush, each pursuing his own best interest in a society that believes in the freedom of the commons. Freedom in a commons brings ruin to all.[2]

Hardin has identified a market failure where self-interested herdmen spoiled a public "commons." While breaking the commons into tracts of private property may provide a "market" means to solve the problem of overgrazing, one is not able to easily fashion market solutions for "commons" less capable of division into private property, such as the air or water resources. How is the political authority to deal with socially erroneous private decisions that pollute the air or water? The problems of ecological waste resulting from the failure of the "invisible hand" to promote the public interests has been a major economic-political problem of the twentieth century. The progeny of ecological waste has been the development of environmental protection laws adopting a variety of regulatory techniques. All these resulted from society's perception of market failure that needed governmental solution. Even the strongest advocates of reliance on the market system have admitted that certain circumstances require governmental intervention.

JUSTIFICATIONS FOR REGULATION

Most of the market defects that give rise to a demand for regulation can be classified as follows.[3]

Control of Monopoly Power

For the market economy to optimize the allocation of society's resources, the market must be *competitive*. With many buyers and sellers, no individual can control the market price. However, when a single or dominant seller of a good exists, such monopolist may restrict production to increase the product price. The monopolist charges higher prices to consumers while selling less production. By artificially restricting production, the monopolist also employs fewer resources. Such unemployed resources must seek employment in other "competitive" industries. In effect, the higher price paid to the monopolist does not work to the advantage of the consumer by attracting more resources to the monopolist to increase production. In short, the higher price of the monopolist maximizes its profits, but does not serve society by redirecting economic resources to society's advantage. The victims of this market failure have accordingly sought governmental intervention.

Control of "Windfall Profits"

Sudden increases in price may allow those who hold an interest in a commodity to earn a "windfall profit." For example, those who owned large amounts of oil earned huge windfall profits when the Arabs raised the price of oil. Also, owners of natural gas earned windfall profits when the cost of finding new natural gas rose. Similarly, those who own existing housing earned windfall profits when construction costs rise faster than other costs. Any firm that cannot expand its production to satisfy all market demands will earn a windfall profit if it finds an unusually cheap supply source or buys machines when they are cheap. Usually windfall profits are not controlled, but when windfall profits are great in amount and do not reflect any particular talent or skill on the part of the producers, there is sometimes a demand for regulation. The object of the regulation is to transfer these "undeserved" windfall profits from producers or owners of the scarce resources to consumers or taxpayers.

Correction for Externalities

As individuals pursue their self-interest through voluntary market transactions, they may impose costs or bestow benefits on other individuals. Such effects are called *externalities*, which arise whenever the benefits or costs of a transaction do not fall completely on the parties to that transaction. Since individuals normally pursue only their own self-interests, they ignore any externalities associated with their transactions. As a consequence, the market process may lead to a misallocation of society's resources.

For example, a business firm bases its production decisions on the cost of its purchased inputs. It ignores any impact its discharges may have on the surrounding environment. Similarly, consumers who litter the roadside do not consider all the costs of their actions. Both parties focus only on their private costs, which are less than the social costs. Hence, the competitive market overproduces goods that pollute the environment. Since the environment is a "free" good, there is little incentive for a firm (or consumer) to voluntarily restrict its emmission of pollutants. Any firm attempting to "clean" its discharges would be at a disadvantage in comparison with its competitors, which would have lower costs. Hence, the market "fails" to discipline individual participants who pollute the environment. Government intervention seems necessary to deal with the market failures created by either production or consumption externalities.

Correction for Inadequate Information

The effective allocation of economic resources under the market system is dependent on informed consumers. If consumers make decisions based on incomplete information, their selection of goods and services may not necessarily maximize their welfare. For example, incomplete information concerning the effects of cigarette smoking or the ingestion of a particular drug may expand its acceptance among consumers. In contrast, more information of its harmful effects can change consumer behavior and thereby cause a change in the allocation of resources. Consequently, imperfect information represents a market failure causing overproduction or underproduction of some good. Governmental intervention to improve the flow of information to consumers seems warranted.

Correction for "Excessive Competition"

A commonly argued justification for regulation is the need to control "excessive competition." This notion assumes that if prices fall too low, firms will go out of business, and the products will end up being too costly. This particular "justification," however, is usually an "empty box," or unsupported by economic theory. One exception may include an industry with large fixed costs and cyclical demands. The firms in this industry, pricing at incremental cost in the downswing, may find they generate insufficient revenue to maintain full capacity. The reduced capacity during slack periods is inefficient; however, it is more expensive to increase capacity during the next upswing than to maintain it continuously. This rationale is most often used to justify "depression cartels" as are accepted in Europe and in Japan.

Correction for Absence of Restraint on Purchasers

If someone other than a buyer pays for the buyer's purchases, the buyer feels no pocketbook constraint and may purchase a good oblivious to the resource cost he or she imposes on the economy. When moral restraint or institutional constraints fail to control purchases, government regulation may be demanded.

An obvious example of absence of restraint on buyers is the medical care industry. Since medical care is paid ... by the government or by large private insurers without any constraint on the amount demanded by the individual user, medical costs have escalated. If one believes that the lack of buyer restraint prevents higher prices from acting as a check on individual demands for those resources, which in turn reduces the incentive to hold down prices, one might advocate regulation to keep prices down, improve efficiency, or limit the supply or medical treatment.

Correction for Industrywide Irrationalization

It is sometimes argued that firms in an industry lack sufficient rationalization to produce efficiently. Other social or political factors act to counterbalance any tendency for the firms to cooperate on an industrywide plan. If problems make it difficult for firms to plan jointly, government intervention to require industrywide rationalization may be needed.

Correction for Scarcity

Sometimes sudden supply failures, as in the case of the Arab oil boycott, may impose too serious a hardship on many buyers who cannot afford the resulting traumatic price increases. On other occasions, a deliberate decision is made to abandon the market and use regulatory allocation to achieve some "public interest" objective, as in the allocation of licenses for television stations. In cases such as these, the regulation is justified on the basis of scarcity.

Correction for Unequal Bargaining Power

The most efficient allocation of resources is achieved by free market forces when bargaining power is not substantially unequal. If the "unequal bargaining power" of small sellers seems to frustrate the attainment of efficient allocation of resources, governmental response that allows the sellers to organize in order to deal more effectively with the buyers may be demanded. This justification supports the legislation favoring the organization of labor and farm cooperatives.

Governmental Paternalism

Even with full and adequate information available to the decision maker in the marketplace, some may argue that the consumer will nevertheless make the wrong decisions, necessitating governmental protection. This governmental paternalism is based on the notion that the government knows better than the individual what he wants and what is good for him. The distrust of the ability of the purchaser may be based on the inability of the lay person to evaluate the information, as in the case of purchasing professional services. On other occasions, the lay person may possess irrational tendencies that prevent accurate evaluation of information. For example, a person suffering from cancer may purchase a drug even though all reasonably reliable information indicates that it is worthless or even harmful to the user.

MULTIPLE JUSTIFICATIONS

Regulatory programs often rest on not one but several different justifications. For example, one might justify the regulation of workplace safety on several grounds. One could argue that worksite accidents impose cost (*externalities*) on individuals who are not represented at the bargaining table of employers and employees. That bargaining may not produce adequate expenditure for safety devices. Or one might argue that the workers do not know enough about the risk or consequences of accidents to insist on added safety expenditures. This is to argue that there is an *informational* defect in the market. Or one might maintain that the workers are too weak to bargain for the safety they need; that they have *unequal* bargaining power. Additionally, one might claim that the workers are incapable of understanding their future feelings about accidents and, therefore, underestimate the risk. Consequently, safety regulation should be *paternalistically* provided to give them what they "really" want, contrary to their expressed views.

It may be important to clarify justifications for regulation because the differing justifications suggest differing remedies. The identification of an informational problem would suggest an informational remedy. A paternalistic justification for regulation would not. Moreover, a clear differentiation of the justifications argued can suggest the need for empirical study that may bring the parties toward agreement on a single justification, which will aid in choosing the best regulatory weapon to deal with the problem.

DIRECT OR INDIRECT REGULATION

Usually the government decides to operate within the framework of the market system. It attempts to modify firm behavior indirectly by changing the rules of the marketplace. This indirect approach minimizes government interference while preserving business independence and performance. Examples of indirect government intervention include antitrust enforcement and pollution abatement regulations.

When a market solution is not feasible by indirect regulations, the government increases its direct participation in economic decision making. Economic decisions are no longer left to private individuals; instead, the government shares in basic economic decision making. Examples of direct government intervention vary from economic regulations by public utility authorities to government ownership of enterprises.

EVALUATIVE CRITERIA FOR GOVERNMENT INTERVENTION

Since government decisions are a composite of political, social, and economic opinions, government policies may not be selected on economic justifications alone. But from an economic perspective, the government should adopt a policy that improves market performance with a minimum expenditure of society's resources. Such performance can be evaluated by three criteria: (1) efficiency, (2) equity, and (3) stability.

EFFICIENCY

Economic efficiency has several dimensions. *Static efficiency* is concerned with the utilization of society's resources at a given time and involves two parts. First, each firm must use the minimum resources necessary, known as X-efficiency. Second, resources must be allocated optimally throughout the economy, in a process known as allocative efficiency. X-efficiency avoids waste of resources, while allocative efficiency ensures that resources are employed in their most valued use.

Dynamic efficiency is concerned with maximizing society's welfare over time through technological progress. The invention of new goods and production processes enlarges society's consumption possibilities and enables firms to produce more products using fewer resources than before.

EQUITY

Equity implies some notion of fairness and is based primarily on value judgments. Since government intervention may affect the distribution of income and wealth among society's members, the determination of the equity or fairness of the new distribution must be made. In short, the government must guard against the inequity created by political favors in government programs to the detriment of society.

Some writers have pointed out that there is often a deficiency in the political decision-making process similar to the deficiency of externalities in the private market economy. Government may impose a cost on society without providing any offsetting benefits or use governmental power to acquire benefits for which others will have to pay. The ideal government response is to provide only those public services that are worth at least as much as they cost and by preventing some groups from exploiting other groups. In comparison with alternative political systems, democratic institutions perform this task tolerably well. However, narrowly motivated special interests find it relatively easy to use the democratic process to acquire advantages at the expense of the general public. Of course, these special-interest programs will impose costs on the general public in the form of higher taxes and prices. But organizing the general public for the purpose of generating political opposition to these groups is difficult. Some of those suffering from the adverse special-interest program will not contribute to the opposition effort. So when a program is being considered that benefits the few at the expense of the many, our political representatives can expect to hear from the few, but not from the many. This often results in a bias in political results. Just as society suffers from privately imposed market externalities because the private benefits to market participants are paid for, in large part, by the defenseless public, similarly society suffers from *political externalities* when various private benefits received from government programs also are paid for, in large measure, by the defenseless public.

Government policies are often designed to favor the organized interests of the few at the expense of the unorganized interests of the many. These "political externalities" may take the form of higher prices, less efficient allocations of resources between different regions of the country, or less success in dealing with the market externalities than society is paying for. Consequently, caution is advisable before embracing any governmental solution to the problem of market defects. For once political power has been created for the purpose of achieving some objective, it is naive to imagine that those with political influence will not employ this power for their own narrow purposes.

STABILITY

A major economic role of the government is economic *stability* with full employment and minimal inflation. While the government's stabilization policies normally involve some combination of monetary and fiscal policies, government intervention policies may affect the government's ability to achieve macroeconomic stability. For example, the Occupational Safety and Health Administration may promulgate a rule that requires firms to purchase "safe" production equipment. To compensate for these higher costs, firms may raise their prices and thereby aggravate the rate of inflation in the economy.

The economic performance criteria of efficiency, equity, and stability can provide a means for evaluating government intervention policies. The primary rationale for government intervention is to maximize society's use of resources. This goal involves seeking the minimization of static inefficiencies arising from market failures. However, such government intervention policies must not unnecessarily or unreasonably disrupt dynamic efficiency, equity, or economic stability. The conflicts among these criteria often require tradeoffs and difficult choices. Couple these economic criteria with other political goals and the decision process becomes even more difficult and complex. Consequently, the actual government intervention policy chosen by government will undoubtedly be susceptible to criticism and often subject to operational improvement.

CONCLUSION

When the market system fails to achieve society's goals, public policy directives from government attempt to fill the void. Society is free to choose to allocate its resources any way it desires and on the basis of any criteria it regards as appropriate. Government is sufficiently representative of society as a whole and accountable to society through the election process and other means to be the body to formulate public policy for society as a whole. Hence, government has a legitimate right to allocate resources for the production of public goods and services and to formulate public policy for business in response to changing public expectations. Consequently, challenges by business to the legitimacy of government and its public policy pronouncements are inappropriate. Rather, management's responsibility is one of working with government and other groups to solve social problems.

DISCUSSION QUESTIONS

1. What are the fundamental economic questions?

2. How does the market system solve the fundamental economic questions?

3. How does the command system solve the fundamental economic questions?

4. Is the market system "natural" or contrived by government?

5. What is the "invisible hand" concept and what does it suggest is appropriate governmental policy?

6. What is the "tragedy of the commons" and what does it suggest is appropriate governmental policy?

7. Identify market failures that lead to a demand for government regulation. Which seem most persuasive of the need for regulation? Which are less persuasive?

8. Identify an example of direct government regulation and an example of indirect regulation.

9. Contrast static economic efficiency with dynamic economic efficiency.

10. What is meant by the attainment of "equity" in government programs? What is a "political externality"?

11. Can government stabilization policies be frustrated by its own regulations?

12. Besides the theory of monopoly, economic theory is not very helpful in identifying "market failures." Who, instead, identifies market failures for society? Consider the "market failure" of incompetent decisions of consumers. How are such decisions identified? How does society learn of consumers' purchasing adulterated meat or unsafe automobiles?

SUGGESTED READINGS

Breyer, Stephen, "Analysing Regulatory Failure: Mismatches, Less Restrictive Alternatives, and Reform," *Harvard Law Review.* Vol. 92, No. 3, January 1979, pp. 549–609.

Greer, Douglas F., *Business, Government, and Society* (New York: Macmillan Publishing Co., 1983), Chaps. 2 and 3.

Hewitt, Charles M., "Sociological Trends in the Law and Inflation," *American Business Law Journal,* Vol. 17, No. 1, Spring 1979, pp. 77–84.

Slade, Michael, "Towards a Study of Law and Economy," *American Business Law Journal,* Vol. 17, No. 1, Spring 1979, pp. 21–48.

Solo, Robert A., *The Positive State* (Cincinnati, Ohio: South-Western Publishing Co., 1982), Chaps, 1, 2, 3, 4, and 5.

ENDNOTES

1. Adam Smith, *An Inquiry into the Nature and Causes of the Wealth of Nations* (2 vols.; London: printed for W. Strahan and T. Cadell in *The Strand,* 1776), Vol. II, p. 289.

2. Garrett Hardin, "The Tragedy of the Commons," *Science* Vol. 162 (Oct.–Dec. 1968), pp. 1243–1248, 1244. Copyright 1968 by the American Association for the Advancement of Science. Used with permission.

3. This list is derived from Stephen Breyer, "Analyzing Regulatory Failure: Mismatches, Less Restrictive Alternatives, and Reform," 92 *Har. L. Rev.* 3 (January 1979), pp. 549–609.

chapter 3

THE ISSUE OF BUSINESS AND SOCiAL INVOLVEMENT

In the first two chapters we observed the evolving role of business in society and its relationship with society as a whole and with government in particular. This historical review seems to clearly reveal the evolution of social and economic ideologies concerning the proper role and functions of business and government institutions. What was deemed proper governmental policy in one era was judged detrimental to society in another. Those adhering to an outdated ideology in the changed social conditions found their ideology suggesting inappropriate action in the new era. In a similar manner, this chapter discusses the ideological beliefs of businessmen concerning their role in society. It then attempts to illustrate how business philosophy has changed in recent years and focuses attention on the ideological dilemmas likely to be faced in the future. One can be sure that as long as the philosophies of business direct business practices to contribute positively to social goals, society will accept and support contemporary business practices. On the other hand, if business ideology gives rise to business practices that society believes are contrary to the common good, society will initiate and enforce restrictions against those practices.

THE IDEOLOGY OF FREE ENTERPRISE

Important to America's development was a body of social and economic philosophy that was shared by business and social leaders. The ideology of the free enterprise system provided direction and justification for both business and governmental affairs. It provided the key elements that make up *the* ideal way to organize economic life. Basic components of this free enterprise ideology are easy to identify. According to George Cabot Lodge, the traditional ideology consists of five great ideals that were expressed as "natural laws" by John Locke and Adam Smith.[1] These ideals fit well in the vast, underpopulated wilderness of America and have served for hundreds of years. The Lockean ideals are stated as follows.

Individualism.   This atomistic notion holds that each individual is more important than society and its institutions. Social institutions are to protect the interests of individual persons. The community is no more than the sum of the individuals in it. Individual fulfillment lies in an essentially lonely struggle where the fit survive. Individuals are to be free to promote and protect their own personal interests. In economic affairs, this means that individuals should be free to own property and enter into contracts with others whereby they sell their skills and products in the free marketplace. Free choice for the individual becomes a core concept of the ideology of "free enterprise."

Equality of Opportunity.   Closely tied to individualism is the concept of equality, which means "equal opportunity." Because America was free of the European rigidities of social rank and class and because of a general shortage of labor in America to fill the jobs of the expanding economic system, opportunities seemed open for all people and the notion of equal opportunity took firm root in early America. Everyone was felt to have an equal chance to engage in trade and commerce, to make one's own way or to pull up stakes and move to the western frontier if necessary for a new start. While the American Indians, the freed slaves, European immigrants and women found American society to be less than its announced free opportunity for all, the philosophical ideal of equality of opportunity has developed into an enduring ideological principle of free enterprise.

Private Property Rights.   The rights of private property are the legal mechanism for strengthening individualism and preserving free choice. Inherent in private property is the right of the owner to obtain governmental assistance in maintaining exclusive use and enjoyment of his property. The self-sufficiency afforded to citizens through the rights of private property forms the basis by which individuals are able to secure their personal liberties. As John Adams explained, "Property must be secure, or liberty cannot exist." Aristotle said a "moderate and sufficient property" for the great mass of people will maintain liberty. The ownership of property allows one to control one's own destiny, rather than to have important decisions made by someone else.

Private property also becomes the basis for decentralization of political and economic power. The "free enterprise" system is founded on the right of private property and the decentralization of control over national economic resources. Society has delegated to individuals the right to own and use physical property for the production and distribution of goods and services to the public. The right of profit—that is, to increase one's holdings of private property—is dependent upon the ability of businessmen to discharge their production and service responsibilities to the public. Profit is a payment made to owners who use their property for productive purposes. Thus, profits become a powerful incentive for property owners to use their property in productive ways that contribute to their own personal welfare as well as to the well-being of society in general.

Competition. The notion of competition is an indispensable part of the free enterprise system. Individuals are to compete for economic rewards, such as good jobs, promotions and quality goods and services. A competitive system will reward the economically competent and punish those who are incompetent or of little ambition. Competition, therefore, is society's method of encouraging high levels of economic performance from all its citizens. Competition channels the interest of self-seeking individuals into productive enterprise which has socially valuable consequences. This was first expressed by Adam Smith when he said that self-seeking enterprisers would be guided by the "invisible hand" of competition to accomplish social goals as they sought their own selfish purposes. The competitive process also is felt to be a successful process of selecting the most fit for positions of leadership. And beyond these, competition keeps power from being concentrated exclusively in the hands of a few.

Limited Government. If people are to be free to dedicate their private property and energies to working hard and producing needed goods and services to promote their own self-interest, competition is necessary to regulate these individual efforts to maximize the well-being of the entire society also. Consequently, in a free market system with sufficient competition, there is no natural need for governmental interference. Moreover, if government laws and regulations stand in the way of individual initiative and general social welfare, they should be stripped away. Beyond protecting private property, enforcing contracts and providing for general security of the individual, the government has little to do. This philosophical ideal of limited government that follows a "hands-off" policy toward business is still a popular belief of the free enterprise ideology.

Specialization and Fragmentation. Adam Smith had argued that specialization of workers and capital was the method by which increased productivity could be obtained. He also argued for specialization among nations and free international trade to increase the general welfare of all nations. In effect, Smith believed that competition would provide sufficient coordination among the specialized parts to efficiently and effectively run the economic world. Beyond the application of this concept to the economic system, it is argued also that scientific specialization is an effective means to enhance knowledge.

PRESSURES ON TRADITIONAL IDEOLOGY

Over the years and particularly since the Civil War the free enterprise ideology has been tested for usefulness by the major social changes occuring in America. However, time and again Americans handled historic confrontations not so much by the ideological blueprint of free enterprise as through innovative institutional mechanisms that permitted decisions to be made as specific challenges arose. Americans did not intentionally abandon the ideals of free enterprise, but their piecemeal solutions to immediate needs and pressures of different groups added up to an erosion of the fundamental concepts of the free enterprise ideology.

The most important social changes that challenged the free enterprise ideology include the following.

- The growth of big business firms and the formulation of cartel arrangements brought about a reduction in competition and an increase in monopolistic practices. Populous movements to counteract these trends resulted in the antitrust laws and the beginning of the expansion of the power of government.
- The formulation of early interest groups signaled a retreat from the idea of limited government. Farmers sought price supports for farm commodities; workers demanded minimum wages; and small businesses sought protection from big business competition.
- The Great Depression of the 1930s further expanded government programs to offset unemployment and lagging business conditions. The depression seemed to eliminate the idea that unemployment was the result of laziness or lack of individual initiative. Instead, many persons believed the free enterprise system contained flaws that necessitated governmental efforts to support the economic level of operations and the individuals within the system who were not receiving a "fair share." In effect, the concept of *laissez-faire* became unacceptable policy to society.
- The size of government grew even larger as a result of World Wars I and II. The concept of a government limited in size seemed to be gone forever.
- The formulation of the organizational society challenged the ideological concepts of individualism and self-reliance. With the growth of big business came the demand for organized labor. The government welfare operations grew in size. Large-scale farming put tremendous pressure on the family farm and educational institutions became massive. As a result, group membership became more important than property as a means to assuring one's income, health, and other privileges granted through membership. The struggle to achieve one's livelihood through independence and self-reliance seemed to be superseded by the effort to organize and make group demands.
- The group demands of the 1960s and 1970s challenged traditional business ideology even more. Industrial pollution and resource depletion have caused ecological concerns. Environmentalists have pressed for a slowdown from America's unbounded economic expansion. Minorities and women have demanded equality in employment and promotion rights because they feel true equality of opportunity has never existed for them. The consumer movement has pressed for more and truthful information about products; for safe products; and for more competition among firms as an effort to reduce prices. The elderly have pressed for retirement

security. All these group concerns have challenged the traditional ideological concepts of freedom, individual initiative, limited government, and the social effectiveness of competition and the market system itself.

- Big business has grown to accept and seek governmental policies that stabilize the economy and protect domestic firms from foreign competitors. Businesses have also long sought the aid of government in the form of subsidies, loans, or regulatory protection. Such governmental actions erode the concept of a *free* market.

It is hard for managers in either business or government to operate within an environment where old ideals no longer seem to work. It is even more difficult because new concepts or ideology are still unfamiliar and disruptive. There is a need to stand back in order to look at the whole array of problems and not merely at those questions which come one by one.

However, meeting the challenge is not easy. Old ideas die hard. They had glorious associations with the past. And the old ideology is often used to legitimize the seats of power and justify the status quo. Nobody likes to look at the weaknesses of the ideology that justifies his position and privilege. More often than not, arguments are made to "return to the ideas that made America great."

ARGUMENTS AGAINST CHANGE IN BUSINESS IDEOLOGY

The opponents of business social involvement argue for the preservation of the private economic system and its ideological commitment to business decision making according to market stimuli. They fear that the adoption of social responsibilities by business will destroy economic efficiency, managerial competence and legitimacy, and our free and pluralistic political system.

LOSS OF EFFICIENCY

Classical economists argue that business enhances public welfare when it reduces costs and improves efficiency in its efforts to maximize profits. Even though businesspersons are selfishly motivated in their drive for profits, competition forces them to behave in the public interest in the long run by reducing costs and prices. Classical economists argue that businesspersons are more socially responsive when they adhere strictly to their economic interests and thereby achieve economic efficiency in the allocation of scarce economic resources. In contrast, if executives use resources for social purposes, they will have to rely on directives from sources other than the free market in allocating scarce resources to alternate uses. Without the discipline and direction of market stimuli in the allocation of social resources, businesspersons lack appropriate criteria for the direction of those resources. Since the function of business is economic, economic values, rather than social, should be the only criteria used to measure success and direct the use of resources. The use of social criteria will cause a loss of economic efficiency.

Some people feel that the public is being misled about who will pay the costs for such social activities by business. Sometimes the public thinks they are going to get these benefits "free." However, the public must bear the costs of businesses' social involvement. Businesses will pass these costs through the price structure. As the ancient economist has stated: "There is no free lunch." Moreover, society may well demand social programs by companies where the costs of the programs exceed the benefits of the program. This obviously involves a misallocation of economic resources.

MANAGERIAL INCOMPETENCE

Since society's resources are limited, there is a need to set social priorities because not all social goals can be achieved at once. Sometimes unreasonable societal expectations do not allow for the appropriate establishment of priorities among social goals. In either case, there is a severe question concerning the right of private management to make decisions concerning social priorities in the allocation of social resources. Business managers may not possess competence in justifying and settling social issues. Placing the burden of nonmarket responsibilities on businesspersons forces them to abandon their professional competence in the pursuit of a set of skills and perceptions that they do not possess. Consequently, even if social concerns are brought within the purview of management without loss of economic efficiency, managers are not likely to correctly identify and effectively deal with social problems.

LOSS OF LEGITIMACY

The historical character of the business firm has been one of a private entity dealing with private property. When managers divert business property into any activity other than furthering the economic interests of the business owners, they are effectively depriving the owners of their property and thereby weakening the justification both for the manager's own authority and for the existence of the organization itself. Thus, any attempt to transform the business into a more public institution, one acting on some concept of the "public interest" and governed by political processes, only serves to question the basic legitimacy of the firm as a private entity.

Moreover, because the business firm is a private entity, it has no direct lines of accountability to the people. Consequently, many have argued that it is unwise to allow business activities in social areas where the business is not accountable. Arguing against an expanded scope of social responsibility for business, Milton Friedman asked a series of questions: "Can self-selected private individuals decide what burden they are justified in placing on themselves and their stockholders to serve that social interest? Is it tolerable that these public functions . . .

be exercised by the people who happen at the moment to be in charge of a particular enterprise, chosen for those posts by strictly private groups?"[2] The implication of Friedman's questions is that business leaders are illegitimate in the sense that they are not elected as public officials and are not held accountable to the public as long as they remain private entities. The obvious fear of the opponents of the social responsibility doctrine is that its adoption will inevitably lead to cries for the accountability of management and the evolution of a political government system in the organization itself. Such evolution will transform the business firm from a voluntary association into a potentially coercive political institution. For these reasons, Friedman referred to the expanded scope of social responsibility as "a fundamentally subversive doctrine."[3]

THREAT TO POLITICAL PLURALISM

Even if businesses are able to expand their scope of social responsibility without excessive loss of economic efficiency, without taking on tasks for which they are totally incompetent, and without undermining their status of legitimacy, opponents of the social responsibility doctrine insist that it constitutes a threat to social and political pluralism and freedom in America. They argue that if the market system no longer directs the activities of the business firm, political direction from the state will become increasingly necessary as business involves itself in social causes. This will result in a gradual expansion of the political direction over business and an expansion of the centralization of control over society.

Frederick Hayek argued that the increasingly pervasive influence of business will give rise to increasing demand for governmental control.

The more it comes to be accepted that corporations ought to be directed in the services of specific public interests, the more pervasive becomes the contention that, as government is the appointed guardian of public interest, government should also have the power to tell corporations what they must do.[4]

Theodore Levitt added:

Welfare and society are not the corporation's business. Its business is making money, not sweet music. The same goes for unions. Their business is 'bread and butter' and job rights. In a free enterprise system, welfare is supposed to be automatic; and where it is not, it becomes government's job. This is the concept of pluralism. Government's job is not business and business' job is not government. And unless these functions are resolutely separated in all respects, they are eventually combined in every respect. In the end, the danger is not that government will run business, or that business will run government, but rather that the two of them will coalesce . . . into a single power, unopposed and unopposable.[5]

Finally, John K. Galbraith has written:

Given the deep dependence of the industrial system upon the state and . . . its identification with public goals and the adaption of these to its needs, the industrial system will not long be regarded as something apart from government . . . Increasingly, it will be recognized that the mature corporation as it develops, becomes part of the larger administrative complex associated with the state. In time, the line between the two will disappear. Men will look back in amusement at the pretense that once caused people to refer to General Dynamics and North American Aviation and AT&T as *private* businesses.[6]

Besides the merging of business and government, Galbraith suggested the corporation itself may become the principal government structure of society. He argued that the elite of the managerial class, which he termed "the technostructure," will not only control the business firms throughout society, but will gradually come to dominant society as a whole as the large business firms develop interconnections with each other and with government. However, in the process of taking over society, the technostructure itself will be influenced by society so that the technostructure and society tend to merge into a single decision-making system in which social goals are accomplished.

Hence, according to these critics, whether it is government, business, or the "technostructure" that comes to dominate society, political pluralism is threatened by the expansion of the scope of business involvement in social affairs.

ARGUMENTS FOR CHANGES IN BUSINESS IDEOLOGY

Proponents for an expanded scope of social involvement by business suggest there are potential benefits for society and for business. They generally imply that business firms can be effective producers of economic values as well as effective socially minded citizens.

CHANGED SOCIETAL EXPECTATIONS

In the mid 1930s, Ralph Currier Davis articulated the concept that the business firm's primary objective is service, not profits.[7] By producing utility for society, society allows the firm to exist. While the stockholder's objective may be to maximize return, the profit gained by investors is only a collateral side effect of achieving the firm's service objective. Similarly, the wages of labor, the interest of financiers, and so forth, are collateral objectives stemming from the firm's successful accomplishment of its primary service objectives. (See Figure 3-1.) When any collateral objective, whether profits, wages, or managerial benefits, is elevated above and imposed on the primary service objective, the long-term survival of the firm is threatened.

Historically, the "service role" of business was fulfilled by the efficient production of goods and services. However, many authors contend that society's expectations of business have broadened beyond the mere efficient execution of the economic function. A statement of one group of business executives and educators maintains that the economic functions must be exercised with a "sensitive awareness of changing social values and priorities."[8] Thus, the major argument for business assumption of an expanded social involvement is the changing needs and expectations of society.

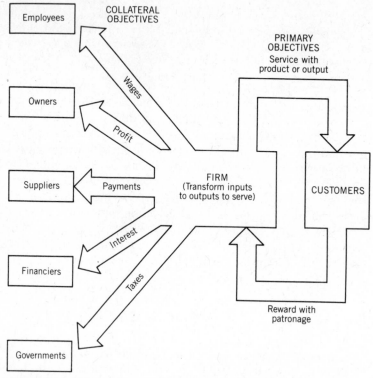

Figure 3-1. The primary objective of business is service.

Society has unquestionable authority to issue or retract grants of privilege, including the basic rights of private property and the decentralization of control over economic resources. The owners of economic resources, in order to maintain a "free" system, are obliged to provide goods and services in the quality and quantity needed by society. The right to profit is dependent on the ability of business organizations to discharge their service responsibilities to the public. To the extent that business is able to comply with this responsibility, it is not necessary for society to modify the rights and privileges of private property and the private management of economic resources. Therefore, if business wishes to remain successful in the long run, it must respond to society's needs and expectations.

Many have argued that the basic economic needs of American citizens have been met by successes of the free enterprise system. However, it is precisely because business has been so successful in meeting these basic economic needs that society has increased its levels of expectation concerning social needs. In short, the production of goods and services alone is no longer sufficient to satisfy society. Society's concern for the "quality of life" requires that business concern itself with social goals as well as production goals.

It has been urged that businesspersons need to recognize that they are part of the complex and interdependent social system in which their decisions may affect the quality of life. Failure to recognize this interdependence may well lead to severe modifications of the business institution. Many argue that businesspersons will commit grievous error if they perceive societal's request for social involvement as a passing fad.[9]

DISCOURAGEMENT OF MORE GOVERNMENT REGULATION

Many argue that if business is socially responsive, the need for additional regulation of the business system by government will be reduced. With reduced regulation, businesses will be free to adopt different courses to solving problems, and decision making itself will be decentralized in keeping with our political philosophy. Moreover, this would keep the decision making at the point where the operating problem occurs and allow a more appropriate remedy to be fashioned without bureaucratic entanglements.

Many social problems will not be solved through the normal processes of the market system. Society long ago recognized that if persons are excluded from the market by institutional barriers such as sex or race discrimination or by the simple fact of poverty, their preferences for the distribution of productive resources will not be registered in the market system. Such arbitrary exclusion of members of society from the economic decision-making process undermines the philosophical basis for pluralistic democracy. The allocation of resources by the market system under such conditions can accepted at a social optimum only if the preferences of the excluded members of society are considered irrelevant. Failure of the business system to modify its discriminatory hiring and training programs resulted in governmental regulations attempting to integrate the excluded members. Other social goods such as environmental qualities are not achieved through the simple market system. Voluntary programs of social involvement in these and other areas were required. Failure to integrate these social goals in the decision-making process for business firms resulted in an enlargement of the governmental regulatory sphere. Business firms reap enlarged public appreciation and reduced governmental regulations when they voluntarily undertake programs that achieve social goals expected by society.

INADEQUACY OF REGULATORY TECHNIQUES

If businesses are acting irresponsibly, people always turn to the government for more laws. But laws do not always seem to solve the problems. Christopher Stone argues that we have put the problem backwards.[10] As a society, since corporations will not behave responsively on their own, we demand new laws. Stone argues that since law doesn't work, we need "social responsibility."

Stone argues that law is not an adequate control of *institutional* behavior, because laws are designed to control individuals. Moreover, he argues that the inadequacy of present regulatory techniques preclude their adoption as the primary means of achieving responsible corporate behavior. He points out that the lawmaking process itself suffers from a time lag problem in identifying behavior that should be outlawed. The legal process also operates under an information gap because the government seldom knows as much as corporate officials. Moreover, legal forums are generally unsuitable to the resolution of complex business-social issues. Stone argues that society's "trust in the legal machinery as a means of keeping corporations in bound is misplaced—and that, therefore, something more is needed." And the "something more," according to Stone, is voluntary moral judgments by responsible people.

According to Stone, the role of the law should be limited to (1) ensuring a representative cross-section of private and public members on the board of directors and (2) mandating the collection and reporting of pertinent social data to the board. This "reformed" board with adequate data of the current corporation-social affairs can be generally relied on for voluntary moral judgments consistent with social expectations.

Laws set standards for general applicability, which establishes minimum standards of behavior. American society has been reluctant to require "excellence" in legal standards. Laws that specify minimum standards of conduct (Thou shalt not steal) seem more legally enforceable than laws of "aspiration" that exhort individuals to realize their fullest potential (Thou shalt do justice). Consequently, law will never be a good mechanism for drawing out of a company the best of what it is capable. Therefore, voluntary efforts to become socially responsive are needed as a better alternative to the governmental directives for behavior.

Connected to the idea that law cannot control the social behavior of business is the notion that "prevention is better than cure." Business firms may well find it to their advantage to tackle social problems in their incipiency, rather than waiting for them to become full-blown social breakdowns requiring governmental intrusions into business practices. If business would "aspire" to higher levels of moral behavior through "prevention" efforts, proponents of social involvement argue that business could use its valuable resources in the design of solutions to social problems. Many have pointed to the managerial, technical, and financial resources that business has that could be utilized in innovative ways to deal with social problems. Instead, many argue that government efforts have often failed in handling social problems and that business may well provide an organizational environment more conducive to achieving social goals. Such assets belie the argument that management lacks competence to deal with social issues. Business neglect of social involvement on the grounds of incompetence is no more tolerable to society than a company's neglect of accounting records on the grounds that their accountant is not fully trained. Business either develops the ability to handle these social tasks or its goes out of business.

SOCIAL INVOLVEMENT CAN BE IN STOCKHOLDER'S INTEREST

While not without critics, some individuals argue that if investors diversified their stock ownership, corporate activities that would not be worthwhile to stockholders in a single firm would become worthwhile to the diversified stock-

Against Social Involvement	For Social Involvement
Loss of economic efficiency	Changed societal expectations
Managerial incompetence	Discouragement of more government regulation
Loss of legitimacy	Inadequacy of regulatory techniques
Threat to political pluralism	Advantages to diversified stockowners

Figure 3-2. Arguments on the issue of business social involvement.

holders.[11] Responsible corporate behavior that would enrich the public sector as a whole would also operate to benefit holders of a diversified stock portfolio. For example, a corporation training program for poorly qualified employees could benefit the business community as a whole. Even if the employees left for another company, the benefit of their training would not be lost to more diversified investors. With more and more individual savings being held by financial institutions with diversified portfolios, this argument gains strength.

Firms are also recognizing that the solution of certain social problems can result in a direct flow of profit. For example, some companies have found that their reclamation of industrial waste can be profitable. Others have noted that failure to become socially involved jeopardizes not only profit but the very survival of the firm itself. Increasingly large numbers of investors and financial institutions are restricting their funds to those socially minded firms who have forestalled the possibility of long-term problems occasioned by socially inept decision making.

A NEW AMERICAN IDEOLOGY

The great social changes of the twentieth century has led George Cabot Lodge to suggest the beginning contours of a new American ideology.[12] He has argued that five new ideological contours, listed as follows, have replaced the old Lockean Five of individualism, property rights, competition, limited state and specialization-fragmentation.

Communitarism. The community has its own special needs. Individual survival and self-esteem depend upon the recognition and enlargement of those community needs. Personal fulfillment is achieved by gaining a place in the community. The individual identifies with the whole, and directs his actions and participation according to the social process of the community. If the community, the work setting or social organization is well designed, its members gain a sense of identity with it. If the social organization is poorly designed, people will become alienated and frustrated. The imperative of individual involvement with social organizations today negates the opportunities for individuals to live in ways Locke or Emerson idealized.

The communitarian organizational style of both corporations and unions have fostered this evolution. Usually the changes have been initiated without consideration of the ideological significance of the change. For example, the teachings of the Protestant Ethic include the notion of individual fulfillment in the worker's secular "calling" or work. However, the traditional beliefs in individualism find little fulfillment on the assembly line or in the factory setting. Consequently, business' extolling the virtues of hard work and obedience to authority is increasingly unacceptable to the community of workers as a means to self-fulfillment. Alternatively, a few workers have sought gratification of their individualistic desires by joining absentee lists, by acting insubordinately toward management, or by finding individual fulfillment away from the job. However, most workers have attained new identity and fulfillment in mutual associations. The result is an organizational style (management and union group) which seeks a "consensus" (a communitarianism ideal) rather than individualistically designed contracts of employment. In short, individuals now achieve status through working with others rather than struggling alone. Rugged individualism and self-reliance are being replaced by new forms of "concensus."

Another example of the evolving contours of communitarianism is in the field of employment opportunity. In the past, individualism demanded no more than *equal opportunity* for workers when gaining employment or seeking promotions. However, if a prohibited type of discrimination has become institutionalized, as in the case of several large corporations, the remedies accepted by the parties involved an *equality of representation* of the minorities at all levels of employment. In the AT&T case, the company agreed to upgrade 50,000 women and 6600 minority group workers and to hire 4000 men to fill traditionally female jobs. Thus, the remedy sought is *equality of result,* not of opportunity. This communitarian idea seems to be supplanting the individualistic one. Since individuals are unequal in many respects, companies must redesign themselves to adapt to these inequalities and to assure a measure of equality of results.

Membership Rights. A new right has come to supercede property rights in political and social importance: the right to enjoy membership in some component of the community. For example, U.S. citizens who have reached the age of 65 or who are blind or disabled have an absolute right to minimum income provided by the government. These rights derive not from the individual's effort or property. Instead, they are communitarian rights that society has judged to be consistent with a "good community." Other "rights," either from membership in the union or in the management team, confer privileges and entitlements associated with the group. These membership "rights" supercede the rights and privileges of owning property; indeed, they are often at the expense of property owners. Membership rights, rather than property rights, tend to guarantee a person's security and well-being.

In addition, the ethical teachings encouraging the individual to practice thrift and to delay gratification have been undermined by the marketing and credit extension policies of business. When coupled with the reality of individuals seeking security from group membership, America has experienced a declining rate of savings for investment purposes. Individuals do not perceive the need to *accumulate* property to enjoy life or secure one's old age.

In the process of social transformation, the utility of property as a legitimizing idea has been eroded also. Large public corporations are not private entities controlled by private owners (stockholders). The shareholders do not control or assume responsibility for company affairs. They are investors who receive an adequate return on their investments or they put their money elsewhere. Nader and his followers who organized "Campaign GM" tried to force shareholders to behave like owners and thus legitimize corporations as property. GM managers labeled such stockholder agitation as radically designed by "an adversary culture . . . antagonistic to our American ideas of private property and individual responsibility." Of course, the reverse is true; GM was the radical. Nader was the conservative, attempting to realign and control the corporation according to its ideological line of authority.

Without the legitimacy of private owners directing the use of their property, corporations have become a "collective" of various interests and amendable to community control. The stockholders, workers, managers, and government claim some "legitimate" interest in corporate resources. Corporate managers become less agents for stockholder-owners and more arbiters of conflicting interests. Instead, managers seek to fashion an agreeable consensus.

Community Needs. Lodge has pointed out that the International Telephone and Telegraph (IT&T) Company in 1977 utilized the concept of "community needs" in its appeal to be freed from the requirements of the antitrust laws. Antitrust laws seek to preserve free trade and competition. However, IT&T argued that the public interest requires a big and strong IT&T at home so that it can withstand the political gyrations abroad. Antitrust policy should be balanced against other public policies, such as the desire for a favorable balance of payments. In effect, the company favored a government-business identification of "community need" over the uniform application of procompetitive laws. This notion is radically different from the traditional idea that the public interest is obtained through the free and vigorous competition among companies trying to satisfy community desires. Nevertheless, more and more business firms seem willing to set aside the old idea of domestic competition so that they can better organize to meet world competition. However, if we abandon competition, "other forces" will be needed to define and preserve the "community" interests. The process to define community needs will doubtlessly involve a larger role for the political authority.

The Active-Planning State. The role of the state is changing radically—it will become the arbiter of community needs. Without effective competition, it will take up the task of coordination, priority setting, and planning. It will decide the contours of the trade-offs that confront us—for example, between environmental purity and energy supplies or between more revenues for auto workers or for computer programmers.

However, the impact of the old ideology of the limited state precludes government from fashioning a coherent and directive plan. An obvious example of the failure of government planning is the "energy crisis." Instead of forthrightly planning, the government attempts to deal with problems through piecemeal solutions. Lodge argues that in the future citizens will come to recognize the planning function of the state and allocate the planning responsibilities between local, regional, centralized, and global authorities.

Systems-Wide Interdependence. The ideas of atomistic competition in economic affairs and of scientific specializations in formulating knowledge seem to have given way to a new consciousness of the interrelatedness of all things. Large business firms dominate industries and multidisciplinary studies are becoming imperative. Business firms must formulate holistic planning techniques in order to comply effectively with governmental regulations on ecology and human rights. These legal requirements must be integrated into traditional business planning that heretofore had limited its horizon to costs and revenues. Likewise, scientific inquiry must accommodate itself to the holistic, rather than specialized, approach to expanding useful knowledge.

In proposing these five notions as the contours of an evolving new ideology, Lodge warned against the dangers of "wishing" communitarianism away or of relegating the accomodation of the communitarianism ideology to posterity. Instead, Lodge advocated forthright ideological analysis that will allow preservation of what is best from the old ideology while consciously adapting to the new communitarian norms.

Old Ideology	Emerging Ideology
Individualism	Communitarianism
equal opportunity	equality of result
contract	consensus
Property rights	Rights of membership
Competition	Cooperation-community need
Limited government	Active, planning government
Atomistic	Holistic
independence	interdependence

Source: Adapted from George Cabot Lodge, "Managerial Implications of Ideological Change," *The Ethics of Corporate Conduct* (Englewood Cliffs, N.J.: Prentice-Hall, Inc., 1977), pp. 79–105.

Figure 3-3. Emerging new ideology.

THE SOCIALIZATION OF BUSINESS

Business recognition of social responsibilities is an evolutionary process. The evolving patterns of new attitude and behavior are reflected in the pragmatic reaction of business to changing circumstances rather than in the adoption of a new coherent ideology. Groping for solutions that "succeed" often entails a compromise of historical ideological commitments to economic functions alone. Therefore, in spite of the historical dominance of this "economic" ideology in American society, the actual practices of management have often deviated from ideological norms. Increasingly, business firms are recognizing that social approval does not flow from the achievement of profits alone. Economic and *social* criteria have become the basis for appraising the role of business in society today.

A MANAGERIAL DILEMMA

In this modern era, neither the traditional economic model nor the social responsibility model is completely satisfying for managers. Operating according to the traditional economic model subjects the firm to all the criticisms usually associated with "profit only" decision making. The economic model simply does not describe reality or offer acceptable prescriptive behavior for business under modern social conditions. Unfortunately, the social responsibility model, as developed to date, also suffers from serious operational problems. It offers no simple decision-making rules for socially minded managers. Confronted by multiple social and economic objectives without defined priorities, the socially responsive manager finds the social responsibility model provides no specific guidance for choosing the appropriate response. Hence, choosing the model for the business firm to follow is a managerial dilemma.

Despite the underdevelopment of effective managerial models, social problems will continue to confront business and to demand managerial response. Precisely because of the lack of specific techniques for value-laden decision making, managers must grope for solutions.

THE "SOCIALIZATION" PROCESS

The process by which new criteria for performance are formed has been identified by Preston and Post as involving three stages.[13] (See Figure 3-4.) The first stage in the socialization process involves the *recognition* or *awareness* of relevant publics affected by the firm's activities. In the second stage, the firm *acknowledges some responsibility* to consider its impact on such publics in the process of making decisions and conducting its activities. When "negative" impacts are identified, decisions ought to be modified to reduce such impact. The third stage in the socialization process involves the firm's *development of a positive stance* or imple-

First stage	Awareness of affected publics	$\left(\begin{array}{c} \text{Receipt of} \\ \text{relevant information} \end{array} \right)$
Second stage	Acknowledgment of some responsibility	$\left(\begin{array}{c} \text{Philosophy of} \\ \text{commitment} \end{array} \right)$
Third stage	Development of a possible program	$\left(\begin{array}{c} \text{Implementing} \\ \text{social policy} \end{array} \right)$

Figure 3-4.   The process of socializing business firms.

menting some program of its own whereby the goals of the "publics" become incorporated into the goals of the firm itself. In essence, the firm becomes "socialized," interacting with the relevant publics in the solution of common problems. As this socialization process proceeds, management develops a new rhetoric to explain its involvement in society. The changes in rhetoric and behavior during the last decades seem to clearly indicate that most businesses are already socially involved, especially larger firms that have a significant impact on society. While "profit pursuit" thinking still dominates the American business consciousness, ideological shifts seem to be evident.

Researchers in the 1950s analyzed the content of many speeches, articles, and books written by business executives.[14] The researchers sought to determine if business ideology had shifted as a result of the events of the Great Depression. They found that two distinct strains of thought among business people existed. The "classical" strain embodied the concepts of traditional economic functions. However, the "managerial" strain emphasized the importance of professional management. These socially minded managers saw themselves as "public trustees" directing their corporations not just for stockholders, but also to promote the public interest. Other researchers in the 1960s confirmed the "managerial" strain.[15]

PROFESSIONAL MANAGEMENT

Professional managerial philosophy accepts the idea that the legitimacy of business is primarily based on economic and legal criteria. Consequently, business behavior must be responsive to market forces and legal directives. These social obligations imposed by the marketplace and by the law are proscriptive of business behavior. Management discharge of its economic and legal obligations begins with a thorough knowledge of the purposes and particulars of those obligations. Therefore, management devotes considerable time and energies to research and investigation of present market conditions and anticipated trends. Similarly, management must understand the legal parameters of its decision-making process. This involves the obtainment of legal advice and professional evaluation of probable future public policies.

In the last two decades, business managers have increasingly encountered problems associated with government regulatory bodies and their requirements of business. The laws and regulations, in effect, have often emerged as determinants of business activities. In many ways, the United States has shifted away from a reliance on the market mechanism to a reliance on state or federal regulation, taxation, or subsidies. These new government regulations apply to virtually all businesses of any size. The problem is further complicated by the often conflicting objectives of various regulations. As a consequence, an understanding of the legal process and its requirements becomes an imperative for professional managers.

In subsequent chapters, the legal obligations of business imposed by the regulatory environment will be explored. Attention will be devoted to the purposes and schemes of regulations, rather than to the details of the rules. This broad public policy approach to legal study will help develop an appreciation of the vast regulatory environment that proscribes managerial decisions. It also emphasizes the necessity of managerial participation in the formulation of public policy to avoid unnecessary and inefficient regulation of business.

As though business compliance with its economic and legal obligations are not difficult enough, society also expects business firms to be socially responsible.

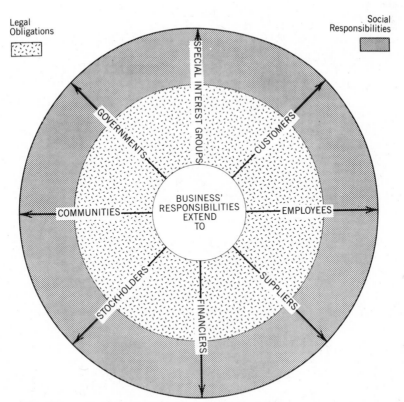

Figure 3-5. The professional manager's conception of the legal and social responsibilities of business.

This implies that business behavior should be "congruent with prevailing social norms, values, and expectations."[16] In contrast to the proscriptive nature of business economic and legal obligations, these social responsibilities are prescriptive in nature, involving the exercise of ethical analysis and discretionary judgment. To uphold its social responsibilities, business firms must be "anticipatory" and "preventive." Effective social responsiveness suggests that business firms must also be action-oriented, not rhetorical alone. (See Figure 3-5.)

Developing business decision-making systems to integrate social values and formulate decisions consistent with social expectations is an enlarged management challenge. Sometimes, social issues arise on the spur of the moment and require a quick managerial response. A typical example might be a protest group arriving at the company's gate and loudly opposing some imminent company action, such as the sponsorship of a controversial television show. Other social issues are long-term and require a reasonably sophisticated response by management. Consequently, management must develop both a short-term and long-term capability to deal effectively with social problems and, thereby, meet its social responsibilities. In dealing with social issues one rational managerial response is to begin with a clarification of the nature of the social issues. Such clarification usually suggests alternative managerial responses that can be rationally evaluated and pragmatically selected.

In subsequent chapters, some social "expectations" of business that exceed the requirements of the law will be explored. Efforts to clarify social issues and explore alternative managerial responses will increase the reader's awareness of business "social responsibilities" and of the possibilities for developing innovative business responses to social change.

CONCLUSION

Free enterprise ideology consists of the basic ideas of the individualism, equality of opportunity, private property rights, competition, limited government, and specialization in economic and scientific affairs. Major economic, political and social changes have occurred since the initial formulation of the free enterprise ideology. These changes have challenged and modified the basic beliefs of the old ideology. The emerging ideology of the modern era seems to stress communitarianism, equality of results, rights of membership, community needs, activist government and systemswide thinking.

Today's business ideology seems to be a mixture of old ideas with new social realities. Corporate managers have adopted new solutions outside the ideological contours of free enterprise. Under the modern era of "responsive capitalism," professional business executives act more like trustees for the public interest than for the limited interest of stockholder-owners. The new ideology seems to be gaining momentum in shaping social policies, while the old ideology clings to the present era through the process of nostalgia and with the hope of revitalization. The debate concerning business's adoption of social responsibilities is largely decided. As one leader of a large corporation has stated:

[T]he corporation is now viewed as having a wide variety of responsibilities transcending the marketplace. Some of those responsibilities are to society at large. Whether a business has social responsibilities is, I know, a subject of widespread debate. But to my mind, it is a debate that continues long after the argument is over. Today I know of no leader of business who sees his function as limited to the pursuit of profit. I know of none who does not realize that the business that for profit's sake ignores the impacts of its actions on society is not likely to make a profit very long.[17]

Business firms, particularly larger ones, have become "socialized," not by having their property appropriated for public ownership and control, but by their own acknowledgement of social responsibilities and development of programs striving for social goals as well as economic goals. The role of business has also been reshaped by laws and regulations that have become important determinants of business behavior. Business's decisions are increasingly altered by legal constraints. This new reality circumscribing business decision making reveals that business operates within two fundamental social processes—the market process and the governmental-legal process. Both processes guide managerial behavior and provide criteria to judge managerial performance.[18] Thus, it is imperative for business management to understand the conceptual differences in the two processes and learn to effectively respond to the demands of both systems. Moreover, the social (ethical/discretionary) responsibilities of management need increased attention as social expectations of business continue to evolve.

DISCUSSION QUESTIONS

1. The traditional "economic model" of business places primary emphasis on production, profit, exploitation of resources, market-based decisions, and limited government. How would a "socially responsible" model of business contrast with these attributes?

2. What are the basic arguments against business assumption of social responsibilities?

3. What are the basic arguments supporting business assumption of social responsibilities?

4. Concerning business' social responsibilities, what are the views of the following people?
   (a) Milton Friedman
   (b) Frederick Hayek
   (c) John K. Galbraith
   (d) Christopher Stone

5. Explain and comment of Ralph C. Davis' argument that the primary objective of business is service, not profits.

6. "We can choose either to understand and move with the tides of history, whatever that may be—or attempt to resist them." Which choice is business adoption of social responsibilities?

7. Compare your ideological beliefs about business with that of (a) your parents and (b) your boss. Can you explain the reasons for any differences or similarities?

8. Which ideal of the free enterprise ideology seems most crucial? Can you rank the other ideals of the free enterprise ideology?

9. Identify a change in American society that has challenged the free enterprise ideology and explain its modification.

10. Given the emergence of a new ideology as described by Lodge, what guidance does it provide for business decision making?

11. Are the financial loans and guarantees provided to Chrysler Corporation a challenge to the free enterprise ideology?

12. What are the obligations of business under the traditional economic model when it closes a plant? Under a socioeconomic model, what are its obligations?

13. Prepare a three-part model of business' responsibilities to society.

14. What are the two major processes that develop guidelines that business is obliged to follow?

15. How are criteria developed to judge the social performance of business in areas where business is not obligated to respond, but discretionarily decides to act?

16. Is corporate legitimacy derived solely from its stockbrokers? Neil Chamberlain has answered:

    "Less and less it can rest its claim to power on a fictional stockholder election; more and more it is forced to seek legitimacy by demonstrating its responsiveness to its publics . . ." Explain.

17. ABC Corp. builds a widget that is stamped out by a w-machine. ABC's w-machines are aging and need replacement. ABC has narrowed its selection of new machines to either Amer-built or Euro-built. Union leaders have written ABC Corp. demanding it "buy American" to protect American jobs.

    What are the responsibilities of ABC Corp. in this instance? Economic? Legal? Ethical?

18. Prepare a statement explaining *your* philosophy of management responsibilities.

SUGGESTED READINGS

Carroll, Archie B., *Business and Society: Managing Corporate Social Performance* (Boston: Little, Brown and Company, 1981), Chap. 2.

Davis, Keith, William C. Frederick, and Robert L. Blomstrom, *Business and Society: Concepts and Policy Issues*, 4th ed. (New York: McGraw-Hill Book Co., 1980), Chaps. 2, 3, and 7.

Friedman, Milton, "The Social Responsibility of Business Is to Increase Its Profits," *The New York Times Magazine*, September 13, 1970, pp. 33, 122–126.

George, Claude, *The History of Management Thought*, 2nd ed. (Englewood Cliffs, N.J.: Prentice-Hall, Inc., 1972), p. 134.

Johnson, M. Bruce, *The Attack on Corporate America: The Corporate Issues Sourcebook* (New York: McGraw-Hill Book Co., 1978), Part I, Chaps. 1 and 4.

Levitt, Theodore, "The Dangers of Social Responsibility," *Harvard Business Review*, September-October 1958, p. 44.

Lodge, George Cabot, "Business and the Changing Society," *Harvard Business Review*, Vol. 52, No. 2, March–April 1974, pp. 59–73.

Lodge, George Cabot, "Managerial Implications of Ideological Change," *The Ethics of Corporate Conduct*, (Englewood Cliffs, N.J.: Prentice-Hall Inc., 1977), pp. 79–105.

ENDNOTES

1. George Cabot Lodge, "Managerial Implications of Ideological Change," *The Ethics of Corporate Conduct* (Englewood Cliffs, N.J.: Prentice-Hall, Inc., 1977), pp. 84–86.

2. Milton Friedman, *Capitalism and Freedom* (Chicago: University of Chicago Press, 1963), pp. 133–134.

3. *Ibid.*

4. Frederick Hayek, "The Corporation in a Democratic Society," in *Management and Corporations, 1985.* ed. Melvin Anshen and George Bach (New York: McGraw-Hill Book Co., 1960), p. 116.

5. Theodore Levitt, "The Dangers of Social Responsibility," *Harvard Business Review*, September–October, 1958, p. 41.

6. John Kenneth Galbraith, *The New Industrial State* (Boston: Houghton-Mifflin Co., 1967), p. 393.

7. Ralph C. Davis, *The Fundamentals of Top Management* (New York: Harper and Row, 1951), pp. 97–106.

8. Committee for Economic Development, *Social Responsibilities of Business Corporations* (New York: CED, 1971).

9. Dow Votaw, "Genius Becomes Rare: A Comment on the Doctrine of Social Responsibility, Pt. II," *California Management Review*, Spring 1973, pp. 16–17.

10. Christopher D. Stone, *Where The Law Ends: The Social Control of Corporate Behavior* (New York: Harper and Row Publishers, 1975).

11. Henry C. Wallich and John J. McGowan, "Stockholder Interest and the Corporation's Role in Social Policy," in William J. Baumol *et al.*, *A New Rationale for Public Policy* (New York: Committee for Economic Development, 1970), pp. 39–59.

12. Lodge, *op. cit.*

13. Lee E. Preston and James E. Post, *Private Management and Public Policy* (Englewood Cliffs, N.J.: Prentice-Hall, Inc., 1975), pp. 46–47.

14. Francis X. Sutton *et al.*, *The American Business Creed* (Cambridge, Mass.: Harvard University Press, 1956).

15. Robert F. Heilbroner, "The View From The Top," in Earl F. Sheit (ed.), *The Business Establishment* (New York: Wiley, 1964), pp. 1–36.

16. S. Prakash Sethi, "Dimensions of Corporate Social Performance: An Analytical Framework," *California Management Review,* Spring 1975, pp. 58–64.

17. John D. deButts, "A Strategy of Accountability," *Running the American Corporation,* William R. Dill, ed. (Englewood Cliffs, N.J.: Prentice-Hall, 1978), p. 146.

18. Preston and Post, *supra,* proposed this notion in their "Principle of Public Responsibility," which requires business to respond affirmatively to the "public policy" process. However, they maintain that public policy is not always congruent with the laws of government. They argue that public policy may either exceed the requirements of laws or, because of nonenforcement, become more relaxed than the laws. In contrast, the author has limited businesses' primary obligation to legal compliance.

part II
THE LEGAL PROCESS

Each society has its own set of values reflected in the goals that its legal system promotes. The substance of the law recognizes certain priorities and defines the legal limits in which they will be permitted to operate. These goals, priorities, and limitations must change as societies evolve and become more complex.

The role of law in American history has been unique. Our legal environment has evolved over a period of approximately two centuries and has been fashioned by the public policies of three basic eras. It began with English common law, which was adopted and refined to meet the problems of a new nation. These laws were modified by the impact and values of the Industrial Revolution and were radically adjusted in the modern era of social awareness and welfare consciousness.

An understanding of the role of law in fashioning governmental "working rules" for the economic affairs of American productive enterprise requires a basic comprehension of Western jurisprudence, both in its theoretical content and in its practical application for social policy. Accordingly, the following materials discuss legal philosophy, lawmaking processes, and the basic structure and decision-making process of the American legal system. Also, a historical perspective of the interaction of the legal system with the evolving American society provides useful insights of the power and limitations of law in molding or reacting to social change.

chapter 4
THE NATURE AND SOURCES OF LAW

What is law? What are its nature and origin? Who creates or determines law? These might be called jurisprudential or philosophical questions of law. They pose appropriate initial inquiries for study of the legal environment of business.

The materials in this chapter suggest explanations of the nature and sources of law. Some readings represent different time periods, which implies that contemporary legal philosophy has evolved from numerous sources, societies, and scholars. This chapter should help the reader achieve a broader understanding of the several philosophies of law that attempt to fashion public policies in American society. Also, the fundamental means of making law are explained.

PHILOSOPHIES OF LAW

Studying jurisprudence or philosophies of law can be a valuable experience. The American judicial decision-making process, for example, devolves considerable discretion on justices as they resolve disputes brought before the courts. Their philosophical tendencies have an impact on their decisions. In other instances, political leaders often argue positions that are premised on a particular legal theory. Philosophical strengths and weaknesses of such political positions can be discerned by understanding more of legal philosophy itself.

Although there are a variety of legal philosophies, a particular few are most often discussed and widely known. An understanding of some of these basic philosophies will help the reader evaluate the impact of legal philosophies on the formulation of "rules" for a society.

NATURAL LAW: LAW AS HIGHEST HUMAN REASON OR DIVINE JUSTICE

Natural law theories have their origin in the political thought of the Greeks and its later incorporation into the Roman law. The Greeks conceptualized the *jus naturale,* which meant "the sum of those principles which ought to control human conduct, because founded in the very nature of man as a rational and social being."[1] This was largely synonymous with the Roman concept of law, which consisted of those principles that were regarded "as so simple and reasonable that . . . they must be recognized everywhere and by everyone."[2]

Medieval lawyers and theologians added the concept that the law of nature was an expression of the Divine Will. They viewed the ultimate origin and final justification of the law to be God, since the law of nature is that part of God which is discoverable by human reason. They believed that natural law is not only that which is natural but also that which is known through connaturality (by being inborn). As such, natural law is dependent on divine reason and therefore "binds men in conscience, and is the prime foundation of human law."[3] The great English lawyer, Blackstone, reasoned, "The will of the Maker is called the Law of Nature. . . . This law, being . . . dictated by God himself, is obligatory upon all. No human laws are of any validity if contrary to this, as they derive their force and authority from this original."[4] The great Roman lawyer, Cicero, wrote:

There is in fact a true law—namely, right reason—which is in accordance with nature, applies to all men, and is unchangeable and eternal. By its commands this law summons men to the performance of their duties; by its prohibitions it restrains them from doing wrong. Its commands and prohibitions always influence good men, but are without effect upon the bad. To invalidate this law by human legislation is never morally right, nor is it permissible ever to restrict its operation, and to annul it wholly is impossible. Neither the senate nor the people can absolve us from our obligation to obey this law, and it requires no . . . [great lawyer] to expound and interpret it. It will not lay down one rule at Rome and another at Athens, nor will it be one rule today and another tomorrow. But there will be one law, eternal and unchangeable, binding at all times upon all peoples; and there will be, as it were, one common master and ruler of men, namely God, who is the author of this law, its interpreter, and its sponsor.[5]

J. L. Brierly, in 1928, attempted to distinguish contemporary natural law from the notions expressed by Roman and medieval writers. His writing attempts to establish a variable content for the "absolutes" of natural law.

When a modern lawyer asks what is reasonable, he looks only for an answer that is valid now and here, and not for one that is finally true; whereas a medieval writer might have said that if ultimate truth eludes our grasp, it is not because it is undiscoverable, but because our reasoning is imperfect. Some modern writers have expressed this difference by saying that what we have a right to believe in today is a law of nature with a *variable content*.[6]

The English lawyer, Sir Frederick Pollock, reasoned that "the law of nature . . . is a living embodiment of the collective reason of civilized mankind."[7] These modern-day natural law philosophers seem to agree with Jerome Hall, who argued that "value is an essential element" in American jurisprudence.[8] Nevertheless, the more modern proponents of natural law reject the notion that the content of natural law is specific, permanent, and unchangeable.

LEGAL POSITIVISM: LAW AS THE EXPRESSION OF POLITICAL POWER

Legal positivists argue that law is the command of the highest political authority. To posit means to put, place, or impose something. Hence, legal positivists view law as that which is laid down or "posited" by the highest authority. The nineteenth-century English lawyer, John Austin, wrote, "The subject matter of jurisprudence is positive law: . . . law set by political superiors to political inferiors."[9] Legal positivists assert that law is derived from some "basic norm" or superior lawful authority. For example, a judicial decision is lawful if it has been rendered in conformity with the Constitution. The legal positivists, therefore, believe that laws are the logical and consistent rules derived from the "basic norm." The philosophical writings of a positivist are either the logical analysis of a derived rule or the continuous searching for a basic norm on which to base the derived legal rule. The basic norm can take a variety of forms: a constitution, an assembly, a sovereign (king), or a mere acknowledgment of existing authority in some particular code or idea such as the Magna Carta. For example, Hans Kelsen has written the following.

If we ask why the constitution is valid, perhaps we come upon an older constitution. Ultimately we reach some constitution that is the first historically and that was laid down by an individual usurper or by some kind of assembly. The validity of this first constitution is the last presupposition, the final postulate, upon which the validity of all the norms of our legal order depends.[10]

Legal positivists also believe that ethical principles have no relevance to the study of law. Their concern is with the law "as it is" and not with law "as it should be." In contrast to the natural law proponents, they believe that value judgments have no place in the study of law.

THE HISTORICAL SCHOOL: LAW AS CUSTON AND TRADITION

German jurists were among the first to state that law is not something that can be developed by a mind that understands and knows law (as in natural law theory) independent of experience. Likewise, to them a rule could not be put forth arbitrarily by a political authority (as in legal positivism). Law was to be understood only in terms of the history of a particular race. Such an approach was clearly a challenge to both the natural law theory and legal positivism.

One of the earliest German advocates of the historical conception of law, Friedrich Karl Von Savigny, has written:

In the earliest times to which authentic history extends, the law will be found to have already obtained a fixed character, peculiar to the people, like their language, manners and constitution. Nay, these phenomena have no separate existence, they are but the particular facilities and tendencies of an individual people inseparably united in nature, and only wearing the semblance of distinct attributes in our view. That which binds them into one whole is the common conviction of the people, the kindred consciousness of an inward necessity, excluding all notion of an accidental and arbitrary origin. . . .

But this organic connection of law with the being and character of the people, is also manifested in the progress of the times; and here again, it may be compared with language. For law, as for language, there is no moment of absolute cessation; it is subject to the same movement and development of every other popular tendency; and this very development remains under the same law of inward necessity, as in its earliest states. Law grows with the growth, and strengthens with the strength of the people, and finally dies away as the nation loses its nationality.[11]

Consequently, historical jurisprudence holds that law develops with the social development of the people or nation. For example, they argue that law is often older than the nation itself; that national government is a subsequent development representing a more mature legal system that was matured with the society itself. Thereafter, as customs and cultural values change, law evolves also. As the great American jurist, Oliver Wendell Holmes, Jr., expounded:

The life of the law has not been logic; it has been experience. The felt necessities of the time, the prevalent moral and political theories, intuitions of public policy, avowed or unconscious, even the prejudices which judges share with their fellow men, have had a good deal more to do than the syllogism in determining the rules by which men should be governed. The law embodies the story of a nation's development through many centuries, and it cannot be dealt with as if it contained only the axioms and corollaries of a book of mathematics. In order to know what it is, we must know what it has been, and what it tends to become. We must alternately consult history and existing theories of legislation. But the most difficult labor will be to understand the combination of the two into new products at every stage. The substance of the law at any given time pretty nearly corresponds, so far as it goes, with what is then understood to be convenient; but its form and machinery, and the degree to which it is able to work out desired results, depend very much upon its past.[12]

INSTRUMENTALISM: LAW AS AN INSTRUMENT OF SOCIAL ORDER

The historical school of legal philosophy resulted in many derivative philosophies. One such derived philosophy could be labeled *instrumentalism*. A modern exponent of instrumentalism is Wolfgang Friedmann, who wrote that "law is not a brooding omnipresence in the sky, but a flexible instrument of social order, dependent on the political values of the society which it purports to regulate." Moreover, he contends, "law must . . . respond to social change if it is to fulfill its function as a paramount instrument of social order."[13]

Besides being adaptable to new social conditions, the law, according to instrumentalists, must be understandable to the public so that it will be respected and followed. However, since much of today's law has become so complex and largely unknown to the public, it is the public's faith in the "ideals" of the law that cause them to continue to uphold and respect the law. If the citizens retain their faith that the law is rational and philosophically sound, law will remain an instrument of social order.

In addition, instrumentalists believe law is the pragmatic decision making of the processes that make or enact the law. A pragmatist follows a trial-and-error methodology to develop an acceptable solution to a social problem. Legal pragmatists likewise use a trial-and-error technique to formulate the most appropriate law. Moreover, the pragmatist views law as a social instrument for the direction and control of individuals and group activities. Bently commented that, "The law at bottom can only be what the mass of people actually does and tends to some extent to make other people do by means of governmental agencies."[14]

Questions

1. How do you define law? Does your definition depend on your legal philosophy? Would the organized mass murders of the Nazi regime qualify as law to the positivist? To the theorist of natural law?
2. If you were the leader of a revolution against a tyrannical government, which legal philosophy would you probably declare to your followers?
3. Can you differentiate between law and justice?
4. Do natural law philosophers think all laws come from "highest reason" or God? What about a traffic law to drive on the right side of the road?
5. Karl Llewellyn's notion that law is created by officials' manipulation of rules is an expression similar to which basic philosophy?

THE AMERICAN SYSTEM OF LAWMAKING

The philosophical underpinnings of the United States combine English and natural law ideals with American pragmatism and the desire to be ruled by the governed. The American legal system is effective not so much because of its power to levy penalties on those who interfere with the legal rights of others, but because Americans generally believe in the American ideals embodied in their legal system and its evolutionary processes of lawmaking.

CONSTITUTIONS

Constitutions allocate power to govern among governmental departments and impose limitations on the exercise of governmental powers. For example, the Constitution of the United States is the supreme law of the land. One basic objective of this "supreme law" is to allocate governing power between the federal and state governments, the results of which are referred to as *federalism*. A second objective is to allocate governing power between three separate federal departments, that is, the legislative, the executive, and the judicial. A third objective of the Constitution is to protect the civil rights of persons within the United States by designating specific limitations on the powers of government.

State constitutions achieve similar objectives at the state level.

Federalism

Many of the colonies had drawn up their own constitutions before the colonies declared war to achieve independence. In contrast, the first national constitution (the Articles of Confederation) was adopted after the war of independence and was in substance a document regulating a league or group of independent states that were joined together but not controlled by the union.

Subsequent problems between the states on matters of boundaries and economic affairs led to the creation of a new national constitution that not only specified the structure and powers of the national government but also contained limitations and restrictions on the powers of the state governments. The new national constitution also took away certain powers from the states and gave them to the national government.

Under the U.S. Constitution all powers not delegated to the United States or prohibited by the Constitution are reserved to the states. This reservation merely confirms the fact that the states only surrendered to the national government those powers expressly delegated by the Constitution. The states retained the powers of policing, taxation, and eminent domain, as well as other powers that may be exercised by a sovereign. Perhaps the broadest power possessed by the states to control business affairs is the police power, which is defined as the power of the state to enact laws for the health, safety, morals, and general welfare of its citizens. In a general sense, this is the power to govern.

In contrast, the national government has enumerated, limited powers. It may act only on those powers that the Constitution grants to it in Article I, Section 8. State governments, however, possess concurrent powers with the national government when the enumerated national powers are not made exclusively the domain of the national government. As long as a state law does not conflict with any national laws in these areas, the states may concurrently regulate the same subject area. However, when state laws attempt to regulate in an area exclusively delegated to the federal government or when their laws conflict with a federal government regulation in those areas in which concurrent regulation is allowed, state regulations become void. The differing factual issues that may concern the extent of national preemption in the area of concurrent powers often creates conflicting views as to the proper balance of power between the federal and state governments.

Separation of Powers

The separation of powers in the Constitution involves the creation of and the vesting of legislative (Article I), executive (Article II), and judicial (Article III) powers of government in three separate and independent branches. The purpose of the separation of powers, in the words of Justice Brandeis, is "not to promote efficiency but to preclude the exercise of arbitrary power. The purpose is, not to avoid frictions, but, by means of the inevitable friction incident to the distribution of the governmental power among the departments, to save the people from autocracy."[15]

Each branch is independent in that persons holding office in one branch do not owe their tenure to the will or preferences of persons in the other branches. Also, the Constitution makes clear that the office in one branch may not usurp or encroach on the powers vested in another branch. However, this constitutional prohibition does not limit the voluntary delegation by the legislature of some of its functions. Because statutes, of necessity, must be drafted in general terms, Congress leaves to the executive, the judiciary, or some administrative agencies the task of making detailed secondary rules to enforce the general mandate expressed in the statute. Also, Congress created courts, such as the Customs Court, and administrative agencies, which embody judicial functions that are not within the judicial branch of government. These apparent violations of the separation of powers doctrine have been tolerated by the Supreme Court as a "quasi-judicial" function, different from a purely judicial task. These deviations illustrate that the separation of powers is a general constitutional principle or ideal that was never conceived or made operational as a rigid rule. Sometimes the pragmatic desire for efficiency overshadows the ideal of separation of powers, especially where no sacrifice of independence is observed.

Constitutional Limitations

A third objective of the U.S. Constitution is to protect the civil rights of persons within the United States by designating specific limitations on the powers of government. These limitations protect individuals from arbitrary and unjust treatment by governmental officials. Besides the lesser known limitations contained in the Constitution, such as prohibitions against *ex post facto* laws and bills of attainder, the first 10 Amendments to the Constitution (Bill of Rights) contain the more generally known limitations on governmental powers. The First Amendment contains protections for speech, press, assembly, and religion. Other amendments protect the rights to bear arms and to have jury trials. The Fourth Amendment protects persons from unreasonable searches and seizures. Amendment Five requires the *federal* government to follow "due process of law"before any person's "life, liberty, or property" may be taken. Amendments

Thirteen through Fifteen, added after the Civil War, eliminate slavery and require *state* governments, like the federal government, to grant persons "due process of law" before depriving them of life, liberty, or property. If any state officials deny due process of law to any person, the federal judiciary is available to correct the state officials.

LEGISLATIVE LAWMAKING

A legislature is an organized body of persons having the authority to make laws for a political unit. While the concept of representative legislative bodies is as old as the Greek philosophers, the existence of such legislative bodies in America is less the result of Greek philosophy and more the result of the evolutionary growth of power by the "privy council" of the English monarchs. The monarchs selected certain aristocrats to serve on the privy council and provide the monarch with advice or financial assistance. As the power of the council grew in comparison with that of the monarchs, the legislative method of lawmaking began in England. Ultimately, the members of the legislatures became elected representatives of the people, rather than appointed by the monarchs.

In America, conventions of representatives of the people have prepared written constitutions. All legislative bodies were constitutionally created. Article I, Section I of the U.S. Constitution provides, "All legislative power herein granted shall be vested in a Congress of the United States, which shall consist of a Senate and House of Representatives." State legislative bodies were created by the respective state constitutions. The laws created by such legislative bodies are variously called statutes, enactments, acts, or legislation.

The process by which Congress enacts a federal statute is typical of most legislative procedures. Congress is divided into two chambers, the "upper house" or Senate and "lower house" or House of Representatives. Each house sets its own procedural rules, determines the qualifications of its members, and may discipline its own members. Each also has special powers of its own; for example, the House of Representatives alone has the power to impeach civil officers of the United States, including the President. Officers impeached by the House of Representatives are tried by the Senate, which may convict on a vote of two thirds of its members. The Senate alone may consent to treaties with foreign nations and approve or disapprove of presidential nominations to most offices, civil or military. Bills, which are proposed laws, may originate in either house, except that all revenue-raising legislation (tariffs and tax bills) must, according to the U.S. Constitution, originate in the House of Representatives. By custom, bills of appropriations originate there as well.

The Senate is composed of 100 members, two for each State of the Union. Senators are elected by their home states for six-year terms.

Figure 4-1. How a bill becomes law. (Reprinted with the permission of Congressional Quarterly Inc.)

HOW A BILL BECOMES LAW

This graphic shows the most typical way in which proposed legislation is enacted into law. There are more complicated, as well as simpler, routes, and most bills fall by the wayside and never become law. The process is illustrated with two hypothetical bills, House bill No. 1 (HR 1) and Senate bill No. 2 (S 2).

Each bill must be passed by both houses of Congress in identical form before it can become law. The path of HR 1 is traced by a solid line, that of S 2 by a broken line. However, in practice most legislation begins as similar proposals in both houses.

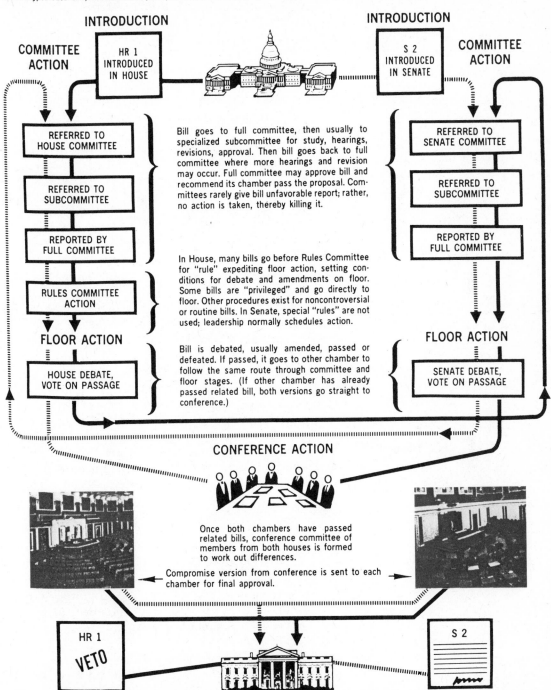

INTRODUCTION

HR 1 INTRODUCED IN HOUSE

COMMITTEE ACTION

REFERRED TO HOUSE COMMITTEE

REFERRED TO SUBCOMMITTEE

REPORTED BY FULL COMMITTEE

RULES COMMITTEE ACTION

FLOOR ACTION

HOUSE DEBATE, VOTE ON PASSAGE

INTRODUCTION

S 2 INTRODUCED IN SENATE

COMMITTEE ACTION

REFERRED TO SENATE COMMITTEE

REFERRED TO SUBCOMMITTEE

REPORTED BY FULL COMMITTEE

FLOOR ACTION

SENATE DEBATE, VOTE ON PASSAGE

Bill goes to full committee, then usually to specialized subcommittee for study, hearings, revisions, approval. Then bill goes back to full committee where more hearings and revision may occur. Full committee may approve bill and recommend its chamber pass the proposal. Committees rarely give bill unfavorable report; rather, no action is taken, thereby killing it.

In House, many bills go before Rules Committee for "rule" expediting floor action, setting conditions for debate and amendments on floor. Some bills are "privileged" and go directly to floor. Other procedures exist for noncontroversial or routine bills. In Senate, special "rules" are not used; leadership normally schedules action.

Bill is debated, usually amended, passed or defeated. If passed, it goes to other chamber to follow the same route through committee and floor stages. (If other chamber has already passed related bill, both versions go straight to conference.)

CONFERENCE ACTION

Once both chambers have passed related bills, conference committee of members from both houses is formed to work out differences.

Compromise version from conference is sent to each chamber for final approval.

HR 1 VETO

S 2

Compromise version approved by both houses is sent to President who can either sign it into law or veto it and return it to Congress. Congress may override veto by a two-thirds majority vote in both houses; bill then becomes law without President's signature.

The number of members of the House of Representatives is set at 435, each representing a district. Districts are reapportioned following each decennial census, so that their populations are, as nearly as is practical, equal. Consequently the various states are not equally represented in the House of Representatives. A Representative serves a two year term.

The Vice President of the United States serves as presiding officer of the Senate, as its President. His functions are primarily procedural; he votes only in the event of a tie. His presence during sessions is not necessary, and the Senate elects a President Pro Tempore to serve in his absence. The President of the Senate refers bills to Senate committees according to their respective jurisdictions for consideration.

The Speaker of the House of Representatives, its presiding officer, is a more powerful figure than the President of the Senate. He is elected by the House and is sure to be a senior member of the majority party. He conducts the proceedings when the House is in session, assigns bills to committees, and appoints members of select and conference committees.

Lobbyists

Only members of Congress may introduce bills, but only rarely is a bill the handiwork of a sponsoring Congressman. When the executive branch of government prepares legislative programs, they are introduced by friendly members of Congress. Special-interest groups and reform organizations also draw up legislative proposals and seek congressional members for sponsorship. Lobbyists, persons paid to gain support for the interests they represent, seek legislative sponsors for their clients. After a bill is introduced, lobbyists advise and encourage legislators to support the introduced bill. Lobbyists, if their principal paid occupation is to affect legislation, must register with the federal government. They provide legislators with logical arguments and information in an effort to convince the legislators not only to vote in favor of a particular piece of legislation, but to support it in congressional deliberations and to convince other legislators to approve it as well. Lobbyists can be a useful source of reliable information, and if they are not, they normally find their effectiveness is slight.

Committees

Once a bill is introduced in either house of Congress, it is referred by the presiding officer to a committee for consideration. Because of the bulk of proposed legislation, and the technical nature of much of it, Congress could not function without the use of specialized committees. Congress utilizes standing committees, but often resorts to a select or special committee. Joint or conference committees are composed of members from both houses. Any of these committees may be further divided into subcommittees. (See Figure 4-2.)

The standing legislative committees review legislative proposals and eventually report out bills, indicating the action they recommend be taken. While holding the bill the committee or subcommittee, or both consecutively, may hold public hearings on the merits of the bill, require the testimony of individuals and the production of documents, and make expenditures for its investigation.

Select committees do not report out legislation. They are formed to investigate specific problems and make recommendations to the full House or Senate.

Joint committees coordinate activities of the separate houses during the committee-hearing phase of the legislative cycle, but they do not report out legislation. A conference committee is formed when the House and Senate have each passed similar but not identical legislation. The committee's task is to work out the differences in the bills and send a compromise bill to both houses for enactment.

The real work of Congress takes place in the committees. Most bills "die" in committee from inaction, but better than two thirds of those bills reported out of a committee are ultimately passed.

Each political party chooses its members for the standing committees through its own Committee on Committees. The committee elects a chairman, customarily the majority party member with the most seniority on the committee. The chairman sets committee meeting times, controls the agenda, creates subcommittees and determines which bills to refer to those subcommittees, and hires the professional committee staff. A majority of a committee may schedule meetings without the agreement of the chairman, but ordinarily will not. The chairman will support his committee's action before the Rules Committee in the House, may lead the floor debate on bills reported by his committee, and will serve on a conference committee dealing with a bill from his committee.

A committee chairman can wield considerable power over proposed legislation in his committee by referring to subcommittees matters he knows will be favorable or unfavorable to a particular proposal, by failing to put on the agenda matters that he opposes, and by making use of political influence over other committee members. Committee and subcommittee hearings can attract a substantial amount of public attention. The committee may call on witnesses for information or opinion, and a failure to testify is punishable by imprisonment until the end of the session of Congress. On important legislation, hearings can extend for weeks or months.

A subcommittee may amend or modify the bill, or even rework it completely before referring it back to the full committee for consideration. The full committee may then hold additional public hearings and make further amendments, deletions, or modifications even though its own subcommittee has already done so. The full committee can also simply refuse to consider the bill, despite a favorable recommendation from a subcommittee. It is a committee function to screen out those bills that it deems unworthy of consideration by the full chamber. Once a majority of a committee votes in support of a bill, in its original form or as amended or modified, it is "reported out," or referred to the full house along with a report expressing both the views of the majority who supported it and the minority who opposed it.

In the House of Representatives, the bill is then referred to the Rules Com-

Senate Standing Committees	Number of members	Number of subcommittes
Agriculture, Nutrition and Forestry	17	7
Appropriations	29	13
Armed Services	15	7
Banking, Housing and Urban Affairs	17	6
Budget	22	0
Commerce, Science and Transportation	17	7
Energy and Natural Resources	20	6
Environment and Public Works	16	6
Finance	20	9
Foreign Relations	17	7
Governmental Affairs	17	8
Judiciary	18	9
Labor and Human Resources	16	7
Rules and Administration	12	0
Small Business	17	8
Veterans' Affairs	12	0
<u>Select and Special</u>		
Ethics	6	0
Indian Affairs	7	0
Intelligence	15	4
Aging	15	0

House Standing Committees		
Agriculture	43	8
Appropriations	55	13
Armed Services	44	7
Banking, Finance and Urban Affairs	43	8
Budget	30	9*
District of Columbia	12	3
Education and Labor	34	8
Energy and Commerce	42	6
Foreign Affairs	36	8
Government Operations	40	7
House Administration	20	6
Interior and Insular Affairs	42	6
Judiciary	28	7
Merchant Marine and Fisheries	36	5
Post Office and Civil Service	24	7
Public Works and Transportation	46	6
Rules	16	2
Science and Technology	40	7
Small Business	39	6
Standards of Official Conduct	12	0
Veterans' Affairs	29	5
Ways and Means	35	6

Figure 4-2. Committees of Congress

<u>Select and Special</u>		
Federal Government Service Task Force	4	0
House Recording Studio	3	0
(Permanent) Intelligence	14	0
Aging	54	4
Narcotics Abuse and Control	18	0
Joint Committtees		
Library of Congress	10	
Printing	10	
Taxation	10	
Economic	20	

*These subdivisions are called "task forces" rather than subcomittees.

Source: Congressional Directory, 1981.

Figure 4.2 Committees of Congress

mittee. The Rules Committee schedules the business to be considered by the House and sets rules for the conduct of business; it limits the time allowed for debate on a bill and limits the number of amendments that may be made to the bill on the floor. The Rules Committee does not put bills on the calendar in the order they are reported out, but in whatever order it finds expedient. The Rules Committee may hold a reported bill indefinitely and thus delay or block its passage. Although the House may deliver a "discharge petition," which requires that a bill be brought out of any committee, including the Rules Committee, a discharge petition must bear the signature of 218 Representatives. Such a petition's passage would be a considerable political feat, given the power of Rules Committee members. The Speaker may order a bill out of the Rules Committee under the "21 Day Rule"; if 21 or more days have elapsed since the matter was referred to the Rules Committee. The 21 Day Rule is only in effect, however, if it was adopted on the opening day of the session.

The Senate has no counterpart to the Rules Committee. The Senate itself determines which reported bills to consider. Once a bill is on the Senate floor, its rules permit unlimited debate on the measure. Once a Senator has the floor, he may speak without interruption until his remarks are concluded, whether or not they are relevant to the matter under debate. Consequently, a Senator or group of Senators may delay or block action on proposed legislation by continuously speaking and refusing to yield the floor, a "filibuster." The filibuster is often used to prevent action on a proposal before the end of a session, or to force the Senate to act favorably on some other matter before returning to the suspended debate. A filibuster may be stopped if three fifths of all Senators (60) vote for cloture. The cloture rule has been used only rarely; the votes are difficult to gather.

Floor Proceedings

Once a bill is on the floor of either house of Congress, further amendments may be attached. An extraneous amendment, or rider, may be attached for practical purposes or to assist or impede passage of the bill. An unpopular rider may be attached to a bill that has strong support from the administration, thereby attempting to force its approval by the President. A bill might become so crippled by amendments and riders that it never passes the house, or so watered down that it is ineffective.

The proceedings on the floors of both houses of Congress are recorded in full and published each day that Congress is in session in the *Congressional Record.* Legislators may "extend their remarks in the *Record*" by submitting for publication in the *Record* material that was never presented on the floor. This is one technique legislators use to firmly establish their position on issues.

Besides the *Congressional Record,* unofficial commercial publications, such as the *Congressional Quarterly* and the *Congressional Digest,* contain information concerning pending legislation and other materials, such as reports of lobbying expenditures and appropriations of funds to various committees.

One of the more important agencies of Congress is the General Accounting Office (GAO). It was created to assist the Congress in controlling the receipt, disbursement, and application of public funds by conducting studies and audits of federally funded programs. The reports of the GAO often have substantial impact on Congress, which may modify federal funding or "powers" of the various authorities studied by the GAO.

Questions
1. What are the two houses of Congress? Which house originates legislation to raise revenue or to appropriate funds?
2. What is the duration of the term of a Senator? A Representative?
3. What official is the presiding officer of the Senate? Of the House?
4. What functions does a lobbyist perform?
5. What are the functions of congressional committees?
6. Why is a committee chairman a powerful position?
7. What is the function of a conference committee?
8. What is the Rules Committee?
9. What is a "filibuster"? How might other members of Congress terminate a filibuster?
10. Which journal publishes the proceedings of Congress?
11. What is the function of the General Accounting Office?

EXECUTIVE LAWMAKING

Article II of the U.S. Constitution provides that "the executive power shall be vested in a president." The office of the President is often referred to as "the world's most demanding job." Clinton Rossiter identified the following ten functions performed by the President: (1) Chief of State (by serving as the ceremonial head of government); (2) Chief Executive (in administering the day-to-day activities of the Executive Branch); (3) Commander in Chief (of the military forces); (4) Chief Diplomat (in executing foreign policy); (5) Chief Legislator (in urging particular legislation to Congress); (6) Chief of the Party (by directing his party); (7) Voice of the People (in emphasizing the nation's "unfinished business"); (8) Protector of the People (by maintaining domestic order); (9) Manager of Prosperity (by suggesting policies to maintain full employment, high production levels, economic growth, price stability, etc.); and (10) World Leader (in acting as the leader of the "Free World").[16] These functions are clearly important in understanding the role of the President as a formal source of social change and of change in the laws governing economic activities.

Obviously, the President cannot be familiar with the detailed operation of every governmental department, program, or agency. The President must rely on the advisors and assistants who make up the Executive Office of the President. (See Figure 4-3.) Beside the assistants in the Executive Office of the President, there are also 12 Executive Departments that make up the Cabinet. (See Figure 4-4.) It is easily observed that personal Presidential oversight of the executive branch is impossible. The President depends on the delegation of authority to subordinates and the selection of effective, competent individuals to administer the delegated authority.

Presidential Lobbying

While the President may submit proposals for legislation to Congress, he cannot force Congress to adopt his proposals. Consequently, he must use informal techniques, including persuasion, the granting and withholding of favors, and television broadcasts to encourage the electorate to exert pressure on members of Congress.

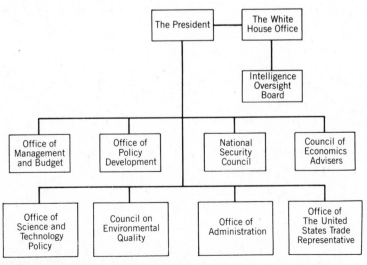

Figure 4-3. Executive Office of the President.

Organization	Total Paid Employees (as of January 1, each year)		
	1980	1970	1960
Executive Office of the President	1,897	4,044	2,814
Executive Departments	1,706,938	2,570,109	2,017,487
1. Department of Agriculture	122,259	106,484	86,508
2. Department of Commerce	42,142	30,823	62,531
3. Department of Defense	960,063	1,272,800	1,052,262
Office of the Secretary of Defense	76,891	69,546	1,759
Department of the Air Force	233,471	321,849	316,294
Department of the Army	343,773	469,297	385,905
Department of the Navy	305,928	402,108	348,304
4. Department of Energy	20,988	—	—
5. Department of Health, Education and Welfare	163,883	106,280	59,898
6. Department of Housing and Urban Development	16,862	14,777	—
7. Department of the Interior	79,905	67,880	50,002
8. Department of Justice	55,737	36,505	29,996
9. Department of Labor	24,220	10,479	6,182
10. Department of State	23,738	41,547	36,715
11. Department of Transportation	73,364	62,189	—
12. Department of Treasury	123,777	88,884	74,200
Independent Agencies	1,118,186	335,401	331,485
1. Consumer Product Safety Commission	927	—	—
2. Environmental Protection Agency	12,891	—	—
3. Equal Employment Opportunity Commission	3,622	645	—
4. Federal Communications Commission	2,233	1,487	1,277
5. Federal Deposit Insurance Corporation	3,598	2,242	1,234
6. Federal Emergency Management Agency	2,300	—	—
7. Federal Home Loan Bank Board	1,524	1,216	961
8. Federal Reserve System	1,456	—	—
9. Federal Trade Commission	2,032	1,268	735
10. General Services Administration	37,936	37,894	27,326
11. International Communications Agency	8,235	—	—
12. International Development Cooperation Agency	6,004	—	—
13. Interstate Commerce Commission	2,092	1,813	2,316
14. National Aeronautics and Space Administration	23,179	32,882	9,665
15. National Labor Relations Board	3,032	2,239	1,624
16. National Science Foundation	2,477	1,735	803
17. Nuclear Regulatory Commission	3,078	—	—
18. Occupational Safety and Health Review Commission	183	—	—
19. Office of Personnel Management	8,069	—	—
20. Securities and Exchange Commission	2,155	1,390	945
21. Small Business Administration	6,225	4,202	2,122
22. Tennessee Valley Authority	49,930	20,677	13,916
23. U.S. Postal Service	683,242	741,461	559,193
24. Veterans Administration	230,538	166,502	172,954
25. Others (38 agencies)	21,228	30,720	25,247

Figure 4-4. Federal executive departments and agencies.

Total, Executive Branch	2,827,021	2,909,554	2,351,786
Total, Legislative Branch	39,334	28,349	22,242
Total, Judicial Branch	14,117	6,713	4,933
Total	2,880,472	2,944,616	2,378,961

Source: Derived from the chart, Organization of Federal Executive Departments and Agencies, DOC Y4.G 74/9: Ex 3/980/Chart.

Figure 4.4 Federal Executive Departments and Agencies

Proposals for legislation may be initiated by any of the departments or agencies within the Executive Branch. Also, under existing law, bills introduced in Congress without the prior consultation of the executive branch must be sent by the relevant committee chairman to the relevant executive agency for comment.

The Office of Management and Budget (OMB) is a part of the Executive Office of the President. The OMB's administrative functions include an examination of *all* proposed legislation, and clearing and coordinating departmental advice on proposed legislation. In this manner, differences between the various departments within the Executive Branch are ironed out, if possible. The OMB attempts to ensure that the administration speaks with a single voice to the Congress.

Once a bill has been passed by both houses of Congress, it is forwarded to the President for his signature. Under the Constitution, the President may sign the bill into law or may veto the bill by returning it to the house in which it originated. If the President takes no action within 10 days following his receipt of the bill, it becomes law "unless the Congress by their Adjournment prevent its Return, in which Case it shall not be a Law." Thus, congressional adjournment after transmittal of the bill to the President affords the President with the opportunity of a "pocket veto" by simply doing nothing.

While a presidential veto may be overriden by Congress, it takes a two-thirds vote of each house to override the President's veto. Accordingly, the veto power is a formidable weapon in the arsenal of the President that may be used to urge Congress to adopt legislation he favors and to avoid legislation he dislikes.

Presidential "Legislating"

Besides lobbying Congress to support legislation desired by the President, there is another sense in which the President may engage in legislative activity. The President may issue orders or legislate directly in performing his duties.

Executive orders are legislative acts performed by the executive branch. Such orders result from the congressional adoption of broad legislative policy statements and the delegation of authority to the executive branch for the implementation of such policies. This implementation generally takes the form of an executive order, published in the *Federal Register*.

For example, Executive Order 11246 charges the Secretary of Labor with ensuring that corporations that benefit from government contracts provide equal employment opportunity regardless of race or sex. Consequently, regulations promulgated by the Department of Labor's Office or Federal Contract Compliance Programs require government contractors to furnish reports about their Affirmative Action Programs and the general composition of their workforces. Also, pursuant to Executive Order 11246, such records must be made available for public inspection if not otherwise prohibited by law. One can easily surmise the impact on corporations that the disclosure of these reports may have. Likewise, one can recognize the significant power residing in the President to issue these kinds of executive orders and thereby significantly modify the operative rules of economic activity.

The handling of the foreign relations of this country is also an executive function. As such, the President has the power to enact executive agreements with other nations or with international organizations without the specific approval of Congress or the Senate in particular. In addition, some international executive agreements may be made pursuant to some expressed delegation of power by Congress.

In exercising this power to make executive agreements, the President engages in legislative functions that may bring about changes in the rules governing economic affairs. For example, reciprocal trade agreements have been implemented by means of an executive agreement. The General Agreement on Tariffs and Trade (GATT) is an executive agreement program that has become a permanent part of the Executive Office of the President. The tariff negotiations conducted under this executive agreement have been undertaken pursuant to a delegation of authority contained in an amendment to the Tariff Act of 1934. Such international agreements also have prohibited the exportation of arms and ammunition from the United States to certain countries.

Thus, it appears clear that changes in law can result from activities of the executive branch. The theory of the separation of powers has limited application in the real world of executive lawmaking.

Questions
1. What variety of functions is performed by the Office of the Presidency?
2. Why is the Office of Management and Budget important to the Presidency?
3. What does it take for Congress to override a presidential veto or legislation?
4. How does the President "legislate"?

JUDICIAL LAWMAKING

The judiciary is also a source of law. Judges "make law" when they interpret a statute or constitutional provision. The court's interpretation of the statute or the Constitution and its application of that interpretation to the particular factual setting of the case before it gives meaning to the statute or the Constitution. Such interpretations can have more importance than the actual legislative provision itself.

Much judge-made law predates the rise to power of the legislature in England. The "lords" of the manors settled controversies between residents of the manor and, in effect, made laws that were to apply to similar controversies in the future. The doctrine under which past judicial decisions are used to decide present controversies is called *stare decisis* ("let the decision stand"). The effect of the doctrine of *stare decisis* is to cause judicial decisions to have a prospective effect as law for subsequent, similar cases. Judge-made law is traditionally referred to as "common law"—a name first given to the rules fashioned by royal judges, who rode throughout England creating rules that were to be common for all Englanders.

Judicial laws are largely formulated in appellate courts. Appellate courts attempt to obtain uniformity in law by resolving conflicting lower court decisions that differ on the interpretation of law. This appellate review necessitates a written opinion by the court to explain exactly which legal questions it is resolving, on which facts, and which reasons are given for the decision. The result of these appellate decisions is to clarify the court's conception of the current state of the law or to declare new law as modern social conditions warrant. The process of issuing written opinions subjects the appellate court's decision to public scrutiny and criticism. Once a legal principle is accepted and cited as precedent, it is continually tested and refined by the courts in light of any changes that may have occurred in technology, social conditions, economic theory, or concepts of morality. Nevertheless, the application of the principle of *stare decisis* creates stability in the judge-made law and provides discipline in the judicial system. Lower court judges are bound to follow precedents in their jurisdictions or to face reversal by a higher court. Similarly, the doctrine tends to prevent appellate courts themselves from vacillating in the application of legal principles. The appellate courts recognize that "adherence to precedent must . . . be the rule rather than the exception if litigants are to have faith in the evenhanded administration of justice in the courts."[17]

ADMINISTRATIVE LAWMAKING

The rapid development and complexity of the American economy gave rise to a public concern for the regulation of industry and trade to prevent abuses that might be detrimental to society. Initially, Congress attempted to legislate rules of proper conduct and have the attorney general's office enforce the laws. It soon became apparent, however, that this form of regulation was neither adequate nor effective, and in some instances was impossible. The constant supervision and inspection necessary to ensure compliance with the rules of regulation could not be fulfilled by either the legislature, the executive, or the judicial branches of government. Thus, there was a recognized need for a government body that was equipped for continuous supervision and that had the particular expertise required to cope with the technicalities of a dynamic economy. The complexity of the business environment, therefore, dictated the choice of the device of the administrative agency as a necessary instrument for the effective supervision and regulation of business activities. An administrative agency is any governmental authority other than courts and legislative bodies. Such an agency may be called a commission, bureau, authority, board, office, department, administration, division, or agency.

The administrative process is the combination of methods and procedures used by administrative agencies in carrying out their tasks. Administrative law attempts to control governmental machinery and programs. Administrative law does not include the substantive law produced by the administrative agencies, such as tax law, labor law, securities law, and so forth.

The administrative agency is normally embodied with functions usually carried out by the three separate branches of government. An administrative agency may exercise the legislative function by formulating rules to govern a particular trade or a specific business practice. The agency exercises an executive function when it investigates business activities and enforces its rules of proper conduct. Finally, the agency is empowered with the judicial function to hold a hearing and to determine if a particular defendant has violated any of the agency's rules.

INTERACTION OF LAWMAKING PROCESSES

It has already been noted that the purpose of the Separation of Power Doctrine is to prevent autocratic rule. Separating the powers and providing a system of checks and balances protects the people from autocracy, but requires frequent interaction among the branches of government in the formulation of laws. For example, a congressional enactment needs presidential approval to become law, unless Congress is able to override a Presidential veto. Likewise, a treaty negotiated by the executive branch needs Senate ratification. It should also be noted that the legislative branch has the power to change judge-made "common law" by enacting legislation. Moreover, if the legislature disapproves of judicial interpretation of a statute, the legislature may amend the statute to overturn the court's interpretation. However, the judiciary has the power of constitutional interpretation, which may restrict the other branches of government. It is explicitly stated in the Constitution that the laws of the federal government in those areas enumerated by the Constitution are supreme over conflicting state laws. However, there is no clause in the Constitution granting supremacy of the judicial branch in determining whether or not an action by another branch (executive or legislative) is constitutional. Accordingly there have been great debates since the earliest date of the Union concerning the right of the judiciary to require the legislative and executive branches to conform to the judiciary's conceptions of constitutional requirements. The power of judicial review of the legislative branch was first asserted in the *Marbury* case of 1803.

Writing for the court, Chief Justice Marshall declared:

[T]he people have an original right to establish . . . their . . . government. . . . This original and supreme will organizes the government, and assigns to different departments their respective powers. It may either stop here, or establish certain limits not to be transcended by those departments.

The government of the United States is of the latter description. The powers of the legislature are defined and limited; and that those limits may not be mistaken, or forgotten, the constitution is written. To what purpose are powers limited, and to what purpose is that limitation committed to writing, if these limits may, at any time, be passed by those intended to be restrained? The distinction between a government with limited and unlimited powers is abolished, if those limits do not confine the persons on whom they are imposed. . . .

The constitution is either a superior paramount law, unchangeable by ordinary means, or it is on a level with ordinary legislative acts, and, like other acts, is alterable when the legislature shall please to alter it.

If the former part of the alternative be true, then a legislative act, contrary to the constitution, is not law: if the latter part be true, then written constitutions are absurd attempts on the part of the people, to limit a power, in its own nature, illimitable.

Certainly, all those who have framed written constitutions contemplate them as forming the fundamental and paramount law of the nation, and consequently, the theory of every such government must be that an act of the legislature, repugnant to the constitution, is void.

This theory is essentially attached to a written constitution, and is, consequently, to be considered, by this court, as one of the fundamental principles of our society. . . .

It is, emphatically, the province and duty of the judicial department to say what the law is. Those who apply the rule to particular cases, must of necessity expound and interpret that rule. If two laws conflict with each other, the courts must decide on the operation of each.

* * *

If then, the courts are to regard the constitution, and the constitution is superior to any ordinary act of the legislature, the constitution, and not such ordinary act, must govern the case to which they both apply. . . .

It is also not entirely unworthy of observation, that in declaring what shall be the *supreme* law of the land, the constitution itself is first mentioned; and not the laws of the United States generally, but those only which shall be made in *pursuance* of the constitution, have that rank.

Thus, the particular phraseology of the constitution of the United States confirms and strengthens the principle, supposed to be essential to all written constitutions, that a law repugnant to the constitution is void. . . . [18]

Questions

1. According to Chief Justice Marshall, why was the U.S. Constitution written?
2. What particular phraseology of the Constitution suggests that "a law repugnant to the constitution is void"?
3. Oliver Wendell Holmes, Jr., in *The Common Law* reminds us of errors often made by students: "that of supposing, because an idea seems very familiar and natural to us, that it has always been so. Many things which we take for granted have had to be laboriously fought out or thought out in past times." Has the judiciary always had the power to declare acts of

Congress unconstitutional? Do any precedents exist in England? The English Supreme Court is the House of Lords. Can the House of Lords declare acts of the House of Commons to be null and void because they are unconstitutional? Does England have a written constitution?

CONCLUSION

The ultimate source of law varies with one's philosophy of law and determines one's agreement or disagreement with existing rules enforced by the political authority. Yet, beyond these philosophical beliefs of the nature or correctness of law, it can scarcely be doubted that law does serve as an instrument of social policy. It provides a mechanism for assigning priorities and resolving disputes between individuals and between individuals and the society as a whole.

The American system of law is largely the result of prior social experiences whereby legal precedents have been developed. Yet the law involves a dynamic process by which rules are initially created, subsequently abandoned, or imaginatively adapted to fit new and unique situations of the modern era. Such knowledge and understanding of the lawmaking processes is necessary for all educated persons but is particularly important for the business leaders of tomorrow in our complex and highly regulated society.

DISCUSSION QUESTIONS

1. In the early 1970s, Texas had a statute making it a crime to obtain an abortion. In considering the constitutionality of this statute, the Supreme Court stated the following.

   We forthwith acknowledge our awareness of the sensitive and emotional nature of the abortion controversy, of the vigorous opposing views, even among physicians, and of the deep and seemingly absolute convictions that the subject inspires. One's philosophy, one's experiences, one's exposure to the raw edges of human existence, one's religious training, one's attitudes towards life and family and their values, and the moral standards one establishes and seeks to observe, are all likely to influence and to color one's thinking and conclusions about abortion. . . .

   Our task, of course, is to resolve the issue by constitutional measurement free of emotion and predilection.

   The court's assertion could best be characterized as an expression of which legal philosophy?

2. Compare the following quotes. Can you identify the legal philosophy of the writer? Which of the systems would you prefer to live under (if either)?

   [T]here will not be different laws at Rome or at Athens, or different now and in the future. . . .[O]ne eternal and unchangable law (shall) . . . be valid for all nations at all times, and there will be one master and ruler, that is, God, over us all, for He is the author of this law, its promulgator, and its enforcing judge. Whoever is disobedient is fleeing from himself and denying his human nature, and by reason of this very fact he will suffer the worst penalties, even if he escapes what is commonly considered punishment.

Law is the totality (a) of the rules of conduct, expressing the will of the dominant class and established in legal order, and (b) of customs and rules of community life sanctioned by state authority—their application being guaranteed by the compulsive force of the state in order to guard, secure, and develop social relationships and social orders advantageous and agreeable to the dominant class.

3. In *United States v. Nixon* (418 U.S. 683 [1974]), counsel for the President urged under the Separation of Powers Doctrine that the President of the United States should have absolute privileged communication, which precludes the courts from issuing a subpoena for presidential records that may reveal criminal activity. Do you agree?

4. In his book, *The Symbols of Government,* Judge Thurman Arnold wrote the following.

In the science of jurisprudence all of the various ideals which are significant to the man on the street must be given a place. It must prove that the law is certain and at the same time elastic; that it is just, yet benevolent; economically sound, yet morally logical. It must show that the law can be dignified and solemn, and at the same time efficient, universal and fundamental, and a set of particular directions. Jurisprudence must give a place to all of the economic, and also ethical, notions of important competing groups within our society, no matter how far apart these notions may be. In its method, it must make gestures of recognition to the techniques of each separate branch of learning which claims to have any relation with the conduct of individuals, no matter now different these techniques may be.

   Such a task can only be accomplished by ceremony, and hence the writings of jurisprudence should be considered as ceremonial observances rather than as scientific observances. This is shown by the fact that the literature of jurisprudence performs its social task most effectively for those who encourage it, praise it, but do not read it. For those who study it today it is nothing but a troubling mass of conflicting ideas. However, it is not generally read, so that its troubles are known only to the few people who read it for the purpose of writing more of it. For most of those who reverence the law, the knowledge that there is a constant search going on for logical principles is sufficient.

   . . . There is comfort in such a literature, but there is no progress and no discovery.

To Arnold, what is the value of jurisprudential writings?

5. The Declaration of Independence begins:

When in the Course of human events it becomes necessary for one people to dissolve the political bands which have connected them with another, and to assume among the powers of the earth, the separate and equal station to which the Laws of Nature and of Nature's God entitle them, a decent respect to the opinions of mankind requires that they should declare the causes which impel them to the separation. We hold these truths to be self-evident, that all men are created equal, that they are endowed by their Creator with certain unalienable Rights, that among these are Life, Liberty and the pursuit of Happiness.

What Philosophy of law is embodied in this statement?

6. Outline the basics of your philosophy of law.

7. What is the purpose of establishing government by a written constitution?

8. What are the basic allocations of power in the U.S. Constitution? Are the principles embodied in the Constitution appropriate for a business firm?

9. Identify strengths and weaknesses of the federal legislative, executive, and judicial process.

10. Explain your understanding of the "common law."

SUGGESTED READINGS

Bonsignore, John, "Lacunarian Law," *American Business Law Journal,* Vol. 15, No. 1, Spring 1977, pp. 52–60.

Fisher, Bruce D., "A Role for Jurisprudence in the Business Law Curriculum," *American Business Law Journal,* Vol. 15, No. 1, Spring 1977, pp. 38–45.

Hartzler, H. Richard, "The Legal System Process for Goal Achievement," *American Business Law Journal,* Vol. 17, No. 1, Spring 1979, pp. 122–123.

Levenson, Howard, "Some Reflections on Civil Liberty in the English Legal System," *American Business Law Journal,* Vol. 17, No. 1, Spring 1979, pp. 1–20.

Liebhafsky, H. H., *American Government and Business* (New York: Wiley, 1971), Chaps. 2 and 3.

ENDNOTES

1. J. L. Brierly, *The Law of Nations* (London: Oxford University Press, 1928), p. 10.
2. *Ibid.*
3. Jacques Maritain, *The Range of Reason* (New York: Scribner's, 1952), p. 28.
4. Sir William Blackstone, *Commentaries on the Laws of England,* ed. William Hardcastle Browne (New York: L. K. Strouse, 1892), pp. 7–8.
5. Cicero, *On the Common Wealth,* trans. Sabine and Smith (Indianapolis, Ind.: Bobbs-Merrill, 1976), pp. 215–16.
6. Brierly, *Law of Nations,* pp. 14–15 (author's italics).
7. Frederick Pollock, "The Law of Reason," I *Mich. L. Rev.* 173 (1903).
8. Jerome Hall, *Studies in Jurisprudence and Criminal Theory* (New York: Oceana Pub., 1958), p. 14.
9. John Austin, *Lectures on Jurisprudence or the Philosophy of Positive Law,* rev. and ed. Robert Campbell, 2 vols., 5th ed. (London: John Murray, 1929), Vol. 1, p. 86.

10. Hans Kelsen, *General Theory of Laws and State* (Cambridge, Mass.: Harvard University Press, 1945), p. 115.
11. Friedrich K. von Savigny, *Of the Vocation of Our Age for Legislation and Jurisprudence* (1831), trans. A. Hayward (London: Littlewood, 1982), pp. 24, 27.
12. O. W. Holmes, Jr., *The Common Law* (Boston: Little, Brown & Co., 1881), pp. 1–2.
13. W. Friedmann, *Law in a Changing Society* (London: Stivens and Sons, and Berkeley: University of California Press, 1959), p. ix.
14. Arthur F. Bently, *The Process of Government* (Bloomington, Ind.: Principia Press, 1935), p. 276.
15. *Myers* v. *U.S.*, 272 U.S. 52 (1926), Justice Brandeis's dissent at p. 293.
16. Clinton P. Rossiter, *The American Presidency*, 2d ed. (New York: Harcourt, Brace and World, Inc., 1960).
17. Benjamin Cardozo, *The Nature of the Judicial Process* (New Haven: Yale University Press, 1921), p. 34.
18. *Marbury* v. *Madison*, 5 U.S. (1 Cranch) 137 (1803).

chapter 5

THE ADJUDICATORY PROCESS

The adjudicatory process is a *system* of regularized and institutionalized procedures creating judicial *power* for resolving public and private disputes. The power of the judiciary is derived from its constitutional or statutory creation and historical practices. The following materials emphasize the basic elements of the adjudicatory process and should assist the student in understanding the judicial process of solving a legal controversy.

COURT SYSTEMS

A general familiarity with the court systems is necessary to understand the adjudicatory process. Initially, one should recognize that there is a distinction between a trial court and an appellate court. Trial courts, or courts of original jurisdiction, are courts where the cases are first heard and decided. It is in this arena that the opposing parties present their evidence and the jury determines its verdict. Ordinarily, a single judge presides over this hearing.

Although most cases go no further than the trial court, a party dissatisfied with the outcome of the trial may usually request an appellate court to review the process and decisions of the trial court. The appellate court ordinarily consists of a number of judges who read the record or transcript of the proceedings in the trial court and review the written arguments filed by counsel outlining the supposed error that occurred in the trial court. The appellate court justices make their decisions from these written transcripts and arguments. There are no new

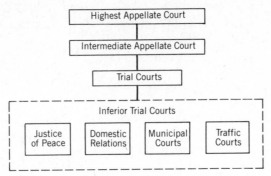

Figure 5-1. State court systems.

trials before the appellate courts. Rather, the appellate court will determine whether the lower court misinterpreted the law or committed some procedural error which necessitates a new trial in the lower court.

Each of the 50 states of the United States has its own court system. There are many differences in functions and labels given to the trial courts in the various states. Each state also has at least one appellate court. Some states provide intermediate appellate courts to relieve the highest appellate court of an excessive workload of appeal requests (see Figure 5-1).

The federal court system is comparatively simple. The basic trial court at the federal level is the U.S. District Court. Appeals from these district courts are taken to the U.S. Court of Appeals which is divided into eleven circuits. Each circuit court hears appeals from decisions of district courts in its circuit. The highest appellate court in the federal system is the Supreme Court of the United States (Figure 5-2).

Some cases can be appealed to the Supreme Court as a *right* granted in legislation. The Supreme Court may also select cases that it regards as of particular public importance for its review by granting special permission to appeal. Since legislative rights to appeal are infrequent, litigants cannot normally force

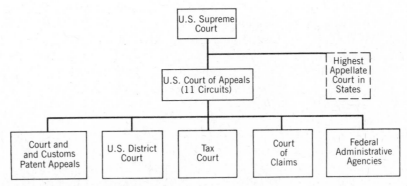

Figure 5-2. Federal court systems.

the Supreme Court to hear their appeal. Instead, they petition the Court through the *writ of certiorari* begging for the privilege to appeal. The decision to grant *certiorari* is at the court's discretion.

PROCEDURAL DUE PROCESS

The states maintain courts in which individuals may seek appropriate legal remedies when their lawful rights have been violated. Each court is governed by procedural rules that seek to ensure that any party that properly comes before the court will be granted his or her "day in court." The rules of the court provide for a systematic resolution of legal controversies. The rules may vary from one court system to another, but they must comply with U.S. constitutional requirements. However, mandatory compliance with the U.S. Constitution has not always been required. Historically, the Bill of Rights and its protections for the individual were added to the U.S. Constitution to limit the power of the *federal* government to prevent it from exercising an oppressive power similar to the crown's exercise of power over its subjects in the colonies. Each of the states already had its own constitution, which afforded similar protections to state citizens from oppressive state action. Consequently, the Bill of Rights was not applicable as a limitation on powers of *state* government.

After the Civil War, however, the Fourteenth Amendment was added to the U.S. Constitution to limit the power of *state* governments and to ensure the power of the federal government to protect individuals in certain instances from state governments. This amendment's basic purpose was to provide federal protection to the freed slaves of the South from oppressive state governments. One protection afforded to individuals in the Fourteenth Amendment is the provision that no state shall deprive an individual of life, liberty, or property without following the requirements of "due process of law." This means, among other things, that the procedural rules used by state courts must conform to the requirements of due process of law as defined by the federal courts. Inevitably, this raises questions as to the proper definition of "due process."

Some have suggested that the Fourteenth Amendment "due process" clause embodies all the protections granted in the U.S. Bill of Rights and that the protections for individuals afforded in the Bill of Rights are, therefore, binding on the states as well as on federal authorities. The Supreme Court rejected this notion and, instead, adopted a selective approach in defining the substance of the Fourteenth Amendment's "due process."[1] This approach is called the "incorporation" or "absorption" theory, which means that the due process clause incorporates or absorbs, in whole or in part, various of the amendments in the Bill of Rights. In this manner, the incorporated amendment or portion thereof becomes applicable to the states also.

Those safeguards in the Bill of Rights that have only limited validity, such as the right to trial by a jury of 12 or immunity from prosecution unless initiated by a grand jury, are not so fundamental as to be implied or absorbed into the due process clause of the Fourteenth Amendment. However, freedom of the press, freedom of religion, and freedom from condemnation without a fair trial are rights that express those "fundamental principles of liberty and justice which lie at the base of all our civil and political institutions" and, therefore, are implied in the comprehensive concept of due process of law. Denial of these rights by federal or state authorities would be repugnant to the conscience of a free people. In this manner, the selective incorporation process has helped define the contours of due process.

Whether a criminal conviction deprives the defendant of due process of law is determined by the court reviewing "the whole course of proceedings in order to ascertain whether they offend those canons of decency and fairness which express the notions of justice of English speaking peoples."[2] Indeed, the safeguards of due process of law summarize the history of freedom of English-speaking peoples running back to the Magna Carta. As Justice Douglas has commented, "The history of American freedom is, in no small measure, the history of procedure."[3]

Shaughnessy v. United States
345 U.S. 206 (1953)
Supreme Court of the United States

Justice Black, dissenting

No society is free where government makes one person's liberty depend upon the arbitrary will of another. Dictatorships have done this since time immemorial. They do now. Russian laws of 1934 authorized the People's Commissariat to imprison, banish and exile Russian citizens as well as "foreign subjects who are socially dangerous." Hitler's secret police were given like powers. German courts were forbidden to make any inquiry whatever as to the information on which the police acted. Our Bill of Rights was written to prevent such oppressive practices. Under it this Nation has fostered and protected individual freedom. The Founders abhorred arbitrary one-man imprisonments. Their belief was—our constitutional principles are—that no person of any faith, rich or poor, high or low, native or foreign, white or colored, can have his life, liberty or property taken "without due process of law." This means to me that neither the federal police nor federal prosecutors nor any other governmental official, whatever his title, can put or keep people in prison without accountability to courts of justice. It means that individual liberty is too highly prized in this country to allow executive officials to imprison and hold people on the basis of information kept secret from courts.

* * *

Justice Jackson, concurs with dissent.

Procedural fairness and regularity are of the indispensable essence of liberty. Severe substantive laws can be endured if they are fairly and impartially applied. Indeed, if put to the choice, one might well prefer to live under Soviet substantive law applied in good faith by our common-law procedures than under our substantive law enforced by Soviet procedural practices. Let it not be overlooked that due process of law is not for the sole benefit of an accused. It is the best insurance for the Government itself against those blunders which leave lasting stains on a system of justice but which are bound to occur on *ex parte* consideration.

* * *

The most scrupulous observance of due process, including the right to know a charge, to be confronted with the accuser, to cross-examine informers and to produce evidence in one's behalf, is especially necessary where the occasion of detention is fear of future misconduct, rather than crimes committed. [P]roceeding[s] . . . [of] "preventive detention" are safeguarded with full rights to judicial hearings for the accused. On the contrary, the Nazi regime in Germany installed a system of "protective custody" by which the arrested could claim no judicial or other hearing process, and as a result the concentration camps were populated with victims of summary executive detention for secret reasons. That is what renders Communist justice such a travesty. There are other differences, to be sure, between authoritarian procedure and common law, but differences in the process of administration make all the difference between a reign of terror and one of law.

Questions

1. What does it mean that government officials are held accountable to courts of justice?
2. What specific rights of procedural due process are granted to a person detained by government authorities?
3. What test or standard does the court use to determine if the defendant received due process of law?
4. Technically, "procedural" due process refers to the regularity of the proceedings, that is, whether the court rules of procedure were properly and uniformly followed by the court. "Substantive" due process refers to the fairness of the procedure employed by the court, that is, assuming the rule is regularly and uniformly followed, whether that rule is fair or just. With these distinctions in mind, what kind of a violation of due process would it be to jail an unpopular political person without a trial? What if the jailing occurs after a regular trial that followed the court rule that defendants do not have the right to cross-examine the accusers?

JURISDICTION

Jurisdiction refers to the power of a court to hear and decide a particular controversy. A court has power to decide cases when it has jurisdiction over the subject matter of the case and jurisdiction over the parties to the case. A court's jurisdiction over the dispute or subject matter is usually determined by a constitution or by some legislation. Either of these will specify the types of controversies that the particular court can resolve. State courts of general jurisdiction are normally empowered to hear all types of cases that are not specifically assigned to courts of limited or inferior jurisdiction. Inferior state courts (such as justice of the peace courts, mayor's courts, or municipal courts), hear cases involving limited periods of punishments and fines. However, even if the court possesses subject matter jurisdiction, it still may not resolve the controversy if it is unable to achieve jurisdiction over the parties.

Jurisdiction over the parties to the controversy must be obtained before the court has the power to render a judgment. Jurisdiction over the person of the plaintiff is easily obtained. The plaintiff's filing of the suit is a voluntary submission to the power of the court. However, jurisdiction over the person of the defendant may be obtained by a variety of means in which a summons is delivered to the defendant. The summons contains a copy of the complaint against the defendant. This "service of process" may be delivered by a private person or a deputy sheriff, or the defendant may voluntarily pick up the "service" at the courthouse. "Service" is more often accomplished by delivery of the summons through registered mail.

Historically, the U.S. Supreme Court ruled that service of process by state courts could not be delivered beyond the borders of the state. However, in the 1940s this concept of territorial restrictions on the issuance of the summons was modified. Many states enacted what have been called "long-arm" statutes that provide for service of process beyond the state boundaries.

Out-of-state service was challenged in the U.S. Supreme Court as a denial of due process of law under the Fourteenth Amendment in the case of *International Shoe Company v. Washington*, 326 U.S. 310 (1945). International Shoe contended that the company itself was not present in the state of Washington and that the notice sent by registered mail to the company was not a personal service that would have any force and effect outside the borders of the state of Washington. The Supreme Court denied the company's contention and said "due process requires only that in order to subject the defendant to a judgment *in personam,* if he is not present within the territory of the form, he have certain minimum contacts with it such that the maintenance of the suit does not offend traditional notions of fair play and substantial justice." Subsequent to the *International Shoe* decision, many states adopted statues giving extraterritorial effect to their service of process. The following case illustrates the utilization of an Illinois long-arm statute in an attempt to compel an Indiana corporation to defend itself in an Illinois court.

Clements v. Barney's Sporting Goods Store

406 N.E. 2d 43 (1980)
Illinois Court of Appeals

This appeal raises the frequently litigated question of when has a foreign corporation submitted itself to the jurisdiction of our courts by the transaction of business within the State. Plaintiff, Thomas Clements, brought this action to recover damages for breach of warranty against defendant, Signa Corporation. According to plaintiff's complaint, he purchased a motor boat from Barney's Sporting Goods, an Illinois corporation, in 1974. The boat was manufactured by defendant, and defendant has allegedly breached its warranty of fitness for a particular purpose. Plaintiff further alleges that defendant, an Indiana corporation, is subject to the jurisdiction of Illinois courts under the "transaction of business" section of the Illinois Long-Arm Statute because of its sale of this boat to Barney's Sporting Goods in Illinois. Although defendant was served with summons, it failed to enter an appearance in this case. A default order was entered against defendant and, subsequently an *ex-parte* judgment of $6,220 was entered against defendant. Approximately one month later, defendant filed a special and limited appearance and affidavit contesting the jurisdiction of the trial court to enter a default judgment against defendant.

After a hearing on defendant's motion, the trial court ruled for . . . [plaintiff]. Defendant's subsequent motion for rehearing was denied by the trial court. Defendant now appeals.

Plaintiff seeks to sustain jurisdiction over defendant under the Illinois Long-Arm Statute. Section 17 provides a pertinent part:

(1) Any person, whether or not a citizen or resident of this State, who in person or through an agent does any of the acts hereinafter enumerated, thereby submits such person, and, if an individual, his personal representative, to the jurisdiction of the courts of this State as to any cause of action arising from the doing of any such acts:

(a) The transaction of any business within this State;

* * *

(3) Only causes of action arising from acts enumerated herein may be asserted against a defendant in an action in which jurisdiction over him is based upon this Section.

The purpose of section 17 is to exert *in personam* jurisdiction over non-resident defendants to the extent permitted by the due process clause of the Fourteenth Amendment to the United States Constitution. Due process requires the existence of sufficient "minimum contacts" between the forum state and the non-resident defendant so that the exercise of personal jurisdiction is consistent with traditional notions of fair play and substantial justice. This determination is to be made on the facts of each case and turns on an assessment of the quality and nature of defendant's activities. Thus, we must decide whether defendant has by some voluntary act or conduct purposely availed itself of the privilege of conducting business within Illinois and thereby invoked the benefits and protection of Illinois law. By displaying its boats and distributing literature at the Chicago Boat Show, advertising in magazines which have Illinois subscribers, and selling its boats to Illinois retailers, defendant has entered the Illinois marketplace and invoked the benefits and protection of Illinois law. Defendant's conduct constitutes direct solicitation of Illinois customers. Solicitation of business inside the State of Illinois has been found sufficient to sustain personal jurisdiction over a non-resident defendant. Additionally, defendant has indirectly entered the Illinois marketplace through the sale of its boat to the Illinois corporation, Barney's Sporting Goods Store. Although defendant was not a participant in the sale of this boat to the plaintiff, we believe defendant cannot insulate itself from the jurisdiction of our courts by using an intermediary or by professing ignorance of the ultimate destination of his goods. In *Gray v. American Radiator & Standard Sanitary Corp.* (1961), 22 Ill.2d 432, 176 N.E. 2d 761, our supreme court said:

As a general proposition, if a corporation elects to sell its products for ultimate use in another State, it is not unjust to hold it answerable there for any damage caused by defects in those products. Advanced means of distribution and other commercial activity have made possible these modern methods of doing business, and have largely effaced the economic significance of State lines. By the same token, today's facilities for transportation and communication have removed much of the difficulty and inconvenience formerly encountered in defending lawsuits brought in other States.

Unless they are applied in recognition of the changes brought about by technological and economic progress, jurisdictional concepts which may have been reasonable enough in a simpler economy lose their relation to reality, and injustice rather than justice is promoted. Our unchanging principles of justice, whether procedural or substantive in nature, should be scrupulously observed by the courts. But the rules of law which grow and develop within those principles must do so in the light of the facts of economic life as it is lived today. . . .

Although the *Gray* court was applying the "commission of a tortious act" section of the Long-Arm Statute, we believe its analysis is equally applicable to the "transaction of business" section of that statute. Accordingly, we believe that defendant has transacted business as provided in section 17(1)(a) of the Civil Practice Act.

Section 17(3) of the Long-Arm Statute mandates that plaintiff's cause of action arose from the jurisdictional acts of defendant. A cause of action arises from a defendant's jurisdictional acts where it lies in the wake of defendant's commercial activities by which defendant submitted to the jurisdiction of the Illinois courts. We have previously held that "[w]here the jurisdictional activities consist of the solicitation of sales, a cause of action arising from the consequences of such a sale comes within the statutory definition of section 17(3)." In this case, plaintiff's purchase of the defective boat was, at least in part, a result of defendant's solicitation in Illinois. Therefore, we hold that defendant has submitted itself to the jurisdiction of our courts under section 17(1)(a) of the Illinois Long-Arm Statute. The order of the circuit court denying defendant's motion to reconsider is hereby affirmed.

Questions

1. What does due process require before a state can force an out-of-state defendant to answer a suit in the state? How was this requirement met in this instance?

2. What reasons did the court cite for extending the state's jurisdictional powers over nonresident defendants?

3. The Illinois statute "mandates that the plaintiff's cause of action" must arise "from the jurisdictional acts of the defendant." What does this mean?

4. Another type of jurisdiction is called jurisdiction *in rem*. In the case of *Pennington v. Fourth National Bank*, 243 U.S. 269 (1917), the Supreme Court said:

   The 14th Amendment did not, in guaranteeing due process of law, abridge the jurisdiction which a state possessed over property within its borders, regardless of the residence or presence of the owner. That jurisdiction extends alike to tangible and to intangible property. . . . The thing belonging to the absent defendant is seized and applied to the satisfaction of his obligation. The Federal Constitution presents no obstacle to the full exercise of this power.

   Why is jurisdiction *in rem* necessary?

5. The importance of possessing jurisdiction is that without it the state court's judgment is void, and with it the judgment is entitled to "full faith and credit" (i.e., enforcement) throughout the 50 states. A state court's judgment that possessed both subject matter and person jurisdiction is enforceable in all states because the U.S. Constitution requires all states to grant "full faith and credit" to the court judgments of the other states in the Union. Does the "full faith and credit" clause suggest a reason for the out-of-state defendant to return and defend himself or herself in a state court from which a summons has been received?

6. Subject matter jurisdiction for federal courts falls into one of two catego-

ries: (1) cases involving "federal questions" (questions concerning a provision of the federal Constitution, a federal statute, or an international treaty) and (2) cases involving "diversity of citizenship" (the respective parties are citizens of different states). All cases in the latter category could be tried in state courts. However, the apprehension of possible state court bias against the out-of-state party inspired the framers of the Constitution to allow such cases to be brought into federal courts. In addition to diversity of citizenship, the amount in controversy must exceed $10,000. Would overcrowding of federal courts with "diversity actions" suggest another reason why the Supreme Court upheld long-arm statutes as satisfying due process requirements?

THEORY OF PLEADINGS

The pleadings, or documents in a case, serve (1) to set the limits within which the litigation will operate and (2) to give notice of the plaintiff's claim to the defendant to gain personal jurisdiction over the defendant. In the written complaint filed with the clerk of the court, the plaintiff's attorney will present the client's version of what transpired and relate the particular relief the plaintiff is seeking from the defendant. In contesting the plaintiff's case, the defendant's attorney will file an answer with the court denying all or some of the plaintiff's allegations about what occurred. These documents isolate the issues of fact—that is, where the parties' version of the facts differ. This divergence of alleged events must be resolved by a trial.

Historically, the rules of pleading were burdened with intricacies and technicalities. The emphasis was on pleading "facts," which required elaborate documents with great detail. However, reform efforts brought about "notice" pleading and its corresponding "discovery" system.

Notice pleading requires the pleadings merely to give "notice" to the opposing parties of their respective claims. The "complaint" and "answer" in the following dispute of *Student v. Worker* illustrate the simplicity of notice pleading.

The "discovery" process allows the opposing parties to seek out further refinements or elaboration in the facts through the use of techniques separate from the pleading documents themselves. These privileges of discovery allow the parties to learn what sort of evidence the other party has that relates to the suit. Certain matters are not subject to discovery but, for the most part, any relevant matter may be ascertained. The techniques of discovery usually are written interrogatories, inspection of documents, physical examination of persons, and depositions. Such procedures allow for proper preparation for trials and aid pretrial settlements. They also eliminate most "surprises" at the trial, which might allow suits to be won or lost by tricks rather than on the merits of the case. The broadest discovery processes are available in civil suits. Many states allow a limited aspect of discovery in criminal suits also.

A "COMPLAINT"

A COMPLAINT

IN THE COURT OF COMMON PLEAS
SUMMIT COUNTY, OHIO

Ernest Student 221 North Street Akron, Ohio 44304 and Dolly Student 221 North Street Akron, Ohio 44304	))) No. _____))
Plaintiffs v. Herbert A. Worker 2631 East Market Street Kent, Ohio 43204 and Worldwide Flush, Inc. 343 Industry Street Kent, Ohio 43204	)) COMPLAINT)))
Defendants	)

COUNT ONE

1. On May 6, 1982, plaintiff, Ernest Student, was driving an automobile, owned jointly by Ernest Student and his wife, plaintiff Dolly Student, southwardly in the left traffic lane of Exchange Street, a multilane public highway in Akron, Ohio.
2. At the same time defendant, Herbert Worker, was driving an automobile, leased by defendant Worldwide Flush, Inc., southwardly in the traffic lane of Exchange Street.
3. Negligently and without warning, defendant, Herbert Worker, shifted from the right traffic lane to the left traffic lane of Exchange Street immediately in front of plaintiff Ernest Student, thus causing plaintiff, Ernest Student, to strike the left rear of defendant, Herbert Worker's automobile.
4. At the time of the impact defendant, Herbert Worker, was the agent of defendant, Worldwide Flush, Inc., and was acting within the scope of his agency and authority.
5. As a direct result of the impact plaintiff, Ernest Student, has suffered a rib fracture, a contusion over the sternum, and a rupture of an intervertebral disk at L-5, S-1. To date, he has expended $767.58 in medical expenses and has lost intermittently a total of 23 days of work. He has suffered great pain of body and mind and in the future will continue to do so and in the future

will be compelled to expend additional sums for medical treatment and hospitalization and will suffer intermittently loss of wages. In addition, the automobile owned by plaintiffs, Ernest Student and Dolly Student, was damaged in the amount of $411.00. Being deprived of the use of the automobile for three weeks, plaintiff, Ernest Student, was required to expend $60.00 for public transportation.

WHEREFORE, plaintiffs demand judgment against defendant, Herbert Worker, or against Worldwide Flush, Inc., or against both of them as follows:

    (a)   In behalf of plaintiffs, Ernest Student and Dolly Student, for damage to their automobile in the sum of $411.00.

    (b)   In behalf of the plaintiff, Ernest Student, in the sum of $15,000.00, together with the costs of this action.

COUNT TWO

1.   For a second claim plaintiff, Dolly Student, restates all that is alleged in paragraphs 1 through 4 of Count One.
2.   Plaintiff, Dolly Student, further states that she is the wife of Ernest Student and that as a direct result of the injuries suffered by Ernest Student as set forth in paragraph 4 of Count One, plaintiff, Dolly Student, has been and will be deprived of the consortium of her husband, Ernest Student.

WHEREFORE, plaintiff, Dolly Student, demands judgment against defendant, Herbert Worker, or against Worldwide Flush, Inc., or against both of them in the sum of $5,000.00, together with the costs of this action.

_____

Chester Goodfellow, Attorney for
  Plaintiffs
Goodfellow, Nice & Easy, Attorneys at
  Law
221 West Market Street
Akron, Ohio 44304

TO THE CLERK:

Please issue summons, plus a copy of this complaint to the Sheriff of Summit County, Ohio, for personal service upon the defendants at their respective addresses, noted in the caption to this complaint, and make return of the same, according to law.

_____

Chester Goodfellow, Attorney for
  Plaintiffs
Goodfellow, Nice & Easy, Attorneys at
  Law
221 West Market Street
Akron, Ohio 44304

AN "ANSWER"

AN ANSWER

IN THE COURT OF COMMON PLEAS
SUMMIT COUNTY, OHIO

Ernest Student   )
221 North Street
Akron, Ohio 44304   ))No. _____
   and
Dolly Student   )
221 North Street
Akron, Ohio 44304   )

      Plaintiffs   )ANSWER
   v.   )
Herbert A. Worker
2631 East Market Street   )
Kent, Ohio 43204
   and   )
Worldwide Flush, Inc.
343 Industry Street   )
Kent, Ohio 43204

Defendant Herbert A. Worker:

1. Admits the allegations contained in paragraphs 1 and 2 of Count One of the complaint, and admits these same paragraphs as incorporated by reference in Count Two of the complaint.
2. Denies the allegations contained in paragraph 3 of Count One of the complaint, and denies the same paragraph as incorporated by reference in Count Two of the Complaint.
3. Alleges that he is without knowledge or information sufficient to form a belief as to the truth of the allegations contained in paragraphs 4 and 5 of Count One of the complaint, and alleges that he is without knowledge or information sufficient to form a belief as to the truth of the allegations contained in paragraph 4 as incorporated by reference in paragraph 1 of Count Two of the complaint, and further alleges that he is without knowledge or information sufficient to form a belief as to the truth of the allegations contained in paragraph 2 of Count Two of the complaint.

                _____

                William Williams, Attorney for
                   Defendant, Herbert Worker
                Williams, Jones & Smith, Attorneys at
                   Law
                225 North High Street
                Akron, Ohio 44304

CERTIFICATE OF SERVICE

A copy of this answer has been mailed, via ordinary U.S. mail, to the attorney for plaintiffs, Chester Goodfellow, Goodfellow, Nice & Easy, Attorneys at Law, 221 West Market Street, Akron, Ohio 44304, this _____ day of _____, 1982.

_____
William Williams,
Attorney for Defendant

Questions
1. What is the controversy in *Student v. Worker?* Which facts are admitted? Which "facts" are in dispute?
2. What additional "facts" might the parties want to discover? What discovery techniques might the parties utilize?

SUMMARY JUDGMENT

One of the recognized purposes of a summary judgment by the judge is to expedite the disposition of civil cases where no issue of material fact is presented to justify a trial. If the pleadings of both parties disclose no real factual issue, the court may find that no triable issue exists and grant summary judgment. With no genuine issues of fact, the court avoids the trial and thereby saves the parties the time and expense of the trial while helping the court clear its congested calendar. Of course, the court can grant a summary judgment in favor of either the plaintiff or the defendant.

THE TRIAL

The purpose of the trial is to resolve all controversy over questions of fact, that is, what events actually transpired. It is the function of the jurors to issue a verdict that determines the "facts" from which the controversy arose. Collectively, the jury must determine which of the opposing versions alleged and testified to is correct. Thus, the jury is the "finder" of the facts.

Except for giving the jury instructions, the judge is normally not allowed to interfere with the jury's fact-finding process. The judge is, however, the sole authority on the law that is to be applied to the facts as the jury found them. In addition, the judge directs the pace of the litigation and administers the rules of procedures for the orderly operation of the hearing.

The trial is conducted under the adversary method. The parties to the controversy, through their lawyers, have the obligation for investigating, initiating, and maintaining the litigation. The court has no other means of obtaining the necessary information to resolve the controversy. The lawyers for each side must select the evidence essential to their cause. They attempt to present evidence that will convince the jury that their version of the facts is correct. The lawyers plan the sequence of the presentation of their witnesses, the questions that will be raised, and the evidence that will be needed to substantiate their claim. The theory of the adversary method is that the best decision will be rendered by the judge or jury if the parties presenting their views are real adversaries. If the parties have a real stake in the outcome of the case, they will present their case in a manner most favorable to their claim. Accordingly, the judge and jury can reach a better decision after having heard the best arguments on each side of the controversy.

The pleadings serve to notify each party of the questions that each must be prepared to meet with the best evidence available. As the party that initiated the action, the plaintiff is obligated to proceed first in presenting his or her case. Following the plaintiff's presentation of evidence, the defendant will attempt with contra evidence to create doubt in the minds of the jurors concerning the plaintiff's version of the controversy. At the conclusion of the presentation of the evidence, the jury will return a verdict (finding of facts) in resolution of that portion of the legal controversy. In civil (noncriminal) cases, the plaintiff must present proofs to convince the jury by the preponderance of the evidence. This is a burden of proof that is much lower than the prosecutor's burden in a criminal case to convince the jury "beyond a reasonable doubt."

JURY SELECTION PROCESS

Prospective jurors are selected from a list of residents in the judicial district of the court. They are summoned to the courthouse and assigned to various trials. Prospective jurors are questioned concerning any possible connection with any of the participants in the trial or the possibility of some bias on the questions before the court. The opposing counsel may demand the exclusion of any prospective juror who demonstrates a specific cause for rejection. Moreover, opposing counsel have a limited number of "preemptory challenges" which allow prospective jurors to be dismissed without giving any reason. This privilege enables opposing counsel to exclude jurors who they feel may be hostile to their client's cause. Once the jury is empaneled, the lawyers present their opening statements. Then, the evidence is presented before the jury.

RULES OF EVIDENCE

Since the jurors are not expert factfinders, they may have considerable difficulty in determining the truth from the evidence. Because the jurors are laypersons, the rules of evidence have been shaped over time to protect the jury from irrelevant, misleading, and unreliable evidence. Repetitious evidence and evidence that may be in violation of certain confidential relationships are also excluded. These rules of evidence have been developed over the years and are too numerous and complex for full discussion here. Indeed, even judges themselves often commit error by introducing inappropriate evidence or failing to admit evidence that should have been presented to the jury.

POST-TRIAL

After the jury renders its verdict, one of the parties is likely to be dissatisfied with the outcome. There are a number of alternatives available to test the correctness of the jury's verdict or the court's judgment. The judgment is the final decision of the court (judge) determined by applying the proper law to the facts as found by the jury. In civil cases, the losing party may ask the judge to rule against the jury's verdict because it is clearly contrary to the evidence (judgment *non obstante veredicto*). In addition, the losing party may seek a new trial if there was some irregularity in the trial proceedings. Also, the losing party may appeal to determine whether the law that was applied in the case was properly applied or whether the law itself is a proper law for contemporary conditions. After the case has been argued before the appeals court and it renders a judgment, the legal controversy is usually terminated. If no appeal is advanced, it is terminated at the conclusion of the proceedings in the trial court.

Appeals beyond the first apellate court are normally not available as a matter of "right." Rather, the highest courts usually determine at their own discretion which of the lower court decisions they wish to review. This procedure usually involves the filing of a petition by the party desiring an appeal with the highest court. The petition asks the high court to issue a writ of *certiorari* to the lower court. The writ of *certiorari* is an order by the high court to the lower court to certify a record of its proceedings for review by the high court. Of course, if the high court grants *certiorari*, this is not a determination of how the court will finally rule on the merits of the lower court decision. The decision on the merits will be decided only after a full hearing before the high court.

APPEAL FOR A NEW TRIAL

Batchoff v. Craney
172 P.2d 308 (1946)
Supreme Court of Montana

[Plaintiff brought this action to recover damages for personal injuries sustained by him while riding as a guest in an automobile alleged to have been owned and controlled by defendant and his agent, the driver of the car. Plaintiff's evidence consisted of his sole testimony, which was contradicted by his own prior statements.

Defendant produced witnesses who testified that he lent his car to Wheeler for his use and that the driver was acting as agent of Wheeler in returning the car when the accident occurred. In other words, the evidence was in sharp conflict. The jury found for the plaintiff and the defendant appealed on the basis that the plaintiff's testimony was not worthy of belief.]

. . . [I]n *Wallace* v. *Wallace*, 85 Mont. 492, 279 P. 374, 377, this court said:

A jury may believe the testimony of one witness and disbelieve that of another, or any numbers of others, and the determination of the jury in this regard is final; having spoken, this court must assume that the facts are as stated by the witnesses believed by the jury, and claimed by the prevailing party. The preponderance of the evidence may be established by a single witness as against a greater number of witnesses who testify to the contrary.

It follows that wherever there is a conflict in the evidence this court may only review the testimony for the purpose of determining whether or not there is any substantial evidence in the record to support the verdict of the jury, and must accept that evidence there found as true, unless that evidence is so inherently impossible or improbable as not to be entitled to belief; and, where a verdict is based upon substantial evidence which, from any point of view, could have been accepted by the jury as credible, it is binding upon this court, although it may appear inherently weak.

* * *

It should be noted that the statements made by plaintiff before the Industrial Accident Board and other declarations contrary to his testimony in this case may not be considered as substantive evidence in this case. . . . The only effect of declarations made by plaintiff at other times and places is to impeach him,

leaving the question of his credibility for the jury.

Speaking of the effect of prior statements inconsistent with present testimony, this court in *State v. Peterson*, 102 Mont. 495, 59 P. 2d 61, 63, said:

These matters tend to discredit, but not destroy, the testimony of the [plaintiff]. 'A witness false in one part of his testimony is to be distrusted in others' and 'a witness may be impeached' by contradictory evidence that his general reputation for truth and integrity is bad, or that he has made at other times statements inconsistent with his present testimony; but while proof of falsity is one part of a witness' testimony, inconsistent statements at other times, contradictory evidence, and reputation may discredit the witness, such proof goes only to the credibility of the witness, of which the jury remains the sole judge, as well as the weight to be given thereto.

It follows that, although the jury may reject the false testimony and "assume, regarding the rest of it, an attitude of distrust," the jurors may render a verdict based upon the testimony of such witness if after examination they find it worthy of belief. And the extent to which impeaching evidence impaired the credibility of a witness assailed is a question exclusively for the jury.

* * *

. . . Our province is to ascertain whether the evidence viewed in the light most favorable to the prevailing party sustains the verdict. If it does we must sustain the action of the trial judge. It was the jury's province to pronounce between conflicting views contained in the evidence. There being substantial evidence to sustain the verdict, the court properly denied the motion for new trial.

We find nothing in the record to warrant us in saying that the court erred in not finding that the jury was actuated by passion and prejudice. . . .

The judgment is accordingly affirmed.

Questions
1. What is a "preponderance" of evidence? Does the side with the greatest number of witnesses win?
2. On review, must the appellate court always accept the verdict of the jury? Do appellate courts "second guess" the jury? If the evidence is conflicting, should the appeals court pick the version of facts it prefers or leave the selection to the jury? Why?
3. Does evidence of "prior inconsistent statements" destroy a witness's testimony?

APPEAL FOR REVERSAL

State v. Liska
  32 Ohio App. 2d 317 (1971)
  Court of Appeals of Ohio

This action comes here from the Berea Municipal Court on appeal from the appellant's conviction and fine of One Hundred Dollars ($100) for an alleged violation of R. C. 2921.05, the so-called "flag desecration" statute. For the reasons stated below, the judgment of the trial court is reversed as being contrary to law.

The appellant, Liska, a student at Baldwin-Wallace College, was arrested and charged with unlawfully and willfully exposing a contemptuous representation of the American flag on the rear window of his automobile. The alleged contemptuous representation consisted of a decal composed of thirteen red and white stripes with a peace symbol appearing on a blue field.

There is nothing in the record to indicate that the appellant was in violation of any traffic laws, nor that he was behaving in a disorderly manner when arrested. The appellant described himself at trial as a conscientious objector to the Viet Nam War and a pacifist, and testified that his purpose in displaying the decal in question was to make a political state-ment of peace. The state's evidence consisted only of the testimony of the arresting officer and a photograph of the offending decal as it appeared on appellant's car.

Appellant assigned the following as error:

(1) The court erred in concluding that appellant's conduct was contemptuous as required by Section 2921.05 of the Revised Code of Ohio. . . .

Allowing the state's evidence its most favorable stance, it is apparent that the most this appellant has done is to display a decal composed of thirteen red and white stripes and a blue square upon which is superimposed a peace symbol. On the evidence in this case that configuration indicates only the appellant's aspiration for peace for his country. We hold that the symbolic indication indicated by the facts of this case, without more, was, as a matter of law, not a contemptuous act within the meaning of R.C. 2921.05.

The conviction is reversed and the appellant discharged.

Questions
1. Did the appellant challenge the facts? Does this explain why he asked for a reversal and not a new trial?
2. In seeking a reversal, what is the appellant asserting as error by the trial court?

RES JUDICATA

Commissioner of Internal Revenue vs. Sunnen
333 U.S. 591 (1948)
Supreme Court of the United States

Justice Murphy

It is first necessary to understand something of the recognized meaning and scope of *res judicata,* a doctrine judicial in origin. The general rule of *res judicata* applies to repetitious suits involving the same cause of action. It rests upon considerations of economy of judicial time and public policy favoring the establishment of certainty in legal relations. The rule provides that when a court of competent jurisdiction has entered a final judgment on the merits of a cause of action, the parties to the suit and their privies are thereafter bound "not only as to every matter which was offered and received to sustain or defeat the claim or demand, but as to any other admissible matter which might have been offered for that purpose." *Cromwell v. County of Sac.* 94 U.S. 351, 352. The judgment puts an end to the cause of action, which cannot again be brought into litigation between the parties upon any ground whatever, absent fraud or some other factor invalidating the judgment.

Questions
1. What is *res judicata?* Does it apply to the same parties or to different parties?
2. Does *res judicata* prohibit an appeal?
3. When will a decision not be protected by the doctrine of *res judicata?*

CONCLUSION

The adjudicatory process involves a series of interrelated actions that result in the resolution of legal controversies. The basic elements of this process are the courts, pleadings, trial, appeal, and ultimate decision (judgment). The courts are created by a constitution or a statute that determines its subject matter jurisdiction. The court's service of process gains personal jurisdiction over the defendant. The pleadings and the trial collectively "determine" the facts, and the judgment of the trial judge is the application of the law to those facts so as to render a decision. Appellate courts determine whether the trial judge properly handled the trial hearing and attempt to ensure uniform interpretation of the laws.

The adjudicatory process can be a long and drawn-out process with numerous technicalities. However, the delays are often built into the process to encourage proper reflection on the issues. In addition, technicalities often are designed to protect specific rights of the parties. It is precisely this "due process of law" that forms the basis of protecting the rights of a free people.

DISCUSSION QUESTIONS

1. Explain the concept of jurisdiction. How is it acquired? How can it have a "long arm"?

2. What are the purposes of pleadings?

3. Diagram a typical state court system and the federal court system.

4. Explain the process of the writ of *certiorari*.

5. Are rules of substance or procedure move valuable to a free society?

6. England has eliminated the jury system. Should we?

7. Why is it necessary to have rules of evidence?

8. Explain the "absorption" theory in Supreme Court interpretation of the Fourteenth Amendment.

9. Distinguish between "substantive" and "procedural" due process.

10. What is *in rem* jurisdiction? Why is it necessary?

SUGGESTED READINGS

Collins, John W., "Creative Analysis of Judicial Decisions," *American Business Law Journal,* Vol. 19, No. 3, Fall 1981, pp. 360–369.

Driscoll, James, "The Decline of the English Jury," *American Business Law Journal,* Vol. 17, No. 1, Spring 1979, pp. 99–112.

Henkel, Jan W., "The Civil Jury—Modification or Abolition," *American Business Law Journal,* Vol. 14, No. 1, Spring 1976, pp. 97–110.

Tankersley, Irvin L., "Utility Cut-offs and Due Process," *American Business Law Journal,* Vol. 16, No. 3, Winter 1979, pp. 365–368.

ENDNOTES

1. *Malinski v. New York,* 324 U.S. 501 (1945).
2. *Ibid.*
3. *Ibid.*

chapter 6
THE ADMINISTRATIVE PROCESS

An administrative agency is any governmental authority other than courts and legislative bodies. Such an agency may be called a commission, bureau, authority, board, office, department, administration, division, or agency. The administrative process is the combination of methods and procedures used by administrative agencies in carrying out their tasks.

The average person is much more directly and more often affected by the administrative process than by the judicial process. A large proportion of our population goes through life without ever becoming a party to a lawsuit. However, the administrative process affects nearly everyone in many different ways almost every day. Administrative agencies protect people from numerous problems: air and water pollution; excessive prices for utility services or transportation rates; unwholesome meats; unfair labor practices by employers and unions; false advertising; and physically unsafe airplanes, bridges, and elevators. The list includes a wide range of items with which we have become so accustomed that we take them for granted.

Administrative agencies are as old as Congress itself. The first Congress conferred power on the President to establish an agency that provided military pensions for "invalids . . . wounded and disabled during the late war."[1] Such payments were to be made "under such regulations as the President of the United States may direct." Administrative law has been growing ever since. Such familiar acronyms as the ICC, the FTC, the EPA, the SEC, and the NLRB became part of America's vocabulary as the government increasingly sought to handle social and economic problems through the administrative process.

LEGISLATIVE AND EXECUTIVE CONTROLS

The administrative agency is embodied with functions usually carried out by three separate branches of government. An administrative agency may exercise the legislative function by formulating rules to govern a particular trade or a specific business practice. The agency exercises an executive function when it investigates business activities and enforces its rules of proper conduct. Finally, the agency is empowered with the judicial function to hold a hearing and to determine if a particular defendant has violated any of the agency's rules.

A problem posed by the unique status of administrative agencies involves the nature of the powers that may be delegated to them. Final rulings are frequently contested on grounds that the work of the agency constituted an unconstitutional delegation of legislative power. In these cases the courts are concerned with whether sufficient limits and boundaries are placed on the powers and actions of the administrative agencies. The following case illustrates this problem.

LEGISLATIVE STANDARDS

South Terminal Corp. v. Environmental Protection Agency
501 F. 2d 646 (1974)
U.S. Court of Appeals (1st Cir.)

Several petitioners have argued that the powers of EPA (Environmental Protection Agency), as construed by us, constitute an unconstitutional delegation to an agency of legislative powers. We do not find the argument persuasive. The last time that a delegation of power to an administrative agency was upset occurred in *A.L.A. Schechter Poultry Corp.* v. *United States*, 295 U.S. 495, (1935), and the unique conditions of that case are not repeated here.

In *Schechter* Congress had delegated to the President the power to approve industry "codes" drawn up by local businessmen. Congress had not prescribed a purpose to be served by the codes, nor had it set boundaries on the provisions the codes could contain. The Court consequently characterized the delegation as utterly without standards and impermissible. Justice Cardozo, concurring, wrote that the legislation was unconstitutional because the power granted was "not canalized within banks that keep it from overflowing. It is unconfined and vagrant. . . . Here in effect is a roving commission to inquire into evils and upon discovery correct them."

The power granted to EPA is not "unconfined and vagrant." The Agency has been given a well defined task by Congress—to reduce pollution levels "requisite to protect the public health," in the case of primary standards. The Clean Air Act outlines the approach to be followed by the Agency and describes in detail many of its powers. Perhaps because the task is both unprecedented and of great complexity, and because appropriate controls cannot all be anticipated pending the Agency's collection of technical data in different regions, the Act leaves considerable flexibility to EPA in the choice of means. Yet there are many benchmarks to guide the Agency and the courts in determining whether or not the

EPA is exceeding its powers, not the least of which is that the rationality of the means can be tested against goals capable of fairly precise definition in the language of science.

Administrative agencies are created by Congress because it is impossible for the Legislature to acquire sufficient information to manage each detail in the long process of extirpating the abuses identified by the legislation;

the Agency must have flexibility to implement the congressional mandate. Therefore, although the delegation to EPA was a broad one, including the power to make essentially "local" rules and regulations when necessary to achieve the national goals, we have little difficulty concluding that the delegation was not excessive.

Questions

1. Since 1935 the Supreme Court has not invalidated a single legislative delegation to an administrative agency. Does this suggest that this matter is no longer of concern to the Court? According to the Supreme Court, what must the Congress do in order to make delegation of legislative power constitutional?

2. Does the standard in the EPA—"to protect the public health"—set boundaries on the agency and prevent "a roving commission to inquire into evils and upon discovery correct them"?

3. In *State* v. *Marana Plantations, Inc.,* 252 P. 2d 87 (1953), the Arizona Board of Health was given the power to "formulate general policies affecting public health" and "to regulate sanitation and sanitary policies in the interests of public health." The Arizona Supreme Court said this was unconstitutional because it would allow the board to "flood the field with such sanitary laws as its unrestrained discretion may dictate." Could the same argument be made against the EPA?

CONGRESSIONAL CONTROLS

Other means of legislative control of administrative agencies have developed besides congressional design of the primary standard and boundaries.

Appropriations

The power of the purse has become a traditional method of legislative check on agency administration. In spite of the substantive declarations of Congress in many enactments, their enforcement and observance can be substantially weakened by refusal to appropriate funds for an adequate staff. Second, amendments to the original statutes creating agency powers can be added onto appropriation acts and thereby restrict future agency activities. Likewise, conditions attached to the spending of appropriated funds can modify the range of practical policy choices available to the agency.

Standing Committees

First, there exists the "subject matter" committees, one from each branch of Congress. These are charged with supervision of the content and substance of the relevant agency's assigned duties. The committee may act as a "watchdog" over the agency to determine whether additional legislation might be necessary to either expand or contract agency authority and influence. Second, a committee concerning government operations exists in both the House and Senate and is charged with the responsibility to ensure that the agencies operate with "economy and efficiency." When these committees are added to the appropriations committee, the result is that all agencies are answerable in certain contexts to at least six committees and maybe more.

EXECUTIVE CONTROLS

What is the extent of power of the executive, the President, to direct and supervise administrative action? The power to appoint the agency chief is the President's most effective weapon of control. Although this power is shared with the Senate, the President's nominees are most often accepted. Therefore, the President can be successful at changing the tempo and emphasis of the regulatory programs by the appointment process. Congress has often sought to diminish this presidential influence by providing certain statutory terms of office that require particular "cause" for removal from office. The question then arises: could the President ignore these constraints on the presidential leadership role?

In the early part of this century, Congress enacted a provision that postmasters were only to be removed with the Senate's consent. President Wilson removed Myers from his postmastership without asking for the Senate's approval. Myers sued for the salary he would have earned except for his "illegal" removal from office. The Supreme Court relied on Article II of the Constitution. "The executive power shall be vested in a President," and that the President "shall take care that the laws be faithfully executed." Then, the Court concluded that the President may properly supervise administrators "in order to secure that unitary and uniform execution of the laws which Article II of the Constitution evidently contemplated in vesting general executive power in the President alone. . . ." The President may remove any officer "on the ground that the discretion regularly entrusted to the officer by statute has not been on the whole intelligently or wisely executed." In this manner the President discharges the constitutional duty of seeing that the laws are "faithfully executed." Consequently, the Court ruled that the provision of the statute that restricted the president's power of removal was in violation of the Constitution and invalid.[2]

Humphrey's Executor v. United States

295 U.S. 602 (1935)
Supreme Court of the United States

[Humphrey, a Federal Trade Commissioner and a Republican, was removed from office by President Franklin D. Roosevelt who desired to staff the Commission with personnel of his own selection. Humphrey began suit for his salary, and after his death it was continued by his executor.]

Justice Sutherland

[The holding of the *Myers* case] goes far enough to include all purely executive officers, [but it does not] include an officer who occupies no place in the executive department and who exercises no part of the executive power vested by the Constitution in the President. . . . The Federal Trade Commission is an administrative body created by Congress to carry into effect legislative policies embodied in the statute in accordance with the legislative standard therein prescribed, and to perform other specified duties as a legislative or as a judicial aid. Such a body cannot in any proper sense be characterized as an arm or an eye of the executive. Its duties are performed without executive leave and, in the contemplation of the statute, must be free from executive control. In administering the provisions of the statute in respect of "unfair methods of competition"—that is to say in filling in and administering the details embodied by that general standard—the commission acts in part quasi-legislatively and in part quasi-judicially. . . .

We think it plain under the Constitution that illimitable power of removal is not possessed by the President in respect of officers of the character of those just named. The authority of Congress, in creating quasi-legislative or quasi-judicial agencies, to require them to act in discharge of their duties independently of executive control cannot well be doubted; and that authority includes, as an appropriate incident, power to fix the period during which they shall continue in office, and to forbid their removal except for cause in the meantime. For it is quite evident that one who holds his office only during the pleasure of another, cannot be depended upon to maintain an attitude of independence against the latter's will.

Questions

1. What is a "quasi-legislative" body? A "quasi-judicial" body?
2. Wiener, a war claims commissioner nominated by President Truman, was removed by President Eisenhower, who desired personnel of his own selection. Wiener sued for his salary and the Supreme Court said, "Judging . . . the claim that the President could remove a member of an adjudicatory body like the War Claims Commission merely because he wanted his own appointees on such a commission, we are compelled to conclude that no such power is given to the President directly by the Constitution, and none is impliedly conferred upon him by statute simply because Congress said nothing about it. The philosophy of *Humphrey's Executor,* in its explicit language as well as its implications, precludes such a claim." *Wiener* v. *U.S.,* 357 U.S. 349 (1958). How is the fact that this was "an adjudicatory body" relevant and helpful in making the decision?

3. When are agencies independent of presidential control? Why could Myers be replaced in spite of congressional restraint on his removal and Humphrey could not?

The Reagan Presidency has used budgetary control as its basic means of effecting regulatory change. After increasing nearly 240 percent in real (constant-dollar) terms during the 1970s, outlays of the 57 major federal regulatory agencies experienced only 1 percent real growth in 1981. The overhaul of the government's regulatory establishment is further confirmed by a substantial decline in staffing at the major agencies. Personnel was reduced by 4 percent in 1981.

INVESTIGATIVE PROCEDURES

The stages of administrative agency procedures are depicted in Figure 6-1. Since the executive powers of administrative agencies normally include the power to investigate, the preliminary procedural steps often begin with some pressure being exerted on the agency to investigate some problem. Individual members of the public or congressional representatives may complain or suggest to the administrative agency that they investigate a particular activity. Moreover, the administrative agency on its own initiative may begin an investigation.

The agency, in exercising its executive powers, may follow either of two approaches to investigating an alleged problem. It may proceed against an individual defendant when it feels that the activity involved is peculiar to that defendant or it may proceed with an investigation of the entire industry if it believes the questionable practice is widespread. The Supreme Court affirmed this practice in *Moog Industries* v. *Federal Trade Commission*, 355 U.S. 414 (1958), when it said:

[A]lthough an alledgedly illegal practice may appear to be operative throughout an industry, whether such appearances reflect fact and whether all firms in the industry should be dealt with in a single proceeding or should receive individualized treatment are questions that call for discretionary determination by the administrative agency. . . . Furthermore . . . the Commission alone is empowered to develop that enforcement policy best calculated to achieve the ends contemplated by Congress and to allocate its available funds and personnel in such a way as to execute its policy efficiently and economically.

Agencies normally possess a staff of attorneys, accountants, economists, or other appropriate specialists to aid in gathering the necessary information. In addition, to accomplish their purposes Congress conferred broad powers of investigation on the regulatory agencies. A set of judicially determined constitutional principles has been developed based on the idea that administrative power of investigation is a necessity for modern administrative government.

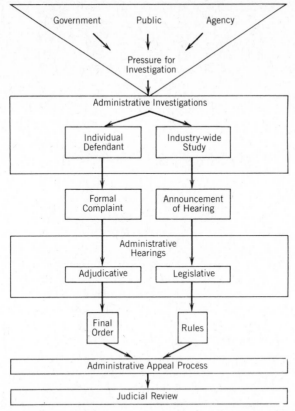

Figure 6-1.   Stages of administrative agency procedures.

ADMINISTRATIVE SUBPOENA POWER

Many administrative investigations are accomplished voluntarily and without reliance on compulsory process. However, since the need for information is sometimes resisted, administrative agencies may enforce their request by seeking a subpoena from the appropriate court. The agency may call for a subpoena to seek the testimony of a person (*ad testificandum*) or to request records (*duces tecum*). A subpoena, if ignored, subjects the recipient to charges of "contempt of court."

When the administrative agency is seeking judicial enforcement of its subpoena, the federal court may consider appropriate questions to determine whether the subpoena should be enforced. The Fourth Amendment protects "the people" from "unreasonable searches and seizures." It also prohibits court issuance of search warrants unless "probable cause" for the search is shown. If issued, the warrant must particularly describe the place to be searched and the person or things to be seized. Therefore, the court must determine whether the subpoena sought is overly broad and excessive in its request for information. Of course, the material sought also must be "subjects" that Congress has authorized the agency to investigate. However, Congress sought to avoid the protections of the Fourth Amendment in the following case.

WARRANTLESS SEARCH

Marshall v. Barlow's, Inc.
436 U.S. 307 (1978)
Supreme Court of the United States

Justice White

Section 8(a) of the Occupational Safety and Health Act of 1970 (OSHA or Act) empowers agents of the Secretary of Labor (Secretary) to search the work area of any employment facility within the Act's jurisdiction. The purpose of the search is to inspect for safety hazards and violations of OSHA regulations. No search warrant or other process is expressly required under the Act.

On the morning of September 11, 1975, an OSHA inspector entered the customer service area of Barlow's, Inc., an electrical and plumbing installation business located in Pocatello, Idaho. The president and general manager, Ferrol G. "Bill" Barlow, was on hand; and the OSHA inspector, after showing his credentials, informed Mr. Barlow that he wished to conduct a search of the working areas of the business. Mr. Barlow inquired whether any complaint had been received about his company. The inspector answered no, but that Barlow's, Inc., had simply turned up in the agency's selection process. The inspector again asked to enter the nonpublic area of the business; Mr. Barlow's response was to inquire whether the inspector had a search warrant. The inspector had none. Thereupon, Mr. Barlow refused the inspector admission to the employee area of his business. He said he was relying on his rights as guaranteed by the Fourth Amendment of the United States Constitution.

Three months later, the Secretary peti-

tioned the United States District Court for the District of Idaho to issue an order compelling Mr. Barlow to admit the inspector. The requested order was issued . . . and was presented to Mr. Barlow. . . . Mr. Barlow again refused admission, and he sought his own injunctive relief against the warrantless searches assertedly permitted by OSHA. A three-judge court was convened. . . . [I]t ruled in Mr. Barlow's favor. Concluding that *Camara* v. *Municipal Court,* 387 U.S. 523 (1967), controlled this case, the court held that the Fourth Amendment required a warrant for the type of search involved here and that the statutory authorization for warrantless inspections was unconstitutional. An injunction against searches or inspections pursuant to Section 8(a) was entered. The Secretary appealed, challenging the judgment.

The Warrant Clause of the Fourth Amendment protects commercial buildings as well as private homes. To hold otherwise would belie the origin of that Amendment, and the American colonial experience. . . . The general warrant was a recurring point of contention in the Colonies immediately preceding the Revolution. The particular offensiveness it engendered was acutely felt by the merchants and businessmen whose premises and products were inspected for compliance with the several parliamentary revenue measures that most irritated the colonists. . . . Against this background, it is untenable that the ban on warrantless searches was not intended to shield places of business as well as of residence.

This court has already held that warrantless searches are generally unreasonable, and that this rule applies to commercial premises as well as homes. . . .

These same cases also held that the Fourth Amendment prohibition against unreasonable searches protects against warrantless intrusions during civil as well as criminal investigations. . . . If the government intrudes on a person's property, the privacy interest suffers whether the government's motivation is to investigate violations of criminal laws or breaches of other statutory or regulatory standards. It therefore appears that unless some recognized exception to the warrant requirement applies, *See* v. *City of Seattle* would require a warrant to conduct the inspection sought in this case.

The Secretary urges that an exception from the search warrant requirement has been recognized for "pervasively regulated business[es]," and for "closely regulated" industries "long subject to close supervision and inspection." These cases are indeed exceptions, but they represent responses to relatively unique circumstances. Certain industries have such a history of government oversight that no reasonable expectation of privacy could exist for a proprietor over the stock of such an enterprise. Liquor and firearms are industries of this type; when an entrepreneur embarks upon such a business, he has voluntarily chosen to subject himself to a full arsenal of governmental regulation.

* * *

Whether the Secretary proceeds to secure a warrant or other process, with or without prior notice, his entitlement to inspect will not depend on his demonstrating probable cause to believe that conditions in violation of OSHA exist on the premises. Probable cause in the criminal law sense is not required. For the purposes of an administrative search such as this, probable cause justifying the issuance of a warrant may be based not only on specific evidence of an existing violation but also on a showing that "reasonable legislative or administrative standards for conducting an . . . inspection are satisfied with respect to a particular [establishment]."

* * *

Nor do we agree that the incremental protections afforded the employer's privacy by a warrant are so marginal that they fail to justify the administrative burdens that may be entailed. The authority to make warrantless searches devolves almost unbridled discretion upon executive and administrative officers, particularly those in the field, as to when to search and whom to search. A warrant, by contrast, would provide assurances from a neutral officer that the inspection is reasonable under the Constitution, is authorized by statute, and is pursuant to an administrative plan containing specific neutral criteria. Also, a warrant would then and there advise the owner of the scope and objects of the search, beyond which limits the inspector is not expected to proceed. These are important functions which underlie the Court's prior decisions that the Warrant Clause applies to inspections for compliance with regulatory statutes. We conclude that the concerns expressed by the Secretary do not suffice to justify warrantless inspections under OSHA or vitiate the general constitutional requirement that for a search to be reasonable a warrant must be obtained.

We hold that Barlow's was entitled to a declaratory judgment that the Act is unconstitutional insofar as it purports to authorize inspections without warrant or its equivalent and to an injunction enjoining the Act's enforcement to that extent.

Questions
1. What industries are identified as subject to warrantless searches? Why?
2. What must OSHA administrators show to a court to obtain a warrant?
3. What advantages are achieved by a system of issuing warrants only on a court's approval?

COMPELLED SELF-INCRIMINATION

The Fifth Amendment protects individuals from being compelled to testify against themselves. This right protects not only compelled oral testimony, but one's possession of documents, records, or other objects that might be incriminating in nature. The following case illustrates some of the limitations of the Fifth Amendment rights in relation to business operations.

United States v. White
322 U.S. 694 (1944)
Supreme Court of the United States

Justice Murphy

*   *   *

Respondent contends that an officer of an unincorporated labor union possesses a constitutional right to refuse to produce, in compliance with a subpoena *duces tecum*, records of the union which are in his custody and which might tend to incriminate him. He relies upon the . . . explicit guarantee of the Fifth Amendment that no person shall be compelled in any criminal case to be a witness against himself. . . .

The Constitutional privilege against self-incrimination is essentially a personal one, applying only to natural individuals. It grows out of the high sentiment and regard of our jurisprudence for conducting criminal trials and investigatory proceedings upon a plane of dignity, humanity and impartiality. It is designed to prevent the use of legal process to force from the lips of the accused individual the evidence necessary to convict him or to force him to produce and authenticate any personal documents or effects that might incriminate him. . . .

Since the privilege against self-incrimina-

tion is a purely personal one, it cannot be utilized by or on behalf of any organization, such as a corporation. . . . Moreover, the papers and effects which the privilege protects must be the private property of the person claiming the privilege, or at least in his possession in a purely personal capacity. But individuals, when acting as representatives of a collective group, cannot be said to be exercising their personal rights and duties nor to be entitled to their purely personal privileges. Rather they assume the rights, duties, and privileges of the artificial entity or association of which they are agents or officers and they are bound by its obligations. In their official capacity, therefore, they have no privilege against self-incrimination. And the official records and documents of the organization that are held by them in a representative rather than in a personal capacity cannot be the subject of the personal privilege against self-incrimination, even though production of the papers might tend to incriminate them personally. . . .

Such records and papers are not the private records of the individual members or officers of the organization. Usually, if not always, they are open to inspection by the members and this right may be enforced on appropriate occasions by available legal procedures. They therefore embody no element of personal privacy and carry with them no claim of personal privilege.

* * *

Basically, the power to compel the production of the records of any organization, whether it be incorporated or not, arises out of the inherent and necessary power of the federal and state governments to enforce their laws, with the privilege against self-incrimination being limited to its historic function of protecting only the natural individual from compulsory incrimination through his own testimony or personal records.

It follows that labor unions, as well as their officers and agents acting in their official capacity, cannot invoke this personal privilege. This conclusion is not reached by any mechanical comparison of unions with corporations or with other entities nor by any determination of whether unions technically may be regarded as legal personalities for any or all purposes. The test, rather, is whether one can fairly say under all the circumstances that a particular type of organization has a character so impersonal in the scope of its membership and activities that it cannot be said to embody or represent the purely private or personal interests of its con-

stituents, but rather to embody their common or group interests only. If so, the privilege cannot be invoked on behalf of the organization or its representatives in their official capacity. Labor unions—national or local, incorporated or unincorporated—clearly meet the test. . . .

These various considerations compel the conclusion that respondent could not claim the personal privilege against self-incrimination under these circumstances. The subpoena *duces tecum* was directed to the union and demanded the production only of its official documents and records. Respondent could not claim the privilege on behalf of the union because the union did not itself possess such a privilege. Moreover, the privilege is personal to the individual called as a witness, making it impossible for him to set up the privilege of a third person as an excuse for a refusal to answer or to produce documents. . . . Nor could respondent claim the privilege on behalf of himself as an officer of the union or as an individual. The documents he sought to place under the protective shield of the privilege were official union documents held by him in his capacity as a representative of the union. No valid claim was made that any part of them constituted his own private papers. He thus could not object that the union's books and records might incriminate him as an officer or as an individual.

Questions

1. The Court indicated that the protection of the Fifth Amendment is personal. What does the Court mean by an essentially *personal* privilege against self-incrimination?
2. What basic reason did the Court use for restricting the constitutional protection of the Fifth Amendment to individuals?
3. Are the records of all "collective groups" subject to administrative investigative powers? May an administrative agency gain information from a corporation? From a nonincorporated entity? From a religious organization? From a communist organization? From the National Association of Colored People?

PUBLIC RECORDS

The privilege against self-incrimination does not apply to records required to be kept by statute or some valid regulation. In *Shapiro* v. *United States*, 335 U.S. 1 (1948), the Supreme Court held that all business records, if required to be kept, are "public" and therefore subject to agency investigation and utilization in criminal prosecutions. The Court declared that "the Privilege which exists as to private papers cannot be maintained in relation to 'records required by law to be kept in order that there may be suitable information of transactions which are the appropriate subjects of governmental regulation and the enforcement of restrictions validly established.'" Moreover, in *California* v. *Byers*, 402 U.S. 424 (1971) the Court ruled that the privilege against self-incrimination cannot be invoked to prevent compelled disclosures unless the disclosures involve "substantial hazards of self-incrimination." Since the defendant had been charged with failure to stop and identify himself at the scene of an auto accident as required by law, the Court had to determine whether such disclosures with respect to automobile accidents entailed a risk of self-incrimination. The Court answered in the negative and emphasized that the statutory purpose was noncriminal and that self-reporting was indispensable to the fulfillment of the statute. The Court said, "A name, linked with a motor vehicle, is no more incriminating than the tax return linked with the disclosure of income. It identifies but does not by itself implicate anyone in criminal conduct."

IMMUNITY STATUTES

The privilege against self-incrimination has been limited by congressional enactment of "immunity" statutes. These statutes compel testimony and production of records even when the privilege of the Fifth Amendment applies. However, the statute confers immunity from prosecution for any offense disclosed in such testimony and records. The Compulsory Testimony Act of 1892 provides the following.

No person shall be excused from . . . testifying or from producing . . . papers . . . before the [administrative agency], or in obedience to the subpoena of the [agency] . . . on the ground . . . that the . . . evidence . . . may tend to incriminate him . . . but no person shall be prosecuted or subject to any penalty or forfeiture for or on account of any transactions, matter or thing, concerning which he may testify, or produce evidence, documentary or otherwise, before said [agency], or in obedience to its subpoena.

In 1970 an amendment was added to this statute that requires that anyone who refuses to testify or to produce records may be fined or imprisoned. All major regulatory agencies have a similar provision to aid in the enforcement of their regulatory powers. The Supreme Court has ruled that such statutes are constitutional because prosecution for crimes revealed by such testimony may not be maintained. Other penalties, such as loss of job, expulsion from organizations, requirement of state registration, or passport ineligibility, do not affect the constitutionality of the statute.

ADMINISTRATIVE HEARINGS

The Administrative Procedure Act (APA) contains provisions that pertain to the procedural aspects of activities by regulatory agencies. The APA prescribes procedures to be followed by administrative agencies in rulemaking (legislative) and in adjudicatory proceedings. The cases in this section contrast the differences between rulemaking and adjudicatory hearings.

After preliminary investigations, an agency may begin an adjudicatory hearing by issuing a formal complaint against a particular defendant or defendants. The agency issues a complaint when it has "reason to believe" that the law has been violated in some manner. The defendants have a number of days in which to answer the complaint. Often the defendant may be interested in having the issue settled by the entry of a "consent order." The defendant is given an opportunity to negotiate an agreement with the agency, which, if accepted, may become a consent order. In such consent orders, it is understood that the agreement is for purposes of settlement of the controversy and does not constitute an admission by the defendant of having violated the law. However, when a consent order is issued by the agency, it carries the force of law with respect to future behavior by the defendant. Any violations of such order by the defendant may result in civil penalties, such as a fine, for each violation. If the parties are not able to negotiate an agreement, an adjudicatory hearing is held to determine if a violation of the law as alleged in the complaint has, in fact, occurred.

NEED FOR ADJUDICATIVE HEARING

Often administrative officials act against a person without first affording the individual a hearing. Such instances are increasingly challenged as a denial of due process of law. For example, in 1961 it was held that due process requires notice and some opportunity for hearing before students at a tax-supported college could be expelled for misconduct.[3] Whether a hearing is required prior to administrative action depends on the circumstances and the interests of the parties involved. The students' "interest" was the right to remain at a public institution of higher learning without interruption of studies. On the other hand, the government's "interest" involved "no consideration of immediate danger to the public or of peril to the national security," which would prevent the school board from exercising at least the fundamental principle of fairness by giving the accused students an opportunity to be heard in their own defense. In effect, the Court ruled that the interest advanced by the students outweighed the interest of the state school system and, therefore, entitled the students to a hearing *prior* to administrative action.

In contrast, the Supreme Court held that a student dismissed for poor academic performance was not entitled to a hearing *prior* to dismissal.[4] The Court said that "there is a . . . significant difference between the failure of a student to meet academic standards and the violation by a student of valid rules of conduct. This difference calls for far less stringent procedural requirements in the case of an academic dismissal." The Court felt that the student had been awarded as much due process as was required because the school had fully informed the student of the faculty's dissatisfaction with her progress and the danger this posed to continued enrollment. The Court concluded:

Academic evaluations of a student, in contrast to disciplinary determinations, bear little resemblance to the judicial and administrative factfinding proceedings to which we have traditionally attached a full hearing requirement.

The decision to dismiss respondent . . . rested on the academic judgment of school officials that she did not have the necessary . . . ability to perform adequately . . . and was making insufficient progress toward the goal. Such a judgment is by its nature more subjective and evaluative than the typical factual questions presented in the average disciplinary decision. Like the decision of an individual professor as to the proper grade for a student in his course, the determination whether to dismiss a student for academic reasons requires an expert evaluation of cumulative information and is not readily adapted to the procedural tools of judicial or administrative decision-making.

Under such circumstances, we decline to ignore the historic judgment of educators and thereby formalize the academic dismissal process by requiring a hearing.

In short, the Court was not convinced that this type of decision could be better handled in a formal hearing. Without sufficient benefits to be expected from the imposition of the hearing requirement and recognizing the burdens imposed on the educational institution by the hearing requirement, the Court ruled that the student's interest was sufficiently protected by the present process of warnings of possible academic dismissal.

Using the same "balancing" process in a business setting, the Court has ruled that in "extraordinary situations" it is necessary for administrative officials to seize business property or otherwise act immediately without an opportunity for a *prior* hearing. The Court has held that immediate administrative action is needed "to collect internal revenue of the United States, to meet the needs of the national war effort, to protect against economic disaster of a bank failure, and protect the public from misbranded drugs and contaminated food."[5] In each of these situations, the public's interest outweighs the private interest and justifies the summary action by the government. In most instances, a *subsequent* hearing is held to determine if the administrative official acted within his or her authority and reasonably in the circumstances. If not, the individual whose property was confiscated or whose interest was interfered with is entitled to compensation from the governmental official.

NEED FOR LEGISLATIVE HEARINGS

Pharmaceutical Manufacturers Association v. Finch

307 F. Supp. 858 (1970)
U.S. District Court (Del.)

In this action for declaratory and injunctive relief, the Pharmaceutical Manufacturers Association ("PMA"), on behalf of its members, seeks a preliminary injunction restraining the Secretary of Health, Education and Welfare [HEW] and the Commissioner of Food and Drugs from taking any action in reliance upon the regulations contained in the Commissioner's Order of September 19, 1969. The September regulations promulgated new standards of evidence necessary to demonstrate the effectiveness of drug products and applied those standards retroactively so as to place in jeopardy the continued marketing of thousands of drug products introduced before 1962 with Food and Drug Administration ("FDA") approval and effectiveness of which FDA has not yet challenged. . . .

. . . PMA contends that the regulations are invalid because they were issued without notice and opportunity for comment in violation of the Administrative Procedure Act. . . .

. . . [T]he Administrative Procedure Act requires the rule-making by an agency be preceded by "general notice of proposed rule-making" in the Federal Register at least thirty days before the effective date of the proposed rule, and further requires that the agency afford interested persons "an opportunity to participate in the rule-making through submission of written data, views or arguments with or without opportunity for oral presentation." That procedure was not followed in this case. The September regulations were made effective by the Commissioner upon their publication in the Federal Register without prior notice or an opportunity for submission of comments by interested parties.

Exempt from the general requirements of notice and opportunity for comment are "in-terpretative rules, general statements of policy, or rules of agency organization, procedure, or practice." The Commissioner has characterized the September regulations as "procedural and interpretative" and thus contends that they fall within the exception to the notice and comment requirement. But the label placed on the September rules by the Commissioner does not determine whether the notice and comment provisions are applicable. As the Supreme Court has emphasized, in holding that a regulation of the Federal Communications Commission constituted an order subject to judicial review, "[T]he particular label placed upon it by the Commission is not necessarily conclusive, for it is the substance of what the Commission has purported to do and has done which is decisive."

. . . [T]hat determination must be made in the light of the basic purpose of those statutory requirements. The basic policy of Section 4 at least requires that when a proposed regulation of general applicability has a substantial impact on the regulated industry, or an important class of the members of the products of that industry, notice and opportunity for comment should first be provided. . . .

The all pervasive and substantial impact which the September regulations have upon the drug industry and in turn upon prescribing physicians and their patients, makes it imperative that the Commissioner comply with the notice and comment provisions of Section 4 before such regulations become effective.

Questions

1. The Administrative Procedure Act requires an agency to give notice and an opportunity to participate to those individuals affected by the creation of a new rule. However, the Administrative Procedure Act contains some exemptions. What exemptions did the secretary of HEW rely on to negate the necessity of providing notice and opportunity to participate? Why did the district court not agree with the secretary's determination on the status of this exemption?

2. Can a decision (rule) announced in an adjudicatory proceeding become a substitute process for announcing "rules"? The Supreme Court said the following.

The rule-making provisions of . . . [the Administrative Procedure Act] . . . were designed to assure fairness and mature consideration of rules of general application. They may not be avoided by the process of making rules in the course of adjudicatory proceedings. There is no warrant in law for the Board to replace the statutory scheme with a rule-making procedure of its own invention. Apart from the fact that the device fashioned by the Board does not comply with statutory command, it obviously falls short of the substance of the requirements of the Administrative Procedure Act. The "rule" created in *Excelsior* was not published in the Federal Register which is the statutory and accepted means of giving notice of a rule as adopted; only selected organizations were given notice of the "hearing," whereas notice in the Federal Register would have been general in character; under the Administrative Procedure Act, the terms of substance of the rule would have to be stated in the notice of hearing, and all interested parties would have an opportunity to participate in the rule making. . . . Adjudicated cases may and do, of course, serve as vehicles for the formulation of agency policies, which are applied and announced therein. They generally provide a guide to action that the agency may be expected to take in future cases. Subject to the qualified role of *stare decisis* in the administrative process, they may serve as precedents. But this is far from saying . . . that commands, decisions, or policies announced in adjudication are "rules" in the sense that they must, without more, be obeyed by the affected public. *NLRB* v. *Wyman-Gordon Co.*, 394 U.S. 759 (1969).

PARTICIPATION IN HEARINGS

Administrative agencies are increasingly faced with the demand for a wider participation in the hearings. Various parties, often consumer groups, request the right to be heard in hearings usually reserved exclusively for the agency and the party under the agency's jurisdiction. The following case illustrates the issues involved.

Hahn v. Gottlieb
430 F. 2d 1243 (1970)
United States Court of Appeals (1st Cir.)

In this appeal, we are asked to decide whether tenants in housing subsidized under the National Housing Act (NHA) have the right to an administrative hearing. . . .

Plaintiffs are members of a tenants' association at the Castle Square project in Boston (the project), a development of low- and middle-income housing financed under NHA. Defendants Gottlieb and Druker (the landlord) are the current owners of the project. Prior to the expiration of the plaintiffs' leases in July 1969, the landlord filed a proposed monthly rent increase of $28 per apartment with the Federal Housing Administration (FHA). Plaintiffs sought an opportunity to be heard on the proposed increase; and, when the FHA failed to satisfy their request, they brought suit in federal district court. . . .

. . . [T]he statute confers broad discretion on the Secretary of HUD. The Secretary is authorized to approve mortgagors and to supervise their operations "under a regulatory agreement or otherwise, as to rents, charges, and methods of operation, in such form and in such manner as in the opinion of the Secretary will effectuate the purposes of this section."

Implementing these broad grants of authority, the Secretary has promulgated regulations concerning priories and income limits for occupancy in FHA projects. The Secretary also regulates the landlord's return on his investment by strictly supervising accounting practices, and, in the case of limited distribution mortgagors like defendants Gottlieb and Druker, by setting a six percent ceiling on return. Applications for rent increases must be submitted to the FHA, which takes into account the rental income necessary to maintain a project's economic soundness and "to provide a reasonable return on the investment consistent with providing reasonable rentals to the tenants." FHA's agreement with the landlord in this case further provides that rental increases will be approved if necessary to compensate for increases in expense "over which the owners have no effective control."

The regulations illustrate that the success of a FHA project requires a flexible exercise of administrative discretion. The ultimate goal of the program is housing for low- and middle-class families, but this goal is to be achieved by expanding the range of housing needs which can be met by private enterprise. To provide low-income housing maintaining a sound investment requires considerable adaptability. We think Congress recognized this need for adaptability when it authorized the Secretary to regulate mortgagors by individual agreement as well as by general rule. Of course, the need for administrative flexibility does not of itself preclude an agency hearing or judicial review, but we must take care lest we kill the goose in our solicitude for the eggs.

Plaintiffs' initial claim is that they are entitled to a formal hearing before the FHA prior to the approval of any rent increase. This contention finds no support in the text of the National Housing Act. Plaintiffs claim, however, that both the right to a hearing and its procedural characteristics can be derived from the

Due Process Clause of the Fifth Amendment. . . .

The proceeding in which plaintiffs seek to assert their interest is basically an informal rate-making process. The landlord who seeks a rent increase submits documentation to the FHA showing his expenses, return on investment, and the like. The FHA staff then examines his proposal in the light of the terms of the regulatory agreement, the broad criteria of the regulations, and current economic conditions. Plaintiffs seek to encumber these negotiations with a formal hearing, the right to cross-examine adverse witnesses, and an impartial decision-maker, who must state the reasons for his decision and the evidence on which he relies. These procedural safeguards are characteristic of adjudicatory proceedings, where the outcome turns on accurate resolution of specific factual disputes. Such safeguards are not, however, essential in "legislative" proceedings, such as rate-making, where decision depends on broad familiarity with economic conditions. . . .

The distinction between "legislative" and "adjudicative" facts is particularly apt in this case, where it is the tenants rather than the landlord who seek a hearing. The tenants are unlikely to have special familiarity with their landlord's financial conditions, the intricacies of project management, or the state of the economy in the surrounding area. Hopefully, the FHA can check the accuracy of the landlord's documentation without their assistance. They may be aware of construction defects in their own living areas, but if, contrary to [law], a building has been approved which does not conform to applicable standards, there would seem to be limited utility in rehearsing old mistakes each time a rental increase is sought. Of course, tenant's complaints about maintenance and living conditions ought to be heard, but such grievances can be dealt with without requiring a trial-type hearing with each rent increase. Indeed, an effective grievance system should be operable at all times, not merely when the landlord seeks to raise his rents. Thus, the elaborate procedural safeguards which plaintiffs demand are unlikely to elicit essential information in the general run of cases.

These procedures would, however, place a significant burden on the relationship between the landlord and the FHA. At present, applications for rent increases are merely one aspect of an on-going relationship between insured and insurer. Plaintiffs would turn these applications into occasions for full-scale review of the relationship, as their conduct in the hearing they have already received illustrates. Such reconsideration may delay economically necessary rent increases and discourage private investors from entering the FHA program at all.

Equally important the project in question contains some 500 tenants, each of whom has the same interest in low-rent housing.

Applying the constitutionally relevant test, therefore, it seems to us that the government interest in a summary procedure for approving rent increases outweighs the tenants' interest in greater procedural safeguards. The procedures demanded by plaintiffs would place substantial additional burdens on the insurer-insured relationship without necessarily improving the fundamental fairness of the proceedings. We, therefore, hold that tenants in housing financed under the National Housing Act are not constitutionally entitled to an administrative hearing on their landlord's proposals for increased rents.

Questions

1. What statutory authority does the FHA have over the owners of tenements in which the FHA has supplied funds? What factors does the FHA consider in determining the appropriate rental rates for FHA housing?

2. Why did the Court rule that the tenants were not entitled to a hearing when FHA is considering rental increases? Do you agree with the reasoning?

3. In *Hahn* the Court was faced with a hearing that was to establish "legislative" facts for the purpose of determining appropriate rental rates. Although it may be appropriate to deny tenants a hearing in regard to ratemaking, would the Court feel differently if the dispute concerned "adjudicative" facts? Consider *Escalera* v. *New York City Housing Authority,* 425 F. 2d 853 (2d. Cir., 1970) in which the housing authority terminated tenancies on the ground of nondesirability of the tenants. The procedural system to terminate included conversations between the project manager and the tenant; tenant hearings before the Tenant Review Board, which allowed the tenant to summarize his or her position but not to present any witness; and a Review Board decision based on items in the tenant's file that may be unknown to the tenant. No findings or reasons for the termination were released to the tenant. Would the Court consider this procedural system to be sufficient for the establishment of adjudicative facts with which to make a fair determination of the tenant's rights?

Despite the rationale of *Hahn,* the imbalance of consumer advocacy in administrative hearings that determine policy has been increasingly recognized in judicial decisions and legislative debates and proposals. In *United Church of Christ* v.

FCC, 359 F. 2d 994 (D.C. Cir. 1966), an allegedly racist Mississippi radio station was applying for a renewal of its license before the Federal Communication Commission (FCC). The church petitioned for a right to intervene and present evidence and arguments in opposition to the relicensing. The FCC refused to hear the church on grounds that the listening public had not suffered an injury and that if the listeners had "standing to sue" in these cases, it would pose great administrative burdens on the agency. The court of appeals disagreed with the FCC and remanded the case back to the FCC with the provision that some "audience participation" be allowed in the new proceedings before the commission. The court determined that unless consumers could be heard, there might be no one to bring program deficiencies or offensive commercialization to the attention of the commission in an effective manner. As this case indicates, there is a growing body of case law in which the courts are requiring federal agencies to consider the consumer groups that are being affected by the agency's decisions.

The concept of intervention before regulatory bodies by state attorney generals is also growing. Since attorney generals are generally charged with the responsibility of representation before various bodies of state government, the attorney general may intervene to present various sides of an issue before a commission. It is not uncommon for two assistant attorney generals to appear on opposite sides on the same case before a commission.

Regulatory agencies that oversee public utilities are charged with protecting the public interest. Since the services and goods produced by these regulated industries are paid for by the consumer, the agencies seek to balance a "fair price" to the consumer for these services and products with a "fair return" to the supplier. Regulation seeks, like competition, to provide satisfactory services at rates that make efficient use of natural resources. However, historically the performance of regulatory agencies has not always been satisfactory from the consumer's point of view. The regulatory agencies usually set price levels on a cost-plus basis and interfere little in the development of standards of quality for service or products. Many feel this performance was the result of agencies being susceptible to great private pressures from the industries they regulate. To compensate for these industry pressures in the electric utility area, Congress enacted the Public Utility Regulatory Policies Act (PURPA) of 1978. PURPA entitles any consumer to intervene and participate as a matter of right in electric utility ratemaking proceedings. PURPA also establishes alternative methods to compensate such consumer representatives if they substantially contribute to the approval of a rate incorporating their views.

ADMINISTRATIVE APPEALS

In larger administrative agencies, adjudicatory hearings are often held before independent administrative law judges. These individuals are civil servants performing judicial duties on assignment to various agencies. The decision of the administrative law judge articulates the "findings of fact" and "interpretations of law," which are later reviewed by the top officials of the agency. This review by the agency commissioners or board members is an internal appeal process to correct or affirm the decisions of the hearing judge. Consequently, a final decision or order by the agency is not rendered until the entire process has been completed. On completion, the decision of the agency is subject to review by the courts, which usually involves an appellate court because the agency served as the "trial court." To allow the agency to correct its own internal errors and avoid unnecessary court congestion, the courts generally review only the "final orders" of the agencies. Sometimes a party may attempt an earlier review by the courts. Such efforts are most often denied "on the long settled rule of judicial administration that no one is entitled to judicial relief for a supposed or threatened injury until the prescribed administrative remedy has been exhausted."[6] This rule requiring exhaustion of the administrative remedy "cannot be circumvented by asserting that the charge on which the complaint rests is groundless" or "that the mere holding of the prescribed administrative hearing would result in irreparable damage." Trials are sometimes necessary to establish that the suit is groundless.

Questions
1. May a defendant obtain a court injunction to stop an administrative hearing that is outside the agency's statutory power?
2. What is the purpose of the rule requiring an exhaustion of administrative remedies prior to obtaining judicial review?

JUDICIAL REVIEW

Judicial review is employed as a control device over an administrative agency's actions on completion of the administrative proceedings. The function of judicial review is not to examine the correctness of an administrative decision but rather to determine whether an agency has done the following:

1. Acted within its delegated authority.
2. Conducted a fair proceeding.
3. Made a reasonable decision supported by substantial evidence.

The function of judicial review may be restricted. The statute, for example, may provide that the agency's determination shall be final and not subject to judicial review. Congress, for example, has often established draft boards whose selection of young people for the armed forces is not subject to judicial review.

Also, there are practical limits on judicial review. Court review is expensive, it involves delay, and there is perhaps a fear of adverse publicity. Moreover, even if the court reverses the agency decision and remands the case, the agency can reach essentially the same decision again and merely correct its court-declared error.

STANDARDS FOR REVIEW

Citizens To Preserve Overton Park, Inc. v. Volpe

401 U.S. 412 (1971)
Supreme Court of the United States

Justice Marshall

Section 4(f) of the Department of Transportation Act and § 138 of the Federal-Aid Highway Act are clear and specific directives. Both provide that the Secretary "shall not approve any program or project" that requires the use of any public parkland "unless (1) there is no feasible and prudent alternative to the use of such land, and (2) such program includes all possible planning to minimize harm to such park. . . . " This language is a plain and explicit bar to the use of federal funds for construction of highways through parks—only the most unusual situations are exempted. . . .

For that we must look to § 706 of the Administrative Procedure Act, which provides that a "reviewing court shall . . . hold unlawful and set aside agency action, findings, and conclusions . . ." if the action was "arbitrary, capricious, an abuse of discretion, or otherwise not in accordance with law" or if the action failed to meet statutory, procedural, or constitutional requirements. . . .

The court is first required to decide whether the Secretary acted within the scope of his authority. This determination naturally begins with a delineation of the scope of the Secretary's authority and discretion.

As has been shown, Congress has specified only a small range of choices that the Secretary can make. Also involved in this initial inquiry is a determination of whether on the facts the Secretary's decision can reasonably be said to be within that range. The reviewing court must consider whether the Secretary properly construed his authority to approve the use of parkland as limited to situations where there are no feasible alternative routes or where feasible alternative routes involve uniquely diffi-

cult problems. And the reviewing court must be able to find that the Secretary could have reasonably believed that in this case there are no feasible alternatives or that alternatives do involve unique problems.

Scrutiny of the facts does not end, however, with the determination that the Secretary has acted within the scope of his statutory authority. Section 706 (2) (A) requires a finding that the actual choice made was not "arbitrary, capricious, an abuse of discretion, or otherwise not in accordance with law." To make this finding the court must consider whether the decision was based on a consideration of the relevant factors and whether there has been a clear error of judgment.

Although this inquiry into the facts is to be searching and careful, the ultimate standard of review is a narrow one. The court is not empowered to substitute its judgment for that of the agency.

The final inquiry is whether the Secretary's action followed the necessary procedural requirements. Here the only procedural error alleged is the failure of the Secretary to make formal findings and state his reason for allowing the highway to be built through the park.

Undoubtedly, review of the Secretary's action is hampered by his failure to make such findings, but the absence of formal findings does not necessarily require that the case be remanded to the Secretary. Neither the Department of Transportation Act nor the Federal-Aid Highway Act requires such formal findings. Moreover, the Administrative Procedure Act requirements that there be formal findings in certain rule-making and adjudicatory proceedings do not apply to the Secretary's action here. . . .

Thus it is necessary to remand this case to the District Court for plenary review of the

Secretary's decision. That review is to be based on the full administrative record that was before the Secretary at the time he made his decision. But since the bare record may not disclose the factors that were considered or the Secretary's construction of the evidence it may be necessary for the District Court to require some explanation in order to determine if the Secretary acted within the scope of his authority and if the Secretary's action was justifiable under the applicable standard. The court may require the administrative officials who participated in the decision to give testimony explaining their action. Of course, such inquiry into the mental processes of administrative decisionmakers is usually to be avoided. But . . . it may be that the only way there can be effective judicial review is by examining the decisionmakers themselves.

The District Court is not, however, required to make such an inquiry. It may be that the Secretary can prepare formal findings that will provide an adequate explanation for his action. Such an explanation will, to some extent, be a "*post hoc* rationalization" and thus must be viewed critically. If the District Court decides that additional explanation is necessary, that court should consider which method will prove the most expeditious so that full review may be had as soon as possible.

Questions

1. What should the Court consider in deciding whether the secretary acted within the scope of this authority?
2. Assuming that the secretary did act within the scope of his statutory authority, the Court must determine whether the actual decision made by the secretary was not "arbitrary, capricious, an abuse of discretion, or otherwise not in accordance with law." How is the Court to determine whether the decision made by the secretary was arbitrary?
3. The Court on review can also determine whether the secretary followed any necessary procedural requirements. What procedural error was alleged to have been violated by the secretary? Did the Court conclude that this procedural requirement existed?

DISCLOSING INFORMATION

Administrative agencies in their regulatory functions accumulate a great deal of information concerning individuals in business enterprises. The chief administrative agent, the President, has from the beginning of our nation asserted a constitutional right to withhold information. Presidents have withheld information from Congress and others under the doctrine of executive privilege. Issues concerning the extent of executive privilege are complex and continuing, but executive privilege unquestionably exists. The courts have jurisdiction to consider problems concerning the privilege and in determining its scope.

The Freedom of Information Act (FOIA) is a 1966 amendment of the Administrative Procedure Act. It requires disclosure of governmental records to anyone unless the governmental records are specifically exempted by the statute.

District courts are given jurisdiction to enforce its provisions. The act requires that each agency shall make available to the public information in the following manner.

1. Substantive rules and general policies of general applicability adopted by the agency must be published in the *Federal Register.*
2. An agency must make available to the public its opinions, statements of policy, interpretations, staff manuals, and instructions.
3. Each agency on request shall make the records concerning facts compiled by the agency in the course of investigation or facts filed with the agency promptly available to any person.

These disclosures must be made regardless of the motive, interest, or intent of the individual making the request. The request might include the right to inspect, copy, or suggest corrections in the records. The federal district court shall determine whether the record shall be disclosed or amended, with the burden of proof on the agency to justify its refusal to disclose or amend. Failure to obey district court orders would result in contempt of court citations for noncompliance against the administrative officials.

Strangely, the act did not mention executive privilege. Instead, the act made the following exemptions from disclosure for matters:

(1) specifically required by Executive order to be kept secret in the interest of the national defense or foreign policy;
(2) related solely to the internal personnel rules and practices of an agency;
(3) specifically exempted from disclosure by statute;
(4) trade secrets and commercial or financial information obtained from a person and privileged or confidential;
(5) inter-agency or intra-agency memorandums or letters which would not be available by law to a party other than an agency in litigation with the agency;
(6) personnel and medical files and similar files the disclosure of which would constitute a clearly unwarranted invasion of personal privacy;
(7) investigatory files compiled for law enforcement purposes except to the extent available by law to a party other than an agency;
(8) contained in or related to examination, operating, or condition reports prepared by, on behalf of, or for the use of an agency responsible for the regulation or supervision of financial institutions; or
(9) geological and geophysical information and data, including maps, concerning wells.

The nine exemptions of the act are not the only law that protects against required disclosure. Administrative officers may be governed by other statutory law, by the common law, by executive privilege, by executive orders, and agency-made law in the form of regulations, orders, or instructions. Often legislation confers discretionary powers on agency officers to disclose or not disclose specified information. Consequently, the courts often have to balance the Information Act with other statutes that may apply to the situation. These confusing rules and contradictory enactments have caused many commentators to assert that Congress created a rather shabby product in the Information Act. They maintain that many deficiencies in the act result from congressional inattention and indifference. Perhaps, this is because Congress prepared this legislation rather than following the lead of the executive branch of government. Legislation originated and promoted through Congress by the executive branch often appears more coherent and internally consistent than legislation prepared by Congress alone. Although the principle of open government with citizenry access to governmental information is vital to a free system of government, it is unfortunate that Congress was not able to achieve these goals in a more satisfactory fashion. However, the first steps in any new frontier are usually small.

INFORMATIONAL PIRACY

Chrysler Corp. v. Brown
441 U.S. 369 (1979)
Supreme Court of the United States

Justice Rehnquist

The expanding range of federal regulatory activity and growth in the Government sector of the economy have increased federal agencies' demand for information about the activities of private individuals and corporations. These developments have paralleled a related concern about secrecy in Government and abuse of power. The Freedom of Information Act (hereinafter "FOIA") was a response to this concern, but it has also had a largely unforeseen tendency to exacerbate the uneasiness of those who comply with governmental demands for information. For under the FOIA third parties have been able to obtain Government files containing information submitted by corporations and individuals who thought the information would be held in confidence.

This case belongs to a class that has been popularly denominated "reverse-FOIA" suits, The Chrysler Corporation seeks to enjoin agency disclosure on the grounds that it is inconsistent with the FOIA. . . .

As a party to numerous Government contracts, Chrysler is required to comply with Executive Orders 11246 and 11375, which charge the Secretary of Labor with ensuring that corporations who benefit from Government contracts provide equal employment opportunity regardless of race or sex. The U.S. Department of Labor's Office of Federal Contract Compliance Programs (OFCCP) has promulgated regulations which require Government contractors to furnish reports and other information about their affirmative action programs and the general composition of their work forces.

* * *

Regulations promulgated by the Secretary of Labor provide for public disclosure of information from records of the OFCCP and its compliance agencies. Those regulations state that notwithstanding exemption from mandatory disclosure under the Freedom of Information Act.

records obtained or generated pursuant to Executive Order 11246 [as amended] . . . shall be made available for inspection and copying if it is determined that the requested inspection or copying furthers the public interest and does not impede any of the functions of the OFCC[P] or the Compliance Agencies except in the case of records disclosure of which is prohibited by law.

It is the voluntary disclosure contemplated by this regulation, over and above that mandated by the FOIA, which is the gravamen of Chrysler's complaint in this case.

* * *

We have decided a number of FOIA cases in the last few years. . . . We have, moreover, consistently recognized that the basic objective of the Act is disclosure.

In contending that the FOIA bars disclosure of the requested equal employment opportunity information, Chrysler relies on the Act's nine exemptions and argues that they require an agency to withhold exempted material. In this case it relies specifically on Exemption 4:

(b) [FOIA] does not apply to matters that are—
(4) trade secrets and commercial or financial information obtained from a person and privileged or confidential. . . .

Chrysler contends that the nine exemptions in general, and Exemption 4 in particular, reflect a sensitivity to the privacy interests of private individuals and nongovernmental entities. That contention may be conceded without inexorably requiring the conclusion that the exemptions impose affirmative duties on an agency to withhold information sought. In fact, that conclusion is not supported by the language, logic, or history of the Act.

The organization of the Act is straightforward. Subsection (a) places a general obligation on the agency to make information available to the public and sets out specific modes of disclosure for certain classes of information. Subsection (b), which lists the exemptions, simply states that the specified material is not subject to the disclosure obligations set out in subsection (a). By its terms, subsection (b) demarcates the limits of the agency's obligation to disclose; it does not foreclose disclosure.

That the FOIA is exclusively a disclosure statute is, perhaps, demonstrated most convincingly by examining its provision for judicial relief. Subsection (a)(4)(b) gives federal district courts "jurisdiction to enjoin the agency from withholding agency records and to order the production of any agency records improperly withheld from the complainant." That provision does not give the authority to bar disclosure, and thus fortifies our belief that Chrysler, and courts which have shared its view, have incorrectly interpreted the exemption provisions to the FOIA. The Act is an attempt to meet the demand for open government while preserving workable confidentiality in governmental decisionmaking. Congress appreciated that with the expanding sphere of governmental regulation and enterprise, much of the information within Government files has been submitted by private entities seeking Government contracts or responding to unconditional reporting obligations imposed by law. There was sentiment that Government agencies should have the latitude, in certain circumstances, to afford the confidentiality desired by these submitters. But the congressional concern was with the agency's need or preference for confidentiality; the FOIA by itself protects the submitter's interest in confidentiality only to the extent that this interest is endorsed by the agency collecting the information.

Enlarged access to governmental information undoubtedly cuts against the privacy concerns of nongovernmental entities, and as a matter of policy some balancing and accommodation may well be desirable. We simply hold here that Congress did not design the FOIA exemptions to be mandatory bars to disclosure.

This conclusion is further supported by the legislative history. The FOIA was enacted out of dissatisfaction with Section 3 of the Administrative Procedure Act, which had not resulted in as much disclosure by the agencies as Congress later thought desirable. Statements in both the Senate and House Reports on the effect of the exemptions support the interpretation that the exemptions were only meant to permit the agency to withhold certain information, and were not meant to mandate nondisclosure. . . .

We therefore conclude that Congress did not limit an agency's discretion to disclose information when it enacted the FOIA. It necessarily follows that the Act does not afford Chrysler any right to enjoin agency disclosure.

Questions
1. What reason might Chrysler have for desiring to keep its submitted information private?
2. Is the agency empowered to label the information received from Chrysler as "confidential" and therefore exempt from disclosure?
3. Is Chrysler able to force the agency not to disclose the company's submitted information?

According to some authors, the FOIA has implanted "uncertainty in the minds of business about government's willingness and ability to protect against the privacy of proprietary information."[7] Although Congress believed the major beneficiaries of the FOIA would be journalists, scholars, and public interest groups seeking to scrutinize government behavior and remedy public injustices, researchers have found that over two thirds of all requests for government information have come from corporations or their law firms. The FOIA has become a vehicle for business firms to survey, at the public's expense, the private affairs and activities of business competitors. A small industry of FOIA middlemen now exists in the greater Washington, D.C., area. Such companies, for a fee, will make a freedom of information request on a client's behalf, thus masking the client's identity. Although this effect was unintended by Congress, the FOIA has become as a means to abrogate some of the rights of business privacy. This result and uncertainty about the government's future policies in this regard have created an economic disincentive for firms to spend funds on studies that ultimately will be shared with business competitors. Some authors have come to the following conclusion.

Should business be unable to limit diffusion or to command a price for [productivity studies], marginal projects will either be abandoned or will be developed by overseas firms operating under a different government environment thereby promoting foreign, rather than U.S. productivity.[8]

CONCLUSIONS

During the twentieth century, and particularly since the 1930s, detailed regulations of business affairs have mushroomed. Congress has sought to solve or prevent various business-social problems through the use of regulatory agencies. Consequently, administrative law and procedure have become increasingly important as government attempts to carry out its policies and programs through regulatory agencies. The Administrative Procedures Act has established the basic guidelines for agency behavior and provided the people with opportunities to comment on proposed regulations. Moreover, the act assists individuals who seek to force agencies to meet their legal responsibilities or challenge the agency when they exceed their authority.

Ever-expanding regulation-related litigation has brought forth numerous suggestions for change of the regulatory system. One recomendation is for more specialized courts or special technical assistants for judges. However, the greatest regulatory relief comes from the process of deregulation itself. The advocates for greater reliance on the market system have been heeded by Congress in recent years. For example, Congress has legislated the gradual deregulation of the airline and trucking industries and limited the regulatory powers of the Federal Trade Commission in certain areas. Congress has even enacted the Regulatory Flexibility Act, which is designed to reduce the regulatory burden on small business. The balance between regulatory and market processes is difficult to achieve and continually evolving.

DISCUSSION QUESTIONS

1. The Amalgamated Meat Cutters seek to require the major meatpacking companies to perform their obligations, under their 1970 collective bargaining agreements with the union, to grant a general wage increase of 25 cents an hour effective September 6, 1971. The employers respond that the implementation of the wage increase obligation would violate Executive Order 11615, promulgated by President Nixon on August 15, 1971, which establishes a 90-day price-wage freeze. The union's position is that this defense is insufficient as a matter of law because the act authorizing the freeze is unconstitutional and the executive order is invalid because the act unconstitutionally delegates legislative power to the president, in violation of the general constitional principle of the separation of powers, and in contravention of Article I, Section I of the Constitution, which provides that "All legislative Powers herein granted shall be vested in a Congress of the United States."

   The union's position is that the act's broad authority to the President "to issue such orders and regulations as he may deem appropriate to stabilize prices, rents, wages and salaries" vests "unbridled legislative power in the President," a naked grant of authority to determine whether they "will be controlled, and the scope, manner and timing of those controls." Evaluate the union's assertion and decide.

2. James Gould, the operator of a sole proprietorship refused to allow access by the Interstate Commerce Commission (ICC) to his transportation-related records. The ICC petitioned the district court to enforce its demand.

   Gould contends that his operations are not within ICC jurisdiction and that he need not respond to the ICC's demands unless it demonstrates probable cause for a belief that he has violated federal law or he has been adjudicated to be subject to ICC jurisdiction.

The ICC claims that it has the authority to determine its own jurisdiction by summary inspection procedures.

What are the ICC's powers?

3. Gould also resists the ICC's demands with an assertion of the Fifth Amendment privilege against self-incrimination, because his personal records are inextricably entwined with his business records. The ICC agents would require Gould to point out, segregate, assemble, and turn over certain documents for examination on his premises.

Will Gould prevail?

4. A dispute heard by an administrative law judge for the Federal Communications Commission (FCC) involved an application by two attorneys named Johnson for a permit to establish a radio station. Opposition from an existing station (Faulkner) raised issues regarding the truth of representations made by the applicants to the commission. The applicants made counterallegations that the existing station was attempting merely to delay the entry of a competitor. In deciding the facts, the administrative law judge commented:

> It may be said, finally, that there is nothing more precious and vital to a practicing lawyer than his "good name"; that the Johnsons evidently are attorneys of some distinction in Carrolton, Georgia; and that the Commission, thus, has at least a presumptive basis for preferring the veracity of Mr. Hollis Johnson's testimony over Mr. Thorburn's [representative of Faulkner], absent a persuasive justification to the contrary.

The commission accepted the findings of the judge and not only granted the Johnsons a permit but also denied the existing station's application for renewal, partly because the administrative law judge had decided that it had made serious misrepresentations in the matter with the Johnsons.

On appeal from the denial of its renewal application, Faulkner contends that the findings of the administrative judge were tainted because he favored the Johnsons' testimony merely because they were lawyers. The commission urges the established rule that, on appeal, a court must accept the facts as found initially by the commission.

Are the findings of the commission final?

5. A Red Lion Broadcasting Company radio station carried a 15-minute program criticizing the author of a book dealing with a U.S. Senator. The minister who made the broadcast charged that the author had been fired from a newspaper for making false charges against city officials, had worked for a Communist-affiliated publication, had attacked J. Edgar Hoover and the Central Intelligence Agency (CIA), and had written his book in order to destroy the Republican Senator. The FCC supported the author in his demand for free reply time on the station, because he had been personally

attacked. According to the FCC, this opportunity for response is required by the "fairness doctrine."

In its legislative scheme, Congress delegated to the FCC the power to prescribe conditions and restrictions as may be necessary to administer the laws relating to public communications. The FCC is further directed to "consider the demands of the public interest." The Red Lion license contained the condition that operation of the station be carried out in the public interest. By later legislation, Congress made plain that the "public interest" requirement imposed a duty on broadcasters to discuss both sides of controversial public issues. Knowing the FCC's position on personal attacks, Congress never amended this language.

Red Lion contends that the FCC is exceeding the authority granted to it by Congress by requiring that Red Lion provide free response time.

What result?

6. Transco, a supplier of natural gas subject to the authority of the Federal Power Commission (FPC), was denied approval by the FPC of its plans to curtail deliveries in order to cope with a natural gas shortage being experienced by Transco. Transco sought review of the FPC's determination, and on review the Court of Appeals "desiring to be more fully informed about the 'crisis'" ordered that additional information be produced regarding the level of Transco's natural gas reserves. The Commission was specifically ordered to investigate the matter by a subpoena of Transco's books and records pertaining to gas supplies and by field investigation, and to report to the court within 30 days.

The FPC sought immediate review by the Supreme Court of this order and was granted relief in the form of a vacation of the appellate court's order. On what ground?

7. The Consumer Product Safety Commission (CPSC) obtained accident reports from various manufacturing companies, which claimed the information was confidential.

CPSC received requests under the Freedom of Information Act from the Consumers' Union and agreed to release the information, including the claimed "confidential" accident reports. The manufacturers seek an injunction to avoid the disclosure. What result?

8. The National Institute for Occupational Safety and Health (NIOSH) suspected, as a result of a walk-through inspection of an electric insulator manufacturing plant, that a chemical used in the plant might be causing an allergic reaction in some workers. NIOSH demanded that the company, Westinghouse Electric Corp., provide it access to the medical records of all past and present employees in the area where the suspect chemical was used. Westinghouse refused, asserting that medical records are confidential.

NIOSH conducted interviews with some of the present employees and found some symptoms of allergic reaction to the chemical. NIOSH subpoenaed the medical records; Westinghouse refused unless it was presented with written consent from the employees; NIOSH filed an action in district court to enforce the subpoena.

Westinghouse provides a company doctor who treats employees for problems not related to their employment as well as for those that are employment-related. A reaction to the suspect chemical can be life-threatening. Symptoms would be revealed by pulmonary function tests, blood tests, and general allergic reactions.

Should Westinghouse be required to respond to the subpoena without employee consents?

9. Midwest TV claimed that Los Angeles television transmissions were being broadcast into San Diego by Southwestern Cable, adversely affecting Midwest's San Diego station. The FCC reviewed the petition of Midwest and the written responses of Southwestern but did not conduct hearings before ordering that Southwestern must restrict its carriage of Los Angeles signals to those areas it served on February 15, 1966, the date of the order, until hearings were held to determine whether the carriage of such signals into San Diego contravenes the public interest. Southwestern believes that the FCC exceeded its authority by issuing the order without a hearing.

The Communications Act grants the FCC authority to issue "such order, not inconsistent with the [Act], as may be necessary in the execution of its functions." The Act applies to all interstate and foreign communication by wire or radio (including signals, pictures, and sounds of all kinds), and the FCC's function is to "make available to all the people of the United States a rapid, efficient . . . wire and radio communication, whether a telephone, telegraph, cable, or radio."

Did the FCC exceed its authority?

10. Industrial Molded Plastic Inc (IMP), is a long-standing client of yours. The following events have recently transpired and IMP's president has asked you to prepare an opinion letter on the legal ramification for IMP and all parties concerned:
   (a) An OSHA inspector attempted to inspect IMP's plant 1 yesterday. The plant manager refused to allow the inspector in without a warrant.
   (b) IMP's accountant received a subpoena *duces tecum* from the FTC. The accountant has refused to produce any corporate records, citing Fifth Amendment protection of both the corporation and himself.
   (c) The EPA has filed an administrative complaint against IMP. Can IMP obtain a court injunction to halt the proceedings because the EPA lacks jurisdiction over this type of pollution?

SUGGESTED READINGS

Flippen, Edward L., "The Internal Revenue Service Summons: An Unreasonable Expense Burden on Banks and an Invasion of Depositors' Privacy?" *American Business Law Journal*, Vol. 12, No. 3, Winter 1975, pp. 249–280.

Reed, O. Lee, "Must Quasi-Legislators, Like Caesar's Wife, Be Above Suspicion?: Recusal of Rulemakers for Prejudice and Bias," *American Business Law Journal*, Vol. 19, No. 1, Spring 1981, pp. 1–30.

Reed, O. Lee, "The Sunshine Society and The Legal Regulation of Business Through Compulsory Disclosure," *American Business Law Journal*, Vol. 16, No. 1, Spring 1978, pp. 83–101.

Simet, Donald P., "Constructing Criteria for the Evaluation of Pre-Deprivation Procedures: The Task Forgotton in *Board of Curators v. Horowitz*," *American Business Law Journal*, Vol. 18, No. 3, Fall 1980, pp. 337–370.

Tucker, Edwin W., "New Dimensions of Official Liability and Immunity," *American Business Law Journal*, Vol. 14, No. 1, Spring 1976, pp. 85–96.

END NOTES

1. K. C. Davis, *Administrative Law and Government* (St. Paul, Minn.: West Publishing Co., 1960), p. 25.
2. *Myers* v. *U.S.*, 272 U.S. 52 (1926).
3. *Dixon* v. *Alabama State Board of Education*, 294 F. 2d 150 (5th Cir., 1961).
4. *University of Missouri* v. *Horowitz*, 98 S. Ct. 948 (1978).
5. *Fuentes* v. *Shevin*, 407 U.S. 67 (1972).
6. *Myers* v. *Bethelehem Corp.* 303 U.S. 41 (1938).
7. William L. Casey, Jr., John E. Marthinsen, and Laurence S. Moss, "Businesses Move to Get Low-Cost Government Information about Competitors," *Collegiate Forum* (Dow Jones and Co., Inc.), Fall 1980, p. 3.
8. *Ibid.*

chapter 7

THE INTERACTION OF LAW AND SOCIETY

To accommodate social change, the legal system must be a dynamic process by which laws are constantly being created, altered, and adapted to meet the needs of contemporary society. Indeed, for the legal system to be effective in a democratic society, laws must be kept relevant to the "felt necessities" of society's members. The pressures for changes in law come from many sources. Technological advances that bring about new business methodologies or new institutional arrangements to exploit the new technology often necessitate new laws that support or limit the new technology. Economic upheaval, such as that precipated by the Great Depression or World Wars, produce crises to which the government must respond.

The speed with which new laws (public policies) for economic affairs are adopted depends on many factors. Often, customary practices or the ideology of the proponents of the existing policies of law operate to delay the response of the legal process to new social pressures. The legal or governmental system itself may act either to speed up or delay the response of the law to technological and social change. In an unlimited monarchy (or modern dictatorship) in which there is no restraint on governmental power, the sovereign may regulate business or refrain from regulation as the sovereign may be so influenced. However, the American system of constitutional law often constrains the governing body and restricts the government's power to regulate and its speed of enactment.

In the following materials, the dynamic character of the legal system is explored. First, the field of tort law and its evolutional qualities are presented. Additional cases show how the courts modify or change legal standards to fit current social conditions. Finally, a review of Supreme Court decisions illustrates how the Court's attitudes on adhering to current policy in spite of changing social conditions can frustrate the efforts of Congress to change public policies.

THE THEORY OF TORT LAW

A body of law commonly called *torts* is primarily judge-made law and is concerned with compensating victims who are injured because of the "fault" of someone else. The Latin word *tortus* means twisted, implying that someone's conduct is twisted away from society's norm of acceptable behavior. This "unreasonable" conduct causes the individual to be labeled at fault and, as such, he or she must pay compensatory money damages to any victim injured as a result of this wrongful behavior.

A tort is not the same as a crime, though the same action by a person may constitute both a tort and a crime. The crime is an offense against the public at large which is prosecuted by the state. The purpose of such proceedings is to protect and vindicate the interest of the public by punishing violators, by eliminating them from society, by reforming their behavior, or by deterring others from imitating their actions. The only role of the victim of criminal behavior is to serve as an accuser and witness in the criminal prosecution. In contrast, the victim of a tort brings a civil action against the tort-feasor to gain compensation for sufferings caused by the tort. The court will aid the successful litigant in the collection of any monies awarded for his or her sufferings.

Liability for tortious behavior has been imposed by judges on the following three fundamental grounds or legal theories:

1. *Intent* of the defendant to interfere with legally protected interests of the plaintiff.
2. *Negligence* of the defendant that causes harm to the plaintiff.
3. *Strict liability* (without "fault"), which is the imposition of liability for policy reasons, despite the absence of wrongful intent or negligence.

Under the common law, almost all torts have been categorized under some legal theory and given a name. However, some torts may not have a name and, of course, initially all of today's torts were without names. Observe the following language employed by a judge in an 1896 case:

While no precedent is cited for such action, it does not follow that there is no remedy for the wrong, because every form of action, when brought for the first time, must have been without a precedent to support it. Courts sometimes of necessity abandon their search for precedents, and yet sustain a recovery upon legal principles clearly applicable to the new state of facts, although there was no direct precedent for it, because there had never been an occasion to make one. . . . For instance, the action for enticing away a man's wife, now well established, was at first earnestly resisted upon the ground that no such action had ever been brought. . . . As we recently said by this court in an action then without precedent, "If the most that can be said is that the case is novel, and is not brought plainly within the limits of some adjudged case, we think such fact not enough to call for a reversal of the judgment." The question therefore is not whether there is any precedent for the action, but whether the defendant inflicted such a wrong upon the plaintiff as resulted in lawful damages. (*Kujek* v. *Goldman et al.,* 150 N.Y. 176).

INTENTIONAL TORTS

Tortious intent is the desire to bring about physical results or consequences that are disapproved by law. By voluntarily (intentionally) contracting muscles in his or her body, the actor "intends" a result. If the desire of the muscular contraction is to bring about an invasion of the legally protected interest of another, the actor's intent is tortious whether the actual consequences were intended or not. For example, pulling a chair out from under a person about to be seated is intentionally desiring the consequence of physical impact of the person with the ground. As such, the defendant's assertions of intending no more than a practical joke or not intending to injure the plaintiff would not be acceptable as defenses because they describe the defendant's "motive" (inspiration for the act), rather than the "intent." The voluntary act (pulling away the chair) and the desire of particular results which invades another's personal interest (defendant's hitting the ground) is the relevant "intent" in determination of intentional torts.

Litigation involving the interests of persons to have their physical self and property free of intentional invasion by others has created a number of specifically named torts. Some intentional torts are described as follows:

Battery

The intentional and offensive contact with another person without consent is a battery. It is clear that persons are to be protected from indecent and hostile contact, but other relatively trivial contacts made without consent can be a battery also. An unappreciated kiss, joke, or physical assistance can be a battery. Since a certain amount of personal contact is inevitable in a crowded world, consent to ordinary contacts is assumed. Time, place, and circumstances of the touching will affect its characterization as being reasonable or unpermitted.

Assault

The intentional act to arouse apprehension of immediate harmful or offensive contact in the mind of another is an assault. No actual contact is necessary; rather the individual is to be compensated for purely mental disturbance caused by the defendant's actions. It is an assault on another to raise a fist to strike, to aim a weapon, or to corner with a display of force. Because menacing actions are necessary to create the fear of "immediate" contact, mere words or threats are usually not assaults because no reasonable apprehension of immediate contact results.

Mental Distress

The law has been slow to accept the notion that peace of mind is entitled to legal protection. However, in recent years the intentional infliction of mental distress by extreme or outrageous conduct has been recognized as a tort. The actions necessary to establish this tort must be especially calculated to cause serious mental distress. Spreading false rumors that the plaintiff's son had hanged himself, or wrapping up a gory dead rat in place of a loaf of bread for the plaintiff to open are examples of the kind of outrageous conduct that forms this kind of action. Moreover, prolonged and extreme measures to collect debts, evict tenants, or adjust insurance claims can be defined as this type of tortious conduct.

False Imprisonment

A false imprisonment, or false arrest, is an intentional restraint on the free movement of another. "Imprisonment" doesn't mean only iron bars and the like; restraint on freedom of movement may suffice. Free movement could be constrained by locking the plaintiff in a room or out of a room, by refusing him or her the right to exit from an automobile or a store, or by compelling the plaintiff to accompany the defendant. The "imprisonment" need not last more than an appreciable amount of time. It is essential that the restraint be imposed against the plaintiff's will, though he or she need not resist to the point of physical violence. Under the common law, a storekeeper's detention of a suspected shoplifter who was ultimately found innocent can amount to a false arrest and subject the storekeeper to liability. However, most states have enacted legislation that protects the storekeeper from liability if the detention is reasonable and in good faith.

Trespass

Intentional trespass to land may be committed by entry on the land, by casting objects on it, or by remaining on the land after a right to entry has terminated. A similar trespass may be committed to personal properties also.

Conversion

A major interference with the personal property of another may be so serious as to justify the court, at the plaintiff's request, to order the intruder to buy the property from the plaintiff. The extent of interference is determined by many relevant factors, namely, the extent and duration of the interference, the defendant's intent, the harm done to the property, the degree of interference to the plaintiff, and the expense and inconvenience caused the plaintiff. The conversion occurs when the defendant intends to exercise control over another's personal property that is inconsistent with the owner's property rights and such exercise of control is determined to be a substantial interference.

Defamation

Defamation is the intentional publication to a third person of defamatory information that causes injury to the plaintiff's reputation. Defamatory information is any communication that tends to diminish the esteem, respect, and goodwill in which the plaintiff is held. Language that causes contempt, derogatory, or unpleasant feelings against the plaintiff is likewise defamatory. However, if the defendant can establish the truthfulness of his or her remarks, no liability attaches to the words. In addition, certain defamatory communications are qualifiedly privileged and immune from prosecution, such as publications fairly made by a person in the discharge of some public or private duty, as an employee remark to a superior to protect the employer from the believed criminal behavior of another employee.

Privacy

Interferences with the right of the plaintiff "to be let alone" can amount to the tort of privacy. This tort is a creation of this century. Four kinds of invasions of plaintiff's right to privacy are embodied in this tort. The four invasions are (1) intrusion on the plaintiff's physical and mental solitude or seclusion (such as placing secret recording devices in plaintiff's bedroom); (2) public disclosure of private facts (such as publicly exhibiting films of a caesarean operation); (3) publicity that places the plaintiff in a false light in the public eye (such as using the face of an honest cab driver in a story about the cheating propensities of taxi drivers); (4) appropriation, for the defendant's advantage, of the plaintiff's name or likeness (such as using plaintiff's name or picture without consent in an advertisement).

THE TORT OF NEGLIGENCE

An unavoidable accident is an event that was not intended, and that, under the circumstances, could not have been foreseen or prevented by exercise of reasonable precautions. There is no liability in such a case because there is no wrongful intent or failure to exercise proper care. However, if the event could have been prevented by the exercise of reasonable care, then the defendant's failure to be careful causes him or her to be liable under the tort of negligence.

Negligence, as a cause of action, is established by the plaintiff when four elements are proven.

1. A duty of care was owed by the defendant to those foreseeable individuals who would be exposed to unreasonable risk if the defendant didn't exercise due care in whatever he or she was doing. When the risk of injury to others is greater than the burden to take adequate precautions, the defendant is under the lawful duty to take those precautions.
2. The defendant failed to exercise reasonable care as a reasonable person would have done under similar circumstances.

3. There was a reasonably close causal connection between the defendant's failure to exercise due care and the plaintiff's injury. This is commonly known as "proximate cause."
4. Actual injury or damage to the plaintiff occurred. Such injury to the plaintiff may include property damage, medical bills, loss of wages, and pain and suffering.

Although many courts prefer not to attempt to define different degrees of negligence, various statutes often require such definitions. The distinctions usually made are as follows: slight negligence is the failure to exercise the great care that persons of extraordinary prudence and foresight are accustomed to use, and gross negligence is the failure to exercise even scant care. Courts have difficulty in drawing a distinction between gross negligence and "reckless" conduct, which is willful conduct in disregard of a known and probable risk.

Two usual defenses to a charge of negligence are contributory negligence and assumption of risk. Contributory negligence is negligence by the plaintiff that contributed to his or her own injuries. In the eyes of the law, both plaintiff and defendant are at "fault," and consequently, the plaintiff is unable to recover from the defendant. A few states require the courts by statute to compare the negligence of each party, and if the defendant's negligence outweighs the plaintiff's, the plaintiff is allowed to recover losses minus an amount attributed to his or her own negligence. This process of comparative negligence, in effect, apportions the loss between the unequally negligent parties.

The assumption of risk defense means the plaintiff, with knowledge of the risk, voluntarily entered some activity or relation agreeing to take his or her own chances. The legal result is that the defendant is not under a duty to the plaintiff as to those known and assumed risks.

STRICT LIABILITY TORTS

The last hundred years have witnessed the overthrow of the doctrine of "no liability without fault." As one writer put it, there is "a strong and growing tendency, where there is blame on neither side, to ask, in view of the exigencies of social justice, who can best bear the loss and hence to shift the loss by creating liability where there has been no fault."[1] The courts are weighing various factors in our complex and dangerous civilization to determine, as a matter of social policy, which party is best able to shoulder the loss. The defendant is held liable on the court's conclusion that the responsibility *should* be the defendant's, as a matter of social adjustment of losses. This approach by the courts is a far cry from the common law determination of individual fault on the basis of intent or failure to exercise proper care. Rather, the normal basis of strict liability is the creation of undue risk of harm to other members of the community while personally exercising ordinary care and intending no harm. For example, keeping a pet bear creates undue risk of harm to others if the bear escapes. Though intending no harm and taking care to prevent escape, the owner would, nevertheless, be held strictly liable for any damages resulting from the bear's escape. It is usually said that legal liability for "ultrahazardous activities" by the defendant that necessarily involve a risk of serious harm cannot be eliminated by the exercise of utmost care. The liability normally extends to the limits of the risk on society imposed by that dangerous activity. However, the plaintiff's assumption of risk will normally relieve the defendant of strict liability.

Strict liability theory has been extended into many fields of law. Sellers of goods have found increasing court propensities to find them strictly liable for defective goods that cause harm to the purchasers. Carriers and innkeepers are strictly liable for goods entrusted to their care unless statutes have modified such responsibility. However, strict liability theory is employed more often in legislation. Workers' compensation laws, pure foods acts, child labor statutes, and numerous other enactments utilize strict liability theory.

JUDICIAL DEVELOPMENT OF NEW LAWS

As a primary arena for the fair adjustment of conflicting claims by litigating parties, the law of torts is a continuous battleground of social theory with increasing realization that the interests of society are necessary ingredients in the resolution of private disputes. The notion of public policy in private cases is not new to tort law but is certainly a more important variable in today's cases. Consequently, the courts are making more conscientious efforts to direct the law along lines that will achieve desirable social results. The legal process may be a slow, confusing, and often a painful progress toward achieving the best rule for society, but ultimately the rules formulated must coincide with public opinion or the continuing processes of evolution in legal theory will be pushed at a faster pace.

Numerous cases in this and other chapters contain illustrations of how public policy is granted an expanding influence in the determination of the court's decision.

Nader v. General Motors Corporation
255 N.E. 2d 765 (1970)
Court of Appeals of New York

Chief Judge Fuld

The complaint, in this action by Ralph Nader, pleads four causes of action against General Motors Corporation (GMC), and three other defendants allegedly acting as its agents. The first two causes of action charge an invasion of privacy. . . .

The plaintiff, an author and lecturer on automotive safety, has, for some years, been an articulate and severe critic of General Motors' products from the standpoint of safety and design. According to the complaint—which, for present purposes, we must assume to be true—[GMC], having learned of the imminent publication of the plaintiff's book "Unsafe at Any Speed," decided to conduct a campaign of intimidation against him in order to "suppress plaintiff's criticism of and prevent his disclosure of information" about its products. To that end, [GMC] authorized and directed the other defendants to engage in a series of activities which, the plaintiff claims . . . violated his right to privacy.

Specifically, the plaintiff alleges that the GMC agents (1) conducted a series of interviews with acquaintances of the plaintiff, "questioning them about, and casting aspersions upon [his] political, social, . . . racial, and and religious views . . . ; his integrity; his sexual proclivities and inclinations; and his personal habits"; (2) kept him under surveillance in public places for an unreasonable length of time; (3) caused him to be accosted by girls for the purpose of entrapping him into illicit relationships; (4) made threatening, harassing and obnoxious telephone calls to him; (5) tapped his telephone and eavesdropped, by means of mechanical and electronic equipment, on his private conversations with others; and (6) conducted a "continuing" and harassing investigation of him. In point of fact, the parties have agreed—at least for purposes of this motion—that the sufficiency of these allegations is to be determined under the law of the District of Columbia. The District is the jurisdiction in which most of the acts are alleged to have occurred, and it was there, too, that the plaintiff lived and suffered the impact of those acts. It is, in short, the place which has the most significant relationship with the subject matter of the tort charged.

Turning, then, to the law of the District of Columbia, it appears that its courts have not only recognized a common-law action for invasion of privacy but have broadened the scope of that tort beyond its traditional limits. Thus, in the most recent of its cases on the subject, *Pearson* v. *Dodd* 133 U.S. App. D.C. 279, the Federal Court of Appeals for the District of Columbia declared:

We approve the extension of the tort of invasion of privacy to instances of intrusion, whether by physical trespass or not, into spheres from which an ordinary man in a plaintiff's position could reasonably expect that the particular defendant should be excluded.

Quite obviously, some intrusions into one's private sphere are inevitable concomitants of life in an industrial and densely populated society, which in law does not seek to proscribe even if it were possible to do so. "The law does not provide a remedy for every annoyance that occurs in everyday life." However, the District of Columbia courts have held that the law should and does protect against certain types of intrusive conduct, and we must, therefore, determine whether the plaintiff's allegations are actionable as violations of the right to privacy under the law of that jurisdiction. . . .

It should be emphasized that the mere gathering of information about a particular individual does not give rise to a cause of action under this theory. Privacy is invaded only if the information sought is of a confidential nature and the defendant's conduct was unreasonably intrusive. Just as a common-law copyright is lost when material is published, so, too, there can be no invasion of privacy where the information sought is open to public view or has been voluntarily revealed to others. In order to sustain a cause of action for invasion of privacy, therefore, the plaintiff must show that the appellant's conduct was truly "intrusive" and that it was designed to elicit information which would not be available through normal inquiry or observation.

* * *

Turning, then, to the particular acts charged in the complaint, we cannot find any basis for a claim of invasion of privacy, under District of Columbia law, in the allegations that the [defendant], through its agents or employees, interviewed many persons who knew the plaintiff, asking questions about him and casting aspersions on his character. Although those inquiries may have uncovered information of a personal nature, it is difficult to see how they may be said to have invaded the plaintiff's privacy. Information about the plaintiff which was already known to others could hardly be regarded as private to the plaintiff. Presumably, the plaintiff had previously revealed the information to such other persons, and he would necessarily assume the risk that a friend or acquaintance in whom he had confided might breach the confidence. If, as alleged, the question tended to disparage the plaintiff's character, his remedy would seem to be by way of an action for defamation, not for breach of his right to privacy.

Nor can we find any actionable invasion of privacy in the allegations that the [defendant] caused the plaintiff to be accosted by girls with illicit proposals, or that it was responsible for the making of a large number of threatening and harassing telephone calls to the plaintiff's home at odd hours. Neither of these activities, howsoever offensive and disturbing, involved intrusion for the purpose of gathering information of a private and confidential nature.

Apart, however, from the foregoing allegations which we find inadequate to spell out a cause of action for invasion of privacy under District of Columbia law, the complaint contains allegations concerning other activities by [GMC] or its agents which do satisfy the requirements for such a cause of action. The one which most clearly meets those requirements is the charge that [GMC] and its codefendants engaged in unauthorized wiretapping and eavesdropping by mechanical and electronic means. In point of fact, the [defendant] does not dispute this, acknowledging that, to the extent the two challenged counts charge it with wiretapping and eavesdropping, an actionable invasion of privacy has been stated.

There are additional allegations that the [defendant] hired people to shadow the plaintiff and keep him under surveillance. In particular, he claims that, on one occasion, one of its agents followed him into a bank, getting sufficiently close to him to see the denomination of the bills he was withdrawing from his account. From what we have already said, it is manifest that the mere observation of the plaintiff in a public place does not amount to an invasion of his privacy. But, under certain circumstances, surveillance may be so "overzealous" as to render it actionable. Whether or not surveillance in the present case falls into this latter category will depend on the nature of the proof. A person does not automatically make public everything he does merely by being in a public place, and the mere fact that Nader was in a bank did not give anyone the right to try to discover the amount of money he was withdrawing. On the other hand, if the plaintiff acted in such a way as to reveal that fact to any casual observer, then, it may not be said that the [defendant] intruded into his private sphere. In any event, though, it is enough for present purposes to say that the surveillance allegation is not insufficient as a matter of law.

Questions

1. How did the legal right of privacy develop? The source of the district's common law action for invasion of privacy is the classic article by Warren and Brandeis ("The Right to Privacy," 4 *Harv. L. Rev.* 192). It was premised, to a large extent, on principles originally developed in the field of copyright law. The authors based their thesis on a right granted by the common law to "each individual . . . of determining, ordinarily, to what extent his thoughts, sentiments, and emotions shall be communicated to others." Their principal concern appeared to be not with a broad "right to be let alone" but, rather, with the right to protect oneself from having one's private affairs known to others and to keep secret or intimate facts about oneself from the prying eyes or ears of others.

2. What activities did the court feel were actionable "intrusions" to privacy? Which activities were not actionable? What criteria did the court use to decide?

Troppi v. Scarf
187 N.W. 2d 511 (1971)
Court of Appeals of Michigan

In August 1964, plaintiffs were the parents of seven children, ranging in age from six to sixteen years of age. John Troppi was 43 years old, his wife 37.

While pregnant with an eighth child, Mrs. Troppi suffered a miscarriage. She and her husband consulted with their physician and decided to limit the size of their family. The physician prescribed an oral contraceptive, Norinyl, as the most desirable means of insuring that Mrs. Troppi would bear no more children. He telephoned the prescription to defendant, Frank H. Scarf, a licensed pharmacist. Instead of filling the prescription, Scarf negligently supplied Mrs. Troppi with a drug called Nardil, a mild tranquilizer.

Believing that the pills she had purchased were contraceptives, Mrs. Troppi took them on a daily basis. In December 1964, Mrs. Troppi became pregnant. She delivered a well-born son on August 12, 1965.

Plaintiff's complaint alleges four separate items of damage: (1) Mrs. Troppi's lost wages; (2) medical and hospital expenses; (3) the pain and anxiety of pregnancy and childbirth, and (4) the economic cost of rearing the eighth child. . . .

We begin by noting that the fundamental conditions of tort liability are present here. The defendant's conduct constituted a clear breach of duty. A pharmacist is held to a very high standard of care in filling prescriptions. When he negligently supplied a drug other than the drug requested, he is liable for resulting harm to the purchaser.

We assume, for the purpose of appraising the correctness of the ruling dismissing the complaint, that the defendant's negligence was a cause in fact of Mrs. Troppi's pregnancy. The possibility that she might become pregnant was certainly a foreseeable consequence of the defendant's failure to fill a prescription for birth control pills; we therefore could not say that it was not a proximate cause of the birth of the child.

Setting aside, for the moment, the subtleties of the damage question, it is at least clear that the plaintiffs have expended significant sums of money as a direct and proximate result of the defendant's negligence. The medical and hospital expenses of Mrs. Troppi's confinement and her loss of wages arose from the defendant's failure to fill the prescription properly. Pain and suffering, like that accompanying childbirth, have long been recognized as compensable injuries.

This review of the elements of tort liability points up the extraordinary nature of the trial court's holding that the plaintiffs were entitled to no recovery as a matter of law. We have here a negligent, wrongful act by the defendant, which act directly and proximately caused injury to the plaintiffs. . . .

In *Shaheen* v. *Knight* (1957), a Pennsylvania court ruled that a physician who violated his promise to perform an elective sterilization operation was not liable for the consequences of his breach of contract. . . .

Underlying the *Shaheen* opinion are two principal ideas. The first is that the birth of a healthy child confers such an undoubted benefit upon the plaintiff as to outweigh, as a matter of law, the expenses of delivering and rearing the child. The second is that if the child is really unwanted, plaintiff has a duty to place him for adoption, in effect to mitigate damages. . . .

Our review has been conducted to determine whether the defendant in this case should be exempted from the consequences of his negligence. We conclude that there is no valid reason why the trier of the fact should not be free to assess damages as it would in any other negligence case. . . .

Overriding Benefit. It is arguable that the birth of a healthy child confers so substantial a benefit as to outweigh the expenses of his birth and support. In the great majority of cases, this is no doubt true, else, presumably, people would not choose to multiply so freely. But can we say, as a matter of law, that a healthy child always confers such an overriding benefit?

Thus, if the defendant's tortious conduct conferred a benefit to the same interest which was harmed by his conduct, the dollar value of the benefit is to be subtracted from the dollar value of the injury in arriving at the amount of damages properly awardable.

Since pregnancy and its attendant anxiety, incapacity, pain and suffering are inextricably related to child bearing, we do not think it would be sound to attempt to separate those segments of damage from the economic costs of an unplanned child in applying the "same interest" rule. Accordingly, the benefits of the unplanned child may be weighed against all the elements of claimed damage.

The trial court evidently believes, as did the court in *Shaheen* v. *Knight,* that application of the benefits rule prevents any recovery for the expenses of rearing an unwanted child. This is unsound. Such a rule would be equivalent to declaring that in every case, as a matter of law, the services and companionship of a child have a dollar equivalent greater than the economic costs of his support, to say nothing of the inhibitions, the restrictions, and the pain and suffering caused by pregnancy and the obligation to rear the child.

There is a growing recognition that the financial "services" which parents can expect from their offspring are largely illusory. As to companionship, cases decided when "loss of companionship" was a compensable item of damage for the wrongful death of a child reveal no tendency on the part of juries to value companionship so highly as to outweigh expenses in every foreseeable case. . . .

What must be appreciated is the diversity of purposes and circumstances of the women who use oral contraceptives. Unmarried women who seek the pleasures of sexual inter-

course without the perils of unwed motherhood, married women who wish to delay slightly the start of a family in order to retain the career flexibility which many young couples treasure, married women for whom the birth of another child would pose a threat to their own health or the financial security of their families, all are likely users of oral contraceptives. Yet it is clear that in each case the consequences arising from negligent interference with their use will vary widely. A rational legal system must award damages that correspond with these differing injuries. The benefits rule will serve to accomplish this objective.

Consider, for example, the case of the unwed college student who becomes pregnant due to a pharmacist's failure to fill properly her prescription for oral contraceptives. Is it not likely that she has suffered far greater damage than the young newlywed who, although her pregnancy arose from the same sort of negligence, had planned the use of contraceptives only temporarily, say, while she and her husband took an extended honeymoon trip? Without the benefits rule, both plaintiffs would be entitled to recover substantially the same damages.

Application of the benefits rule permits a trier of fact to find that the birth of a child has materially benefitted the newly wed couple, notwithstanding the inconvenience of an interrupted honeymoon, and to reduce the net damage award accordingly. Presumably a trier of fact would find that the "family interests" of the unmarried coed have been enhanced very little.

The essential point, of course, is that the trier must have the power to evaluate the benefit according to all the circumstances of the case presented. Family size, family income, age of the parents, and marital status are some, but not all, the factors which the trier must consider in determining the extent to which the birth of a particular child represents a benefit to his parents. That the benefits so conferred and calculated will vary widely from case to case is inevitable.

Mitigating Damages. It has been suggested that parents who seek to recover for the birth of an unwanted child are under a duty to mitigate damages by placing the child for adoption. If the child is "unwanted," why should they object to placing him for adoption, thereby reducing the financial burden on defendant for his maintenance?

However, to impose such a duty upon the injured plaintiff is to ignore the very real difference which our law recognizes between the avoidance of conception and the disposition of the human organism after conception. . . . At the moment of conception, an entirely different set of legal obligations is imposed upon the parents. A living child almost universally gives rise to emotional and spiritual bonds which few parents can bring themselves to break.

Once a child is born he obviously should be treated with love regardless of whether he was wanted when he was conceived. Many, perhaps most, persons living today are conceptional accidents in the sense that their parents did not desire that a child result from the particular intercourse in which the person was conceived. Nevertheless, when the child is born, most parents accept him with love. That the plaintiffs accepted their eighth child does not change the fact that the birth of another child, seven years younger than the youngest of their previously born children, unbalanced their life style and was not desired by them.

The doctrine which requires a plaintiff to take measures to minimize the financial consequences of a defendant's negligence requires only that reasonable measures be taken. . . .

In determining reasonableness, the best interests of the child must be considered. The law has long recognized the desirability of permitting a child to be reared by his natural parents. The plaintiffs may have believed that the hazards of adoption would damage the child.

A child will not be taken from his mother without her consent. . . . The mother's right to keep the child is not dependent on whether she desired the conception of the child.

As a matter of personal conscience and choice parents may wish to keep an unwanted child. Indeed, parents have been known to keep children that many think should be institutionalized, e.g., mentally retarded children, not because of any anticipated joy or happiness that the child will bring to them but out of a sense of obligation. So, too, the parents of an unplanned, healthy child may feel, and properly so, that whether they wanted the child or not is beside the point once the child is born and that they have an obligation to rear the child as best they can rather than subject him to rearing by unknown persons.

Further, even though the parents may not want to rear the child they may conclude that the psychological impact on them of rejecting the child and placing him for adoption, never seeing him again, would be such that, making the best of a bad situation, it is better to rear the child than to place him for adoption.

Many women confronted with an unwanted pregnancy will abort the fetus, legally or illegally. Some will bear the child and place him for adoption. Many will bear the child, keep and rear him. The defendant does not have the right to insist that the victim of his negligence have the emotional and mental makeup of a woman who is willing to abort or place a child for adoption. If the negligence of a tortfeasor results in conception of a child by a woman whose emotional and mental makeup is inconsistent with aborting or placing the child for adoption, then, under the principle that the tortfeasor takes the injured party as he finds him, the tortfeasor cannot complain that the damages that will be assessed against him are greater than those that would be determined if he had negligently caused the conception of a child by a woman who was willing to abort or place the child for adoption.

While the reasonableness of a plaintiff's efforts to mitigate is ordinarily to be decided by the trier of fact, we are persuaded to rule, as a matter of law, that no mother, wed or unwed, can reasonably be required to abort (even if legal) or place her child for adoption. The plaintiffs are entitled to have the jurors instructed that if they find that negligence of the defendant was a cause in fact of the plaintiff's injury, they may not, in computing the amount, if any, of the plaintiff's damages, take into consideration the fact that the plaintiffs might have aborted the child or placed the child into adoption.

Uncertainty of Damages. Of the four items of damage claimed by plaintiffs, each is capable of reasonable ascertainment. The medical and hospital expenses and Mrs. Troppi's lost wages may be computed with some exactitude. Plaintiff's claimed pain and anxiety, if not capable of precise determination, is a component of damage which triers of fact traditionally have been entrusted to ascertain. As to the costs of rearing the child until his majority, this is a computation which is routinely performed in countless cases.

It should be clear that ascertainment of *gross* damages is a routine task. Whatever uncertainty attends the final award arises from application of the benefits rule, which requires that the trier of fact compute the dollar value of the companionship and services of an unwanted child. Placing a dollar value on these segments may well be more difficult than assessing damages for, say, Mrs. Troppi's lost wages. But difficulty in determining the amount to be subtracted from the gross damages does not justify throwing up our hands and denying recovery altogether.

The assessment of damages in this case is properly within the competence of the trier of fact. The element of uncertainty in the net recovery does not render the damages unduly speculative.

Reversed and remanded for trial.

Questions

1. Did the analogous area of a physician's liability for failure of a non-therapeutic sterilization operation resulting in the birth of an unwanted child provide relevant precedent?
2. What actual loss or injury resulted in *Troppi*?
3. In *Shaheen* v. *Knight* (1957) the court concluded that "we are of the opinion that to allow damages for the normal birth of a normal child is foreign to the universal public sentiment of the people." Do sentiments change?
4. Mitigation of damages involves the responsibility of the injured party to take reasonable steps to avoid or minimize further loss. In order to mitigate their damages, must the plaintiff place her unwanted newborn child for adoption?
5. The court concluded that although the benefits of having the child are to be deducted from the gross damages, such benefits do not as a matter of law override the damages suffered. Can you give any examples?
6. Would the awarding of damages to the parents for "wrongful conception" cause the child to feel unwanted and emotionally like a "bastard"?

   The first case to expressly reject [this] . . . argument and to hold that the parents of an unplanned normal child could recover all damages proximately caused by a negligently performed sterilization operation was *Custodio* v. *Bauer*, 251 Cal. App. 2d 303 (1967).

   Rejecting the argument that an award of damages could reduce the child to an emotional bastard, the court found that the possibility of psychological harm was no greater than in any other case where a child learns that his existence is the result of his parents' ineptitude at birth control. Most persuasively, the court observed that modern attitudes with respect to family establishment and the use of contraceptives had changed, and further insinuated that the birth of an unplanned child may not be viewed by some as something less than a "blessed event."

Sherlock v. *Stillwater Clinic*, 260 N.W. 2d 169 (Minn., 1977).

JUDICIAL ECONOMIC POLICYMAKING

In the nineteenth century, the judiciary, as well as the other branches of government, was devoted primarily to providing and, if necessary, creating the legal devices necessary for the economic expansion of the American continent. The government created a legal framework that encouraged individual initiative by establishing private property rights. It also guaranteed that the reasonable expectations arising from freely negotiated contracts were protected. Hence, business laws reflected society's notion of appropriate policy for the economic system. Protection against those who might exploit or abuse society in the production and distribution of the nation's goods and services was to be effectuated through the forces of competition. So strong was this faith in competition as an efficient regulator, that the government, influenced by a laissez-faire philosophy, offered little, if any interference with the operation of the economy.

Substantial governmental interference with trade activities largely began in the last two decades of the nineteenth century. Of course, the decisions concerning a change in the role of government and the variety of methods to be employed in trade regulation have not been accomplished without opposition. At the outset, debate centered on the nature of the "power" of the government to legislate or regulate economic affairs. Of course, the Supreme Court decided the constitutional extent of the governmental powers over economic matters.

Initially, the Supreme Court was committed to the ideology of laissez-faire. Hence, it utilized its power of judicial review to protect the free capitalistic system from the legislative or executive branches of government that attempted interferences with the fundamental basis of capitalism; that is, private property and the freedom to contract. The Supreme Court interpreted general clauses of the Constitution to restrict both state and federal legislative bodies to a laissez-faire policy.

JUDICIAL RESTRICTIONS ON STATE LEGISLATURES

Efforts of the state legislatures to regulate their economic affairs is founded on the state's "police power," which empowers the state to protect the health, safety, morals, or general welfare of the state citizenry. However, the Supreme Court has utilized constitutional interpretation to limit state legislation over economic affairs. Since the commerce clause of the U.S. Constitution grants to the federal government the power to regulate interstate commerce, by implication the states were denied this power. The purpose of inserting the commerce clause in the Constitution was to prevent the states from imposing tariffs or duties on imports into their state or otherwise discriminating against interstate merchants transporting goods into the state. The commerce clause was intended to create a "free market" throughout the states of the Union. Consequently, the Supreme Court could utilize the clause to prohibit state governments from regulating certain aspects of commerce that the Court deemed to be interstate, and beyond the reach of state governments. The Supreme Court has stated that whenever the subject of economic regulation requires a national or uniform plan, Congress possesses *exclusive* power for legislative solution. And even if no uniformity of regulation is required, the Court has held that state regulations may not discriminate against interstate commerce or substantially and unduly burden interstate commerce. Only if the economic affair was not one requiring uniformity and the state law did not discriminate against or unduly burden interstate commerce, was the state free of this judicial trap that restricted state legislative efforts to regulate economic activity.

A second judicial constraint was imposed on the state governments in their efforts to regulate economic affairs. Originally, the Bill of Rights and its protections for the individual were added to the U.S. Constitution to limit the power of the *federal* government from becoming an oppressive central government similar to the crown's exercise of power over its subjects in the colonies. Each of the states already had its own constitution, which afforded similar protection to state citizens from oppressive state actions. Consequently, the Bill of Rights was not applicable as a limitation on powers of *state* government. After the Civil War, however, the Fourteenth Amendment was added to the U.S. Constitution as a limitation on the power of *state* government and as a source of power to the federal government to protect individuals in certain instances from unwarranted state actions. This amendment's basic purpose was to provide federal protection to the freed slaves of the South from oppressive state government.

One protection afforded to individuals in the Fourteenth Amendment is that no state shall deprive an individual of his life, liberty, or property without following the requirements of "due process of law." Initially, process was a synonym for procedure and "due process of law" meant that appropriate procedure of law must be followed in depriving an individual of life, liberty, or property. Legislative due process would require that state legislative bodies follow their respective constitutional and statutory procedures before and during the enactment of law. However, the Supreme Court extended the power of the "due process" clause of the Fourteenth Amendment from a "procedural" constraint to a "substantive" restraint on legislators. "Substantive" due process involves the Court's declaration of the unconstitutionality of those state regulatory statutes that the Court determines to be unreasonable interferences with liberty or property. In this sense, the due process clause was utilized to eliminate state regulations whenever the Court was convinced the statute was unreasonable or did not conform to the justices' concept of laissez-faire philosophy. The Supreme Court, in effect, had the last word or veto power over state legislatures by virtue of "substantive due process" interpretation.

Substantive due process restrictions on state legislatures began with a Supreme Court decision that adopted the common law tradition that the prices charged in certain industries and trades were properly subject to public (state) regulation.

In *Munn* v. *Illinois* 94 U.S. 113 (1876), the Supreme Court declared:

[I]t has been customary in England from time immemorial, and in this country from its first colonization, to regulate ferries, common carriers, hackmen, bakers, millers, wharfingers, innkeepers, . . . , and in so doing to fix a maximum of charge to be made for services rendered, accommodations furnished, and articles sold. . . .

From this it is apparent that, down to the time of the adoption of the Fourteenth Amendment, it was not supposed that statutes regulating the use, or even the price of the use, of private property necessarily deprived an owner of his property without due process of law. Under some circumstances they may, but not under all. The amendment does not change the law in this particular: it simply prevents the States from doing that which will operate as such a deprivation.

This brings us to inquire as to the principles upon which this power of regulation rests, in order that we may determine what is within and what without its operative effect. Looking then, to the common law, from whence came the right which the Constitution protects, we find that when private property is "affected with a public interest, it ceases to be *juris privati* only." This was said by Lord Chief Justice Hale more than two hundred year ago . . . and has been accepted without objection as an essential element in the law of property ever since. Property does become clothed with a public interest when used in a manner to make it of public consequence, and affect the community at large. . . .

According to the reasoning of *Munn* v. *Illinois*, the states were freed of the constitutional barrier of due process and permitted to regulate those industries that were "affected with the public interest." Other industries, not so affected with the public interest, remained beyond the authority of the state government to impose public regulations.

There were two categories of industry considered to be "affected with the public interest" and, hence, subject to state regulation. First, as was indicated in *Munn* v. *Illinois,* it included those industries where buyers or sellers were apt to be caught in a "distress position" that subjected them to extreme price exploitation. Examples include the grain elevators in *Munn* v. *Illinois* or stockyards, hotels, and docks. Secondly, there are the "natural monopolies," where the economies of large-scale operation necessitated concentration of the industry into a single business entity in order to produce units at lowest average cost. Obvious examples of these industries include electric and gas companies, telephone companies, and urban transit.

Within these two categories of industries, the legislatures of the states were empowered to regulate industry prices. However, the Court did not fully retreat from its activist policy of protecting laissez-faire economic philosophy. Instead, the Court undertook to protect the regulated companies from a regulated price level that was so low as to constitute a deprivation of the utility's property rights.[2] The Court determined that rates must allow a "fair return" on the invested value of property in such organizations. In these instances, the Court acted as a "supra legislature" and reviewed the reasonableness of the rates on any regulated industry.

In those industries not "affected with the public interest" the Court adopted a policy of protecting these industries from "unreasonable" regulations. In *Allgeyer* v. *Louisiana* 165 U.S. 578 (1897), the Court invalidated state statutes that prohibited their citizens from contracting with companies outside of the state. In the field of labor relations, numerous state statutes designed to aid workers were held to be "unreasonable" interferences with liberty and, consequently, in violation of the due process clause. In *Lochner* v. *New York* 198 U.S. 45 (1905), the Court held a New York statute unconstitutional because it limited the hours of work by those employed in bakeries. The Court opinion stated:

In every case that comes before this court, therefore, where legislation of this character is concerned, and where the protection of the Federal Constitution is sought, the question necessarily arises: Is this a fair, reasonable, and appropriate exercise of the police power of the state, or is it an unreasonable, unnecessary arbitrary interference with the right of the individual to his personal liberty, or to enter into those contracts in relation to labor which may seem to him appropriate or necessary for the support of himself and his family . . . ?

We think the limit of the police power has been reached and passed in this case. There is, in our judgment, no reasonable foundation for holding this to be necessary and appropriate as a health law to safeguard the public health or the health of individuals who are following the trade of baker.

Justice Holmes dissented from the *Lochner* decision and began an attack on the use of substantive due process to void state economic regulations:

This case is decided upon an economic theory which a large part of the country does not entertain. If it were a question whether I agreed with that theory, I should desire to study it further and long before making up my mind. But I do not conceive that to be my duty, because I strongly believe that my agreement or disagreement has nothing to do with the right of a majority to embody their opinions in law . . . [A] Constitution is not intended to embody a particular legal theory, whether of paternalism and the organic relation of the citizen to the state or of *laissez-faire*. It is made for people of fundamentally different views, and the accident of our finding certain opinions natural and familiar, or novel, and even shocking, ought not to conclude our judgment upon the question whether statutes embodying them conflict with the Constitution of the United States.

In spite of Holmes' dissent, the Supreme Court continued to use substantive due process to void many state statutes attempting to regulate economic affairs. Thus, many statutory economic controls that the state legislatures desired were held to be unconstitutional during the era from 1890 to 1934.

JUDICIAL RESTRICTIONS ON CONGRESS

In the early history of the federal government there were only limited efforts in economic regulation. Substantial federal economic regulation actually began as a result of the Supreme Court decision invalidating state regulation of the railroads. The Court held that the interstate nature of the railroads required *uni-*

form regulations, which states could not supply. Therefore, Congress found it necessary to pass the Interstate Commerce Commission (ICC) Act of 1887 to deal with growing monopolistic abuses in the railroad industry. The Supreme Court upheld the ICC Act because railroads were involved in interstate commerce. The Supreme Court has upheld other federal regulations of interstate trade that have involved questions of immorality or "harmful products." For example, the Court allowed Congress to prohibit interstate lotteries, interstate shipment of adulterated food or drugs, interstate transport of prostitutes, or interstate transportation of stolen motor vehicles. However, there were other Supreme Court interpretations of the commerce clause that were calculated to restrict the power of the federal government to regulate economic activities. For example, the Court restricted the meaning of interstate commerce to transportation of goods from one state to another. The effect of this interpretation was to limit the commerce clause to those activities surrounding transportation. Consequently, any federal legislation designed to deal with a particular subject area other than transportation were held to be beyond the powers of Congress. Insurance was held not to be "commerce" and not subject to federal regulation. The Sherman Antitrust Act was initially held not to apply to local "manufacturing" activities. One of the greatest impacts of the Supreme Court's narrow interpretation of the commerce clause was in labor relations. In the famous case of *Hammer* v. *Dagenhart* 247 U.S. 251 (1918), the Court held the Federal Child Labor Act to be unconstitutional. The Act attempted to prohibit the shipment in interstate commerce of articles manufactured in factories in which children under 14 years of age were employed in production. The Court concluded that this "manufacturing" was beyond the reach of the "interstate commerce" power. Moreover, since the manufactured articles were not "harmful," the Court reasoned that Congress was really attempting to regulate social problems (child labor abuses), not commerce. Hence, the Court concluded that these social problems in manufacturing were not part of the federal government's constitutional powers over "transportation."

During the economic depression of the 1930s, despite public demands for increased federal action, the Supreme Court struck down the National Industrial Recovery Act as unconstitutionally extending beyond the power conferred under the commerce clause. The Supreme Court also invalidated the Railroad Retirement Act of 1934 because the statute was said to deal with purely social ends without any "direct" relation to interstate commerce. The Bitumunous Coal Conservation Act of 1935, which set minimum wages and minimum hours for miners whose coal production was subsequently shipped in interstate commerce, was held unconstitutional. Mining was said to precede "commerce" and had only an "indirect" effect on interstate commerce, and, consequently, was beyond the federal powers to control.

In total, the Supreme Court frustrated both state and federal legislative attempts to deal with perceived economic problems. The Court's decisions seem to be based on its belief that its conception of economic theory and policy was best suited for America. It used its power of judicial review in an effort to preserve a governmental policy (laissez-faire), which the state and federal legislatures felt was no longer appropriate to the era.

NEW ERA OF LEGISLATIVE ECONOMIC POLICY

In the mid-1930s the Court declined to use substantive due process to veto *state* economic legislation and thereby began abandoning its policy of promoting laissez-faire economic philosophy. The change in policy was announced in the 1934 case of *Nebbia* v. *New York* 291 U.S. 502, in which the Court admitted:

The phrase 'affected with the public interest' can, in the nature of things, mean no more than that an industry, for adequate reasons, is subject to control for the public good. In several of the decisions of this Court wherein the expression 'affected with the public interest,' . . . [has] been brought forward as the criteri[on] of the validity of price control, it has been admitted that [it is] not susceptible of definition and form[s] an unsatisfactory test of the constitutionality of legislation directed at business practices or prices.

Since the Court rejected the "affected with the public interest" criterion for determining the power of the states to impose regulation, a new test for violation of "due process" was needed. Therefore, the Court asserted:

Neither property rights nor contract rights are absolute; for government cannot exist if the citizen may at will use his property to the detriment of his fellows, or exercise his freedom of contract to work them harm. Equally fundamental with the private right is that of the public to regulate it in the common interest.

So far as the requirement of due process is concerned . . . a state is free to adopt whatever policy may reasonably be deemed to promote public welfare, and to enforce that policy by legislation adapted to its purpose. The Courts are without authority either to declare such policy, or, when it is declared by the legislative arm, to override it. If the laws passed are seen to have a reasonable relation to a proper legislative purpose, and are neither arbitrary nor discriminatory, the requirements of due process are satisfied. . . . With the wisdom of the policy adopted, with the adequacy or practicability of the law enacted to follow it, the courts are both incompetent and unauthorized to deal.

In 1941 the Supreme Court wrote:

We are not concerned, however, with the wisdom, need, nor appropriateness of the legislation. Differences of opinion on that score suggest a choice which 'should be left where . . . it was left by the Constitution—to the states and to Congress.'[3]

Later, the Court ruled:

This court . . . has consciously returned closer and closer to the earlier Constitutional principle that states have power to legislate against what are found to be injurious practices in their internal commercial and business affairs, so long as their laws do not run afoul of some specific federal constitutional prohibition, or of some valid federal law. . . . Under this doctrine the Due Process Clause is no longer to be so broadly construed that the Congress and the state legislatures are put in a strait-jacket when they attempt to suppress business and industrial conditions which they regard as offensive to the public welfare.[4]

By 1955, the Supreme Court was of the opinion:

The day is gone when this Court uses the Due Process Clause of the Fourteenth Amendment to strike down state laws, regulatory of business and industrial conditions, because they may be unwise, improvident, or out of harmony with a particular school of thought.[5]

Consequently, the constitutional door was open for state legislatures to regulate all forms of business activity. The only constitutional restraints remaining are the requirements that the law have a "reasonable relation to a proper legislative purpose" and not be "arbitrary nor discriminatory." In effect, the states have broad regulatory powers over all industries.

In 1937, another series of Supreme Court decisions began that broadly interpreted the commerce clause, and thereby expanded the *federal* congressional power to deal with economic affairs. In the *National Labor Relations Board* v. *Jones & Laughlin Steel Corp.* 301 U.S. 1 (1937), the Supreme Court upheld the National Labor Relations Act and its application in a *manufacturing* setting. In effect, the Supreme Court was abandoning its restrictive interpretation of "interstate commerce" as transportation only. In *U.S.* v. *Darby Lumber* 312 U.S. 100 (1941), the Supreme Court upheld the legislative exercise of the "commerce" power in the Fair Labor Standards Act of 1938 and applied its provisions to an *intrastate* merchant who paid less than the federal minimum wage. In that case, the Supreme Court concluded that the "commerce" power may be utilized to exclude any article from interstate commerce whether the product itself is harmful or not. This conclusion permits Congress to regulate "social problems," like abusive labor practices, which were previously considered beyond congressional reach. As a consequence of *Darby Lumber,* Congress was empowered to eliminate from commerce items manufactured without payment of the minimum federal wage or, alternatively, impose a fine on those who violated the federal minimum wage law. Additional comprehensive federal regulation of a purely local commercial activity was proposed in the Agricultural Adjustment Act of 1938, which was challenged in the following case.

Wickard v. Filburn
> 317 U.S. 111 (1942)
> Supreme Court of the United States

JACKSON, Mr. Justice:

It is urged that under the Commerce Clause of the Constitution, Congress does not possess the power . . . [to fix a wheat] quota that the farmer may harvest for sale or for his own farm needs, and [to] . . . declare that wheat produced on excess acreage may neither be disposed of nor used except upon payment of [a] . . . penalty. . . .

Defendant says that this is a regulation of production and consumption of wheat. Such activities are, he urges beyond the reach of Congressional power under the Commerce Clause, since they are local in character, and their effects upon interstate commerce are at most "indirect." In answer the Government argues it is sustainable as a "necessary and proper" implementation of the power of Congress over interstate commerce.

* * *

The Court's recognition of the relevance of the economic effects in the application of the Commerce Clause . . . has made the mechanical application of legal formulas no longer feasible. Once an economic measure of the reach of the power granted to Congress in the Commerce Clause is accepted, questions of federal power cannot be decided simply by finding the activity in question to be "production," nor can consideration of its economic effects be foreclosed by calling them "indirect." The present Chief Justice has said in summary of the present state of the law: "The commerce power is not confined in its exercise to regulation of commerce among the states. . . . The power of Congress over interstate commerce is plenary and complete in itself, may be exercised to its utmost extent, and acknowledges no limitations other than are prescribed in the Constitution. . . . It follows that no form of state activity can constitutionally thwart the regulatory power granted by the commerce clause to Congress. Hence the reach of that power extends to those intrastate activities which in a substantial way interfere with or obstruct the exercise of the granted power."

Whether the subject of the regulation in question was "production," "consumption," or "marketing" is, therefore, not material for purposes of deciding the question of federal power before us. That an activity is of local character may help in a doubtful case to determine whether Congress intended to reach it. The same consideration might help in determining whether in the absence of Congressional action it would be permissible for the state to exert its power on the subject matter, even though in so doing it to some degree affected interstate commerce. But even if (defendant's) activity be local and though it may not be regarded as commerce, it may still, whatever its nature, be reached by Congress if it exerts a substantial economic effect on interstate commerce, and this irrespective of whether such effect is what might at some earlier time have been defined as "direct" or "indirect."

The effect of consumption on home-grown wheat on interstate commerce is due to the fact that it constitutes the most variable factor in the disappearance of the wheat crop. Consumption on the farm where grown appears to vary in an amount greater than 20 per cent of average production. The total amount of wheat consumed as food varies but relatively little, and use as seed is relatively constant.

The maintenance by government regulation of a price for wheat undoubtedly can be accomplished as effectively by sustaining or increasing the demand as by limiting the supply. The effect of the statute before us is to restrict the amount which may be produced for market and the extent as well as to which one may forestall resort to the market by producing to meet his own needs. That defendant's own contribution to the demand for wheat may be trivial by itself is not enough to remove him from the scope of federal regulation where, as here, his contribution, taken together with that of many others similarly situated, is far from trivial.

It is well established by decision of this Court that the power to regulate commerce includes the power to regulate the prices at which commodities in that commerce are dealt in and practices affecting such prices. One of the primary purposes of the Act in question was to increase the market price of wheat, and to that end to limit the volume thereof that could affect the market. It can hardly be denied that a factor of such volume and variability as home-consumed wheat would have a substantial influence on price and market conditions. This may arise because being in marketable condition such wheat overhangs the market and, if induced by rising prices, tends to flow into the market and check price increases. But if we assume that it is never marketed, it supplies a need of a man who grew it which would otherwise be reflected by purchases in the open market. Home-grown wheat in this sense competes with wheat in commerce. The stimulation of commerce is a use of the regulatory function quite as definitely as prohibitions or restrictions thereon. This record leaves us in no doubt that Congress may properly have considered that wheat consumed on the farm where grown, if wholly outside the scheme of regulation, would have a substantial effect in defeating and obstructing its purpose to stimulate trade therein at increased prices.

It is said, however, that this Act, forcing some farmers into the market to buy what they could provide for themselves, is an unfair promotion of the market and prices of specializing wheat growers. It is of the essence of regulation that it lays a restraining hand on the self-interest of the regulated and that advantage from the regulation commonly fall to others. The conflicts of economic interest between the regulated and those who advantage by it are wisely left under our system to resolution by the Congress under its more flexible and responsible legislative process. Such conflicts rarely lend themselves to judicial determination. And with the wisdom, workability, or fairness, of the plan of regulation we have nothing to do.

Questions

1. Under the interstate commerce clause, may the federal government regulate "marketing"? "Production"? Consumption"?
2. How far does the interstate commerce power extend into the states?
3. May the Court inquire into congressional purposes for passing legislation in order to determine if Congress is regulating "economic affairs" and not some "social or moral" problem? *In the Heart of Atlanta Motel, Inc.* v. *U.S.* 379 US 241 (1964), the Supreme Court ruled:

> In framing [the Civil Rights Act of 1964] . . . Congress was also dealing with what is considered a moral problem. But that fact does not detract from the overwhelming evidence of the disruptive effect that racial discrimination has had on commercial intercourse. It was this burden which empowered Congress to enact appropriate legislation, and, given this basis for the exercise of its power, Congress was not restricted by the fact that the particular obstruction to interstate commerce with which it was dealing was also deemed a moral and social wrong. It is said that the operation of the motel here is of a purely local character. But, assuming this to be true, "(i)f it is interstate commerce that feels the pinch, it does not matter how local the operation which applies the squeeze." *United States* v. *Women's Sportwear Mfrs. Assn.*, 336 U.S. 460, 464 (1949). . . .Thus the power of Congress to promote interstate commerce also includes the power to regulate the local incidents thereof, including local activities in both the States of origin and destination, which might have a substantial and harmful effect upon that commerce. One need only examine the evidence . . . to see that Congress may—as it has—prohibit racial discrimination by motels serving travelers, however "local" their operations may appear. Nor does the Act deprive appellant of liberty or property under the Fifth Amendment. The commerce power invoked here by the Congress is a specific and plenary one authorized by the Constitution itself. The only questions are (1) whether Congress had a rational basis for finding that racial discrimination by motels affected commerce, and (2) if it had such a basis, whether the means it selected to eliminate that evil are reasonable and appropriate. If they are, appellant has no "right" to select its guests as it sees fit, free from governmental regulation.

CONCLUSION

The legal system attempts to resolve controversies. It involves an analysis of the relevant facts in the case, selecting past cases for guidance, evaluating alternative solutions, and reaching a conclusion with articulated reasoning. Understanding this process of legal analysis begins with an appreciation for the dynamic quality of the case-law method—how changing factual situations bring about different legal conclusions and how a new rule is formulated when the reasons for the rule become outdated or no longer serve societal needs. Consequently, the application of the rules of law to various factual situations have been reviewed to gain understanding of the framework for legal analysis and the changing nature of law.

Since the landmark *Marbury* announcement that it is for the courts "to say what the law is," the Justices of the Supreme Court have played an important role in fashioning the "rules" of the American economic system. After society's commitment to a laissez-faire philosophy of government had terminated, the Supreme Court's ideological commitment to laissez-faire resulted in decisions that fought against society's efforts to regulate private economic affairs. As such, the Court was a potent force in retarding the legal response to social change. However, the Supreme Court has ultimately abdicated its commitment to laissez-faire philosophy. In contrast, it has expanded the reach of legislative powers. The Court, through expansive definitions of interstate commerce, has created a federal legislative preeminence in the fashioning of national economic policy. Indeed, the new ideological commitment of the Court in the modern age appears to be one of governmental imperative in economic affairs. Justices, like members of society, may differ as to the kinds and degree of governmental action, but, by far, the majority of individuals and Justices consider governmental action to be a necessity. However, in the modern age the policy choices of governmental action will largely remain a legislative function, rather than judicial. The Court has removed itself from the role of second-guessing legislative policies. Its role will be more restricted to statutory interpretation.

DISCUSSION QUESTIONS

1. The plaintiff was in the process of moving her furniture out of her apartment when the landlord appeared with a pistol. He threatened her and told her not to move anything out of the apartment since he had a lien on the goods because of the unpaid rent. The gun was unloaded, but the plaintiff didn't know that. The plaintiff sued for assault. If the defendant meant no actual harm and the gun was unloaded, would this be an assault?

2. Roberts took his Oldsmobile into Breisig's for repairs. Roberts asked when the car would be ready. Breisig said he hoped the repairs would be completed by the end of the day and that he would park the car in the parking lot of his shop so Roberts could pick it up that evening.

Breisig finished the work and parked the car in the lot, leaving the keys in the car. Soon thereafter two teenage boys stole the car and, while driving, negligently struck George, the plaintiff, who suffered serious injuries.

George brought an action against Breisig, claiming that the keys in the unattended automobile constituted an act of negligence. Breisig denied that his conduct constituted negligence, contending that his action was not the proximate cause of plaintiff's injuries. Decide.

3. Jacques entered a Sears store in New York to purchase business supplies. He picked up 19 reflectorized letters and numbers worth 10 cents apiece and put them in his pocket. He also selected a mailbox and had two extra keys made. He paid for the mailbox and keys, but left the store without paying for the letters and numbers. At the time he had over $600 in cash and a $400 check in his wallet.

A Sears' security officer observed Jacques putting the items in his pocket and leaving the store without paying for them. As Jacques approached his car in the store parking lot, the officer stopped him and told him that he was under arrest. He took Jacques back to a security office, where Jacques admitted having taken the letters without paying for them. He said he wished to pay for the letters, that he was "sorry about the whole thing," and that he "would never do anything like this again."

Sears' security officers called the New York police, who took Jacques to police headquarters, booked him, and later released him on bail.

Jacques brought this action for damages against Sears, alleging false imprisonment and false arrest. Sears contended that its detention of Jacques was "reasonable." Decide.

4. Mrs. Garner went into a drugstore to buy some soap. Her father, who was ill, remained in her car in the parking lot in front of the store. She found the bar of soap, took it to the cashier, paid for it, and received a sales ticket. The cashier put the soap in a small bag. Mrs. Garner's sister was with her and had not finished shopping. Mrs. Garner said that she was going out to the car to see if their father was all right. She walked out of the store, but before she got to her car, the manager of the store yelled at her, telling her to stop, and accused her of stealing the bar of soap. She denied it, but he told her she would have to go back into the store with him to prove that she hadn't stolen the soap. There were a number of people in the parking lot who heard the manager's loud and rude accusations. When the manager and Mrs. Garner got back to the store, the cashier verified that Mrs. Garner had paid for the soap. Mrs. Garner was then released. Is the store liable to the plaintiff for slander and false imprisonment?

5. Montgomery Ward, Inc. sold 2200 one-day-old chickens to Paul, who placed them in his newly constructed, modern, hygienic coop, to raise them as egg-layers. Paul had raised chickens all his life, and tended the new chicks day and night, sleeping in the coop for the first six months. In their third week the chicks developed signs of illness which worsened over time, until a form

of avian cancer was diagnosed that destroyed the entire flock before it reached one year of age.

A jury concluded, in a suit of breach of implied warranties instituted by Paul, that the birds carried the disease at the time they were delivered to Paul. The defendant, Ward, protested and expert testimony established, that this form of avian cancer is not detectable in newborn chicks, cannot be prevented, and has no cure; Ward thus had no knowledge that the chicks were defective at the time of delivery. Under what theory of tort liability might Ward be liable?

6. Mrs. Johnson received a prescription for Equanil, a tranquilizer, from her physician. The original prescription was for three capsules per day and was marked "P.R.N.," or prescription refillable as needed. Mrs. Johnson frequently had the prescription refilled and soon was taking 7 to 10 pills per day. Mrs. Johnson's pharmacist refilled the prescription on her request because of the P.R.N. notation on the original prescription. The pharmacist was dispensing 100 pills every 9 to 10 days to Mrs. Johnson. Eventually the plaintiff began having convulsions and additionally suffered brain and liver damage due to prolonged overdoses of equanil. The evidence shows that much of the harm to Mrs. Johnson occurred after she became addicted to equanil. Mrs. Johnson's niece (also her guardian) has asked you to assist her in obtaining some type of recovery for the permanent injuries her aunt has suffered. On what tort cause of action might the pharmacist be liable under the above facts? What elements of the tort action must be proven? What affirmative defenses might the pharmacist raise? Are any of these affirmative defenses likely to be upheld?

7. Hughes holds a Texas license to operate a commercial minnow business near Wichita Falls, Texas. An Oklahoma game ranger arrested him on a charge of violating Section 4-115(b) by transporting from Oklahoma to Wichita Falls a load of minnows purchased from a minnow dealer licensed to do business in Oklahoma. Hughes's defense that Section 4-115(b) was unconstitutional because it was repugnant to the commerce clause was rejected, and he was convicted and fined. What is the result on appeal?

8. Is the power of judicial review unreasonable? Is it necessary to maintain some constitutional flexibility over time?

9. Contrast the tort theories of intentional, negligent, and strict liability. Which theory involves more "social engineering"?

10. How broad is the "commerce" power? Has it always been the same?

SUGGESTED READINGS

Jentz, Gaylord A. and Thomas A. Collins, "Extension of Strict Liability to All Third Persons," *American Business Law Journal*, Vol. 12, No. 3, Winter 1975, pp. 231–248.
Kempin, Frederick G., Jr., "Why Legal History," *American Business Law Journal*, Vol. 15, No. 1, Spring 1977, pp. 88–100.

Lantry, Terry L., "An Expanding Legal Duty: The Recovery of Damages for Mental Anguish by Those Observing Tortious Activity," *American Business Law Journal,* Vol. 19, No. 2, Summer 1981, pp. 214–226.

Mass, Michael A., "Garbage As Commerce: Must We Swim or Sink in it Together," *American Business Law Journal,* Vol. 17, No. 2, Summer 1979, pp. 211–220.

Miller, Arthur Selwyn, *The Modern Corporate State: Private Governments and the American Constitution* (Westport, Conn.: Greenwood Press, 1976).

Stevens, George E., "'Insult and Outrage' In the Employer-Employee Relationship," *American Business Law Journal,* Vol. 16, No. 1, Spring 1978, pp. 103–106.

Stevens, George E., "The Publicity Requirement and the Right to Privacy," *American Business Law Journal,* Vol. 16, No. 3, Winter 1979, pp. 360–364.

Tucker, Edwin, W., "Interest Analysis in Conflict of Laws," *American Business Law Journal,* Vol. 17, No. 1, Spring 1979, pp. 128–129.

ENDNOTES

1. Ezra Pound, "The End of Law as Developed in Legal Rules and Doctrines," 27 *Harv. L. Rev.* 195 (1914); p. 223.
2. *Smyth* v. *Ames* 169 U.S. 466 (1898).
3. *Olsen* v. *Nebraska* 313 U.S. 236, 246–247, (1941).
4. *Lincoln Federal Labor Union* v. *Northwestern Iron & Metal Co.* 335 U.S. 325, 536–537, (1949).
5. *Williamson* v. *Lee Optical of Okla.* 348 U.S. 483, 487–488. (1955).

part III
THE COMPETITIVE PROCESS

From earliest U.S. history, American society has placed a firm faith in the workings of a free market economy. Protection against those who might exploit or abuse society in the production and distribution of the nation's goods and services was to be effectuated through the forces of competition. While this belief in competition as a virtue for society continues even today, the government has found it necessary to change its role from passive observer of economic activity into modern-day protector of "competition"; the theory being that by protecting and preserving competition, America will continue to reap the benefits of a free economy except for the historical role of a limited government.

In the last part of the nineteenth century, a device known as a trust became popular as a technique of gaining monopolistic control of industries. The majority of the stock of competing companies would be transferred to a board of trustees and the previous stockholders would receive trust certificates naming them as beneficiaries entitled to dividends coming from the companies through the trust to them. The trustee board would be composed of various directors from the companies in the industry. The board would then make policy decisions for the supposedly competing companies and, in effect, run the legally separate companies in a monopolistic manner. It was this use of the trust device that brought in an era known as "trust busting" (i.e., eliminating this type of trust purpose, not eliminating the trust device itself). The laws enacted to eliminate monopolistic practices in industry likewise became known as antitrust laws. The laws do not outlaw legitimate uses of trusts; rather, the laws are designed to promote competition.

Of course, the decisions concerning a change in the role of government and the variety of methods to be employed in regulation of competition have not been accomplished without opposition. Certainly, the policy choices selected to preserve "competition" have not received universal acceptance.

The materials in Part III scan the historical development of antitrust laws and present the various viewpoints concerning appropriate antitrust policy. The basic substantive rules relating to the structure of industries and the conduct of firms are discussed.

chapter 8
THE GOALS OF ANTITRUST

The years before the Civil War were the Golden Age for small businesses. After the war, however, the tendency was for firms to consolidate. Economists have debated whether the consolidation of smaller units into larger firms was the inevitable result of the conditions brought about by the Industrial Revolution. Many of the witnesses appearing before the Industrial Commission in 1899 believed the chief motivating force for business consolidation was the cutthroat competition, which wiped out profits.[1] Others felt smaller firms suffered in comparison with large ones in securing the best management or in bargaining with labor, bankers, and transportation companies. Despite these opposing views, the invention of labor-saving machinery made large-scale production profitable and often required consolidation.

As the size of the business units increased, the older methods of organizing a business by means of individual proprietorships or partnerships became inadequate. The capital needs for buildings, equipment, and inventories were too great for individuals to supply and the risk was too great to be undertaken by single proprietors. Consequently, the corporate form of business was adopted following the Civil War as a vehicle to raise sufficient amounts of risk capital and limit the liability of the owners. The corporate form had been resisted in earlier times because it had been associated with the monopolistic practices of the mercantilistic trading companies. Many also argued that corporations could grow to a size that would rival the state itself. Their efforts to impose legal constraints on the size and purposes of corporations became ineffective as time passed, and the corporation became the dominant form of business organization.

While many large firms achieved their size by internal growth and natural expansion, many more grew through the process of consolidation. Initial efforts to consolidate an industry usually involved a "pool." A pool was an organization of differing business units whereby members sought to control prices by apportioning the available business in some way. Another form of pool was that in which territory and market were allocated. However, the pool represented a mere federation of the parties and lacked an effective process to discipline members into adherence to the plan. To form a more permanent bond that controlled the membership, the trust became the most favorite form of combination. A trust was a form of organization in which the stockholders under a trust agreement transfered a controlling portion of their stock to a Board of Trustees in exchange for trust certificates. The trust certificates entitled the former shareholders to receive dividends and beneficial enjoyment of their property, except that technical ownership and power to direct the business firm resided with the Board of Trustees. The Board of Trustees was composed of representatives from each of the firms. For example, the Standard Oil Company of Ohio developed a scheme in 1882 in which the stockholders of 40 companies placed their shares in the hands of nine trustees who dictated the policies of the constituent companies. The public, in general, had no difficulty in understanding the purpose of this new organization. So obvious was it that the trusts were organized to eliminate competition that the term "trust" became commonly used to designate any large combination that approached a monopoly. Public opinion became aroused and by 1884 the antimonopolists had convinced the leading political parties to incorporate into their platforms a call for government action to prevent or control monopolies. In 1890, the federal government passed the Sherman Antitrust Act.

LEGISLATIVE HISTORY

In 1940, the Temporary National Economic Committee conducted a study and investigation with respect to the concentration of economic power in the production and distribution of goods and services in America. Two members of the committee filed the following report,[2] which characterized the legislative history of the Sherman Act.

Antitrust in Action
Walter H. Hamilton and Irene Till

The Sherman Act is a weapon of policy from another age. As the eighties became the nineties, the Nation was becoming uncomfortably conscious of an industrial revolution. . . . The land was dotted with factories using simple mechanical processes; yet, chemistry and biology had not been subdued into technologies and electricity had just ceased to be a toy. The telephone was still a novelty; the electric light had just passed its eleventh birthday; the wonders that lie within the vacuum tube were still to be explored. The automobile was a rather impious hope; the airplane, an adventurous flight in wishful thinking. The motion picture and the radio broadcast were as yet hardly tangible enough to be subjects of fancy. Agriculture, once the foundation of national wealth, was being driven back country. Petty trade had been forced to make a place beside itself for a big business which seemed to masses of the people to be strange, gigantic, powerful.

The unruly times offered opportunity to the swashbuckling captains of industry, whose ways were direct, ruthless, and not yet covered over by the surface amenities of a later age. In sugar, nails, tobacco, copper, jute, cordage, borax, slate pencils, oilcloth, gutta percha, barbed fence wire, castor oil they bluntly staked out their feudal domains. The little man caught in a squeeze play—the independent crowded to the wall by "the Octopus"—the farmer selling his wheat, corn, or tobacco under the tyranny of a market he did not understand—the craftsman stripped of his trade by the machine—the consumer forced to take the ware at an artificial price or go without—here were dramatic episodes. Industry was in the clutch of radical forces—and of iniquity. It was a period in which the ordinary man was confused, disturbed, resentful.

Of this confusion, disturbance, resentment, Congress became aware. It was led by protest and petition to the necessity of doing something about it. Yet a number of obstacles blurred the vision and arrested the action of the Fifty-first Congress. At the time there had been little experience with administration. The regulatory commission was almost unknown. The Interstate Commerce Commission, but 3 years old, had not yet found its footing: the dominant purpose behind it was not to regulate the railroads but to put an end to rebates and discriminations upon which favored shippers thrived. Some of the State commissions were a bit older, but they had little to offer in the way of usage, device, invention. Just as little was known about industry, whose curious ways had not yet become a subject of detailed study; a speculative account of how competition was supposed to work was enough. Since, barring collusion, the general theory was applicable to any ware of trade, the bewildering variety of industrial activity was hardly suspected.

*   *   *

To men of simple faith the ends came easily. As text of bill and gloss of debate indicate, their aim was to make monopoly in all its forms as odious at law as morally it was outrageous. In terms of a public policy, not yet overcharged with legalisms, they proclaim the norm of a free competition too self-evident to be debated. . . .

*   *   *

Back to the Common Law

As a creature of such currents of thought the statute took shape. The original Sherman bill was a very tentative proposal. It professed to outlaw all arrangements which prevented "full and free competition," [and] to open the Federal courts to suits by parties damnified by such agreements, . . . Its terms were uncertain, it invited constitutional attack, its author was timid in its defense. Twice it was rewritten by the Committee on Finance; yet, it remained the target for the kind of shafts which the statesmen of that generation loved to hurl. The author, confused, yielding, anxious to placate, time after time would concede objection and accept amendment. As thus from many desks rather incongruous bits came into place, members became quite uncertain as to the objective and content of the proposed measure. . . .

But a posse of Senators on the warpath was not enthusiastic about so lukewarm a measure. . . . [To] Senator Reagan, of Texas, . . . a "trust" was a crime; the persons perpetrating it, criminals; and he wanted the United States statutes bluntly to say so. In a bill untainted by decorous compromise he drove at the heart of the mischief. In concrete terms it set down a list of activities any one of which tended to create a trust; made participation in any plan to abridge unrestricted competition a "high misdemeanor"; punished with a fine not to exceed $10,000 or imprisonment at hard labor for five years or both; and, that the punishment might be worthy of the crime, made each day of violation a separate offense. Senator Ingalls, of Kansas, who knew what the farmer was up aginst, sponsored an elaborate porposal . . . For a time Senators Reagan and Ingalls each sought to amend the Sherman bill by replacing it with his own. In the course of debate a colleague suggested that the Reagan measure was a complement, not a substitute, for the original bill. So bright an idea was bound to prevail. . . . Among statutes-to-be competition gave way to combination; the three bills became one.

Step by step all seemed right. Yet somehow the whole of the resolve seemed different from the sum of the motions. A majority had gone along, yet only a straggling of supporters remained faithful to the completed work. Once—and then again—a motion had been made to recommit the bill, not to the Finance Committee whence in lean form it had come, but to the Judiciary Committee. On former occasions the proposal "to deliver the child for nurture to persons who have most interest in its death" had been voted down and for the time the measure was saved from "this great mausoleum of senatorial literature." Now for the third time the motion for reference was put and carried; and the Judiciary Committee—stung by criticism or avid to exploit an opportunity—within six days returned to the Senate a bill with the same caption. The committee had scrapped all that had been sent along; and, with Senator Hoar of Massachusetts as draftsman, had written its own law.

The new bill simply recited for "commerce among the several States," the rule of the common law against restraint of trade. . . . The statement was framed in familiar legal symbols, not in the language of industry or the idiom of public policy. The prohibitions, which had grown out of the experience with petty trade, were taken over intact. . . .

*   *   *

[There was no] . . . attempt to devise new machinery of enforcement. In the thought of the nineties the law should be as nearly self-enforcing as possible. The main reliance seems to have been placed upon the private suit. A man knew when he was hurt better than an agency or government above could tell him. Make it worth their while—as the triple-damage clause was intended to do—and injured members could be depended upon to police an industry. If more were needed, the resort was to the usual course of Federal justice. Another duty was added to the overlarge obligations of the Attorney General and of the several district attorneys scattered throughout the land.

After the briefest of discussions the Senate adopted the Hoar bill. Its sponsors were apologetic for the very little distance the statute went; but the zeal for argument had long since been spent. It was accepted as a "first installment," presently to be amended as experience pointed the way. In the House a time limit forced an early vote; leave to print crowded the inaudible debate from the floor into the Congressional Record. A single amendment led to a struggle in conference and was eventually abandoned; the text was left intact. There was no enthusiasm; but here was something at least for the people back home—and the congressional campaign was warming up. Besides there were matters of real consequence, such as the McKinley Tariff Act, which wanted legislative attention. So, with only a single vote in dissent—though in both Houses members answered "present" or were conveniently absent—on the 2d of July 1890, the bill became the law of the land. It is to this day strangely called the Sherman Act—for no better reason, according to its author, than that Senator Sherman had nothing to do with it whatever.

The Intent—if any—of Congress

A great deal has been said about the purpose of Congress in passing the act. At best legislative intent is an evasive thing. It is wrapped in the conditions, the problems, the attitudes, the very atmosphere of an era that is gone. But aside from saying that the act reflects its date, there is little more to recite. Instead, as a creation of the process of legislation, the statute bears the confused marks of its origin. . . . In this case a scattered mass of opinion and of feeling was never distilled into an articulate statement. . . .

In search for intent the record has been thumbed through with meticulous care and to little purpose. The debates exhibit heat, passion, righteous indignation against the devil of monopoly. The bills proposed went much farther than the Hoar Act. . . .

A ruse, whose cleverness only legislative experts can appreciate, drove a barrier between debate and eventual statute. The matter went to a committee notoriously hostile to the legislation. The committee turned a deaf ear to all that the Senate had said and done and went its own way. Intent, therefore, forsakes the Congressional Record for the capacious recesses of that flexible corpus called the common law. . . .

The Fifty-first Congress sensed the rush of an oncoming industrialism. Its task, facing the future, was to create a barrier against shock, a road to order, a guaranty of justice. In debate it laid bare evils within the emerging national economy, but could bring itself to do something about it only in a babble of voices. Except for words, it made no thrust at present dangers; it came to no grip with the trends of the times; it made no attempt to chart a course for American industry. When the voters would no longer tolerate delay, it acted. When the need was to shape the future, it looked to the past. On the eve of the greatest of industrial revolutions, the National Government was fitted out with a weapon forged to meet the problems of petty trade. Out of an inability of Congress to face the economic problems of its day the "charter of freedom" for American industry was born.

Questions

1. Which special interest groups cried out for antitrust laws against big business consolidations?
2. Had society studied the operations and working practices of big industries so as to more appropriately fashion a public policy with respect to big business? Without factual understanding, are ideological beliefs sufficient to develop public policy?
3. Did the people of the 1880s consider the use of an administrative agency of specialists to control the intricate affairs of big business?
4. Was Congress able to fashion a consensus to support the original Sherman Bill? What were the critics of the Sherman Bill attempting to accomplish?
5. How would you characterize the Hoar Bill? Did it recite new requirements for industry or propose mere legislation of the rules against restraint of trade contained in the common law? Did it devise any new machinery of enforcement or attempt to make the laws self-enforcing?
6. Why was there no extensive debate concerning the provisions of the Hoar Bill? What "legislative history" is available to aid in interpreting congressional intent in passing the Sherman Act?
7. Without extensive legislative history, where could the court turn for aid in interpreting the Sherman Act?
8. How would you characterize the congressional effort in trying to deal with the evils of monopoly? Does Congress seem any different today in dealing with the economic problems of the modern age?

PURPOSES OF THE SHERMAN ACT

It is a well-established principle that "courts should construe the law with a view to effecting the object of its enactment."[3] Since Congress in 1890 enacted only the barest of statutory language with little actual legislative history to aid in interpretation, the courts have had to fashion the substance of antitrust law on a case-by-case basis. In so doing the courts have recognized two basic purposes of antitrust laws. In *Northern Pacific Railway Co.* v. *United States,* Mr. Justice Black expressed the two basic purposes of the antitrust laws as follows.

The Sherman Act was designed to be a comprehensive charter of economic liberty aimed at preserving free and unfettered competition as the rule of trade. It rests on the premise that the unrestrained interaction of competitive forces will yield the best allocation of our economic resources, the lowest prices, the highest quality, and the greatest material progress, while at the same time providing an environment conducive to the preservation of our democratic, political and social institutions.[4]

ECONOMIC PURPOSES

The courts have recognized that the Congress enacted the Sherman Act in substantial part because of its belief that a competitive economy would best ensure a prosperous nation. The general economic objective of the antitrust laws, therefore, is the promotion of free and open competition. In determining whether a particular restraint impairs competition, the Supreme Court has indicated that courts should look to the prinicpal concerns that gave rise to the enactment of the Sherman Act. In *The Standard Oil Company* v. *United States,* the Supreme Court expressed these concerns as:

(1) The power . . . to fix the price and thereby to injure the public;
(2) [The power to impose some] . . . limitation on production; and
(3) The danger of deterioration in quality . . . which [is] the inevitable resultant of the monopolistic control over . . . [an article's] production and sale.[5]

The Court felt that Congress was opposed to the "power" to fix prices, limit production, or reduce quality, whether that "power" arose by the collusion of competitors or the outright monopolization of a single firm. These practices cause a loss of *economic efficiency,* which has become a basic standard with which to measure a restraint to determine whether or not it offends the Sherman Act.

SOCIAL PURPOSES

Preservation of Small Business Units. The Sherman Act was passed by Congress not only to achieve a competitive economy but also to preserve a social structure that protects the political life of the nation from control by trusts and business combinations. It was believed that the best safeguard against such control was the preservation of a Jeffersonian society of many small, independent businessmen. With this atomistic market structure, the problems of resource allocation and income distribution are to be solved through the impersonal mechanism of the market, and not through the conscious exercise of power held in private hands (as in monopoly), or in government hands (as in state enterprise or governmental regulation). This political purpose underlying the Sherman Act has been reflected in subsequent decades in the enactment of additional antitrust statutes that attempt to curb the power of large businesses and to halt the perceived trend toward concentration of the economy.

Some courts have concluded that a decentralized market composed of numerous small business units is socially desirable even where such markets are economically inefficient. Judge Learned Hand in *United States* v. *Alcoa Company of America,* wrote:

Throughout the history of [the antitrust laws] it has been constantly assumed that one of their purposes was to perpetuate and preserve for its own sake in spite of possible cost, an organization of industry in small units which can effectively compete with each other.[6]

This social goal of antitrust enforcement to protect small business units in spite of possible economic cost has been a frequent theme of the basic antitrust philosophy.

Preservation of Economic Liberty and Opportunity. Some courts and commentators have suggested that another social purpose of the antitrust laws is the preservation of individual liberty and freedom of action. Under free and competitive conditions without barriers to entry, individuals are free to enter whatever trade or profession they prefer. While it has been said that "restraints upon the freedom of economic units to act according to their own choice and discretion . . . run counter to antitrust policy,"[7] freedom of choice also implies the freedom to enter into contracts and agreements deemed useful by the participants. As the Supreme Court stated in *Standard Oil Co. of N.J.* v. *United States:*

[The framers of the Sherman Act recognize that] the freedom of the individual right to contract, when not unduly or improperly exercised, was the most efficient means for prevention of monopoly. . . . In other words, that freedom to contract was the essence of freedom from undue restraint on the right to contract.[8]

Consequently, the courts have held that the Sherman Act was not intended to outlaw all restraints limiting a firm's freedom of action, but only those that *unduly* or *unreasonably* restrain competition. Justice Brandeis stated this "rule of reason" in *Chicago Board of Trade* v. *United States.*

Every statement concerning trade, every regulation of trade, restrains. To bind, to restrain, is of their very essence. The true test of legality is whether the restraint imposed is such as merely regulates and perhaps promotes competition or whether it is such as may suppress or even destroy competition.[9]

Others have stated, however, that any restraint on an individual's freedom of action is to be condemned under the antitrust laws whether or not such restraint has the effect of unreasonably suppressing competition. This view has been particularly apparent in cases concerning vertical restrictions on distribution where the manufacturer often has been denied the right to impose any limitation on the distributor, regardless of the economic effect of such restrictions.

It is not difficult for the reader to determine that the two basic antitrust purposes may often be in conflict. The debate over whether economic efficiency or social purposes should have priority goes to the heart of the controversy surrounding the *approach* that antitrust laws should take in dealing with any restraint on competition.

WORKABLE COMPETITION

An ideological commitment to competition permeates society and is often supported by an almost religious fervor. It is not surprising, therefore, that statutory and common law reflect this ideological commitment to the competitive market system. However, while nearly everyone is in favor of competition, there is a great deal of debate concerning the degree or type of competition sufficient to bring about its benefits—in other words, what type of competition is to be accepted as a public policy *norm* against which to judge whether an industry is sufficiently competitive. There are basically three schools of economic thought (approaches) concerning the appropriate norm of "workable competition."

THE MODEL OF INDUSTRIAL ORGANIZATION ANALYSIS

The application of the economic models of price theory to industries in the real world is a subject of economics called "industrial organization." Most of the economists in the field of industrial organization believe it is the *market organization* of those business units (or industry structures) that affects the performance of the market or industry as a whole. In short, economists try to ascertain how market processes direct the activities of producers in meeting consumer demands. They attempt to identify how these processes break down and how they can be adjusted through government intervention to make actual business performance more closely conform to society's ideals.

A simple descriptive model of the overall approach of most industrial organization studies was conceived by Edward S. Mason during the late 1930s.[10] Other scholars have extended the model, which is illustrated in Figure 8-1.[11]

As indicated in Figure 8-1, the principal components of market analysis are structure, conduct, and performance.

The elements of market *structure* tend to be stable over time. However, they can be altered by either private or government policy. The structure of the relevant market embraces such features as the number and size distribution of sellers and buyers, the degree of physical or subjective product differentiation,

Figure 8-1. A Model of industrial organization analysis.

the conditions of entry of new firms, and the degree of diversification of the individual firms' product lines.

The word *conduct* denotes behavior and actions on the part of the firms in the market. The several items listed under conduct in Figure 8-1 reflect action, not static conditions. The conduct of sellers and buyers involves such matters as pricing policies and practices, overt and tacit interfirm cooperation, advertising strategies, research and development commitments, investment in production facilities, legal tactics, and so on.

Finally, *performance* relates to the achievements or end results of the firms' conduct. Did the firms achieve the social goals of efficiency, technological advancements, full employment and equitable distribution of income? More succinctly, structure and conduct relate to *how* the market functions whereas performance relates to *how well* the market functions in terms of societal goals.

The arrows in Figure 8-1 indicate that traditional industrial organization theory assumes a causal flow running from structure to conduct to performance. For example, a changing structural characteristic, such as a change in the number and size distribution of firms, may cause changes in price and production policies (conduct) that result in favorable or unfavorable effects on inflation, employment, technological innovations, or allocative efficiency (performance). Stated in reverse order, Figure 8-1 reveals that the performance of a particular industry is dependent on the conduct of the sellers in that market. Furthermore, the conduct of the sellers depends on the structure of the relevant market. Thus, the market structure-conduct-performance paradigm provides the basis for analysis and appraisal of the extent to which the market structure and conduct in various markets yields satisfactory economic performance.

While the reader will not be presented with all the myriad interrelationships of the industrial organization model, this limited exposition of the model is helpful in understanding the theoretical underpinnings of any public policy measure designed to improve performance by manipulating structure or conduct variables.

STRUCTURALIST APPROACH

Structuralists believe that a norm of workable competition can be formulated from classical economic theory, which can be modified for a realistic economic setting. They maintain that certain structural characteristics of an industry can be identified and that these characteristics can be applied to any specific industry on a case-by-case basis to determine whether antitrust enforcement is needed. Industries lacking these characteristics should be restructured through dismemberment orders. Such structural characteristics of a workably competitive market would include the following.

1. An appreciable number of traders (absence of concentration) so that consumers could readily turn away from any particular trader and find a variety of other alternatives.
2. An equitable distribution of size and power so that no firm is powerful enough to coerce a rival nor so large that the remaining traders lack the capacity to absorb a substantial proportion of its trade.
3. Responsiveness of market participants to economic incentives rather than political and social purposes.
4. Independence of traders in determining commercial policy.
5. Reasonable opportunity of entry for new traders without the handicap of artificial barriers.
6. Minimization of persuasive advertising, brand, and product differentiation.

These market structure tests place primary emphasis on limiting the economic power in the hands of private parties. Structuralists seek to employ antitrust laws to ensure the continued existence of the competitive system, with checks and balances against any private attempts to control the market. Structuralists also favor alternative governmental policies that encourage small businesses, the use of government procurement and surplus property programs to establish competing firms, and the imposition of taxes on increased advertising expenditures that can destroy the independence of consumers. However, correctives, such as the divestiture of existing firms, would be the more desired remedy of the structuralists.

CONDUCT APPROACH

Advocates of the conduct approach argue that certain business practices that interfere with the efficient operation of the competitive marketplace should be reasonably identified and outlawed. They argue that standards of illegal "conduct" must be identified so that business managers will have "fairly definite standards" to guide their behavior. They conclude that the criterion of *intent* to commit these illegal acts establishes a sensible test for determining antitrust enforcement. In effect, prohibition of illegal overt actions and behaviors should be the only basis for judicial action in the field of antitrust. Since attorneys, who enforce antitrust law, are trained and conditioned to prosecute against behavior or conduct rather than mere status, the conduct approach has had a definite impact on the evolving antitrust laws.

PERFORMANCE APPROACH

The pure economic performance test to determine appropriate antitrust policy includes criteria such as the following.

1. Is the industry economically efficient?
2. Is it technologically progressive?
3. Does it show a reasonable and socially useful profit pattern?
4. Does it have as much freedom of entry as the nature of the industry will permit?
5. Is it well suited to serve national defense needs?

Negative answers to these questions suggest the need for antitrust action; positive answers suggest immunity from antitrust attack. However, it is extremely difficult for these performance tests to be applied by the courts. The literature of performance economists summarizes more specific tests, as follows.

1. Whether the firm is progressive in product and process innovation.
2. Whether cost reductions are passed on to consumers promptly.
3. Whether investment is excessive in relation to output.
4. Whether the profits are continually and substantially higher than in industries exhibiting similar trends in sales and costs and innovations.
5. Whether competitive effort concentrates mainly on selling activities rather than improvements in services and products and price reductions.

To the extent that the performance of the firm or industry, as measured by these criteria, is determined to be acceptable, antitrust attack on the industry is deemed inappropriate. Obviously, the spokespeople of large firms adopt the performance criteria and argue that their particular firm should not be subjected to antitrust action because their performance is acceptable.

Many believers in performance criteria for "workable competition" do not emphasize competition between sellers and buyers *within* an industry, but rather a more dynamic concept of interindustry or technological competition. Their argument, first expressed by Joseph Schumpeter, is that classical, intraindustry competition tends to promote maximum output, minimum prices, and optimum allocation efficiency, but that this efficiency is static and unprogressive.[12] While they concede that the competitive model abhors concentration, they argue that it makes no allowance for the research, development, and innovation required for economic growth. To have progress, they say, more concentration must be tolerated. They contend that only big firms can provide the sizable funds necessary for technological experimentation and innovation. In turn, these firms rely on the certainty of a short-run monopolistic position to recapture their research expenditures. Finally, they argue that while progress may require higher levels of concentration in many industries, such concentration should not be a concern to society because technological development in the long run will erode short-run monopolistic positions. In sum, they argue that the consumer is protected, not by static competition between large numbers of small firms, but in the long run by technological competition by a small number of large firms, which through research and innovation eventually erode the power basis of short-term monopolies.

Connected to this theory of technological and interindustry competition and its toleration of short-term monopolies is the belief that bigness and concentration will be controlled by the "right" people. A. A. Berle, Jr. has asserted that the great power possessed by some corporations is forcing their officers to develop a "corporate conscience" and behave in a socially responsible manner.[13] David E. Lilienthal has argued that antitrust philosophy is no longer needed and that the antitrust laws are, in fact, crippling American industries. He feels that the newer type of big businessman is an industrial statesman who embraces the ideals of social responsiblity and enlightened self-interest.[14] Lilienthal believes the present managers of giant corporate enterprises have demonstrated their capacity for exercising industrial stewardship.

RETORT OF THE STRUCTURALISTS

The structuralists object to the arguments presented by the performance economists. For one, structuralists have pointed out that the industry's performance as directed by the "corporate conscience" may not have been *compelled* by competition, but represents the dispensations of management who for the moment may be benevolent. However, structuralists reiterate that there is no assurance that the acceptable performance of today may not be transformed into the abusive monopoly or oppressive conspiracies of tomorrow. Without competition or detailed government supervision, what guarantees does society have that economic performance will continue to serve the public interest? In retort to the "corporate conscience" control of the American economy, Professor Ben Lewis has testified:

It isn't going to happen; if it did happen it wouldn't work; and if it did work it would still be intolerable to free men. I am willing to dream, perhaps selfishly, of a society of selfless men. Certainly, if those who direct our corporate concentrates are to be free from regulation either by competition or government, I can only hope that they will be conscientious, responsible, and kindly men; and I am prepared to be grateful if this proves to be the case. But, I shall still be uneasy and a little ashamed, with others who are ashamed, to be living my economic life within the limits set by the gracious bounty of the precious few. If we are to have rulers, let them be men of good will; but above all, let us join in choosing our rulers—and in ruling them.[15]

Structuralists also challenge the basic assumption of the thesis that industrial giantism is *inevitable* under modern technological conditions. Economists favoring large firms argue that such firms are able to obtain the maximum economies of scale. In contrast, the structuralists argue that more size generally means more efficiency, but only up to a point. They argue that, except for some of the utilities, there is apparently no industry in the United States in which a firm needs a full 100 percent of the domestic market in order to reach the maximum in productive efficiency—to keep unit costs down to the technological minimum. Structural economists point out that our larger country with geographically broad markets in a large, affluent population makes it possible for most of our manufacturing firms to reach a quite large absolute size without becoming large in relation to the size of the particular industries they operate within. A 1956 study of 20 large industries concluded that only one of them (typewriters) required a market share as high as 20 percent in order to realize all potential economies at the plant level.[16] Only two other such industries (tractors and copper) were found to require market shares of more than 10 percent in order to realize the lowest possible production cost. In 10 of those 20 major industries, all economies of scale in the production process were exhausted at a market share of no more than 2 percent. After that point, the unit cost remained at that same level in spite of the increasing size of the firm. Indeed, structural economists argue that inefficiencies may start to set in.

Structuralists have explored this question of size inefficiencies by looking at the profitability of firms of different sizes in the same industry. If the very largest producer is the most profitable, one can of course argue that this superior profitability is due either to (1) superior efficiency or (2) monopoly power. However, if the largest firm in the industry is not the most profitable, the general conclusion can only be that size and efficiency are unrelated in the production of that particular product. Since it can hardly be contended that the largest firms possess less monopoly power than their smaller rivals, the poor profit performance must be poor efficiency.

A study by John Blair of 30 major American industries reported that, in 16 of them, there was no discernible relationship between size and profitability; i.e., the largest firms in those industries were no more profitable on the average than their smaller competitors.[17] In the other 14 industries, the biggest firms in 6 industries were also the most profitable, but in 8 of them the smaller firms were more profitable than the giants. While General Motors was the most profitable company in the auto industry, the largest firm in the aluminum industry, Alcoa, was the least profitable of the aluminum producers. Anaconda was the least profitable firm in its industry. In liquor, meatpacking, and plumbing fixtures, firms one-fifth the size of the industry leader were the most profitable.

Structuralists argue that the very largest firms are not only less efficient than their middle-sized competitors, but also tend to be technologically inferior. While structuralists freely admit that larger firms spend more on research and development, they quickly point out that the larger firms spend the bulk of their research expenditures on "marketing" innovations rather than basic scientific research. For example, one famous study of 61 important inventions of this century reported that only 16 of those inventions came from large corporations.[18] Well over half of these key inventions were the work of the solitary inventor. Structuralists maintain that invention is essentially a thinking process, the act of a single person rather than an organization.

Beyond the invention process itself, structuralists point out that it is the smaller or medium-sized firm, not the industry leader, that is the general innovator of new technology. The larger firms, they argue, are too anxious to protect their investments in existing technology to be receptive to the real inventors, who often approach the large corporations with their inventions. For example, the man who invented xerography, Chester F. Carlson, was repeatedly turned away by IBM, Eastman Kodak, and Remington Rand. The firm that finally accepted him was the Haloid Company, a tiny enterprise with declining sales and a net income at the time (1946) of roughly $100,000. Structuralists point out that Haloid, now known as Xerox, took a chance on Carlson's invention precisely because of its relative poverty, not in spite of it.[19]

In brief, the structuralists maintain that the prescription of the performance economists that large firms are inevitable and economically and technically efficient is not sustained by the available evidence. Instead, structuralists argue that America should go slowly in letting the smaller firms be gobbled up or driven out of business by larger business enterprises.

CONCLUSION

The consolidation of business units following the Civil War led to a populous movement for legislation against monopolies. Congressional reaction was a statutory enactment of common law principles against restraint of trade and monopolization. It has been the courts' task to put "flesh" on the statute through case-by-case interpretation. The courts have emphasized two basic purposes for antitrust laws: (1) competitive markets for economic efficiency and (2) political and social freedoms resulting from the decentralization of economic power.

Economists, in their theoretical models, have demonstrated the advantages of competition and the disadvantages of monopolies. Yet the qualifications and doubts of many concerning the assumptions of the economic models have caused questions concerning the appropriateness of the models as blueprints for public policy. Nevertheless, industrial organization economists believe modifications in the models can be made so that the theoretical relationships more closely correspond to real settings and become acceptable for public policy formulation. Continuing debate among economists over the proper definition of "workable competition" and the appropriate approach for antitrust enforcement make the development of a public consensus almost impossible. No matter how the courts decide in an antitrust issue, some group with an opposing theory will criticize the conclusion.

DISCUSSION QUESTIONS

1. In his book, *The Antitrust Paradox* (1978), Robert H. Bork discusses the historical foundations of antitrust and concludes that antitrust was originally intended to advance consumer welfare only. Do you agree?

2. Bork advises the courts to ignore any social discontent resulting from "moral aversion" to higher prices for consumers that give producers greater profits. Bork concedes that consumers who continue to buy after a monopoly is formed pay more for the same output and that this shifts income from purchasers to the monopoly and its owners. He points out, though, that in such a case both purchasers and owners are consumers and the resulting shift in income distribution does not lessen total wealth.

    Therefore, he claims, the income distribution effects of an economic activity should be completely excluded from the determination of the antitrust legality of the activity; disapproval of any such income redistribution could only rest on "a tenuous moral ground."

    What is your reaction? Were the populists in the 1880s concerned about income redistribution resulting from "trust" combinations?

3. Bork recommends that the courts permit small competitors to be acquired through horizontal mergers up to market shares that leave "three significant companies" in an industry. Moreover, he argues the courts should never interfere with the absorption of these oligopolies, by other forms of merger, into conglomerates.

    Would the adoption by the courts of these recommendations lead to social contentment?

4. Bork has also recommended that the judiciary approve price fixing, the division of territories, and other restraints that are ancillary to integrating productive economic efficiency. Is economic efficiency the sole purpose of antitrust?

5. Professor Lawrence Sullivan of the University of California, Berkeley, has written "To argue, as do the Chicago economists, that antitrust ought to be used solely to inhibit expressions of market power in a technical economic sense, is not only to miss much in the history and development of the law, but to ignore much of its potential. . . . The political consensus that supports antitrust comes from other sources. Americans continue to value institutions the scale and the workings of which they can comprehend. Many continue to value the decentralization of decisionmaking power and responsibility. Many favor structures in which power in one locus may be checked by power in another. Antitrust, broadly conceived and sensitively administered, may contribute to the realization of these values."[20] Do you agree?

6. Outline the basic model of analysis in the economic field of industrial organization. Then, contrast the views of the "structure" and "performance" economists in relation to the unit of economic efficiency (plant versus firm), number of sellers, branding, entry, and methods of technological invention and innovation.

7. What is the basic tenet of Joseph Schumpeter's theory of dynamic competition?

8. What are A. A. Berle's views concerning appropriate antitrust policy? What was Ben Lewis's reaction to Berle's argument of "corporate conscience"?

9. Is industrial giantism inevitable? Are large firms more economically efficient and technologically progressive than small firms?

10. Robert Bork argues that market or industry structure is the result of individuals (firms) seeking efficient scales of operations and that private parties cannot create "artificial" entry barriers. Moreover, he finds no empirical or theoretical basis for believing that high market concentrations as they exist in oligopolies would result in output restrictions or higher prices. Consequently, in the absence of outright conspiratorial collusion, Bork would not have antitrust attack oligopolic situations. How would a structuralist react to Bork's conclusions?

SUGGESTED READINGS

Bork, Robert, *The Antitrust Paradox* (New York: Basic Books, 1978).

Bork, R. H., W. S. Bowman, Jr., H. M. Blake, and W. K. Jones, "The Goals of Antitrust: A Dialogue on Policy," *Columbia Law Review,* March 1965, pp. 363–443.

Caves, Richard, *American Industry: Structure, Conduct, Performance,* 4th ed. (Englewood Cliffs, N.J.: Prentice-Hall, Inc. 1977).

Elzinga, Kenneth G., "The Goals of Antitrust: Other Than Competition and Efficiency, What Else Counts," *University of Pennsylvania Law Review,* June 1977, p. 1198.

McGee, John S., *In Defense of Industrial Concentration* (New York: Praeger Publishers, 1971).

Peltzman, Sam, "The Gains and Losses from Industrial Concentration," *Journal of Law & Economics,* October 1977, pp. 229–263.

Pitofsky, Robert, "The Political Content of Antitrust," *University of Pennsylvania Law Review,* April 1979, p. 1063.

Posner, Richard A., *Antitrust Law: An Economic Perspective* (Chicago: University of Chicago Press, 1976).

Scherer, F. M., "The Causes and Consequences of Rising Industrial Concentration," *Journal of Law & Economics,* April 1979, pp. 191–208.

Scherer, F. M., A. Beckenstein, E. Kaufer, and R. D. Murphy, *The Economics of Multi-Plant Operation* (Cambridge, Mass.: Harvard University Press, 1975), p. 339.

Stewart, William S., "Federal Antitrust Enforcement," *American Business Law Journal,* Vo. 17, No. 1, Spring 1979, pp. 127–128.

Sullivan, Lawrence A., *Handbook of the Law of Antitrust* (St. Paul, Minn.: West Publishing, 1977).

Weiss, Leonard W., "The Structure-Conduct-Performance Paradigm and Antitrust," *Univ. of Pennsylvania Law Review,* April 1979, pp. 1124–1130.

ENDNOTES

1. Preliminary Report of the Industrial Commission, p. 9.
2. Walter H. Hamilton and Irene Till, *Antitrust in Action,* Monograph 16, Temporary National Economic Committee (Washington, D.C.: U.S. Government Printing Office, 1941), exerpted from pp. 5–11.
3. *United States* v. *Union Pacific R.R. Co.,* 226 U.S. 61, 87 (1912).
4. 365 U.S. 1,4 (1958).
5. *Standard Oil Co.* v. *United States,* 221 U.S. 1, 52 (1911).
6. 148 F 2d 416 (2d Cir. 1945).
7. *U.M.W.* v. *Pennington,* 381 U.S. 657, 668 (1965).
8. 221 U.S. 1, 62 (1911).
9. 246 U.S. 231, 238 (1918).
10. Edward Mason, "Price and Production Policies of Large-Scale Enterprise," *American Economic Review Supplement,* 29 (March, 1939), pp. 61–74.
11. Joe Bain, *Industrial Organization* (New York: Wiley & Sons, 1959); J. M. Clark, *Competition as a Dynamic Process* (Washington, D.C.: Brookings Institute, 1961); and F. M. Scherer, *Industrial Market Structure and Economic Performance* (Chicago: Rand McNally, 1970).
12. Joseph A. Schumpeter, *Capitalism, Socialism, and Democracy* (New York: Harper, 1942), pp. 88, 103.
13. Adolf A. Berle, Jr., *The 20th Century Capitalist Revolution* (New York: Harcourt, Press and World, 1954), pp. 172–173.
14. David E. Lilienthal, *Big Business: A New Era* (New York: Harper & Brothers, 1953).
15. "Administered Price Inflation: Alternative Public Policy" (Hearing on administered prices before the Subcommittee on Antitrust and Monopoly of the Senate Judiciary Committee, 86th Congress, 1st session). (Washington, D.C.: U.S. Government Printing Office, 59), Part 9, p. 4717.
16. Joe S. Bain, *Barriers to New Competition* (Cambridge, Mass.: Harvard University Press, 1956), p. 84. Bain's findings are summarized in Sherman and Tollison, "Public Policy Toward Oligopoly: Dissolution and Scale Economies," 4 *Antitrust Law & Economics Review* (Summer 1971). pp. 83–84.
17. John M. Blair, *Economic Concentration: Structure, Behavior, and Public Policy* (New York: Harcourt Brace, 1972), p. 181.
18. *Ibid.,* p. 209.
19. Erwin A. Blackstone, "The Copying-Machine Industry: Innovations, Patents, and Pricing," *Antitrust Law & Economics Review,* Vol. 6, No. 1 (1972).
20. Sullivan, "Economics and More Humanistic Disciplines: What Are The Sources of Wisdom for Antitrust?" 125 *University of Pennsylvania Law Review* 1214, 1222–23 (1977).

chapter 9
REGULATION OF MONOPOLIES

Monopoly, or *monopoly power,* has been defined by the Supreme Court as the power or ability to fix or control prices in, or exclude competitors from, a relevant market. Not all monopolies, however, have been declared illegal. In certain situations a monopoly or exclusive privileges, such as in patent or licensing situations, may be granted by federal, state, or local government. In other cases, monopoly may occur when only one firm survives a competitive struggle because of its efficiency in production or the quality of its products. What is legally proscribed, therefore, is the act of or attempt at "monopolization," which proscription involves an analysis of the intent of the firm whose large market control and practices are questioned.

MONOPOLIZATION

Section 2 of the Sherman Act outlaws monopolizations, attempts to monopolize, and conspiracies to monopolize. Congress outlawed monopolization and then, in effect, passed the buck to the courts to further articulate this law in specific situations. The courts have had a difficult time applying this law. One reason for this is that economic theory, as illustrated by the differing views of the conduct, structuralist, and performance schools of thought, has been little help. In addition, a public consensus concerning specific cases has been lacking. As a result, the courts' decisions have been subjected to criticism and ridicule by those holding to one or more of the opposing economic viewpoints.

Section 2 of the Sherman Act uses the word *monopolize*. The statutory language does not say that monopoly is prohibited but rather that "to monopolize" is to transgress the law. "Monopolize" was not defined by the statute, so such definition had to be determined by the courts. The Supreme Court has indicated that monopolization exists when two elements are present. First, the possession of monopoly power in the relevant market must be established, and second, the willful (intentional) acquisition or maintenance of that power must be shown.

In *Standard Oil* v. *U.S.*, 221 U.S. 1 (1911) the Supreme Court determined that Standard Oil's unification of power and control over petroleum and its products was the result of combinations, not of normal methods of industrial development. These large combinations afforded Standard Oil better than 90 percent control of the oil market, which equaled monopoly power. Coupled with these combinations were certain patterns of conduct that were essentially predatory. The Standard Oil trust had gained control of the country's oil pipeline system and thereby became practically the sole purchaser of crude oil. Because of the large shipments of oil required by this largest purchaser of oil, Standard Oil was able to exact preferential rebates from railroads. Standard Oil, in addition, caused the railroads to charge discriminatorily higher rates to Standard Oil competitors in the shipment of their refined products. In addition, Standard Oil was accused of conducting industrial espionage and of waging predatory price warfare to drive rivals out of business or to "encourage" them to join the trust. These predatory actions were sufficient evidence to establish Standard Oil's intent to monopolize. The use of predatory behavior as evidence of "intent" established a behavioral or conduct approach to the determination of illegality under Section 2.

In *U.S.* v. *U.S. Steel Corp.*, 251 U.S. 417 (1920), the Supreme Court found no violation of Section 2 and asserted the following:

The corporation is undoubtedly of impressive size and it takes an effort of resolution not to be affected by it or to exaggerate its influence. But we must adhere to the law and the law does not make mere size an offense or the existence of unexerted power an offense. It, we repeat, requires overt acts.

This statement, when coupled with the previous case against Standard Oil, has been characterized as the "abuse theory" of monopoly. Under this theory the government must establish the monopolistic intent of the defendant with proof of overt acts and conduct that abuse the competitors. Without actions by the defendant indicating a wrongful intent, the government is unable to prove the abuse of monopoly power.

The abuse theory of monopoly is consistent with the conduct approach for antitrust laws. Only the abusive practices and conduct of the defendant are outlawed. To the structural economists, a monopoly that restricts production and raises its price is contrary to the public interest, whether overt predatory conduct can be shown or not. It matters not how the monopolist obtained power or maintains its position. Consequently, the criticisms of structural economists and the growing public concern over the inadequacy of the abuse theory (the conduct approach) caused the government to consider a different approach in the Alcoa case.

THE ALCOA CASE

In 1937 the Justice Department charged the Aluminum Company of America, Alcoa, with illegal monopolization. Alcoa was formed in 1888 to exploit patents it held on the basic process for producing aluminum. After the basic patents expired in 1909, there were several attempts by others to enter the industry, but none were successful. During these early years, Alcoa had been involved in various litigations involving patents, merger disputes, international cartelization, and price discrimination.

The District Court absolved Alcoa on the charge of monopolization on the basis of the *U.S. Steel* decision. The Justice Department appealed, but a quorum of six justices could not be obtained in the Supreme Court. Four Supreme Court justices disqualified themselves because they had been associated with the prior litigation against Alcoa. A congressional amendment of the Judicial Code established a court of appeals to serve, in such circumstances, as the court of last resort. The case was then sent to the Court of Appeals in the second circuit. A three-member panel of judges, with Judge Learned Hand presiding, heard the appeal. As in all monopolization cases, the court had to determine if Alcoa possessed monopoly power in the relevant market and if that power was intentionally obtained and maintained.

The determination of whether Alcoa possessed monopoly power turned on how the market in which Alcoa operated was defined. This is so because monopoly power cannot be measured in the abstract. It has significance only in relation to a defined market within meaningful boundaries. Consequently, the issues of monopoly and market are intertwined. Proper delimitation of the market involves a consideration of what set of near substitutes should be considered as the "product" market. The market definition also requires an inquiry into substitution, both in production and in use of the items traded in the market.

In the Alcoa case the court dismissed the possibility of substitution on the production (supply) side. The court felt that the highly specialized aluminum refining facilities precluded the possibility of other companies converting their plants to produce aluminum. Moreover, on the demand side, aluminum's unique properties led the court to summarily exclude other metals such as steel, copper, and magnesium. Although such exclusion was perhaps unjustified by the facts (some users viewed other metals as substitutes for aluminum in many applications), the court nevertheless limited its analysis to alternative definitions of Alcoa's aluminum ingot market share (none of which need be discussed). Suffice it to say that Judge Hand concluded that Alcoa's 90 percent control of the virgin aluminum market "is enough to constitute a monopoly." Having found that Alcoa possessed a monopoly of the aluminum market, the court had to determine whether Alcoa's intent to achieve that position was sufficiently proven to establish a monopolization violation under Section 2.

United States v. Aluminum Co. of America
148 F. 2d 416 (1945)
U.S. Court of Appeals, 2d Cir.

Circuit Judge Hand

It is undisputed that throughout [a 28-year] period "Alcoa" continued to be the single producer of "virgin" ingot in the United States; and the plaintiff argues that this without more was enough to make it an unlawful monopoly. . . . "Alcoa's" [defense] . . . is that its monopoly was not retained by unlawful means, but was the result of a growth which the Act does not forbid, even when it results in a monopoly. . . .

The [trial] judge found that, over the whole half century of its existence, "Alcoa's" profits upon capital invested, after payment of income taxes, had been only about ten percent. . . . [Hence] it would be hard to say that "Alcoa" had made exorbitant profits on ingot. . . . But the whole issue is irrelevant anyway, for it is no excuse for "monopolizing" a market that the monopoly has not been used to extract from the consumer more than a "fair" profit. The Act has wider purposes. . . . Congress did not condone "good trusts" and condemn "bad" ones; it forbad all. Moreover, in so doing it was not necessarily actuated by economic motives alone. It is possible, because of its indirect social or moral effect, to prefer a system of small producers, each dependent for his success upon his own skill and character, to one in which the great mass of those engaged must accept the direction of a few. These considerations, which we have suggested only as possible purposes of the Act, we think the decisions prove to have been in fact its purposes. . . .

It does not follow because "Alcoa" had such a monopoly, that it "monopolized" the ingot market: it may not have achieved monopoly; monopoly may have been thrust upon it. If it had been a combination of existing smelters which united the whole industry and controlled the production of all aluminum ingot, it would certainly have "monopolized" the market. . . . We may start therefore with the premise that to have combined ninety percent of the producers of ingot would have been to "monopolize" the ingot market; and, so far as concerns the public interest, it can make no difference whether an existing competition is put an end to, or whether prospective competition is prevented. . . . Nevertheless, it is unquestionably true that from the very outset the courts have at least kept in reserve the possibility that the origin of a monopoly may be critical in determining its legality. . . . This notion has usually been expressed by saying that size does not determine guilt; that there must be some "exclusion" of competitors; that the growth must be something else than "natural" or "normal"; that there must be a "wrongful intent," or some other specific intent; or that some "unduly" coercive means must be used. . . .

What engendered these compunctions is reasonably plain; persons may unwittingly find themselves in possession of a monopoly, automatically so to say: that is, without having intended either to put an end to existing competition, or to prevent competition from arising when none had existed; they may become monopolists by force of accident. . . . A market may, for example, be so limited that it is impossible to produce at all and meet the cost of production except by a plant large enough to supply the whole demand. Or there may be changes in taste or in cost which drive out all but one purveyor. A single producer may be the survivor out of a group of active competitors, merely by virtue of his superior skill, foresight, and industry. In such cases, a strong argument can be made that, although the result may expose the public to the evils of monopoly, the Act does not mean to condemn the resultant of those very forces which it is its prime object to foster. The successful competitor, having been urged to compete, must not be turned upon when he wins. . . .

It would completely misconstrue "Alcoa's" position in 1940 to hold that it was the passive beneficiary of a monopoly, follwoing upon an involuntary elimination of competitors by automatically operative economic forces.

There were at least one or two abortive attempts to enter the industry, but "Alcoa" effectively anticipated and forestalled all competition, and succeeded in holding the field alone. True, it stimulated demand and opened new uses for the metal, but not without making sure that it could supply what it had evoked. There is no dispute as to this; "Alcoa" avows it as evidence of the skill, energy and initiative with which it has always conducted its business; as a reason why, having won its way by fair means, it should be commended, and not dismembered. . . .

The only question is whether it falls within the exception established in favor of those who do not seek, but cannot avoid, the control of a market. It seems to us that that question scarcely survives its statement. It was not inevitable that it should always anticipate increases in the demand for ingot and be prepared to supply them. Nothing compelled it to keep doubling and redoubling its capacity before others entered the field. It insists that it never excluded competitors; but we can think of no more effective exclusion than progressively to embrace each new opportunity as it opened, and to face every newcomer with new capacity already geared into a great organization, having the advantage of experience, trade connections and the elite of personnel. Only in case we interpret "exclusion" as limited to manoeuvers not honestly industrial, but actuated solely by a desire to prevent competition, can such a course, indefatigably pursued, be deemed not "exclusionary." So to limit it would in our judgment emasculate the Act; would permit just such consolidations as it was designed to prevent. . . .

In order to fall within Section 2, the monopolist must have both the power to monopolize, and the intent to monopolize. To read the passage as demanding any "specific" intent, makes nonsense of it, for no monopolist monopolizes unconscious of what he is doing. So here, "Alcoa" meant to keep, and did keep, that complete and exclusive hold upon the ingot market with which it started. That was to "monopolize" that market, however innocently it otherwise proceeded.

Questions

1. Is the approach in the *Alcoa* case a conduct approach (abuse theory)?
2. What was the court's response to Alcoa's assertion that it was a "good" monopoly and charged only "fair" prices? Is this assertion relevant to a structuralist? To a performance economist?
3. Did Alcoa "intend" to monopolize? What proof of intent did the court require? Is the court's approach that of a structuralist or of a performance economist?
4. What is a "thrust upon" defense? Can you give examples? Was the monopoly of Alcoa "thrust upon" it? Is a newspaper firm in a town with only one newspaper an illegal monopoly?

Remedial action in the *Alcoa* case was deferred until after World War II. During the war, the government built aluminum-producing plants that were operated by Alcoa. After the war, the government's plants were sold to the newly formed Reynolds Metals Company and the Kaiser Aluminum Company. Thereafter, the district court concluded that with the two new competitors, Alcoa did not need to be fragmented.

The *Alcoa* decision was broadly endorsed by the Supreme Court in subsequent decisions. The approach in *Alcoa* overturned the *Standard Oil* and *U.S. Steel* precedents. It became possible to infer illegal monopolization from the mere possession and continuation over time of monopoly power without evidence of unreasonable (abusive) practices driving competitors from the market. In 1948 Justice Douglas, in speaking for a 6-1 majority upholding a monopolization charge, stated that "monopoly power, whether lawfully of unlawfully acquired, may itself constitute an evil and stand condemned under Section 2 even though it remains unexercised."[1]

THE duPONT CASE

The decision in *United States* v. *duPont* in 1956 shattered the hard-line structuralist approach against dominant firms of the *Alcoa* decision. In *duPont*, the Justice Department argued for a narrow definition of the market embracing only cellophane sales. The government emphasized cellophane's unique properties, the substantial price differences between cellophane and other packaging materials, and the unusually high profits realized by cellophane sales. However, duPont argued that the relevant market included all "flexible wrapping materials" because there was a high cross-elasticity of demand between cellophane and other flexible wrapping materials. Within this broadly defined market, cellophane embraced only an 18 percent share.

duPont dominated the cellophane market by virtue of patents acquired from abroad and from its own improvement inventions. duPont also settled with an American company that had challenged duPont's patent claims by working out a licensing arrangement. The government argued that these patent arrangements justified an inference of illegal intent to monopolize. The district court disagreed with both the government's definition of the market and its proof of intent to monopolize.

United States v. duPont & Co.
351 U.S. 377 (1956)
Supreme Court of the United States

Justice Reed

. . . Market delimitation is necessary . . . to determine whether an alleged monopolist violates § 2. The ultimate consideration in such a determination is whether the defendants control the price and competition in the market for such part of trade or commerce as they are charged with monopolizing. Every manufacturer is the sole producer of the particular commodity it makes but its control in the above sense of the relevant market depends upon the availability of alternative commodities for buyers: i.e., whether there is a cross-elasticity of demand between cellophane and the other wrappings. This interchangeability is largely gauged by the purchase of competing products for similar uses considering the price, characteristics and adaptability of the competing commodities. . . .

If a large number of buyers and sellers deal freely in a standardized product, such as salt or wheat, we have complete or pure competition. Patents, on the other hand, furnish the most familiar type of classic monopoly. As the producers of a standardized product bring about significant differentiations of quality, design, or packaging in the product that permit differences of use, competition becomes to a greater degree incomplete and the producer's power over price and competition greater over his article and its use, according to the differentiation he is able to create and maintain. A retail seller may have in one sense a monopoly on certain trade because of location, as an isolated country store or filling station, or because no one else makes a product of just the quality or attractiveness of his product, as for example in cagarettes. Thus one can theorize that we have monopolistic competition in every nonstandardized commodity with each manufacturer having power over the price and production of his own product. However, this power that, let us say, automobile or soft-drink manufacturers have over their trademarked products is not the power that makes an illegal monopoly. Illegal power must be appraised in terms of the competitive market for the product.

Determination of the competitive market for commodities depends on how different from one another are the offered commodities in character or use, how far buyers will go to substitute one commodity for another. For example, one can think of building materials as in commodity competition but one could hardly say that brick competed with steel or wood or cement or stone in the meaning of Sherman Act litigation: the products are too different. This is the interindustry competition emphasized by some economists.

On the other hand, there are certain differences in the formulae for soft drinks but one can hardly say that each one is an illegal monopoly. Whatever the market may be, we hold that control of price or competition establishes the existence of monopoly power under § 2. Section 2 requires the application of a reasonable approach in determining the existence of monopoly power. . . . This of course does not mean that there can be a reasonable monopoly.

* * *

. . . [W]here there are market alternatives that buyers may readily use for their purposes, illegal monopoly does not exist merely because the product said to be monopolized differs from others. If it were not so, only physically identical products would be a part of the market. To accept the Government's argument, we would have to conclude that the manufacturers of plain as well as moistureproof cellophane were monopolists, and so with films such as Pliofilm, foil, glassine, polyethylene, and Saran, for each of these wrappings materials is distinguishable. These were all exhibits in the case. New wrappings appear, generally similar to cellophane: is each a monopoly? What is called for is an appraisal of the "cross-elasticity" of demand in the trade. . . . The varying circumstances of each case determine the result. In considering what is the relevant market for determining the control of price and competition, no more definite rule can be declared than that commodities reasonably interchangeable by consumers for the same purposes make up that "part of the trade or commerce," monopolization of which may be illegal. . . .

It may be admitted that cellophane combines the desirable elements of transparency, strength and cheapness more definitely than any of the others. . . .

But, despite cellophane's advantages, it has

to meet competition from other materials in every one of its uses. . . . Thus, cellophane shares the packaging market with others. The overall result is that cellophane accounts for 17.9% of flexible wrapping materials, measured by the wrapping surface. . . .

An element for consideration as to cross-elasticity of demand between products is the responsiveness of the sales of one product to price changes of the other. If a slight decrease in the price of cellophane causes a considerable number of customers of other flexible wrappings to switch to cellophane, it would be an indication that a high cross-elasticity of demand exists between them; that the products compete in the same market. The court below held that the "[g]reat sensitivity of customers in the flexible packaging markets to price or quality changes" prevented duPont from possessing monopoly control over price. The record sustains these findings.

We conclude that cellophane's interchangeability with the other materials mentioned suffices to make it a part of this flexible packaging material market.

The Government stresses the fact that the variation in price between cellophane and other materials demonstrates they are noncompetitive. As these products are all flexible wrapping materials, it seems reasonable to consider, as was done at the trial, their comparative cost to the consumer in terms of square area. Cellophane costs two or three times as much, surface measure, as its chief competitors for the flexible wrapping market, glassine and greaseproof papers. Other forms of cellulose wrappings and those from other chemical or mineral substances, with the exception of aluminum foil, are more expensive. The uses of these materials, . . . are largely to wrap small packages for retail distribution. The wrapping is a relatively small proportion of the entire cost of the article. Different producers need different qualities in wrappings and their need may vary from time to time as their products undergo change. But the necessity for flexible wrappings is the central and unchanging demand. We cannot say that these differences in cost gave duPont monopoly over prices in view of the findings of fact on that subject. . . .

The facts above considered dispose also of any contention that competitors have been excluded by duPont from the packaging material market. That market has many producers and there is no proof duPont ever has possessed power to exclude any of them from the rapidly expanding flexible packaging market. . . . The record shows the multiplicity of competitors and the financial strength of some with individual assets running to the hundreds of millions.

The "market" which one must study to determine when a producer has monopoly power will vary with the part of commerce under consideration. The tests are constant. That market is composed of products that have reasonable interchangeability for the purposes for which they are produced—price, use and qualities considered. While the application of the tests remains uncertain, it seems to us that duPont should not be found to monopolize cellophane when that product has the competition and interchangeability with other wrappings that this record shows.

Questions

1. By a narrow definition of the market, the courts may find a monopoly (as in the *Alcoa* case) or they may determine that no monopoly exists (as in *duPont*) when a broad definition of the market is accepted. What is the test to define the "product market"? Does the application of this test in any factual situation afford considerable leeway to the court?

2. The *Alcoa* decision emphasized the lack of interchangeability of production facilities, which provided Alcoa with the illegal monopolization power to exclude competitors or to control price. In contrast, the *duPont* decision emphasized the interchangeability of various producers' goods despite the inability of others to produce cellophane. Which of these two cases creates a better approach for Section 2?

3. Does the company that produces Dr. Pepper soft drink possess an illegal monopoly?

4. Is interindustry competition to be included in the definition of the product market?

5. Why did the Supreme Court not consider the issue of whether duPont's patent practices justified an inference of intent to monopolize?

WILLFUL AND EXCLUSIONARY PRACTICES

The principal litigated victory of the government in the late 1960s was the *Grinnell* case.[2] This case restated the elements that constitute monopolization under Section 2, that is, "the possession of monopoly power in the relevant market and . . . the willful acquisition or maintenance of that power as distinguished from growth or development as a consequence of a superior product, business acumen, or historic accident." *Grinnell*'s requirement to separate "willful acquisition or maintenance" of monopoly power from "growth or development" through superior products, business acumen, or historic accident has become a difficult task in subsequent cases.

The Grinnell test makes it clear that mere possession of monopoly power to control market prices is not sufficient to establish a violation of Section 2. It must also be shown that the power was *willfully* acquired or maintained. The cases have established that a firm that has monopoly control of a market may not engage in practices that are designed to continue such control. The principal conduct attributed to Alcoa in support of the assertion that it had monopolized the market for aluminum ingots was its practice of expanding existing plants and constructing new facilities in anticipation of increased demand for the product. This expansion of capacity had the effect of discouraging and frustrating entry into the field by other firms. Judge Learned Hand delineated the proper means of analyzing the conduct of a firm with monopoly power by writing, "The only question is whether it falls within the exception established in favor of those who do not seek, but cannot avoid, the control of the market."[3] Reviewing Alcoa's expansion policy, the court stated that it could "think of no more effective exclusion than to embrace every new opportunity as it opened."[4]

One point made clear by the *Alcoa* decision is that the conduct of firms with monopoly power is viewed differently from that of firms without such power. It leads to the conclusion that firms with monopoly power may not maintain that power through means that are not economically inevitable. This conclusion follows naturally from the strong policy of the antitrust laws to which monopoly is repugnant. Some monopolies must be tolerated because they are inevitable, natural, or "thrust upon" their owners. But where a firm with monopoly power interferes with natural economic forces that would otherwise dissipate its monopoly, the law rightfully condemns it.

The question of defining appropriate limits on permissible business behavior by a monopoly is perplexing. On one hand, monopoly power and the market dislocations it generates are abhorrent to an effective competitive system. On the other hand, it is fundamental to Section 2 enforcement that a monopolist will not be penalized if its success derives solely from its superior skill, foresight, and industry. However, these eloquent statements are difficult to apply sensibly and consistently in specific situations. For example, the word *willful* suggests that intent is the critical element in determining whether conduct by a monopolist is legal or not. Although many have argued that intent is an ambiguous indicator, the courts nevertheless accept testimony and corporate documents of plans and correspondence that may reveal corporate intent to monopolize.

Also, the language in the *Alcoa* case suggests that *any* exclusionary business behavior, at least where not economically inevitable, would violate Section 2. Some have pointed out that there are many forms of conduct not economically inevitable that can have an exclusionary effect and that it would clearly be unwise policy to deter. For example, a monopolist may improve its product and succeed thereby in obtaining additional business. Or the monopolist may improve its production facilities so as to become more efficient and then pass that efficiency along to consumers in the form of lower prices. Such conduct, it is argued, may actually exclude existing or potential rivals but surely should not be considered illegal under Section 2.[5]

Perhaps a fairer and more effective description of permissible behavior by a monopolist must proceed beyond loose language dealing with intent or exclusion and come to grips with the specific conduct engaged in by the monopolist. A description of permissible behavior by a monopolist must inquire whether the conduct at issue is *unreasonably* exclusionary or anticompetitive, that is, whether the anticompetitive effects of a practice outweigh its procompetitive consequences, taking into account whether the same procompetitive consequences could have been achieved through a less restrictive alternative action. The search for clear guidelines to identify only *unreasonable* exclusionary behavior, however, is continuous but rarely satisfying to all. For example, consider the following discussion concerning the appropriate pricing policies of a monopolist.

PRICING POLICIES OF A MONOPOLIST

It frequently occurs that a business rival (sometimes a new entrant) cuts price significantly below the price of a monopolist in order to take away part of its market. Assuming the monopolist desires to respond with a price cut of its own, in what circumstances would such behavior violate Section 2 of the Sherman Act?

No Price Response

It is possible to argue that a monopolist should not be permitted to engage in responsive price cuts at all when a new, smaller challenger appears on a scene. If a legally mandated price were imposed on the monopolist, smaller rivals would eventually cut into the market share of the monopolist until its market position fell below the monopoly level. At that point the monopolist would be free to respond with any price strategy it felt would be effective.

New entrants protected by a legally mandated umbrella price of the monopolist may themselves charge higher prices than would otherwise be the case. The whole industry could become economically inefficient for the period of time the administered price umbrella was in effect. Also, the legally mandated umbrella price creates extremely burdensome administrative problems in supporting the monopolist's pricing policy. For example, suppose the monopolist improves the quality of its products. The court would have to judge what constitutes a fair increase in price to take into account the more attractive features introduced. No increase in price for a better quality item would have the same effect on the new entrant as a price cut. These and other objections to the no-response rule has led to its rejection by the courts.

Discriminatory Pricing

One rule could require that a monopolist not respond to a new challenge by lowering prices strategically in competitive markets. This rule requires that the monopolist not discriminate in price between geographic markets or between product categories. Consequently, if there is to be a price reduction, it must be across the board.

The district court in *Grinnell* discussed the issue of discriminatory pricing, and the Supreme Court affirmed the district court's decision with little more than a passing reference to this issue. The Court acknowledged that Grinnell had reduced its prices in competitive markets and raised prices in markets in which it faced no competition. Accordingly, the Court approved of the government's proposal to require Grinnell to sell on nondiscriminatory terms. In the *United Shoe Machinery* case, the Court acknowledged that a discriminatory pricing policy may not be "predatory, abusive, or coercive," but nevertheless could be "in economic effect, exclusionary" and hence a violation of Section 2.[6] Although the authority of precedents is not overwhelming, it could be a dangerous practice for a monopolist to engage in discriminatory pricing, which may have the "exclusionary effect" of eliminating the new competition.

Predatory Pricing

Professors Areeda and Turner have argued that predatory or exclusionary pricing by a monopolist should be assessed by a series of cost-based rules.[7] Their rule states that a monopolist should be held to be violating Section 2 only when it sells "below cost," defining cost as average *variable* cost. They assert that a firm that is selling at a short-term profit-maximizing price is clearly not a predator even though it may be selling below its full cost. On the other hand, when a firm sells at less than average variable cost, it is taking an out-of-pocket loss on every unit sold. Such conduct can only be explained as part of a strategy to drive rivals out of business and then recoup the earlier losses with larger than competitive prices. Also, sales at such low prices raise the specter that success in the market will depend not on the relative efficiency of rivals, but on which seller has a sufficiently long purse to subsidize these unit-by-unit competitive losses. Thus, Areeda and Turner argue that a price at or above average variable cost is presumed nonpredatory; a price below is conclusively presumed unlawful. This rule provides sufficient guidance as to permissible pricing behavior for a monopolist and the courts alike. Several courts of appeal and district courts have recently adopted the below-average variable-cost rule to test for predatory pricing, but in limited circumstances.[8]

A different cost-based rule is suggested by Professor Posner, who defines predatory pricing as (1) selling below average variable cost (Areeda-Turner rule) or (2) "pricing at a level calculated to exclude from the market an equally or more efficient competitor" (Posner's rule).[9] Posner adopts a rebuttable presumption that predation is selling below average *total* cost with intent to exclude a competitor. A defendant could rebut the *prima facie* case of predation by showing, because of change in supply and demand, that its average total costs were not the correct guide to efficient pricing. This formulation apparently is predicated on the belief that an average variable-cost rule (Areeda-Turner rule) would be too permissive and would allow a monopolist to eliminate a competitor whose long-run cost may be equal to or lower than the monopolist's. Short-term costs are invariably lower than long-run costs because the former may not include a variety of past expenses that have become a fixed cost for existing competitors but are yet to be incurred by the new entrant. Allowing existing firms to ignore previous fixed costs by pricing according to their present variable costs will force a new entrant to absorb losses on its initial fixed costs.

Several courts have recognized the problem identified by Posner and attempted to deal with it by adopting a two-step test for predatory pricing.[10] The first standard to determine predation is whether the price is below the average variable cost (Areeda-Turner rule). Even if it is not, a violation can still occur if it is below the average total cost and barriers to entry are high. The theory appears to be that if entry barriers are high, a monopolist can drive equally efficient or nearly as efficient rivals out of business (or discipline them into a compliant posture through price wars), and then raise its price to above competitive levels to reap monopoly profits before new entrants can create a competitive market.

Professor Scherer has concluded that it may be socially undesirable to allow price cutting to eliminate competitors when the monopolist's position is attained by an "image advantage." When image superiority is created in the consumers' minds by advertising and trademarking an item, the firm is able to maintain a price premium. Professor Scherer has written as follows.

An image advantage . . . enhances the dominant firm's incentive to cut prices temporarily to exclude less favored rivals. What society obtains following successful image-induced exclusionary pricing is not the freeing of resources that can be employed more effectively elsewhere, but rather, higher prices and profits accompanied by increased consumption of the "premium" product. . . . I find it hard to avoid a value judgment that temporary price cutting to eliminate producers handicapped only by an inferior brand image is socially undesirable.[11]

Scherer's conclusion and Posner's rule were applied in the Federal Trade Commission (FTC) case against Borden and its monopolization of the processed lemon juice market.[12] In 1978 the FTC concluded that the 30 percent price advantage achieved through successful differentiation of the ReaLemon brand served as an instrument by which Borden could control prices and entry into the processed lemon juice market. The FTC found that although Borden did not sell below average variable cost, it did price below average total cost with the intent to exclude competitors (in violation of Posner's rule). The FTC concluded that "the effect of Borden's spurious product differentiation, making it necessary for competitors to sell considerably below ReaLemon, created a circumstance where [Borden's reduced prices, which were still above average variable] . . . cost could, as the record indicates, be predatory in the sense that even equally efficient competitors could be driven from the market."

The ReaLemon case, apparently utilizing Posner's rule for predatory pricing, was affirmed by the Sixth Circuit Court of Appeals in 1982. While the defendant's request for *certiorari* was pending before the Supreme Court, the FTC agreed to a proposed settlement in which Borden would not be allowed to sell its ReaLemon for less than the product's variable cost. By a 3-2 vote, the newly aligned (three Reagan appointees) comission asked the Supreme Court to let the commission substitute a new version of predatory pricing standards because the original ruling, according to the new commission, did not set forth "a satisfactory, cost-based standard" for what constitutes predatory price setting. The original order prohibited Borden from selling ReaLemon at "unreasonably low prices" but did not define "unreasonable." Therefore, the commission believed that the public interest would not be served by defending its earlier opinion in the Supreme Court. Under the new order, Borden must not price ReaLemon so that the product's net revenue for any fiscal quarter in any sales district is less that the variable cost for that quarter and district. The cost formula would not include all the costs associated with developing and marketing the product.

FTC ACT, SECTION 5

The basic authority of the FTC is enforcement of all antitrust laws and of Section 5 of the FTC Act, which outlaws "unlawful methods of competition" among competitors. This latter provision was conceived as protection for honest businesses from competitors utilizing unfair competitive practices. The FTC is empowered by the statute to conduct investigations to determine if any business firm is in violation of Section 5. Whenever the commission has "reason to believe" that any party is violating Section 5, it is authorized to issue a complaint against the party. The courts have upheld the authority of the FTC to outlaw a practice as an "unfair method of competition" though the practice is not yet a full-blown antitrust violation under the Sherman Act.[13]

The FTC instigated some actions beginning in the late 1960s to reorganize monopolistic industries. For example, one FTC action involved a complaint against the Xerox Corporation for its monopolization of the plain paper copier business. Xerox settled through a consent order and agreed to make its extensive portfolio of copying machine patents available for licensing at a royalty rate not exceeding 1.5 percent (to all except IBM).[14]

In an effort to extend its authority under Section 5 even further, the FTC issued a complaint against a "shared monopoly" situation, which would not normally be a provable violation under Section 2 of the Sherman Act.[15] None of the firms alone could be charged with monopolization under Section 2 of the Sherman Act because no firm by itself controlled a dominant share of the market. The case involved the three leading ready-to-eat (i.e., cold) breakfast cereal manufacturers. During the late 1960s, 81 percent of the total sales of cereal were made by the three leading sellers. As usual, the cereal makers urged a much broader market definition that would encompass such other breakfast foods as hot cereals, toast, waffles, and bacon and eggs.

The behavior of the three leading cereal makers embodied a high degree of parallelism and respect for mutual interdependence. Kellogg exercised price leadership and the other firms followed. List price reductions were rare and secret price cutting was unknown. As a result, the cereal makers maintained prices at twice the level of their manufacturing costs. Prices were high enough for them to spend 16 cents per sales dollar on advertising and still realize an after-tax return on assets between 1958 and 1970 of roughly twice the average for all manufacturing corporations.

Kellogg and General Mills had always refused to engage in private label cereal production. Post quit the private brand distribution in the 1960s even though internal analyses showed sizable private label accounts to be quite profitable.

With the leading cereal producers charging high prices and realizing supranormal profits, one may well wonder why new firms did not enter to erode these high profits. Economies of scale do not appear to be the answer, because minimum optimum scale appears to involve no more than 4 to 6 percent of the market.[16] Consequently, the FTC concluded and argued that opportunities for profitable new entry had been preempted largely by the existing sellers' proliferation of product brands. A firm attempting to gain a product differentiation advantage to facilitate its entry found that the established sellers had created such a diversity of product variants that a new brand entrant would hardly be noticed without enormous promotional expenditures. There may be little evidence of explicit intent by the cereal makers to preclude entry by the proliferation of products, but the entry-deterring *effects* of brand proliferation have been widely known to marketing managers since the 1960s, if not earlier.

The evidence of parallel noncompetitive behavior in private brands, overall monopolistic profits, persistently high concentration levels, and a plausible mechanism (brand proliferation) of collective market share maintenance was deemed insufficient to conclude the practice of illegal monopolization under Section 5 of the FTC Act. The administrative law judge dismissed the FTC complaint in September 1981, saying FTC counsel had not proved the charge that the companies' conduct illegally interfered with the ability of new firms to enter the market. The judge said that brand proliferation is "nothing more than the introduction of new brands, which is a legitimate means of competition. [The companies] engaged in intense, unrestrained and uncoordinated competition in the introduction of new products."[17] The judge's decision was not reversed by the full commission.

If monopolization had been found, the FTC indicated that a structural reorganization would be required. The FTC wanted three new competitors spun off from Kellogg, one from General Mills, and one from General Foods. Beyond this, the FTC asked that many of the cereal formulas and trademarks be made available for licensing to rivals. Licensees would thereby be able to use, for example, the name Cheerios and indicate that they had followed the original formula under strict quality-control standards. Companies would distinguish their Cheerios with a prominent company name identification. Consequently, it would be possible to have Jones' Cheerios and Smith's Cheerios as well as General Mills' Cheerios. The FTC felt that this would encourage new price-oriented competition.

It is clear that the cereal case was uncommonly innovative. For one, it alleged monopolization by oligopolists rather than by a dominant firm. Second, the theory of entry preclusion argued (brand proliferation) was novel. And, third, the request for a trademark licensing remedy to enhance price competition was unusual.

PROPOSALS OF REFORM

It is difficult to determine the impact of the existing monopolization doctrines on American industries. Many suppose that they have at least discouraged the more blatant predatory behavior. Also, many have argued that the fear of Section 2 may have induced some leading sellers to restrain their competitive efforts so as not to exceed the range of a 60 to 64 percent market share that Judge Learned Hand had identified as the threshold of monopoly.

Apart from these behavioral modifications, the direct impact of the Sherman Act, Section 2, in lessening market concentration has been more modest. Scherer has indicated that between 1890 and 1970 "the courts have ordered structural reorganization in only 32 Section 2 cases—all but 7 of them before 1950."[18] One reason for this relatively small reorganization effort is judicial reluctance to impose structural remedies. The courts often perceive the monopolists as "efficient and progressive." The courts often seem unconvinced that restructuring will bring about the theoretical benefits of workable competition.

Another factor that has hindered the enforcement of Section 2 is the complexity and cost of major monopolization suits. The Justice Department is believed to have expended at least $10 million in the IBM suit alone. IBM was believed to have spent $100 million in legal fees and related expenses in defending itself against charges of Section 2 violations.[19] Presentation of the government's case against IBM took nearly three years, and that does not include the time IBM took to present its defense. Widespread dissatisfaction with the protracted litigation has resulted in a series of proposals to streamline the procedures. The National Commission for the Review of Antitrust Laws and Procedures issued its first report in January 1979.[20] Some of the views expressed therein were enacted in the antitrust procedural improvements legislation of 1980. As one improvement, the statute broadened the range of practices that a delaying attorney could be personally liable for if the practices in question are engaged in "unreasonably and vexatiously." Although these procedures may be helpful in moving the case along, it may well be nearly impossible to vastly speed up the handling of large antitrust cases if the estimates are correct that IBM gained at least $2 million a day for each day of delay.[21]

Proposals have also been made suggesting changes in the substantive law itself. A task force established by President Johnson recommended in 1968 a new concentrated industries act. This proposal would have set up structural criteria to judge whether oligopolistic industries needed to be reorganized and established a specially constituted court of economic, legal, and organizational specialists. In 1972 and in 1973, the late Senator Phillip Hart introduced an industrial reorganization bill. In his proposal the existence of a monopoly power would be presumed if a company's after-tax return on stockholders' equity exceeded 15 percent for five consecutive years. Other precise tests were included to identify monopoly power. The proposal required divestiture of firms possessing monopoly power and would be enforced by a specially constituted industrial reorganization commission. Neither the concentrated industries bill nor the industrial reorganization bill were able to attract sufficient votes for congressional passage.

In 1976 Senator Hart proposed a "no-fault" monopolization bill which would amend the Sherman Act, Section 2, by eliminating the government's burden to prove intent to monopolize. His proposal allowed two defenses for the companies found to possess monopoly power. They could escape fragmentation only by demonstrating that their power came solely from legally acquired and used patents or that divestiture would cause a loss of substantial scale economies. Senator Hart's proposal did not gain sufficient congressional support to be voted out of committee. However, the first report of the National Commission for the Review of Antitrust Laws and Procedures indicated that the no-conduct (or no-fault) monopolization concept needed further study.

Structurally oriented senators have also proposed legislation to deal specifically with a single industry or firm. One bill proposed breaking up AT&T prior to AT&T's settlement of divestiture with the Justice Department in 1982. The petroleum industry competition bill called for the oil industry to eliminate its vertically integrated status among the 18 largest oil firms in the United States. Another bill proposed that the oil industry be prohibited from acquiring firms in other basic energy areas, such as coal or atomic energy.

CONCLUSION

Governmental regulation of industrial structure seems to favor the maintenance of the existing industry structure. Such conservatism is based on the recognition that the U.S. economic system performs relatively well in comparison with other systems throughout the world. Instead of utilizing the antitrust law for structural reform, alternative governmental policies (as explored in subsequent chapters) have been utilized to modify business behavior. Nevertheless, structuralists maintain that the rising tide of economic concentration threatens economic and political liberties as much as it erodes economic efficiencies. The continuing debate between structuralists and performance economists has been manifested in the bills placed before Congress. These proposals and others that are sure to be presented in the future deserve attention by business people. Increased research and more information are surely needed to formulate future public policies on the critical issues of appropriate industry structure.

DISCUSSION QUESTIONS

1. IBM marketed electronic data processing equipment that consisted of central processing units plus various peripheral devices such as magnetic tapes, disk and drum information storage components, memory units, and terminal devices such as printers. The peripheral devices are connected by plugs to the central processing units, and several other companies market peripheral components that are plug-compatible with IBM central processing units (CPUs). Peripheral devices are not interchangeable on CPUs of various manufacturers, but at a modest cost, manufacturers can alter the plug interfaces so as to make their devices plug-compatible with the products of other CPU manufacturers such as Univac, Burroughs, and Honeywell.

   IBM launched a marketing strategy to meet the competitive threat of plug-compatible suppliers of peripheral devices. One such supplier, which specialized in producing devices plug-compatible with IBM CPUs, brought a Section 2 action to prevent IBM from implementing its marketing strategy.

   Apply the *duPont* decision to determine the relevant market. What would be the effect of the existence of relatively high cross-elasticity of demand between IBM CPU plug-compatible and nonplug-compatible devices?

2. IBM has obtained a position of monopoly power in the peripheral equipment market by research and technical innovations. In response to the

challenge of Telex and other producers of peripheral equipment, IBM lowered its prices on peripheral equipment. What facts and tests would be relevant in deciding if IBM's actions were lawful?

3. For 15 years, the *Lorain Journal* was the only daily newspaper in a town of 52,000 and served 99 percent of Lorain families. When a local radio station was established, the *Journal* refused to publish advertisements for businesses that advertised over the radio station as well. Does the *Journal,* as a monopolist, have the right to refuse to deal with whatever advertisers it chooses? Does the Sherman Act apply to competition between industries? Would the *Journal's* actions constitute a violation of Section 2 of the Sherman Act?

4. Kodak, a film and camera monopolist, was in a position to set industry standards. Competitors argued that because of Kodak's dominant position, it must make sufficient advance information of its product innovations available to its competitors so that they can also introduce copies of the new product at the same time as Kodak introduces its new product. In support of a Section 2, Sherman Act, charge, the competitors argued that Kodak's failure to "predisclose" its new products to competitors is anticompetitive conduct.

5. Yoder Brothers, Inc. was in the business of breeding new varieties chrysanthemums and producing cuttings of new varieties for sale to growers. A competing propagator and distributor of cuttings, California-Florida Plant Corporation (CFPC) brought a Section 2 action against Yoder Brothers.

   Yoder had a 20 percent share of the market for all ornamental plants, a 49.6 percent share of all chrysanthemums grown, and a 58.1 percent share of chrysanthemum cuttings taken and sold. Once a new chrysanthemum variety was developed, its purity was perserved by asexual reproduction, i.e. by the taking of cuttings, which are grown into new plants. In setting the prices for its cuttings, Yoder did not consider the prices of other ornamental plants.

   Adjustments in greenhouse layouts, watering systems, and the use of lights must be made in order for growers of mature plants to switch from one type of ornamental plant to another, but growers often shift crops depending on consumer demand. A large number of growers handle a wide assortment of ornamentals and they allocate greenhouse space depending on the demand by ultimate consumers. Multicrop growers shift production within the year in response to shifts in price and demand.

   Consumer demand fluctuates rapidly and is responsive to price, and the demand by growers for cuttings corresponds with the demand by ultimate consumers for the mature plants or cut flowers.

   During the time subject to suit, the price of chrysanthemum cuttings did not change at the same times or in the same amounts as the price of carnation cuttings, and there was no relationship between price changes of chrysanthemum cuttings and carnation cuttings.

   Given the above facts, what market would be relevant to a claim of attempted monopolization against Yoder Brothers?

6. In 1949 the International Boxing Club of New York and the International Boxing Club of Illinois obtained control of all major boxing arenas in the United States, and contracts with the heavyweight, middleweight, and welterweight champions of the world. They controlled the promotion of 81 percent of all championship fights held between June 1949 and May 1953. As defendants in a suit for violation of the Sherman Act, Section 2, the Clubs claimed that the relevant market was the business of promoting all professional boxing events, as opposed to *championship* events exclusively, saying that "the physical identity of the products here would seem necessarily to put them in one and the same market." Do championship boxing contests constitute a "separate, identifiable market?"

7. May an electric power company holding a national monopoly refuse to sell power or transmit power over its lines from other suppliers to a newly established, municipal power system that would serve the power company's former customers?

8. IBM has been charged with restraining competitors from entering or remaining in the general-purpose digital computor market "by announcing future production of new models for such markets where it knew that it was unlikely to be able to complete production within the announced time." How might this conduct be anticompetitive? What remedy could be imposed?

9. IBM has been charged with dominating the education market for general-purpose digital computors "by granting exceptional discriminatory allowances in favor of universities and other education institutions." How might this conduct be anticompetitive? What remedy could be imposed?

10. American Telephone & Telegraph Company (AT&T) was charged with monopolizing the telecommunications service and equipment markets (and submarkets thereof) in violation of Section 2 of the Sherman Act. Among other things, AT&T was charged with obstructing the interconnection of equipment provided by other firms with the equipment in the Bell System, which hindered the sales of telecommunications equipment in competition with Western Electric, a wholly owned subsidiary of AT&T.

    Was this conduct a violation of Section 2?

SUGGESTED READINGS

Areeda, P. and Turner, D. *Antitrust Law* (Boston: Little Brown and Co., 1978).

Baumol, William J., "Quasi-Permanence of Price Reductions: A Policy for Prevention of Predatory Pricing," *Yale Law Journal*, Vol. 89, No. 1, 1979.

Greer, D. F., "A Critique of Areeda and Turner's Standard for Predatory Practices," *Antitrust Bulletin*, Summer 1979, pp. 233–261.

Joskow, Paul L. and Alvin K. Klevorick, "A Framework for Analyzing Predatory Pricing Policy," *Yale Law Journal*, Vol. 89, No. 213, 1979.

Koller, Roland H. II, "When Is Pricing Predatory?" *Antitrust Bulletin*, Summer 1979, pp. 283–306.

Maher, John A., "Draining the *ALCOA* 'Wishing Well.' The Section 2 Conduct Requirement after *Kodak* and *Calcomp*," *Fordham Law Review*, December 1979, pp. 294–295.

National Commission for the Review of the Antitrust Laws and Procedures, *Report to the President and the Attorney General* (Washington D.C.: January 1979).

Posner, Richard A., *Antitrust Law: An Economic Perspective* (Chicago: University of Chicago Press, 1976), pp. 184–195.

Scherer, F. M., "Predatory Pricing and the Sherman Act: A Comment," *Harvard Law Review*, Vol. 89, No. 869, 1976.

Stein, Alvin M. and Barry J. Brett, "Market Definition and Market Power in Antitrust Cases—an Empirical Primer on When, Why, and How," *New York University Law Review*, Vol. 24, 1979, pp. 639–676.

The Industrial Reorganization Act, Hearings before the U.S. Senate Subcommittee on Antitrust and Monopoly of the Committee on the Judiciary, Part I (1973).

Waldman, Don E., "Economic Benefits in the *IBM*, *AT&T*, and *Xerox* cases: Government Antitrust in the 70's," *Antitrust Law and Economics Review*, No. 2, 1980, pp. 75–92.

Williamson, Oliver, "Predatory Pricing: A Strategic and Welfare Analysis," *Yale Law Journal*, Vol. 87, No. 284 (1977).

ENDNOTES

1. *U.S.* v. *Griffith Amusement Company*, 334 U.S. 100, 105 (1948).
2. *U.S.* v. *Grinnell Corp.*, 384 U.S. 563 (1966).
3. *U.S.* v. *Alcoa*, 148 F. 2d at 431.
4. *Ibid.*
5. *Ibid.*, p. 21, 518.
6. *U.S.* v. *United Shoe Machinery Corp.*, 110 F. Supp. 295, 340–41.
7. P. Areeda and D. Turner, "Predatory Pricing and Related Practices Under Section 2 of the Sherman Act," 88 *Harv. L. Rev.* 697 (1975).
8. See, *Janich Bros., Inc.* v. *American Distilling Co.*, 570 F. 2d 848 (9th Cir., 1977), cert. denied, 47 U.S.L.W. 3195 (Oct. 2, 1978); *Pacific Engr. & Prod. Co.* v. *Kerr-McGee Corp.*, 551 F. 2d 790 (10th Cir.), cert. denied, 98 S. Ct. 234 (1977).
9. R. Posner, *Antitrust Law: An Economic Perspective*, 188 (1976).
10. See, *International Air Industries, Inc.* v. *American Excelsior Co.*, 517 F. 2d 714, 734 (5th Cir., 1975), cert. denied, 424 U.S. 940 (1976). *I.L.C. Peripherals Leasing Corp.* v. *IBM* (1978–2), Trade Cases, Para. 62,177 (N.D. Cal., 1975) at 75,256–57.
11. Scherer, "Predatory Pricing and the Sherman Act: A Comment," 89 *Harv. L. Rev.* 869, 889 (1976).
12. *FTC* v. *Borden*, 92 F.T.C. 669 (1978).
13. *FTC* v. *Brown Shoe Co.*, 384 U.S. 316 (1965).
14. *In re Xerox Corp.*, 86 F.T.C. 364 (1975).
15. *In re Kellogg et al.*, filed January 25, 1972.
16. F. M. Scherer, *Industrial Market Structure and Economic Performance*, 2d ed. (Chicago, Ill.: Rand McNally, 1980), p. 539.
17. *FTC News Summary*, Vols. 50–81, September 18, 1981.
18. *Ibid.*, p. 540.
19. *Ibid.*, p. 541.
20. L. Lempert, "Antitrust Reform Faces Long, Winding Road," *Legal Times*, September 15, 1980.
21. W. Shepherd and C. Wilcox, *Public Policy Toward Business* (Homewood, Ill.: Richard D. Irwin, Inc., 1979), pp. 148–49.

chapter 10
REGULATION OF MERGERS

A *merger* is the uniting of formerly independent enterprises under a single ownership. It involves the complete acquisition of the stock of another corporation and then the termination of the acquired corporation as a corporate entity. A merger may also be effected through the outright purchase of the assets of another enterprise. If the acquiring and acquired firms continue their existence, the union of the firms is technically referred to as an acquisition, not a merger.

Absent any attempt to monopolize, internal growth of assets is generally recognized as a legitimate method of corporate expansion. However, external growth through mergers and acquisitions of separate firms that were formerly independent enterprises often has the effect of reducing competition and tending toward a monopoly.

HISTORICAL PERSPECTIVES

TYPES OF MERGERS

A *horizontal* merger unites the ownership of side-by-side competitors. It combines like plants (such as steel mills) that produce the same product and sell in the same geographic market. A *vertical* merger unites suppliers and users in the chain of production and distribution. It brings under one ownership the control of unlike plants producing different products but related in the successive stages of production or marketing. Vertical mergers are usually referred to as "integration." A *conglomerate* merger may be classified as one of three main forms: (1) product extension, (2) market extension, or (3) pure diversification. (See Figure 10-1.) When the acquired and acquiring firm are in allied or closely related

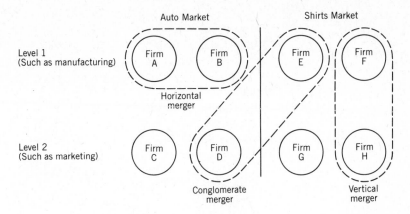

Figure 10-1. Types of mergers.

fields, so that the acquisition extends the acquired company's product line (for example, a soap company acquiring a liquid bleach firm), the combination is referred to as a product extension merger. A market extension merger involves the acquisition of a like firm that operates in a different geographic market (for example, a beer firm in the Midwest acquiring a beer firm in California). A pure conglomerate merger is one in which the acquiring firm and the acquired firm are in totally unrelated fields (for example, an oil firm and a fire insurance company).

MOTIVES FOR MERGERS

Merger actions are taken for different reasons of business advantage. The main categories of gains to the firm include the following.

1. Market power. The merger may increase the combined firm's market power by increasing its market share or by erecting higher entry barriers. Market power, in turn, provides opportunities for higher prices and profits for the firm.
2. Technical economies. A merger may help firms achieve economies of scale and lower average unit costs. There may be economies of scale in conducting research and development as a firm expands. The combined firm may be able to economize on management services by having a common central pool of financial planners, accountants, market researchers, labor relations specialists, lawyers, and the like. Vertical economies achieved through vertical integration may avoid the cost of extra material handling, uncertainty, or reprocessing. It may also be possible to obtain some economies by pooling diverse enterprises to reduce risks.
3. Pecuniary economies. Mergers may create pecuniary gains by the firm's larger purchases of raw materials, advertising space, managerial talent,

capital, or other inputs. Tax benefits of the merger may enhance pecuniary gain also.

4. New market entry. Entry into new markets is usually easier through mergers than by "starting from scratch." Such mergers may not confer market power or achieve technical or pecuniary economies but merely provide the nucleus for the acquiring firm to venture into new areas.

5. Salvage of failing companies. Many mergers involve the absorption of a failing company. Failure, of course, means imminent bankruptcy, which often involves a financial insolvency of a short-term nature. The infusion of new capital by the acquiring firm revives the failing company.

6. Takeovers. A takeover involves an action by one firm to seize, or take over, another firm whose management appears inefficient. The firm attempting the takeover typically makes a tender offer for a controlling block of the stock of the acquired company at a price above the current market price. The acquiring company believes it can manage the company so much better that profits in the acquired firm will rise sufficiently to offset the premium paid for the stock.

In many instances, mergers have increased industrial efficiency and improved a firm's position as a competitor. On the other hand, mergers often result in larger firms that gain discretionary control over prices through the elimination of smaller competitors. The separation of economically efficient mergers from mergers that enhance market power to the detriment of society is not always easy. Moreover, differing economic perspectives (structuralists or performance economists) have made consensus on a merger policy even more difficult to obtain.

MERGER ACTIVITY

There have been three major periods of merger activity in the United States.[1] The first great boom was from 1897 to 1904. The mergers of this period were primarily horizontal and resulted in the formation of firms with 60 to 90 percent control of the market in many industries. It was the era of financial capitalism and of the creation of dominant firms in major industries. This merger wave stopped primarily because of changing stock market and economic conditions but also because of Theodore Roosevelt's antitrust enforcement in 1902.

The second active merger period occurred in the 1920s. It mainly resulted in the formation of oligopolies that replaced the industry structure of one large dominant firm. The mergers of this period tended to create second- and third-ranking firms to compete with the existing dominant firms. This merger activity, like the first, came to an end with a change in economic conditions, in this case the depression that occurred in the 1930s.

The third merger period, in the 1960s, mainly involved conglomerate mergers. Although horizontal and vertical mergers continued, conglomerate mergers became very popular. This merger activity took a pronounced dip in the late

1960s as the stock market dropped over 40 percent. In addition, antitrust enforcement against mergers, particularly conglomerate mergers during the period 1969–1971, helped reverse the continuing growth in conglomerate mergers. (See Figure 10-2).

THE EVOLUTION OF STATUTORY LAW

Mergers were initially challenged under the Sherman Act. Early government successes in prohibiting mergers were largely limited to railroad consolidations.[2] Subsequent efforts to use the Sherman Act against mergers were unsuccessful. The most famous defeat for the Justice Department occurred in 1948 when it lost its suit against the U.S. Steel Corporation's acquisition of the Consolidated Steel Corporation. The merger was allowed by the Supreme Court even though Consolidated accounted for 11 percent of the structural steel and plate fabrication activity in the Pacific and Mountain states and U.S. Steel controlled 39 percent of all raw steel ingot capacity.[3]

In contrast to the Supreme Court's unwillingness to interpret the Sherman Act as an effective weapon against industrial consolidation by mergers, Congress expressed consternation about mergers and acquisitions and their effect in reducing competition or tending toward a monopoly. Congress first attempted to formulate a merger policy in the Clayton Act of 1914. Section 7 of the Clayton Act established guidelines as to when mergers were to be held illegal. It differed from the Sherman Act in that "actual" restraints or monopolization did not have to be proven. The Clayton Act was designed to stop anticompetitive mergers before they resulted in the creation of a monopoly. This purpose was to be

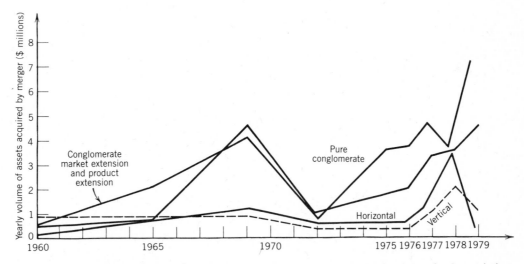

Figure 10-2. Trends in U.S. mergers, by type. [*Source:* Federal Trade Commission, Statistical Report on Mergers and Acquisitions (Washington, D.C.: U.S. Government Printing Office, annual.]

accomplished by the method of making illegal those mergers that "may" lessen competition. By lowering the government's burden of proof from an *actual* anticompetitive effect to a *probable* anticompetitive effect, Congress anticipated that anticompetitive activities, such as mergers, would be arrested in their early stages. This concept of attacking evil practices in their incipiency is carried throughout the major sections of the Clayton Act.

Despite the intentions of Congress, the original language of Section 7 of the Clayton Act possessed several loopholes that vastly reduced its effectiveness in preventing mergers. The original text included language that made it necessary for the merger to eliminate competition between the "acquiring" and the "acquired" firms in order to be illegal. If competition *between* these two firms is eliminated, they must first be in competition with one another. Consequently, the acquiring-acquired language indicated that Section 7 applied only to horizontal mergers (that is, those companies that compete with one another). Therefore, vertical or conglomerate mergers were felt to be free of Section 7 attack until the Justice Department decided to test this language in the late 1940s. In addition, the original language prohibited only the acquisition of *stock* in another company if the probable effect would be to substantially lessen competition. Therefore, any combination of companies, including horizontal, that wanted to avoid Section 7 would not acquire the *stock* of the acquired firm. Instead, acquisition of *assets* was used to avoid Section 7's prohibition of *stock* acquisitions. As a consequence, Section 7 of the Clayton Act had only a minimal effect in prohibiting mergers. Indeed, so ineffective was Section 7 that antitrust enforcement officials reverted to the use of the Sherman Act in an effort to prohibit mergers. For example, the government's attempt to prohibit the previously discussed merger of U.S. Steel with Consolidated Steel in the 1940s was prosecuted under the Sherman Act rather than Section 7 of the Clayton Act. However, in that case and in others the Sherman Act was also found inadequate for preventing mergers.

In 1950, the Celler-Kefauver Amendment modified Section 7 of the Clayton Act. This amendment omitted the acquiring-acquired language to indicate that horizontal, vertical, or conglomerate mergers were illegal if they had the probable effect of substantially lessening competition. In addition, the acquisition of stock or *assets* was made illegal if it had the prohibited anticompetitive effect. The two major loopholes of the original Section 7 language consequently were closed by the Celler-Kefauver Amendment. The amended Section 7 now reads, in part, as follows.

That no person engaged in commerce, or in any activity affecting commerce shall acquire, directly or indirectly, the whole or any part of the stock or other share capital [or] . . . the whole or any part of the assets of another person engaged also in commerce or in any activity affecting commerce, where in any line of commerce or in any activity affecting commerce in any section of the country, the effect of such acquisition may be substantially to lessen competition, or to tend to create a monopoly.

From the legislative history and from the omission of the acquiring-acquired language, it was clear that the amended Section 7 was intended to apply to mergers of every type. Any type of merger that has the probability of lessening competition "in any line of commerce" (product market) or "in any section of the country" (geographic market) was declared illegal. Accordingly, any use of Section 7 to challenge a merger begins with the definition of the relevant product and geographic markets, followed by the determination of the probable effect of the merger in the relevant markets.

In spite of Congress's recognition that some mergers might bring about economic efficiencies, it outlawed mergers that had the probable effect of substantially reducing competition in the relevant product or geographic markets. Congress made no provision for an "economic efficiencies" defense to a Section 7 charge. Consequently, the courts have not generally made substantial inquiry into the economic efficiencies alleged to have been accrued by virtue of any proposed merger. Instead, the court's analysis has concentrated on the probable anticompetitive impact of the merger.

HORIZONTAL MERGERS

To observe the principles applied by the courts in interpreting the new Section 7 of the Clayton Act, it is necessary to examine the leading decisions. Often the decisions of the courts involve mergers that contain a mixture of horizontal, vertical, and conglomerate characteristics. Nevertheless, the basic policies and principles enunciated by the court for the various types of mergers can be discussed separately, beginning with the basic horizontal type of merger.

BETHLEHEM-YOUNGSTOWN

The first major government victory under the new Section 7 involved Bethlehem Steel Corporation's proposed merger with Youngstown Sheet and Tube.[4] Bethlehem Steel Corporation, the nation's second largest producer of steel, handled 16.3 percent of total U.S. ingot capacity. Youngstown Sheet and Tube Company was the sixth largest producer, with 4.6 percent of national ingot capacity. Bethlehem argued that the merger did not have the probability of substantially lessening competition because the two companies essentially sold in two different geographical submarkets. Bethlehem argued that this was essentially a market extension merger because Bethlehem, which sold most of its output in the East, did not directly compete with Youngstown, which primarily sold in the Midwest. Only about 10 percent of the combined output of Bethlehem and Youngstown was shipped to customers in overlapping geographic territories. The trial court rejected this characterization of the proposed merger and held that the freight cost barriers to interpenetration of regional markets were overcome sufficiently to view the market as nationwide in scope. Accordingly, the court felt a merger combining 16.3 and 4.6 percent of national capacity had the probability of substantially lessening competition in the national market.

Bethlehem attempted to justify the merger by arguing that it would enable Bethlehem to compete more effectively with the largest steel producer, U.S. Steel. In particular, Bethlehem argued that it had no plant in the Chicago area and shipped into Chicago less than 1 percent of its output. Bethlehem argued that the acquisition of the Chicago facilities of Youngstown would create more vigorous competition with U.S. Steel in this area. Furthermore, Bethlehem declared that it would not otherwise enter this geographical market.

The trial judge rejected Bethlehem's pro-competitive argument by asserting that Congress "made no distinction between good mergers and bad mergers. It condemned all which came in reach of the prohibition of Section 7." Furthermore, the court was not convinced that the merger was the only means to increase the supply of steel in the Chicago area. Accordingly, the trial court enjoined the merger. Bethlehem did not appeal. A few years later, Bethlehem developed a modern steel-making facility in the Chicago area and Youngstown invested $450 million to modernize its Chicago works.

BROWN-KINNEY

The first Supreme Court case interpreting the new Section 7 of the Clayton Act was decided in 1962. It involved the effort of Brown Shoe Company to merge with G. R. Kinney Company. Brown was the fourth largest shoe manufacturer in the United States in 1955, with approximately 4 percent of the national output. Kinney was the 12th largest manufacturer, with 0.5 percent of output. There was no contention in the suit that the merger posed a threat to horizontal competition in shoe manufacturing. Instead, debate centered on competition in shoe retailing. Brown owned and operated approximately 470 of the nation's 22,000 retail shoe outlets, and franchised 760 other independent retail outlets. Kinney owned and operated more than 350 retail stores. The Supreme Court's analysis of the boundaries of the product and geographic markets has provided the basic criteria for determination of relevant markets.

Brown Shoe Co. v. United States
370 U.S. 296 (1962)
Supreme Court of the United States

Chief Justice Warren

This suit . . . [alleges] that a contemplated merger between the G. R. Kinney Company, Inc. (Kinney), and the Brown Shoe Company, Inc. (Brown) . . . would violate § 7 of the Clayton Act. . . . The complainant sought injunctive relief . . . to restrain consummation of the merger.

* * *

The Product Market

The outer boundaries of a product market are determined by the reasonable interchangeability of use or the cross-elasticity of demand between the product itself and substitutes for it. However, within this broad market, well-defined submarkets may exist which, in themselves, constitute product markets for antitrust purposes.

. . . The boundaries of such a submarket

may be determined by examining such practical indicia as industry or public recognition of the submarket as a separate economic entity, the product's peculiar characteristics and uses, unique production facilities, distinct customers, distinct prices, sensitivity to price changes, and specialized vendors. Because § 7 of the Clayton Act prohibits any merger which may substantially lessen competition "in *any* line of commerce," it is necessary to examine the effects of a merger in each such economically significant submarket to determine if there is a reasonable probability that the merger will substantially lessen competition. If such a probability is found to exist, the merger is proscribed.

Applying these considerations to the present case, we conclude that the record supports the District Court's finding that the relevant lines of commerce are men's, women's, and children's shoes. These product lines are recognized by the public; each line is manufactured in separate plants; each has characteristics peculiar to itself rendering it generally noncompetitive with the other; and each is, of course, directed toward a distinct class of customers.

* * *

The Geographic Market
The criteria to be used in determining the appropriate geographic market are essentially similar to those used to determine the relevant product market. . . . Moreover, just as a product submarket may have § 7 significance as the proper "line of commerce," so may a geographic submarket be considered the appropriate "section of the country." The geographic market selected must, therefore, both "correspond to the commercial realities" of the industry and be economically significant. Thus, although the geographic market in some instances may encompass the entire Nation, under other circumstances it may be as small as a single metropolitan area. . . .

The District Court found that the effects of [the retail] . . . aspect of the merger must be analyzed in every city with a population exceeding 10,000 and its immediate contiguous surrounding territory in which Brown and Kinney sold shoes at retail through stores they either owned or controlled. . . .

We therefore agree that the District Court properly defined the relevant geographic markets in which to analyze this merger as those cities with a population exceeding 10,000 and their environs in which both Brown and Kinney retailed shoes through their own outlets. Such markets are large enough to include the downtown shops and suburban shopping centers in areas contiguous to the city, which are the important competitive factors, and yet are small enough to exclude stores beyond the immediate environs of the city, which are of little competitive significance.

The Probable Effect of the Merger
The market share which companies may control by merging is one of the most important factors to be considered when determining the probable effects of the combination on effective competition in the relevant market. In an industry as fragmented as shoe retailing, the control of substantial shares of the trade in a city may have important effects on competition. If a merger achieving 5 percent control were now approved, we might be required to approve future merger efforts by Brown's competitors seeking similar market shares. The oligopoly Congress sought to avoid would then be furthered and it would be difficult to dissolve the combinations previously approved. Furthermore, in this fragmented industry, even if the combination controls but a small share of a particular market, the fact that this share is held by a large national chain can adversely affect competition. Testimony in the record from numerous independent retailers, based on their actual experience in the market, demonstrates that a strong, national chain of stores can insulate selected outlets from the vagaries of competition in particular locations

and that the large chains can set and alter styles in footwear to an extent that renders the independents unable to maintain competitive inventories. . . .

Other factors to be considered in evaluating the probable effects of a merger in the relevant market lend additional support to the District Court's conclusion that this merger may substantially lessen competition. One such factor is the history of tendency toward concentration in the industry. As we have previously pointed out, the shoe industry has, in recent years, been a prime example of such a trend. . . .

. . . By the merger in this case, the largest single group of retail stores still independent of one of the large manufacturers was absorbed into an already substantial aggregation of more or less controlled retail outlets. As a result of this merger, Brown moved into second place nationally in terms of retail stores directly owned. Including the stores on its

franchise plan, the merger placed under Brown's control almost 1,600 shoe outlets, or about 7.2 percent of the Nation's retail "shoe stores" as defined by the Census Bureau, and 2.3 percent of the Nation's total retail shoe outlets. We cannot avoid the mandate of Congress that tendencies toward concentration in industry are to be curbed in their incipiency, particularly when those tendencies are being accelerated through giant steps striding across a hundred cities at a time. In the light of the trends in this industry we agree with the Government and the court below that this is an appropriate place at which to call a halt.

. . . We hold that the District Court was correct in concluding that this merger may tend to lessen competition substantially in the retail sale of the men's, women's and children's shoes in the overwhelming majority of those cities and their environs in which both Brown and Kinney sell through owned or controlled outlets.

Questions
1. What criteria did the Court identify for determination of a relevant product submarket?
2. What geographic submarket did the Court adopt?
3. What "probable anticompetitive effects" of this proposed merger did the Court identify?

DEFINING THE MARKET

In *Brown Shoe* the Supreme Court established criteria for defining markets. These criteria provide considerable latitude for the courts in determining the relevant market. Review of two decisions applying the *Brown Shoe* criteria can illustrate the eclectic approach of the Court.

The first case involves the acquisition of the Rome Cable Corporation by the Aluminum Company of America.[5] Alcoa produced various types of aluminum electrical conductor cable, and Rome specialized in copper conductor cable but used aluminum in about 10 percent of its cables. The district court found Rome's share (0.3 percent) of the *bare aluminum* cable market to be too small to threaten any substantial lessening of competition when added to Alcoa's 32.5 percent share. When the *insulated and bare aluminum* was combined with the *insulated and bare copper,* again the market shares were too small for illegality. Nevertheless, the Supreme Court reversed the district court decision and held that the *combined insulated and bare aluminum* wire and cable market, with all copper products excluded, could be utilized to test the legality of the merger. The Court argued that the price of aluminum conductors was generally less than the price of comparable copper conductors and a price change for copper conductors did not cause a responsive change in the aluminum conductor prices or vice versa. The Court concluded that the addition of Rome's 1.3 percent share of this market to Alcoa's 27.8 percent share constituted a substantial lessening of competition.

The second case involves a proposed merger between the Continental Can Company, second largest maker of tin cans in the United States, and the Hazel-Atlas Glass Company, the third largest bottle manufacturer.[6] Continental held 33 percent of the market for tin cans and Hazel-Atlas held 10 percent of the market for glass bottles. The trial court found cans and bottles to be separate product markets and, hence, concluded that competition was not substantially reduced by the merger. On appeal, the Supreme Court pointed out that tin cans and glass bottles were closely competitive in many applications with buyers switching from one type of container to another. The Court wrote that

In defining the product market . . . we must recognize meaningful competition where it is found to exist. . . . [T]hough the interchangeability of use may not be so complete and the cross-elasticity of demand not so immediate as in the case of most intraindustry mergers, there is over the long run the kind of customer response to innovation and other competitive stimuli that brings the competition between these two industries within § 7's competition-preserving proscriptions. . . . That there are price differentials between the two products or that the demand for one is not particularly or immediately responsive to changes in the price of the other are relevant matters but not determinative of the product market issues. . . . Where the area of effective competition cuts across industry lines, so must the relevant line of commerce.[7]

In the relevant market of metal cans and glass bottles combined, Continental held second place, with a 22 percent share, and Hazel-Atlas held sixth place with a 3 percent share. According to the Court, these percentages were too high for the merger to be legal.

These two decisions of the Supreme Court illustrate the wide extremes (some say inconsistency) that the courts are willing to accept in defining "sensitive competitive relations" that courts feel are worthy of preservation. It appears that "markets" can be easily gerrymandered to accomplish the overall philosophical desires of the Court either to stem the concentration of economic power through mergers or to permit mergers perceived to enhance economic efficiencies.

DETERMINING "PROBABLE EFFECT"

The *Brown Shoe* decision indicated that several basic elements should be reviewed in determining the "probable effect" of a proposed merger. The Court felt the combination of the percentages of the defined market held by the two merging parties was one of the most important factors to be considered. Second, the combined market share must be functionally viewed in terms of the industry. In a fragmented industry, even small market shares by the merging parties can adversely affect competition, particularly if the relatively small combination involves one of the largest firms in that industry. Third, the Court pointed out that "the history of tendency toward concentration in the industry" is an important factor to be considered.

These factors, first articulated in *Brown Shoe,* became determinative standards in subsequent cases. The court was willing to use the statistical market data and industry trends toward concentration for a determination of "probable effect." The dissenting justices criticized the Court's approach as amounting to an almost *per se* rule. Structuralists, of course, have favored this approach to halt the continuing trend toward concentration. Performance economists, on the other hand, argue that several procompetitive mergers or mergers advancing the levels of economic efficiency have also been prohibited and, consequently, society's interests are not being advanced by an almost *per se* illegality based on percentages alone. Nevertheless, the success of the Justice Department in gaining verdicts that outlawed mergers during the 1960s led to the establishment of the Department of Justice Merger Guidelines.

MERGER GUIDELINES

The 1968 Merger Guidelines emphasized market structure as the basic determinant of whether mergers would be challenged by the Department of Justice. The guidelines distinguished between concentrated industries. In less concentrated industries, mergers may be allowed that would not be tolerated in oligopolistic industries (see Figure 10-3). The guidelines were not law but were criteria for use by the Department of Justice in its determination of which mergers to challenge in the courts. However, because the Justice Department had been so successful in gaining favorable verdicts during the 1960s, many merger proposals were forestalled when the parties determined that they would be challenged under the guidelines. The guidelines were revised by the Department of Justice in 1982. A summary explanation of the new guidelines is presented at the end of this chapter. But before a discussion of these new guidelines is proper, other types of mergers should be examined.

VERTICAL MERGERS

When a firm has successive stages in the production or distribution of finished goods or services, it is said to be *vertically integrated.* On the positive side, vertical integration may generate economies of scale. However, competition must remain effective after the merger if society is to share such cost savings through

Once the several appropriate markets ("product" and "geographic") in which to test the anticompetitive effects of a merger are determined:

a. In highly concentrated markets (over 75 percent in the four largest firms), these shares will ordinarily be challenged.

Acquiring Firm	Acquired Firm
4%	4% or more
10%	2% or more
15% or more	1% or more

b. In less highly concentrated markets (less than 75 percent in the four largest firms), these shares will ordinarily be challenged.

Acquiring Firm	Acquired Firm
5%	5% or more
10%	4% or more
15%	3% or more
20%	2% or more
25% or more	1% or more

c. If market concentration has been increasing, any merger involving over 2 percent will also be challenged.

d. Any merger with a firm that has "an unusual competitive advantage" or is an "unusually competitive factor in the market" will be challenged.

e. Failing firms are exempt if prospects for rehabilitation are clearly remote and "good faith efforts" for mergers within the Guidelines have failed.

f. Normally, economies will not prevent a challenge under these Guidelines because alternate routes to achieve such economies (which are difficult to measure) are available.

Source: Abstracted from Department of Justice, *Merger Guidelines*, May 30, 1968.

Figure 10.3 Horizontal merger guidelines (1968).

lower prices for consumers. Unfortunately, vertically integrated firms may also follow business practices that weaken or destroy their nonintegrated or less integrated rivals. For example, the vertically integrated firm may be in a position to exclude less integrated firms from the best sources of supply or from retail outlets. This is referred to as a supply squeeze and involves either a refusal to sell to less integrated firms or a preferential allocation of raw materials to the subsidiaries of the integrated firms. Second, the vertically integrated firm may be in a position to control the prices and profits of its less integrated rivals by employing a price squeeze. The vertically integrated firm either (1) sells to its distributor at a lower price than to independent rivals, while maintaining the price at the retail level, or (2) reduces its price (and profit) at the retail level when consumer demand declines, but maintains the prices for the primary materials sold to less integrated rivals.

To provide equal access to suppliers and outlets, public policy could prohibit vertical integration altogether. Already the federal government and many states have laws that prohibit distillers from engaging in the retailing of liquors. It is possible that Congress could decide that divestiture is appropriate policy in many highly integrated industries, such as aluminum, copper, oil, or steel. Without outright prohibition, Congress has found it necessary in certain instances to require integrated firms to give fair allocation of supplies to nonintegrated or less integrated rivals.[8] Absent specific legislation of prohibition or allocation, Congress has permitted vertical integration, particularly if achieved without mergers. However, vertical mergers may have an exclusionary *effect*, which has led Congress to include such vertical mergers in the amended Section 7 of the Clayton Act.

The firm seeking a vertical merger argues that its purpose is to assure itself of a source of supply or of an outlet. However, the courts must be careful to weigh this "legitimate business purpose" for an ensured supply for the merged firm against the *effect* of the merger on the ability of the nonintegrated or less integrated firms to obtain supplies or outlets.

BROWN-KINNEY

The first decision applying the new language of Section 7 of the Clayton Act to a vertical acquisition involved the merger of the Brown Shoe Company with G. R. Kinney Company. The horizontal aspects (in retailing) of this merger were discussed previously. However, because Brown was primarily engaged in manufacturing and Kinney in retailing, the vertical aspects of this merger were even more important to the companies involved and to the Court.

Brown Shoe Co. v. United States
370 U.S. 296 (1962)
Supreme Court of the United States

Chief Justice Warren   *   *   *

The District Court found a "definite trend" among shoe manufacturers to acquire retail outlets. . . .

And once the manufacturers acquired retail outlets, the District Court found there was a "definite trend" for the parent-manufacturers to supply an ever increasing percentage of the retail outlets' needs, thereby foreclosing other manufacturers from effectively competing for the retail accounts. Manufacturer-dominated stores were found to be "drying up" the available outlets for independent producers.

Brown Shoe

Brown Shoe was found not only to have been a participant, but also a moving factor, in these industry trends. . . . [I]n 1951, Brown . . . began to seek retail outlets by acquisitions. . . .

The acquisition of these corporations was found to lead to increased sales by Brown to the acquired companies. . . .

During the same period of time, Brown also acquired the stock or assets of seven companies engaged solely in shoe manufacturing. As a result, in 1955, Brown was the fourth largest shoe manufacturer in the country, producing about 4% of the Nation's total footwear production.

Kinney

Kinney is principally engaged in operating the largest family-style shoe store chain in the United States. At the time of trial, Kinney was found to be operating over 400 such stores in more than 270 cities. These stores were found to make about 1.2% of all national retail shoe sales by dollar volume. . . .

The Vertical Aspects of the Merger

Economic arrangements between companies standing in a supplier-customer relationship are characterized as "vertical." The primary vice of a vertical merger or other arrangement tying a customer to a supplier is that, by foreclosing the competitors of either party from a segment of the market otherwise open to them, the arrangement may act as a "clog on competition," . . . which "deprive[s] . . . rivals of a fair opportunity to compete." Every extended vertical arrangement by its very nature, for at least a time, denies to competitors of the supplier the opportunity to compete for part of or all of the trade of the customer-party to the vertical arrangement. However, the Clayton Act does not render unlawful all such vertical arrangements, but forbids only those whose effect "may be substantially to lessen competition, or to tend to create a monopoly" "in any line of commerce in any section of the country." . . .

* * *

. . . [W[e conclude that the record supports the District Court's finding that the relevant lines of commerce are men's, women's, and children's shoes. These product lines are recognized by the public; each line is manufactured in separate plants; each has characteristics peculiar to itself rendering it generally noncompetitive with the other; and each is, of course, directed toward a distinct class of customers.

TheGeographic Market

. . . [T]he relevant geographic market is the entire Nation. The relationships of product value, bulk, weight and consumer demand enable manufacturers to distribute their shoes on a nationwide basis, as Brown and Kinney, in fact, do. . . .

The Probable Effect of the Merger

* * *

Since the diminution of the vigor of competition which may stem from a vertical arrangement results primarily from a foreclosure of a share of the market otherwise open to competitors, an important consideration in determining whether the effect of a vertical arrangement "may be substantially to lessen competition, or to tend to create a monopoly" is the size of the share of the market foreclosed. . . .

[Another] . . . important such factor to examine is the very nature and purpose of the arrangement. . . .

* * *

. . . In 1955, the date of this merger, Brown was the fourth largest manufacturer in the shoe industry while Kinney . . . owned and operated the largest independent chain of family shoe stores in the Nation. Thus, in this industry, no merger between a manufacturer and an independent retailer could involve a larger potential market foreclosure. Moreover, it is apparent both from past behavior of Brown and from the testimony of Brown's President, that Brown would use its ownership of Kinney to force Brown shoes into Kinney stores. . . .

Another important factor to consider is the trend toward concentration in the industry. . . .

The existence of a trend toward vertical integration, which the District Court found, is well substantiated by the record. Moreover, the court found a tendency of the acquiring manufacturers to become increasingly important sources of supply for their acquired outlets. The necessary corollary of these trends is the foreclosure of independent manufacturers from markets otherwise open to them. . . .

* * *

The District Court's findings, and the record facts . . . convince us that the shoe industry is being subjected to just such a cumulative series of vertical mergers which, if left unchecked, will be likely "substantially to lessen competition."

Questions
1. Kinney held 1 percent of the national sales of men's shoes, 1.5 percent of the national sales of women's shoes, and 2 percent of the national sales of children's shoes. Since Brown supplied 7.9 percent of Kinney's requirements following the merger, the share of the market foreclosed ranged from 0.08 percent for men's shoes (1 percent times 7.9 percent) to 0.16 percent for children's shoes (2 percent times 7.9 percent). Are these shares substantial? Is there any indication that Brown would continue to limit its supply to Kinney to the 7.9 percent?
2. Why is the existence of a trend toward vertical integration an important criterion in determining the probable effect of the merger?

CONGLOMERATE MERGERS

Economic analysis reveals that conglomerate mergers may adversely affect competition.

First, conglomerate mergers may *entrench* oligopoly in various industries by weakening the competitive ability of the independent firms. The large acquiring firm uses nonprice forms of competition (brand differentiation) to enhance the market power of the acquired company. Independents, without sufficient financial resources to compete on nonprice terms, lose their competitiveness, for, if the smaller firms attempt to compete too vigorously on price, the larger merged firm can utilize discriminatory and exclusionary practices to discipline its smaller rival. Large multiproduct firms can utilize (a) product discrimination, in the form of either saturation advertising or one-product price cutting, (b) geographic price discrimination, (c) business reciprocity, or (d) tie-in sales as retaliation against any smaller rivals showing some price independence. Thereafter, fear of these retaliatory practices can force smaller firms into compliant postures and discourage potential entrants. In either case, oligopoly is solidified and oligopolistic nonprice competition replaces price competition.

Second, a conglomerate merger may lessen competition by eliminating the potential entrance of the merging party into the industry on an independent basis. This is usually referred to as the elimination of a "potential competitor." In addition, present members of the industry may perceive the potential entrant as on the edge of the industry and about to enter. Such perception can exert a competitive effect on the performance of the present members of the industry. This "edge effect" is eliminated when the firm enters the industry by merger.

Third, the Supreme Court held that the "reciprocity" made possible by some acquisitions introduces "an irrelevant and alien factor" into the choice among competing products. Reciprocity, at the least, creates "a priority on the business at equal prices." Reciprocal trading may not involve bludgeoning or coercion but may flow from more subtle arrangements. Threatening withdrawal of orders if products of an affiliate cease to be bought or basing future purchases on the condition of receipt of orders for products of that affiliate are examples of subtle, but nonetheless, anticompetitive reciprocal practices. Reciprocity in trading as a result of an acquisition violates Section 7 if the probability of a lessening of competition is shown.

Congress, in passing the Celler-Kefauver Act of 1950, recognized the potential anticompetitive effects that may follow from a conglomerate merger. However, since 1950 the antitrust enforcement agencies have challenged comparatively few conglomerate mergers. The two major victories of the government enunciated the three basic doctrines outlawing conglomerate mergers.[9] When conglomerate mergers create probabilities of (1) reciprocity, (2) oligopolistic entrenchment, or (3) elimination of *potential* competitors or the "edge effect," they may be illegal.

FTC v. Procter & Gamble Co.
386 U.S. 568 (1966)
Supreme Court of the United States

Justice Douglas

This is a proceeding by the Federal Trade Commission charging . . . that Procter's acquisition of Clorox might substantially lessen competition or tend to create a monopoly in the production and sale of household liquid bleaches.

At the time of the merger, in 1957, Clorox was the leading manufacturer in the heavily concentrated household liquid bleach industry. It is agreed that household liquid bleach is the relevant line of commerce. The product is used in the home as a germicide and disinfectant, and, more importantly, as a whitening agent in washing clothes and fabrics. It is a distinctive product with no close substitutes. Liquid bleach is a low-price, high-turnover consumer product sold mainly through grocery stores and supermarkets. The relevant geographical market is the Nation and a series of regional markets. Because of high shipping costs and low sales price, it is not feasible to ship the product more than 300 miles from its point of manufacture. Most manufacturers are limited to competition within a single region since they have but one plant. Clorox is the only firm selling nationally; it has 13 plants distributed throughout the Nation. Purex, Clorex's closest competitor in size, does not distribute its bleach in the northeast or mid-Atlantic States; in 1957, Purex's bleach was available in less than 50% of the national market.

At the time of the acquisition, Clorox was the leading manufacturer of household liquid bleach, with 48.8% of the national sales—annual sales of slightly less than $40,000,000. Its market share had been steadily increasing for the five years prior to the merger. Its nearest rival was Purex, which . . . accounted for 15.7% of the household liquid bleach market. The industry is highly concentrated; in 1957, Clorox and Purex accounted for almost 65% of the Nation's household liquid bleach sales, and, together with four other firms, for almost 80%. The remaining 20% was divided among over 200 small producers. . . .

Since all liquid bleach is chemically identical, advertising and sales promotion are vital. In 1957 Clorox spent almost $3,700,000 on advertising, imprinting the value of its bleach in the mind of the consumer. In addition, it spent $1,700,000 for other promotional activities. The Commission found that these heavy expenditures went far to explain why Clorox maintained so high a market share despite the fact that its brand, though chemically indistinguishable from rival brands, retailed for a price equal to or, in many instances, higher than its competitors.

Procter is a large, diversified manufacturer of low-price, high-turnover household products sold through grocery, drug, and department stores. Prior to its acquisition of Clorox, it did not produce household liquid bleach. . . . Procter has been marked by rapid growth and diversification. It has successfully developed and introduced a number of new products. Its primary activity is in the general area of soaps, detergents, and cleansers. . . . Procter was the dominant factor in this area. It accounted for 54.4% of all packaged detergent sales. The industry is heavily concentrated—Procter and its nearest competitors, Colgate-Palmolive and Lever Brothers, account for 80% of the market.

In the marketing of soaps, detergents, and cleansers, as in the marketing of household liquid bleach, advertising and sales promotion are vital. In 1957, Procter was the Nation's largest advertiser, spending more than $80,000,000 on advertising and an additional $47,000,000 on sales promotion. Due to its tremendous volume, Procter receives substantial

discounts from the media. As a multi-product producer Procter enjoys substantial advantages in advertising and sales promotion. Thus, it can and does feature several products in its promotions, reducing the printing, mailing, and other costs for each product. It also purchases network programs on behalf of several products, enabling it to give each product network exposure at a fraction of the cost per product that a firm with only one product to advertise would incur. . . .

The decision to acquire Clorox was the result of a study conducted by Procter's promotion department designed to determine the advisability of entering the liquid bleach industry. The initial report noted the ascendancy of liquid bleach in the large and expanding household bleach market, and recommended that Procter purchase Clorox rather than enter independently. Since a large investment would be needed to obtain a satisfactory market share, acquisition of the industry's leading firm was attractive. . . .

All mergers are within the reach of Section 7, and all must be tested by the same standard, whether they are classified as horizontal, vertical, conglomerate or other. As noted by the Commission, this merger is neither horizontal, vertical, nor conglomerate. Since the products of the acquired company are complementary to those of the acquiring company and may be produced with similar facilities, marketed through the same channels and in the same manner, and advertised by the same media, the Commission aptly called this acquisition a "product-extension merger":

By this acquisition . . . Procter has not diversified its interests in the sense of expanding into a substantially different, unfamiliar market or industry. Rather, it has entered a market which adjoins, as it were, those markets in which it is already established, and which is virtually indistinguishable from them insofar as the problems and techniques of marketing the product to the ultimate consumer are concerned. As a high official of Procter put it, com-menting on the acquisition of Clorox, "While this is a completely new business for us, taking us for the first time into the marketing of a household bleach and disinfectant, we are thoroughly at home in the field of manufacturing and marketing low priced, rapid turn-over consumer products." . . .

The anticompetitive effects with which this product-extension merger is fraught can easily be seen: (1) the substitution of the powerful acquiring firm for the smaller, but already dominant, firm may substantially reduce the competitive structure of the industry by raising entry barriers and by dissuading the smaller firms from aggressively competing; (2) the acquisition eliminates the potential competition of the acquiring firm.

The liquid bleach industry was already oligopolistic before the acquisition, and price competition was certainly not as vigorous as it would have been if the industry were competitive. Clorox enjoyed a dominant position nationally, and its position approached monopoly proportions in certain areas. The existence of some 200 fringe firms certainly does not belie that fact. Nor does the fact, relied upon by the court below, that, after the merger, producers other than Clorox "were selling more bleach for more money than ever before." In the same period, Clorox increased its share from 48.8% to 52%. The interjection of Procter into the market considerably changed the situation. There is every reason to assume that the smaller firms would become more cautious in competing due to their fear of retaliation by Procter. It is probable that Procter would become the price leader and that oligopoly would become more rigid.

The acquisition may also have the tendency of raising the barriers to new entry. The major competitive weapon in the successful marketing of bleach is advertising. Clorox was limited in this area by its relatively small budget and its inability to obtain substantial discounts. By contrast, Procter's budget was much larger; and, although it would not devote its entire budget to advertising Clorox, it could divert a large portion to meet the short-term threat of a new entrant. Procter would be able to use its volume discounts to advantage in advertising Clorox. Thus, a new entrant would be much more reluctant to face the giant Procter than it would have been to face the smaller Clorox.

Possible economies cannot be used as a defense to illegality. Congress was aware that some mergers which lessen competition may also result in economies but it struck the balance in favor of protecting competition.

The Commission also found that the acquisition of Clorox by Procter eliminated Procter as a potential competitor. The Court of Appeals declared that this finding was not supported by evidence because there was no evidence that Procter's management had ever intended to enter the industry independently and that Procter had never attempted to enter. The evidence, however, clearly shows that Procter was the most likely entrant. Procter has recently launched a new abrasive cleaner in an industry similar to the liquid bleach industry, and had wrested leadership from a brand that had enjoyed even a larger market share than had Clorox. Procter was engaged in a vigorous program of diversifying into product lines closely related to its basic products. Liquid bleach was a natural avenue of diversification since it is complementary to Procter's products, is sold to the same customers through the same channels, and is advertised and merchandised in the same manner. Procter had substantial advantages in advertising and sales promotion, which, as we have seen, are vital to the success of liquid bleach. No manufacturer had a patent on the product or its manufacture, necessary information relating to manufacturing methods and processes was readily available, there was no shortage of raw material, and the machinery and equipment required for a plant of efficient capacity were available at reasonable cost. Procter's management was experienced in producing and marketing goods similar to liquid bleach. Procter had considered the possibility of independently entering but decided against it because the acquisition of Clorox would enable Procter to capture a more commanding share of the market.

It is clear that the existence of Procter at the edge of the industry exerted considerable influence on the market. First, the market behavior of the liquid bleach industry was influenced by each firm's predictions of the market behavior of its competitors, actual and potential. Second, the barriers to entry by a firm of Procter's size and with its advantages were not significant. There is no indication that the barriers were so high that the price Procter would have to charge would be above the price that would maximize the profits of the existing firms. Third, the number of potential entrants was not so large that the elimination of one would be insignificant. Few firms would have the temerity to challenge a firm as solidly entrenched as Clorox. Fourth, Procter was found by the Commission to be the most likely entrant.

Questions

1. What is a product-extension merger?
2. What were the anticompetitive effects of the "deep pockets" of Procter & Gamble? In other words, what would be the competitive effect if Procter & Gamble's financial resources were made available to Clorox to market a product that involves extensive promotional expenditures to differentiate its otherwise competitively identical product?
3. What is a potential competitor? How is a potential competitor eliminated by a merger?

THE "EDGE EFFECT"

One of the earliest cases concerning "potential competition"involved a firm that had repeatedly considered entering the market into which it merged.[10] The fact that this firm had tried to enter the new market independently made its status as a source of competition clear. However, most potential entry cases are not so simple. In *Procter & Gamble* (P&G), the appellate court had found that there was no evidence P&G intended to enter the liquid household bleach market on its own. The Supreme Court disagreed, as previously mentioned, concluding that P&G had all the resources needed to enter on its own, had entered similar markets without mergers, and was the most likely entrant into the liquid bleach market.

In 1971, the Supreme Court further defined the potential competition doctrine. Falstaff Brewing Co., the fourth largest producer of beer in the United States, acquired the Narragansett Brewing Co., the leading seller in New England.[11] Since Falstaff executives testified they would not have built a brewery on their own in New England, the district court ruled that Falstaff had no intent to enter the New England market and, therefore, could not be eliminated as a potential competitor by merging. On appeal, the Supreme Court said the following.

The specific question . . . is not what Falstaff's internal company decisions were but whether, given its financial capabilities and conditions in the New England market, it would be reasonable to consider it a potential entrant into that market. . . . [I]f it would appear to rational beer merchants in New England that Falstaff might well build a new brewery . . . then its entry by merger becomes suspect. . . . The district court should therefore have appraised the economic facts about Falstaff in the New England market in order to determine whether in any realistic sense Falstaff could be said to be a potential competitor . . . so positioned on the edge of the market that it exerted beneficial influence on competitive conditions in that market.[12]

On remand, the trial court reconsidered the evidence and concluded that Falstaff was not a *perceived* potential entrant and, therefore, the merger was allowed to stand. The lower court felt that brewers in New England were too involved in an intense rivalry among themselves to be influenced by Falstaff's remote threat.

A year later, the Supreme Court restated its view of the edge effect of the potential competition doctrine.

Unequivocable proof that an acquiring firm actually would have entered *de novo* but for a merger is rarely available. . . . Thus, . . . the principal focus of the doctrine is on the likely effects of the premerger position of the acquiring firm on the fringe of the target market. . . . [A] market extension merger may be unlawful if the target market is substantially concentrated, if the acquiring firm has the characteristics, capabilities, and the economic incentive to render it a perceived potential *de novo* entrant, and if the acquiring firm's premerger presence on the fringe of the target market in fact tempered oligopolistic behavior on the part of the existing participants in the market.[13]

This instruction from the Supreme Court requires lower courts to determine whether the acquiring firm's premerger posture as a possible entrant constrained the pricing policies of the firms already in the industry. This is a difficult burden of proof imposed on the antitrust enforcers, who attempt to utilize the potential competition doctrine to stop market extension and product extension mergers. It is likely to reduce the effectiveness of the potential competition doctrine to forestall conglomerate mergers.

"TOEHOLD" ACQUISITIONS

The Supreme Court has not yet been subjected to one version of the potential competition doctrine referred to as the "toehold" acquisition. Under this doctrine, a large conglomerate acquisition of a leading seller in a concentrated industry would be challenged because a less anticompetitive entry is available. The large conglomerate could have acquired a smaller industry participant (a toehold) and built its acquisition into a competitive challenger. Although without Supreme Court endorsement, the toehold theory has been widely discussed in the lower courts and among antitrust authorities. Its purpose, like the potential competition doctrine itself, is to preserve the opportunity for deconcentration of oligopolistic markets by requiring likely entrants to enter *de novo* or by toehold acquisition rather than by acquisition of competitive significant firms in those markets. The lower courts, in applying this doctrine, have looked to a variety of factors, including concentration level, entry barriers, the capacity of the outside firm to enter *de novo* or by toehold acquisition, the deconcentration effect of such entry, and the number of other potential entrants.

NEW MERGER GUIDELINES

In June 1982, theJustice Department announced new guidelines that outline the standards now in use by the Department of Justice in determining what mergers it will challenge. The new guidelines replace those issued by the Department in 1968.

MARKET CONCENTRATION

One significant change from the 1968 guidelines is the use of a different index to measure market concentration. The 1968 guidelines used the four-firm concentration ratio to measure market shares. The four-firm concentration ratio is the sum of the percentage market shares of the top four firms in the market. The new guidelines use the Herfindahl index instead. That index is calculated by squaring the percentage market share of each firm in the market and then adding those squares. The Department maintains that the Herfindahl index was chosen because it gives a more accurate measure of market structure than the four-firm concentration ratio. For instance, if there were a market in which 4 firms each had a 15 percent share and 40 firms each had a 1 percent share, and a second market where 1 firm had 57 percent of the market and the remaining 43 firms one percent each, the four-firm concentration ratios would be identical— 60 percent each. (See Figure 10-4.) The Herfindahls for those two markets would be far from the same, however. The first market would have an index of 940 and the second an index of 3292—more than three times as great. In the first market, the Department's concern about mergers would be relatively low, and in the second, quite high. In actually applying the Herfindahl index to a merger situation two figures are important—the index of concentration after the merger, and how much that differs from the index before the merger.

Four-Firm Ratios	Herfindahl Index
$15\% + 15\% + 15\% + 15\% = 60$	$15^2 + 15^2 + 15^2 + 15^2 + 1^2 \ldots$ (for 40 firms) $= 940$
$57\% + 1\% + 1\% + 1\% = 60$	$57^2 + 1^2 \ldots$ (for 43 firms) $= 3292$

Figure 10.4 Contrasts of four-firm concentration ratios with Herfindahl index.

In analyzing market concentration in a horizontal merger the new guidelines use the post-merger Herfindahl index to set forth three levels of concentration.

- Where the post-merger market is "unconcentrated," that is, where even after the merger the Herfindahl is below 1000, the Department would be unlikely to challenge any merger. An index of 1000 indicates the level of concentration that exists, for instance, in a market shared equally by 10 firms.
- Where the post-merger market is "moderately concentrated," with an index between 1000 and 1800, a challenge would still be unlikely, provided the merger increases the index by less than 100 points. If the merger increases the index by more than 100 points, a challenge by the Antitrust Division would be more likely than not, with the decision being based on the extent of the increase, the ease of entry, and the presence or absence of other relevant factors specified in the guidelines.
- Where the post-merger market is "highly concentrated," resulting in an index above 1800, challenge is unlikely where the merger produces an increase of less than 50 points. If the merger produces an increase in the index between 50 and 100 points, challenge is more likely than not, again depending on the size of the increase, ease of entry and other factors as specified. If the merger produces an increase in the index of more than 100 points, challenge is likely. An index of 1800 indicates the level of concentration that exists, for instance, in a market shared equally by approximately six firms (5.56 equally sized firms, to be precise).

In addition, if the leading firm in the market has a market share of 35 percent or more and is about twice as large as the second largest firm or larger, the Department is likely to challenge a merger by the largest firm with any firm having at least 1 percent of the market. In such a case, the only possible mitigating factor to be considered by the Department would be ease of entry.

Converted into the Herfindahl measurement, the 1968 guidelines stated that a challenge was likely for mergers that increased concentration by 30–40 points in highly concentrated markets (four-firm concentration of 75 percent or more) and by 50–90 points in less highly concentrated markets (four-firm concentration of less than 75 percent). Unlike the new guidelines, however, the old guidelines did not state that mergers producing smaller increases in concentration would not be challenged. Similarly, the old guidelines did not recognize an unconcentrated region where challenges were generally unlikely. (See Figure 10-5.)

New Entry

The inferences drawn from the concentration numbers above may be adjusted to take account of very easy entry to the market. The reason that ease of entry is so important is that where firms not already in the market can enter it very

1968 Guidelines[a]		1982 Guidelines
(Four-firm ratio of 75 percent or more)	Highly concentrated market	(Herfindahl Index above 1800 points)
Challenge if Herfindahl Index increases by 30–40 points		Challenge if Herfindahl Index increases by 50 points
(Four-firm ratio of less than 75 percent)	Moderately concentrated market	(Herfindahl Index between 1000 and 1800 points)
Challenge if Herfindahl Index increases by 50–90 points		Challenge if Herfindahl Index increases by 100 points
(Not specifically defined)	Unconcentrated market	(Herfindahl Index less than 1000 points)
If market concentration has been increasing, any merger involving 2 percent market share will be challenged		No challenge

[a]Decision criteria have been converted into Herfindahl measurement.

Figure 10.5 The contrasting decision criteria of 1968 and 1982 merger guidelines.

easily, inferences drawn from the post-merger concentration index can be misleading. Because ease of entry cannot be expressed in market statistics, it must be looked at as an independent consideration, but one that the guidelines make clear is very significant.

Other Factors

Compared with the old guidelines, the new guidelines identify a much larger number of additional factors that the Department will consider in deciding whether to challenge a merger.

The other factors to be considered are ones that might warrant some adjustment to the inferences drawn from the level of post-merger concentration. The guidelines state that, where relevant, these factors will be used to resolve close cases. These factors generally deal with the ease and profitability of collusion among sellers to raise prices above competitive levels. For instance, with homogeneous products, the number of issues on which competitors must agree in order to raise prices is smaller, thus making effective collusion more likely. Similarly, a challenge would be more likely if there was evidence of prior horizontal collusion among firms in the market.

NONHORIZONTAL MERGERS

The guidelines make clear that although nonhorizontal mergers are less likely to harm competition, they are not always innocuous. They make plain that much of what is said about horizontal mergers could also be applied to nonhorizontal mergers—such as the discussion of market concentration, ease of entry, and other factors—and they discuss five nonhorizontal theories of liability.

The five nonhorizontal theories of liability under which such mergers might be challenged are:

- The elimination of specific potential entrants into the market.
- The creation of barriers to entry to the market through vertical mergers.
- The facilitation of collusion through vertical mergers that integrate the firms to include the retail level.
- The elimination through vertical merger of a disruptive buyer.
- The evasion of rate regulation.

For each of the five theories the guidelines describe the possible harm and the conditions necessary for that harm to occur.

DEFENSES

In a concluding section dealing with defenses to an antitrust challenge to a merger, the guidelines indicate that only in extraordinary cases will the Department consider a claim of efficiencies as a mitigating factor to a merger that would otherwise be challenged. They also indicate that a stringent analysis will be applied to the so-called "failing firm" defense, a doctrine that may immunize otherwise anticompetitive mergers. To recognize the defense, the Department will require that the failure of the firm be very likely and that no less anticompetitive acquisition be available.

Questions
1. What does the Herfindahl Index measure?
2. In a horizontal merger situation, what three standards are applied to determine if the merger should be challenged?
3. When is a market considered unconcentrated, moderately concentrated, or highly concentrated?
4. Why is ease of entry significant in determining whether to challenge a merger?
5. What other factors should be reviewed to determine whether to challenge a merger?
6. What are the five theories of liability under which nonhorizontal mergers may be challenged? Can you relate any of these theories to any previously decided cases?
7. What defenses are available for merging firms?

CONCLUSION

Since the early 1960s, merger policy in the United States has become more strict and consistent. The lines defining illegal mergers have become reasonably clear.

Horizontal mergers that appreciably increase market shares, especially if in concentrated industries, are likely to be held illegal. Vertical mergers that substantially foreclose competitors from suppliers or outlets or raise entry barriers are normally decreed illegal. Conglomerate mergers involving reciprocity or the elimination of potential entrants will likewise be challenged.

U.S. merger policy attempts to retain industries with firms possessing small market shares and to promote entry. However, industry structure predating this new merger policy has not been affected. Merger policy has not sought to restructure existing firms. Instead, it seeks to avoid increasing levels of industry concentration. Consequently, one major criticism of U.S. merger policy is its *status quo* hardening of industrial structure. Large firms are privileged to retain their size while gaining an unintended immunity from the takeover process. Critics further argue that the strict rules of U.S. merger policy have prevented smaller firms from merging to gain the size that firms predating this policy have obtained.

On the other hand, structuralists have argued that the looseness of the conglomerate merger guidelines allows more conglomerate mergers than it prohibits. They point out that the failure to retard conglomerate mergers has led to an increase in the overall aggregate economic concentration. This increased concentration is achieved with little evidence that conglomerate mergers enhance industrial efficiency.[14] Consequently, these critics call for congressional intervention to stop conglomerate mergers that confer little social benefit but conflict with the societal goal of decentralizing economic power.

Merger policy is not wanting for critics who suggest reform, but no group of critics has been successful in convincing Congress of the need to modify its legislative policy on mergers. This congressional inactivity suggests general approval by Congress of the merger policy that has been fashioned through legislative, judicial, and enforcement processes.

DISCUSSION QUESTIONS

1. Brunswick Corporation is one of the two largest manufacturers, distributors, and financiers of bowling alley equipment. Until the early 1960s it did not operate recreational bowling centers itself.

    In the early 1960s the bowling recreation industry began a decline and an alarming number of Brunswick's customers defaulted on payments. Rather than repossess the equipment for resale, Brunswick began to take over the failing bowling centers by purchase of stock or assets, and keep them operating when they otherwise would have failed. Brunswick carried out such takeovers where its new Bowling Centers Operations Division determined that a center could produce a positive cash flow.

    A competing operator of bowling centers in several cities over the country sued Brunswick, alleging a Section 7 violation by a "deep pocket" manufacturer integrating vertically forward into local markets, causing a potential lessening of horizontal competition on the local level. Because of Brunswick's acquisitions, the local competitors did not realize the increase in their market shares they had anticpated, and, it was contended, reduced the income they would have made as a result of failures of bowling houses within local markets.

Did the plaintiff sustain an injury that Section 7 was intended to prevent, entitling the plaintiff to treble damages?

2. Arrow Brands, Inc., was in the business of purchasing aluminum foil in large quantities from manufacturers and converting it into "florist foil" by coloring and embossing it. The converted foil was then sold to wholesale florist supply houses. Although 200 companies in the United States were engaged in the business of converting foil into decorative foil, only 8 served the florist industry, with the remainder converting foil for innumerable other decorative wrapping purposes. Arrow accounted for 33 percent of annual florist foil wholesale sales in the United States market.

Theoretically, any of the 200 foil converters could supply florist foil, used for covering clay and plastic pots and as decoration in arrangements, because decorative foil used in the florist trade is physically not distinguishable from foil decorated by coloring, laminating, or embossing but used for potato wrap, cheese wrap, medicine containers, and so on. However, of the 192 million pounds of converted aluminum foil shipped annually in the United States, 9.7 million pounds consisted of decorative foil, and of that decorative foil, less than 1.5 million pounds went to the florist trade, virtually all of which was shipped by the eight firms, including Arrow, catering to that trade. Also, users of decorative foil, other than florists and florist supply houses, do not purchase from the florist foil converters.

A lower price prevails in the market for florist foil than for colored or embossed aluminum foil sold in the same weight units and gauged at the same thickness. Florist foil brings $.75 to $.85 per unit, whereas other decorative foils are priced at approximately $1.15 to $1.22 per unit.

Arrow and other florist foil converters purchased their plain foil from Reynolds Metals Company, among other producers. Plain or raw foil costs contribute 70 percent of the total cost of production.

Following Reynolds acquisition of Arrow, Arrow lowered its prices, and by 1957 it had increased sales 18.9 percent over its 1955 sales volume. Five of Arrow's seven competitors' sales in 1957 were 14 to 47 percent below 1955 sales.

The FTC found a violation of Section 7 of the Clayton Act and ordered divestiture. Reynolds appealed, arguing that the converting and supplying of florist foil is not a "line of commerce" distinct from the converting and supplying of other decorative foils. It was not contended that Reynolds' acquisition of Arrow was likely to have an anticompetitive effect on the market for *all* decorative foils.

What is the relevant "line of commerce"?

3. In the mid-1970s, Atlantic Richfield Company (Arco) was the 13th largest publicly held corporation in terms of assets and ranked 15th in terms of

sales and revenues. It produced petroleum products and natural gas, and had never engaged in the copper business. Since the late 1960s, high-level Arco management recognized a need for diversification and favored diversification into the copper industry only if it could be accomplished by large acquisition rather than by original entry or toehold acquisition.

The Anaconda Company was a fully integrated copper and aluminum company, ranking third in the industry for the mining of copper ore, and fourth in the refined copper market. Anaconda's market shares were 8.27 percent for copper ore and 9.78 for refined copper. The three leaders in the refined copper market controlled 60 percent of the market.

Original entry into the copper industry entailed outlays from $200 million to $450 million for the discovery and development of an exploitable ore deposit, which could take 10 years or more, the development of technical expertise, and the construction of smelting facilities. Total entry time could range up to 20 years.

In 1967, Arco and Anaconda agreed to merge, with Anaconda to become a wholly owned subsidiary of Arco. The Federal Trade Commission sought to enjoin the merger on the basis that a violation of Section 7 of the Clayton Act would result, on the theory of actual potential entry.

Was Arco a potential *de novo* entrant?

4. Cargill Inc., a huge, privately owned corporation, had been involved for over 100 years in grain trading in the midwest and had acquired river barges and towboats that were used to carry not only grain but also other bulk commodities. By 1973 Cargill was involved in vegetable oil processing, sugar trading, ore and metal mining, ocean shipping, flour milling, corn wet milling, industrial chemical manufacturing, animal feed, fertilizer, and poultry product production, and salt mining. After forming a planning committee and receiving its recommendations for company expansion, Cargill made a tender offer for all outstanding shares of stock in Missouri Portland Cement Co. (MP), a cement manufacturer operating three plants on the Missouri and Ohio Rivers.

Missouri Portland Cement sold its cement in an 11-state area, along with several dozen competitors including 8 of the 10 largest cement producers in the country. MP was the 20th largest national producer, possessing 2 percent of national cement production capacity and 8 percent of capacity in its 11-state area. The cement industry could be characterized as oligopolistic.

MP sued Cargill to enjoin the acquisition, on the basis that such an acquisition or merger would result in a violation of Section 7 of the Clayton Act. MP argued that Cargill was attempting a "product-extension merger" as was attempted by Proctor & Gamble with Clorox. MP further analogized that Cargill's "deep pocket" would enable it to raise entry barriers or discourage competition in the cement industry.

How would you characterize the acquisition of Missouri Portland Cement by Cargill? What economic effect would you expect it to have on the cement market? Would a Section 7 violation result? Is *Proctor & Gamble* applicable to this situation?

5. BOC recently acquired a 35 percent interest in Airco by stock purchase. BOC is a multinational corporation and is the world's second largest producer of industrial gases but has never produced or sold industrial gases in the United States. Airco was the third largest industrial gas producer in the United States, with a 16 percent share of the market, and the two market leaders in the U.S. control 26 and 18 percent.

Based on findings that there was a reasonable probability that BOC would have eventually entered the U.S. industrial gas market by internal expansion, the FTC found a violation of Section 7 of the Clayton Act, and ordered that BOC divest itself of the Airco stock. The FTC opinion gave no indication of when such an entry might be expected to occur. BOC denied any intent to enter the market either *de novo* or by toehold acquisition.

On appeal by BOC, the FTC conceded that at the time of the acquisition, BOC, as a potential market entrant, was having no present procompetitive effect on the U.S. industrial gases market. Decide.

6. Steiger Tractor, Inc. was a manufacturer of four-wheel-drive farm tractors. It marketed this product through 236 of its own dealers and acted as supplier for International Harvester, Allis-Chalmers Corp., and Canadian Co-operation Implements, Ltd. (CCIL). Steiger ranked third among the 10 shippers of four-wheel-drive farm tractors in the United States and its total four-wheel-drive tractor production was 19 percent of industry production. International Harvester Co. (Harvester), in addition to buying from Steiger, itself produced four-wheel-drive tractors, accounting for 6 percent of the industry. The top four firms shipping four-wheel-drive farm tractors accounted for 73 percent of industry shipments.

In 1974 Steiger and Harvester executed a stock purchase agreement giving Harvester 39 percent of Steiger's common stock and the right to appoint three of Steiger's nine directors, and a manufacturing agreement under which Steiger was to assemble four-wheel-drive tractors for Harvester using Harvester components, and requiring Harvester to purchase a certain minimum of such tractors, up to a maximum of 48 percent of Steiger's annual production. It also prohibited Harvester from limiting Steiger's contractual obligations to Allis-Chalmers and CCIL, and Harvester could not prevent Steiger from undertaking sound business activities. The United States sued under Section 7 of the Clayton Act to force a divestiture of the stock and to cancel the stock purchase agreement. The government claimed that the planned arrangement would substantially lessen competition in the production and sale of four-wheel-drive tractors.

Steiger's financial position before this agreement with Harvester had been precarious for some time. In 1970 its supplier had refused to ship parts and it sustained a $525,971 loss and ended the year with working capital of $82,755, cash of $4914, and current liabilities of $1,111,841.

In May 1971, Steiger obtained bank financing on the strength of a contract to produce five tractors per month for CCIL, plus an assignment of CCIL's accounts receivable as security, plus the personal endorsement of Steiger's Chairman/Chief Executive Officer. In August 1971, that bank discontinued credits, citing Steiger's lack of equity. Steiger then borrowed $750,000 from a business investment firm. In November 1971, the bank was persuaded to again lend funds to Steiger when it received a contract to produce 60 units for Allis-Chalmers and offered inventory and accounts receivable as security, plus the Chairman's personal guarantee.

By the end of 1971, losses were $852,922. Working capital was a negative $456,642 and shareholders' equity was negative $334,296. Steiger borrowed $450,000 from customers, overdrew its bank account by as much as $500,000, and submitted all of its corporate activities to the approval of a commercial credit firm. A small upturn occurred at the end of 1973, but Steiger's condition was the worst in the industry.

After Steiger's agreements with Harvester became effective, Harvester's investment allowed Steiger to build a new manufacturing facility, which enabled Steiger to enter foreign markets with the increased production. Steiger escaped the control of the commercial credit firm and once again obtained normal lines of credit from banks.

In 1975 Steiger ranked second in four-wheel-drive tractor production. Harvester had increased its share of four-wheel-drive sales from 8.4 percent in 1973 to 10.2 percent in 1975.

Evaluate the probable effect on competition in the four-wheel-drive farm tractor market of the Harvester-Steiger agreements.

Are the data relating to Steiger's financial condition relevant to a Section 7 charge, in view of its ranking in the market?

7. In 1978 Beatrice Food Company, the 37th largest industrial corporation in the country, acquired Tropicana products, the nation's leading processor of chilled orange juice, with over 30 percent of the sales in grocery stores. The Administrative Law Judge ruled that the evidence overwhelmingly showed a separate relevant product market for chilled orange juice sold to the retail market. Ready-to-drink chilled orange juice (COJ) is sold in cartons, bottles, or plastic containers and is distinguished from frozen concentrate and canned, single-strength orange juice. Orange juice is regularly processed in dairies across the country. Beatrice has 37 dairies and the widest geographical sales area of any dairy in the country. At the time of the merger Beatrice processed COJ at 12 plants and held about 35 percent of the market as measured in gallons of COJ sold to grocery stores. The evidence indicated a trend toward concentration of the COJ industry with the top four companies controlling 55 percent of the gallon sales in 1975, 60 percent in 1978, and 64 percent shortly after the merger. Beatrice and Tropicana sold or tried to sell their products to the same chain food stores and vied for sales in at least 48 metropolitan areas.

The Administrative Law Judge held that the merger violated Section 7 of the Clayton Act and ordered the divestiture of Tropicana within one year of the date of the order. Moreover, the judge ordered that all of Tropicana's profits during the time that it was held by Beatrice be turned over to the U.S. Treasury to "avoid unjust enrichment" and "to prevent illegal practices in the future."

Comment on the judge's remedy regarding the divestiture of profits.

SUGGESTED READINGS

Cann, Wesley A., Jr., "The New Merger Guidelines: Is the Department of Justice Enforcing the Law?", *American Business Law Journal*, Vol. 21, No. 1, Spring 1983, pp. 1–48.

McDonald, James L. and Marcia J. Staff, "Bank Mergers After the Omnibus Banking Bill: Is *Philadelphia National Bank* Finally Dead?", *American Business Law Journal*, Vol. 20, No. 3, Fall 1982, pp. 421–434.

Marinelli, Arthur J., "Judicial Reexamination of Section 7 of the Clayton Act," *American Business Law Journal*, Vol. 20, No. 2, Summer 1982, pp. 203–222.

Mueller, Willard F., *The Celler-Kefauver Act: The First 27 Years*, U.S. House of Representatives, Committee on the Judiciary, Subcommittee on Monopolies and Commercial Law, Nov. 7, 1979, pp. 7–8.

ENDNOTES

1. See Ralph L. Nelson, *Merger Movements in American Industry—1890–1956* (Princeton: Princeton University Press, 1962).
2. *U.S.* v. *Northern Securities Co.*, 193 U.S. 197 (1904).
3. *U.S.* v. *Columbia Steel Co.*, 334 U.S. 495 (1948).
4. *U.S.* v. *Bethlehem Steel Co.*, 168 F. Supp. 576 (1958).
5. *U.S.* v. *Aluminum Company of America*, 377 U.S. 271.
6. *U.S.* v. *Continental Can Co.*, 217 F. Supp. 761 (1963); 378 U.S. 441 (1964).
7. 378 U.S. 441, 449, 455, 457 (1964).
8. During the oil shortage of the 1970s, Congress mandated that large vertically integrated oil companies share their scarce supplies of crude oil with refineries that had little or no crude oil production (Energy Petroleum Act of 1973).
9. The two cases are *FTC* v. *Consolidated Foods*, 380 U.S. 592 (1965), which outlawed probable reciprocity, and *FTC* v. *Procter & Gamble*, 386 U.S. 568 (1966), which utilized "entrenchment" and "potential competition" doctrines.
10. *U.S.* v. *El Paso Natural Gas Co.*, 376 U.S. 651 (1964).
11. *U.S.* v. *Falstaff Brewing Corp.*, 332 F. Supp. 970 (1971), 410 U.S. 526 (1973).
12. 410 U.S. 526, 533–534, 532 (1973).
13. *U.S.* v. *Marine Bancorporation*, 418 U.S. 602, 624–625 (1974).
14. F. M. Scherer, *Industrial Market Structure and Market Performance*, 2d ed. (Chicago: Ill.: Rand McNally, 1980), p. 563.

chapter 11

HORIZONTAL COMBINATIONS

One of the premises of an effective competitive system is that rivals act independently in determining price, quality, and other terms of trade. Such competitive action among sellers affords the buyers an opportunity to find the lowest price offered by the suppliers.

On the other hand, profit-oriented competitors are tempted to unite on price or other terms of trade. By avoiding price or other types of competition, it is possible for the firms to raise prices above the level that would result from independent competitive action. Even Adam Smith, the often-quoted author of the *Wealth of Nations* who proclaimed the virtues of freely competitive enterprise, warned, "people of the same trade seldom meet together, even for merriment and diversion, but the conversation ends in a conspiracy against the public, or in some contrivance to raise prices."[1]

Only if rivals act independently in regard to competitive matters, can society be assured that the efficiency, equity, and progress associated with a competitive system will be achieved. Accordingly, public policy has long recognized that joint action that restrains competition should normally be prohibited. However, society has not always been successful in identifying and suppressing joint actions in the form of contracts, trusts, conspiracies, or other collusions.

RULE OF REASON

The rules of law governing competition collusion followed by the courts prior to the adoption of the federal and state antitrust statutes were based on English common law. The common law permitted restraints on competition that were merely ancillary to some legitimate business purpose, but voided those contracts whose main object was to restrict competition. For example, a contract of employment restraining an employee, should he or she quit or be terminated, from subsequently competing with the employer was held lawful if the restraint imposed was reasonable in time (limited to a number of years) and in area (limited to a geographical area). This restraint was considered ancillary to the basic employment contract, that is, it allowed the employer to train the employee without fear of the employee's immediate exit as a competitor. Likewise, a restraint on one's freedom to exercise one's trade, if accepted in selling the business, was held valid if it was reasonable in time and area because it was ancillary to the sale of the business. Because social purposes, such as employment training or the sale of businesses, were being furthered by these contracts and because they did not involve substantial restraints on competition, the common law allowed enforcement. In contrast, the common law courts would not enforce contracts among competitors to fix prices on their goods. These types of contracts were considered contrary to the public interest. Therefore, the basic rule of reasonableness (rule of reason) governed the enforcement of the common law restraint of trade. However, as agreements among competitors found alternative means of private enforcement through pools or the trust arrangement, it became apparent that the passive approach of nonenforceability of the contract followed by the common law was an inadequate protection for the public. A positive approach was needed to combat the problem of the trusts and collusion in American industries. Consequently, Congress enacted the Sherman Act.

Section 1 of the Sherman Act provides that "every contract, combination, . . . or conspiracy, in restraint of trade or commerce . . . is . . . illegal." This section imposes the positive duty on the federal government to enforce the policy of maintaining the principles of market price (competitively determined) in the conduct of business. Since expressed standards for identifying a "restraint of trade" were not specified in the law, the federal courts have had to develop and apply such standards as were found necessary to preserve competition.

Section 1 of the Sherman Act declares "every" contract, combination, or conspiracy in restraint of trade to be illegal. In interpreting this provision, the obvious question arises: Are *reasonable* restraints of trade that were lawful under the common law made unlawful by Section I? In other words, does the word *every* in Section 1 mean "every"—including those reasonable common law restraints—and thereby outlaw *all* restraints on trade? Initially, the Supreme Court answered this question affirmatively.

[T]he plain and ordinary meaning of such language is not limited to that kind of contract alone which is in unreasonable restraint of trade, but all contracts are included in such language, and no exception or limitation can be added without placing in the Act that which has been omitted by Congress. *U.S.* v. *Trans-Missouri Freight Association*, 166 U.S. 290 (1896).

This language by the Supreme Court indicates that the justices were following a "plain meaning" rule of statutory interpretation. They believed the plain meaning of the words as employed in the statute were the best evidence of the intention of Congress. They argued that if the legislators had meant something else, different words would have been used to indicate the alternative meaning. The dissenting justices favored a "purpose construction." They felt the statute should be interpreted in light of its purpose rather than the strictly literal meaning of the language employed in the statute.

In 1911, the Court decided to adopt the purpose approach. The Court determined that the elimination of reasonable restraints of trade that were lawful under the common law was not within the purpose of the Sherman Act. Consequently, a "rule of reason" approach was accepted as the proper method of interpreting the Sherman Act. So, though the act itself may say "every" restraint of trade, the judicial interpretations of the act have added the requirement of "unreasonableness" before the restraint of trade is to be ruled illegal. This rule of reason was first enunciated in the monopolization case against the Standard Oil trust in 1911. However, one of the most frequently cited statements of the rule of reason is that of Justice Brandeis in *Chicago Board of Trade* v. *U.S.*, 246 U.S. 231, 238 (1918).

The true test of legality is whether the restraint imposed is such as merely regulates and perhaps thereby promotes competition or whether it is such as may suppress or even destroy competition. To determine that question the court must ordinarily consider the facts peculiar to the business to which the restraint is applied; its condition before and after the restraint was imposed; the nature of the restraint and its effect, actual or probable. The history of the restraint, the evil believed to exist, the reason for adopting the particular remedy, the purpose or end sought to be attained, are all relevant facts. This is not because a good intention will save an otherwise objectionable regulation or the reverse; but because knowledge of the intent may help the court to interpret facts and to predict consequences.

PRICE-FIXING

Business people freely accept and publicly proclaim the advantages of competition and the free market. They maintain that the self-regulating aspects of competition promote the public welfare by ensuring lower prices and greater productivity. However, business people also recognize that in planning for productive operations and in the development of marketing strategy, cooperation among competitors may reduce the hazards associated with the competitive process. When such agreements are made between competitors at the same level of the distribution process, the agreements are considered horizontal combinations. Obvious examples include the agreements of manufacturers to fix prices they charge to the public, or of wholesalers not to sell competing goods in each other's assigned territory. Such horizontal combinations eliminate competition between competing rivals. Society is then faced with higher prices and no alternative source of supplies. Because most of these practices present obvious harm to the competitive process, the courts have treated them as containing no redeeming social or economic value and, hence, unreasonable *per se.* However, in many instances the consipring merchants have attempted to convince the court that they set or fix only "reasonable" prices and achieve only "reasonable" profits as a result of the price-fixing agreement. In the following case, the conspirators also argued that their buying program to support prices merely eliminated "ruinous competition."

U.S. v. Socony-Vacuum Oil Co.
310 U.S. 150 (1939)
Supreme Court of the United States

Justice Douglas

The court charged the jury that it was a violation of the Sherman Act for a group of individuals or corporations to act together to raise the prices to be charged for the commodity which they manufactured where they controlled a substantial part of the interstate trade and commerce in that commodity. The court stated that where the members of a combination had the power to raise prices and acted together for that purpose, the combination was illegal and that it was immaterial how reasonable or unreasonable those prices were or to what extent they had been affected by the combination. . . .

In *United States* v. *Trenton Potteries Co.,* 273 U.S. 392, this Court sustained a conviction under the Sherman Act where the jury was charged that an agreement on the part of the members of a combination, controlling a substantial party of an industry, upon the prices which the members are to charge for their commodity is in itself an unreasonable restraint of trade without regard to the reasonableness of the prices or the good intentions of the combining units. . . . This court reviewed the various price-fixing cases under the Sherman Act . . . and said ". . . it has since often been decided and always assumed that uniform price-fixing by those controlling in any substantial manner a trade or business in interstate commerce is prohibited by the Sherman Law, despite the reasonableness of the particular prices agreed upon." This Court pointed

out that the so-called "rule of reason" had not affected this view of the illegality of price-fixing agreements. And in holding that agreements "to fix or maintain prices" are not reasonable restraints of trade under the statute merely because the prices themselves are reasonable, it said . . .

The aim and result of every price-fixing agreement, if effective, is the elimination of one form of competition. The power to fix prices, whether reasonably exercised, or not, involves power to control the market and to fix arbitrary and unreasonable prices. The reasonable price fixed today may through economic and business changes become the unreasonable price of tomorrow. Once established, it may be maintained unchanged because of the absence of competition secured by the agreement for a price reasonable when fixed. Agreements which create such potential power may be held to be in themselves unreasonable or unlawful restraints, without the necessity of minute inquiry whether a particular price is reasonable or unreasonable as fixed and without placing on the government in enforcing the Sherman Law the burden of ascertaining from day to day whether it has become unreasonable through the mere variation of economic conditions. . . .

Thus, for over forty years this Court has consistently and without deviation adhered to the principle that price-fixing agreements are unlawful *per se* under the Sherman Act and that no showing of so-called competitive abuses or evils which those agreements were designed to eliminate or alleviate may be interposed as a defense.

Questions

1. Did the Court accept the notion that reasonable prices and reasonable profits are justifications for price-fixing?
2. Is the elimination of "ruinous competition" a justification for establishing a price-fixing scheme?
3. If the Supreme Court accepted reasonable prices and profits as justification for price-fixing and ruled that such pricing and profits were reasonable, what would have to be done if the parties later changed their price structure? Would the Supreme Court become like a price control board? Do you think the Court wanted to get into such an activity?
4. When is an activity considered "unreasonable *per se*"? What reasons can be given for having such a rule? The Supreme Court said the following.

[T]here are certain agreements or practices which because of their pernicious effect on competition and lack of any redeeming virtue are conclusively presumed to be unreasonable and therefore illegal without elaborate inquiry as to the precise harm they have caused or the business excuse for their use. This principle of *per se* unreasonableness not only makes the type of restraints which are proscribed by the Sherman Act more certain to benefit everyone concerned, but it also avoids the necessity for an incredibly complicated and prolonged economic investigation into the entire history of the industry involved, as well as related industries, in an effort to determine at large whether a particular restraint has been unreasonable—an inquiry so often wholly fruitless when undertaken. *Northern Pac. R. Co.* v. *United States*, 356 U.S. 1 (1957).

PROOF OF CONSPIRACY

Price-fixing has been ruled unreasonable *per se* since *U.S.* v. *Trenton Potteries* (1927). Enforcement officials have consistently taken legal action against schemes to rig, control, or stabilize prices. No anticompetitive scheme is frowned on more than a price-fixing combination. Consequently, the Department of Justice believes that everyone should understand the illegality of price-fixing. Therefore, the Department often brings *criminal* charges against participants of a price-fixing conspiracy. A criminal violation of the Sherman Act can be a felony and result in imprisonment for up to three years. The act authorizes the imposition of fines of $100,000 per count for an individual and a $1,000,000 fine per count for a corporation. These criminal penalties were upgraded in 1976 from more lenient provisions in the original Sherman Act. The increase in the level of penalties and the increased willingness of enforcement officials to proceed with criminal suits suggest that more prosecution and stiff sentencing of antitrust violators may well occur in the future. Business executives have been imprisoned for participation in price-rigging schemes.

Some business people attempt to circumvent the price-fixing prohibitions by concealing their conspiracy from the public. Historically, some conspiracies have been proven by presenting in evidence the actual documents or contracts of the price-fixing scheme. When such documents are not prepared or not discovered, circumstantial evidence is presented to establish the conspiracy. Meetings of competitors are often used as evidence of a conspiracy. In addition, business firms that sell their products at the same price are behaving "parallel," and such behavior may imply a conspiracy. "Conscious parallelism" of the competitors in following the same practices is often asserted as evidence of conspiracy. The following case deals with the question of evidence of conspiracy and whether the "parallel behavior" of several competitors was the result of the independent business judgment by each competitor or the result of a conspiracy.

Esco Corporation v. United States

340 F. 2d 1000 (1965)
U.S. Court of Appeals (9th Cir.)

This is an appeal from a jury verdict convicting appellant corporation of violating Section 1 of the Sherman Act by means of its participation in an alleged price-fixing conspiracy, admittedly a *per se* violation of the Act. . . .

The "central criminal design" charged herein was the restraint of trade by fixing prices on stainless steel pipe and tubing within the described market area. But, it is contended, Esco's "relationship" to the two . . . [Los Angeles] meetings and the Salt Lake City meeting of the competitors was "perfectly legal. . . ." [Defendant's] counsel [argues] "there is a compelled inference" that Tubesales, the biggest competitor, called the meeting "not to ask for agreement, but simply to announce" its own pricing plans. Were we triers of fact, we might well ask if this were so, what purpose was to be served by a meeting of competitors?

Nor are we so naive as to believe that a formal signed-and-sealed contract or written resolution would conceivably be adopted at a meeting of price-fixing conspirators in this day and age. In fact, the typical price-fixing agreement is usually accomplished in a contrary manner.

While particularly true of price-fixing conspiracies, it is a well recognized law that any conspiracy can ordinarily only be proved by inferences drawn from relevant and competent circumstantial evidence, including the conduct of the defendants charged. . . . A knowing wink can mean more than words. Let us suppose five competitors meet on several occasions, discuss their problems, and one finally states—"I won't fix prices with any of you, but here is what I am going to do—put the price of my gidget at X dollars, now you all do what you want." He then leaves the meeting. Competitor number two says—"I don't care whether number one does what he says he's going to do or not; nor do I care what the rest of you do, but I am going to price my gidget at X dollars." Number three makes a similar statement—"My price is X dollars." Number four says not a word. All leave and fix "their" prices at "X" dollars.

We do not say the foregoing illustration compels an inference in this case that the competitors' conduct constituted a price-fixing conspiracy, including an agreement to so conspire, but neither can we say, as a matter of law, that an inference of no agreement is compelled. As in so many other instances, it remains a question for the trier of fact to consider and determine what inference appeals to it (the jury) as most logical and persuasive after it has heard all the evidence as to what these competitors had done before such meetings, and what actions they took thereafter, or what actions they did not take.

An accidental or incidental price uniformity, or even "pure" conscious parallelism of prices is, standing alone, not unlawful. Nor is an individual competitor's sole decision to follow a price leadership standing alone, a violation of law. But we do not find that factual situation here.

It is not necessary to find an express agreement, either oral or written, in order to find a conspiracy, but it is sufficient that a concert of action be contemplated and that defendants conform to the arrangement. . . . Mutual consent need not be bottomed on express agreement, for any conformance to an agreed or contemplated pattern of conduct will warrant an inference of conspiracy. . . . An exchange of words is not required. . . . Thus not only

action, but even a lack of action, may be enough from which to infer a combination or conspiracy. . . .

Applying these rules to the facts at hand, the jury came to an opposite conclusion from that which [Esco] urges, and the fact that Esco's involvement was in but two of ten allegedly conspiratorial situations does not absolve Esco from participation in the entire conspiracy if its involvement in the two was unlawful and knowingly and purposely performed. We hold that sufficient evidence existed for the jury to find participation in a price-fixing conspiracy.

Questions
1. How many different types of evidence of a conspiracy or agreement are discussed in *Esco?*
2. Is pure "conscious parallelism" illegal? Is it evidence? Is it enough evidence to have a jury decide? What can the defendants do to rebut the evidence of their "parallel" behavior to avoid an adverse jury verdict?
3. Is price leadership illegal?
4. Do you think it is wise to attend your competitor's announcement of new pricing plans? Is it ever wise to consult with your competitors concerning prices?

MODERN PRICE-FIXING

The prices for many public purchases and construction projects are set by competitive bidding. Specifications for the project are published and bids are invited. Later, the sealed bids are opened, with the lowest bid winning. Sometimes bidding rings are formed whereby the bids are rigged so that the ring's chosen winner submits the lowest bid (but a bid higher than under a truly competitive bidding process). These rings are clearly illegal under Section 1 of the Sherman Act.

The most famous bidding ring involved the makers of heavy electrical equipment, prosecuted and convicted in 1960.[2] The conspirators, including General Electric and Westinghouse, had met under assumed names in various meeting places, ranging from luxury hotels to backwoods cabins in Canada. They had utilized codes in written correspondence, which was sent to their home addresses rather than to their offices. Oral communications were limited to public telephones. Despite their efforts to maintain secrecy, 29 companies and 45 of their officers pleaded guilty or offered no defense in criminal suits when faced with the evidence the government had acquired. Seven officers served brief jail sentences and the companies were fined $1.9 million. Thereafter, over 1900 private treble-damage suits were filed by victims of the illegal price-rigging, and over $405 million was paid out by the conspirators to settle the suits.

Thereafter, to avoid the strong price competition in the turbine-generator market following the breakup of the conspiracy, General Electric (GE) announced in 1963 a new pricing system. The price system involved the publication of a price formula, publication of all orders and prices offered, and a "price protection" clause in all sales contracts, which guaranteed customers that discounts from the formula system would be retroactively applied to all sales during the preceding six months. This self-penalty provision and publication of pricing data assured GE's competitors that it would not give selective price discounts. Westinghouse immediately copied GE's plan, and identical price levels followed. The Justice Department did not challenge this arrangement until the 1970s. Finally, a consent decree was negotiated in December 1976, in which the pricing scheme was withdrawn, but no penalties or damages were assessed against General Electric or Westinghouse.[3]

Questions

1. The private utilities that purchased the electrical generators from the price-fixers did not complain of the high prices. In addition, the damage claims of the utilities were regarded by many as meek. Can you offer an explanation of why these regulated utilities were not more aggressive?
2. Which method of "price-fixing" is safer for the company—GE's secret rendezvous with competitors or its announced pricing systems? Is either method acceptable to the public?

Beyond the big case against GE and Westinghouse, other price-fixing agreements were prosecuted in the 1960s on a wide range of national markets, such as eyeglasses, soap, cheese, watches, electrical lamps, explosives, typewriters, ball bearings, newspaper print, stainless steel, fertilizer, and chemicals. Even small-scale price-fixing arrangements were attacked in such markets as auto body repairs, fire extinguishers, ready-mix cement, Hawaiian package tours, paper labels, Korean wigs, timber, Utah egg dealers, construction firms, gypsum, industrial laundries, school dairy products, travel agents, and bakeries.

One of the larger cases in the 1970s involved 23 major producers of paper board boxes used for food, drugs, household supplies, and textiles.[4] The criminal suits against 48 corporate officials resulted in *nolo contendere* pleas or convictions. In prosecuting these cases, the Department of Justice announced new and tougher guidelines for price-fixing penalties. The guidelines call for an average 18-month jail term, an average $50,000 fine, and fines on the company equaling 10 percent of sales in the product. Nevertheless, the judge refused the Department of Justice's recommendation and set jail sentences that averaged 10 days for 15 of the 49 managers found guilty. Fines assessed by the judge averaged $5000.

Questions
1. Is the variety of products involved in price-fixing schemes surprising? Is this "record" embarrassing to the business community?
2. Are the Department of Justice's guidelines for price-fixing penalties too tough? Were the sentences imposed by the trial judge too lenient?

UNRECOVERABLE DAMAGES

In the *Illinois Brick*[5] case, consumers of concrete block sued to recover damages caused by price-fixing by producers. The consumers were represented by the attorney general of Illinois. The Supreme Court held that these consumers could not recover because they were only "indirect" purchasers who had bought from wholesalers. The Court held that the wholesalers, the direct purchasers, could sue because they were in privity with the price-fixers. The Court was fearful of "multiple liability" if it permitted the consumer, the remote purchaser, to recover damages also. The Court avoided this possibility by ruling that the remote purchaser could not recover any damages passed on by the wholesalers.

The *Illinois Brick* decision could restrict the deterrent force of private treble-damage claims against price-fixers. It is conceivable that wholesalers could pass on the price-rigging charges and suffer no harm. Such wholesalers would lack incentive to file antitrust claims against their suppliers. And if the wholesalers chose not to sue to recoup their "higher costs," the final consumer would have no recourse.

Questions
1. Should the difficulty of assigning damages between the wholesalers and consumers preclude the consumers' right to sue?
2. Should Congress, by amending the antitrust laws, overturn the *Illinois Brick* decision?

EXCHANGE OF PRICE INFORMATION

U.S. v. Container Corp.
393 U.S. 333 (1968)
Supreme Court of the United States

Justice Douglas

This is a civil antitrust action charging a price-fixing agreement in violation of Section 1 of the Sherman Act.

The case as proved is unlike any other price decisions we have rendered. There was here an exchange of price information but no agreement to adhere to a price schedule as in . . . *United States* v. *Socony-Vacuum Oil Co.* . . . There was here an exchange of information concerning specific sales to identified customers, not a statistical report on the average cost to all members, without identifying the parties to specific transactions. Here all that was present was a request by each defendant of its competitor for information as to the most recent price charged or quoted, whenever it needed such information and whenever it was not available from another source. Each defendant on receiving that request usually furnished the data with the expectation that it would be furnished reciprocal information when it wanted it. That concerted action is of course sufficient to establish the combination or conspiracy, the initial ingredient of a violation of Section 1 of the Sherman Act.

There was of course freedom to withdraw from the agreement. But the fact remains that when a defendant requested and received price information, it was affirming its willingness to furnish such information in return.

* * *

The result of this reciprocal exchange of prices was to stabilize prices though at a downward level. Knowledge of a competitor's price usually meant matching that price. The continuation of some price competition is not fatal to the Government's case. The limitation or reduction of price competition brings the case within the ban, for as we held in *United States* v.

Socony-Vacuum Oil Co., interference with the setting of price by free market forces is unlawful *per se*. Price information exchange in some markets may have no effect on a truly competitive price. But the corrugated container industry is dominated by relatively few sellers. The product is fungible, and the competition for sales is price. The demand is inelastic, as buyers place orders only for immediate, short-run needs. The exchange of price data tends toward price uniformity. For a lower price does not mean a larger share of the available business but a sharing of the existing business at a lower return. Stabilizing prices as well as raising them is within the ban of Section 1 of the Sherman Act. As we said in *United States* v. *Socony-Vacuum Oil Co.*, "in terms of market operations stabilization is but one form of manipulation." The inferences are irresistible that the exchange of price information has had an anticompetitive effect in the industry, chilling the vigor of price competition.

Price is too critical, too sensitive a control to allow it to be used even in an informal manner to restrain competition.

Questions
1. Is the exchange of price information by competitors illegal *per se?* Is the purpose of the exchange to fix prices? Is the effect of the exchange to fix prices?
2. The first element of a Section 1 violation, the joint action, is clearly established by the agreement to exchange price information. However, the government has to establish that the effect of the exchange of price information is to stabilize or fix prices. What proofs were offered in *Container Corporation* of price stabilization?

A trade association is a voluntary association of business competitors existing for the purpose of promoting their businesses through cooperative activity. Most trade associations engage in collecting and disseminating price information. A trade association of hardwood manufacturers operated an interchange of reports on inventory, production, prices, and sales, with a commentary added by the compiler of statistics. In reporting their information to the association, the members disclosed prices on closed transactions, current prices being offered, and future price intentions. The association reports identified sellers and their price quotations and the names of buyers associated with particular purchases. Moreover, the reports of the association were not available to buyers. When the Department of Justice charged the plan constituted a combination to restrain pricing in hardwood lumber, the association members argued that "perfect competition," as economic theory explains, requires those participating in the market to have complete knowledge of market conditions. This information exchange, they argued, was simply the means of providing market information to industry sellers.

The Supreme Court rejected the defendants' arguments and held the association's activities in violation of Section 1. The Court remarked that the published reports were not available to both sellers and buyers as is theorized in "perfect competition." Moreover, the Court pointed out that the competitive market process and its market information flow do not include a "skilled interpretor . . . to insistently recommend harmony of action likely to prove profitable in proportion as it is unitedly pursued."[6]

Questions
1. If a trade association is to have a price-reporting service, what ingredients should it avoid in order to be lawful?
2. Many have argued that nonmembers of a trade association cannot be certain that the data furnished by a group of sellers is correct. Accordingly, they have urged that price-reporting in industries become a public function to be handled by the government or a regulated enterprise. Do you agree?

ALLOCATING MARKETS

Agreements between competitors to divide markets on a customer or geographic basis are often referred to as horizontal customer or territorial allocations. These agreements can have a greater anticompetitive effect than price-fixing among competitors because price-fixers may still compete on product quality or additional services rendered. In contrast, competitors who agree not to compete in geographic markets or for different customers completely eliminate competition.

Almost from the beginning, the Court has declared that allocation of markets among competitors is illegal *per se*. Two modern cases have reaffirmed that position.

In 1967 the Supreme Court held the division of markets accomplished by a trademark licensing system was illegal.[7] There were 30 licensees who owned substantially all the stock of the licenser, Sealy. Sealy's board of directors was composed of five members from the licensee-stockholder group. The Court characterized the licenser as a joint venture of the stockholder-licensees and, therefore, a horizontal combination. Since the licenser, dominated by the licensees, allocated exclusive territories to the licensees, the Court found this territorial arrangement to be a horizontal market allocation by the licensees and illegal *per se*.

In the *Topco* case, regional supermarket chains joined together to form Topco Associates, Inc., as a group-buying operation.[8] Topco thereafter obtained private label brands for its members. Members of the Topco combination limited the location of their stores to designated territories, which eliminated intrabrand competition between them. They argued that there were still plenty of other grocery stores within the territories where they had eliminated competition among themselves. Topco members argued that their arrangement enabled them to compete more vigorously with the private labels of the national chains (inter-brand competition). The lower court agreed with Topco and dismissed the case. The Supreme Court reversed in 1972 and found the allocation of territories to be a horizontal restraint and, therefore, a *per se* violation of Section 1. The Supreme Court noted that Topco had no authority under the Sherman Act to determine the respective values of intrabrand and interbrand competition. The Court, in both *Sealy* and *Topco,* was not willing to balance the procompetitive effects in the interbrand market against the elimination of intrabrand competition among private brand sellers.

GROUP BOYCOTTS

Klor's v. Broadway-Hale Stores
359 U.S. 207 (1959)
Supreme Court of the United States

Justice Black

Klor's, Inc., operates a retail store on Mission Street, San Francisco, California; Broadway-Hale Stores, Inc., a chain of department stores, operates one of its stores next door. The two stores compete in the sale of radios, television sets, refrigerators and other household appliances. . . .

Klor's brought this action to treble damages and injunction in the United States District Court.

In support of its claim Klor's . . . [alleged]: [M]anufacturers and distributors of such well-known brands as General Electric, RCA, Admiral, Zenith, Emerson and others have conspired among themselves and with Broadway-Hale either not to sell to Klor's or to sell to it only at discriminatory prices and highly un-

favorable terms. Broadway-Hale had used its "monopolistic" buying power to bring about this situation. . . . The concerted refusal to deal with Klor's has seriously handicapped its ability to compete and has already caused it a great loss of profits, goodwill, reputation and prestige.

The defendants did not dispute these allegations, but sought summary judgment and dismissal of the complaint for failure to state a cause of action. They submitted unchallenged affidavits which showed that there were hundreds of other household appliance retailers, some within a few blocks of Klor's who sold many competing brands of appliances, including those the defendants refused to sell to Klor's. From the allegations of the complaints, and from the affidavits supporting the motion for summary judgment, the District Court concluded that the controversy was a "purely private quarrel" between Klor's and Broadway-Hale, which did not amount to a "public wrong proscribed by the [Sherman] Act." On this ground the complaint was dismissed and summary judgment was entered for the defendants. . . . [I]t held that here the required public injury was missing since "there was no charge or proof that by any act of defendants the price, quantity, or quality offered the public was affected, nor that there was any intent or purpose to effect a change in, or an influence on, prices, quantity, or quality. . . ." The holding, if correct, means that unless the opportunities for customers to buy in a competitive market are reduced, a group of powerful businessmen may act in concert to deprive a single merchant, like Klor, of the goods he needs to compete effectively. . . .

We think Klor's allegations clearly show one type of trade restraint and public harm the Sherman Act forbids, and that defendants' affidavits provide no defense to the charges. Section 1 of the Sherman Act makes illegal any contract, combination, or conspiracy in restraint of trade. . . . In the landmark case of *Standard Oil Co.* v. *United States,* 221 U.S. 1, this court read Section 1 to prohibit those classes of contracts or acts which the common law deemed to be undue restraints of trade and those which new times and economic conditions would make unreasonable. . . . The Court recognized that there were some agreements whose validity depended on the surrounding circumstances. It emphasized, however, that there were classes of restraints which from their "nature or character" were unduly restrictive, and hence forbidden by both the common law and the statute. . . . Group boycotts, or concerted refusals by traders to deal

with other traders, have long been held to be in the forbidden category. They have not been saved by allegations that they were reasonable in the specific circumstances, nor by a failure to show that they "fixed or regulated prices, parcelled out or limited production, or brought about a deterioration in quality."

* * *

Plainly the allegations of this complaint disclose such a boycott. This is not a case of a single trader refusing to deal with another, nor even of a manufacturer and a dealer agreeing to an exclusive distributorship. Alleged in this complaint is a wide combination consisting of manufacturers, distributors and a retailer. This combination takes from Klor's its freedom to buy appliances in an open competitive market and drives it out of business as a dealer in the defendants' products. It deprives the manufacturers and distributors of their freedom to sell to Klor's at the same prices and conditions made available to Broadway-Hale, and in some instances forbids them from selling to it on any terms whatsoever. It interferes with the natural flow of interstate commerce. It clearly has, by its "nature" and "character" a monopolistic tendency. As such it is not to be tolerated merely because the victim is just one merchant whose business is so small that his destruction makes little difference to the economy. Monopoly can as surely thrive by the elimination of such small businessmen, one at a time, as it can by driving them out in large groups. In recognition of this fact the Sherman Act has consistently been read to forbid all contracts and combinations "which 'tend to create a monopoly,'" whether "the tendency is a creeping one" or "one that proceeds at full gallop."

Questions

1. The district court ruled that these facts merely demonstrated the existence of a "private dispute" without any "public wrong." What did the court mean by no "public wrong proscribed by the Act"?

2. Why did the Supreme Court feel these facts reveal a "public wrong"?
3. Would there be illegal behavior if each distributor independently refused to deal with Klor?

RELATIONS WITH COMPETITORS

Cases have revealed that Section 1 of the Sherman Act prohibits conspiracies that unreasonably restrain trade. Some kind of *joint or concerted* action between two or more persons or companies must exist for Section 1 of the Sherman Act to apply. But there need not be anything so formal as a written contract; "understandings" are enough, and these can be inferred by the court or jury from the way the parties have conducted themselves. Any kind of a mutual understanding that gives the parties a basis for expecting that a business practice or decision will be adopted by one and all, or at least not opposed by the others, is sufficient to establish joint action.

For Section 1 to be violated, the joint action must have as its *purpose or effect* an unreasonable restraint of trade. If the *purpose* is unreasonable, it does not matter whether the action taken by the parties is successful or fails. Such restraints of trade that are in their purpose considered unreasonable are identified as *per se* violations. Federal enforcement policy allows criminal prosecution for these *per se* offenses, which include the following.

Price-Fixing.   This agreement need not be on a specific price. The law is violated by agreements on maximums or minimums, on a common sales agent, on terms or conditions of sale such as credit terms or discounts, or even on the mere exchange or price information if this has a stabilizing effect on prices. The agreement of price-fixing schemes can be inferred from a course of conduct or from a history of telephone calls, meetings, and the like between competitors followed by uniform price action. Price-fixing, in whatever form, is the antitrust violation most frequently prosecuted criminally.

Dividing Territory.   Competitors may not agree as to geographical areas in which each will or will not sell. Any course of action whereby competitors avoid each other's territory may be a basis for a court finding of such an illegal agreement.

Dividing Customers.   Competitors may not agree that each will sell to a particular customer or class of customers and not to another. Neither may competitors agree on which of them will make any specific sales.

Dividing Products.   Basically, competitors may not agree that one will not make or sell products made or sold by another.

Limiting Production.   Competitors may not agree to restrict or limit production or production capacity. Violations of this form often involve a quota system.

Boycotting.   Competing sellers must not agree among themselves not to sell to a particular customer or reseller, whatever the reason.

Suppression of Quality Competition.   Competitors may not agree to restrict the development of improvements in the quality of their products. Nor may competitors agree to limit research for quality improvements. Most agreements of this type are, in effect, agreements not to compete and are contrary to the basic purpose of antitrust laws.

To avoid suspicion of a *per se* violation, there should be no conversations or communications of any kind with competitors concerning these kinds of agreements. If any communications are made, a document should be prepared indicating the extent of the conversation and how the conversation was limited to avoid any violation of antitrust law. If one of these subjects comes up in conversation at a trade meeting attended by company employees, employees should terminate the conversation immediately or leave the gathering. Again, documentation of the incident should be recorded indicating the facts and the employee's noninvolvement. In all *per se* situations it makes no difference that an apparently sound business consideration may be involved also. There are no acceptable excuses or such a thing as being just a "little bit" guilty.

Besides the *per se* offenses under the Sherman Act, the legality of other joint action by competitors turns on the reasonableness, under the circumstances, of any restraint on competition. Reasonableness of such restraints is measured in terms of both the purpose of the restraint and its effect on competition. All these potential restraints must be tested on an individual basis. However, one should remember that a reasonable business purpose will not excuse joint action that has an unreasonable effect on competition.

INTERLOCKING DIRECTORATES

Corporate law does not prohibit directors from being directors also with competing corporations. However, such common interlocking directorships pose threats to the level and vigor of competition between the interlocking firms. While common or interlocking directorates could be prohibited by the Sherman Act, the difficulties of proof under that Act normally preclude successful prosecution.

CLAYTON ACT, SECTION 8

The attitude against "interlocks" was sufficiently pervasive among members of Congress in 1914 to pass Section 8 of the Clayton Act. However, the enforcement of Section 8 of the Clayton Act has not been spectacular. The first definitive interpretation of Section 8 by the Supreme Court did not occur until 1953.[10]

Moreover, Section 8 of the Clayton Act has limited coverage. For one, it applies only to horizontal interlocks, rather than to vertical or conglomerate interlocks. Corporations that have common directors, and that buy and sell from each other, are not uncommon. Yet such vertical interlocks are not covered by Section 8. Likewise, an interlock between banks and commercial or industrial corporations is not prohibited.

In addition, "indirect" interlocks are lawful. For example, partners of an investment banking house could each be directors of different competing corporations. Finally, it should be noted that only directors are covered under Section 8. Therefore, an officer or an employee who is not a director of the corporation, could be on the board of directors of any other corporation, competitor or not. The Federal Trade Commission has complained of these "loopholes" in Section 8. It has argued that these alternatives provide enterprises with means to "link together" as strongly as through common directors.

FUTURE LEGISLATION?

In January 1978, the staff of the Subcommittee on Reports, Accounting and Management of the Senate issued a study on "Interlocking Directorates Among the Major U.S. Corporations."[11] The following excerpt from the study identifies some continuing concerns with interlocking relationships and possible courses of legislative action in the future.

Part II. Summary, Conclusions and Recommendations

*   *   *

From the study, the staff has concluded that American business is highly concentrated across industry lines—perhaps more concentrated today than it was in 1913 when Louis Brandeis wrote of the "endless chain," and in 1955 when C. Wright Mills spoke of the "power elite."

The 130 major companies in the study represented assets totalling over $1 trillion, about 25 percent of the assets of all U.S. corporations. According to the computer analysis, these companies at the top of corporate America were heavily concentrated through interlocking directorates. Except for 7 investment advisory companies, each of the 123 major firms connected on an average with half of the other companies in the study through a total of 530 direct and 12,193 indirect interlocks. These corporate connections were intensified at the upper end of the scale: 9 firms reached 90–99 companies; 22 firms reached 80–89 companies; and 22 firms reached 70–79 companies.

A more striking picture of corporate concentration appeared among the 13 largest companies in the study. With few exceptions, each of these firms directly or indirectly interlocked with each other. In addition, each of the top 13 reached an average of 70 percent of the other major companies through a total of 240 direct and 5547 indirect interlocks. This is a conservative statistic since the data base did not include the director interlocks of the top 13 firms' 486 subsidiaries.

*   *   *

The 16 leading financial institutions were heavily linked. Commercial banking directors clustered on insurance company boards and insurance directors met on banking company boards. Banking and insurance company directors also interlocked substantially on the boards of the largest industrials, utilities, transportation, and retailing organizations.

* * *

Among the eight major energy companies, three of the largest firms were indirectly interlocked with each of their competitors. One industrial, Caterpillar Tractor, hosted as many as five of the eight energy majors on its board. The No. 1 energy company, Exxon, directly interlocked with the first, third, fourth, fifth, sixth largest corporations in the United States.

In the rapidly changing telecommunications industry the giant, A.T.&.T., indirectly linked with its closest rival, IBM, 22 times. Directly represented at the A.T.&T. board table were 8 of the 13 largest companies in the nation.

* * *

All four broadcasting organizations (ABC, CBS, NBC and Westinghouse) were represented on the board of the country's largest international banker, Citicorp, and the network companies linked with each other on the boards of other financial companies and industrials.

Such interlocking directorates among the Nation's very largest corporations may provide mechanisms for stabilizing prices, controlling supply and restraining competition. They can have a profound effect on business attempts to influence Government policies. They can impact on corporate decisions as to the type and quality of products and services to be marketed in the United States and overseas. They can influence company policies with respect to employee rights, compensation and job conditions. They can bear on corporate policies with respect to environmental and social issues and possibly, control the shape and direction of the Nation's economy.

Recommendations for Legislative Consideration

The staff believes that the matters disclosed in this study justify congressional oversight and examination of new legislation directed toward breaking up the close directorate ties among the larger corporations and providing the public with a better understanding of how corporate policies are made and who is responsible for making them.

Accordingly, the following proposals are recommended for consideration:

First, Congress should enact a general prohibition against any officer or director of a company with over $1 billion in assets or sales from being an officer or director of any other company of similar size.

This proscription would apply to all lines of business, including regulated and non-regulated enterprises. It would be a flat prohibition against multiple management representation involving two or more companies above the $1 billion threshold.

This may sound like a harsh proposal. Indeed, it is, because its purpose is to effect dynamic changes in the composition of major company boards. Its objective is to separate the larger corporate managements in order to encourage more innovative and competitive corporate policies and to avoid possible conflicts of interest.

The idea is not a new one. It emerged from the recommendations of Louis Brandeis in 1913 after his study of the Pujo Committee report. It was suggested by a top official of the Antitrust Division in 1950 and by Senator Humphrey in 1951. It was implicit in the recommendations of the staff of the Celler Antitrust Subcommittee in 1965.

The statutory restriction would be easier to enforce than existing antitrust statutes since it is a flat prohibition without exceptions. Furthermore, such legislation may be more palatable to both the business and political sectors since it seeks to reach concentration by restructuring the composition of major corporate boards rather than the corporate organizations themselves. At least, it would be a first step in meeting the problems of shared monopolies and unbalanced competition.

The reasoning behind this proposal is that, on analysis, those companies with the closest directorate ties are the industry leaders with over $1 billion in sales or assets, and it is at this level that the potentials for abuse reach their intensity on a national scale, and the impact on corporate policies can be the most severe.

Second, Congress should amend Section 8 of the Clayton Act and other relevant interlocking directorate statutes, to prohibit all types of interlocks between actual and potential competitors, and to prohibit interlocks involving actual and potential customers, suppliers and sources of credit or capital. Such prohibitions may have to be specially tailored to meet the interlock problems within the regulatory jurisdictions, but in the nonregulated areas, they should be given a sweeping effect. Legislation along this line was recommended in the Celler Antitrust Subcommittee staff report. It has recently received renewed interest in the subcommittees of the Judiciary and Commerce committees of the House.

Such prohibitions should be made applicable to any corporation in interstate commerce which has sales or assets over a prescribed amount. The million dollar threshold in Section 8 of the Clayton Act is too low. But a $100 million limit may be too high. Further investigation is needed as to an appropriate cutoff.

Third, the regulatory agencies should require current and complete reporting of interlocking directorships by the companies under their respective jurisdictions and make the information publicly available. The agencies have the general authority to obtain the data. There is nothing confidential about it. . . .

* * *

Fourth, the appropriate regulatory agencies should adopt rules for requiring diversified representation on the boards of companies under their jurisdictions. For instance, consideration should be given to insisting that at least one-third of the board membership be representative of consumers, minorities, employees and the public generally. A company should be required to submit its balanced slate annually to the jurisdictional agency for approval. Companies continuing to do business without agency approval should be subject to penalties and administrative action. Again, an appropriate cutoff may be necessary for effective enforcement.

This also may be a harsh proposal. But it is justifiable. . . . Each of the 130 major boards, and those major and minor boards with which they directly interlock, are composed primarily of corporate officials or directors or partners in firms whose basic orientation is from the business sector. There are few voices from the people to establish a broader dialogue as to board decisions.

* * *

Finally, consideration should be given to rulemaking and, where necessary, legislation seeking to make board meetings of the larger U.S. corporations open to the public. These entities have as great a responsibility to the people as do the Federal agencies which are required to open their meetings by the Government in the Sunshine Act [enacted in 1976]. Perhaps, there should be a "Business in the Sunshine Act" requiring board openness, but like the Federal statute, containing provisions for closure of the meetings when trade secrets, privileged and/or financial information, or personnel matters are to be discussed.

The staff understands that open discussions of corporate plans and policies can have significant effects on a company's securities or on its business reputation. However, the value of a major corporate board being open to public understanding may far outweigh the potential adverse impact of open deliberations.

In conclusion, the staff appreciates the sincere interests on the part of corporate executives to surround themselves with experienced advisors from the business community. It understands that representatives from the financial sector can be helpful on the boards of nonfinancial corporations, and that officers and directors of industrial and commercial entities can be useful to financial institutions. However, the staff feels that the use of the interlocking directorate as a management device may have gone too far. As shown in the analysis and material produced by this study, it may have already crossed the threshold of private enterprise and entered the domain of private government.

Questions

1. Identify potential dangers associated with the 530 direct and 12,193 indirect directorate interlocks between 123 major firms in the United States.
2. Should Congress prohibit the officers and directors of any company with over $1 billion dollars in assets or sales from being an officer or director of any other company of similar size?
3. Should Section 8 of the Clayton Act be amended to prohibit all types of interlocks, whether actual or potential, horizontal or vertical?
4. Should regulatory agencies require current and complete reporting of interlocking directorships?
5. Should the law require diversified representation of society on the boards of companies?
6. Should the board meetings of large U.S. corporations be open to the public?

CONCLUSION

The long trend of cases against anticompetitive horizontal combinations has created rather clear lines against price-fixing and related collusive activities. However, the continuing successful prosecutions against these practices reveal that outright collusion still exists. The remedies imposed by the courts include fines and injunctive orders to stop conspiring. Many criticize these remedies as too weak and call for higher fines against conspirators to eliminate the profits obtained by conspiracy.

Beyond these underground conspiracies, implicit or tacic collusion is widespread. The horizontal merger movements of past eras have made a significant portion of American industry oligopolistic. When a small group of firms make up an industry, coordinated selling and pricing become not only possible but probable in light of the sellers' recognition of their interdependence. Price cuts are not made because competitors can easily retaliate, and all sellers would gain less revenue if the demand for the product was not sufficiently elastic. Likewise, price increases are followed, and identical prices result from these supposedly independent but concurrent actions of the major sellers. Smaller sellers are not likely to be aggressive price competitors because of their fear of retaliation by the giants. The result of this interdependence is often characterized as noncompetitive price-fixing. And as the cases reveal, present antitrust laws do not afford much opportunity of relief for the public.

Structural economists have criticized the failure to dissolve dominant firms in oligopolistic situations. However, the Department of Justice has been rebuffed by the courts in its effort to secure divestiture of oligopolistic firms. Moreover, Congress has not seen fit to modify the Sherman Act to apply to price leadership, oligopolistic industry structure, or indirect interlocking directorates. Consequently, antitrust efforts against horizontal combinations forming joint price and marketing policies have been mixed—lenient penalties have been given in cases of strict illegality for conspiracies and no success has resulted against the problem of oligopoly.

DISCUSSION QUESTIONS

1. A shipyard on Staten Island was sold by Bethlehem Steel to a trading company. The deed included a covenant, binding on all subsequent purchasers, that the property would not be used for the construction or repair of ships or harbor craft (except pleasure craft) for 20 years. Sound Ship Company, a corporation in the business of building and repairing barges, wanted to purchase the shipyard from the trading company and sought a waiver of the deed restriction by Bethlehem, which was refused unless Sound Ship paid an additional $250,000. Sound Ship leased property elsewhere and eventually went out of business.

    Bethlehem had remained in the ship construction and repair business in New York harbor at another site but sold the Staten Island yard because of a decline in the shipbuilding industry.

    Sound Ship claims that the deed covenant violates Section 1 of the Sherman Act, entitling Sound Ship to treble damages. What is the result?

2. In order to "protect the manufacturer, laborer, retailer and consumer" from the marketing of copies of original clothing and textile designs, textile and garment manufacturers formed the Fashion Originators' Guild of America. To prevent the practice they characterized as "style piracy," guild members obtained agreements from retailers across the nation under which the retailers were to cooperate with the guild by refusing to stock "copies" of guild members' original designs. In addition, member textile manufacturers agreed to sell fabric only to garment manufacturers dealing with cooperating retailers. Members' prices and production were not regulated or affected, nor did the quality of their products deteriorate. "Copies" consistently sold at lower prices than originals. Garment and textile designs are not protected under copyright or patent law.

    Are the guild's practices lawful?

3. The American Medical Association (AMA) restricts a doctor's solicitation of patients by advertising. It also restricts competition among doctors for a job in a hospital or business. Further, the AMA labels unethical the participation of a doctor with nonphysicians such as dentists or psychologists in the ownership or management of a health care organization. Are these restraints on physicians by the AMA in violation of antitrust?

4. Beer wholesalers generally extended credit to their retailers in the Fresno area for periods between 30 and 42 days at no interest, and precise credit terms for various individual retailers varied considerably. The wholesalers then began to restrict the credit they offered, and eventually stopped extending credit at all.

   A group of beer retailers contends that these actions constitute an illegal *per se* horizontal agreement to fix prices. The wholesalers believe that the elimination of credit terms is not price-fixing.

   What is your analysis?

5. dupont Company and Ethyl Corporation were the leading producers among four manufacturers of lead-based gasoline antiknock compounds. dupont and Ethyl followed a practice whereby they would announce new price increases several days in advance of a 30-day notice that they had contracted to give customers. Competitors then would decide whether to match the increase announced. This early warning allowed all competitors to reach the same price level by the day the contractual notice was required. The government charged the companies with price-signaling, which informally, but effectively, set prices.

   What decision?

6. Sears, Roebuck and Co. and the BF Goodrich Co. are competitors in the sale of home appliances, automotive supplies, sporting goods, tires, radio and television sets, and toys. They compete in 97 communities located in 31 states through 110 retail stores of Sears and 112 retail stores of Goodrich, located in the same communities. Sidney Wineburg has been director of both Sears and Goodrich for many years. Are the directorships held by Wineburg lawful?

7. Ernest Martin was a stockholder and director of F & M Productions, a corporation that produced musical comedies on Broadway and in other legitimate theaters. Martin and two others acquired control of Paramount Pictures by a purchase of 9 percent of Paramount stock.

   Paramount has invested money in stage plays as a backer, has acquired motion picture rights to certain Broadway plays, and has granted stage production rights to others for plays based on Paramount motion pictures.

   Paramount Pictures sued Martin, claiming a violation of Section 8 of the Clayton Act. What position would Martin take?

8. Herbert Siegel and two others acquired control of Paramount Pictures by a purchase of 9 percent of Paramount stock. Siegel was then chairman of the

board of directors and principal stockholder in Baldwin-Montrose, a chemical company. Baldwin-Montrose owned 70 percent of the stock of General Artists Corporation (GAC), a large talent agency. Siegel was a director of GAC. GAC had an ownership interest in one television program. As a talent agency, GAC finds positions for clients and negotiates contracts on their behalf, and also acts as agent for television program producers, helping them to sell programs to the networks. GAC has supplied talent to Paramount.

Through its subsidiary corporations Paramount develops, produces, and packages television programs and licenses television exhibition of feature films.

On May 20, 1965, Siegel resigned as director of GAC. On May 26, 1965, Siegel was elected to Paramount's board of directors.

Paramount sued Siegel under Section 8 of the Clayton Act. What result?

SUGGESTED READINGS

Elzinga, K. G. and W. Breit, *The Antitrust Penalties: A Study in Law and Economics* (New Haven, Conn.: Yale University Press, 1976).

Kamerschen, David R., "An Economic Approach to the Detection and Proof of Collusion," *American Business Law Journal,* Vol. 17, No. 2, Summer 1979, pp. 193–210.

Loescher, Samuel M., "Economic Collusion, Civil Conspiracy, and Treble Damage Deterrents: The Sherman Act Breakthrough with Southern Plywood," *The Quarterly Review of Economics and Business,* Winter 1980, pp. 6–35.

Loutzenhiser, Janice, "The ERA Boycott and the Sherman Act," *American Business Law Journal,* Vo. 17, No. 4, Winter 1980, pp. 507–519.

Siedel, George J., III, "Multiple Listing Services and the Sherman Act: A New Chapter," *American Business Law Journal,* Vol. 20, No. 2, Summer 1982, pp. 267–276.

Sonnenfeld, J. and P. L. Lawrence, *Harvard Business Review,* July–August 1978, pp. 145–157.

Sullivan, Lawrence A., *Handbook of the Law of Antitrust* (St. Paul: West Publishing Co., 1977).

Whitman, Douglas, "Advertising By Professionals," *American Business Law Journal,* Vo. 16, No. 1, Spring 1978, pp. 39–66.

ENDNOTES

1. Adam Smith, *An Inquiry into the Nature and Causes of the Wealth of Nations* (London: J. M. Dent and Sons, Ltd., 1970), Vol. 1, Book 1, Chapter 10, Part II, p. 117.
2. See John G. Fuller, *The Gentlemen Conspirators* (New York: Grove Press, 1962).
3. *U.S.* v. *General Electric Co.,* "plaintiff's memorandum in support of a proposed modification to the final judgment entered on October 1, 1962, against each defendant," December 1976.
4. *U.S.* v. *Alton Box Board Co.,* 76 CR 199, N.D. Ill. (1977).
5. *Illinois Brick Co.* v. *Illinois,* 431 U.S. 720 (1977).
6. *American Column and Lumber Co.* v. *U.S.,* 257 U.S. 377, 394–412 (1912).

7. *U.S.* v. *Sealy, Inc.*, 388 U.S. 350 (1976).

8. *U.S.* v. *Topco Associates, Inc.*, 405 U.S. 596 (1972).

9. *California Motor Transport Co.* v. *Trucking Unlimited*, 404 U.S. 508 (1972).

10. *United States* v. *Sears, Roebuck and Co.*, 111 F. Supp. 614 (SD NY 1953).

11. Staff Study, Subcommittee on Reports, Accounting and Management of the Committee on Governmental Affairs, United States Senate, "Interlocking Directorates Among the Major U.S. Corporations" (Washington: U.S. Government Printing Office, 1978) pp. 1–999. Excerpt pp. 6–7.

chapter 12
VERTICAL COMBINATIONS

Since the manufacturer, wholesaler, and retailer are not operating at the same level of distribution, they are often not in direct competition with each other. However, the manufacturer and distributor may desire to enter into contractual relations that restrict competition. For example, a manufacturer may desire to impose resale restrictions on the distributors, thereby controlling the distributors' resale price, the territorial area of resale, or the customers to whom the distributor may resell. Beyond these efforts to impose resale policies, the manufacturer may also desire to restrict the distributors' freedom to sell competing brands, known as an exclusive dealing arrangement. These vertical resale restrictions and exclusive dealing arrangements are vertical agreements between manufacturers and distributors and, as such, are different from the horizontal agreements studied in Chapter 11.

As noted in Chapter 11, joint action by sellers or by buyers to eliminate competition among themselves is illegal. However, joint action by a seller and a buyer, a vertical arrangement, may also result in a lessening of competition, as was suggested in the analysis of vertical mergers in Chapter 10. Consequently, vertical contractual arrangements often have been challenged as contrary to antitrust goals. Vertical arrangements usually involve vertically imposed price control, consumer or territorial divisions, or exclusive dealings.

REASONS FOR VERTICAL COMBINATIONS

It should first be made clear that no manufacturer desires to allow its retailers to make above-normal profits. Such a position would imply that the manufacturer is willing to pay more than necessary for retailing services. Above-normal profits can be achieved by retailers only if they restrict sales to gain higher prices. Such sales restrictions could reduce the manufacturer's sales and, in effect, take money out of the manufacturer's own pocket. Consequently, when manufacturers attempt to impose vertical restraints on resale, it is because they believe such policies will induce dealer behavior that will make the distribution process more efficient. Additional profits for the retailer resulting from the manufacturer-imposed restrictions are gained at the retail level in exchange for distribution efficiencies or expanded sales efforts, which also accrue to the advantage of the manufacturer. The expanded sales through retail promotion may reduce unit costs for the manufacturer. The consumer may share these lower costs through long-term price reductions and obtain more services from the retail outlets.

The most common justification raised for vertical restraints is the optimization of sales effort by dealers through the elimination of "free riding." Selling involves the provision of information and persuasion. It is in the nature of some products that dealers may need to invest money and time in carrying a full line of models for display, instructing sales personnel in the product's features and comparative advantages, and explaining the product and its uses to potential consumers. The dealer, of course, will do these things only if the cost can be recaptured in the price at which the product is sold. Nevertheless, some dealers will perceive the opportunity to avoid these costs and capture the consumer by offering a lower price. Such dealers take a "free ride" on the other dealers' sales efforts. If free riding becomes common, no dealer will find it worthwhile to provide the sales effort that the manufacturer believes is optimal in the distribution of the products.

For the manufacturer to ensuer optimal dealer sales effort and avoid free riding, the manufacturer may divide dealer territories or fix minimum resale prices. When the product is of such a nature that it can be sold effectively through one or a few outlets in a given area, the manufacturer may employ the use of a few outlets with restricted market areas. However, where using many outlets in an area is a preferable marketing strategy, the manufacturer may choose to maintain the resale price charged by dealers. Such resale restrictions eliminate competition between the dealers who sell the manufacturer's brand. Alternative brands of other manufacturers continue to compete in the marketplace for the consumers' dollars. Consequently, vertical restraints eliminate *intrabrand* competition, but may enhance *interbrand* competition.

Many economists suggest that the degree to which vertical restraints are exercised should be left to the free determination of the marketplace. However, other economists have asserted that the elimination of intrabrand competition by the use of vertical restraints may be part of a method or means to achieve conspiratorial horizontal restraints by the manufacturer. If manufacturers agree to fix prices, they would have the ability, if vertical restraints were lawful, to impose their price-fixing scheme not only at the manufacturing level but also at the retail level. Consequently, they argue that it is preferable to disallow intrabrand restrictions at the retail level to frustrate manufacturer efforts to extend their conspiratorial price-fixing scheme all the way through the distribution channels. This is especially true, they argue, because the courts have been unwilling to eliminate monopolistic and oligopolistic industry structure at the manufacturing level. Consequently, tacit collusion and follow-the-leader pricing of competitors in oligopolistic industries make it easy for the manufacturer-competitors to achieve parallel behavior without being condemned by antitrust laws. With lawful vertical price-fixing, they can extend their power to the retail level. On the other hand, those in favor of vertical arrangements argue that the conspiracies by manufacturers should be detected at their source. Efficient distribution operations created by vertical restraints should not be outlawed as a technique to frustrate alleged conspiratorial conduct on a horizontal level.

Many opponents of vertical arrangements have argued that in some industries the intrabrand competition eliminated by vertical restraints is significant competition that should not be lost. The elimination of any intrabrand competition in industries where only a few brands exist would have adverse effects on consumer welfare. Even where brands proliferate, it is often asserted that intrabrand competition, for example in the auto industry, is significant. A vertical arrangement for an auto brand (Chevrolet, for instance) would eliminate significant price competition between dealerships selling the same brand. It is argued that such competition is too significant to be eliminated.

It is also argued that the higher profits achieved for retailers under a resale price maintenance program make possible larger expenditures for nonprice forms of competition only in the short run. In the long run, the higher prices and profits may simply invite proliferation of outlets or the entry of minor brands. Excess capacity thus develops at the distributor's level, with rising average costs and falling profits. Thereafter, distributors press the manufacturer to provide wider margins by raising the resale price or by reducing the factory price. Usually, argue the opponents to vertical price-fixing, higher prices for consumers would result. They point to the studies that have found that certain branded items could be purchased at prices averaging 19 percent lower in those areas where *intrabrand* price competition was possible than in those areas where the manufacturer eliminated such competition.

Finally, opponents argue that the independent judgment of small retailers is destroyed by vertical restraints and America's "free" economy is thereby eroded. Also, resale price maintenance is argued to contain an inflationary bias. All the arguments, both for and against vertical arrangements, have gained some constituency and force in the fashioning of antitrust rules. (See Figure 12-1.) Since economists have differed in their prescriptions regarding vertical arrangements, lawmakers have also vacillated and developed inconsistent rules.

VERTICAL PRICE RESTRAINTS

Vertical price control involves a manufacturer imposing a fixed price on the wholesaler or retailer as the product travels through the distribution channel to its final consumers. Such vertical control of prices after the manufacturer has

For	Against
Eliminate "free riding"	Facilitate collusion
Maximize sales promotion	Erode "free" economy
Maximize production to lower unit costs	Injure independents: price or supply squeeze
	May develop excess capacity

Figure 12.1 Arguments for and against vertical combinations.

passed title to others is often called *resale* price maintenance. This practice is usually limited to a manufacturer that is able to identify its product in the resale market in order to enforce compliance with its resale pricing policy. Therefore, resale price maintenance is usually applied in the sale of brand name products.

Usually, vertical price control is affected by means of a contract between a manufacturer and its distributors. The manufacturer inserts its desired resale price in the sales-purchase agreement, and the buyer promises to abide by the seller's desires. If the buyer fails to adhere to the fixed price, the seller can sue for damages if this type of provision is upheld as lawful.

FAIR TRADE LAWS

The antitrust authorities have historically argued that vertical contracts to fix resale prices are illegal restraints of trade in violation of Section 1 of the Sherman Act. As early as 1911, in *Dr. Miles Medical Co. v. John D. Part & Sons*, the Supreme Court held that contractual agreements designed to maintain retail prices after the manufacturer had parted with title to the goods were injurious to the public interest and illegal.[1] However, proponents of the practice of resale price maintenance have made various attempts to persuade Congress to legalize the practice. The impact of the Great Depression and the growth of chain and cut-rate stores solidified the efforts of various groups of small retailers and wholesalers (particularly druggists) for legalization of resale price maintenance, which they designated as "fair trade." The first "fair trade" act was passed by the California Legislature in 1931. In 1933 the California statute was amended so that a single agreement between a manufacturer and a distributor to fix the resale price of a trademarked product was to be applicable to all other distributors in the state even though the other distributors did not sign the price-maintenance contract. This *nonsigners* provision made the resale price control law a potent method for enforcing resale price maintenance on distributors. Any distributor having notice of the contractual arrangement with other dealers and not conforming to the resale prices so fixed was subject to legal suit for violating the price-fixing provision.

Since the initial resale price control laws applied only to intrastate transactions, the trade groups sought legalization of resale price maintenance contracts in the course of interstate commerce. Congress reacted with the passage of the Miller-Tydings Act in 1937 and added a nonsigner provision in the McGuire Act in 1952. These acts legalized resale price agreements in interstate commerce and removed these contracts from the prohibitions of the Sherman Act.

The fair trade movement was successful in obtaining laws in all states except Missouri, Texas, and Vermont and in the District of Columbia. The movement peaked in the early 1950s with 1600 manufacturers enforcing fair trade agreements.[2] However, legal setbacks at the state level and the growing pressures of competition slowly eroded the successes of the fair trade movement.

Besides the states that never passed the fair trade laws, several additional states, through their courts, ruled the fair trade statute legally unenforceable. Over a dozen other states refused to enforce the nonsignor provisions, which were declared to be an unconstitutional deprivation of due process of law for the nonsignors. Consequently, retailers in more than 20 states were able to ignore the manufacturers' prescribed minimum prices. Moreover, enterprising business people opened mail order houses in nonfair trade areas and shipped branded merchandise at reduced prices to customers in the fair trade states. Federal courts had ruled that the states could not enjoin the shipment of interstate merchandise into their area.[3] Moreover, in the fair trade states, the more aggressive retailers chose to ignore fair trade laws and forced the manufacturers to decide whether to initiate legal proceedings to enforce compliance and alienate an important, high-volume retailer or to ignore the retailers' actions. With some large retailers ignoring the price minimum and with the out-of-state mail order houses undercutting the price minimum, many manufacturers abandoned the retail price maintenance program completely. Others introduced new product lines to be sold at uncontrolled retail prices in competition with their fair traded items. By 1974, the value of fair traded items fell from the estimated 10 percent of retail sales in 1959 to 4 percent.[4] In 1975, so few supported the fair trade laws that 15 states repealed their statutes and Congress repealed the Miller-Tydings and McGuire Acts.[5] The abolition of the fair trade laws did not seem to have a perceptible effect, because the forces of competition had already eroded the effects of the fair trade laws.

REFUSALS TO DEAL

As previously mentioned, the Supreme Court held in the 1911 *Dr. Miles* case that contracts designed to maintain resale prices after the manufacturer had parted with title to the goods were illegal. However, in 1919 the Supreme Court allowed resale price maintenance in *U.S. v. Colgate & Co.*, 250 U.S. 300 (1919). Colgate did not have contractual agreements with its dealers to maintain the resale price. Instead, it announced that it would refuse to deal with those distributors that did not cooperate with the announced resale price expected by Colgate. The Supreme Court held that Colgate could not be charged with an *agreement* to vertically fix prices. The Colgate decision was distinguished from previous cases that were based on contracts between the manufacturer and the dealer. Thus, although the results (resale price maintenance) were the same in *Dr. Miles* and *Colgate,* the techniques used to achieve those results were different. Consequently, vertical price-fixing was both legal and illegal, depending on the technique employed.

The following case represents an effort by the Supreme Court to cut back the utilization of the *Colgate* doctrine to achieve resale price maintenance.

United States v. Parke, Davis & Co.

363 U.S. 29 (1960)
Supreme Court of the United States

Justice Brennan, Jr.

The Government . . . [alleged] that Parke Davis conspired and combined, in violation of Section 1 of the [Sherman] Act, with retail and wholesale druggists . . . to maintain the wholesale and retail prices of Parke Davis pharmaceutical products. . . .

Parke, Davis makes some 600 pharmaceutical products which it markets nationally through drug wholesalers and drug retailers. The retailers buy these products from the drug wholesalers or make large quantity purchases directly from Parke Davis. Sometime before 1956 Parke Davis announced a resale price maintenance policy in its wholesalers' and retailers' catalogues. . . .

There are some 260 drugstores in Washington D.C., and some 100 in Richmond, Virginia. . . : There are five drug wholesalers handling Parke Davis products in the locality who do business with the drug retailers. The wholesalers observed the resale prices suggested by Parke Davis. However, during the spring and early summer of 1956, drug retailers in the two cities advertised and sold several Parke Davis vitamin products at prices substantially below the suggested minimum retail prices. . . . The Baltimore office manager of Parke Davis in charge of the sales district which included the two cities sought advice from his head office on how to handle this situation. The Parke Davis attorney advised that the company could legally "enforce an adopted policy arrived at unilaterally" to sell only to customers who observed the suggested minimum resale prices.

He further advised that this meant that "we can lawfully say, 'we will sell you only so long as you observe such minimum retail prices' but cannot say 'we will sell you only if you agree to observe such minimum retail prices,' since . . . agreements as to resale price maintenance are invalid." Thereafter in July the branch manager put into effect a program for promoting observance of the suggested minimum retail prices by the retailers involved. The program contemplated the participation of the five drug wholesalers. In order to insure that retailers who did not comply would be cut off from sources of supply, representatives of Parke Davis visited the wholesalers and told them, in effect, that not only would Parke Davis refuse to sell to wholesalers who did not adhere to the policy announced in its catalogue, but also that it would refuse to sell to wholesalers who sold Parke Davis products who did not observe the suggested minimum retail prices. Each wholesaler was interviewed individually but each was informed that his competitors were also being apprised of this. The wholesalers without exception indicated a willingness to go along.

Representatives called contemporaneously upon the retailers involved, individually, and told each that if he did not observe the suggested minimum retail prices, Parke Davis would refuse to deal with him, and that furthermore he would be unable to purchase any Parke Davis products from the wholesalers. Each of the retailers was also told that his competitors were being similarly informed.

Several retailers refused to give any assurances of compliance and continued after the July interviews to advertise and sell Parke Davis products at prices below the suggested minimum retail prices. Their names were furnished by Parke Davis to the wholesalers. Thereafter, Parke Davis refused to fill direct orders from such retailers and the wholesalers likewise refused to fill their orders. This ban was not limited to the Parke Davis products being sold below the suggested minimum prices but included all the company's products, even those necessary to fill prescriptions. . . .

* * *

The program upon which Parke Davis embarked to promote general compliance with its suggested resale prices plainly exceeded the limitations of the *Colgate* doctrine and . . . effected arrangements which violated the Sherman Act. Parke Davis did not content itself with announcing its policy regarding retail prices and following this with a simple refusal to have business relations with any retailers who disregarded that policy. Instead, Parke Davis used the refusal to deal with the whole-

salers in order to elicit their willingness to deny Parke Davis products to retailers and thereby help gain the retailers' adherence to its suggested minimum retail prices. The retailers who disregarded the price policy were promptly cut off when Parke Davis supplied the wholesalers with their names. . . . In thus involving the wholesalers to stop the flow of Parke Davis products to the retailers, thereby inducing retailers' adherence to its suggested retail prices, Parke Davis created a combination with the retailers and the wholesalers to maintain retail prices and violated the Sherman Act. Although Parke Davis' originally announced wholesalers' policy would not under *Colgate* have violated the Sherman Act if its action thereunder was the simple refusal without more to deal with wholesalers who did not observe the wholesalers' Net Price Selling Schedule, that entire policy was tainted with the "vice of . . . illegality," when Parke Davis used it as the vehicle to gain the wholesalers' participation in the program to effectuate the retailers' adherence to the suggested retail prices. . . .

Questions
1. What was the advice of the Parke Davis attorney? Was it correct in light of the *Colgate* doctrine?
2. What did Parke Davis do that "went beyond" a mere refusal to deal and transformed their unilateral behavior into bilateral or group practice?
3. Considering the *Parke Davis* decision, is it possible to utilize the *Colgate* doctrine to achieve resale price maintenance when the manufacturer sells through wholesalers?

CONSIGNMENTS

A manufacturer may send goods to a dealer for sale to the public with the understanding that the manufacturer is to remain the owner of the goods and the dealer is to act as the manufacturer's agent in making the sale. The device of entrusting another person with the possession of property for the purpose of sale is commonly referred to as *selling on consignment*. Since the goods are still the property of the manufacturer, may the manufacturer set the dealer's resale price of the items? In other words, may selling on consignment provide an alternative means of achieving resale price maintenance? The Supreme Court has said that the use of a consignment device in connection with a short-term lease to coerce administered resale prices in a vast distribution system is illegal under the antitrust laws.[6] Hence, the manufacturer's use of the consignment device to maintain resale prices will not necessarily protect the consignor from a charge of violation of Section 1.

CRIMINAL CHARGES AND COSTS

It should be noted that the Justice Department has obtained criminal indictments against business firms that conspire to maintain resale prices. Historically, utilization of criminal proceedings for price-fixing has been restricted generally to horizontal price-fixing. But a recent grand jury indictment against a manufacturer for arranging price-fixing among the parties of a vertical supply chain serves as a stark reminder that vertical price-fixing is perceived by some (the Carter Administration) to be just as obnoxious to society as horizontal price-fixing.[7] However, Reagan Administration officials have announced that they do not regard vertical price-fixing as obnoxious. Consequently, antitrust enforcement by the Justice Department against vertical price maintenance during Reagan's term of office has been relaxed.

The cost of vertical price-fixing can be substantial. The aforementioned distributor who was indicted for vertical price-fixing also has been sued for violation of the Sherman Act by the attorney general in Massachusetts.[8] Bringing the action on behalf of the state as *parens patriae* for all natural persons residing in Massachusetts, the attorney general charged that the price-fixing conspiracy resulted in higher prices in Massachusetts, which entitled the attorney general to seek treble damages on behalf of all natural persons residing within Massachusetts. In addition, the attorney general is seeking an injunction to stop the vertical price-fixing practices as well as the cost of the suit, which includes a reasonable attorney's fee. This state action, and others of the same kind, illustrate the critical dangers associated with agreements to vertically fix prices. For example, it is reported that attorney generals in six states have won more than $12 million in settlements from Levi Strauss & Co. since its settlement with the Federal Trade Commission on charges that it fixed the resale price of its jeans.[9]

VERTICAL NONPRICE RESTRAINTS

Vertical arrangements between a seller and a customer can give rise to the imposition of *customer limitations* on resale. This restraint involves a manufacturer granting a distributor the right to sell its product and binding the retailer not to resell to particular customers, such as discount houses, public agencies, or industrial users. The manufacturer may want to reserve these accounts for itself without competition from its distributors.

Vertical arrangements also can be used by the seller to impose *territorial limitations* on sales made by its customers. This restraint involves a manufacturer giving a distributor exclusive sales rights in a particular area on the distributor's promise not to sell in another dealer's territory. This arrangement restricts the final purchaser to buying the brand from the distributor that serves its particular territory. This arrangement has various names, such as exclusive agency, exclusive selling, closed territory, or territorial safety.

The courts have permitted manufacturers to contractually make a buyer primarily responsible for adequately serving a given territorial area, even though the buyer thereby may not have the time and resources to trade elsewhere outside the assigned area. The manufacturer thereby achieves some informal but practical territorial division. The courts also allow the seller to insist on delivery to a designated location only and to prohibit "branching" by the dealer. This "location" clause also provides a form of territorial division of the market at the retail level. Either a "primary responsibility" clause or a "location" clause in sales contracts can provide sellers with a semblance of territorial division, which is normally lawful because neither clause involves a complete restriction on the buyer from making sales elsewhere. Only practical constraints, brought about by the primary responsibility or location clauses, restrict the buyer to the assigned area or to the store location.

Some manufacturers, however, attempt to impose more complete territorial and customer resale restraints on their buyers. In *U.S. v. Schwinn*, 388 U.S. 365 (1967), the Supreme Court ruled that customer and territorial restrictions on buyers' resale policies were *per se* unreasonable. Strangely, the Court ruled that Schwinn's consignment sales, which imposed the same customer and territorial restraints, were to be tested by the rule of reason. On application of the reasonableness test in the bicycle market, the Court determined that Schwinn's use of customer and territorial restrictions in consignment sales were lawful because interbrand competition was sufficiently strong and the intrabrand restriction imposed by Schwinn was insignificant in the bicycle market. Though the customer and territorial restrictions imposed on the outright sales were the same as those imposed in the consignment sales in terms of market effect, the Court ruled the restraints in the outright sales to be unreasonable *per se* without any analysis of the market effect. This dichotomy in approach, which determines legality by the contractual method of sale, was highly criticized in the legal and economic literature. Lower courts increasingly displayed ingenuity in finding interpretive ways around the *Schwinn* rule for *per se* illegality of vertical restraints in *sale* situations. Finally, the Supreme Court decided to reconsider *Schwinn's* strict *per se* rule of illegality in *sale* situations.

Continental T.V., Inc. v. GTE Sylvania, Inc.
433 U.S. 36 (1977)
Supreme Court of the United States

[In an attempt to improve its market position by attracting more aggressive and competent retailers, Sylvania limited the number of retail franchises granted for any given area and required each franchisee to sell its products only from the location at which it was franchised. Petitioner, one of Sylvania's franchised retailers, claimed that Sylvania had violated Section 1 of the Sherman Act by entering into and enforcing franchise agreements that prohibited the sale of Sylvania's products other than from specified locations.]

Justice Powell

Both Schwinn and Sylvania sought to reduce but not to eliminate competition among their respective retailers through the adoption of a franchise system. . . . [T]he Schwinn franchise plan included a location restriction similar to the one challenged here. These restrictions allowed Schwinn and Sylvania to regulate the amount of competition among their retailers by preventing a franchisee from selling franchised products from outlets other than the one covered by the franchise agreement. To exactly the same end, the Schwinn franchise plan included a companion restriction, apparently not found in the Sylvania plan, that prohibited franchised retailers from selling Schwinn products to nonfranchised retailers. In *Schwinn* the Court expressly held that this restriction was impermissible under the broad principle stated there. In intent and competitive impact, the retail customer restriction in *Schwinn* is indistinguishable from the location restriction in the present case. In both cases the restrictions limited the freedom of the retailer to dispose of the franchised products as he desired. The fact that one restriction was addressed to territory and the other to customers is irrelevant to functional antitrust analysis, and indeed, to the language and broad thrust of the opinion in *Schwinn*.

* * *

In essence, the issue before us is whether *Schwinn's per se* rule can be justified. . . .

The market impact of vertical restrictions is complex because of their potential for a simultaneous reduction of intrabrand competition and stimulation of interbrand competition. . . .

Vertical restrictions reduce intrabrand competition by limiting the number of sellers of a particular product competing for the business of a given group of buyers. Location restrictions have this effect because of practical constraints on the effective marketing area of retail outlets. Although intrabrand competition may be reduced, the ability of retailers to exploit the resulting market may be limited both by the ability of consumers to travel to other franchised locations and, perhaps more importantly, to purchase the competing products of other manufacturers. . . .

Vertical restrictions promote interbrand competition by allowing the manufacturer to achieve certain efficiencies in the distribution of his products. These "redeeming virtues" are implicit in every decision sustaining vertical restrictions under the rule of reason. Economists have identified a number of ways in which manufacturers can use such restrictions to compete more effectively against other manufacturers. For example, new manufacturers and manufacturers entering new markets can use the restrictions in order to induce competent and aggressive retailers to make the kind of investment of capital and labor that is often required in the distribution of products unknown to the consumer. Established manufacturers can use them to induce retailers to engage in promotional activities or to provide service and repair facilities necessary to the efficient marketing of their products. Service and repair are vital for many products, such as automobiles and major household appliances. The availability and quality of such services affect a manufacturer's good will and the competitiveness of his product. Because of market imperfections such as the so-called "free rider" effect, these services might not be provided by retailers in a purely competitive situation, despite the fact that each retailer's benefit would be greater if all provided the services than if none did. . . .

The question remains whether the *per se* rule stated in *Schwinn* should be . . . abandoned in favor of a return to the rule of reason. . . .

. . . Such restrictions, in varying forms, are

widely used in our free market economy. As indicated above, there is substantial scholarly and judicial authority supporting their economic utility. There is relatively little authority to the contrary. Certainly, there has been no showing in this case, either generally or with respect to Sylvania's agreements, that vertical restrictions have a "pernicious effect on competition" or that they "lack . . . any redeeming virtue." Accordingly, we conclude that the *per se* rule stated in *Schwinn* must be overruled. . . .

In sum, we conclude that the appropriate decision is to return to the rule of reason that governed vertical restrictions prior to *Schwinn*.

Questions
1. When is a *per se* unreasonable rule appropriate?
2. Why was Schwinn's *per se* rule against resale restraints considered inappropriate?
3. What business reasons or procompetitive effects did the court identify that may result from vertical resale restrictions?
4. The Court in a footnote in *Continental T.V.* provided this analysis in upholding Sylvania's vertical restriction under the rule of reason.

> Interbrand competition is the competition among the manufacturers of the same generic product—television sets in this case—and is the primary concern of antitrust law. The extreme example of a deficiency of interbrand competition is monopoly, where there is only one manufacturer. In contrast, intrabrand competition is the competition between the distributors—wholesale or retail—of the product of a particular manufacturer.
>
> The degree of intrabrand competition is wholly independent of the level of interbrand competition confronting the manufacturer. Thus, there may be fierce intrabrand competition among the distributors of a product produced by a firm in a highly competitive industry. But when interbrand competition exists, as it does among television manufacturers, it provides a significant check on the exploitation of intrabrand market power because of the ability of consumers to substitute a different brand of the same product.

> Does this suggest the circumstances under which the courts would prohibit an intrabrand restraint?

EXCLUSIVE SUPPLY ARRANGEMENT

Supply contracts often contain a clause requiring the buyer not to handle the products of a competitive supplier. The buyer is required by the exclusive supply contract to buy all of its supplies of the product from the contractually designated supplier. This vertical arrangement is termed an exclusive supply or an exclusive dealing contract. Another form of exclusive supply contract is a requirements contract, which commits a buyer to purchase from the seller all (or substantially all) of its requirements of a product and, thus, by *implication* to promise not to buy elsewhere. Consequently, the buyer's commitment not to buy elsewhere may be embodied in a clause of the exclusive supply contract itself or it may be implied, as in a requirements contract. Nevertheless, the effect of the various types of contracts is the same.

The commercial purpose of exclusive dealing contracts is to secure the undivided attention of the distributor in promoting the product of the manufacturer to the consumer. Distributors enter into exclusive dealing contracts to secure a dependable source of supply or to obtain assistance from the manufacturer in sales promotion.

Exclusive supply contracts can also operate to lessen competition through the *exclusion* of rival suppliers. If the exclusive supply contract is for a long duration, competing suppliers are denied access to the buyer for a long period of time. The rival suppliers lose the buyer as an outlet for their products. Exclusive dealing can be especially detrimental to small suppliers, who lack the large volume of sales required for a dealer to maintain its business on an exclusive basis without selling competitive brands. Also, if all or most of an industry is utilizing exclusive dealing arrangements, entry of new firms at the manufacturing level is impossible without the new entrant's creation of its own distribution outlets. This fact, of course, raises the cost of entry and reduces the potential of new competitors.

CLAYTON ACT, SECTION 3

Congressional concern with the potential anticompetitive effects of exclusive dealing arrangements led to the enactment of a provision in the Clayton Act that limits its practice. Section 3 of the Clayton Act makes it illegal for any person "to lease or make a sale . . . of . . . commodities, whether patented or unpatented, . . . on the condition, agreement or understanding that the lessee or purchaser thereof shall not use or deal in the . . . commodities of a competitor . . . of the lessor or seller, where the effect of such . . . [arrangement] may be to substantially lessen competition or tend to create monopoly in any line of commerce." Consequently, whether any particular exclusive dealing agreement is prohibited by Section 3 depends in each case on the determination of the *probable effect* of the agreement in substantially lessening competition in the relevant product market. Early Supreme Court cases determining the *substantiality* of the "probable effect" have been characterized as follows.

Where the alleged violator dominated or was a leader in the industry, proof of such fact was . . . determined to be a sufficient predicate from which to conclude that the use of exclusive-dealing contracts was violative of Section 3 and other factors appeared to have been largely ignored. [Later] . . . the Supreme Court extended the rule to business organizations enjoying a powerful, though clearly not dominant, position in the trade and doing a substantial share of the industry's business by means of these contractual provisions and [the Court] tacitly approved the trial court's refusal to consider other economic effects or merits of the system employed. *Dictograph Products v. FTC*, 217 F. 2d 812 (1954).

The Supreme Court's utilization of such tests as "dominance of the seller" or a "powerful position," which included a "substantial share of the industry's business," without inquiry into the economic effects or merits of the exclusive dealing system amounts to an almost *per se* test of illegality by a firm that has a substantial share of the market. This test of substantiality was so strict that almost all exclusive dealings were illegal. This test became known as the "quantitative substantiality" test because the Court emphasized the dollar volume of commerce tied up in the exclusive-dealing contracts. The court said that if a "not insubstantial amount of commerce was affected," then the exclusive-dealing contracts were illegal. The Court made no further inquiry concerning economic effects and made no market analysis of the impact of the exclusive-dealing arrangements. This quantitative substantiality test and its almost *per se* determination of illegality received mixed reviews in the legal and economic literature. The Supreme Court retreated from this strict test in the following case and approved a more lenient test, which is generally referred to as "qualitative substantiality."

Tampa Electric Co. v. Nashville Co.
365 U.S. 320 (1960)
Supreme Court of the United States

[Tampa Electric Co., a public utility in Florida, contracted with Nashville Coal Company for its expected coal requirements for two new electrical generating units to be constructed. The agreement required Tampa Electric to purchase all its requirements of coal for a period of 20 years. Before the first shipment of coal was to be delivered, Nashville Coal Company advised Tampa Electric that the contract was illegal under the antitrust laws and that no coal would be delivered. Tampa Electric purchased its coal requirements elsewhere and sued Nashville Coal for breach of contract.]

Justice Clark

. . . [The District Court and the Court of Appeals] . . . admitted that the contract "does not expressly contain the 'condition'" that Tampa Electric would not use or deal in the coal of [defendant's] competitors. Nonetheless, they reasoned, the "total requirements" provision had the same practical effect, for it prevented Tampa Electric for a period of 20 years from buying coal from any other source. . . . [B]oth courts found that the "line of com-

merce" on which the restraint was to be tested was coal. . . . Both courts compared the estimated coal tonnage as to which the contract pre-empted competition for 20 years, namely, 1,000,000 tons a year by 1961, with the previous annual consumption of peninsular Florida, 700,000 tons. Emphasizing that fact as well as the contract value of the coal covered by the 20-year term, i.e., $128,000,000, they held that such volume was not "insignificant or insubstantial" and that the effect of the contract would "be to substantially lessen competition," in violation of the [Clayton] Act. Both courts were of the opinion that in view of the executory nature of the contract, judicial enforcement of any portion of it could not be granted without directing a violation of the Act itself, and enforcement was, therefore, denied.

Application of Section 3 of the Clayton Act

* * *

In practical application, even though a contract is found to be an exclusive-dealing arrangement, it does not violate the section unless the court believes it probable that performance of the contract will foreclose competition in a substantial share of the line of commerce affected. Following the guidelines of earlier decisions, certain considerations must be taken. *First,* the line of commerce, i.e., the type of goods, wares, or merchandise, etc., involved must be determined, where it is in controversy on the basis of the facts peculiar to the case. *Second,* the area of effective competition in the known line of commerce must be chartered by careful selection of the market area in which the seller operates, and to which the purchaser can practically turn for supplies. In short, the threatened foreclosure of competition must be in relation to the market affected. . . .

Third, and last, the competition foreclosed by the contract must be found to constitute a substantial share of the relevant market. That is to say, the opportunities for other traders to enter into or remain in that market must be significantly limited. . . .

To determine substantiality in a given case, it is necessary to weigh the probable effect of the contract on the relevant area of effective competition, taking into account the relevant strength of the parties, the proportionate volume of commerce involved in relation to the total volume of commerce in the relevant market area, and the probable immediate and future effects which preemption of that share of the market might have on effective competition therein. It follows that a mere showing that the contract itself involves a substantial number of dollars is ordinarily of little consequence.

The Application of Section 3 Here

In applying these considerations to the facts of the case before us, it appears that both the Court of Appeals and the District Court have not given the required effect to a controlling factor in the case—the relevant competitive market area. This omission, by itself, requires reversal, for, as we have pointed out, the relevant market is the prime factor in relation to which the ultimate question, whether the

contract forecloses competition in a substantial share of the line of commerce involved, must be declared. . . .

Relevant Market of Effective Competition
*   *   *

We are persuaded that on the record in this case, neither peninsular Florida, nor the entire State of Florida, nor Florida and Georgia combined constituted the relevant market of effective competition. . . . By far the bulk of the overwhelming tonnage marketed from the same producing area as serves Tampa is sold outside of Georgia and Florida, and the producers were "eager" to sell more coal in those States. While the relevant competitive market is not ordinarily susceptible to a "metes and bounds" definition, . . . it is of course the area in which [defendant] and the other 700 producers effectively compete.

The record shows that, like the [defendant], they sold bituminous coal "suitable for [Tampa's] requirements," mined in parts of Pennsylvania, Virginia, West Virginia, Kentucky, Tennessee, Alabama, Ohio and Illinois. We take notice of the fact that the approximate total bituminous coal product in the year 1954 from the districts in which these 700 producers are located was 359,289,000 tons, of which some 290,567,000 tons were sold on the open market. Of the latter amount, some 78,716,000 tons were sold to electric utilities. . . . From these statistics it clearly appears that the proportionate volume of the total relevant coal product as to which the challenged contract pre-empted competition, less than 1%, is, conservatively speaking, quite insubstantial. A more accurate figure, even assuming pre-emption to the extent of the maximum anticipated total requirements, 2,250,000 tons a year, would be .77%.

Effect on Competition in the Relevant Market

It may well be that in the context of antitrust legislation protracted requirements contracts are suspect, but they have not been declared illegal *per se.* . . . It is urged that the present contract pre-empts competition to the extent of purchases worth perhaps $128,000,000, and that this "is, of course, not insignificant or insubstantial." While $128,000,000 is a considerable sum of money, even in these days, the dollar volume, by itself, is not the test, as we have already pointed out.

The remaining determination, therefore, is whether the pre-emption of competition to the extent of the tonnage involved tends to substantially foreclose competition in the relevant coal market. We think not. That market sees an annual trade in excess of 250,000,000 tons of coal and over a billion dollars—multiplied by 20 years it runs into astronomical figures. There is here neither a seller with a dominant position in the market as in *Standard Fashions;* nor myriad outlets with substantial sales volume, coupled with an industrywide practice of relying upon exclusive contracts, as in *Standard Oil.* . . .

On the contrary, we seem to have only that type of contract which "may well be of economic advantage to buyers as well as to sellers." *Standard Oil Co. v. United States.* In the case of the buyer it "may assure supply," while on the part of the seller it "may make possible the substantial reduction of selling expenses, give protection against price fluctuations, and . . . offer the possibility of a predictable market." The 20-year period of the contract is singled out as the principal vice, but at least in the case of public utilities the assurance of a steady and ample supply of fuel is necessary in the public interest. In weighing the various factors, we have decided that in the competitive bituminous coal marketing area involved here, the contract sued upon does not tend to foreclose a substantial volume of competition.

Questions

1. How did the lower courts define the competitive geographical market? Did the Supreme Court agree?
2. How did the lower courts determine the "substantiality" of the probable anticompetitive effect? What is the proper test to determine "substantiality" of the probable anticompetitive effect?

REFUSAL TO SELL TO NONEXCLUSIVE DEALERS

Many large suppliers achieve exclusive dealing arrangements without contractual provisions prohibiting the dealer from buying elsewhere. Instead, the manufacturers, relying on the *Colgate* doctrine, refuse to sell to dealers that will not handle only their products. Any dealers that stock competing lines of merchandise have their supplies cut off by these manufacturers.

Most firms, in dropping the contractual provisions for exclusive dealing to avoid Section 3 of the Clayton Act, have inserted an "adequate representation" clause that requires the dealer to adequately represent the manufacturer's interest in an assigned area. Any number of reasons, such as failure to promote sales or to secure a certain volume of sales, may provide grounds for the manufacturer to assert that the dealer is not adequately representing the manufacturer, and therefore cancel their trading relationship. Often, manufacturers argue that the handling of products provided by rival suppliers precludes the dealer from adequately representing the manufacturer's interest. Consequently, the "adequate representation" clause in combination with the *Colgate* right of refusing to deal provides an alternative method of securing an effective exclusive dealing arrangement.

FRANCHISES

The typical franchise contract involves a franchisor who grants the franchisee the right to operate a business in a certain manner in a designated area and to use the franchisor's trademark or trade name in the operation. Because the franchisor normally has substantially more bargaining power than the franchisee, the franchise agreements contain provisions that restrict the franchisee's freedoms. Franchisees often agree not to compete with other franchised dealers in another territory. Franchisees also often agree not to sell competitors' brands from the franchised outlet. Franchise agreements sometimes require the franchisee to purchase supplies and services from the franchisor. Often the restrictions imposed in franchise contracts violate the antitrust laws. However, Congress has also enacted the federal trademark statute, the Lanham Act. This act requires franchisors to exercise control over the use of their trademark so as not to misrepresent the source of trademarked goods. Consequently, franchisors must exercise stringent quality control to maintain consistency in all franchised outlets to protect the product represented by the trademark. Quality variance would negatively affect the public's attitude toward the mark in an economic sense and conflict with the policies of the Lanham Act. Consequently, some of the restrictions placed on franchisees may be motivated by the franchisor's desire to maintain quality control as required by the Lanham Act.

TIE-IN ARRANGEMENTS

A tie-in agreement is a refusal by a seller to sell or lease one product or service unless another product or service is also bought or leased. In effect, the distributor forces its buyers to take a less desirable product or service (the tied product) in order to obtain a more wanted item (the tying product). The courts have said that ordinarily there can be hardly any reason for tying two goods together except to use one's power over the tying product or service to gain a market for the tied product. Tie-in agreements limit competition in the market for the tied product in that rival sellers in the tied product must overcome their competitor's economic power over the tying product to gain access to the available buyers of tied products. Because of this anticompetitive effect, tie-in arrangements receive close scrutiny by the courts, which find the tie-in illegal if the firm (1) has sufficient economic power in the tying product (2) to restrict competition in the tied product market. For example, it is normally unreasonable to require that a buyer finance his or her purchase through the seller or to require that lessees of equipment use the lessor's supplies in the equipment. The courts generally give tie-ins an almost *per se* status of illegality unless the seller can produce an exceptional justification.

The tie-in may be justified if the seller can prove that the new technology involved in a sensitive piece of equipment functions properly only if the seller's repair parts and service are used. If this is true, and only as long as this is true, the tie-in for repair parts and service would not be unreasonable. Besides this new technology justification, which was first expressed in *Jerrold Electronics*,[10] and the quality control justification made by the Lanham Act, other tie-ins have received a rather inhospitable reception by the courts.

Principe v. McDonald's Corp.
631 F. 2d 303 (1980)
U.S. Court of Appeals (4th Cir.)

This appeal presents the question of whether a fast food franchise that requires its licensees to operate their franchises in premises leased from the franchisor is guilty of an illegal tying arrangement in violation of Section 1 of the Sherman Act. . . .

I

The . . . Principes . . . are franchisees of McDonald's hamburger restaurant[s] in Hopewell, Virginia . . . [and] in Colonial Heights. . . .

They filed this action . . . alleging . . . McDonald's violated federal antitrust laws by tying store leases and $15,000 security deposit notes to the franchise rights at the Hopewell and Colonial Heights stores. . . .

II

At the time this suit was filed, McDonald's consisted of at least four separate corporate entities. McDonald's Systems, Inc. controlled franchise rights and licensed franchisees to sell hamburgers under the McDonald's name. Franchise Realty Interstate Corporation (Franchise Realty) acquires real estate, either by purchasing or long term lease, builds McDonald's hamburger restaurants, and leases them either to franchisees or to a third corporation, McOpCo. McOpCo, which is not a party to this suit, operates about one-fourth of the McDonald's restaurants in the United States as company stores. Straddling this triad is McDonald's Corporation, the parent, who owns all the stock of the other defendants.

McDonald's is not primarily a fast food retailer. While it does operate over a thousand stores itself, the vast majority of the stores in its system are operated by franchisees. Nor does McDonald's sell equipment or supplies to its licensees. Instead its primary business is developing and collecting royalties from limited menu fast food restaurants operated by independent business people.

McDonald's develops new restaurants according to master plans . . . and . . . uses demographic data generated by the most recent census and its own research in evaluating potential sites. . . .

* * *

After the specifics of each proposed new restaurant are approved, McDonald's decides whether the store will be company operated or franchised. If the decision is to franchise the store, McDonald's begins the process of locating a franchisee. . . .

Meanwhile, Franchise Realty acquires the land, either by purchase or long term lease and constructs the store. Acquisition and development costs averaged over $450,000 per store in 1978. All McDonald restaurants bear the same distinctive features with a few exceptions due to architectural restrictions: the golden arches motif, the brick and glass construction and the distinctive roofline. According to the defendants, these features identify the stores as a

McDonald's even where zoning restrictions preclude other advertising or signs.

As constructed, McDonald's restaurants are finished shells; they contain no kitchen or dining room equipment. Furnishing store equipment is the responsibility of the operator, whether a franchisee or McOpCo. McDonald's does provide specifications such equipment must meet, but does not sell the equipment itself.

Having acquired the land, begun construction of the store, and selected an operator, McDonald's enters into two contracts with the franchisee. Under the first, the franchise agreement, McDonald's grants the franchisee the rights to use McDonald's food preparation system and to sell food products under the McDonald's name. The franchisee pays a $12,500 franchise fee and agrees to remit three percent of his gross sales as a royalty in return. Under the second contract, the lease, McDonald's grants the franchisee the right to use the particular store premises to which his franchise pertains. In return, the franchisee pays a $15,000 refundable security deposit (as evidence of which he receives a twenty year non-negotiable non-interest bearing note) and agrees to pay eight and one half percent of his gross sales as rent. These payments under the franchise and lease agreements are McDonald's only sources of income from its franchised restaurants. The franchisee also assumes responsibility under the lease for building maintenance, improvements, property taxes and other costs associated with the premises. Both the franchise agreement and the lease generally have twenty year durations, both provide that termination of one terminates the other, and neither is available separately.

III

The Principes argue McDonald's is selling not one but three distinct products, the franchise, the lease, and the security deposit note. The alleged antitrust violation stems from the fact that a prospective franchisee must buy all three in order to obtain the franchise.

As evidence that this is an illegal tying arrangement, the Principes point to the unfavorable terms on which the franchisees are required to lease their stores. Not only are franchisees denied the opportunity to build equity and depreciate their property, but they must maintain the building, pay for improvements and taxes, and remit 8.5 percent of their gross sales as rents. In 1978 the gross sales of the Hopewell store generated about $52,000 in rent. That figure nearly equalled Franchise Realty's original cost for the site and corresponds to more than a fourth of the original cost of the entire Hopewell restaurant complex. At that rate of return, the Principes argue, Franchise Realty will have recouped its entire investment in four years and the remainder of the lease payments will be pure profit. The Principes contend that the fact the store rents are so high proves that McDonald's cannot sell the leaseholds on their own merits.

Nor has McDonald's shown any need to forbid its licensees to own their own stores, the Principes say. Appellants contend that McDonald's is the only fast food franchisor that requires its licensees not only to pay royalties but to lease their own stores. McDonald's could maintain its desired level of uniformity by requiring franchisees to locate and construct stores according to company specifications. The company could even provide planning and design assistance as it apparently does in connection with food purchasing and restaurant management. The Principes argue McDonald's has not shown that the success of its business or the integrity of its trademarks depends on company ownership of all store premises.

A separate tied product is the note that evidences the lesee's $15,000 security deposit, according to the appellants. The Principes argue the security deposit really is a mandatory contribution to McDonald's working capital, not security against damage to the store or breach of the lease contract. By tying the purchase of these $15,000 twenty year non-negotiable non-interest bearing notes to that of the franchise, McDonald's allegedly has generated a capital fund that totalled over $45 million in 1978. It is argued that no one would purchase such notes on their own merits. The Principes assert that only by requiring franchisees to purchase the notes as a condition of obtaining a franchise has McDonald's been able to sell them at all.

McDonald's responds that it is not in the business of licensing use of its name, improving real estate for lease, or selling long term notes. Its only business is developing a system of hamburger restaurants and collecting royalties from their sales. The allegedly tied products are but parts of the overall bundle of franchise benefits and obligations. According to McDonald's, the appellants are asking the court to invalidate the way McDonald's does business and to require it to adopt the licensing procedures of its less successful competitors. Federal antitrust laws do not compel such a result, McDonald's contends.

* * *

IV

As support for their position, the Principes rely primarily on the decision of the Ninth Circuit in *Siegel v. Chicken Delight, Inc.,* one of the first cases to address the problem of franchise tie-ins. Chicken Delight was what McDonald's characterizes as a "rent a name" franchisor: it licensed franchisees to sell chicken under the Chicken Delight name but did not own store premises or fixtures. The company did not even charge franchise fees or royalties. Instead, it required its franchisees to purchase a specified number of cookers and fryers and to purchase certain packaging supplies and mixes exclusively from Chicken Delight. These supplies were priced higher than comparable goods of competing sellers. A class composed of franchisees challenged the tying arrangements as a violation of the Sherman Act. The

district court held for the franchisees and Chicken Delight appealed.

In addressing Chicken Delight's argument that the allegedly tied products all were essential components of the franchise system, the Ninth Circuit looked to the "function of the aggregation." Viewing the essence of a Chicken Delight franchise as the franchisor's trademark, the court sought to determine whether requiring franchisees to purchase common supplies from Chicken Delight was necessary to ensure that their operations lived up to the quality standards the trademark represented. Judged by this standard, the aggregation was found to consist of separate products:

This being so, it is apparent that the goodwill of the Chicken Delight trademark does not attach to the multitude of separate articles used in the operation of the licensed system or in the production of its end product. It is not what is used, but how it is used and what results that have given the system and its end product their entitlement to trademark protection. It is to the system and the end product that the public looks with the confidence that established goodwill has created.

In the court's view, Chicken Delight had attempted to "extend trademark protection to common articles (which the public does not and has no reason to connect with the trademark)," a classic kind of illegal tying arrangement.

The Principes urge this court to apply the *Chicken Delight* reasoning to invalidate the McDonald's franchise lease note aggregation. They urge that McDonald's can protect the integrity of its trademarks by specifying how its franchisees shall operate, where they may locate their restaurants and what types of buildings they may erect. Customers do not and have no reason to connect the building's owner with the McDonald's operation conducted therein. Since company ownership of store premises is not an essential element of the trademark's goodwill, the Principes argue, the franchise, lease and note are separable products tied together in violation of the antitrust laws. In *Philips v. Crown Central Petroleum Corporation*, this court . . . noted that "the very essence of a franchise is the purchase of several related products in a single competitively attractive package." Franchising has come a long way since the decision in *Chicken Delight*.

Without disagreeing with the result in *Chicken Delight*, we conclude that the Court's emphasis in that case upon the trademark as the essence of a franchise is too restrictive. Far from merely licensing franchisees to sell products under its trade name, a modern franchisor such as McDonald's offers its franchisees a complete method of doing business. It takes people from all walks of life, sends them to its management school, and teaches them a variety of skills ranging from hamburger grilling to financial planning. It installs them in stores whose market has been researched and whose location has been selected by experts to maximize sales potential. It inspects every facet of every store several times a year and consults with each franchisee about his operation's strengths and weaknesses. Its regime pervades all facets of the business, from the design of the menu board to the amount of catsup on the hamburgers, nothing is left to chance. This pervasive franchisor supervision and control benefits the franchisee in turn. His business is identified with a network of stores whose very uniformity and predictability attracts customers. In short, the modern franchisee pays not only for the right to use a trademark but for the right to become a part of a system whose business methods virtually guarantee his success. It is often unrealistic to view a franchise agreement as little more than a trademark license.

Given the realities of modern franchising, we think the proper inquiry is not whether the allegedly tied products are associated in the public mind with the franchisor's trademark, but whether they are integral components of the business method being franchised. Where

the challenged aggregation is an essential ingredient of the franchised system's formula for success, there is but a single product and no tie in exists as a matter of law.

Applying this standard to the present case, we hold the lease is not separable from the McDonald's franchise to which it pertains. McDonald's practice of developing a system of company owned restaurants operated by franchisees has substantial advantages, both for the company and for franchisees. It is part of what makes a McDonald's franchise uniquely attractive to franchisees.

First, because it approaches the problem of restaurant site selection systematically, McDonald's is able to obtain better sites than franchisees could select. Armed with its demographic information, guided by its staff of experts and unencumbered by preferences of individual franchisees, McDonald's can wield its economic might to acquire sites where new restaurants will prosper without undercutting existing franchisees' business or limiting future expansion. Individual franchisees are unlikely to possess analytical expertise, undertake elaborate market research or approach the problem of site selection from an area wide point of view. Individual franchisees benefit from the McDonald's approach because their stores are located in areas McDonald's has determined will produce substantial fast food business and on sites where that business is most likely to be diverted to their stores. Because McDonald's purposefully locates new stores where they will not undercut existing franchisees' business, McDonald's franchisees do not have to compete with each other, a substantial advantage in the highly competitive fast food industry.

Second, McDonald's policy of owning all of its own restaurants assures that the stores remain part of the McDonald's system. McDonald's franchise arrangements are not static: franchisees retire or die; occasionally they do not live up to their franchise obligations and must be replaced; even if no such contingency intervenes, the agreements normally expire by their own terms after twenty years. If franchisees owned their own stores, any of these events could disrupt McDonald's business and have a negative effect on the system's goodwill. Buildings whose architecture identified them as former McDonald's stores would sit idle or be used for other purposes. Replacement franchisees would have to acquire new and perhaps less desirable sites, a much more difficult and expensive process after the surrounding business area has matured. By owning its own stores, McDonald's assures its continued presence on the site, maintains the store's patronage even during management changes and avoids the negative publicity of having former McDonald's stores used for other purposes. By preserving the goodwill of the system in established markets, company store ownership produces attendant benefits for franchisees.

Third, because McDonald's acquires the sites and builds the store itself, it can select franchisees based on their management potential rather than their real estate expertise or wealth. Ability to emphasize management skills is important to McDonald's because it has built its reputation largely on the consistent quality of its operations rather than on the merits of its hamburgers. A store's quality is largely a function of its management. McDonald's policy of owning its own stores reduces a franchisee's initial investment, thereby broadening the applicant base and opening the door to persons who otherwise could not afford a McDonald's franchise. Accordingly, McDonald's is able to select franchisees primarily on the basis of their willingness to work for the success of their operations. Their ability to begin operating a McDonald's restaurant without having to search for a site, negotiate for the land, borrow hundreds of thousands of dollars and construct a store building is of substantial value to franchisees.

Finally, because both McDonald's and the franchisee have a substantial financial stake in the success of the restaurant, their relationship becomes a sort of partnership that might be impossible under other circumstances. McDonald's spends close to half a million dollars on each new store it establishes. Each franchisee invests over $100,000 to make the store operational. Neither can afford to ignore the other's problems, complaints or ideas. Because its investment is on the line, the Company cannot allow its franchisees to lose money. This being so, McDonald's works with its franchisees to build their business, occasionally financing improvements at favorable rates or even accepting reduced royalty payments in order to provide franchisees more working capital.

All of these factors contribute significantly to the overall success of the McDonald's system. The formula that produced systemwide success, the formula that promises to make each new McDonald's store successful, that formula is what McDonald's sells its franchisees. To characterize the franchise as an unnecessary aggregation of separate products tied to the McDonald's name is to miss the point entirely. Among would be franchisees, the McDonald's name has come to stand for the formula, including all that it entails. We decline to find that it is an illegal tie in.

Questions

1. What is the main argument of the plaintiff that the lease is an illegal tie-in with the franchise? What is the argument that the security deposit is an illegal tie-in with the franchise?
2. Does the court disagree with the result obtained in the *Chicken Delight*

decision? How did the court justify its treatment of the franchise-lease-deposit aggregation as a single product?

3. Would this court approve of a situation where McDonald's required all franchises to purchase their meat supplies from McDonald's?

CONCLUSION

In light of the differing economic arguments both supporting and condemning vertical arrangements, it is not surprising that lawmakers have vacillated in the formulation of public policy positions concerning vertical arrangements.

For one, the law has condemned vertical price-fixing through contracts, but permitted such control if accomplished by the right to refuse to deal. At the same time, Congress allowed vertical price-fixing for a period of time in the "fair trade" laws. Presently, the fair trade laws have been repealed and the *Colgate* doctrine is so restricted that few firms would rely on it as authority for vertical price-fixing. Consequently, historical vacillation has been replaced in the post-war years with a clear public policy denunciation of vertical price controls. However, this certainty has again been shaken by the doubts expressed by the Reagan Administration concerning the appropriateness of outlawing vertical price restraints.

Second, the courts have ruled that vertical nonprice restraints are to be judged by the rule of reason, which generally permits intrabrand restraints as long as sufficient interbrand competition exists. This permissiveness allows some customer territorial division, which protects distributors' margins as much as a resale price maintenance program would. This *per se* condemnation of high retail margins through vertical price-fixing but rule-of-reason permissiveness for such margins accomplished through customer or territorial divisions is inconsistent, though apparently explained by the less restrictive nature of the latter technique.

Exclusive supply contracts were interpreted to be almost *per se* illegal in the 1950s. Subsequent litigation relaxed this strict illegality. In addition, the "adequate representation" clause and the right to refuse to deal have provided an alternative method of securing exclusive dealing.

The modern relaxation of the rules against nonprice resale restraints and exclusive dealing is perhaps partially explained by the fact that contractual vertical arrangements are less obtrusive than vertical mergers. Vertical mergers are even more restrictive than simple contractual restriction. It eliminates the independent status of the distributor altogether and enhances the overall level of economic concentration. Yet historically, vertical mergers were not outlawed as rigidly as contractual vertical arrangements. Inadvertently, the strict posture of the law against contractual vertical arrangements fostered the vertical merger movement as an alternative to contractual vertical control. Recognition of this unintended consequence may partially explain the relaxation of the rules against contractual restraints.[11] Now, the more generally lawful and less restrictive contractual combinations may replace the feeling by manufacturers that only through vertical mergers were they able to achieve retailer control.

Finally, the courts seem to be developing a more lenient attitude toward tie-ins in franchise situations. The court's adoption of an "essential ingredient" test to avoid the existence of a tied product provides wide latitude for franchisors in developing franchise packages.

DISCUSSION QUESTIONS

1. The B&R Ice Cream franchise requires the franchisee not to carry any other brands of ice cream for sale from the B&R franchise outlet. What questions would you ask to determine if this practice is lawful?

2. A licensor of patents, trademarks, and tradenames on bedding products sells advertising and promotional goods and products to its licensees, as well as mattress ticking, inner spring assemblies, labels, and so on. Each licensee is required to execute a franchise agreement that prescribes a territory in which the licensee will operate, called its "area of primary responsibility."

   Each licensee is required by the franchise to participate in a "pass-over" plan. Under this plan a licensee is not prohibited from selling outside its area of primary responsibility, but if it should do so, the licensee making the sale must pay 7 percent of its gross receipts from the sale to the licensee in whose area the sale was made.

   An independent accounting firm had examined the expenses of the licensees at the request of the licensor, and found that the licensees' fixed selling expenses were 2 percent and its fixed advertising expenses were 5 percent. The licensor believes that a licensee should be compensated for these expenses if a competitor sells in its area.

   Is this plan lawful? What effect would it have on your evaluation if the profit margin on each sale was 4 percent or if the fixed selling expenses totaled only 5 percent?

3. Clairol markets Miss Clairol hair coloring products through two distinct channels of trade. Miss Clairol "salon" product is sold through distributors only to beauty salons and beauty schools. Miss Clairol "retail" product is sold by the company either directly to large retail chains or to wholesalers who in turn sell to retail stores for ultimate resale to the general public for home use. This dual distribution system has existed since Clairol entered the retail market in the 1950s.

   Clairol charges a substantially lower price for its salon product ($6.12 per dozen) than it charges for the products it sells to the retail trade ($11.67 per dozen) for resale to the general public.

   Each bottle of the retail Miss Clairol is enclosed in an individual yellow carton, bearing the conspicuous cautionary statement of possible skin irritation and the necessity of a preliminary test. It also indicates the product must not be used for dyeing the eyelashes or eyebrows; to do so may cause blindness. Each retail carton also contains a carefully prepared and copyrighted booklet providing detailed information and instructions to enable the untrained consumer to obtain safe and satisfactory results.

Clairol packages its Miss Clairol salon product in a six-pack carton with only one sheet of instructions describing the antiallergy test. The salon instructional sheet does not contain the warning that preliminary patch and strand tests should be given before each application of the product.

Clairol wrote letters to each salon distributor threatening termination if they sell the salon product to retailers. Are Clairol's policies lawful?

4. U.S. Steel Home Credit Corp., a wholly owned subsidiary of U.S. Steel Corp., was offering 100 percent financing to home developers in the Louisville, Kentucky, area during a period of years when no other lending institution in that area could match U.S. Steel Home Credit Corp. credit terms and interest rates. One such developer alleged, in a suit against U.S. Steel and the U.S. Home Credit Corp., that in order to obtain loans from the credit corporation, it had to use the funds to purchase prefabricated homes from U.S. Steel Corp. at "unreasonably high prices" and erect the homes on lots also purchased with borrowed funds.

The plaintiff-developer alleged that the credit corporation's lending arrangements were considered "uniquely advantageous" to developers and were used to tie in U.S. Steel's prefab homes.

What arguments might U.S. Steel and its subsidiary raise in defense?

5. Chevrolets, manufactured by General Motors, ordinarily are purchased by dealers from the manufacturer pursuant to a comprehensive uniform dealer-selling agreement. The agreement contains a clause prohibiting a dealer from moving to or establishing "a new or different location, branch-sales office, or place of business." Is this location clause lawful?

6. In the sales agreements for plain paper copiers, X-box stipulated that all services and parts required for the repair and maintenance of the copier must be provided by X-box. Without these service and parts contracts, X-box believes that its copiers would not function properly. Consequently, X-box has been using these contractual stipulations since the introduction of its products in 1964. Discuss the legality of this contractual provision.

7. Fotomat Corporation is engaged in the retail sale of film processing, film, and camera-related products, which are sold from small (9' × 5'), "drive-thru" kiosks located generally in shopping center parking lots. Some kiosks are operated by franchisees. According to the franchise contract, Fotomat is obligated to run a pickup and delivery service to the kiosks from a central area office. A route driver runs a daily pickup and delivery circuit of all the kiosks in the area, delivering the previous day's developed film and picking up that day's film. At the end of the route, the driver delivers the film to the processor.

In 1968, Photovest purchased 15 franchises to operate 15 Fotomat stores in Marion County, Indiana. Initially, the franchise agreement included a contractual clause prohibiting Photovest from buying film processing from anyone other than Fotomat. Then in June 1971, Fotomat wrote to its franchisees, apparently with knowledge of the then-recent opinion in *Siegel* v. *Chicken Delight,* advising them that they could use any processor they wished despite the provision in their agreements to the contrary. This letter, however, also assured the franchisees that Fotomat was selling processing at its cost without any markup whatsoever. Fotomat then adopted a policy that any franchisee who did switch print processors would have to supply its own pickup and delivery. When Photovest decided to switch processors in September 1974, Fotomat responded, consistent with this policy, by demanding that Photovest do its own pickup and delivery and customer service. Is Fotomat's policy lawful?

8. A consignment agency system of marketing employed by General Electric Co. sets the price at which lightbulbs can be sold by GE agents. These agents are thousands of independent businesses such as hardware, grocery, and drug stores that have entered into agreements of agency with GE whereby they handle the GE product on consignment, title passing from GE to the retail customer. Seventy-five percent of GE bulbs are sold by this method, the remainder going to nonagent dealers without restriction as to resale price. Is this practice in violation of the Sherman Act?

9. XYZ sold wearing apparel with suggested resale prices. In designing its system of maintaining resale prices, XYZ considered (1) using various forms of coercion, discipline, and surveillance; (2) terminating dealers it believed would not comply with these restrictions; or (3) prohibiting dealers from being reimbursed under its cooperative advertising program for ads offering XYZ's merchandise at other than its suggested prices. Are any of these enforcement methods illegal?

10. Russell Stover Candies, Inc., a major maker of boxed chocolates, refuses to deal with retailers who charge less than the manufacturer-suggested prices, and Stover communicates this policy to its dealers. Stover refuses to do business with stores that discount. As a result, Russell Stover Candy is sold at or above the suggested prices virtually everywhere. Is Stover violating the law?

SUGGESTED READINGS

Barrett, St. J., "Restrictive Distribution and the Assault of the 'Free Riders," *Journal of Corporation Law,* Vol. 7, Spring 1982, pp. 467–487.

Behringer, John W. and Monica A. Otte, "Liability and the Trademark Licensor: Advice for the Franchisor of Goods or Services," *American Business Law Journal,* Vol. 19, No. 2, Summer 1981, pp. 109–152.

Goldberg, Victor, "Enforcing Resale Price Maintenance: The FTC Investigation of Lenox," *American Business Law Journal,* Vol. 18, No. 4, Winter 1981, pp. 225–258.

Leete, Burt A., "An Analysis of the Standard for Determining the Requisite Economic Control Necessary for a Tying Contract to Amount to a Violation of the Sherman Act: The Lessons of Fortner I and II," *American Business Law Journal*, Vol. 16, No. 2, Fall 1978, pp. 189–202.

Williamson, Oliver, "Assessing Vertical Market Restrictions," *University of Pennsylvania Law Review*, April 1979, pp. 960–966.

Zelek, Jr., E. F., L. W. Stern, and T. W. Dunfee, "A Rule of Reason Model After Sylvania," *California Law Review*, January 1980, pp. 13–47.

ENDNOTES

1. *Dr. Miles Medical Co.* v. *John D. Park & Sons Co.*, 220 U.S. 373 (1911).
2. James C. Johnson and Louis E. Boone, "Farewell to Fair Trade," *MSU Business Topics*, Spring 1976, p. 25.
3. *Bissell Carpet Sweeper Co.* v. *Masters Mail Order Co. of Washington*, 240 F. 2d 684 (1957); and *General Electric Co.* v. *Masters Mail Order Co. of Washington*, 244 F. 2d 681 (1957), cert. denied.
4. See "Fair-Trade Laws May Be Retired by Congress," *Chicago Tribune*, February 10, 1975, citing a Consumer Union's estimate.
5. Public Law 94-145.
6. *Simpson* v. *Union Oil Co.*, 377 U.S. 13 (1964).
7. *U.S.* v. *Cuisinarts, Inc.*, Crim No. H-80-49; Civ. No. H-80-559, D. Conn., Sept. 17, 1980.
8. *Massachusetts* v. *Cuisinarts, Inc.*, Dkt. No. 80-2430-K, D. Mass., Oct. 10, 1980.
9. Robert E. Taylor, "Litvack Gets Attention of Business with Novel Antitrust Prosecution," *Wall Street Journal*, Oct. 31, 1980.
10. *U.S.* v. *Jerrold Electronics Corp.*, 365 U.S. 567 (1961).
11. Justice Douglas (dissenting) felt the requirements contracts employed by Standard Stations, Inc., were relatively less innocuous than the alternatives (agency devices or acquisition) available to the large oil companies. *Standard Oil Co. of Calif.* v. *United States*, 337 U.S. 293, 320 (1949).

chapter 13
PRICE DISCRIMINATION

Price discrimination is usually associated with some degree of market power and the absence of market forces. In markets with *open* price publicity, a seller would not normally be able to make some buyers pay a higher price while giving others a lower price for the same commodity. Instead, buyers asked to pay the higher price would turn to another seller. However, when *covert* price concessions are granted, buyers are unaware of the discrimination and do not pressure the seller to set uniform prices for all customers. Moreover, if price discrimination is openly practiced, unfavored buyers who continue to patronize the seller must have no alternative source of supply; that is, the seller possesses some monopoly power. Consequently, price discrimination is either an indicator of some degree of monopoly power or of incomplete (covert) competition.

There are three basic methods by which price discrimination may be exercised. First, the seller may discriminate between *customers* by charging a higher price to those who can afford to pay or who lack the power to buy from a substitute seller. Second, a seller may discriminate between purchasers in *different localities*. This geographic price discrimination may involve the practice of charging higher prices on a national basis while the seller receives a reduced price on shipments into a particular local market, or higher prices on domestic sales than on international sales (dumping). Third, price discrimination may be practiced by selling substantially identical products under *different labels or brands* at substantial differences in price. For example, petroleum refineries sell gasoline under different brand names, one at a higher price than the other.

EFFECTS ON COMPETITION

Price discrimination can affect market structure and the vigor of competition. It may strengthen or weaken competition, depending on the type of price discrimination utilized.

Some economists have argued that price discrimination can enhance competition by facilitating experimentation in pricing. Sellers will be willing to experiment with prices if such changes can be restricted to test markets. In this way, the seller can reduce the consequences of an adverse reaction by consumers or a business rival.

Another procompetitive effect is often called the "erosion theory." It maintains that unsystematic price discrimination has a tendency to undermine oligopolistic discipline. Sellers who are eager to utilize excess capacity may grant secret, discriminatory price concessions. But as word leaks out, other sellers match or undercut the secret discounts. As the price concessions spread, list prices become increasingly unrealistic and sellers may lose confidence in their rivals' willingness to cooperate to achieve a common price policy. In effect, the discriminatory lower price made available to one or a few buyers, it is said, may thereupon erode the published or uniform oligopolistic price and eventually become a price reduction available to all.

Those who do not accept the erosion theory argue that if the seller made the discriminatory lower price to retain or obtain a buyer's patronage, the buyer must at present have an alternative source of supply at a lower price. Either the buyer could obtain the product from another firm in the industry, probably one of the smaller independents, or the buyer could vertically integrate to produce the good for itself. If the buyer has these options, opponents of the erosion theory argue, then price discrimination is unnecessary as a competitive process because the real competition is the alternative available to the buyer. Therefore, instead of eroding the oligopolistic price structure, the price discrimination will more likely erode the enlargement of the alternative options available to the buyer; that is, it will eliminate the small independent seller or discourage the buyer from vertical integration. Consequently, opponents of the erosion theory view price discrimination as a technique utilized by oligopolistic firms to lower prices in certain product or geographic areas as a competitive response to the smaller firms. They lower prices in a discriminatory fashion rather than uniformly to all buyers. This price discrimination becomes a disciplinary action against a smaller firm. Therefore, price discrimination enables the large firm to "erode" small, independent competing sellers rather than the oligopolistic price structure.

Moreover, the erosion theory does not consider that the secret price concessions may be obtained only by large buyers who thereby obtain substantial cost advantages over smaller competing buyers. Consequently, the smaller competitors faced with higher purchasing costs and lower profits may be forced out of business without regard to their efficiency.

Even the proponents of the erosion theory recognize that discriminatory price concessions must be granted on an unsystematic basis. This is conceded because systematic price discrimination is likely to weaken competition by entrenching firms in their position of power. For example, a firm's dominant position in an industry could be entrenched if it received discriminatory price concessions from suppliers and granted discriminatory price reductions to large buyers. Competitors of the dominant firm that do not receive the price concessions from the suppliers would be at an obvious cost disadvantage. Moreover, the dominant firm's price concessions to large purchasers make it difficult for competing sellers to secure orders. In this manner, American Can Company was able to maintain its dominant position in the tin can industry by both receiving from suppliers and granting to large customers *systematic* discriminatory price concessions.[1]

Another sort of systematic discriminatory pricing involves the acceptance of lower rates of return on product lines that face competition and maintaining high margins on product lines that do not face stiff competitors.

In summation, various types of systematic price discrimination can strengthen monopoly positions by permitting large firms (1) to enjoy input costs lower than their smaller rivals (2) by foreclosing other sellers from buyers who receive special discounts for concentrated purchases from the monopolist and (3) by making entry into narrow segments of the market difficult or impossible because of narrow profit margins. On the other hand, economists differ as to whether *unsystematic* price discrimination can have a procompetitive effect by undermining oligopolistic discipline. Instead, some economists insist *unsystematic* price discrimination is a "disciplinary" technique used by large firms to force smaller firms into compliance policies.

PUBLIC POLICY ON PRICE DISCRIMINATION

With so many types and effects of price discrimination, it is difficult to form a consensus on appropriate public policy and to draft a discerning statute that would discourage undesirable price discrimination while permitting desirable ones.

Besides congressional efforts in the Interstate Commerce Act to eliminate price discrimination by railroads, the first statutory prohibition of price discrimination was embodied in Section 2 of the 1914 Clayton Act. It outlawed price discrimination where the effect "may be to substantially lessen competition or tend to create a monopoly." Price discrimination based on differences in the grade, quality, or quantity of the commodity sold was exempted. The quantity exemption proved to be a giant loophole, so that enforcement of the law was not spectacular. Of the 43 complaints by the FTC charging illegal price discrimination between 1914 and 1936, in only 8 was the government able to claim success.[2]

The growth of chain stores in the 1920s and 1930s led to a Federal Trade Commission investigation of chain store practices. The FTC report concluded that one reason for the decline of independent retailers was the ability of giant chains to obtain discriminatory price concessions from their suppliers. The chains passed the savings from these lower costs on to the consumer in lower prices, which drew away customers from smaller retailers. The report concluded that 15 percent of the chain's selling price advantage over independents was accountable to the induced price discrimination.[3] To eliminate this advantage derived from exerting purchasing leverage, the commission recommended strengthening of the law.

Congressional reaction to the FTC report was the amendment of Section 2 of the Clayton Act through the enactment of the Robinson–Patman Act of 1936. Congress sought to protect small independent enterprises from the price discrimination practices of large firms in both their sales and purchasing functions. Consequently, many assert that the purpose of the act is to reduce price discrimination as a competitive weapon and preserve small businesses. The preservation of small businesses, however, may be inconsistent with economic efficiency and consumer welfare. Although the appropriateness of the goals of the Robinson–Patman Act are still debated, the greater prosecutorial success of the FTC under the amended Section 2 cannot be disputed. Since its enactment, the FTC has issued over a thousand cease and desist orders against price discrimination practices.[4]

ROBINSON–PATMAN ACT

The Robinson–Patman Act has two main purposes, which are as follows.

1. The prevention of a seller from using its profits on higher priced interstate sales to unfairly subsidize its lower price in a regional market in competition with a regional seller.
2. The prevention of buyers from using their large purchasing power to exact discriminatory prices from suppliers to the unfair disadvantage of smaller buyers.

To protect these small sellers and buyers, the Robinson–Patman Act makes it illegal to charge different prices for different buyers for goods of like grade and quality when the effect of the differences in prices may substantially lessen competition. To determine whether a Robinson–Patman violation is present under Section 2(a) of the act, one should ask the following questions.

1. Has the company made sales at different prices within a reasonably contemporaneous time period. (This time period may vary depending on the competitive market, but six months is a good rule of thumb.)
2. Has one of the two sales involving different prices occurred in interstate commerce? (Price discrimination occurring totally intrastate is not covered by the Act.)
3. Are the products sold of like grade and quality (that is, of substantial physical and chemical identity without any significant difference from the commercial standpoint and regardless of different "branding")?

4. Have the sales resulted in probable injury to competition at the seller, buyer, or subbuyer level?

If any of these elements is absent, no Robinson–Patman violation has occurred. Even if the four criteria of a Section 2(a) violation are present, the defendant may still avoid conviction of violation of the law if he or she is able to prove a "justification" for the price discrimination. The act authorizes three justifications.

One justification for price discrimination under the law is "difference in cost of manufacturer, sale, or delivery resulting from the differing methods or quantities in which such commodities are . . . sold or delivered." However, this defense is largely an illusion.

In determining costs, the FTC considers only "full cost," that is, variable costs plus an appropriate share of total overhead. Full costing does not permit a seller to demonstrate that the lower price is justified because it completely covers variable cost and makes some partial contribution to overhead costs. The FTC feels variable cost pricing would defeat the purpose of the Robinson–Patman Act. Consequently, the FTC argues that the Robinson–Patman Act requires each customer to bear its proportionate share of the total cost. The imposition of the full-cost rule leads to inherently arbitrary judgments, since accounting theory provides no uniquely correct way of prorating fixed or joint costs.

Because of the difficulty in proving that the accounting standards utilized in the cost defense are the only or most appropriate standards, the defendant normally cannot establish the defense with acceptable evidence. Because of the debates concerning techniques of overhead cost allocation, the seller often fails to carry the burden of proof that the lower price was cost-justified. Between 1936 and 1954 only 11 attempts were made to utilize the cost defense in cases brought before the FTC. Of these, only two were fully successful.[5] Apart from the difficult task of proving the defense in litigation, the defendant may find more success in convincing the FTC at the informal investigatory stage that its cost data justify its price differential.

A second justification provided under the law is the privilege of charging different prices because of "changing conditions affecting the market for or the marketability of the goods concerned." This defense can be easily demonstrated by actual or eminent deterioration of perishable goods or obsolescence of seasonal goods. It also covers price changes resulting from inflation or other changing market conditions. Distress sales under court order or discontinuance of business would likewise be protected.

The last justification under the Act is embodied in Section 2(b). This section grants the seller the privilege of lowering a price in good faith to meet a price offered by a competitor. This defense has received considerable use in litigated cases and will be more fully discussed in the cases to follow.

Section 2(c) of the Robinson–Patman Act outlaws "phoney brokerage." Brokerage payments may not be paid by a seller to a buyer or an agent of the buyer except for services rendered to the seller. Often buyers attempt to bypass brokers of the seller and then seek the commission the broker normally earns from the seller. However, the buyer has not rendered services to the seller and is not entitled to such brokerage commission. The buyer has rendered service to himself or herself in bypassing the broker. These "phoney brokerage" allowances are illegal *per se*.

As the interpretations to Section 2(c) have evolved, mediaries are likely to be classified as wholesalers entitled to a wholesalers' functional discount if they customarily take title to goods being distributed, assume the risk of price fluctuations, and maintain warehouses and inventories. Any firm performing less than these functions is apt to be called a broker. Such brokers can earn a fee only for services rendered to the seller. Drawing a line between services rendered to the seller or buyer is obviously difficult and tends to eliminate any payments except to clearly recognized wholesalers or to bona fide brokers. Phoney brokers owned and set up by large buyers in order to obtain a brokerage commission (discount) from the seller are illegal.

Many large companies, nevertheless, are able to escape Section 2(c) violation by purchasing the entire output of their suppliers or by purchasing only from suppliers who employ no brokers. As a consequence, Section 2(c) may operate to the disadvantage of medium-sized buyers who have less flexibility in choosing sources of supply. Moreover, Section 2(c) may cause the unnecessary preservation of possibly uneconomic brokerage functions. Because of these and other shortcomings, there is rather widespread sentiment for the repeal of Section 2(c).

COMPETITIVE INJURY

Price discrimination of goods of like grade and quality is illegal only if (1) the effect of such discrimination in any line of commerce may substantially lessen competition or (2) injure or prevent competition with any person who either (a) grants or (b) knowingly receives the benefit of such discrimination or (c) customers of either of them. This language appears to indicate, and the effect of court decisions seems to support, that the first part of this law protects against injury to competition whereas the second part covers injury to a competitor. However, the courts have never officially recognized the concept of injury to a competitor unless such injury is a substantial injury to competition also. Rather than to merely protect a competitor, the FTC has chosen to use the test of injury to competition. Of course, private litigants favor the use of the more easily proven injury to a competitor (namely, themselves) test. Some courts tend to find competitive injury whenever an injury to a competitor occurs, which causes some confusion as to which legal standard is to be applied.

From the language of the Act, it is possible to have competitive injury on various levels of business operations. For example, if interstate seller A's price discrimination causes his or her (probably smaller, regional) competitive seller B to suffer injury, this would be primary-line or seller-level injury. Seller A could sell in most markets at a high price to subsidize the lower price in the market competing with Seller B. This seller-level injury is illustrated in Figure 13-1.

If the manufacturer sells his or her products at different prices to buyers

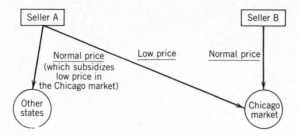

Figure 13-1.   Seller-level (primary-line) injury.

who compete with each other, the price discrimination will cause competitive injury at the buyers' level. This is called secondary-line injury and is diagrammed in Figure 13-2.

A third-line injury occurs when the customers of the supplier's buyer are discriminated against in prices. This level is a more controversial means of showing competitive injury, and lawsuits alleging third-line injuries rarely occur. Theoretically, it is possible for price discrimination to exist where no primary-line injury is present and the secondary-level buyers do not compete with each other, so that secondary-level injury is absent also. Nevertheless, if a lower price to a secondary-level buyer allows that buyer to pass on a lower price to customers who compete with customers of another secondary-level supplier, competitive injury occurs on the third level, as diagrammed in Figure 13-3.

Injury to the vigor of competition from the practice of price discrimination is clear when individual competitors are so lethally injured that they withdraw from the market, leaving fewer rivals competing more cautiously thereafter. However, courts have been willing to infer competitive injury even though rivals have not been literally driven from the market. The evidence needed to determine the requisite competitive injury has varied in court decisions, and its adequacy is continually debated.

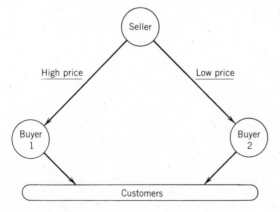

Figure 13-2.   Buyer-level (secondary-line) injury.

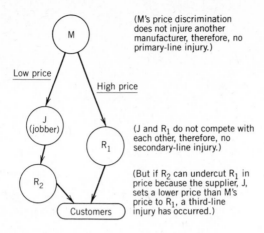

Figure 13-3. Subbuyer level (third-line) injury.

PROOF OF COMPETITIVE INJURY

Utah Pie Co. v. Continental Baking Co.
386 U.S. 685 (1967)
Supreme Court of the United States

Justice White

This suit for treble damages . . . was brought by petitioner, Utah Pie Company, against [defendants], Continental Baking Company, Carnation Company and Pet Milk Company. The complaint charged . . . violations by each [defendent] of Section 2(a) of the Clayton Act as amended by the Robinson–Patman Act. . . . The jury found for petitioner on the price discrimination charge. . . .

The product involved is frozen dessert pies. . . . The period covered by the suit comprised the years 1958, 1959, and 1960 and the first eight months of 1961. Petitioner is a Utah corporation which for 30 years has been baking pies in its plant in Salt Lake City and selling them in Utah and surrounding States. It entered the frozen pie business in late 1957. . . . Utah Pie's share of this market in those years was 66.5%, 34.3%, 45.5%, and 45.3%, respec-

tively, its sales volume steadily increasing over the four years. Its financial position also improved. Petitioner is not, however, a large company. . . .

Each of the [defendants] is a large company and each of them is a major factor in the frozen pie market in one or more regions of the country. Each entered the Salt Lake City frozen pie market before petitioner began freezing dessert pies. None of them had a plant in Utah. . . . They sold primarily on a delivered price basis.

The major competitive weapon in the Utah market was price. The location of petitioner's plant gave it natural advantages in the Salt Lake City marketing area and it entered the market at a price below the then going prices for [defendant's] comparable pies. For most of the period involved here its prices were the lowest in the Salt Lake City market. It was, however, challenged by each of the [defendants] at one time or another and for varying periods. There was ample evidence to show that each of the [defendants] contributed to what proved to be a deteriorating price structure over the period covered by this suit, and each of the [defendants] in the course of the ongoing price competition sold frozen pies in the Salt Lake market at prices lower than it sold pies of like grade and quality in other markets considerably closer to its plants. . . .

Petitioner's case against Continental is not complicated. . . . Effective for the last two weeks of June it offered its 22-ounce frozen apple pies in the Utah area at $2.85 per dozen. It was then selling the same pies at substantially higher prices in other markets. The Salt Lake City price was less than its direct cost plus an allocation for overhead. . . .

The Court of Appeals concluded that Continental's conduct had had only minimal effect, that it had not injured or weakened Utah Pie as a competitor, that it had not substantially lessened competition and that there was no reasonable possibility that it would do so in the future.

We differ with the Court of Appeals. Its opinion that Utah was not damaged as a competitive force apparently rested on the fact that Utah's sales volume continued to climb in 1961. . . . But this retrospective assessment fails to note that Continental's discriminatory below-cost price caused Utah Pie to reduce its price to $2.75. The jury was entitled to consider the potential impact of Continental's price reduction absent any responsive price cut by Utah Pie. . . . The jury could rationally have concluded that had Utah not lowered its price, Continental, which repeated its offer once, would have continued it. . . . It could also have reasonably concluded that a competitor who is forced to reduce his price to a new all-time low in a market of declining prices will in time feel the financial pinch and will be a less effective competitive force. . . .

Section 2(a) does not forbid [all] price com-petition. . . . But Congress has established some ground rules for the game. Sellers may not sell like goods to different purchasers at different prices if the result may to be injure competition in either the sellers' or the buyers' market unless such discriminations are justified as permitted by the Act. This case concerns the sellers' market. In the context, the Court of Appeals placed heavy emphasis on the fact that Utah Pie constantly increased its sales volume and continued to make a profit. But we disagree with its apparent view that there is no reasonably possible injury to competition as long as the volume of sales in a particular market is expanding and at least some of the competitors in the market continue to operate at a profit. Nor do we think that the Act only comes into play to regulate the conduct of price discriminators when their discriminatory prices consistently undercut other competitors. It is true that many of the primary line cases that have reached the courts have involved blatant predatory price discriminations employed with the hope of immediate destruction of a particular competitor. On the question of injury to competition such cases present courts with no difficulty, for such pricing is clearly within the heart of the proscription of the Act. Courts and commentators alike have noted that the existence of predatory intent might bear on the likelihood of injury to competition. In this case there was some evidence of predatory intent with respect to each of these [defendants]. There was also other evidence upon which the jury could rationally find the requisite injury to competition. . . . We believe that the Act reaches price discrimination that erodes competition as much as it does price discrimination that is intended to have immediate destructive impact. In this case, the evidence shows a drastically declining price structure which the jury could rationally attribute to continued or sporadic price discrimination. The jury was entitled to conclude that "the effect of such discrimination," by each of these [defendants], "may be substantially to lessen competition . . . or to injure, destroy, or prevent competition with any person who either grants or knowingly receives the benefit of such discrimination. . . ." The statutory test is one that necessarily looks forward on the basis of proved conduct in the past.

Questions
1. What evidence did the Court of Appeals rely on to determine that there was no "probable injury to competition"?
2. Must a predatory price discrimination be employed with the hope of immediate destruction of a particular competitor?
3. What evidence existed as to Continental's predatory intent? What motive could Continental have in selling its pies below cost?
4. Would Pet Milk's insertion of an "industrial spy" into Utah Pie's plant be evidence of predatory intent?

The *Utah Pie* decision has been criticized for protecting a seller whose cost advantage (lower transportation cost) made it quite able to protect itself. The controversy in this case also includes the argument over what constitutes predatory pricing. Below total cost pricing was accepted as evidence of predatory intent. However, recent cases reveal some appellate courts have rejected primary-line injury claims because prices had not been cut below average *variable* costs (see Areeda–Turner test in Chapter 9).[6] The Areeda–Turner test has been criticized by Posner and others when the pricing decision of the seller is supported by substantial monopoly power (entry barriers), as in the *Borden* ReaLemon case. Consequently, the controversy over predatory pricing formulas continues unabated, and Supreme Court clarification is sorely needed.

SECONDARY-LINE INJURIES

In secondary-line cases a clearer standard of competitive injury has been adopted. Beginning with the *Morton Salt* cash in 1948, the Supreme Court observed that Morton established a quantity discount schedule that lowered the price for carload lots and lowered the price even further on the basis of total annual purchases. The discount schedule permitted the largest buyers to gain prices below those of smaller rivals. The Court found the price scheme to be an illegal injury to competition and wrote the following.

The legislative history of the Robinson–Patman Act makes it abundantly clear that Congress considered it to be an evil that a large buyer could secure a competitive advantage over a smaller buyer solely because of the large buyer's quantity purchasing ability. . . . [I]n enacting the Robinson–Patman Act Congress was especially concerned with protecting small businesses which were unable to buy in quantities, such as the merchants here who purchased in less-than-carload lots. . . . That respondents quantity discounts did result in price differentials between competing purchasers sufficient in amount to influ-ence their resale price of salt was shown by evidence. This showing in itself was adequate to support the Commission's appropriate finding that the effect of such discriminations "may be substantially to lessen competition . . . and to prevent competition."[7]

Subsequent secondary-line cases have indicated that the price differentials must be large enough and given over a sufficient period of time to have a significant effect on sales and market shares before an inference of a competitive injury can be made. A 1965 appellate court has written as follows.

[I]t seems well established that where the record indicates a price differential substantial enough to cut into the purchaser's profit margin and discloses a reduction which would afford the favored buyer a significant aggregate saving that, if reflected in a resale price cut, would have a noticeable effect on the decisions of customers in the retail market, an inference of injury may properly be indulged.[8]

THE 2(b) DEFENSE

When a *prima facie* Section 2(a) price discrimination violation has been found, Section 2(b) of the Robinson–Patman Act permits a seller to rebut the *prima facie* presumption of illegality by showing that its lower price was "made in good faith to meet an equally low price of competitor."

The *Standard Oil of Indiana* case[9] established the meeting competition de-fense as a complete defense to a charge of injurious price discrimination. The FTC had charged Standard Oil with illegal discrimination in selling its Red Crown gasoline in the Detroit area to four independent gasoline dealers who received a price lower than that charged to other Red Crown dealers competing with the favored four dealers. Standard insisted it was simply meeting the lower price quoted by competitors, namely, a small independent refinery named Red Indian. Red Indian sold on a uniform price basis and normally had lower prices than the giant oil firms in order to secure retail outlets. The FTC refused to accept Standard's defense as an absolute defense where the discriminatory pric-ing caused competitive injury at the retail level.

The court of appeals upheld the Commission's decision that the probable injury to competition was to be weighed against the claimed advantage of the business practice of price discrimination. If the government could show that substantial injury to competition was reasonably probable, this would outweigh the need for Standard Oil of Indiana to retain customers by price discrimination. Standard Oil appealed this decision to the Supreme Court.

Prior to the Supreme Court's decision, the commission changed its attitude and in substance adopted the erosion theory. It felt price discrimination should be permitted in industries in which economic power had become concentrated in the hands of a few sellers. In such oligopolistic industries, the FTC recognized that price competition is almost nonexistent. Usually the only form of price competition is secret price concessions, such as Standard Oil made to the four independent retailers. The commissioners reasoned that if the Robinson–Patman Act was applied so as to require equal treatment of all customers, it might stifle this limited price competition in oligopolistic industries. By permitting some price discrimination, the commissioners accepted the erosion theory and its notion that some price competition would develop by allowing secret price discriminations. Consequently, in June 1949, the commission publicly announced its preference that the good faith meeting of competition defense be made absolute.[10] The Commission's new policy reduced the likelihood of success by the government's attorneys in defending the court of appeals' decision.

In 1951, the Supreme Court reversed the court of appeals in the *Standard Oil of Indiana* decision.[11] The Court ruled that even though competition among customers is injured, a seller may justify a lower discriminatory price to some customers if it showed that the lower price was made in good faith to meet the equally low price of a competitor.

Those who reject the erosion theory believe the *Standard Oil of Indiana* decision was a mistake.[12] They contend that price discrimination by a large seller discourages price competition by small competitors, such as Red Indian. Their argument is as follows.

Red Indian is faced with the consequence of continuing to lower its price in a financial war with Standard Oil of Indiana which is supporting its selective price reductions with higher prices charged elsewhere. In time, Red Indian will learn not to wage financial warfare with giant firms and will adopt a compliant price policy consistent with the pricing policies dictated by the larger firms. The real competitive factor, Red Indian, will be eroded by allowing the large firms the privilege of price discrimination. There will not be, as the erosion theory predicts, an erosion of the price level adopted by oligopolistic firms. Instead, the price discrimination becomes a tool for large firms to discipline smaller rivals who "dare" to lower their price below that level considered tolerable by the giants. Real price competition from smaller firms will "erode" away.

Despite the continuing debate, the good faith meeting of competition defense is an absolute defense, regardless of the existence of any competitive injury. The following case, *Cadigan* v. *Texaco*, is illustrative of the present policy.

Cadigan v. Texaco, Inc.
492 F. 2d 383 (1974)
U.S. Court of Appeals (9th Cir.)

[A former operator and lessee of Texaco service station brought suit against Texaco alleging that Texaco's sale of gasoline to Wickland Oil, a station across the street, at prices lower than the prices paid to Texaco by the plaintiff was a violation of the Robinson–Patman Act.]

* * *

Section 2(b) provides a complete defense to a *prima facie* case of price discrimination, despite any adverse effect on competition created by the price differential. The sole permissible inference which may be drawn from the uncontroverted facts is that Texaco offered the discriminatory discounts in a good faith effort to secure Wickland's business by matching prices offered by Texaco's competitors, Humble and American. . . . Plaintiff . . . contends that . . . defendants, not having shown that the prices of Texaco's competitors were lawful, failed to bring themselves within the Section 2(b) proviso. We reject this contention. A defendant need not prove the actual lawfulness of his competitor's price in order to secure the protection of the proviso. The well established rule is that Section 2(b) is satisfied unless it appears that the defendant either knows the price being met is unlawful or that it is inherently unlawful.

Plaintiff has offered no proof to suggest that the competitor's prices were unlawful, much less that Texaco knew them to be such.

Finally, [plaintiff] argues that the Section 2(b) defense can be asserted only when the price discrimination is made to retain old customers, and not, as in this case, when a seller meets competitive prices in order to obtain a new customer. The distinction is unsound and

has been rejected by the courts, *Sunshine Biscuits, Inc.* v. *FTC*, 306 F. 2d 48 (7th Cir., 1962); and is not applied by the Federal Trade Commission, *see* Beatrice Foods Co., Trade Reg. Rep. 19,045 (FTC 1970).

We agree with the Seventh Circuit that:

If, in situations where the Section 2(b) proviso is applicable, sellers could grant good faith competitive price reductions only to old customers in order to retain them, competition for new customers would be stifled and monopoly be fostered. In such situations an established seller would have a monopoly of his customers and a seller entering the market would not be permitted to reduce his price to compete with his established rivals unless he could do so on a basis such as cost justification. Moreover, the distinction would create a forced price discrimination between a seller's existing customers to whom he had lawfully lowered his price under Section 2(b) and a prospective new customer. These results, we believe, are incompatible with the purpose for which the Robinson–Patman Act was enacted.

Questions

1. Is the "good faith meeting of competition" defense a complete defense to a *prima facie* case of price discrimination?
2. To take advantage of the 2(b) defense must the seller prove the lawfulness of the competitor's price that it is meeting?
3. May the 2(b) defense be utilized "aggressively" to obtain new customers? Or is the 2(b) defense limited to the retention of old customers (defensive use)?

BUYER LIABILITY

Section 2(f) of the Robinson–Patman Act reveals that "it shall be unlawful for any person engaged in commerce, in the course of such commerce, knowingly to induce or receive a discrimination in price which is prohibited by this section."

From this language, it is easy to determine that the *buyer* may be in violation of this Act also. The buyer has committed a violation if he or she (1) receives an unlawful price discrimination and (2) has knowledge of its illegality. From the landmark *Automatic Canteen* case, the Court ruled that the FTC has the burden of "coming forward with evidence" on the buyer's knowledge of illegality and that this burden extends to establishing that the buyer lacked knowledge of cost justification of the price discrimination.[13] However, the FTC may establish its burden by "trade experience" evidence. In an FTC decision, it was established that the FTC need only show that the buyer "should have known" that the price discrimination received was not justified by costs or by meeting competition and, therefore, that the buyer had a "duty to inquire."[14]

Great A&P Tea Co. v. FTC
440 U.S. 69 (1979)
Supreme Court of the United States

Justice Stewart

The question presented in this case is whether the petitioner, the Great Atlantic and Pacific Tea Company (A&P), violated Section 2(f) of the Robinson–Patman Act, by knowingly inducing or receiving illegal price discriminations from the Borden Company (Borden).

The alleged violation was reflected in a 1965 agreement between A&P and Borden under which Borden undertook to supply "private label" milk to more than 200 A&P stores in a Chicago area that included portions of Illinois and Indiana. This agreement resulted from an effort by A&P to achieve cost savings by switching from the sale of "brand label" milk (milk sold under the brand name of the supplying dairy) to the sale of "private label" milk (milk sold under the A&P label).

To implement this plan, A&P asked Borden, its longtime supplier, to submit an offer to supply under private label certain of A&P's milk and other dairy product requirements. After prolonged negotiations, Borden offered to grant A&P a discount for switching to private label milk provided A&P would accept limited delivery service. Borden claimed that this offer would save A&P $410,000 a year compared to what it had been paying for its dairy products. A&P, however, was not satisfied with this offer and solicited offers from other dairies. A competitor of Borden, Bowman Dairy, then submitted an offer which was lower than Borden's. [Court footnote reads:

"The Bowman bid would have produced estimated annual savings of approximately $737,000 for A&P as compared with the first Borden bid, which would have produced estimated annual savings of $410,000."]

At this point, A&P's Chicago buyer contacted Borden's chain store sales manager and stated, "I have a bid in my pocket. You [Borden] people are so far out of line it is not even funny. You are not even in the ball park." When the Borden representative asked for more details, he was told nothing except that a $50,000 improvement in Borden's bid "would not be a drop in the bucket."

Borden was thus faced with the problem of deciding whether to rebid. A&P at the time was one of Borden's largest customers in the Chicago area. Moreover, Borden had just invested more than five million dollars in a new dairy facility in Illinois. The loss of the A&P account would result in underutilization of this new plant. Under these circumstances, Borden decided to submit a new bid which doubled the estimated annual savings to A&P, from $410,000 to $820,000. In presenting its offer, Borden emphasized to A&P that it needed to keep A&P's business and was making the new offer in order to meet Bowman's bid. A&P then accepted Borden's bid after concluding that it was substantially better than Bowman's.

* * *

Section 2(f) provides:

That it shall be unlawful for any person engaged in commerce, in the course of such commerce, knowingly to induce or receive a discrimination in price *which is prohibited by this section.* (Emphasis added.)

Liability under Section 2(f) thus is limited to situations where the price discrimination is one "which is prohibited by this section." While the phrase "this section" refers to the entire Section 2 of the Act, only subsections (a) and (b) dealing with seller liability involve discriminations in price. Under the plain meaning of Section 2(f), therefore, a buyer cannot be liable if a *prima facie* case could not be established against a seller or if the seller has an affirmative defense. In either situation, there is no price discrimination "prohibited by this section."

The derivative nature of liability under Section 2(f) is dependent on seller liability under Section 2(a).

The derivative nature of liability under Section 2(f) was recognized by this Court in *Automatic Canteen Co. of America* v. *FTC,* 346 U.S. 61. In that case, the Court stated that even if the Commission has established a *prima facie* case of price discrimination, a buyer does not violate Section 2(f) if the lower prices received are either within one of the seller's defenses or not known by him not to be within one of those defenses. . . . The Court thus explicitly recognized that a buyer cannot be held liable under Section 2(f) if the lower prices received are justified by reason of one of the seller's affirmative defenses.

The petitioner, relying on this plain meaning of Section 2(f) and the teaching of the *Automatic Canteen* case, argues that it cannot be liable under Section 2(f) if Borden had a valid meeting competition defense. The respondent, on the other hand, argues that the petitioner may be liable even assuming that Borden had such a defense. The meeting competition defense, the respondent contends, must in these circumstances be judged from the point of view of the buyer. Since A&P knew for a fact that the final Borden bid beat the Bowman bid, it was not entitled to assert the meeting competition defense even though Borden may have honestly believed that it was

simply meeting competition. Recognition of a meeting competition defense for the buyer in this situation, the respondent argues, would be contrary to the basic purpose of the Robinson–Patman Act to curtail abuses by large buyers.

The short answer to these contentions of the respondent is that Congress did not provide in Section 2(f) that a buyer can be liable if the seller has a valid defense. The clear language of Section 2(f) states that a buyer can be liable only if he receives a price discrimination "prohibited by this section." If a seller has a valid meeting competition defense, there is simply no prohibited price discrimination.

* * *

In the *Automatic Canteen* case, the Court warned against interpretations of the Robinson–Patman Act which "extend beyond the prohibitions of the Act and, in so doing, help give rise to a price uniformity and rigidity in open conflict with the purposes of other antitrust legislation." Imposition of Section 2(f) liability on the petitioner in this case would lead to just such price uniformity and rigidity.

In a competitive market, uncertainty among sellers will cause them to compete for business by offering buyers lower prices. Because of the evils of collusive action, the Court has held that the exchange of price information by competitors violates the Sherman Act. *United States* v. *Container Corp.,* 393 U.S. 333. Under the view advanced by the respondent, however, a buyer, to avoid liability, must either refuse a seller's bid or at least inform him that his bid has beaten competition. Such a duty of affirmative disclosure would almost inevitably frustrate competitive bidding and, by reducing uncertainty, lead to price matching and anticompetitive cooperation among sellers.

* * *

As in the *Automatic Canteen* case, we decline to adopt a construction of Section 2(f) that is contrary to its plain meaning and would lead to anticompetitive results. Accordingly, we hold that a buyer who has done no more than accept the lower of two prices competitively offered does not violate Section 2(f) provided the seller has a meeting competition defense.

* * *

Under the circumstances of this case, Borden did act reasonably and in good faith when it made its second bid. The petitioner, despite its longstanding relationship with Borden, was dissatisfied with Borden's first bid and solicited offers from other dairies.

* * *

Thus Borden was informed by the petitioner that it was in danger of losing its A&P business in the Chicago area unless it came up with a better offer. It was told that its first offer was "not even in the ball park" and that a $50,000 improvement "would not be a drop in the [bucket]." In light of Borden's established business relationship with the petitioner, Borden could justifiably conclude that A&P's statements were reliable and that it was necessary to make another bid offering substantial concessions to avoid losing its account with the petitioner.

Borden was unable to ascertain the details of the Bowman bid. It requested more information about the bid from the petitioner, but this request was refused. It could not then attempt to verify the existence and terms of the competing offer from Bowman without risking Sherman Act liability. Faced with a substantial loss of business and unable to find out the precise details of the competing bid, Borden made another offer stating that it was doing so in order to meet competition. Under these circumstances, the conclusion is virtually inescapable that in making that offer Borden acted in a reasonable and good-faith effort to meet its competition, and therefore was entitled to a meeting competition defense.

Since Borden had a meeting competition defense and thus could not be liable under Section 2(b) the petitioner who did no more than accept that offer cannot be liable under Section 2(f).

Questions

1. The FTC argued that the purpose of the Robinson–Patman Act is to curtail abuses by large buyers. Does the result of the A&P decision curtail the opportunities for abuses by large buyers? Does it offer the seller an easily proven affirmative defense that may be utilized also by the big buyer to the potential harm of other competing buyers? Will large buyers be able to receive substantial price concessions as a result of the A&P decision without incurring Robinson–Patman Act liability?

2. The Supreme Court warned that the FTC's interpretation of the act would extend beyond the prohibitions of the Robinson–Patman Act and lead to price uniformity and rigidity. How does the Court reach this conclusion?

3. The Supreme Court in a footnote indicated that A&P was not a "lying buyer" and the Court, therefore, did not need to decide whether such a buyer could be liable under Section 2(f) even if the seller had a meeting competition defense. In addition, a dissenting justice argued that a buyer who induces the lower bid by *misrepresentation* should not escape Robinson–Patman Act liability. Do these statements imply a warning to buyers as to the negotiation ploys that they might utilize?

EQUALITY IN PROMOTION

Sections 2(d) and 2(e) of the Robinson–Patman Act seek to afford equitable treatment to competing customers of the seller. These sections require that promotional payments, services, or facilities (such as advertising allowances or display materials) must be extended by the seller on proportionately equal terms to all the seller's customers who compete with each other. The law does not require that probable adverse competitive effect be shown for violation of these sections to occur. Rather, damages from the loss of the promotional service or allowance or to the buyer's "business stature" will suffice for the award of a pecuniary recovery to the buyer. Equitable promotional services to all customers should be the general rule of the seller, unless the seller can justify failure to provide equitable treatment of promotional services on the ground that it was meeting in good faith a competing offer of assistance by a competitor.

CONCLUSION

Price discrimination is a widespread business practice that has both favorable and unfavorable effects on competition. Consequently, the purpose of the law prohibiting price discrimination was to be specifically aimed only at the anticompetitive evils created by the buying power and selling practices of big business that injure smaller competitors. By overprotecting these competitors, the Robinson–Patman Act has become controversial because it is in conflict with the accepted antitrust purpose of protecting competition, not competitors.

In addition, many argue that the Act is conceptually complex, resulting in myriad interpretations, some of which have expanded the law beyond its narrowly conceived purpose and caused a chilling effect on the vigor of price flexibility and competition.

Efforts to repeal or reform the Robinson–Patman Act have consistently met with stern opposition from the lobbies of small business. In its present form, the Act is difficult to comply with, particularly in industries with sensitive price competition. To avoid violating the Act, a fundamental understanding of the provisions of the law by all levels of management is imperative.

DISCUSSION QUESTIONS

1. Hanson, a glass retailer, sued Pittsburgh Plate Glass Industries, Inc. (PPG), under the Robinson–Patman Act, claiming that PPG sold to Hanson's competitors at prices lower than those offered to Hanson. Hanson purchased glass at 62 cents per foot, which was cut to his size specifications. A competitor purchased standard stock sizes of identical glass at 35 cents per foot. Does PPG have a defense to this price discrimination charge?

2. Borden produced evaporated milk, canned the product, and marketed it bearing several labels, including Borden's own brand label and those for several customers' private brands. Evaporated milk bearing the Borden brand was sold at prices above that bearing private brand labels, both at wholesale and retail levels. At the retail level, a definite brand preference for Borden milk was found to exist, a certain segment of the market being willing to pay a higher price for the Borden label. The FTC charged Borden Co. with price discrimination, and Borden argued that the consumer brand preference rendered the products commercially different and, therefore, of different "grades" even though the canned milk was physically identical and of equal quality. Are Borden's products of "like grade and quality"?

3. Central Ice Cream Co. sued Golden Road Ice Cream Co. under the Robinson–Patman Act. Central claims Golden Road offered special price concessions to Central's customers in order to secure their patronage. Both companies manufacture ice cream in Illinois, and they compete in selling to retailers in the Chicago area. Does the Robinson–Patman Act apply?

4. Forelco sold its pocket calculator throughout the United States for around $100 a unit. The retailers then would mark up from that price and sell to the consuming public. In an effort to improve its market penetration in the South, Forelco implemented the policy of a reduced price in the southern states. What questions would you ask to determine if Forelco's pricing policies violated the Robinson–Patman Act?

5. Synflex, a division of Samuel Moore, manufactures plastic hydraulic hose and associated parts that are used in industry and agriculture. In August 1970, Bernard and Paul Schaben began selling Synflex products in the so-called agricultural aftermarket. The Schabens purchased these products from Samuel Moore at the prices established by Samuel Moore for its distributors. The Schabens set their own resale prices; frequently, they were higher than those suggested by Samuel Moore.

   Couplamatic, Inc., a wholly owned subsidiary of Samuel Moore, manufactures couplers, dies, and other hydraulic hose accessories. Couplamatic sold Samuel Moore products through a network of independent distributors. In June 1973, Couplamatic began distributing Synflex hose and accessories through "wagon jobbers," its own traveling distributors, in direct competition with the Schabens. Couplamatic obtained the Synflex products at factory cost plus a percentage add-on. No money was exchanged between the corporations; the transfer prices were merely bookkeeping entries.

   The Schabens allege that Samuel Moore engaged in discriminatory pricing. They argue that Couplamatic was a purchaser of Samuel Moore products, and that it enjoyed favorable prices unlawful under Section 2(a) of the Robinson–Patman Act. What result?

6. In the early 1970s, Borden departed from its uniform nationwide pricing system and divided the nation into three zones for pricing purposes. Borden

maintained a lower price in Zone 2 than in the other two zones. Zone 2 is where Borden faced the most serious competitive challenge by Golden Crown. Borden's lower prices in Zone 2 are not attributable to lower costs. How might Borden's pricing practices be illegal under the Robinson–Patman Act?

7. Kony sells its radio headset throughout the United States to retailers. To improve its sales in California, Kony reduced the price to California retailers. Kony received complaints from other retailers throughout the rest of the United States demanding the same reduced price. Is Kony running any legal risk in refusing to grant the same price reduction to buyers outside of California?

8. Since 1955 American Oil Co. had operated a marketing system in Chicago whereby it divided the city into sales zones for its dealers (gasoline station operators). The zones numbered in the hundreds and zone boundaries had never been changed. Although no market studies were done, each zone was intended to encompass the area from which a dealer drew his customers. When a lower retail price for a competing brand appeared in a zone, causing the American dealer to lose sales volume, American investigated its competitor's tank prices and determined if an allowance for the dealer in the affected zone was needed. The allowance took the form of a discount on American's tank wagon price to that dealer only. Some dealers received advertising allowances, and some received credits against rent payments, depending on their lease agreements with American. American did not always use the system, even when it received information as to lowered prices by competitors.

    Bargain Car Wash, a gas station and car wash, was an American dealer in Chicago whose arena of direct competition included its own zone and 12 surrounding zones. Bargain competed to some degree with gasoline stations in 22 additional zones.

    During 1968 Bargain received a \$.013-per-gallon allowance for the months of February and May. American dealers in the zones in which Bargain competed received allowances for those months, and most received allowances for several more months, with the amount of discount ranging up to \$.02 per gallon.

    On the average, Bargain's American competitors received allowances covering 136 days in 1968, to Bargain's 50 days. Some competing dealers received up to a \$.02 advertising or rental allowance per gallon sold.

    Bargain sued American under Section 2(a) of the Robinson–Patman Act. American raised two defenses. One defense involved the claim that the lower prices for individual dealers were granted in order to meet an equally low price offered by a competitor of American to individual competitors of American dealers. The second defense argued that the discounts and advertising and rent allowances were granted because of declining retail gasoline prices, which constituted "changing conditions" in the gasoline market.

    What result?

SUGGESTED READINGS

Blair, John M., *Economic Concentration: Structure, Behavior and Public Policy*, (New York: Harcourt Brace Jovanovich, Inc., 1972), pp. 342–347.

Bowman, W. S., "Restraint of Trade by the Supreme Court: The Utah Pie Case," *Yale Law Journal*, November 1967, p. 70.

Kintner, Earl W., *A Robinson–Patman Primer* (New York: Macmillan, 1970). U.S., Congress, House, Committee on Small Business, Ad Hoc Subcommittee on Antitrust, Robinson–Patman Act, and Related Matters Hearings, *Recent Effort to Amend or Repeal the Robinson–Patman Act*, Pt. 2, 94th Cong., 1st. sess., (1975), pp. 282–312.

ENDNOTES

1. *U.S.* v. *American Can Co.*, 230 F. 859, 256 U.S. 706 (1921); and see James W. McKie, *Tin Cans and Tin Plate* (Cambridge, Mass.: Harvard University Press, 1959), pp. 58–64, 160–82.

2. See Corwin D. Edwards, *The Price Discrimination Law* (Washington, D.C.: Brookings Institution, 1959), p. 6.

3. U.S. Federal Trade Commission, *Final Report on the Chain Store Investigation* (Washington, D.C.: U.S. Government Printing Office, 1934), p. 55.

4. U.S., Congress, House, Committee on Small Business, Ad Hoc Subcommittee on Antitrust, Robinson–Patman Act, and Related Matters Hearings, *Recent Effort to Amend or Repeal the Robinson–Patman Act*, Pt. 2, 94th Cong., 1st. sess., 1976, pp. 186–91.

5. See the *Report of the Attorney General National Committee to Study Antitrust Laws* (1955), p. 171.

6. See *Pacific Eng. & Prod. Co. of Nev.* v. *Kerr-McGee Corp.*, 551 F. 2d 790 (10th Cir., 1977), and *International Air Inds.* v. *American Excelsior Co.*, 517 F. 2d 714 (5th Cir., 1975), cert. denied in both cases.

7. *FTC* v. *Morton Salt Co.*, 334 U.S. 37, 43, 47 (1948).

8. *Foremost Dairies, Inc.* v. *FTC*, 348 F. 2d 674, 680 (1965).

9. *Standard Oil Co.* v. *FTC*, 340 U.S. 231 (1951).

10. Hearings before Subcommittee No. 1 of the House Committee of the Judiciary on S. 1008, 81st Cong. 1st. sess., June 8 and 14, 1949, p. 61.

11. *Standard Oil Co.* v. *FTC*, 340 U.S. 231 (1951).

12. Ronald H. Wolf and Vernon A. Mund, *Business and Government* (Advocate Publishing Group, 1980), p. 196.

13. *Automatic Canteen Co. of Am.* v. *FTC*, 346 U.S. 61 (1953).

14. *Fred Meyer, Inc.* v. *FTC*, 359 F. 2d 351 (9th Cir. 1966).

chapter 14

UNFAIR COMPETITIVE PRACTICES

By now, it is certainly clear that the American community has adopted the basic policy of competition as one of the means of social betterment. America has fashioned the antitrust laws in an attempt to protect the free competitive market from single firm monopolies and from competitor cartels. The competitive philosophy has even recognized and tolerated the more rigorous levels of competition that often cause harsh consequences to befall weaker or less efficient firms. These consequences are viewed as essential reallocations of the nation's scarce economic resources that in the long run bestow more gains on society than the losses occasioned by the reallocating process.

While the competitive process of trade warfare may be waged ruthlessly to the bitter end, there are certain rules of combat that must be observed. In the interest of the public and the competitors themselves, limits have been set by the law. Numerous practices have been designated as "unfair" competition; that is, beyond the traditional boundaries of reasonable business behavior. The courts have fashioned this body of laws that attempt to prohibit unfair competitive practices by either forcing violators to compensate competitors injured by the "unfair" competitive tactics or by issuing injunctions against the continuation of the unfair practices. Some of the law of unfair competition antedates the antitrust laws or other statutory regulations of business that involve enforcement by an administrative agency of government.

PRIVATE ENFORCEMENT

A brief categorization of unfair competition would include the following.

1. Injurious falsehoods by competitors that result in the diversion of patronage from the victim or otherwise injures his goodwill.
2. Infringement of another's trade secrets, patents, or trademarks.
3. Unauthorized interference with contracts or economic expectations.

These common law rules against unfair competition have also been reinforced by federal and state statutes.

The tort of injurious falsehoods includes defamation of the competitor, his goods, and his business methods. The following case illustrates a situation of injurious falsehoods, commonly referred to as trade disparagement.

TRADE DISPARAGEMENT

Testing Systems, Inc. v. Magnaflux Corp.
251 F. Supp. 286 (1966)
United States District Court (E.D. Pa.)

This is an action for trade libel or disparagement of property. . . .

Essentially the facts are these. Both plaintiff, Testing Systems, Inc., and the defendant, Magnaflux Corp., are engaged in the manufacture and sale of equipment, devices and systems, including chemical products, for use in the nondestructive testing of commercial and industrial materials. . . . The complaint contains allegations that both written and oral statements disparaging plaintiff's product were circulated by the defendant's agents to plaintiff's current and prospective customers. Specifically, in the former category, it is alleged that the defendant did on or about May 6, 1965, through its agents, publish an allegedly false report to the effect that the United States Government had tested plaintiff's product, and found it to be only about 40% as effective as that of the defendant.

It appears further from the complaint that on or about May 23, 1965, while in attendance at a manufacturer's convention in Phila-

delphia, defendant's agent, in the presence of plaintiff's current and prospective customers, "did in a loud voice state that . . . [plaintiff's] . . . stuff is no good," and that "the government is throwing them out."

[D]efendant admits the . . . [facts], but asserts that the action must nevertheless be dismissed because the defendant did no more than make an unfavorable comparison of plaintiff's product with its own.

* * *

It would serve no useful purpose to dwell at length on the issue of unfavorable comparison. Suffice it to say, as the defendant properly points out, that a statement which takes the form of an unfavorable comparison of products, or which "puffs" or exaggerates the quality of one's own product is not ordinarily actionable. This has long been the rule in England, where the action originated, and is now well established in the vast majority of United States jurisdictions.

However, this Court is not convinced by

the defendant's arguments, that his comments amounted to mere unfavorable comparison. The modern history of the doctrine of unfavorable comparison and its permissible use in the conduct of business traces its origin to the leading English case of *White* v. *Mellin* (1985). There the defendant had advertised his product as being far more healthful than plaintiff's. In refusing relief the Court established the precedent that irrespective of their truth or falsity, statements by one competitor which compare his product with that of another are not actionable.

It does not follow from this, however, that every trade disparagement is protectible under the guise of unfavorable comparison merely because the perpetrator was canny enough to mention not only the product of his competitor but also his own. The decision in *White* v. *Mellin*, was founded on the near impossibility of ascertaining the truth or falsity of general allegations respecting the superiority of one product over another. To decide otherwise, explained Lord Herschell, would turn the courts "into a machinery for advertising rival productions by obtaining a judicial determination [as to] which of the two was better."

* * *

The fine line that separates healthy competitive effort from underhanded business tactics is frequently difficult to determine. Apart from the tradesman's right of free speech, which must be vigorously safeguarded, the public has a genuine interest in learning the relative merits of particular products, however that may come about. To advance these interests the law of the marketplace gives the competitor a wide berth in the conduct of his business.

Nonetheless, there is an outer perimeter to permissible conduct. The tradesman must be assured that his competitors will not be suffered to engage in conduct which falls below the minimum standard of fair dealing. "[I]t is no answer that they can defend themselves by

also resorting to disparagement. A self-respecting business man will not voluntarily adopt, and should not be driven to adopt, a selling method which he regards as undignified, unfair, and repulsive. A competitor should not, by pursuing an unethical practice force his rival to choose between its adoption and the loss of his trade."

The defendant's comments in the case presently before this Court do not entitle him to the protection accorded to "unfavorable comparison." There is a readily observable difference between saying that one's product is, in general, better than another's and asserting, as here, that such other's is only 40% as effective as one's own. The former, arguably, merely expresses an opinion, the truth or falsity of which is difficult or impossible of ascertainment. The latter, however, is an assertion of fact, not subject to the same frailties of proof, implying that the party making the statement is fortified with the substantive facts necessary to make it. This distinction has never been seriously questioned. The defendant in this case admittedly circulated to plaintiff's present and prospective customers false statements to the effect that the government had tested both products and found the defendant's to be 60% more effective than the plaintiff's. This is not the sort of "comparison" that courts will protect.

Apart from this, there is at least one additional factor which withdraws the defendant's comments from the category of unfavorable comparison. Not content with making the admittedly false statements and allowing them to be evaluated independently of all extraneous influence, the defendant here gave added authenticity to its assertions by invoking the reputation of a third party, the United States Government. It is unnecessary to speculate on the additional force the defendant's remarks must have had when coupled with the purported approval of so highly credible a source. This, of course, is to say nothing of the statements to the effect that the plaintiff had been "thrown out," which by no stretch of the imagination could be termed mere comparison.

For all of the above reasons, it is the judg-

ment of this Court that the defendant's remarks are actionable. . . .

Questions
1. What is the defense to the allegations of trade disparagement in *White* v. *Mellin?*
2. What public policy is supported in the decision in *White* v. *Mellin?*
3. Why was the rationale of *White* v. *Mellin* not applicable in this instance?

"PALMING OFF"

One large area of unfair competition is the fraudulent (false) marketing of one person's goods as those of another. This unlawful marketing tactic is often referred to as "palming off" or "passing off." It consists of false representations to the public that are likely to induce them to believe that the goods of the misrepresentor are those of another. This is often done by some sort of counterfeiting or imitating of the plaintiff's containers, trademark, tradenames, the appearance of his or her place of business, or the physical appearance of the product sold. The test utilized in such cases is whether the resemblance is so great as to deceive the ordinary customer acting with the caution usually exercised in such transactions. If the customer could mistake one product for the other *because* of the false representation, this likelihood of confusion or deception is sufficient for the plaintiff to gain injunctive relief against the defendant's false representations. On the other hand, if the imitation does not involve a misrepresentation or a passing off, the result will be different, as illustrated in the following case.

Sears, Roebuck & Co. v. Stiffel Co.
376 U.S. 225 (1964)
Supreme Court of the United States

Justice Black

The question in this case is whether a State's unfair competition law can, consistently with the federal patent laws, impose liability for or prohibit the copying of an article which is protected by neither a federal patent nor a copyright. The respondent, Stiffel Company, secured design and mechanical patents on a "pole lamp"—a vertical tube having lamp fixtures along the outside, the tube being made so

that it will stand upright between the floor and ceiling of a room. Pole lamps proved a decided commercial success, and soon after Stiffel brought them on the market, Sears, Roebuck & Company put on the market a substantially identical lamp, which it sold more cheaply, Sears' retail price being about the same as Stiffel's wholesale price. Stiffel then brought this action against Sears in the United States District Court . . . claiming in its first count that by copying its design Sears had infringed Stiffel's patents and in its second count that by selling copies of Stiffel's lamp Sears had caused confusion in the trade as to the source of the lamps and had thereby engaged in unfair competition under Illinois law. There was evidence that identifying tags were not attached to the Sears lamp although labels appeared on the cartons in which they were delivered to customers, that customers had asked Stiffel whether its lamps differed from Sears' and that in two cases customers who had bought Stiffel lamps had complained to Stiffel on learning that Sears was selling substantially identical lamps at a much lower price.

The District Court, after holding the patents invalid for want of invention, went on to find as a fact that Sears' lamp was "a substantially exact copy" of Stiffel's and that the two lamps were so much alike, both in appearance and in functional details, "that confusion between them is likely, and some confusion has already occurred." On these findings the court held Sears guilty of unfair competition, enjoined Sears "from unfairly competing with [Stiffel] by selling or attempting to sell pole lamps identical to or confusingly similar to" Stiffel's lamp, and ordered an accounting to fix profits and damages resulting from Sears' "unfair competition."

The Court of Appeals affirmed. That court held that, to make out a case of unfair competition under Illinois law, there was no need to show that Sears had been "palming off" its lamps as Stiffel lamps; Stiffel had only to prove that there was a "likelihood of confusion as to the source of the products"—that the two articles were sufficiently identical that customers could not tell who had made a particular one. Impressed by the "remarkable sameness of appearance" of the lamps, the Court of Appeals upheld the trial court's findings of likelihood of confusion and some actual confusion, findings which the appellate court construed to mean confusion "as to the source of the lamps." The Courts of Appeals thought this enough under Illinois law to sustain the trial court's holding of unfair competition, and

thus held Sears liable under Illinois law for doing no more than copying and marketing an unpatented article. We granted *certiorari* to consider whether this use of a State's law of unfair competition is compatible with the federal patent law.

* * *

In the present case the "pole lamp" sold by Stiffel has been held not to be entitled to the protection of either a mechanical or a design patent. An unpatentable article, like an article on which the patent has expired, is in the public domain and may be made and sold by whoever chooses to do so. What Sears did was to copy Stiffel's design and to sell lamps almost identical to those sold by Stiffel. This it had every right to do under the federal patent laws. That Stiffel originated the pole lamp and made it popular is immaterial. "Sharing in the goodwill of an article unprotected by patent or trade-mark is the exercise of a right possessed by all—and in the free exercise of which the consuming public is deeply interested." To allow a State by use of its law of unfair competition to prevent the copying of an article which represents too slight an advance to be patented would be to permit the State to block off from the public something which federal law has said belongs to the public. The result would be that while federal law grants only 14 to 17 years' protection to genuine inventions, States could allow perpetual protection to articles too lacking in novelty to merit any patent at all under federal constitutional standards. This would be too great an encroachment on the federal patent system to be tolerated.

Sears has been held liable here for unfair competition because of a finding of likelihood of confusion based only on the fact that Sears' lamp was copied from Stiffel's unpatented lamp and that consequently the two looked exactly alike. Of course there could be "confusion" as to who had manufactured these nearly identical articles. But mere inability of the public to tell two identical articles apart is not enough to support an injunction against copying or an award of damages for copying that which the federal patent laws permit to be copied. . . . [B]ecause of the federal patent laws a State may not, when the article is unpatented and uncopyrighted, prohibit the copying of the article itself or award damages for such copying. The judgment below did both and in so doing gave Stiffel the equivalent of a patent monopoly on its unpatented lamp. That was error, and Sears is entitled to a judgment in its favor.

Questions

1. Why was Stiffel not able to succeed in its first count of patent infringement?
2. Was Sears palming off its lamps as Stiffel's?
3. Illinois law of unfair competition did not require a showing of palming off before the plaintiff was entitled to an injunction. Instead, an injunction was issued to prevent confusion. Did the Supreme Court feel Illinois' version of the law was compatible with the federal patent laws?
4. What two basic public policies are in conflict in this case—the fruits of competition versus the avoidance of consumer confusion? Which policy won? When would the other policy win?

TRADE SECRETS

Many businesses have secret information, formulas, processes, or methods used in the production of goods. These "trade secrets" are often known by employees who acquire the information in performance of their duties. Since employees have a duty of loyalty to their employer, they are to hold these trade secrets in confidence. It is illegal for a competitor to obtain trade secrets from an employee by bribery or by urging the employee to quit his job for subsequent employment by the competitor. While the employee is free to leave his employment, he must not make use of the trade secret of his former employer in his new job.

The following case involves an action for the misappropriation of trade secrets and the potential conflict between the law of trade secrets and the patent laws of the United States.

Kewanee Oil Co. v. Bicron Corporation
416 U.S. 470 (1974)
Supreme Court of the United States

[Kewanee Oil Co., petitioner, is a leading manufacturer of a type of synthetic crystal that is useful in the detection of ionizing radiation. As the result of expenditures in excess of $1 million, Kewanee was able to grow a 17-inch crystal, something no one else had done previously. Kewanee considered its manufacturing techniques to be trade secrets. Former employees of Kewanee formed Bicron, defendant, to compete with Kewanee in the production of the 17-inch crystals. Petitioner filed suit, seeking an injunction and damages for the misappropriation of trade secrets. The federal district court, applying Ohio trade secret law, granted a permanent injunction against defendant and its employees, which prohibited the disclosure or use of 20 claimed trade secrets until such time as the trade secrets had been released to the public, had otherwise become available to the public, or had been obtained by defendants from sources having the legal right to convey the information. The Court of Appeals reversed the district court, holding Ohio's trade secret law to be in conflict with the patent laws of the United States.]

Mr. Chief Justice Burger

* * *

The subject of a trade secret must be secret, and must not be of public knowledge or of a general knowledge in the trade or business. This necessary element of secrecy is not lost, however, if the holder of the trade secret reveals the trade secret to another "in confidence, and under an implied obligation not to use or disclose it." These others may include those of the holder's "employees to whom it is necessary to confide it, in order to apply it to the uses for which it is intended." Often the recipient of confidential knowledge of the subject of a trade secret is a licensee of its holder. The protection accorded the trade secret holder is against the disclosure or unauthorized use of the trade secret by those to whom the secret has been confided under the express or implied restriction of nondisclosure or nonuse. The law also protects the holder of a trade secret against disclosure or use when the knowledge is gained, not by the owner's volition, but by some "improper means," which may include theft, wiretapping, or even aerial reconnaissance. A trade secret law, however, does not offer protection against discovery by fair and honest means, such as by independent invention, accidental disclosure, or by so-called reverse engineering, that is by starting with the known product and working backward to divine the process which aided in its development or manufacture.

* * *

The first issue we deal with is whether the States are forbidden to act at all in the area of protection of the kinds of intellectual property which may make up the subject matter of trade secrets.

* * *

The laws which the Court of Appeals in this case held to be in conflict with the Ohio law of trade secrets were the patent laws passed by the Congress in the unchallenged exercise of its clear power under . . . the Constitution. The patent law does not explicitly endorse or forbid the operation of trade secret law. However, . . . if the scheme of protection developed by Ohio respecting trade secrets "clashes with the objectives of the federal patent laws," then the state law must fall. . . .

* * *

Certainly the patent policy of encouraging invention is not disturbed by the existence of another form of incentive to invention. In this respect the two systems are not and never would be in conflict.

The more difficult objective of the patent law to reconcile with trade secret law is that of disclosure, the *quid pro quo* of the right to exclude.

* * *

The interest of the public is that the bargain of 17 years of exclusive use in return for disclosure be accepted. If a State, through a system of protection, were to cause a substantial risk that holders of patentable inventions would not seek patents, but rather would rely on the state protection, we would be compelled to hold that such a system could not constitutionally continue to exist. In the case of trade secret law no reasonable risk of deterrence from patent application by those who can reasonably expect to be granted patents exists.

Trade secret law provides far weaker protection in many respects than the patent law. While trade secret law does not forbid the discovery of the trade secret by fair and honest means, e.g., independent creation or reverse engineering, patent law operates "against the world," forbidding any use of the invention for whatever purpose for a significant length of time. The holder of a trade secret also takes a substantial risk that the secret will be passed on to his competitors, by theft or by breach of a confidential relationship, in a manner not easily susceptible of discovery or proof. Where patent law acts as a barrier, trade secret law functions relatively as a sieve. The possibility that an inventor who believes his invention meets the standards of patentability will sit back, rely on trade secret law, and after one year of use forfeit any right to patent protection, is remote indeed.

* * *

Trade secret law and patent law have coexisted in the country for over one hundred years. Each has its particular role to play, and the operation of one does not take away from the need for the other. Trade secret law encourages the development and exploitation of those items of lesser or different invention than might be accorded protection under the patent laws, but which items still have an important part to play in the technological and scientific advancement of the Nation. Trade secret law promotes the sharing of knowledge, and the efficient operation of industry; it permits the individual inventor to reap the rewards of his labor by contracting with a company large enough to develop and exploit it. Congress, by its silence over these many years, has seen the wisdom of allowing the States to enforce trade secret protection. Until Congress takes affirmative action to the contrary, States should be free to grant protection to trade secrets.

Since we hold that Ohio trade secret law is not preempted by the federal patent law, the judgment of the Court of Appeals for the Sixth Circuit is reversed, and the case is remanded to the Court of Appeals with directions to reinstate the judgment of the District Court.

Questions
1. What lawful means are available to learn a competitor's trade secrets?
2. Do trade secrets promote or hinder competition?
3. Is disclosure of trade secrets as important to society as the disclosure of information concerning patents?
4. Are the state trade secret laws and the U.S. patent laws in conflict?

TRADEMARKS

A trademark is a distinctive mark, word, letter, number, design, picture, or combination thereof that is affixed to goods and used by a business firm to identify the products it manufactures or sells. Trademarks may be registered with the U.S. Patent Office. The Lanham Act (Trademark Act of 1946) permits trademark registration and protection of a mark placed "on the goods or their containers or displays associated therewith or on the tags or labels affixed thereto."

Generally, generic or descriptive designations cannot be used as trademarks. This limitation protects against one firm monopolizing a word that generally describes a product of that industry. The following case further illustrates the issues involved in formulating a trademark and in protecting the mark from infringement. An infringement is a form of passing off, in that the infringer attempts to use the mark or some variation in order to cash in on the goodwill and reputation of the competitor's mark. As such, trademark infringement constitutes unfair competition.

Abercrombie & Fitch Co. v. Hunting World, Inc.
537 F. 2d 4 (1976)
U.S. Court of Appeals (2d Cir.)

This action by Abercrombie & Fitch Company (A&F), owner of well-known stores at Madison Avenue and 45th Street in New York City and seven places in other states, against Hunting World, Incorporated (HW), operator of a competing store on East 53rd Street, is for infringement of some of A&F's registered trademarks using the word "Safari." . . .

I.

The complaint, after describing the general nature of A&F's business, reflecting its motto "The Greatest Sporting Goods Store in the World," alleged as follows: For many years A&F has used the mark "Safari" on articles "exclusively offered and sold by it." Since 1936 it has used the mark on a variety of men's and women's outer garments. A&F has spent large sums of money in advertising and promoting products identified with its mark "Safari" and in policing its right in the mark, including the successful conduct of trademark infringement suits. HW, the complaint continued, has engaged in the retail marketing of sporting apparel including hats and shoes, some identified by use of "Safari" alone or by expressions such as "Minisafari" and "Safariland." Continuation of HW's acts would confuse and deceive the public and impair "the distinct and unique quality of the plaintiff's trademark." A&F sought an injunction against infringement and an accounting for damages and profits.

HW filed an answer . . . that "the word 'safari' is an ordinary, common, descriptive, geographic, and generic word" which "is commonly used and understood by the public to mean and refer to a journey or expedition, especially for hunting or exploring in East Africa, and to the hunters, guides, men, animals, and equipment forming such an expedition" and is not subject to exclusive appropriation as a trademark. . . .

II.

The cases, and in some instances the Lanham Act, identify four different categories of terms with respect to trademark protection. Arrayed in an ascending order which roughly reflects their eligibility to trademark status and the degree of protection accorded, these classes are (1) generic, (2) descriptive, (3) suggestive, and (4) arbitrary or fanciful. The lines of demarcation, however, are not always bright. Moreover, the difficulties are compounded because a term that is in one category for a particular product may be in quite a different one for another, because a term may shift from one category to another in light of differences in usage through time, because a term may have one meaning to one group of users and a different one to others, and because the same term may be put to different use with respect to a single product. In various ways, all of these complications are involved in the instant case.

A generic term is one that refers, or has come to be understood as referring, to the genus of which the particular product is species. At common law neither those terms which were generic nor those which were merely descriptive could become valid trademarks. While, as we shall see, the Lanham Act makes an important exception with respect to those merely descriptive terms which have acquired secondary meaning, it offers no such exception for generic marks. The Act provided for the cancellation of a registered mark if at any time it "becomes the common descriptive name of an article or substance." This means that even proof of secondary meaning, by virtue of which some "merely descriptive" marks may be registered, cannot transform a generic term into a subject for trademark. . . . [N]o matter how much money and effort the user of a generic term has poured into promoting the sale of its merchandise and what success it has achieved in securing public identification, it cannot deprive competing manufacturers of the product of the right to call an article by its name. . . . The pervasiveness of the principle is illustrated by a series of well-known cases holding that when a suggestive or fanciful term has become generic as a result of a manufacturer's own advertising efforts, trademark protection will be denied save for those markets where the term still has not become generic and a secondary meaning has been shown to continue. A term may thus be generic in one market and descriptive or suggestive or fanciful in another.

The term which is descriptive but not generic stands on a better basis. Although section 2(e) of the Lanham Act forbids the registrations of a mark which, when applied to the goods of the applicant, is "merely descriptive," Section 2(f) removes a considerable part of the sting by providing ". . . nothing in this chapter shall prevent the registration of a mark used by the applicant which has become distinctive of the applicant's goods in commerce" and that the Commissioner may accept, as *prima facie* evidence that the mark has become distinctive, proof of substantially exclusive and continuous use of the mark applied to the applicant's goods for five years preceding the application. . . . In the case [of generic terms] any claim to an exclusive right must be denied since this in effect would confer a monopoly

not only of the mark but of the product by rendering a competitor unable effectively to name what it was endeavoring to sell. In the . . . case [of descriptive terms] the law strikes the balance, with respect to registration, between the hardships to a competitor in hampering the use of an appropriate word and those to the owner who, having invested money and energy to endow a word with the good will adhering to his enterprise, would be deprived of the fruits of his efforts.

The category of "suggestive" marks was spawned by the felt need to accord protection to marks that were neither exactly descriptive on the one hand nor truly fanciful on the other. . . . Having created the category the courts have had great difficulty in defining it. . . . [One] court has observed . . . that:

A term is suggestive if it requires imagination, thought, and perception to reach a conclusion as to the nature of goods. A term is descriptive if it forthwith conveys an immediate idea of the ingredients, qualities, or characteristics of the goods.

Also useful is the approach taken by this court . . . that the reason for restricting the protection accorded descriptive terms, namely the undesirability of preventing an entrant from using a descriptive term for his product, is much less forceful when the trademark is a suggestive word since, as Judge Lumbard wrote,

The English language has a wealth of synonyms and related words with which to describe the qualities which manufacturers may wish to claim for their products and the ingenuity of the public relations profession supplies new words and slogans as they are needed.

If a term is suggestive, it is entitled to registrations without proof of secondary meaning. Moreover, . . . the decision of the Patent Office to register a mark without requiring proof of secondary meaning affords a rebuttable presumption that the mark is suggestive or arbitrary or fanciful rather than merely descriptive.

It need hardly be added that fanciful or arbitrary terms enjoy all the rights accorded to suggestive terms as marks—without the need of debating whether the term is "merely descriptive" and with ease of establishing infringement. . . .

III.

We turn first to an analysis of A&F's trademarks to determine the scope of protection to which they are entitled. . . .

It is common ground that A&F could not apply "Safari" as a trademark for an expedition into the African wilderness. This would be a clear example of the use of "Safari" as a generic term. What is perhaps less obvious is that a word may have more than one generic use. The word "Safari" has become part of a family of generic terms which, although deriving no doubt from the original use of the word and reminiscent of its milieu, have come to be understood not as having to do with hunting in Africa, but as terms within the language referring to contemporary American fashion apparel. These terms name the components of the safari outfit well-known to the clothing industry and its customers: the "Safari hat," a broad flat-brimmed hat with a single, large band; the "Safari jacket," a belted bush jacket with patch pockets and a buttoned shoulder loop; when the jacket is accompanied by pants, the combination is called the "Safari suit." Typically these items are khaki-colored.

This outfit, and its components, were doubtless what Judge Ryan had in mind when he found that "the word 'safari' in connection with wearing apparel is widely used by the general public and people in the trade." The record abundantly supports the conclusion that many stores have advertised these items despite A&F's attempts to police its mark. In contrast, a search of the voluminous exhibits fails to disclose a single example of the use of "Safari," by anyone other than A&F and HW, on

merchandise for which A&F has registered "Safari" except for the safari outfit and its components as described above.

What has been thus far established suffices to support the dismissal of the complaint with respect to many of the uses of "Safari" by HW. Describing a publication as a "Safariland Newsletter," containing bulletins as to safari activity in Africa, was clearly a generic use which is nonenjoinable. A&F also was not entitled to an injunction against HW's use of the word in advertising goods of the kind included in the safari outfit as described above. And if HW may advertise a hat of the kind worn on safaris as a safari hat, it may also advertise a similar brim as a minisafari. Although the issue may be somewhat closer, the principle against giving trademark protection to a generic term also sustains the denial of an injunction against HW's use of "Safariland" as a name of a portion of its store devoted at least in part to the sale of clothing as to which the term "Safari" has become generic.

A&F stands on stronger ground with respect to HW's use of "Camel Safari," "Hippo Safari," and Chukka "Safari" as names for boots imported from Africa. As already indicated, there is no evidence that "Safari" has become a generic term for boots. Since, as will appear, A&F's registration of "Safari" for use on its shoes has become incontestable, it is immaterial whether A&F's use of "Safari" for boots was suggestive or "merely descriptive."

HW contends, however, that even if "Safari" is a valid trademark for boots, it is entitled to the defense of "fair use" within Section 33(b)(4) of the Lanham Act. That section offers such a defense even as against marks that have become incontestable when the term charged to be an infringement is not used as a trademark "and is used fairly and in good faith only to describe to users the goods and services of such party, or their geographic origin."

Here, Lee Expeditions, Ltd., the parent company of HW, has been primarily engaged in arranging safaris to Africa since 1959;

Robert Lee, the president of both companies, is the author of a book published in 1959 entitled "Safari Today—The Modern Safari Handbook" and has, since 1961, booked persons on safaris as well as purchased safari clothing in Africa for resale in America. These facts suffice to establish, absent a contrary showing, the defendant's use of "Safari" with respect to boots was made in the context of hunting and traveling expeditions and not as an attempt to garner A&F's good will. The district court here found the HW's use of "Camel Safari," "Hippo Safari," and "Safari Chukka" as names for various boots imported from Africa constituted "a purely descriptive use to apprise the public of the type of product by referring to its origin and use." The court properly followed the course sanctioned by this court in . . . [a previous case] by focusing on the "use of words, not on their nature or meaning in the abstract." When a plaintiff has chosen a mark with some descriptive qualities, he cannot altogether exclude some kinds of competing uses even when the mark is properly on the register. We do not have here a situation similar to those in . . . [previous cases] in . . . which we rejected "fair use" defenses, wherein an assertedly descriptive use was found to have been in a trademark sense. It is significant that HW did not use "Safari" alone on its shoes, as it would doubtless have done if confusion had been intended.

We thus hold that the district court was correct in dismissing the complaint.

Questions

1. Why cannot generic names be trademarked? Can a term that was registered as a fanciful trademark become generic over time and lose its trademark protection?

2. Can you supply examples of the use of the word *ivory* as a generic description of a product and as an arbitrary term applied to a product?

3. In the example of a "deep bowl spoon," which words are descriptive of the article and which are generic? On the other hand, when would "deep bowl" be a generic term?

4. Under what conditions will the Lanham Act allow the registration of a descriptive term as a trademark? What policy supports this rule?

5. If a person is able to register a mark without proof of secondary meaning, the Patent Office must have determined that the term was not merely descriptive. Does the conclusion of the Patent Office aid the registrant in an action against an alleged infringer?

6. A fanciful term usually means words invented solely for their use as trademarks. Can you supply an example?

7. An arbitrary term usually means a common term used in an unfamiliar way. Can you supply an example?

8. What advantages exist for the registrant when fanciful or arbitrary terms are used?

9. Why was the registrant's trademark, "Safari," not enforceable in the sale of safari outfits? Why was the Safari trademark generally enforceable in the sale of safari boots? Is use of the term Safari, in relation to the boots, suggestive or merely descriptive? Is use of the term Safari, in relation to

the boots, an "incontestable" (i.e., continuous five-year use) trademark? What is the effect of incontestability?

10. What is the defense of "fair use"? Why was the defendant entitled to assert this defense?

TRADENAMES

A tradename, like a trademark, identifies the manufacturer or distributor of a product. Unlike a trademark, a tradename may also designate a service or the business conducted by the name holder. Therefore, tradenames have a broader scope than trademarks, but generally follow the same rules for validity and protection from infringement. As one court has written:

We read the Delaware cases as holding that a plaintiff in a trade-name infringement—unfair competition case must show (1) either that its name is capable of exclusive appropriation or that its name, though not capable to exclusive appropriation, has acquired a "secondary meaning" and (2) that the name appropriated by the defendant is of such similarity to that of plaintiff that plaintiff's customers or potential customers are likely to confuse the two.

For public policy reasons, words which are purely descriptive or purely geographical have been held to be non-exclusive. Absent a showing of secondary meaning, no action for unfair competition may be maintained. Where, however, the words are arbitrary or fanciful and could be descriptive of anything, they are not descriptive at all, and the prior user is entitled to the exclusive use thereof. Stated another way: "Rights in names of corporations which are made up of fanciful non-descriptive names are based on priority of use and as between two similar corporate names, not personal or descriptive in character, the one coming into existence last must give way to the prior one."

Questions
1. When can a name, like Akron, not become exclusive? What about the Akron Corporation?
2. Could the Akron Barber Shop preclude another company from calling itself the Akron Door Company? The Akron City Barber Shop?
3. Must the plaintiff and defendant be competitors before the plaintiff is entitled to protection of its tradename?

INTERFERENCE WITH CONTRACTS

Interference with contracts is a tort that began in England by permitting a master to sue one who had forcibly taken away his servants. Subsequently, courts allowed suits where a servant was enticed away without violence and, ultimately, to situations not involving a master-servant relationship. The elements of the tort require proof of intentional (not negligent) interference by the defendant with the contract of the plaintiff with another. The defendant's interference must have been the "proximate cause" of the breach of the plaintiff's contract. If the interference of the defendant involved tortious behavior, like violence, coercion, or fraud, the courts have uniformly found the defendant liable. However, there is not such unanimity of judicial opinion where the defendant uses means that are lawful, in and of themselves. The majority of the courts hold that the action is still maintainable in the absence of justification. Justification (or privilege) for the defendant often includes action by the defendant to protect an equal or superior interest, such as a right to protect his or her own property or contract interest. Also, the defendant may refuse to enter into contracts, even though it results in an interference with the plaintiff's contract. If the interference results from the defendant's performing his or her legal duties, no cause of action will arise. Finally, the defendant's conduct may be justifiable on the grounds of some socially desirable objective. For example, in *Brimelow* v. *Casson,*[1] the defendant's purpose for preventing prostitution was held sufficient justification for his interference with the plaintiff's contracts.

Imperial Ice Co. v. Rossier et al.

112 P. 2d 631 (1941)
Supreme Court of California

The California Consumers Company purchased from S. L. Coker an ice distributing business, inclusive of good will, located in . . . Santa Monica. . . . In the purchase agreement Coker contracted . . . [to] "not engage in the business of selling and or distributing ice . . . in [Santa Monica] so long as the purchasers, or anyone deriving title to the good will of said business from said purchasers, shall be engaged in a like business therein." Plaintiff, the Imperial Ice Company, acquired . . . the California Consumers Company full title to this ice distributing business including the right to enforce the covenant not to compete. Coker subsequently began selling in [Santa Monica] in violation of the contract ice supplied to him by a company owned by W. Rossier, J. A. Matheson, and Fred Matheson. Plaintiff thereupon brought this action in the superior court for an injunction to restrain Coker from violating the contract and to restrain Rossier and the Mathesons from inducing Coker to violate the contract. The complaint alleges that Rossier and the Mathesons induced Coker to violate his contract so that they might sell ice to him at a profit. The trial court . . . gave judgment for those defendants.

Plaintiff has appealed from the judgment on the sole ground that the complaint stated a cause of action against the defendants Rossier and the Mathesons for inducing the breach of contract.

The question thus presented to this court is under what circumstances may an action be maintained against a defendant who has induced a third party to violate a contract with the plaintiff.

It is universally recognized that an action will lie for inducing breach of contract by a resort to means in themselves unlawful such as libel, slander, fraud, physical violence, or threats of such action. Most jurisdictions also held that an action will lie for inducing a breach of contract by the use of moral, social, or economic pressures, in themselves lawful, unless there is sufficient justification for such inducement.

Such justification exists when a person induces a breach of contract to protect an interest which has greater social value than insuring the stability of the contract. Thus, a person is justified in inducing the breach of a contract the enforcement of which would be injurious to health, safety, or good morals. The interest of labor in improving working conditions is of sufficient social importance to justify peaceful labor tactics otherwise lawful, though they have the effect of inducing breaches of contracts between employer and employee or employer and customer. In numerous other situations, justification exists depending upon the importance of the interest protected. The presence or absence of ill-will, sometimes referred to as "malice," is immaterial, except as it indicates whether or not an interest is actually being protected.

It is well established, however, that a person is not justified in inducing a breach of contract simply because he is in competition with one of the parties to the contract and seeks to further his own economic advantage at the expense of the other. Whatever interest society has in encouraging free and open competition by means not in themselves unlawful, contractual stability is generally accepted as of greater importance than competitive freedom. Competitive freedom, however, is of sufficient importance to justify one competitor in inducing a third party to forsake another competitor if no contractual relationship exists between the latter two. A person is likewise free to carry on his business, including reduction of prices, advertising, and solicitation in the usual lawful manner although some third party may be induced thereby to breach his contract with a competitor in favor of dealing with the advertiser. Again, if two parties have separate contracts with a third, each may resort to any legitimate means at his disposal to secure performance of his contract even though the necessary result will be to cause a breach of the other contract. A party may not, however, under the guise of competition actively and affirmatively induce the breach of a competitor's contract in order to secure an economic advantage over that competitor. The act of inducing the breach must be an intentional one. If the actor had no knowledge of the existence of the contract or his actions were not intended to induce a breach he cannot be held liable though an actual breach results from his lawful and proper acts.

* * *

The complaint in the present case alleges that defendants actively induced Coker to violate his contract with plaintiffs so that they might sell ice to him.

The contract gave to plaintiff the right to sell ice in the stated territory free from the competition of Coker. The defendants, by virtue of their interest in the sale of ice in that territory, were in effect competing with plaintiff. By inducing Coker to violate his contract, as alleged in the complaint, they sought to further their own economic advantage at plaintiff's expense. Such conduct is not justified. Had defendants merely sold ice to Coker without actively inducing him to violate his contract, his distribution of the ice in the forbidden territory in violation of his contract would not then have rendered defendants liable. They may carry on their business of selling ice as usual without incurring liability for breaches of contract by their customers. It is necessary to prove that they intentionally and actively induced the breach. Since the complaint alleges that they did so and asks for an injunction on the grounds that damages would be inadequate, it states a cause of action. . . .

The judgment is reversed.

Questions
1. May an individual induce a breach of contract by unlawful means, such as libel, fraud, or threats of violence?
2. May an individual induce a breach of contract by lawful means, such as moral, social, or economic pressures?

3. When is a person "justified" in inducing a breach of contract? Is "competing" a justification?
4. Can a person be liable for inducing a breach of contract if he had no knowledge of the existence of the contract?

PUBLIC ENFORCEMENT

No more than a decade after the Sherman Act had been adopted, bills were being introduced for its amendment. However, it was not until 1914 that Congress was able to pass new antitrust legislation. Critics of the Supreme Court complained of its lenient approach in the "rule of reason" interpretation of the Sherman Act. In addition, the Sherman Act had not sufficiently coped with the problem of increased private concentration of economic power. Consequently, the rise of the political movement, "progressivism," under the leadership of Theodore Roosevelt in the Republican party and Woodrow Wilson of the Democratic party, eventually produced both the Clayton Act and the Federal Trade Commission Act in 1914.

THE FEDERAL TRADE COMMISSION

The Federal Trade Commission Act created the Federal Trade Commission (FTC), consisting of five Commissioners with a staff of Civil Service employees. The basic authority of the Commission is the enforcement of Section 5, which outlaws "unfair methods of competition" among competitors. This broad language obviously conferred discretion on the Commissioners, subject to judicial review, to more particularly define "unfair" competitive practices, a task Congress found impossible.

Investigations by the Commission to determine whether there are violations of Section 5, or of any law administered by the Commission, may be originated at the request of the President, Congress, governmental agencies, or on complaints by members of the public. Of course, the Commission may originate an investigation on its own initiative also. The Commission seeks voluntary cooperation in its investigations, but if the public interest requires, the Commission may invoke compulsory processes.

Whenever the Commission has reason to believe that any party is violating Section 5, it is authorized to issue a complaint against the party. However, when time and the nature of the proceeding permit, the Commission serves a notice on the party of the Commission's determination to institute a formal proceeding against the party. Within the prescribed time period, the party may file with the Secretary of the Commission a reply stating whether he or she is interested in having the proceedings disposed by the entry of a consent order. If the reply is in the negative, or if no reply is filed within the specified time, the complaint will be served. If on the other hand, the reply is in the affirmative, the party will be offered an opportunity to execute an appropriate settlement for consideration by the Commission.

The adjudicative proceedings of the Commission are commenced by the issuance and service of a complaint. The respondent named in the complaint has a specific number of days after service of the complaint to file an answer to the charges contained therein. Should the respondent elect not to contest the allegations of fact set forth in the complaint, he or she files, in effect, an admission answer that constitutes a waiver of hearing. If the answer is a denial of the allegations of fact contained in the complaint, the "case" then is heard by an administrative law judge assigned to the Commission. During the hearings, counsel for the Commission has the burden of proving the allegations contained in the complaint. The judge files an initial decision that includes (1) a statement of findings and conclusions, as well as the reasons or basis therefor, on all the material issues of fact, law, or discretion presented in the record, and (2) an appropriate order.

On appeal from, or review of, an initial decision of the judge, the Commission will consider such parts of the record as necessary to resolve the issues presented. In rendering its decision, the Commission adopts, modifies, or sets aside the findings, conclusions, and order contained in the initial decision of the judge and includes in its decision a statement of the reasons for its actions. Any party required by an order of the Commission to cease and desist may obtain a review of such order by filing a written petition in a circuit court of appeals of the United States. On filing a petition, the Commission files with the court a record of the proceedings.

The appellate court has the power to enter a decree, affirming, modifying, or setting aside the Commission's order. The statute provides that "findings of the Commission as to the facts, if supported by evidence, shall be conclusive." The judgment and decree of the appellate court is final, except that it shall be subject to review by the Supreme Court on *certiorari*.

When an order of the Commission to cease and desist becomes final, either by failure to appeal or through affirmance by court action, and it is violated, the respondent is subjected to a fine of $10,000 per day for each violation. Furthermore, if an order of the Commission is affirmed and adopted by an appellate court, so that the order of the Commission becomes the order of the court, a violation thereof would constitute "contempt of court."

The Commission seeks, whenever possible, to avoid its formal procedures as a method to prevent the continuation of the practices that may violate any of the laws it administers. One method of "voluntary" enforcement is to permit any party to request advice from the Commission as to whether a proposed course of action violates any of its laws. The Commission informs the requesting party of the Commission's views, which will bind the Commission, so that if it changes these views, the inquiring party will be notified and given an opportunity to conform with the new views. However, a request is considered inappropriate (1) when the course of action is already being followed by the requesting party, (2) when the course of action is under investigation by the Commission or another governmental agency, or (3) when the proposed course of action is such that an informed decision could be made only after an extensive investigation. Another method of voluntary compliance is urged by the Commission through its issuance of "guides." These are administrative interpretations of law that aid the Commission's staff as well as businessmen in evaluating certain types of practices.

The rulemaking powers of the FTC were confirmed and clarified in the FTC Improvement Act of 1975. The FTC is empowered to issue substantive rules with the force and effect of law that define and prohibit unfair and deceptive practices. Specific and detailed procedures for creating such rules are outlined in the Act. The FTC typically promulgates rules that relate to entire industries. While the FTC believes rulemaking is a more efficient and a fairer process than the case-by-case procedure, both processes will continue to be utilized by the Commission to fashion laws against unfair competition.

ANTITRUST ENFORCEMENT BY FTC

Initially, the Supreme Court withheld discretion from the FTC by holding: "It is for the courts, not the Commission, ultimately to determine as matter of law what they include . . . [as unfair methods of competition]." *FTC* v. *Gratz* 253 U.S. 421 (1920). The Court then was only willing to hold acts that would constitute violations of the antitrust acts as also constituting "unfair competition." However, the Court was less willing in its interpretation of Section 5 to outlaw practices that did not amount to outright Sherman or Clayton Act violations. The Court did not clearly relax this attitude until it announced its new policy in the following case.

FTC v. Brown Shoe Co.
384 U.S. 316 (1956)
Supreme Courts of the United States

Black, Mr. Justice.

. . . The Federal Trade Commission filed a complaint against the Brown Shoe Co., Inc., one of the world's largest manufacturers of shoes. . . . The unfair practices charged against Brown revolve around the "Brown Franchise Stores' Program" through which Brown sells its shoes to some 650 retail stores. The complaint alleged that under this plan Brown . . . had "entered into contracts or franchises with a substantial number of its independent retail shoe store operator customers which require said customers to restrict their purchases of shoes for resale to the Brown lines and which prohibit them from purchasing, stocking or reselling shoes manufactured by competitors of Brown." Brown's customers who entered into these restrictive franchise agreements, so the complaint charged, were given in return special treatment and valuable benefits which were not granted to Brown's customers who did not enter into the agreements. . . .

The . . . admissions of Brown as to the existence and operation of the franchise program were buttressed by many separate detailed fact findings of [the Administrative Law Judge], one of which findings was that the franchise program effectively foreclosed

Brown's competitors from selling to a substantial number of retail shoe dealers. Based on these findings and on Brown's admissions the Commission concluded that the restrictive contract program was an unfair method of competition within the meaning of §5 and ordered Brown to cease and desist from its use.

Thus the question we have for decision is whether the Federal Trade Commission can declare it to be an unfair practice for Brown, the second largest manufacturer of shoes in the Nation, to pay a valuable consideration to hundreds of retail shoe purchasers in order to secure a contractual promise from them that they will deal primarily with Brown and will not purchase conflicting lines of shoes from Brown's competitors. We hold that the Commission has power to find, on the record here, such an anticompetitive practice unfair, subject of course to judicial review.

In holding that the Federal Trade Commission lacked the power to declare Brown's program to be unfair the Court of Appeals was much influenced by and quoted at length from this Court's opinion in *Federal Trade Commission* v. *Gratz,* 253 U.S. 421. That case, decided shortly after the Federal Trade Commission Act was passed, construed the Act . . . as giving the Commission very little power to declare any trade practice unfair. Later cases of this Court, however, have rejected the *Gratz* view and it is now recognized . . . that the Commission has broad powers to declare trade practices unfair. This broad power of the Commission is particularly well established with regard to trade practices which conflict with the basic policies of the Sherman and Clayton Acts even though such practices may not actually violate these laws. The record in this case shows be-

yond doubt that Brown, the country's second largest manufacturer of shoes, has a program, which requires shoe retailers, unless faithless to their contractual obligations with Brown, substantially to limit their trade with Brown's competitors. This program obviously conflicts with the central policy of both §1 of the Sherman Act and §3 of the Clayton Act against contracts which take away freedom of purchasers to buy in an open market. Brown nevertheless contends that the Commission had no power to declare the franchise program unfair without proof that its effect "may be to substantially lessen competition or tend to create a monopoly" which of course would have to be proved if the Government were proceeding against Brown under §3 of the Clayton Act rather than §5 of the Federal Trade Commission Act. We reject the argument that proof of this §3 element must be made for as we pointed out above our cases hold that the Commission has power under §5 to arrest trade restraints in their incipiency without proof that they amount to an outright violation of §3 of the Clayton Act or other provisions of the antitrust laws. This power of the Commission was emphatically stated in *F.T.C.* v. *Motion Picture Ad. Co.,* 344 U.S. 392, at pp. 394–395:

It is . . . clear that the Federal Trade Commission Act was designed to supplement and bolster the Sherman Act and the Clayton Act . . . to stop in their incipiency acts and practices which, when full blown, would violate those acts. . . .

We hold that the Commission acted well within its authority in declaring the Brown franchise program unfair whether it was completely full blown or not.

Questions

1. May the FTC rule a practice to be "unfair" (illegal) even if the practice is not an antitrust violation? What would the Commission have to show if it was trying to prove that Brown's exclusive dealing contracts violate Sec-

tion 3 of the Clayton Act? What must the FTC establish in order to prove that an exclusive dealing is an "unfair method of competition"?

2. Why did the FTC rule that this exclusive dealing program was "unfair" and other exclusive dealing franchise programs are not "unfair"? Does the answer have any connection with the outlawed Brown-Kinney merger in 1961?

Atlantic Refining Company v. FTC
381 U.S 357 (1965)
Supreme Court of the United States

Clark, Mr. Justice

The Federal Trade Commission has found that an agreement between the Atlantic Refining Company (Atlantic) and the Goodyear Tire & Rubber Company (Goodyear), under which the former "sponsors" the sale of the tires, batteries and accessory (TBA) products of the latter to its wholesale outlets and its retail service station dealers, is an unfair method of competition in violation of Section 5 of the Federal Trade Commission Act. Under the plan Atlantic sponsors the sale of Goodyear products to its wholesale and retail outlets on an overall commission basis. Goodyear is responsible for its sales and sells at its own price to Atlantic wholesalers and dealers for resale; it bears all of the cost of distribution through its warehouses, stores and other supply points and carries on a joint sales promotion program with Atlantic. The latter, however, is primarily responsible for pormoting the sale of Goodyear products to its dealers and assisting them in their resale; for this it receives a commission on all sales made to its wholesalers and dealers. . . .

Section 5 of the Federal Trade Commission Act . . . empowers the Commission, in the first instance, to determine whether a method of competition or the act or practice complained of is unfair. The Congress intentionally left development of the term "unfair" to the Commission rather than attempting to define "the many and variable unfair practices which prevail in commerce." Where the Congress has provided that an administrative agency initially apply a broad statutory term to a particular situation, our function is limited to determining whether the Commission's decision "has 'warrant in the record' and a reasonable basis in law." While the final word is left to the courts, necessarily "we give great weight to the Commission's conclusion."

Certainly there is "warrant in the record" for the findings of the Commission here. Substantial evidence supports the conclusion that notwithstanding Atlantic's contention that it and its dealers are mutually dependent upon each other, they simply do not bargain as equals. Among the sources of leverage in Atlantic's hands are its lease and equipment loan contracts with their cancellation and short-term provisions. . . . It must also be remembered that Atlantic controlled the supply of gasoline and oil to its wholesalers and dealers. This was an additional source of economic leverage, as was its extensive control of all advertising on the premises of its dealers.

Furthermore, there was abundant evidence that Atlantic, in some instances with the aid of Goodyear, not only exerted the persuasion that is a natural incident of its economic power but coupled with it direct and overt threats of reprisal. . . . In 1951, seven months after the sales-commission plan had gone into effect, Goodyear had enjoyed great success in signing contracts with Atlantic dealers despite the fact that a 1946–1949 survey had shown the 67% of the dealers had preferred Lee tires and 76% Exide batteries.

With this background in mind, we consider whether there was a "reasonable basis in law" for the Commission's ultimate conclusion that the sales-commission plan constituted an unfair method of competition.

[N]either . . . the Commission [nor] the Court of Appeals held that the sales-commission arrangement was a tying scheme. What they did find was that the central competitive characteristic was the same—the utilization of economic power in one market to curtail competition in another. Here that lever was bolstered by actual threats and coercive practices. As our cases hold, all that is necessary in Section 5 proceedings to find a violation is to discover conduct that "runs counter to the public policy declared in the" Act.

. . . [The FTC's] use as a guideline of recognized violations of the antitrust laws was, we believe, entirely appropriate. It has long been recognized that there are many unfair methods of competition that do not assume the proportions of antitrust violations. When conduct does bear the characteristics of recognized antitrust violations it becomes suspect, and the Commission may properly look to cases applying those laws for guidance. . . .

Thus the Commission was warranted in finding that the effect of the plan was as though Atlantic had agreed with Goodyear to require its dealers to buy Goodyear products and had done so. It is beyond question that the effect on commerce was not insubstantial. . . .

The short of it is that Atlantic with Goodyear's encouragement and assistance, has marshalled its full economic power in a continuing campaign to force its dealers and wholesalers to buy Goodyear products. The anticompetitive effects of this program are clear on the record and render unnecessary extensive economic analysis of market percentages or business justifications in determining whether this was a method of competition which Congress has declared unfair and therefore unlawful.

Questions

1. Has Goodyear or Atlantic violated Section 1 of the Sherman Act?
2. What economic power did Atlantic possess over its dealers? Could Atlantic refuse the sale of its gasoline to any dealers who refused to purchase Goodyear TBA? Why not? Could it use its economic power to "urge" its dealers to buy Goodyear TBA? Why not?
3. How was this action by Atlantic similar to an antitrust violation?

CONCLUSION

Some competitive tactics have been ruled "out of the bounds" of reasonableness and lacking social justification since the earliest times of the competitive market. Initially, the judicial process of developing compensatory and injunctive remedies for tortious behavior fashioned a body of laws against "unfair competition." The rules of the judicial process have been reinforced by statutory measures such as the Lanhman Act, which strengthens and enlarges the protections against "unfair" competitive tactics. Ultimately, Congress decided that a continuing administrative supervision over the competitive process was needed and, therefore, created the Federal Trade Commission. The FTC and similar state agencies have developed a voluminous set of rules about unfair methods of competition, and the end of the process of identifying unfair practices does not appear in sight.

DISCUSSION QUESTIONS

1. Republic Gear Company was engaged in the sale and distribution of gears for the automobile replacement market in the United States. York manufactured and sold gears in Brazil. In 1955 Republic and York made a written agreement that granted York a license to manufacture and sell the Republic line of gears in Brazil for a term of 15 years.

   Subsequently, Borg-Warner contacted York concerning the manufacture of transmissions in Brazil, items not covered by the Republic agreement.

   Borg-Warner learned that York had a 15-year agreement with Republic. Borg-Warner decided not to license York to manufacture transmissions without licensing it to manufacture gears and would not do so while York had a license from Republic to manufacture gears. York repudiated the Republic agreement after Borg-Warner assured York of gear and transmission licenses. Borg-Warner knew that York had no right to terminate the Republic agreement. In Republic's suit against Borg-Warner, Borg-Warner maintained that its conduct amounted to "normal business competition." Decide.

2. Hannigan became a distributor of metal outdoor storage buildings manufactured by Fabricated. In 1958, Hannigan conceived of a new idea for outdoor storage cabinets. After negotiations, Hannigan and Fabricated entered into an agreement whereby Fabricated contracted to manufacture these cabinets exclusively for Hannigan; in consideration thereof, Hannigan agreed to purchase all such outdoor storage cabinets from Fabricated. The contract placed no limitations on Fabricated's right to manufacture and sell its metal outdoor storage buildings, and Fabricated continued to manufacture and to sell such storage buildings to various customers, including Sears.

   Hannigan, meanwhile, sold the Fabricated manufactured outdoor cabinets to his various customers, which included Sears. Sears became Hannigan's customer in early 1959 and almost immediately attempted by letter to persuade Fabricated's sales manager to sell the lawn cabinets directly to Sears notwithstanding Fabricated's exclusive contractual commitment to Hannigan. Sears' avowed purpose for inviting Fabricated into a direct purchasing relationship was to avoid and to eliminate the profit of the middleman, Hannigan.

   Sears' buyer attempted to persuade Fabricated to sell cabinets directly to Sears or it would go elsewhere for steel storage buildings. At this time Fabricated was in large measure economically dependent on Sears because

60 percent of Fabricated's "business was devoted to Sears as a customer." After Fabricated agreed to Sears' proposal, Hannigan sued Sears. What result?

3. UCC is a computer company that had developed an advanced system designed to maintain information on inventory in retail department stores, called AIMES III. UCC and LYC, a diversified holding company not previously active in the computer markets, agreed to form a new corporation, Lykes/UCC "as a joint venture for the purpose of entering the southeastern U.S., a new market for UCC's computer systems." UCC had previously sold an AIMES III system to a department store in Fort Worth, Texas, subject to an agreement limiting the store to private and confidential use of the system, which was not available from any other source. A UCC vice president who was later to become president of Lykes/UCC met with LYC executives and suggested that LYC could form a wholly owned subsidiary and operate without sharing profits in the joint venture.

LYC formed LYCSC, withdrew from the joint venture, and bribed an employee of the Fort Worth department store to deliver tapes and documents enabling LYCSC to run the system in its entirety. LYCSC then offered the AIMES III system for sale, promoting it with detailed sales presentations, and at one point displayed AIMES III component programs and listings to a computer expert who had the ability to utilize such information in designing his own systems.

UCC sued LYC and LYCSC, claiming misappropriation of a trade secret. The defendants argued that the AIMES III system was not a trade secret, and that even if it were, they had made no commercial use of the secret.

What result?

4. Two companies marketing plastic mattress covers use the same size and shape package, one displaying the word, "Hygient" in a white cross on a green oval, and the other displaying the word, "Hygienic" in a white cross on a red oval. These marks were given identical placement on the packages. The word "Hygient" had been registered and constituted a valid trademark before the "Hygienic" mark came into use. The mattress covers bearing the "Hygienic" mark are in fact hygienic when sold.

What defense would you propose for the company using "Hygienic" to an action for trademark infringement? With what result?

5. A cosmetics manufacturer, A, acquired trademarks for various products containing a part of the aloe vera plant as a principal ingredient. Each product name included ALO-, such as ALO-PLUS, ALO-V SHAMPOO, and ALO-ROUGE. For ten years the company was the only marketer of aloe products. After that time a new producer, B, brought out a line of competing products bearing names such as ALOE ESSENCE, MASQUE OF ALOE and JEL D'ALOE.

A claimed that B's use of "ALOE" infringed on its trademark rights in the various names of A's "family" of products. B claimed that A's trademarks were invalid.

What arguments would A use? Is a secondary meaning necessary in this case?

6. "LaTouraine" Coffee Co. sold coffee to small metropolitan restaurants in the New York/New Jersey area. It built a well-known reputation and a large market. Its name, LaTouraine, is a French province, but LaTouraine Coffee Co. does not process or sell its coffee in France.

Lorraine Coffee Co. was formed 38 years later, and was operated as a family business in New York and northern New Jersey. The founder of Lorraine Coffee took the name from Alsace-Lorraine, another region in France, but that company also has no business connection with France.

LaTouraine Co. claims infringement of its registered trademark "LaTouraine." Lorraine Co. defends, claiming that a geographical name cannot be a valid trademark. What result?

7. A manufacturer of pharmaceutical products marketed a product containing quinine and chocolate under the tradename of "Coco-Quinine." When a competitor brought out a nearly identical product called "Quin-Coco," the original manufacturer claimed infringement.

The two products were used for the same purpose and were indistinguishable by flavor or appearance. Both used chocolate for its color and flavor, and as a suspending medium for the quinine.

What defense should the competitor raise?

8. "Frostie" is a valid trademark aquired in connection with the sale of a root beer concentrate. Thereafter, the Dr. Pepper Company began to use the words "Frosty Pepper," which were prominently printed on the carton of its soft drink product. These cartons also contained a picture of a bottle of Dr. Pepper being poured into a glass containing ice cream and opposite this was the trademark "Dr. Pepper" and the words beneath it, "and ice cream." Frostie brought an action for infringement of its trademark and unfair competition. What result?

9. Miller Brewing Company argued it possessed a common law trademark for its "Lite" beer. Accordingly, Miller sued Heileman Brewing for its use of the word "Light" as a trademark for its beer. What result?

10. Anheuser-Busch, Inc. registered the slogan, "Where there's life . . . there's Bud" under the Lanham Act. The slogan was used in advertising including television advertising portraying people at social gatherings along with vocal and written use of the slogan.

Chemical Corporation of America marketed a floor wax that contained an insecticide. Chemical Corporation began a television advertising campaign also portraying people in social situations, dancing, eating, and drinking, with simultaneous use of the slogan, "Where there's life . . . there's bugs."

Anheuser-Busch sought an injunction, claiming infringement, and Chemical Corporation claimed the right to use a "Where there's life" slogan, especially when the products are quite dissimilar and in no way competitive.

What result?

11. The nation's largest retail newsstand operator demanded and received "display promotional allowances" from various magazines, comic book, and pocket book publishers. The publishers understood that if the allowances were not granted, this company, in a position of dominance in the field, would not continue to handle their publications. Other retailers did not receive such allowances.

The FTC issued a cease and desist order under Section 5 of the FTC Act, labeling it an unfair method of competition for the newsstand operator to induce or receive advertising assistance that is not available on proportionately equal terms to all other customers of the supplier, i.e., to knowingly benefit from a violation of Section 2(d) of the Clayton Act. On appeal, the buyer argued that Section 2(d) prohibits only the *seller* from granting disproportionate advertising allowances, but does not outlaw *buyer* receipts of such allowances.

What should be the result on appeal?

SUGGESTED READINGS

Allison, John R., "Private Cause of Action for Unfair Competition Under the Lanham Act," *American Business Law Journal,* Vol. 14, No. 1, Spring 1976, pp. 1–24.

Averott, N. W., "Meaning of Unfair Acts or Practices in Section 5 of the Federal Trade Commission Act," *Georgetown Law Journal,* Vol. 70, October 1981, pp. 225–296.

Donegan, Jr., T. J., "Section 43(a) of the Lanham Trademark Act as a Private Remedy for False Advertising," *Food, Drug, and Cosmetic Law Journal,* Vol. 37, July 1982, pp. 264–288.

Reich, R. B., "Future of Unfair Methods of Competition," *Antitrust Law Journal,* Vol. 50, 1981/82, pp. 801–810.

ENDNOTE

1. (1924) LR 1 Ch Div 302, (1923) All Eng. 40.

chapter 15

ANTITRUST: INTERNATIONAL TRANSACTIONS AND EXEMPTED ACTIVITIES

Every year, American businesses enter into thousands of international transactions which raise possible antitrust issues. Many of these transactions—indeed, probably most of them—do not raise serious antitrust enforcement issues. Yet avoidance of antitrust problems is important. Consequently, a fundamental understanding of how antitrust relates to international transactions is explored in this chapter.

While antitrust laws are generally applicable to all economic affairs, certain activities have been granted exemptions. Both the legislature and the courts have created exemptions on the basis of some opposing public policy. For example, congressional creation of the patent system requires judicial tolerance for the patent monopoly. The public policy favoring rewards to inventors takes precedence over the antimonopoly laws. In the same fashion, this chapter reveals other favored public policies that result in the creation of exemptions of certain activities from the application of the antitrust laws.

INTERNATIONAL TRANSACTIONS

One way to avoid international antitrust problems is to seek a "business review" by the Justice Department. Under the Business Review Procedure, the Department may issue a statement of enforcement intention with respect to a specific pending transaction. The Business Review Procedure affords the business firm an expression of the views of the Antitrust Division in regard to particular transactions that pose close or difficult international antitrust questions. If appropriate, the firm may make subsequent operational changes to avoid antitrust violations.

As with domestic enforcement, certain types of international agreements are regarded as illegal *per se*. Normal *per se* rules will be applied fully to basic horizontal restraints designed to affect U.S. market prices or conditions or to divide the U.S. market from other markets. Most other restraints are tested by the "rule of reason," which involves a full factual inquiry as to whether they will have any significantly adverse effect on competition, what the justification for them is, and whether that justification could be achieved in a less anticompetitive way.

A special antitrust exemption is provided under the Webb-Pomerene Act for acts of a collective export association of American producers, provided that the association does not (1) artificially or intentionally restrain U.S. domestic trade or affect U.S. domestic prices or (2) restrain the export trade of any U.S. competitor of the association. The Webb-Pomerene Act applies solely to the export of "goods, wares or merchandise" and, therefore, does not explicitly extend to services, such as consulting, engineering, construction, insurance, and finance and other nonvisible trade, which has grown large during the last few decades. Therefore, the Webb-Pomerence Act is too weak for organizing U.S. exporters. When there are possible criminal penalties and civil liabilities for treble damages under the after-the-fact interpretations of antitrust laws, most firms would not assume the risk associated with foreign trade.

Competition for foreign markets often requires exporting firms to handle competing lines of products. Such firms would have to operate under the threat of antitrust litigation each time they dealt in competing lines of products and services. To expand exports, and relieve firms of potential antitrust problems, Congress enacted the Export Trading Company Act of 1982. The Act could reshape the business-government relationship in the United States, making it more compatible with international standards. The Act allows export trading companies to receive prior clearance and exemption from antitrust laws concerning their exportation of competing lines of goods or services or joint exportation efforts with otherwise competing firms. Even if they may later be found in violation of certain antitrust provisions, the damages for aggrieved parties is limited to single damages, rather than the normal treble damages.

ENFORCEMENT POLICY

Antitrust enforcement by the United States government has two major purposes with respect to international commerce. The first is to protect the American consuming public by assuring it the benefit of competitive products and ideas produced by foreign competitors as well as domestic competitors. Competition by foreign producers is particularly important when imports are or could be a major source of a particular product, or where the domestic industry is dominated by a single firm or a few firms. An agreement or set of private agreements designed to raise the price of such imports or to exclude them from the domestic market raises most serious antitrust concerns. Antitrust enforcement can be expected against domestic firms and foreign firms subject to American jurisdiction for participation in such agreements. Moreover, the form of agreement is not controlling; an informal undertaking embodied in a single conversation may be just as punishable as the same undertaking contained in a complete contract. Any type of restraint that limits the competition offered by significant foreign competitors and products in our domestic market will be examined with great care by enforcement officials.

The second major antitrust enforcement purpose is to protect American export and investment opportunities against privately imposed restrictions. The concern is that each U.S.-based firm engaged in the export of goods, services, or capital should be allowed to compete on merit and not be shut out by some restriction imposed by a bigger or less principled competitor. Often, the most objectionable private restrictions involve collective efforts by one group of competitors to exclude another from a particular market.

QUESTIONS OF JURISDICTION

The application of U.S. antitrust law to overseas activities raises some difficult questions of jurisdiction. First, there is the question of subject matter jurisdiction: whether United States antitrust law applies to certain overseas acts that affect U.S. commerce. The acts of U.S. citizens in a foreign nation normally are subject to the law of the country where they occur. Yet U.S. law in general, and U.S. antitrust laws in particular, are not limited to transactions that take place within our borders. When foreign transactions have a substantial and foreseeable effect on U.S. commerce, they are subject to U.S. law regardless of where they take place. A consideration of whether there is sufficient impact on U.S. commerce to confer jurisdiction generally involves practical analysis of "purpose" and "effect" as discussed in the preceding section on enforcement policy. U.S. antitrust law should be applied to overseas transactions that will have a substantial and foreseeable effect on U.S. commerce; however, it should avoid unnecessary interference with the sovereign interests of foreign nations.

For example, to use the Sherman Act to restrain or punish an overseas conspiracy whose clear purpose and effect is to restrain significant commerce in the U.S. market is both appropriate and necessary to effective U.S. enforcement. By contrast, to apply the Sherman Act to a combination of U.S. firms engaged in foreign activities that have no direct or intended effect on U.S. consumers or export opportunities would extend the Act beyond the point Congress must have intended. This could encroach on the sovereignty of a foreign state without any overriding justification based on legitimate United States interests.

Subject matter jurisdiction may sometimes be challenged through the affirmative defense variously referred to as the act of state doctrine or the doctrine of foreign governmental compulsion. These defenses are subject to important limitations, however. A major limitation is territorial. Although the U.S. courts will recognize an antitrust defense for actions taken or compelled by a foreign sovereign within its territory, such recognition will not be afforded with respect to an act inside the United States. The situation where a soveign government attempts to compel an act in third countries is less clear. A second limitation is that the act on which the defense is based must be the act of a truly sovereign entity acting within the scope of its powers under the law of its nationality. The valid decree of a foreign government usually meets this requirement; the action of a nongovernmental agent of a foreign government does not, at least when it is not proved that such agent clearly was authorized to perform the alleged acts of state as a delegated sovereign function. Third, the act of state defense does not apply to the "commercial" actions of a foreign government or instrumentality, but only to its public, political actions.

It is clear that the most important concern of antitrust enforcement is to protect the U.S. domestic market against restraints on competition—restraints on entry, pricing, and terms of sale. In carrying out this effort, no essential distinction is made between domestic and foreign firms. In general, foreign firms, including state-owned or state-controlled firms, will be expected to observe the prohibitions of our antitrust laws, and to benefit from the enforcement of those laws in the same manner as domestically incorporated enterprises.

FOREIGN ANTITRUST LAWS

At the end of World War II, much information became available concerning the extent to which the Axis powers had utilized international cartels to further their imperialistic aims. Accordingly, there were many multilateral attempts after the war to improve overall international trade relations. One proposal involved an International Trade Organization (ITO), which was to investigate and publicize its findings in cases of alleged restrictive practices. This proposal relied on the exploitation of adverse public opinion as a device for dealing with restrictive practices. Numerous efforts to create the ITO failed, but one viable multilateral international antitrust agreement has been created, although the United States is not a party to it. This multinational agreement established the European Economic Community and contains articles prohibiting agreements between enterprises "likely to affect trade between member states and which have the effect of preventing, restraining, or distorting competition in the common market." Beyond this multinational agreement, the adoption and enforcement of antitrust policy has remained within the province of the various nations. And among the nations adopting antitrust rules, the U.S. is clearly the most vigorous enforcer. The enforcement principles utilized by the U.S. Attorney General are clearly enunciated in the Antitrust Guide for International Operations. In conjunction with the United States's antitrust policy, both the Department of State and the Justice Department have emphasized a concurrent policy of advocating that foreign countries adopt antitrust policies comparable to that of the United

States. However, the probability that any such international agreement and organization will be created in the near future is slight, indeed.

EXEMPTED ACTIVITIES

REGULATED INDUSTRIES

Industries that are regulated by federal and state agencies are exempt from direct application of the antitrust laws. In theory, the regulatory body protects the public interest in lieu of competition. Obvious examples include the fields of transportation, electricity, gas, telephone, and broadcasting. Instead of competitively determined prices in these industries, industry prices are set by a regulatory body, which attempts to accommodate the interests of both the industry and the public. However, the exemptions granted to regulated industries are not complete, but relate only to the specific practices of the industry that are regulated. For example, uniform prices by trucking firms may be approved by the regulatory body and exempted from antitrust action, but mergers among trucking firms may still be subject to the Clayton Act.

STATE ACTION

In *Parker* v. *Brown*, 317 U.S. 341 (1943), the Supreme Court established that the Sherman Act does not outlaw state action or official action directed by the state. The Supreme Court has expressed the "state action" exemption as follows: ". . . [W]here a restraint upon trade or monopolization is the result of valid governmental action, as opposed to private action, no violation of the Act can be made out."[1] However, the exemption is not as broad as this language would suggest. The following case is a more modern court pronouncement of the boundaries of the "state action" exemption.

City of Lafayette, LA. v. LA. Power & Light Co.
435 U.S. 389 (1978)
Supreme Court of the United States

Mr. Justice Brennan.

      *   *   *

Petitioner cities are organized under the laws of the State of Louisiana, which grant them power to own and operate electric utility systems both within and beyond their city limits. Petitioners brought this action in the District Court . . . alleging that . . . Louisiana Power & Light Co. (LP&L), an investor-owned electric service utility with which petitioners compete in the areas beyond their city limits, committed various antitrust offenses which injured petitioners in the operation of their electric utility systems. LP&L counterlcaimed, seeking damages and injunctive relief for various antitrust offenses which petitioners had allegedly committed and which injured it in its business and property.

* * *

Petitioners . . . argue that the antitrust laws are intended to protect the public only from abuses of private power and not from actions of municipalities that exist to serve the public weal.

Petitioners' contention that their goal is not private profit but public service is only partly correct. Every business enterprise, public or private, operates its business in furtherance of its own goals. In the case of a municipally owned utility, that goal is likely to be, broadly speaking, the benefit of its citizens. But the economic choices made by public corporations in the conduct of their business affairs, designed as they are to assure maximum benefits for the community constituency, are not inherently more likely to comport with the broader interests of national economic well-being than are those of private corporations acting in furtherance of the interests of the organization and its shareholders. The allegations of the counterclaim, which for present purposes we accept as true, aptly illustrate the impact which local governments, acting as providers of services, may have on other individuals and business enterprises with which they inter-relate as purchasers, suppliers, and sometimes, as here, as competitors.

LP&L alleged that the city of Plaquemine contracted to provide LP&L's electric customers outside its city limits gas and water service only on condition that the customers purchase electricity from the city and not from LP&L. The effect of such a tie-in is twofold. First, the tying contract might injure former LP&L customers in two ways. The net effect of the tying contract might be to increase the cost of electric service to these customers. Moreover, a municipality conceivably might charge discriminatorily higher rates to such captive customers outside its jurisdiction without a cost-justified basis. Both of these practices would provide maximum benefits for its constituents, while disserving the interests of the affected customers. Second, the practice would necessarily have an impact on the regulated public utility whose service is displaced. The elimination of customers in an established service area would likely reduce revenues, and possibly require abandonment or loss of existing equipment the effect of which would be to reduce its rate base and possibly affect its capital structure. The surviving customers and the investor-owners would bear the brunt of these consequences. The decision to displace existing service, rather than being made on the basis of efficiency in the distribution of services, may be made by the municipality in the interest of realizing maximum benefits to itself without regard to extra-territorial impact and regional efficiency.

* * *

In 1972, there were 62,437 different units of local government in this country. Of this number 23,885 were special districts which had a defined goal or goals for the provision of one or several services, while the remaining 38,552 represented the number of counties, municipalities, and townships, most of which have broad authority for general governance subject to limitations in one way or another imposed by the State. These units may, and do, participate in and affect the economic life of this Nation in a great number and variety of ways. When these bodies act as owners and providers of services, they are fully capable of aggrandizing other economic units with which they interrelate, with the potential of serious distortion of the rational and efficient allocation of resources, and the efficiency of free markets which the regime of competition embodied in the antitrust laws is thought to engender. If municipalities were free to make economic choices counseled solely by their own parochial interests and without regard to their anticompetitive effects, a serious chink in the armor of antitrust protection would be introduced at odds with the comprehensive national policy Congress established.

We conclude that these . . . arguments for implying an exclusion for local governments from the antitrust laws must be rejected. We therefore turn to petitioners' principal argument, that . . . *Parker* held that all governmental entities, whether state agencies or subdivisions of a State, are, simply by reason of their status as such, exempt from the antitrust laws.

Parker v. *Brown* involved the California Agricultural Prorate Act enacted by the California Legislature as a program to be enforced "through action of state officials . . . to restrict competition among the growers [of raisins] and maintain prices in the distribution of their commodities to packers." The Court held that the program was not prohibited by the federal antitrust laws since "nothing in the language of the Sherman Act or in its history . . . suggests that its purpose was to restrain a state or its officers or agents from activities directed by its legislature," and "[t]he state . . . as sovereign, imposed the restraint as an act of government which the Sherman Act did not undertake to prohibit."

Goldfarb v. *Virginia State Bar,* 421 U.S. 773 (1975), underscored the significance of *Parker*'s holding that the determinant of the exemption was whether the challenged action was "an act of government" by the State as "sovereign." *Parker* repeatedly emphasized that the anticompetitive effects of California's prorate program derived from "the state['s] command"; the State adopted, organized, and enforced the program "in the execution of a governmental policy." *Goldfarb,* on the other hand, presented the question "whether a minimum-fee schedule for lawyers published by the Fairfax County Bar Association and enforced by the Virginia State Bar," violated the Sherman Act. Exemption was claimed on the ground that the Virginia State Bar was "a state agency by law." The Virginia Legislature had empowered the Supreme Court of Virginia to regulate the practice of law and had assigned the State Bar a role in that regulation as an administrative agency of the Virginia Supreme Court. But no Virginia statute referred to lawyers' fees and the Supreme Court of Virginia

had taken no action requiring the use of and adherence to minimum-fee schedules. *Goldfarb* therefore held that it could not be said that the anticompetitive effects of minimum-fee schedules were directed by the State acting as sovereign. The State Bar, though acting within its broad powers, had "voluntarily joined in what is essentially a private anticompetitive activity," and was not exeucting the mandate of the State. Thus, the actions of the State Bar had failed to meet "[t]he threshold inquiry in determining if an anticompetitive activity is state action of the type the Sherman Act was not meant to proscribe . . ." *Goldfarb* therefore made it clear that, for purposes of the *Parker* doctrine not every act of a state agency is that of the State as sovereign.

Bates v. *State Bar of Arizona,* 433 U.S. 350 (1977), involved the actions of a state agency to which the *Parker* exemption applied. *Bates* considered the applicability of the antitrust laws to a ban on attorney advertising directly imposed by the Arizona Supreme Court. In holding the antitrust laws inapplicable, *Bates* noted that "[t]hat court is the ultimate body wielding the State's power over the practice of law, and, thus, the restraint is 'compelled by direction of the State acting as a sovereign.'" We emphasized, moreover, the significance to our conclusion of the fact that the state policy requiring the anticompetitive restraint as part of a comprehensive regulatory system, was one clearly articulated and affirmatively expressed as state policy, and that the State's policy was actively supervised by the State Supreme Court as the policymaker.

These decisions require rejection of petitioners' proposition that their status as such automatically affords governmental entities the "state action" exemption. *Parker*'s limitation of the exemption, as applied by *Goldfarb* and *Bates,* to "official action directed by the state," arises from the basis for the "state action" doctrine—that given our "dual system of government in which, under the Constitution, the states are sovereign, save only as Congress may constitutionally subtract from their authority," a congressional purpose to subject to antitrust control the States' acts of government will not lightly be inferred. To extend that doctrine to municipalities would be inconsistent with that limitation. Cities are not themselves sovereign; they do not receive all the federal deference of the States that create them. *Parker*'s limitation of the exemption to "official action directed by a state," is consistent with the fact that the States' subdivisions generally have not been treated as equivalents of the States themselves. In light of the serious economic dislocation which could result if cities were free to place their own parochial interests above the Nation's economic goals reflected in the antitrust laws, we are especially unwilling to presume that Congress intended to exclude anticompetitive municipal action from their reach.

On the other hand, the fact that municipalities, simply by their status as such, are not within the *Parker* doctrine, does not necessarily mean that all of their anticompetitive activities are subject to antitrust restraints. Since "[m]unicipal corporations are instrumentalities of the State for the convenient administration of government within their limits," the actions of municipalities may reflect state policy. We therefore conclude that the *Parker* doctrine exempts only anticompetitive conduct engaged in as an act of government by the State as sovereign, or, by its subdivisions, pursuant to state policy to displace competition with regulation or monopoly public service. There remains the question whether the Court of Appeals erred in holding that further inquiry should be made to determine whether petitioners' actions were directed by the State.

The petitioners . . . focus their arguments upon the fact that municipalities may exercise the sovereign power of the State, concluding from this that any actions which municipalities take necessarily reflect state policy and must therefore fall within the *Parker* doctrine. But, the fact that the governmental bodies sued are cities, with substantially less than statewide jurisdiction, has significance. When cities, each of the same status under state law, are equally free to approach a policy decision in their own way, the anticompetitive restraints adopted as policy by any one of them, may express its own preference, rather than that of the State. Therefore, in the absence of evidence that the State authorized or directed a given municipality to act as it did, the actions of a particular city hardly can be found to be pursuant to "the state['s] command," or to be restraints that "the state . . . as sovereign" imposed. The most that could be said is that state policy may be neutral. To permit municipalities to be shielded from the antitrust laws in such circumstances would impair the goals Congress sought to achieve by those laws, without furthering the policy underlying the *Parker* "exemption." This does not mean, however, that a political subdivision necessarily must be able to point to a specific, detailed legislative authorization before it properly may assert a *Parker* defense to an antitrust suit. While a subordinate governmental unit's claim to *Parker* immunity is not as readily established as the same claim by a state government sued as such, we agree with the Court of Appeals that an adequate state mandate for anticompetitive activities of cities and other subordinate governmental units exists when it is found "from the authority given a governmental entity to operate in a particular area, that the legislature contemplated the kind of action complained of."

*   *   *

Today's decision does not threaten the legitimate exercise of governmental power, nor does it preclude municipal government from providing services on a monopoly basis. *Parker* and its progeny make clear that a State properly may, as States did in *Parker* and *Bates*, direct or authorize its instrumentalities to act in a way which, if it did not reflect state policy, would be inconsistent with the antitrust laws. Compare *Bates* with *Goldfarb*. True, even a lawful monopolist may be subject to antitrust restraints when it seeks to extend or exploit its monopoly in a manner not contemplated by its authorization. But assuming that the municipality is authorized to provide a service on a monopoly basis, these limitations on municipal action will not hobble the execution of legitimate governmental programs.

Questions

1. What was the tie-in utilized by the city? How might the tie-in cause a misallocation of economic resources?
2. Why was California's proration system exempt from antitrust laws in *Parker*?
3. Why was Virginia's minimum fee schedule for lawyers not exempt from antitrust laws in *Goldfarb*?
4. Contrast *Goldfarb* and *Bates*.
5. When may a city possess the "state action" exemption?

LOBBYING

Lobbying of itself is not a violation of the antitrust laws. In the 1961 *Noerr* case, the Supreme Court stated: "We think it equally clear that the Sherman Act does not prohibit two or more persons from associating together in an attempt to persuade the legislature or the executive to take particular action with respect to a law that would produce a restraint or monopoly."[2] The Court felt the legislative history of the antitrust laws did not reveal any congressional purpose to regulate political activity. Moreover, to find lobbying an illegal activity would impair the right of individuals to petition the government, a right guaranteed by the Constitution. So, even if the defendant's sole lobbying purpose were to influence the passage of legislation that would eliminate competition, such motive would not transform lobbying activity into a violation of the Sherman Act. The Court reiterated: "The right of the people to inform their representatives in government of their desires with respect to the passage or enforcement of laws cannot properly be made to depend upon their intent. . . "[3] Nevertheless, the Court did suggest that if a publicity campaign was a "mere sham" to cover an attempt to restrain trade, the application of the Sherman Act would be justified. The following case deals with an allegation of just such a "sham."

California Motor Transport Co. v. Trucking Unlimited

404 U.S. 508 (1972)
Supreme Court of the United States

Mr. Justice Douglas

This is a civil suit . . . for injunction relief and damages instituted by [plaintiffs], who are highway carriers operating in California, against [defendants], who are also highway carriers operating within, into, and from California. [Plaintiffs] and [defendants] are, in other words, competitors. The charge is that the [defendants] conspired to monopolize trade and commerce in the transportation of goods in violation of the antitrust laws. The conspiracy alleged is a concerted action by [defendants] to institute state and federal proceedings to resist and defeat applications by [plaintiffs] to acquire operating rights or to transfer or register those rights. These activities, it is alleged, extend to rehearings and to reviews or appeals from agency or court decisions on these matters.

The District Court dismissed the complaint for failure to state a cause of action. The Court of Appeals reversed. . . .

The present case is akin to *Eastern Railroad Presidents Conference* v. *Noerr Motor Freight Inc.*, 365 U.S. 127, where a group of trucking companies sued a group of railroads to restrain them from an alleged conspiracy to monopolize the long distance freight business in violation of the antitrust laws and to obtain damages. We held that no cause of action was alleged insofar as it was predicated upon mere attempts to influence the Legislative Branch for the passage of laws or the Executive Branch for their enforcement.

* * *

The same philosophy governs the approach of citizens or groups of them to administrative agencies (which are both creatures of the legislature, and arms of the executive) and to courts, the third branch of Government. Certainly the right to petition extends to all departments of the Government. The right of access to the courts is indeed but one aspect of the right of petition.

We conclude that it would be destructive of rights of association and of petition to hold that groups with common interests may not, without violating the antitrust laws, use the channels and procedures of state and federal agencies and courts to advocate their causes and points of view respecting resolution of their business and economic interest vis-a-vis their competitors.

We said, however, in *Noerr* that there may

be instances where the alleged conspiracy "is a mere sham to cover what is actually nothing more than an attempt to interfere directly with the business relationships of a competitor and the application of the Sherman Act would be justified."

In that connection the complaint . . . [alleges] . . . the "sham" theory by stating that the power, strategy, and resources of the [defendants] were used to harass and deter [plaintiffs] in their use of administrative and judicial proceedings so as to deny them "free and unlimited access" to those tribunals. The result, it is alleged, was that the machinery of the agencies and the courts was effectively closed to [plaintiffs], and [defendants] indeed became "the regulators of the grants of rights, transfers and registrations" to [plaintiffs]— thereby depleting and diminishing the value of the businesses of [plaintiffs] and aggrandizing [defendants'] economic and monopoly power.

[Defendants] rely on our statement in that "*Noerr* shields from the Sherman Act a concerted effort to influence public officials regardless of intent or purpose." In the present case, however, the allegations are not that the conspirators sought "to influence public officials," but that they sought to bar their competitors from meaningful access to adjudicatory tribunals and so to usurp that decision-making process. It is alleged that [defendants] "instituted the proceedings and actions . . . with or without probable cause, and regardless of the merits of the cases." . . . [S]uch a purpose or intent, if shown, would be "to discourage and ultimately to prevent the [plaintiffs] from invoking" the processes of the administrative agencies and courts and thus fall within the exception to *Noerr*.

The political campaign operated by the railroads in *Noerr* to obtain legislation crippling truckers employed deception and misrepresentation and unethical tactics. We said:

Congress has traditionally exercised extreme caution in legislating with respect to problems relating to the conduct of political activities, a caution which has been reflected in the decisions of this Court interpreting such legislation. All of this caution would go for naught if we permitted an extension of the Sherman Act to regulate activities of that nature simply because those activities have a commercial impact and involve conduct that can be termed unethical.

Yet unethical conduct in the setting of the adjudicatory process often results in sanctions. Perjury of witnesses is one example. Use of a patent obtained by fraud to exclude a competitor from the market may involve a violation of the antitrust laws. . . . Conspiracy with a licensing authority to eliminate a competitor may also result in an antitrust transgression. Similarly, bribery of a public purchasing agent may constitute a violation of Section 2(c) of the Clayton Act, as amended by the Robinson-Patman Act.

There are many other forms of illegal and reprehensible practice which may corrupt the administrative or judicial processes and which may result in antitrust violations. Misrepresentations, condoned in the political arena, are not immunized when used in the adjudicatory process. Opponents before agencies or courts often think poorly of the other's tactics, motions, or defenses and may readily call them baseless. One claim, which a court or agency may think baseless, may go unnoticed; but a pattern of baseless, repetitive claims may emerge which leads the factfinder to conclude that the administrative and judicial processes have been abused. That may be a difficult line to discern and draw. But once it is drawn, the case is established that abuse of those processes produced an illegal result, viz., effectively barring respondents from access to the agencies and courts. Insofar as the administrative or judicial processes are involved, actions of that

kind cannot acquire immunity by seeking refuge under the umbrella of "political expression."

[Defendants], of course, have the right of access to the agencies and courts to be heard on applications sought by competitive highway carriers. That right, as indicated, is part of the right of petition protected by the First Amendment. Yet that does not necessarily give them immunity from the antitrust laws.

It is well settled that First Amendment rights are not immunized from regulation when they are used as an integral part of conduct which violates a valid statute.

* * *

First Amendment rights may not be used as the means or the pretext for achieving "substantive evils" which the legislature has the power to control. Certainly the constitutionality of the antitrust laws is not open to debate. A combination of entrepreneurs to harass and deter their competitors from having "free and unlimited access" to the agencies and courts, to defeat that right by massive, concerted, and purposeful activities of the group are ways of building up one empire and destroying another. . . . If these facts are proved, a violation of the antitrust laws has been established. If the end result is unlawful, it matters not that the means used in violation may be lawful.

What the proof will show is not known, for the District Court granted the motion to dismiss the complaint. We must, of course, take the allegations of the complaint at face value for the purposes of that motion. On their face the above-quoted allegations come within the "sham" exception in the *Noerr* case, as adapted to the adjudicatory process.

Accordingly we affirm the Court of Appeals and remand the case for trail.

Questions
1. What is the principle of the *Noerr* case?
2. How are the plantiffs attempting to avoid the application of the *Noerr* case

in their situation?

3. Identify some unethical conduct in the adjudicatory process that may result in an antitrust violation. What specific unethical conduct is being alleged about these defendants?
4. Why is the First Amendment not an absolute defense for the defendants?

UNIONS

A 1908 case, referred to as the *Danbury Hatters* case, held that union activities in organizing a nationwide boycott of plaintiff's hats to bring about unionization were in violation of the Sherman Act.[4] To avoid further antitrust prosecution of unionizing activities, the labor movement lobbied for protection of legitimate union activities. In 1914 Congress passed Section 6 of the Clayton Act, which provided that "the labor of a human being is not a commodity or article of commerce." Section 6 further provides that antitrust laws shall not be construed to "forbid the existence and operation of labor . . . organizations, instituted for purposes of mutual self-help." Consequently, neither members or labor organizations can be held to be "illegal combinations or conspirarcies in restraint of trade under the antitrust laws." However, Section 6 did not entirely prevent antitrust actions against union activities. Therefore, unions urged and received passage of the Norris LaGuardia Act in 1932, which restricts the use of court injunctions in cases involving union activities and labor disputes. As a result, provisions of the antitrust laws and the labor laws must be considered together in determining the scope of the exemption of union activities from antitrust laws. Generally, the Court has not construed these acts as granting a blanket exemption for all labor union activities. Any combinations in illegal restraint of trade between businessmen and a labor union are not insulated from the Sherman Act.

In *United Mine Workers* v. *Pennington,* the Court held that:

[A] union forfeits its exemption from the antitrust laws when it is clearly shown that it has agreed with one set of employers to impose a certain wage scale on other bargaining units. One group of employers may not conspire to eliminate competitors from the industry and the union is liable with the employers if it becomes a party to the conspiracy. This is true even though the union's part in the scheme is an undertaking to secure the same wages, hours or other conditions of employment from the remaining employers in the industry."[5]

However, the union conspiracy with business firms must be established by clear proof, a task rarely accomplished.

The National Labor Relations Act places beyond the reach of the Sherman Act any union-employer agreements as to "wages, hours, and working conditions." However, a union demanding that prices be set on the products it produces would probably come under the ban of the Sherman Act. Union activity between these extremes is more difficult to label as exempted union activities or prohibited antitrust violations. There have been cases where union demands appear to be an attempt to control prices but which in reality are so closely connected with wages, hours, or other conditions of employment that the union activities will be protected from charges of a Sherman Act violation. For example, in *Amalgamated Meat Cutters & Butcher Workmen* v. *Jewel Tea Company*, the union was charged with attempting to impose marketing hour restrictions on the retail sale of fresh meat before 9 A.M. and after 6 P.M.[6] The Court stated that the marketing hour restrictions were so intimately related to "wages, hours, and working conditions" that the union's successful attempt to obtain these provisions through bona fibe bargaining fell within the labor exemption.

On the other hand, unions have been found to violate antitrust laws when they "agree" with unionized employers not to deal with nonunion employers, where the purpose of the agreement was to exclude nonunion products from competing with union-made products. In short, only "legitimate" union activities pertaining to hours, wages, terms, and conditions of employment are excluded from the antitrust law. Unions going beyond the boundaries of "legitimate" union actions come within the coverage of the Sherman Act. Combinations or agreements solely seeking the elimination of competition or an agreement to control or fix prices are examples of union activities not protected by the labor exemption.

The economic effect of the labor exemption from antitrust law substantially interferes with the obtainment of antitrust goals. There is no difference in economic effect between the union's *agreeing* to impose similar terms on other employers and the union's unilateral efforts to obtain similar terms from those employers. Consequently, the Supreme Court has frankly admitted:

Union success in standardizing wages ultimately will affect price competition among employers, but the goals of federal labor law never could be achieved if this effect on business competition were held a violation of the antitrust laws. The Court therefore has acknowledged that labor policy requires tolerance of the lessening of business competition. . .[7]

COOPERATIVES

Section 6 of the Clayton Act provides that nothing in the antitrust laws is to be construed to forbid the "existence and operation of . . . agriculture or horticultural organizations" that are organized for "mutual help, and not having capital stock or conducted for profit." It also provides that such organizations shall not be deemed illegal combinations or conspiracies in restraint of trade. Section 1 of the Capper-Volstead Act expands the exemption to include agricultural organizations formed with or without capital stock. However, it is possible for an agricultural cooperative to lose its exemption where nonproducer interests are part of the organization other than by way of capital contributions. Therefore, agricultural cooperatives may not combine with others to restrain trade.

The Secretary of Agriculture is authorized to issue a cease and desist order if an agricultural organization or cooperative monopolizes or restrains trade in interstate commerce to the degree that the price of the product is "unduly enhanced."[8] Absent any proceeding by the Secretary of Agriculture, the cooperative is subject to antitrust charges of monopolization or unreasonable restraint of trade. The Supreme Court has stated that the Act "did not leave cooperatives free to engage in practices against other persons in order to monopolize trade, or restrain and suppress competition with the cooperative."[9] Instead, the Act did make "it possible for farmer-producers to organize together, set associations policy, fix prices for which their cooperative will sell their produce, and otherwise carry on like a business corporation without thereby violating the antitrust laws."[10]

Another section of the Capper-Volstead Act applies to certain nonprofit organizations, such as schools, churches, hospitals, and charitable institutions. Such institutions can receive price favoritism from business corporations without causing a violation of the Robinson-Patman Act.[11]

THE BUSINESS OF INSURANCE

Prior to 1944, it had been assumed that insurance was not "commerce" as used in the Commerce Clause.[12] However, in 1944 the Supreme Court held that the word "commerce" did include the insurance business.[13] Consequently, in 1945 the McCarran-Ferguson Act was passed, which declared that the regulation and taxation of the business of insurance by the several states was in the public interest and that the antitrust laws should not apply to the business of insurance. The Supreme Court has held that "the relationship between insurer and insured, the type of policy which could be issued, its reliability, interpretation, and enforcement—these are the core of the 'business of insurance'."[14] Consequently, the fixing of rates, the selling and advertising of policies, and the licensing of companies and their agents are activities of the "business of insurance" and exempt from the antitrust laws. The McCarran-Ferguson Act does not exempt insurance companies, but rather exempts the insurance business if regulated by the states. Activities of insurance companies outside the insurance business are subject to the antitrust laws. Moreover, the McCarran-Ferguson Act specifically indicates that insurance companies are liable for "any agreement to boycott, coerce, or intimidate. . . ." This provision apparently was passed to prevent the blacklisting of agents or companies by other insurance companies.

CONCLUSION

Most exemptions from antitrust law are based on a conflicting public policy. Congress has approved of combinations that improve the economic affairs of labor, agricultural, and charitable organizations. Likewise, federal and state regulation of utilities, the insurance business, and state regulations (under the Parker Doctrine) are considered acceptable substitutes for the competitive process provided through the antitrust laws. Moreover, the Noerr Doctrine protects the rights of business firms to combine for political activities. Even the exemptions provided in the Webb-Pomerene Act, the Export Trading Company Act, and the Patent Act can be explained by recognition of opposing public policies. On the other hand, a few exemptions have less credible support. For example, the Supreme Court has continued to follow its old precedent in which baseball was held not to be a business or "interstate commerce" and, therefore, to be beyond the reach of the antitrust law. This is true in spite of the fact that the other major professional sports are not exempt. However, these unregulated and exempt industries represent a small percentage of business activities. The bulk of economic affairs remains subject to the antitrust laws or to the supervision of regulatory bodies.

DISCUSSION QUESTIONS

1. An American corporation engaged in the manufacture of widgets joined with a British citizen who owned a controlling interest in a British corporation also engaged in the widget business. Together, the corporation and the individual purchased all of the stock in a French company producing widgets in France. In the worldwide market for widgets, the American firm was the largest manufacturer, while the British and French companies each had a substantial percentage of the market sales.

   The three corporations entered into agreements dividing the world into territorial markets. Any product sold by one company in the territory of another (or destined for use in the territory of another) could be sold only at a price approved by the company in whose territory the sale was made, and the controlling company also received a percentage of the net sale from the seller. When possible, the three companies cooperated to protect one another from each other's competition.

   Could this conduct be subject to attack under Section 1 of the Sherman Act?

2. The Canadian government made a private Canadian corporation its exlusive agent for the purchase of vanadium, a material used in steel production. The corporation, acting in concert with an affiliated American company, used its position to exclude a competitor of the American affiliate from the Canadian market. Are the activities of the American affiliate immune from action under the Sherman Act because of the "act of state" doctrine?

3. Previously, Timberland had purchased a milling plant in Honduras that was mortgaged to the Bank of America. Timberland made a substantial cash offer for the Bank's interest in an effort to clear its title, but the Bank refused to sell. Instead, the Bank conveyed the mortgage to Cassanova, who paid nothing, but agreed to pay the Bank a portion of what he collected.

Cassanova immediately assigned the Bank's claim to Caminals, who went to court to enforce the claim, ignoring throughout Timberland's effort to purchase or settle it. Under the laws of Honduras, an "embargo" on property is a court-ordered attachment, registered with the Public Registry, that precludes the sale of that property without a further court order. Hondurian law provides, on embargo, that the court appoint a judicial officer called an "intervenor" to ensure against any diminition in the value of the property. Caminals obtained an embargo, and the intervenor, accused of being on the payroll of the Bank of America, crippled and for a time completely shut down Timberland's milling operation.

Timberland alleged that officials of the Bank of America and others located in Honduras conspired to prevent Timberlane from milling lumber in Honduras and exporting it to the United States, thus maintaining control of the Hondurian export lumber business in the hands of a few select individuals financed and controlled by the Bank. The District Court dismissed the suit on the basis of the "act of state" doctrine. Was the District Court ruling correct?

4. Competing firms in the United States, through meetings held in the United States, entered into an agreement to restrain importation into the United States of a raw material, X-zale. Thereafter, the group instigated and succeeded in gaining legislation from a foreign government to restrict exports of X-zale to the U.S. and world markets. Are these firms subject to punishment under the Sherman Act? Are their actions protected by the "act of state" doctrine?

5. RXI, the second largest of five producers of X-metal in the United States, has entered into preliminary discussions with British Metals Ltd., one of the largest X-metal producers in the Common Market, about a research and development joint venture for the development of a process for producing X-metal from materials other than X-ore. X is available in a variety of domestic shales, but nobody has found an economic way to recover it. Several X-metal producers, including RXI and British Metals Ltd., are trying some research at the laboratory stage, but so far none has been able to develop any workable process.

The parties will form a British company, in which each will own half of the shares and appoint half the directors. The parties agree that all their research operations in this area will be conducted through the joint company. The parties have agreed that if the joint venture's research is successful, the joint company will seek to obtain patents covering its processes. RXI will be given an exclusive license to all patent rights and use of know-how in North America, while British Metals Ltd. will be given similar rights to patents in the United Kingdom, other EEC countries, and all former British colonies and dominions except Canada.

Is this joint research effort likely to violate the Sherman Act?

6. American Company X has licensed a subsidiary in which it has 85 percent of the voting stock to practice certain patents and know-how in foreign Coun-

try A. X requires the foreign subsidiary to grant back title or an exclusive license on any new patents or know-how the foreign subsidiary may obtain or develop related to the licensed technology rights.

Meanwhile, Company X grants a similar license (including the grant-back) in Country B to a licensee in which X has a 30 percent voting stock interest, and the remaining stock is held by the public.

Finally, in Country C, X grants a similar license (including the grant-back) to a leading local firm.

Are any of these exclusive grantback licenses likely to be illegal?

7. International Action Corporation (IAC) is a large, well-known multinational corporation headquartered in New York City. IAC manufactures printing machines in New Jersey. It relies on overseas subsidiaries to manufacture and sell its products throughout the rest of the western world. The IAC subsidiaries develop sales in their own assigned territories. Normally, when an order comes in to one subsidiary from the assigned territory of another, the recipient will send it on or suggest that the consumer contact directly the subsidiary assigned to the territory.

Has IAC violated American antitrust laws?

8. Razors, Inc. (RI), an American company, is the largest manufacturer of razor blades both in the United States and internationally, accounting for about half of all U.S. and world sales. RI proposes to buy Glint, a small German specialty manufacturer, which has developed a cadmium steel razor blade arguably superior to the traditional steel blades offered by RI and the other major companies here and abroad. Glint has started selling these blades in Germany (but on a low advertising budget) and still accounts for less than 1 percent of all razor blade sales in Germany. Its export sales to the United States are insignificant. RI independently possesses the technical capability to manufacture cadmium blades, but it has decided against doing so either in the United States or abroad.

Is the merger lawful under U.S. antitrust laws?

9. Several U.S. electrical equipment manufacturers and engineering firms have established a consortium for the purpose of submitting a bid on an extremely large hydroelectric project in a Latin American country. The consortium consists of the second, third, and sixth largest U.S. electrical equipment manufacturers. The consortium also includes the United States' first, fifth, and eighth largest engineering firms.

The parties have formed the consortium because the project is too large for a smaller group to finance, and a smaller group would not have the technical capabilities necessary to carry out the project. Most of the manu-facturers and engineers have tight capital situations and are already reason-ably busy due to domestic demand and contracts made for sales and con-struction work in other countries. Since the project will take almost 10 years to complete, the parties are also concerned with the long-run political situa-tion in the host country.

The parties believe that they will be competing against similar consortia supported by the Japanese and British governments. The parties have not invited any other American or foreign firms to join the group; and they do not know whether other American engineering or equipment manufacturing firms know about it.

Is the consortium in violation of antitrust laws?

10. Import Metals Company mines X-ore in five countries and sells X-ore and X-product in a number of countries, including the U.S. Import Metals is 75-percent-owned by a diversified investment company, which is mostly owned and controlled by the government of C, the Asian country where Import Metals and its parent are headquartered.

Offshore, Inc., a large multinational corporation incorporated in Delaware, mines X-ore abroad and processes it into X-product, which it sells in the U.S. and a number of other countries. Offshore owns 75 percent of a subsidiary that it organized in C to operate a large X-ore mine there.

Vitamina is a European-based fruit company that sells large quantities of fruit juices in its own stores in the U.S. It recently discovered a very large X-ore deposit on one of its fruit plantations and has been selling X-ore abroad.

Import Metals, Vitamina and the four or five other foreign X-ore producers recently met in Country C to form a cartel, and agreed on quotas and prices for all X-ore production. Import Metals is the only one of these foreign producers that sells X-ore or X-product in the United States, but the others all sell substantial amounts of X-ore to foreign brokers, who resell about 25 percent of world production in the U.S. The government of C has given notice that it wants Offshore to pledge to the cartel members that it will abide by the agreed-upon quotas and prices. Advise Offshore.

11. An association of companies that own and operate processing plants, feed mills, and hatcheries and breeder flocks for the production of broiler chickens claims exemption from antitrust laws on the theory that it is composed of "farmers" within the meaning of the Capper-Volstead Act. The government, in support of its suit against the association to restrain its cooperative activities, established that the broiler chickens are actually grown by independent contractors, hired by the association members, who raise the chicks on their own farms and in their own buildings and who tend them daily. The companies breed and hatch the eggs, provide feed, and slaughter and process the mature broilers.

Should the association be exempt?

12. A state bar association, a state agency under the State Supreme Court, issued rules providing for disciplinary action against any lawyer habitually charging fees below the minimum fees set by any local bar association. Neither the Supreme Court nor the state bar required that all local bar associations, which are voluntary associations of lawyers, issue such schedules, but a county bar association did publish a "suggested minimum fee schedule" that all local attorneys followed in setting fees for routine services.

A purchaser of real estate sued the state and county bar associations under Sherman Act Section 1 when he was unable to locate an attorney to provide a title examination, a service which by law must be performed by a lawyer, for less than the suggested minimum fee.

Are either or both bar associations protected from legal action under the Sherman Act?

13. GM granted a new Oldsmobile dealership franchise to Tober Motors in Springfield, Massachusetts. Reiter Motors, which held a GM Oldsmobile franchise in the same city, applied for an injunction in state court to prevent Tober from operating. Reiter invoked a state law that provides that a manufacturer may not grant a competitive franchise in the relevant market area previously granted to another franchise. If it wishes to grant such a franchise, the manufacturer must give notice to the existing dealer in the area, and unless there is agreement, the matter must be submitted to binding arbitration for a determination of the relevant market area, the adequacy of service in the area, and the propriety of granting an additional dealership. A revision of the law declared it illegal to "arbitrarily" grant a franchise without notice to existing franchisees, such notice to be given 60 days before the grant to existing franchisees within a 20-mile radius of the proposed new location.

GM and Tober claim that the law is void because it conflicts with federal antitrust law, and that the protection of existing dealers from competition is not a legitimate state interest.

What result?

14. A, a corporation organized under the laws of Country X, is a wholly owned subsidiary of AUSA, a U.S. company. A manufactures and sells 25 percent of the widget market in Country X. Two of the other widget suppliers, B and C, are entirely locally owned and together account for about 20 percent of the market in X. The fourth supplier, D, is a majority-owned subsidiary of a manufacturer located in the Federal Republic of Germany, and accounts for about 30 percent of the market. The remaining 25 percent of the X market is accounted for by imports from U.S., Japanese, and Swiss manufacturers.

B and C find the widget market in X unprofitable. The government of X asks A, B, C, and D to form an advisory council to advise it on how to strengthen the local widget manufacturing industry. A joins B, C, and D in advising the X government that the market in X is not large enough to sustain four local manufacturers plus substantial imports; and A, B, C, and D suggest either a tariff increase or an embargo for a specified period. This action, if taken, would affect exports by a second U.S. manufacturer presently accounting for about 6 percent of the market in X. Officers of AUSA are advised of this action of A. Has A or AUSA violated the Sherman Act?

15. *The Seattle Times* is owned by the local Seattle Times Company, and *The Seattle Post-Intelligencer* is published by the Hertz Corporation of New York. These two Seattle newspapers have proposed a joint operating agreement

that combines their operations, except for editorial. The Newspaper Preservation Act gives the U.S. Attorney General power to confer immunity on such arrangements, if such action is needed to prevent one of the newspapers from closing.

While it has not been proven that the *Post-Intelligencer* is failing financially, it is in danger of financial failure because of a 13-year steadily downward trend in circulation and advertising. The Hertz Corporation contends that the *Post-Intelligencer* has been kept alive only by capital spending from the parent organization. At the same time, however, Hertz has rebuffed all offers to buy the paper. Opponents of the agreement argue that the *Post-Intelligencer* could be sold to someone who would continue to publish it independently.

The law calls for the Attorney General to receive public comments for 45 days before making a decision. What would you recommend to the Attorney General?

SUGGESTED READINGS

Ashley, Pamela J., "Vanishing Immunity: The Antitrust Assault on Regulated Industries, *Loyola Law Review*, Vol. 27, Winter 1981, pp. 187–218.

Hewitt, Charles M. and Richards, Eric L., "Will *Detroit Edison* Turn Off *Parker's* Power?", *American Business Law Journal*, Vol. 15, No. 3, Winter 1978, pp. 379–389.

Richards, Eric L., "Reconciling the Tension Between Anticompetitive State Regulations and the Sherman Act: California Retail Liquor Dealers Ass'n v. Midcal Aluminum, Inc.," *American Business Law Journal*, Vol. 19, No. 4, Winter 1981, pp. 539–556.

ENDNOTES

1. *Eastern R. Presidents Conference* v. *Noerr Motor Freight, Inc.*, 365 U.S. 127 (1961).
2. *Ibid.*, p. 136.
3. *Ibid.*, p. 139.
4. *Loewe* v. *Lawlor*, 208 U.S. 274 (1908).
5. 381 U.S. 657 (1965).
6. 381 U.S. 676 (1965).
7. *Connell Co.* v. *Plumbers and Steamfitters*, 421 U.S. 616 (1975).
8. 7 USCS Section 292.
9. *Maryland and Virginia Milk Producers Association* v. *United States*, 362 U.S. 458 (1960).
10. *Ibid.*, p. 466.
11. 15 USCS Section 13c.
12. *Paul* v. *Virginia*, 8 Wall 168 (1869).
13. *U.S.* v. *South-Eastern Underwriters Association*, 322 U.S. 533 (1944).
14. *SEC* v. *National Security, Inc.*, 393 U.S. 453 (1969).

part IV
THE REGULATORY PROCESS

The birth of the United States and the birth of laissez-faire economics occurred in the same era, as a reaction against mercantilism and its government-dictated economic policies. Because of this heritage of a limited role of government, Americans have tended to overlook the fact that governmental domination over economic affairs has been the norm in history and a relatively free market economy the exception. Instead, Americans have viewed their short history, with its reliance on the market mechanism and on relative freedom from governmental restraint, as the natural state of a national economy. Consequently, the subsequent development of government regulations of business has resulted only when the populace perceived failures of the market system.

Adam Smith popularized the "invisible hand" concept: the idea that an individual who "intends only has own gain," is, nevertheless, "led by an invisible hand to promote . . . the public interest." Ever since, there seems to have been a dominant tendency of thought that decisions reached individually will, in fact, be the best decisions for an entire society. But Garrett Hardin's "Tragedy of the Commons" reminds us that "[r]uin is the destination toward which all men rush, each pursuing his own best interest in a society that believes in the freedom of the commons." But how is the political authority to deal with socially erroneous private decisions? One instance in American history is particularly illustrative of the two main political reactions to the "tragedy of the commons."

Under oil and gas law, the "rule of capture" allows the owner of a tract of land to produce oil and gas from beneath his land even if he includes some oil and gas that has migrated from beneath his neighbor's land. Moreover, he will not be liable to his neighbor even if his production has caused the migration. The neighbor's only defense to the rule of capture is to capture the oil or gas first. The result of this rule was a rush to drill by all property owners. However, when a field is developed too rapidly, the natural energy of a reservoir is dissipated in a manner that reduces the total recovery from a reservoir. Is this a tragedy of the commons? Is this "waste" a failure of the market system that can only be prevented by regulation?

Also, the "rule of capture" has the effect of bringing large amounts of oil to the surface for storage and sale in excess of a market demand that will support a price to cover the cost recovery. Is the resulting "destructive competition" in need of regulation for the social good? Are the costs of storing on the surface large amounts of oil that could have been left in the reservoir a waste of economic resources?

The problems of ecological waste and excessive competition resulting from the failure of the "invisible hand" to promote the public interest have been one of the major economic-political problems of the twentieth century. Excessive competition has spawned private cartels, which are then either outlawed by antitrust or socially approved as long as public participation (regulation) is included. The progeny of ecological waste, whether of human or natural resources, has been labor laws and environmental laws adopting a variety of regulatory techniques. All these resulted from society's perception of market failure needing governmental solution. Even the strongest advocates of reliance on the market system have admitted that certain circumstances require governmental intervention.

Indeed, for much of the past century, the central issue of government economic policy has been whether to accept big business with direct governmental control of business policies, or to reject such control and rely on antitrust enforcement and the positive support of competition through encouragement of new entrants and subsidization of marginal producers. The American ambivalence toward big business has been reflected in cycles of expanded antitrust enforcement and then relaxation; or alternatively, of more regulation and then deregulation. The elements of these competing approaches to the problem of market failure can be found in the government policy of almost any period. For example, in the presidential campaign of 1912 Theodore Roosevelt, who had gained a reputation as a "trust buster" in the decade before, accepted the trend toward the consolidation of large enterprises and the existence of monopoly power. Therefore, he argued for regulation, which he felt would achieve the approximate results of competition, rather than the promotion of competition itself. And today, the debate between the political parties concerning the appropriate role of government in dealing with market failures is no less intense, particularly when one notes that regulatory failure seems often as prevalent as market failure.

The chapters in this part contain materials that reveal the separate methods of government regulation dealing with various aspects of market failure. Each chapter will expose the historical movements that led to the societal decision to adopt government regulation over the respective subject area and discuss the substantive provisions of the regulatory techniques employed.

chapter 16

REGULATION OF PUBLIC UTILITIES

A long-accepted rationale for government intervention in the economy is the theory of natural monopoly. It maintains that in certain industries, competition will only produce higher costs, an unnecessary and wasteful duplication of facilities and services, and chronic instability. It is primarily on this theory that almost all public utility regulation has been premised. The following excerpt summarizes the development and acceptance of the theory of natural monopoly, which, in turn, mandates the formation of new regulatory techniques.

MARKET FAILURE AND REGULATORY INTERVENTION

Competition and Monopoly in Public Utility Industries
B. Behling, *The University of Illinois Bulletin,* Vol. xxxv, No. 100, (1938) pp. 18–26.

It was not unnatural that competition should have been accepted as proper in the public service enterprises in the beginning. The country had been built upon the competitive ideal. . . . The country was young and undeveloped, and encouragement to initiative and to business promotion was believed to be imperative. Especially was the latter true of the new public service industries which held so much promise for good in promoting power production. . . . What was not foreseen was that freedom of enterprise may breed strongly entrenched monopolies under some circumstances rather than the competition which often is considered the normal outcome of free enterprise.

Technical limitations in the early days help to explain the existence of several companies in one locality. The use of direct current at low voltages in the electrical industry made distribution over areas exceeding one square mile impossible. With the subsequent improvements in generation and transmission, the previously small and non-competing enterprises in one city sought to expand by encroaching upon one another's territory, and spirited competition began. Difficulty in raising large amounts of capital for utility undertakings also fostered the development of small local companies in this early period. Rivalry between electrical equipment manufacturers, in whose control the development of that industry began, contributed to the location of several production and distribution units in one city. Rapid improvement in technical efficiency and in the investment standing of the industries made larger producing and distributing units possible and accounted for the cut-throat competition which soon appeared.

There was an even stronger reason why competition presented itself in the utility industries, aside from the failure to realize their monopolistic inclination. Law making, which is the source of comprehensive regulation, is slowly evolved. Regulatory mechanisms were not invented in the same laboratories with the electric light and the telephone. Monopoly, then as now, could receive public sanction only upon the provision of an adequate control. The story of the development of that control is the history of the struggle to eliminate uneconomic competition and is at the same time the history of the search for effective regulation. That quest is not yet ended.

There is scarcely a city in the country that has not experienced competition in one or more of the utility industries. Six electric light companies were organized in the one year of 1887 in New York City. Forty-five electric light enterprises had the legal right to operate in Chicago in 1907. Prior to 1895, Duluth, Minnesota, was served by five electric lighting companies, and Scranton, Pennsylvania, had four in 1906.

* * *

The above examples might be multiplied, but those given are typical of a wide-spread condition. More significant are the results which followed competition. . . . Cut-throat competition favored the public for a time with low rates, but invariably at the expense of a deteriorated service. Financial exhaustion of one or more of the companies eventually brought about a complete consolidation, or an agreement as to rates or territory. . . . Competition which was relied upon to insure for the public reasonable rates and satisfactory service proved to be elusive and non-enduring and failed to measure up to expectations. It continually was disappearing as a result of bankruptcies, consolidations, and informal agreements, leaving in its wake torn-up streets, "dead" wires and useless poles and pipes, enormous overcapitalization, and paralyzed service. Whereupon the public paid for the competitive folly in high rates to cover dividends on unused, unnecessary investment, and watered stock. . . .

The experience with competition was the same in water, gas, electric, and telephone enterprises. . . . But the mere realization of the inefficiency of competition in public utility operation came along before its elimination of this country. . . .

* * *

. . . The problem was to achieve an adequate control over monopoly, assuming its acceptance as the logical type of economic organization, after many investigations reported the common conclusion that to attempt to enforce competition was useless and recommended its abandonment. . . .

The first attempts at regulation, after judicial process through the common law had proved inadequate, were by legislative charter. The initial policy was to make the charters of a special nature, granted by legislative authority in each case. In reality, the special charters were often not such at all, being copied from previous grants. . . . A high degree of uniformity resulted from the repetition . . . of the principal provisions, and regulation by special charter soon gave way to regulation by general charter. It is interesting to note that every state went through essentially the same stages in regulatory experimentation. . . . A few states . . . benefited from the experience of their sister states by skipping the period of special charters and beginning with general corporation laws.

The abandonment of the special charter was . . . not a forward step in regulation. The era of general charter regulation was, in fact, one of full and free competition. The issuance of franchises usually was the prerogative of the municipal governments, and the latter were generally of the opinion that their only protection lay in granting competing franchises. In most of the states, in fact, during the latter half of the nineteenth century and on into the present one, the granting of an exclusive franchise was either unconstitutional or contrary to statutory law. The common policy was to grant franchises to all who applied.

The most glaring weakness of regulation by franchise was that it did not provide a continuous control over the utility companies. Minute details as to rates and services were often incorporated in the franchise, but the results were not effective. Due to advancement in the arts of production, to competition, and to declining prices during a part of the period, maximum rate provisions became a farce, because the companies, in an attempt to enlarge their markets, voluntarily charged less than the prescribed rates.

In an effort to make regulation by franchise relatively continuous and effective in restraining the utilities, the terms of franchises were shortened. This policy served only to add to the complexity of the situation. . . . The short-term franchise was a handicap to the companies, also, creating financial insecurity, and making capital wary because of the uncertainty as to whether or not and on what terms the franchise would be renewed. The opposite extreme was the granting of perpetual franchises, but these, like exclusive grants, were unpopular, if not illegal, on the ground that they played into the hands of the monopolists.

Aside from the theoretical weaknesses of franchise regulation which became all too apparent, graft and corruption prevailed. After an early period of promiscuous issuing of franchises based on the conviction that public utiliy development would be encouraged, it began to be realized that franchises were special privileges and worth money. With this realization the way was paved for bribery and corruption. Even honest local officials could not cope with the situation, for they were incapable of understanding the technicalities of a franchise and negotiated blindly. . . .

* * *

The glaring weaknesses of charter and franchise regulation aroused spirited demand for more stringent and continuous control over public utility activities, particularly as to rates and services. Under term franchises there had been little influential control over rates, less over service requirements, and practically none over discrimination. The creation of the mandatory state commission with the power to prescribe rates and service standards and to prevent discrimination has been the response to the demand for adequate and continuous supervision.

Questions
1. Could you identify a natural monopoly? What is your criteria for defining a natural monopoly?
2. Was the theory of natural monopoly justifying government regulation developed by the demands of the populace or by the needs of the producers?

3. Why were the first electric utility firms rather small business units? What brought about "cut-throat" competition in this industry?
4. What were the results of competition in the operation of public utilities?
5. What were the weaknesses of the regulatory technique of granting franchises?
6. What reasons explain the development of regulatory commissions?
7. What type of regulation is generally considered most appropriate for a natural monopoly? A system that attempts to produce the same results as a competitive market? Or should it be allowed to take monopoly profits and turn them over to the government?

RATE REGULATION

In Chapter 7 it was shown how the Supreme Court utilized the Fourteenth Amendment's "due process" clause as a barrier against state governmental meddling in the market economy. There were exceptions, and one major exception was the English and later American common law interpretation that the prices charged in certain industries and trades were properly subject to public regulation. In *Munn* v. *Illinois,* this common law tradition was incorporated into a constitutional interpretation that authorized the states to regulate prices in certain industries.

According to the reasoning of *Munn* v. *Illinois,* the states were freed of the constitutional barrier of due process and permitted to regulate those industries that were "affected with the public interest." Other industries, not so affected with the public interest, remained beyond the authority of the state government to impose public regulations until this policy was abandoned by the Court in the 1930s.

There were two categories of industry considered to be "affected with the public interest" and, hence, subject to state regulation. First, as was indicated in *Munn* v. *Illinois,* there are those industries where buyers or sellers are apt to be caught in a "distress position" that subjects them to extreme price exploitation. The grain elevators discussed in *Munn* v. *Illinois* and the stockyards, hotels, and docks are examples. Second, there are the "natural monopolies," where the economies of large-scale operation necessitate concentration of the industry into a single business entity in order to produce units at lowest average cost. Obvious examples of these industries include electric, gas, telephone, and urban transit companies.

Within these two categories of industries, the legislatures of the states were empowered to regulate industry prices. However, the Court did not fully retreat from its activist policy of protecting laissez-faire economic philosophy. Instead, the Court undertook to protect the regulated companies from a regulated price level that was so low as to constitute a deprivation of the utility's property rights.[1]

The states, and the federal government also, have allowed certain industries to obtain monopoly positions so that the public might realize the advantages of large-scale output and low production costs. It becomes, then, the task of regulation to ensure that low average costs will be reflected in correspondingly low prices to the public. It has been the objective of regulation to fix rates so that the regulated companies will receive no more or no less than a "fair return" on their investments. When profits are greater than "fair returns," rates are to be reduced. When profits are less than "fair returns," the public service commission is obliged under the U.S. Constitution to raise rates so that the investors are not deprived of their property rights.

RATEMAKING

Ratemaking by state utility commissions generally employs an adjudicatory type of procedure, although it will be somewhat less formal than a civil trial in a court. Rates are set on a company basis, not an industry-wide basis. The major exceptions have been the industry-wide price setting by the federal government in the natural gas and crude oil industries.

The purpose of a rate proceeding is to determine whether a request for a rate increase is justified by the evidence given at the hearing. Virtually all ratemaking proceedings involve the application of the following formula:

$$\text{Operating Costs} + [\text{Rate Base} \times \text{Rate of Return}] = \text{Revenues Allowed}$$

In this equation, the revenues allowed to be earned by a regulated firm for a period of time must cover the operating costs of the company and provide a profit or "fair return" on the investments of capital provided by the firm. The rate base, or the investment of capital on which the corporation shareholders are entitled to earn a return, is multiplied by the "rate of return" felt to be appropriate, considering the prevailing rates of return in alternative investments with similar risks. What may be the appropriate rate of return or what may be included in the rate base and how it is to be valued have been the subjects of much controversy in public utilities law.

Evidence is given at the ratemaking proceeding to establish appropriate figures to apply in the formula. Witnesses at that hearing often disagree as to what constitutes a fair and reasonable rate of return under current conditions and what value should be placed on the utility's property. They also may disagree about what should be charged against operating costs. When an expense is disallowed, it generally does not mean that the utility cannot incur such an expense, only that the shareholders themselves must pay the expense out of the amount allowed them as a reasonable return on their investment.

OPERATING COSTS

Operating expenses usually constitute the largest sum of money in the determination of the revenue requirements of the public utility. While most operating expenses incurred by utilities stir little controversy, in recent years there has been an increase in disputes about what constitutes allowable operating expenses. The following excerpt from an opinion of the Ohio Public Utilities Commission illustrates the types of disagreements that can arise concerning operating expenses.

Before the Public Utilities Commission of Ohio
Case No. 80-260-EL-AIR (1981)

This case comes before the Commission upon application of The Cincinnati Gas & Electric Company . . . for authority to increase its rates and charges for electric service to its jurisdictional customers. The applicant alleges that its existing rates are insufficient to afford it reasonable compensation for the service it renders. . . .

* * *

Operating Revenues and Expenses

The applicant and the Staff each submitted an analysis of test year accounts, reflecting the results of the Applicant's operations under its existing rates. These analyses were primarily based on six months of actual data and six months of forecasted data. The adjustments to test year expenses recommended by the various parties are discussed on an item by item basis under appropriate subheadings below.

* * *

Labor Expense The Applicant . . . requests a post-test year adjustment of $3,536,331 to cover increased expenses resulting from wage increases granted after the end of the test year. Approximately 66 percent of that amount involves increases granted under various collective bargaining agreements, and the remainder relates to an increase granted to the Company's supervisory, administrative, and professional (SAP) employees. . . . The Office of Consumer's Counsel (OCC) opposes the adoption of any post-test year adjustment for increased labor expense.

It is now well established that the test year results must be reasonably representative of normal operations. Stated somewhat differently, a utility's allowable expenses should create a representative picture of the costs which the utility will incur in the near-term future. In order to accomplish this, it is imperative that the allowable expenses reflect known cost changes which can be calculated with reasonable certainty, and are beyond the control of the utility.

In recognition of that principle, the Commission has long permitted the annualization of wage increases granted during the test year under the terms of a signed union contract. More recently, the Commission recognized that once a wage increase has been granted, it is highly unrealistic to assume that the increased wage rate will not prevail in the future, simply because it is not governed by the terms of a signed union contract. Since that time, the Commission has generally permitted the annualization of both union and non-union wage increases granted during the test year. Still more recently, the Commission recognized that there is little conceptual difference between annualizing wage increases to test year-end levels and recognizing increases which occurred shortly thereafter. Thus, we specifically approved post-test year adjustments to reflect union wage increases which were granted after the end of the test year. Finally, we approved a post-test year adjustment which reflected both union and non-union wage increases.

* * *

Executive Compensation The Applicant's test year expenses include $4,291 in dues associated with business club memberships for certain top Company executives. The Staff supports the inclusion of this amount. OCC

(Office of Consumer's Counsel) argues that these expenses should be excluded, because there has been no showing that the availability of the club facilities contributes to the rendition of electric service.

This argument is without merit. The record clearly indicates that club facilities are used for business purposes, such as Company board meetings, and even if this were not the case, these expenses clearly constitute a part of the overall compensation paid to these executives. There is nothing in the record indicating that the amounts paid during the test year were unreasonable.

Charitable Contributions The Applicant requests an allowance of $247,000 for charitable contributions. The Ohio Citizens' Council, which represents the various United Way Organizations throughout Ohio, supports the inclusion of a reasonable allowance for this item. OCC (Office of Consumer's Counsel) objects to the inclusion of any allowance for charitable contributions.

A number of public witnesses representing various recipients of the Applicant's charitable contributions appeared at the hearing and explained the nature of the services their organizations provide. Although these services undoubtedly provide valuable benefits to the Cincinnati community, this testimony has essentially been rendered irrelevant by the Supreme Court's decision in *City of Cleveland* v. *Pub. Util. Comm.,* 63 Ohio St. 2d 62 (1980). There, the Court reversed its earlier holding in *City of Cincinnati* v. *Pub. Util. Comm.,* 55 Ohio St. 2d 168 (1978) and held that charitable contributions cannot be included as test year operating expenses. As a result, the Commission is legally prohibited from including an allowance for this item unless and until the General Assembly enacts legislation specifically authorizing such an allowance. OCC's objection must therefore be sustained.

Advertising and Area Development Expense The Applicant requests an allowance of

$501,000 for advertising and area development expense. The Office of Consumers' Counsel opposes any allowance for this item, citing *City of Cleveland* v. *Pub. Util. Comm.,* 63 Ohio St. 2d 62 (1980).

In the *City of Cleveland* case, the Supreme Court found that utilities engage in four basic types of advertising: (1) institutional, which is designed to enhance or preserve the corporate image of the utility, or present it in a favorable light, (2) promotional, which is designed to obtain new utility customers, to increase usage by present customers, or to encourage one form of energy in preference to another, (3) consumer or informational, which is designed to inform the consumer of rates, charges, and conditions of service, of benefits and savings available to the consumer, and of proper safety precautions, emergency procedures, and similar matters, and (4) conservation, which is designed to inform the consumer of the means whereby he can conserve energy and reduce his usage and seeks to encourage him to adopt those means. The Court found nothing objectionable about the inclusion of the costs of informational or conservation advertising, but it expressly held that a utility's institutional and promotional advertising expenses cannot be included in test year operating expenses, unless the utility can demonstrate that those expenditures provide a "direct and primary benefit to its customers."

* * *

Not all utility advertising is readily susceptible to classification under the categories delineated by the Court. Nevertheless, the account descriptions of the various accounts to which advertising expenses are charged provide an appropriate starting point. The evidence in the record of this case indicates that Account 909 includes advertising which informs and instructs the consumer on how to utilize electric service properly and safely, how to conserve energy and reduce peak demand, and how to operate electrical equipment efficiently and economically. This account also includes advertising which provides information regarding service interruptions, safety measures, and emergency procedures. As a result, the Commission believes that expenses charged to this account should qualify for inclusion, unless the evidence in the record demonstrates otherwise.

The evidence further indicates that Account 930, by contrast, includes advertising which provides information concerning the Company's operations, such as the cost of providing service, and the Company's efforts to improve that service. This is precisely the type of advertising which fails to meet the *City of Cleveland* test, and for this reason, the Commission believes that expenditures from Account 930 should not be included as allowable test year expenses unless the record affirmatively demonstrates that they provide a direct and primary benefit to the Company's customers.

The Applicant's test year expenses include $227,000 in Account 930, which is broken down according to various subaccounts. As an example of the advertising included in this account, the Applicant provided a copy of an ad which discusses, among other things, the cost of constructing new capacity and the cost of pollution control. It is apparent that this type of advertising fails to meet the test enunciated by the Court in *City of Cleveland*. Nor is there any other evidence in the record which demonstrates that the expenses included in Account 930 provide a direct and primary benefit to the Applicant's customers. The Commission therefore concludes that these expenses should be excluded in their entirety.

OCC also urges the exclusion of the amounts $110,000 and $56,000 charged to Accounts 912 and 913. Those accounts include the expenses associated with the Company's area development activities, which are designed to encourage new industry to locate in the CG&E service territory, and to encourage existing industry to remain in the area and expand its operations. The record indicates that the Company's efforts in this regard have been

successful. According to Company witness Vandegrift, who is the general manager of the Greater Cincinnati Chamber of Commerce, CG&E played a major role in attracting Ford Motor Company to Clermont County, and was instrumental in convincing Kenner Products Company to maintain its plant in Cincinnati. The opening of the Ford plant created 3,500 new jobs, and the retention of Kenner Products prevented the loss of 2,200 existing jobs.

In urging the exclusion of these expenses, OCC implicity assumes that the *City of Cleveland* test is applicable to area development expenses. We disagree with that assumption. The issue of an area development expense was not even before the Court in the *City of Cleveland* case and these are not the types of activities which the Commission has traditionally classified as promotional advertising. Nor are they properly considered institutional advertising; there is nothing in the record of this case which suggests that these activities are designed to enhance the corporate image of CG&E. The test, then, is simply whether or not the expenses are reasonable, and in view of the obvious benefits these activities provide, such as increased jobs, and increased tax base, and economic growth, the Commission believes that they are.

Assuming, however, only for the sake of argument, that the *City of Cleveland* test applies to these expenditures, they would still qualify for inclusion, since they provide two direct and primary benefits which are specifically related to the provision of electric service. The first benefit involves the retention of load. To the extent that CG&E is successful in persuading existing industries, such as Kenner Products Company, to remain in its service territory, the Company's fixed costs, such as depreciation, property taxes, and return on investment, can be spread over a larger number of customers and kilowatt-hour sales. In turn, this should provide lower unit costs for all customers.

The second benefit involves the concept of load factor. Load factor is a measure of the efficiency of electrical consumption. Customer classes which are composed solely of large industrial customers generally have higher load factors than other customer classes. The record indicates that this is specifically true with respect to the CG&E system. Thus, to the extent that the Company is successful in attracting or retaining large industrial customers, its overall load factor should improve, as should the efficiency with which it utilizes its generating equipment. Such improved efficiency should obviously benefit all of the Company's customers. In view of these considerations, the Commission finds that all of the amounts contained in Accounts 912 and 913 are properly includable in the test year cost of service.

Questions

1. What is meant by the process of annualizing cost? Why is this technique used?
2. If labor expenses can be passed on to utility customers without scrutiny by a commission, what incentive does a regulated industry have for keeping this element of cost to a minimum? Should a commission interject itself into areas of labor-management problems? Should the commission take a side during a strike by utility employees?
3. Should a commission scrutinize executive fringe benefits? With commission review of executive salaries, is it likely that salaries would become comparable to those of the commissioners?
4. Should charitable contributions be allowed as a utility cost of operation?
5. What are the different types of advertising expenditures? Which advertising expenditures does Ohio allow to be recovered from customers?
6. What are area development expenses? Are they closely akin to "promotion" advertising expenditures, which cannot be recovered from customers?

RATE BASE

While the 1876 case of *Munn* v. *Illinois* relieved the state legislators of constitutional restraints against regulation of public utilities, the Supreme Court reasserted judicial supervision of that regulation in the 1898 case of *Smyth* v. *Ames*.[2] The Court held that "the basis of all calculations as to the reasonableness of rates to be charged by a corporation . . . must be the fair value of the property being used by it for the convenience of the public." The regulatory commissions, therefore, must first determine the value of the utility's property that supplies the utility service. This value of the utility's property is called the rate base. To determine the rate base, the regulator must estimate the cost of the productive property.

Original or Replacement Cost?

One of the first legal problems that arose in determining the rate base was the question of whether the regulators must use the original cost of the facilities or the cost that would be incurred in reproducing them at the time the rates are being determined. Because of periodic inflation, public utilities argued for and the courts often required the use of replacement costs. However, in the 1944 case of *Federal Power Commission* v. *Hope Natural Gas Company,* the Court granted wide latitude to the regulatory commissions in the selection of methods to determine the rate base.[3] While some states still use replacement costs, most states employ an evaluation based on the original cost or some variation thereof. The federal commissions usually use original cost for property evaluations also.

Used Property

In *Smyth* v. *Ames,* the Court indicated that fair return must be calculated on property "being used" for the public's benefit. Consequently, a controversy arose as to whether capital allocated to a plant under construction could be included since it is not yet being *used* for the public benefit. Most states have sought some accommodation between the extremes of inclusion or exclusion and have granted some portion of the "work in progress" to be included in the rate base. Other controversial calculations, like an allowance for working capital or depreciation expenses, affect the rate base, but are generally accepted by the courts if they are consistently and fairly applied by the regulatory commission.

RATE OF RETURN

As has been indicated, the public utility's rates must provide sufficient revenue to cover the company's total costs properly incurred in furnishing the particular utility service. The costs include the operating expenses of the utility and a proper "return" on the utility's investment. This return is computed by multiplying a utility's "rate base" by its "rate of return."

Rate of return is expressed as a percentage figure and denotes the annual return to be allowed on the value of the utility's property devoted to public use. It might be considered as the interest rate that the utility earns on its investment in property serving the public. One of the primary functions of utility regulatory agencies in ratemaking proceedings is to determine the appropriate rate of return to be allowed the utilities under their jurisdiction.

The determination of an appropriate rate of return may involve the consideration of a number of factors, the proper application of which has been the subject of considerable disagreement. The rate of return must not be so low as to constitute an unconstitutional confiscation of private property. The Supreme Court has sought to explain what are "just and reasonable" rates so as not to constitute confiscation. The Court has declared:

A public utility is entitled to such rates as will permit it to earn a return on the value of the property which it employs for the convenience of the public equal to that generally being made at the same time and in the same general part of the country of investments in other business undertakings which are attended by corresponding risks and uncertainties; but it has no constitutional right to profits such as are realized or anticipated in highly profit-able enterprises or speculative ventures. The return should be reasonably sufficient to assure confidence in the financial soundness of the utility and should be adequate, under efficient and economical management, to maintain and support its credit, and enable it to raise the money necessary for the proper discharge of its public duties. A rate of return may be reasonable at one time and become too high or too low by changes affecting opportunities for investment, the money market, and business conditions generally. *Blue Water Works & Improv. Co.* v. *West Virginia Pub. Service Commission,* 262 U.S. 679, 692, 693, ...

A variety of factors and methods may be considered by a regulatory agency in determining a fair rate of return. As the Supreme Court has said:

We held in *Federal Power Commission* v. *Natural Gas Pipeline Co. of America,* that the commis-sion was not bound to the use of any single formula or combination of formulae in determining rates. Its rate-making function, moreover, involves the making of "pragmat-ic adjustments." And when the commission's order is challenged in the courts, the ques-tion is whether that order "viewed in its entirety" meets the requirements of the act. Under the statutory standard of "just and reasonable" it is the result reached not the method employed which is controlling. . . . It is not theory but the impact of the rate order which counts. If the total effect of the rate order cannot be said to be unjust and unreasonable, judicial inquiry under the act is at an end. The fact that the method employed to reach that result may contain infirmities is not then important. Moreover, the commission's order does not become suspect by reason of the fact that it is challenged. It is the product of expert judgement which carries a presumption of validity. And he who would upset the rate order under the act carries the heavy burden of making a convincing showing that it is invalid because it is unjust and unreasonable in its conse-quences. . . . *Federal Power Commission* v. *Hope Natural Gas Co.,* 320 U.S. 591 (1944).

New England Telephone & Telegraph Co. v. Maine Public Utilities Commission
390 A.2d 8 (1978)
Maine Supreme Judicial Court

An important method of determining a fair rate of return on investment is by analysis of the utility's cost of capital; i.e., what it must pay to secure financing from equity (stock) and debt investors. Thus, the appropriate rate of return is based upon what the utility must earn to satisfy its investors. . . . Accordingly, it ap-pears to be the practice of the commission, with the tacit approval of this court, to calcu-late rate of return exclusively by means of the cost of capital method. . . .

The cost of capital is calculated by deter-mining the cost of different items of capital. A weighted cost for each item is derived by multi-plying its cost by its ratio to total capital. The sum of these weighted costs then becomes the rate of return.

A simplified example may be helpful at this point. Assume a utility with a capitalization of 25 per cent debt and 75 per cent common equity. Assume, also, that the cost of debt is simply the stated interest which the utility must pay on outstanding debt, say 8 per cent. Be-cause equity investors are subject to greater risks, the cost of common equity is higher, say 10 per cent. Therefore, 25 per cent of the utility's capital requires a return of 8 per cent, thereby necessitating a return of 2.0 per cent

(25 per cent × 8 per cent) on the utility's total capitalization. In other words a 2.0 per cent return is required on 100 per cent of the utility's capital in order to generate a return of 8 per cent on 25 per cent of its capital (2.0 per cent × 100 per cent = 8 per cent × 25 per cent). Similarly, equity has a weighted cost of 7.5 per cent (75 per cent × 10 per cent). Totaling the weighted costs of the individual items of capital we find that the utility requires an overall rate of return of 9.5 per cent in order to meet its cost requirements on the individual items in its capital structure. Such calculations are often expressed thusly:

Item	Capital Structure	Cost	Weighted Cost
Debt	25%	8%	2.0%
Common Equity	75%	10%	7.5%
		Rate of Return:	9.5%

We now turn to three important factors in determining New England's cost of capital and rate of return.

a. Cost of Debt

As we noted in *Mechanic Falls Water Co.* v. *Maine Pub. Utilities Commission*, 381 A.2d at p. 1096: "Ordinarily, the cost of debt is not a complex issue because it involves merely a mechanical computation of the interest rates on a utility's various debt investments." In this case there appears to be no dispute as to the cost assigned by the commission to New England's outstanding debt. . . .

* * *

b. Cost of Equity

In its calculation of New England's cost of capital and rate of return, the commission assigned a cost of 11.5 per cent to New England's common equity. The commission's determination that New England's cost of equity was 11.5 per cent comes against a background of considerable disagreement between the staff's and New England's witnesses. New England argues that the 11.5 per cent figure is unjust, unreasonable, confiscatory, and without sufficient foundation in the evidence before the commission. . . .

As we have indicated, the commission was faced with a considerable amount of testimony with respect to the cost of equity issue. The commission's staff presented one witness on the issue and New England countered with three witnesses, all four advocating different methods with differing results. In *Central Maine Power Co.* v. *Maine Pub. Utilities Commission*, we stated "It will serve no useful purpose in our view to review the mass of testimony from financial experts on the rate of return necessary to support the enterprise and attract new capital. There is no warranty of certainty in matters of this nature." We lack the technical expertise vested in the commission concerning such matters. . . .

* * *

Thus, the commission considered and rejected the testimony of New England's witnesses on cost of equity. Its decree contains a brief summary of the testimony and suggestions of each witness and a statement of the commission's reasons for rejecting each approach. New England suggests that the commission has arbitrarily disregarded this "overwhelming" evidence that the cost of equity was in the range of 14 per cent–15.7 per cent. We hold that the commission's treatment of New England's cost of equity testimony was both reasonable and sufficient. It is the function of the commission to hear the testimony, weigh the evidence, and to reach reasoned conclusions of fact. As the trier of fact, there is no reason in law why the commission could not reject the evidence of certain witnesses and accept the views of another. Our review of the commission's findings of fact is limited to only a determination whether they are supported by substantial evidence. If so, there is no legal error and such findings are final.

In a proper exercise of its discretion, the

commission relied upon the testimony of staff witness David A. Kosh, in determining New England's cost of equity. Mr. Kosh's testimony used the "discounted-cash-flow" (DCF) method to calculate New England's cost of equity. The DCF method involves the combination of anticipated dividends and expected future growth in the value of the equity investor's investment to find a "bare cost of equity." Mr. Kosh analyzed the dividend yield and growth rate of New England, American Telephone and Telegraph, and three other Bell subsidiary operating companies which had a portion of their stock traded in the public market; i.e., "minority" companies. Thus, he gave consideration to the return on equity of other companies with comparable risks.

Mr. Kosh determined that the bare cost of equity was 10.25 per cent for New England (8.75 per cent yield and 1.5 per cent growth rate), 10.44 per cent for American Telephone and Telegraph (6.69 per cent dividend yield and 3.75 per cent growth rate), and 11.05 per cent for the three other Bell operating companies (8.10 per cent dividend yield and 2.95 per cent growth rate). Based on this data he concluded that the bare cost of equity for New England was 10.5 per cent.

However, all parties are agreed that bare cost of equity is not an adequate determination of a utility's cost of equity. Proper consideration must be given to the "market-to-book ratio" of the utility's common stock. Because the bare cost of equity is calculated upon the utility's book value, Mr. Kosh testified that if New England were to earn just 10.5 per cent, the market price of its common equity would tend to equal its book value. However, in order for a utility to be able to sell new issues of common stock, the market value of its stock must exceed its book value. Otherwise, the utility would receive from its new investors less than the book value of its present stock, which has the effect of reducing the overall average value of each share of stock. This results in what is called "dilution" of the investment of the exist-

ing stockholders. The return on common equity must be sufficiently high so as to drive up the market value of the common stock in order to insure that no stock need be issued at less than book value.

The market-to-book ratio is used as a measure of how much greater the market value of the stock must be over its book value so as to prevent dilution. New England's witness testified that it needs a market-to-book ratio of 1.2 to 1.5. On the other hand, Mr. Kosh testified that a market-to-book ratio of 1.1 to 1.15 was sufficient. Based upon his bare cost of equity of 10.5 per cent, he stated that an 11.25 per cent return on the book value of common equity was required to meet this objective market-to-book ratio, and therefore, concluded that New England's cost of equity was 11.25 per cent.

The commission substantially followed Mr. Kosh's recommendations concerning cost of equity, which supplied substantial evidence to support its findings of a cost of equity of 11.5 per cent. The commission stated that it determined a slightly higher cost of equity than that recommended by Mr. Kosh for a number of reasons. It deemed it proper to give slightly more weight to the higher bare cost of equity of the three other Bell operating companies. In addition, the commission reasoned that because in 1976, New England earned 11.1 per cent on its average book equity and its market price was about 5 per cent above book value, its bare cost of equity was closer to 10.75 per cent than the 10.5 per cent recommended by Mr. Kosh. Therefore, the commission concluded, "the appropriate cost of equity to use at this time in the determination of the fair rate of return applicable to the Maine intrastate operations of New England Telephone is 11.5 per cent."

New England's principal objection to the commission's calculation of the 11.5 per cent cost of equity appears to concern its use of a market-to-book ratio of 1.1 to 1.15. New England argues that this figure is unreasonably low and results in dilution of the stockholders' interest and, consequently, confiscation. We find no error in the commission's selection of a market-to-book ratio of 1.1 to 1.5 and hold that its determination was reasonable and supported by substantial evidence.

Mr. Kosh testified that the cost of financing and pressure would act to reduce the proceeds of a stock issue by approximately 5 per cent. Cost of financing includes legal and brokerage fees, accounting expenses, taxes, etc. Pressure describes the tendency of a stock's market price to drop when new stock is issued by the same corporation. Mr. Kosh presented sufficient and detailed testimony to support a finding that a market price of 5 per cent over book value was required to compensate for these effects. Also based upon his studies, Mr. Kosh added another 5 percent as a margin of protection against short-term declines in the market price of New England's stock. He then concluded that the market price of New England's stock must be 10 per cent–15 per cent above its book value in order to prevent dilution. This produces the 1.1 to 1.5 market-to-book ratio used by the commission in its determination of a cost of equity of 11.5 per cent.

We sustain the commission's finding in this respect. Our analysis of the record on this issue has demonstrated that the determination of the cost of equity is one of the most difficult and complex tasks facing the commission. The commission must utilize to the fullest its regulatory expertise and skill to analyze the highly technical economic and financial data presented on this issue. We cannot and will not attempt to second-guess the commission on such matters lying particularly within its area of expertise. Only when its actions are unreasonable or unsupported by substantial evidence may we intervene. . . . Moreover, the burden of proof rests upon New England to demonstrate that the commission has committed legal error. . . .

We hold that New England has failed to meet its burden on this issue. Our review of the record with proper deference being given to the commission, convinces us that its determination of an 11.5 per cent cost of equity was reasonable in result and supported by substantial evidence in the record.

* * *

Capital Structure—The Commission's "Double Leveraging" Adjustment

It can be seen that the cost of capital depends not only upon the individual cost of the different items making up a utility's capitalization, but also upon the proportion of those individual items to the total capital structure. If the earlier example of a hypothetical utility were capitalized at 50 per cent debt and 50 per cent equity, the capital cost calculations would be as follows:

Item	Capital Structure	Cost	Weighted Cost
Debt	50%	8%	4.0%
Equity	50%	10%	5.0%
	Rate of Return:		9.0%

An increase in the "debt ratio" to 50 per cent reduces the hypothetical utility's cost of capital, and rate of return, to 9.0 per cent. This is because of the simple economic fact that debt financing costs less than equity financing. Although a 0.5 per cent reduction in the rate of return may, at first glance, appear somewhat insignificant, it becomes most significant when a utility has a multimillion dollar rate base, as does New England. It is well recognized that "the capital structure of a corporation has a direct influence on the cost of capital." A higher "debt ratio" means lower rate of return and lower rates to the utility's customers.

It appears to be common regulatory practice to disregard the actual book capital structure of a utility when it is deemed to be in the public interest to do so. Instead, a utility commission will adopt a hypothetical capital structure for rate-making purposes.

There are two well-recognized circumstances in which a utility commission might disregard a utility's "actual" capital structure and adopt a "hypothetical" capital structure for rate-making purposes. This first occurs when the utility's actual debt-equity ratio may be deemed to be inefficient and unreasonable, because it contains too much equity and not enough debt, thereby necessitating an inflated rate of return. (On the other hand, the proportion of debt cannot be too high so as to discourage further investment by debt investors.) In such cases the utility commission might adopt a hypothetical ideal capital structure for rate-making purposes. The result is the rates are determined on the basis of a more reasonable and less expensive capital structure. Moreover, the adopting of a hypothetical structure will coerce management to move toward the ideal capital structure in the future because the utility can no longer collect the higher rate of return necessitated by its present capital structure.

The second circumstance occurs when the utility is part of a holding company system. In such cases the utility's book capital structure and capital costs may not be a true reflection of the *system's* capital costs with respect to a particular operating company. It is well settled that "the underlying capital structure of the system must be considered in any parent-subsidiary situation." The double leverage formula adopted by the commission represents one of a number of different approaches which have been utilized by regulatory agencies to account for a utility's status as a subsidiary in a holding company system.

New England is part of the Bell Telephone system, whose parent company is American Telephone and Telegraph Company (AT&T). American Telephone and Telegraph Company owns 86 per cent of New England's common stock, and approximately 45,000 members of the general investing public own the remaining 14 per cent. . . . The double leveraging adjustment was an attempt by the commission to account for New England's status as a subsidiary in the Bell system for purposes of determining cost of capital.

* * *

The principle behind the application of double leveraging adjustments by utility commissions is to account for the parent's alleged use of its low cost debt to purchase stock in its subsidiary, upon which it may earn a higher rate of return than it pays for the debt.

* * *

Unlike any other case in which the double leveraging . . . approach has been applied, the New England Telephone Company is not a wholly owned subsidiary of AT&T. However, the commission considered AT&T's 86 per cent ownership of New England to be sufficient to justify double leveraging. Because AT&T financed its purchase of new England stock with funds it received from its own investors, the commission reasoned that AT&T's return on its investment in New England should reflect AT&T's cost for such funds.

The commission found that AT&T's own capital structure consists of 25 per cent debt, 9 percent preferred stock, and 66 per cent common equity, based upon the testimony of Mr. Kosh. For the costs of these individual items it used 6.5 per cent for debt, 7.8 per cent for preferred stock, and 11.5 per cent for common equity. The commission then calculated AT&T's cost of capital as follows:

Item	Capital Structure	Cost	Weighted Cost
Debt	25%	6.5%	1.63%
Preferred Stock	9%	7.8%	.70%
Common Equity	66%	11.5%	7.59%
	Cost of Capital:		9.92%

Thus, the commission found that AT&T was entitled to a 9.92% per cent return on its investment in New England, this being the Bell system's actual cost for the 86 per cent of New

England's equity owned by AT&T. On the other hand, the 14 per cent minority was to be allocated a 11.5 per cent return upon its investment in New England, as the market cost for New England's common equity held by outside investors. The commission inserted these figures into New England's actual capital structure of 45 per cent debt (which was found to have a cost of 6.99 per cent) and 55 per cent equity (which was proportionally divided between AT&T's and the 14 per cent minority's ownership) as follows:

Item	Capital Structure	Cost	Weighted Cost
Debt	45%	6.99%	3.15%
Common Equity			
AT&T Supplied (55% × 86%)	47.3%	9.92%	4.69%
Minority Supplied (55% × 14%)	7.7%	11.5%	.89%
Rate of Return:			8.73%

Accordingly, the commission found that New England was entitled to a fair rate of return of 8.73 per cent, when proper consideration was given to its double leverage capital structure.

The commission claims that the effect of its decree is to allow a reasonable return of 9.92 per cent to the 86 per cent of New England common equity owned by its parent AT&T and a reasonable return of 11.5 per cent to the 14 per cent of New England owned by some 45,000 members of the investing public. However, the effect of the decree is to allow an average rate of return to all of new England's common equity of 10.14 per cent ([86 per cent × 9.92] + [14 × 11.5 per cent] = 10.1412 per cent). Thus, the overall effect of the commission's decree is to allow AT&T a higher rate of return than the 9.92 per cent deemed to be the proper cost of 86 per cent of New England's common equity, which would appear on its face, to be unfair to the ratepayers. On the other hand, the average return of 10.14 per cent is below the 11.5 per cent found to be reasonable for the 45,000 members of the investing public making up the 14 per cent minority, which New England claims constitutes confisciation.

The parties' briefs and our research fail to disclose any cases, in which a double leveraging adjustment . . . was approved, where the utility was not a wholly owned subsidiary. Thus, the commission's approach appears to be without direct precedent. In every case where a commission attempted to account for a double leveraged capital structure, the only stockholder whose return on common equity was affected was the utility's own parent company. However, in this case there are approximately 45,000 members of the investing public who own 14 per cent of the common stock of New England. The commission determined that the reasonable rate of return on their investment was 11.5 per cent. Yet, as we have noted, the effect of the commission's double leveraging adjustment is to lower the overall return on all shares of New England's common equity to 10.14 per cent. We are unable to find this result reasonable upon the record before us.

What little legal writing exists on the issue suggests that the existence of the 14 per cent minority presents a substantial problem in this case. In the first place, most articles, court and commission decisions imply that double leveraging is appropriate only when the utility is a wholly owned subsidiary. . . .

Moreover, in some cases we find more direct indications that double leveraging . . . (is) inappropriate where a substantial minority exists. . . .

On the other hand, the commission is unable to cite to us any authority in which a double leveraging adjustment . . . has been applied where a substantial minority exists. Our own research discloses very limited circumstances where the interest of minority ownership has been subjugated to the general interest of the ratepayers. . . .

The commission's application of the double leveraging adjustment arises against a general background which discourages such action where a substantial minority interest exists. In the light of these circumstances, the commission cannot summarily dispose of the minority shareholder issue. When claims of confiscation might arise because of a novel approach by the commission, it must make adequate findings of fact and develop sufficient evidence in the record to enable this court to decide upon the reasonableness of its actions. We cannot approve the commission's actions in a factual vacuum. What is needed in this case are findings of fact, supported by substantial evidence, concerning the precise effect of the commission's application of the double leveraging adjustment upon the interests of the 14 per cent minority and, in turn, the ultimate effect, if any, upon New England Telephone. Only then can we determine the reasonableness of the result reached by the commission.

* * *

We hold that the commission cannot apply a double leveraging adjustment to this case. . . .

Questions

1. What is the cost of capital method of determining a "fair rate of return"?
2. What is the adjustment made by calculating a "weighted" cost of capital?
3. What is the method used to determine the cost of debt capital?
4. What is the method used to determine the cost of equity capital?
5. What is the "market-to-book ratio" adjustment for the cost of equity? What is the "cost of finance" adjustment? What is the "pressure" adjustment?
6. How does the capital structure affect the capital cost calculations? When might a regulatory commission adopt a hypothetical capital structure for ratemaking processes?
7. What is the "double leveraging" adjustment? Why was it held to be inappropriate in *New England Telephone & Telegraph*?

RATE STRUCTURE

Once the revenue requirement has been established, the only remaining step is to determine how the rates will be structured—that is, which classes of customer will be charged how much. Historically, that step has been left almost entirely to the discretion of utility management, with the only limitation being that rates not be "unduly discriminatory." Once the rates were approved, it is only the rates, not the total revenues or earnings of the utility, that are fixed and may not be changed without commission authorization. Any excess profits the company earns by charging such rates are not subject to refund.

In the electric utility industry, for example, state commissions initially failed to control rate structures largely because the commissions lacked expertise, time, and access data. Also, in the two decades from 1951 to 1971, the price of electricity was no great concern to the average electrical residential consumer. The real price of electricity actually dropped 43 percent, and as long as rates were falling, consumers were indifferent to how utilities structured their rates. In the absence of consumer complaints, commissions had little incentive to exert systematic control over utility rate structures. Regulators seldom were required to engage in much planning of the economic effects of utility rate structures. That situation was, however, changed dramatically in the 1970s. To understand this change, it is necessary to review the economics of electrical power production and the general method of setting rates.

Electrical Power Production and Pricing

Electrical power cannot be stored. Consequently, power facilities have to be large enough to meet a system's *peak* demands. Peak periods vary by time of day and by season. From an economic efficiency perspective, customers who use power "on-peak" should pay the added (marginal) cost of providing the extra capacity needed to serve them. "Off-peak" users should not be charged for power plant capacity, but only for the cost of the fuel, labor, and materials (variable costs) required for the satisfaction of their demands.

During the development of the electrical industry, when economies of scale could be realized by the construction of larger and larger plants, promotional rates based on volume, not on time of use, seemed appropriate. By promoting use, larger plants were built and the price per kilowatt-hour was lowered. With the maturing of the industry, such opportunities were depleted and promotional rates, where cost per kilowatt-hour declined with increased usage, became difficult to justify.

In setting their rates, electrical utilities divide their costs into three categories: output cost, customer cost, and demand (or capacity) cost. Output costs, often referred to as energy costs, include the cost of fuel, labor, and materials—the short-run variable cost of production. Customer costs are incurred in such activities as reading meters and billing accounts. Demand charges refer to the fixed cost of plant operation to meet a system's peak demand. A system's load factor is the ratio of its average load to its peak load; the higher the load factor, the less idle capacity in the system. According to economists, load factors can be improved by encouraging customers to increase their consumption of power off-peak. Economists maintain that no demand cost should be accessed against any customer for power taken during the off-peak period, because such useage off-peak does not require any additional plant capacity. However, the actual structuring of rates to achieve economic efficiency is more difficult than economic theories suggest.

Federal Intervention

Because Congress felt the state regulatory commissions were remiss in their supervision of "economically efficient" rate structures, it enacted the Public Utility Regulatory Policies Act of 1978 (PURPA) as part of the National Energy Act. Title I of PURPA deals with retail regulatory policies applicable to electric utilities. Section 101 of PURPA states that the purposes of Title I are to encourage:

(1) Conservation of energy supplied by electric utilities;
(2) The optimization of the efficiency of use of facilities and resources by electric utilities; and
(3) Equitable rates to electric consumers.

Section 111 of PURPA then sets forth six "standards" for electric utilities. In essence, the standards provide that:

(1) Rates for service to each class of customers should reflect the cost of providing that service, to the maximum extent practicable;
(2) Declining block rates should not be approved unless they are cost justified;
(3) Time of day rates should be approved unless they are not cost-effective with respect to a given customer class;
(4) Seasonal rates should be approved where they are cost-justified;
(5) Interruptible rates should be offered to industrial and commercial consumers; and
(6) Certain load management techniques should be offered to electric consumers.

Section 111 goes on to require that state regulatory agencies consider each of the standards and determine whether it is appropriate to implement the standard in order to carry out the purposes set forth in Section 101. Section 121 further allows the Secretary of Energy to intervene in state ratemaking proceedings in order to participate in the consideration of the various standards. Consumer and environmental groups are also granted rights to intervene in ratemaking proceedings.

In analyzing PURPA, however, it is important to remember that the provisions are essentially procedural in nature. The Act does, of course, require that state commissions consider the various standards and determine whether their implementation is appropriate, but it does not require that the standards actually be implemented. In fact, it does not even recommend that the standards be implemented. Instead, the ultimate decision on whether or not to implement the standards is clearly left to the discretion of the state regulatory agencies, to be made in accordance with the provisions of otherwise applicable state law. In the following case the specific issues of PURPA standards are discussed in a rate structure hearing.

Before the Public Utilities Commission of Ohio
Case No. 80-260-EL-AIR (1981)

Rates and Tariffs
Allocation of Revenue Responsibility The next step is designing utility rates is to determine how the Applicant's total revenue requirements should be allocated across the various customer classifications. . . .

[Both the Applicant and the Staff] recommend a revenue distribution which is substantially similar to the distribution occurring under existing rates. The Office of Consumers' Counsel concurs in that recommendation and the City of Cincinnati agrees that the existing revenue distribution should be maintained.

The industrial intervenors (and the Retail Merchants Council) generally support the allocation of revenue responsibility on the basis of embedded costs. . . .

The Department of Energy argues that

revenue responsibility should be allocated on the basis of marginal, rather than embedded, costs. . . .

A.

Marginal cost is generally defined as the cost of producing an additional unit of output. A simple example should illustrate the concept. Assume that a utility produces 100 kilowatt-hours of electricity during a given period of time, and that the first 50 kwh cost 4¢ per kwh to produce. Assume further that the next 50 kwh (and any kwh produced thereafter) cost 5¢ per kwh. The company's average, or embedded, cost would be 4.5¢ per kwh, while its marginal, or incremental, cost would be 5¢ per kwh.

The principal argument advanced in support of marginal cost pricing is that it provides accurate price signals to the customers concerning possible changes in their consumption patterns. Assume that a customer in the previously cited example chooses to consume an additional kwh of electricity. The utility will incur an additional cost of 5¢ per kwh (its marginal cost of production). If the customer's rate is based on the company's embedded costs, the customer will pay only 4.5¢ for the additional kwh. The customer will therefore be led to believe that electricity is cheaper to produce than it actually is, and the utility will experience an erosion of earnings, since its incremental costs will exceed its incremental revenues. If, however, the rate is based on the marginal cost of 5¢ per kwh, the rate will provide the customer with accurate information regarding the cost of his increased consumption, and the utility will receive additional revenues equal to its increased costs. From a theoretical standpoint, then, the use of marginal cost pricing would appear to offer certain distinct advantages.

On the practical level, however, there are a number of significant problems associated with the implementation of marginal cost pricing. The first involves the actual determination of marginal costs. While embedded, or average, costs can generally be determined from a utility's accounting or property records, the determination of marginal costs is not so easily accomplished. There are a number of different techniques for making such determinations and the experts disagree over which method is the most appropriate.

Marginal energy costs (costs which vary with energy used), for example, are frequently based on "system Lambda", the incremental cost of generation used by an electric utility in the economic dispatch of its generating units. However, . . . utilities calculate system lambdas in different ways . . . In this proceeding, DOE witness Wilson calculated marginal energy costs by taking the Company's system lambdas for 1979, and applying a weighted escalation factor to reflect fuel price increases through July, 1980. Nowhere, however, has DOE explained precisely how CG&E calculates its system lambdas. In short, the record fails to demonstrate that DOE's calculations in this regard provide a reasonably accurate picture of the marginal energy costs the Company will incur during the near-term future.

The determination of marginal capacity costs (fixed costs to meet peak capacity demands) is no more easily accomplished. In calculating CG&E's marginal cost of capacity, Dr. Wilson used what is commonly referred to as the peaker method. Under this method, the marginal cost of capacity for a system in equilibrium (i.e., having no excess capacity) is assumed to equal the cost of the least capital-intensive type of new generating plant, i.e., an oil-fired combustion turbine peaker. Proponents of this method would argue that the cost of a peaker represents the amount which is properly attributable to marginal capacity costs, irrespective of whether the utility would actually build a peaker if it needed additional capacity. The underlying theory is that even if the utility would actually build a more expensive baseload coal unit instead of a peaker, it would not do so unless its purpose was to provide cheaper energy as well as additional capacity. . . .

The most obvious criticism of this method is that it fails to consider the utility's actual construction plans. . . . The application of the peaker method to the CG&E system would understate demand capacity costs. . . .

The second practical problem associated with marginal cost pricing stems from the fact that the Company's total revenue requirements must be based upon embedded, and not marginal, costs. Thus, if the Company's marginal costs exceed its embedded costs, as they frequently do, especially during periods of inflation, the utility's rates cannot be set *at* marginal costs, or the utility would be granted revenues in excess of the level which is legally permissible. Most advocates of marginal cost pricing attempt to solve this problem by setting . . . the energy (variable) component (of the rate) at marginal cost and scaling down the other components (demand/capacity) by a uniform percentage. . . .

* * *

B.

DOE further argues that the use of a marginal cost analysis is appropriate to carry out the three purposes set forth in Section 101 of PURPA. In a similar vein, DOE claims that the use of an embedded cost analysis would not achieve those objectives. . . .

The first purpose of PURPA is to encourage the conservation of energy supplied by electric utilities. . . .

. . . The parties who have addressed this issue generally agree that conservation means the elimination of wasteful consumption . . . (i.e.) that which the consumer values at less than the value of the resources used in providing it. . . .

DOE's arguments on this issue are essentially summarized by an example. . . . Assume that the average cost of a kilowatt-hour at a given point in time is 27 mills, and that the marginal cost is 34 mills. Assume further that the value to consumers of a portion of the electricity produced at an average cost of 27 mills is 30 mills. According to DOE, charging 27 mills (the average, or embedded, cost) will encourage wasteful consumption, because it would allow the customer to consume additional units which cost 34 mills to produce (and which they value at only 30 mills) for only 27 mills per unit. DOE concludes that only charging the marginal cost of 34 mills will eliminate the wasteful consumption of electricity.

That argument may be valid up to a point, but it ignores the other side of the coin. Not all consumption occurs at the margin, and the utility does not consume resources valued at marginal cost in producing each unit of output. Assume that a customer in DOE's example values *all* of his consumption at 30 mills, and that his demand is totally elastic. Charging the marginal cost of 34 mills would therefore lead that customer to eliminate all of his consumption, even though he values all of the units at more than the total, or average, cost of producing them. This result would be no more desirable than the decreased usage which would result from an arbitrary increase in price. It is therefore apparent that both marginal and embedded cost pricing would encourage conservation, but that neither would do so in a manner which would be characterized as perfect.

The second purpose of PURPA is to encourage the optimization of the efficiency of use of facilities and resources by electric utilities. . . .

* * *

. . . DOE suggests that this objective can only be accomplished by basing utility rates on marginal costs, because costs can be minimized only if some costs are avoided, and only marginal costs can be avoided . . . Witness Brubaker disagrees, arguing that the minimization of costs can best be achieved by providing the customers with balanced price signals, which properly reflect the relative proportions of demand (fixed) and energy (variable) costs. It is obviously difficult to do this if rates are based on marginal costs, since it is frequently necessary to scale down . . . [the demand/fixed] component in order to meet the embedded cost revenue requirement.

The DOE proposal in this proceeding provides an excellent example of that particular problem. DOE witness Wilson calculated marginal energy costs on the basis of system lambdas, and marginal capacity costs on the basis of the cost of an oil-fired peaker. . . . The use of system lambdas overstates the Company's actual (unit) energy costs, while the use of the cost of a peaker understates demand-related (capacity) costs. In addition, Dr. Wilson *reduced* the demand component in order to meet the revenue constraint. . . . The likely customer response to such price signals would be a decrease in kilowatt-hour consumption coupled with an increase in [peak] demand, which would result in a decrease in system load factor, and a less efficient utilization of the Company's invested capital. As a result, it would not appear that the use of marginal cost pricing would lead to an optimizatin of engineering efficiency.

The final purpose of PURPA is to encourage equitable rates to consumers. Although this term, like the others, is not specifically defined in the statute, the parties agree that equitable rates are those which are based on costs, and therefore do not result in the subsidization of one class by another. . . . The problem, of course, is that there are a number of different ways to determine the cost of service, and there is nothing in the record of this case which convincingly demonstrates that rates which are based on marginal costs are any more equitable than rates which are based on embedded costs.

C.

* * *

It is also important to consider the impact of marginal cost pricing on individual classes of customers. Despite the continuity constraint imposed by Dr. Wilson, the Department of Energy's proposed allocation of revenue responsibility would assign approximately $9.2 million more to the residential class than the proposal sponsored by the Company and the Staff. The impact of such a change would obviously be substantial.

D.

In conclusion, the record indicates that marginal cost pricing should not be implemented on the CG&E system at the present time, and that neither the inter-class revenue distribution nor the specific rates to be approved in this proceeding should be based upon an analysis of marginal costs.

* * *

E.

* * *

Time of Day Rates The Department of Energy urges the Commission to adopt the time of day standard set forth in Section 111 of PURPA. . . . Section 115 (b) provides that a time of day rate shall be considered cost effective if:

[T]he long-run benefits of such rate to the electric utility and its electric consumers in the class concerned are likely to exceed the metering costs and other costs associated with the use of such rates.

Specifically, DOE argues that the Commission should approve mandatory time of day rates for transmission and distribution customers consuming more than 1000 mwh per year, and optional time of day rates for all other customers who are willing to pay the associated metering costs.

In theory, it is difficult to quarrel with the concept of time-differentiated rates. To the extent that the cost of providing electric services varies during different periods of the day, such rates should provide the consumers with accurate information concerning the cost consequences of their consumption. If the demand for electricity is relatively elastic, time of day rates should encourage shifts from on-peak to off-peak consumption, thereby deferring or even eliminating the need for future construction of expensive generating facilities. Even if demand is relatively inelastic, time of day rates should still provide the customers with appropriate price signals, and require those who consume electricity during on-peaks periods to pay the associated costs.

In practice, however, a number of significant problems appear. The implementation of time of day rates for all customers would require considerable expense, and there is some question as to whether or not it would be cost-effective. Proposals to implement mandatory time of day rates for limited classes of customers, such as those advanced by DOE . . . raise serious questions of discrimination and basic fairness. Customer reaction is also an important factor to be considered, and the Commission's past experience in this area suggests that such reaction can be negative, or even hostile. Finally, there are certain legal constraints which must be considered. Section 4933.29 of the Revised Code effectively prohibits the application of time-differentiated rates to public school districts.

The Company has already implemented a form of time-differentiated pricing for its industrial and commercial customers. The current Load Management Rider offers lower demand charges to customers whose usage occurs primarily during off-peak hours. The Company has also recently completed two residential time of day rate experiments, and a cost-benefit analysis of those experiments is currently underway.

The Decision on whether to proceed with the implementation of time of day rates obviously rests within the judgment and sound discretion of the Commission. In view of all of the relevant considerations, the Commission believes that further consideration of this issue should be deferred until after the Company's cost-benefit analysis has been completed. The Commission therefore finds that it is not appropriate to implement the PURPA time of day standard for this company at the present time.

Interruptible Rates The Department of Energy recommends that the Commission adopt the interruptible rate standard set forth in Section 111 of PURPA, and require the Company to develop voluntary interruptible rates on a timely basis. . . . DOE witness Hatcher argues that the resource savings are potentially significant, because the Company does not have excess generating capacity.

The Commission believes that the adoption of this recommendation is unnecessary. As Staff witness Groves explained, the Company already offers interruptible rates to those customers who are able to take advantage of them. However, it would obviously be difficult to design a tariff for such service, since the magnitude of the interruptible load and the time and length of the acceptable interruption will obviously vary from customer to customer. Such determinations must clearly be made on an individual basis. It was for this reason that the Commission approved a provision in the Company's current Load Management Rider which states that:

The Company will negotiate an interruptible Service Agreement with a customer provided such customer can demonstrate an interruptible load of at least one thousand (1000) kilowatts upon the request of the Company.

. . . Any resulting agreements are ultimately subject to Commission approval under Section 4905.31 of the Revised Code.

The Staff believes that the implementation of the interruptible rate standard is appropriate and has been accomplished. The Commission finds itself in agreement with the Staff.

Residential Service (RS) The Company's proposed Residential Service (RS) schedule includes a $5.00 customer charge, a flat energy rate during the summer and a two-step declining block rate during the winter. . . .

* * *

The Department of Energy, the Office of Consumers' Counsel, and the Citywide Coalition for Utility Reform all attack the recommendation of the Company and the Staff that a declining block rate be included in the residential rate for the winter months. In essence, these parties argue that the declining block rate is not cost-justified, and is therefore contrary to the declining block standard set forth in Section 111 of PURPA.

* * *

There is no need to recount the testimony which purports to show that the declining block rates are not cost-justified, because no party really contends that they are. There are however, other relevant considerations in designing utility rates, such as the principle of continuity or gradualism, which seeks to minimize the impact of rate changes on individual classes of customers. Congress was aware of this principle when it enacted PURPA, as the Conference Report clearly indicates:

In considering the standards set forth in this section, it is expected that State regulatory authorities . . . take into account the need to protect ratepayers against sudden shifts in electric utility rates which might lead to significant economic hardships.

The Staff believes that the impact on the residential space heating customers justifies the retention of the winter declining block.

The same parties also criticize the residential rates proposed by the Company and the Staff because those rates contain a seasonal differential (without cost justification in violation of) . . . the seasonal rate standard set forth in Section 111 of PURPA.

The Staff recommends that the seasonal differential be retained. In support of this recommendation, the Staff notes that the summer peak has consistently been higher than the winter peak, and that the winter months have had consistently higher load factors than the summer months. As a result of the higher load factors during the winter months, less revenue per unit is required to recover fixed costs. Staff witness Groves specifically argued that the 420 megawatt difference between the summer and winter peaks warrants the price differential between the two seasons.

The Commission believes that the seasonal differential is cost-justified. . . .

Even assuming, however, that the seasonal differential could not be justified on any independent basis, the only actual difference between the winter and summer rate schedules is the existence of the winter declining block, which we have previously found to be justified on other grounds.

Questions

1. Distinguish between the commission's responsibility to determine the "revenue requirement" and its responsibility to determine "rate structure."
2. Give an example of how marginal cost pricing in the electric utility industry would enhance economic efficiency. Why did the Public Utilities Commission of Ohio (PUCO) judge marginal cost pricing inappropriate in Ohio? Under what circumstances might marginal cost pricing be appropriate?
3. What are the theoretical advantages of using "time of day" rates? Why did PUCO refuse to implement this pricing?
4. What advantages could have been achieved by adopting "interruptible" rates? How did PUCO attempt to comply with this PURPA standard?

5. On what basis did PUCO justify its "declining block rates" for residential users during the winter months?
6. How did PUCO justify its granting of a seasonal differential rate?

CONCLUSION

Historical experiences with overly competitive markets have revealed that the alleged benefits of competition are often absent. These inadequacies of the market system lead to the development of theories of regulation to deal with situations of "natural monopoly" or of "destructive competition."

Most supporters of utility regulation have shared a common desire—the desire to be protected. Consumers have sought protection from high rates; liberatarians have sought protection from political corruption and from monopoly; and utility companies have sought protection from governmental ownership and from the effects of competition. Consequently, from its inception, utility regulation has reflected a defensive posture; negating the worst abuses rather than promoting the optimal use of economic resources. As long as the commissions judged the rates of utilities to be "fair and reasonable," the utilities were granted the freedom to make all of the important decisions regarding the production and marketing of utility services. Given the advantages achieved from economies of scale and other technological advances experienced by the utility industries in the past, they were largely free of any other societal complaints.

With the arrival of ecological awareness and the "energy crisis," there were renewed efforts by environmentalists and consumers challenging state regulatory commissions and utility companies concerning the economically optimal use of society's scarce resources. Consumers were shocked at the escalation of utility rates, and environmentalists argued that utilities failed to internalize the social cost of their actions into their pricing structure. Together these groups have urged utility regulators to break with tradition and adopt new theories of rate regulation. Much discussion and continued experimentation in utility regulation will continue in the future.

DISCUSSION QUESTIONS

1. On March 28, 1979, a $100 million nuclear plant was lost through accident for which no negligence on the part of the company could be shown. The Pennsylvania Public Utility Commission ruled that the facility in question, Three-Mile Island, should not be included in the rate base because of the long-term outage arising from the accident. Metropolitan Edison has appealed, claiming that investors should not have to bear the risk of this extraordinary loss. What decision on appeal?

2. Should an electric utility using a nuclear generator be allowed a higher rate of return because of the risk associated with it (i.e. possible failure of the plant)?

3. The Railroad Commission lowered the rate of return to investors in the Market-Street Railway because of the railroad's poor service to customers. What is your opinion to this technique of regulation?

4. According to some authorities, an ideal capital structure for utilities is 60 percent debt, 10 percent preferred stock, and 30 percent stock. A number of commissions take this as a yardstick for an appropriate capital structure for companies subject to their jurisdiction. When would it be appropriate to force the utility into a high debt-equity ratio?

5. The Public Utility Regulatory Policies Act of 1978 addresses the topic of "lifeline" rates and the plight of the poor. PURPA requires the states to determine whether lifeline rates should be adopted by their utilities. If utility rates are outstripping the ability of a significant number of persons to pay for utility services, who should bear the burden of ensuring that individuals receive life-supporting amounts of utility services?

6. Comsat has expenditures in certain nonsocial organizations that are professional organizations whose actions are directly related to Comsat's business. Comsat also has expenses for memberships in social clubs. Comsat's witness testified that these memberships were necessary in order to permit Comsat employees to "carry out the business activities of the corporation in a manner best suited to the successful resolution of matters under discussion or negotiation." Comsat characterized these memberships dues as "small." Are these organizational expenses, or any part, thereof chargeable to ratepayers or investors?

7. The president of Citizens Utilities Company was paid a salary of $70,000 a year. He also received a bonus of $2,000 a year, and additional fringe benefits worth about 40 percent of his salary. He spends an average of two days a week on the affairs of the company, and the balance of his time is devoted to another company of which he is also president. The testimony shows that extra time is on occasion put in by the president on Citizens' affairs. The commission ruled the salary was "far out of line" and "unrealistic." Therefore, the commission determined the sum of $20,000 to be a reasonable salary for the president and reduced the allowable expenses of the utility by $50,000. Citizens objected to this finding on the grounds that it was an arbitrary disallowance, not based on evidence, and an intrusion into the management of the company.
   What result on appeal?

8. Carolina Water Company sought a rate increase, which was denied by the North Carolina Utilities Commission. Thereafter, the water company argued that the rate-case expenses it incurred in attempting to get the rate increase justified a slight rate increase. How should the commission decide?

9. As part of its tax expense for the test year (1976), New England Utilities claims $3 million of "deferred taxes." This amount represents the taxes "deferred" by New England by using an accelerated depreciation method, as opposed to a straight-line depreciation method. New England proposed to "normalize" the taxes by calculating its tax expense for ratemaking purposes as if it had taken straight-line depreciation. Thus, in the early years of an asset's life, the utility collects more from its rates than it actually pays in taxes. This excess amount is then usually credited to a reserve account for deferred taxes because, ultimately, a cross-over point is reached when actual taxes paid by the utility begin to exceed revenues collected for taxes.

However, the commission disallowed the amount of "deferred taxes" as a tax expense, finding that the use of accelerated depreciation resulted in an actual "tax savings," which should be "flowed through" to the ratepayers. Flowthrough is a ratemaking technique by which rates are based on the *actual* taxes to be paid in that year by a utility taking accelerated depreciation. The tax "savings" reduce the utility revenue requirement. In theory, this results in lower rates during the early years of an asset's useful life, but in higher rates after the cross-over point has been reached.

Which ratemaking technique do you favor? Why?

SUGGESTED READINGS

Anderson, Douglas D., *Regulatory Politics and Electric Utilities, A Case Study in Political Economy:* (Auburn House Publishing Co., 1981).

Frishberg, Dov and Uhler, Robert G., "The Neo-Classical Costing Controversy," *Public Utilities Fortnightly,* August 3, 1978, pp. 14–18.

Kelly, Henry C. and Miller, Alan S., "Getting Serious about Utility Regulatory Reform." *Public Utilities Fortnightly,* September 24, 1981, pp. 21–27.

Levy, Paul, F., "Deregulation of Electric Power from a State Perspective," *Public Utilities Fortnightly,* September 16, 1982, pp. 29–33.

Partridge, Waring, "A Road Map to Title I of the Public Utility Regulatory Policies Act of 1978," *Public Utilities Fortnightly,* January 18, 1979, pp. 16–22.

Samprone, Joseph C., Jr. and Riddell-Dudra, Nancy, "State Regulatory Climate: Can it Be Predicted?," *Public Utilities Fortnightly,* October 8, 1981, pp. 41–43.

ENDNOTES

1. *Smyth* v. *Ames,* 169 U.S. 466 (1898).
2. *Ibid.*
3. *FPC* v. *Hope Natural Gas Co.,* 320 U.S. 591 (1944).

chapter 17

REGULATION OF LABOR-MANAGEMENT RELATIONS

The years after the Civil War were a time of building industrial empires. The technological developments of the Industrial Revolution created a need for large-scale industrial establishments. The increasing concentration of economic power was not greatly reduced by the passage of the Sherman Act. However, the growth of the large corporations had significant consequences for workers. It ended the personal relationship that had existed between the employer and employee and put the employee at a considerable bargaining disadvantage. Unionism appeared to be essential to give laborers an opportunity to deal with their employers on an equal basis.

As a consequence of the changing economic conditions, modern labor laws regulate nearly all aspects of the relationship between employer and employee. Employers must concern themselves not only with the National Labor Relations Act but also with fair employment practices, fair labor standards, minimum wage, workers' compensation, unemployment compensation, safety rules, and numerous other legislative prohibitions and regulations. Nevertheless, collective bargaining is the heart of labor law. Despite the detailed regulations provided by law, it is the negotiation and administration of the collectively bargained labor contracts that primarily guarantee the social and economic security that American workers enjoy. As a result, modern unions and collective bargaining have emerged as significant institutions. Moreover, the evolving legal doctrines concerning labor disputes focus attention on the limitations of law. It is largely through the private arena, grievance, and arbitration procedures, that detailed regulations most vitally affecting workers in their daily lives are made.

Within the context of this understanding the question arises, "What role should the court play?" The following cases elaborate some of the history involved in the legislation of labor laws, some of the basic legislative pronouncements themselves, and the appropriate role for the courts. Within the context of particular labor disputes, the reader may gain a more significant understanding of the tremendous social issues involved.

NORRIS–LAGUARDIA ACT

In 1932 Congress passed the Federal Anti-injunction Act (Norris–LaGuardia Act). The act protects legitimate union activity from federal court injunctions attempting to prohibit such activity. The act was passed as a congressional disapproval of the courts' utilization of injunctions in spite of the Clayton Act which had, without clarity, exempted labor activities from the antitrust laws. As a consequence, the provisions of the Norris–LaGuardia Act divest federal courts of injunctive power in cases growing out of a "labor dispute," unless the private complainant can prove in court, under cross-examination, the following elements:

1. Unlawful acts have been threatened or committed.
2. Injury to property will result.
3. Injury to complainant will be greater than injury to defendant unless the unlawful acts are enjoined.
4. Complainant has no adequate "damages" remedy.
5. Public officials (police) are unable or unwilling to provide protection to the complainant's property.
6. Complainant must petition the court with "clean hands" by having made reasonable efforts to negotiate a settlement.

Since all these elements will be difficult to establish, private parties (employers) will most likely be unable to obtain a federal court injunction against labor activities. Even if an injunction is issued, it can enjoin only the specific acts complained of in the petition.

A "labor dispute" is broadly defined in the act to include a list of events in which the federal courts are restricted in the issuance of injunctions against labor activities. Consequently, federal courts are denied the power to issue an injunction to prohibit such "labor disputes" as ceasing or refusing to perform work, joining a labor organization, assembling peacefully, advising others, or giving publicity to any labor dispute. Nor can the federal courts issue injunctions to prohibit the paying of strike or unemployment benefits that may be available to participants in a labor dispute.

The anti-injunction provisions of the Norris–LaGuardia Act establish a policy which is in opposition to the policy of the antitrust laws. Yet, the anti-injunction law does not repeal antitrust laws. Therefore, the courts must "accommodate" or reconcile the two acts. (See Unions in Chapter 15.)

NATIONAL LABOR RELATIONS ACT

Congress determined that the denial by some employers of the right of employees to organize and collectively bargain led to strikes and other forms of industrial strife, which had the effect of obstructing commerce. They felt the inequality of bargaining power between employees who did not possess full freedom of association and employers who were organized in the corporate form substantially burdened the free flow of commerce. Consequently, Congress declared that the policy of the United States, through the National Labor Relations Act of 1932, was to eliminate these obstructions by encouraging the practice and procedure of collective bargaining. This involved the protection of the exercise by workers of the full freedom to self-organize and designate representatives of their own choosing to negotiate terms and conditions of their employment with their employers.

The National Labor Relations Board was created by Section 3 of the act and consists of five members, appointed by the president with the advice and consent of the Senate. The board shall have the authority to make, amend, and rescind such rules and regulations as may be necessary to carry out the provisions of the act.

The two most important portions of the National Labor Relations Act are Sections 7 and 8. Section 7 as originally enacted reads as follows:

Employees shall have the right to self-organization, to form, join or assist labor organizations, to bargain collectively through representatives of their own choosing, and to engage in other concerted activities for the purpose of collective bargaining or other mutual aid or protection.

There are three parts to the right guaranteed by Section 7. First, employees are secured the freedom to form, join, or assist labor organizations. Second, they are guaranteed the right to engage in concerted activities, such as strikes and picketing. Without the right to engage in strikes and picketing, the other rights may have been nothing more than empty slogans. Third, employees are guaranteed the right "to bargain collectively through representatives of their own choosing."

The rights granted to employees in Section 7 are protected against employer interference by Section 8, which details five prohibited practices by employers deemed unfair to labor.

Section 8(a)(1) declares it to be an unfair labor practice for an employer to "interfere with, restrain, or coerce employees in the exercise of rights guaranteed in Section 7." This provision outlaws such antiunion tactics as beating of labor organizers, company lockouts of employees to destroy efforts to organize a union, and other use of the employer's economic power to prevent unionization. This section also prohibits some subtle antiunion tactics, such as carefully timing wage increases to demonstrate to employees that nothing would be gained by joining a union.

Section 8(a)(2) outlaws "company unions" that are dominated and controlled by the company. Such "company unions" granted the employees the *form* of an organization but denied them any substantive rights in control. Section 8(a)(3) prohibits discrimination in the hiring or firing of employees to influence union affiliation. Subsection (4) provides protection for employees against reprisals from the company because of the employee's filing of charges with or giving testimony to the National Labor Relations Board. Section 8(a)(5) declares that it is an unfair labor practice for the company to refuse to bargain collectively with the duly designated representative of the employees.

The National Labor Relations Board has exclusive jurisdiction over both unfair labor practices and questions of which union organization is to represent the employees. The board has the authority to designate or separate the employees into appropriate "bargaining units." The employees of each bargaining unit by majority vote determine if they desire a union and which union will represent the unit. Such elections are controlled by the labor laws. The following cases illustrate situations in which alleged Section 8 violations occurred.

INTERFERENCE WITH UNIONIZING

NLRB v. Gissel Packing Co., Inc.
395 U.S. 575 (1969)
Supreme Court of the United States

Chief Justice Warren

When petitioner's president first learned of the Union's drive in July, he talked with all of his employees in an effort to dissuade them from joining a union. He particularly emphasized the results of the long 1952 strike, which he claimed "almost put our company out of business," and expressed worry that the employees were forgetting the "lessons of the past." He emphasized, secondly, that the Company was still on "thin ice" financially, that the Union's "only weapon is to strike," and that a strike "could lead to the closing of the plant," since the parent company had ample manufacturing facilities elsewhere. He noted, thirdly, that because of their age and the limited usefulness of their skills outside their craft, the employees might not be able to find re-employment if they lost their jobs as a result of a strike. Finally, he warned those who did not believe that the plant could go out of business to "look around Holyoke and see a lot of them out of business." The president sent letters to the same effect to the employees in early

November, emphasizing that the parent company had no reason to stay in Massachusetts if profits went down.

During the two or three weeks immediately prior to the election . . . the president sent the employees a pamphlet captioned "Do you want another 13-week strike?" stating that "We have no doubt that the Teamsters Union can again close the Wire Weaving Department and the entire plant by a strike. We have no hopes that the Teamsters Union Bosses will not call a strike. . . . The Teamsters Union is a strike-happy outfit." Similar communications followed . . . including one stressing the Teamsters' "hoodlum control." . . . He repeated that the Company's financial condition was precarious; that a possible strike would jeopardize the continued operation of the plant; and that age and lack of education would make re-employment difficult. The Union lost the election 7-6, and then filed both objections to the election and unfair labor practice charges which were consolidated for hearing before the [administrative law judge].

The Board agreed with the trial [judge]

that the president's communications with his employees, when considered as a whole, "reasonably tended to convey to the employees the belief or impression that selection of the Union in the forthcoming election could lead [the Company] to close its plant, or to the transfer of the weaving production with the resultant loss of jobs to the wire weavers." Thus, the Board found that under the "totality of the circumstances," petitioner's activities constituted a violation of Section 8(a)(1) of the Act. The Board further agreed with the trial [judge] that petitioner's activities, because they "also interfered with the exercise of a free and untrammeled choice in the election," and "tended to foreclose the possibility" of holding a fair election required that the election be set aside. . . . Consequently, the Board set the election aside, entered a cease-and-desist order, and ordered the Company to bargain on request. . . .

We [must] consider petitioner['s] . . . First Amendment challenge to the holding of the Board. . . .

Any assessment of the precise scope of employer expression, of course, must be made in the context of its labor relations setting. Thus, an employer's rights cannot outweigh the equal rights of the employees to associate freely, as those rights are embodied in §7 and protected by §8(a)(1) and the proviso to §8(c). And any balancing of those rights must take into account the economic dependence of the employees on their employers, and the necessary tendency of the former, because of that relationship, to pick up intended implications of the latter that might be more readily dismissed by a more disinterested ear. Stating these obvious principles is but another way of recognizing that what is basically at stake is the establishment of a nonpermanent, limited relationship between the employer, his economically dependent employee and his union agent, not the election of legislators or the enactment of legislation whereby that relationship is ultimately defined and where the independent

voter may be freer to listen more objectively and employers as a class freer to talk.

Within this framework, we must reject the Company's challenge to the decision below and the findings of the Board on which it was based. The standards used below for evaluating the impact of an employer's statements are not seriously questioned by petitioner and we see no need to tamper with them here. Thus, an employer is free to communicate to his employees any of his general views about unionism or any of his specific views about a particular union, so long as the communications do not contain a "threat of reprisal or force or promise of benefit." He may even make a prediction as to the precise effects he believes unionization will have on his company. In such a case, however, the prediction must be carefully phrased on the basis of objective fact to convey an employer's belief as to demonstrably probable consequences beyond his control or to convey a management decision already arrived at to close the plant in case of unionization. If there is any implication that an employer may or may not take action solely on his own initiative for reasons unrelated to economic necessities and known only to him, the statement is no longer a reasonable prediction based on available facts but a threat of retaliation based on misrepresentation and coercion, and as such without the protection of the First Amendment. We therefore agree with the court below that "conveyance of the employer's belief, even though sincere, that unionization will or may result in the closing of the plant is not a statement of fact unless, which is most improbable, the eventuality of closing is capable of proof." As stated elsewhere, any employer is free only to tell "what he reasonably believes will be the likely economic consequences of unionization that are outside his control," and not "threats of economic reprisal to be taken solely on his own volition."

Equally valid was the finding by the court and the Board that petitioner's statements and communications were not cast as a prediction of "demonstrable economic consequences," but rather as a threat of retaliatory action. The Board found that petitioner's speeches, pamphlets, leaflets, and letters conveyed the following message: that the company was in precarious financial condition: that the "strike-happy" union would in all likelihood have to obtain its potentially unreasonable demands by striking, the probable result of which would be a plant shutdown, as the past history of labor relations in the area indicated; and that the employees in such a case would have great difficulty finding employment elsewhere. In carrying out its duty to focus on the question, "What did the speaker intend and the listener understand," the Board could reasonably conclude that the intended and understood import of that message was not to predict that unionization would inevitably cause the plant to close but to threaten to throw employees out of work regardless of the economic realities. In this connection, we need go no further than to point out (1) that petitioner had no support for its basic assumption that the union, which had not yet even presented any demands, would have to strike to be heard, and that it admitted at the hearing that it had no basis for attributing other plant closings in the area to unionism; and (2) that the Board has often found that employees, who are particularly sensitive to rumors of plant closings, take such hints as coercive threats rather than honest forecasts.

Questions
1. Section 8(a)(1) limits the employer's "free speech" rights. What are the limitations on the employer's speech?
2. How did the Court justify this limitation on the free speech on the employer?
3. What remedies were given to the union for the employer's violation of Section 8(a)(1)?

RUNAWAY SHOP

Section 8(a)(3) prevents an employer from discharging or refusing to hire an employee as a technique to encourage or discourage membership in a labor organization. However, it does not restrict the employer in a normal exercise of its judgment in selecting or discharging employees for proper cause. Nevertheless, the question arises as to whether the employer may close its shop and open another business elsewhere to avoid unionization of the plant, or whether the employer can choose to go out of business altogether in order to avoid unionization. The following excerpt provides some answers.

Textile Workers Union v. Darlington Manufacturing Co.
380 U.S. 263 (1965)
Supreme Court of the United States

Justice Harlan

We are not presented here with the case of a "runaway shop," whereby Darlington would transfer its work to another plant or open a new plant in another locality to replace its closed plant. Nor are we concerned with a shut-down where the employees, by renouncing the union, could cause the plant to reopen. Such cases would involve discriminatory employer action for the purpose of obtaining some benefit in the future from the new employees. We hold here only that when an employer closes his entire business, even if the liquidation is motivated by vindictiveness towards the union, such action is not an unfair labor practice. . . .

The closing of an entire business, even though discriminatory, ends the employer-employee relationship; the force of such a closing is entirely spent as to that business when termination of the enterprise takes place. On the other hand, a discriminatory partial closing may have repercussions on what remains of the business, affording employer leverage for discouraging the free exercise of §7 rights

among remaining employees of much the same kind as that found to exist in the "runaway shop" and "temporary closing" cases. Moreover, a possible remedy open to the Board in such a case, like the remedies available in the "runaway shop" and "temporary closing" cases, is to order reinstatement of the discharged employees in the other parts of the business. No such remedy is available when an entire business has been terminated. By analogy to those cases involving a continuing enterprise we are constrained to hold, in disagreement with the Court of Appeals, that a partial closing is an unfair labor practice under §8(a)(3) if motivated by a purpose to chill unionism in any of the remaining plants of the single employer and if the employer may reasonably have foreseen that such closing will likely have that effect.

Questions
1. What is a "runaway shop"? Is it illegal?
2. Is termination of a business in violation of Section 8(a)3?

BARGAIN IN GOOD FAITH

NLRB v. Katz
369 U.S. 736 (1961)
Supreme Court of the United States

Justice Brennan

Is it a violation of the duty "to bargain collectively" imposed by §8(a)(5) of the National Labor Relations Act for an employer, without first consulting a union with which it is carrying on bona fide contract negotiations, to institute changes regarding matters which are subjects of mandatory bargaining under §8(d) and which are in fact under discussion? The National Labor Relations Board answered the question affirmatively in this case, in a decision which expressly disclaimed any finding that

the totality of the respondents' conduct manifested bad faith in the pending negotiations. . . .

. . . [T]he union['s] charge of unfair labor practices particularly referred to three acts by the company: unilaterally granting numerous merit increases on October 1956 and January 1957; unilaterally announcing a change in sick-leave policy in March 1957; and unilaterally instituting a new system of automatic wage increases during April 1957. As the ensuing litigation has developed, the company has defended against the charges along two fronts:

First, it asserts that the unilateral changes occurred after a bargaining impasse had developed through the union's fault in adopting obstructive tactics. According to the Board, however, "the evidence is clear that the [company] undertook its unilateral actions before negotiations were discontinued, or before, as we find on the record, the existence of any possible impasse." There is ample support in the record considered as a whole for this finding of fact. . . .

The second line of defense was that the Board could not hinge a conclusion that Section 8(a)(5) had been violated on unilateral actions alone, without making a finding of the employer's subjective bad faith at the bargaining table. . . .

The duty "to bargain collectively" enjoined by §8(a)(5) is defined by §8(d) as the duty to "meet . . . and confer in good faith with respect to wages, hours, and other terms and conditions of employment." Clearly, the duty thus defined may be violated without a general failure of subjective good faith: for there is no occasion to consider the issue of good faith if a party has refused even to negotiate *in fact*—"to meet . . . and confer"—about any of the mandatory subjects. A refusal to negotiate *in fact* as to any subject which is within §8(d), and about which the union seeks to negotiate, violates §(a)(5) though the employer has every desire to reach agreement with the union upon an over-all collective agreement and earnestly and in all good faith bargains to that end. We hold that an employer's unilateral change in conditions of employment under negotiation is similarly a violation of §8(a)(5), for it is a circumvention of the duty to negotiate which frustrates the objectives of §8(a)(5) as much as does a flat refusal.

The unilateral actions of the respondent illustrate the policy and practical considerations which support our conclusion. . . . It is clear at a glance that the automatic wage increase system which was instituted unilaterally was considerably more generous than that which had shortly theretofore been offered to and rejected by the union. Such action conclusively manifests bad faith in the negotiations, and so would have violated Section 8(a)(5) even . . . though no additional evidence of bad faith appeared. An employer is not required to lead with his best offer; he is free to bargain. But even after an impasse is reached he has no license to grant wage increases greater than any he has ever offered the union at the bargaining table, for such action is necessarily inconsistent with a sincere desire to conclude an agreement with the union. . . .

. . . Unilateral action by an employer without prior discussion with the union does amount to a refusal to negotiate about the affected conditions of employment under negotiation, and must of necessity obstruct bargaining, contrary to the congressional policy. . . . It will rarely be justified by any reason of substance. It follows that the Board may hold such unilateral action to be an unfair labor practice in violation of Section 8(a)(5), without also finding the employer guilty of over-all subjective bad faith.

Questions

1. What was the 8(a)(5) violation in *NLRB* v. *Katz*?
2. The duty to bargain collectively is defined in Section 8(d). This duty relates only to certain mandatory subjects. What are they?
3. Is the refusal to "meet . . . and confer" about a mandatory subject a violation of 8(a)5?

LABOR-MANAGEMENT RELATIONS ACT

The Labor-Management Relations Act (LMRA) of 1947 (Taft–Hartley Act) was the product of diverse forces. Many business firms continued to attack "unionism" and gladly joined in the effort to develop an antiunion law. Others criticized the unions for abuse of power. John L. Lewis and the United Mine Workers had carried on two long strikes during World War II in defiance of the government. There were news reports that many so-called labor unions were really rackets and controlled by unsavory individuals. Often violence was promoted by union leaders when peaceful measures failed to achieve union objectives. In a few unions the membership rolls were closed to outsiders and jobs passed from father to son. Others criticized the use of secondary boycotts by unions to achieve their purposes. The Taft–Hartley Act attempted to deal with these perceived problems by amending the National Labor Relations Act and in formulating other policies for labor law.

Several changes in labor law were created by the Taft–Hartley Act. First, the labor injunction was revived in a modified and restrictive form. As one example, an injunction could be secured by the National Labor Relations Board to eliminate statutorily defined unfair union practices. Second, Section 7 of the National Labor Relations Act was amended to allow individuals the freedom to refrain from union activities as a right equal to Section 7's previously announced right to join a union. Moreover, Section 8 of the National Labor Relations Act was amended [8(b)(1)] to prohibit union restraint or coercion of workers who attempted to exercise the right not to join the union.

Prior to 1947 the union could secure a "union security" provision in the contract negotiated with the employer whereby the employer would refuse to hire those who were not members of the union. In effect, the union determined who would be hired. This system was called a closed shop and was outlawed by the Taft–Hartley Act. Instead, the Taft–Hartley amendments to the NLRA established that the employer could legally agree to a union membership provision only if it allowed the employer to select employees without regard to pre-hired union membership. Membership in the union could only be required after 30 days of employment. If the employee thereafter refused to pay union initiation fees and dues, the membership provision of the collectively bargained contract would require the employer to discharge the employee. This type of union security agreement is referred to as a union shop.

Although the rules of federal law apply to all employers whose operations affect interstate commerce, Congress has chosen to explicitly exclude employers from the permissible union shop provisions of federal law in those states that have enacted the so-called right-to-work laws. Section 14(b) of the NLRA excludes state employers when state law refuses to enforce any contractual commitments of employers and unions which attempt to mandate membership in labor organizations. Twenty states have enacted such laws which, in effect, outlaw union shops in their jurisdictions.

Besides the amendment of Section 8 to protect the right of the individual worker to refrain from union membership, subsections (2) through (6) of Section 8(b) also outlawed the following concerted union activities:

(2) attempt to cause an employer to discriminate against an employee, except where the employee fails to pay dues,

(3) refusal to bargain in good faith with the employer,

(4) strikes to compel an employer to commit some unfair labor practice or secondary boycotts: i.e. the refusal to work for employer A, unless he ceases to do business with employer B, with whom the union has its real dispute,

(5) requirements of excessive or discriminatory initiation fees,

(6) "feather-bedding" practices of pay without work performed.

The following cases discuss portions of Section 8(b) and relate in more detail some of the particular union practices held to be illegal.

FAIR REPRESENTATION

Local Union, No. 12, United Rubber Workers v. NLRB
368 F. 2d 12 (1966)
U.S. Court of Appeals (5th Cir.)

At the outset it must be reiterated that every union decision which may in some way result in overriding the wishes . . . of . . . even an appreciable number of employees, does not in and of itself constitute a breach of the fiduciary duty of fair representation. Even in the administration stage of the bargaining contract . . . , the union must necessarily retain a broad degree of discretion in processing individual grievances. Thus, where the union after a good faith investigation of the merits of a grievance, concludes that the claim is insubstantial and refuses to encumber further its grievance channels by continuing to process the unmeritorious claim, its duty of fair representation may well be satisfied. Such good-faith effort to represent fairly the interests of individual employees, however, is not evidenced in this controversy. To the contrary, Local 12 in open disregard of the recommendations of its International has continued to refuse to represent the vital interests of a segment of its membership. . . . Undoubtedly, the duty of fair representation can be breached by

discriminatory inaction in refusing to process a grievance as well as by active conduct on the part of the union. . . .

We thus conclude that where the record demonstrates that a grievance would have been processed to arbitration but for arbitrary and discriminatory reasons, the refusal to so process it constitutes a violation of the union's duty to represent its members "without hostile discrimination, fairly, impartially, and in good faith."

Similarly, with respect to the grievances concerning the segregated nature of plant facilities, the union not only refused to process such claims but actively opposed desegregation of shower and toilet facilities. It is impossible for us to look upon such conduct as anything other than an effort to discriminate against Negro employees with respect to conditions of employment. . . . As the Board properly concluded, "whatever may be the bases on which a statutory representative may properly decline to process grievances, the bases must bear a reasonable relation to the Union's role as bargaining representative or its functioning as a labor organization; manifestly racial discrimination bears no such relationship."

. . . Local 12, in refusing to represent the complainants in a fair and impartial manner, thereby violated section 8(b)(1)(A) by restraining them in the exercise of their Section 7 right to bargain collectively through their chosen representatives.

Questions

1. May the union refuse to further prosecute a grievance of an individual union member? What valid justification might be advanced by the union for refusing to prosecute a union member's claim?
2. Why was the refusal to prosecute grievances of union members by Local Union No. 12 in violation of federal law?

SECONDARY BOYCOTTS

NLRB v. Local 825, International Union of Operating Engineers
400 U.S. 297 (1971)
Supreme Court of the United States

Justice Marshall

In this case we are asked to determine whether strikes by Operating Engineers at the site of the construction of a nuclear power generator plant at Oyster Creek, New Jersey, violated §8(b)(4)(B) of the National Labor Relations Act. Although the National Labor Relations Board found the strikes to be in violation of this section, the Court of Appeals refused to enforce the Board's order. . . .

The general contractor for the project, Burns & Roe, Inc., subcontracted all of the construction work to three companies—White Construction Co., Chicago Bridge & Iron Co., and Poirier and McLane Corp. All three employed operating engineers who were members of Local 825, International Union of Operating Engineers. But White, unlike Chicago Bridge and Poirier, did not have a collective-bargaining agreement with Local 825.

In the latter part of September 1965, White installed an electric welding machine and assigned the job of pushing the buttons that operated the machine to members of the Ironworkers Union, who were to perform the actual welding. Upon learning of this work assignment, Local 825's job steward and its lead engineer threatened White with a strike if operating engineers were not given the work. White, however, refused to meet the demand. On September 29, 1965, the job steward and lead engineer met with the construction manager for Burns, the general contractor. They informed him that the members of Local 825 working at the jobsite had voted to strike unless Bruns signed a contract, which would be binding on all three subcontractors as well as Burns, giving Local 825 jurisdiction over all power equipment, including electric welding machines, operated on the jobsite. On October 1, after White and Burns refused to accede to the demands, the operating engineers employed by Chicago Bridge and Poirer as well as those employed by White walked off the job. . . .

Congressional concern over the involvement of third parties in labor disputes not their own prompted §8(b)(4)(B). This concern was focused on the "secondary boycott," which was conceived of as pressure brought to bear, not "upon the employer who alone is a party [to a dispute], but upon some third party who has no concern in it" with the objective of forcing the third party to bring pressure on the employer to agree to the union's demands.

Section 8(b)(4)(B) is, however, the product of legislative compromise and also reflects a concern with protecting labor organizations' right to exert legitimate pressure aimed at the employer with whom there is a primary dispute. This primary activity is protected even though it may seriously affect neutral third parties.

Thus there are two threads to §8(b)(4)(B) that require disputed conduct to be classified as either "primary" or "secondary." And the tapestry that has been woven in classifying such conduct is among the labor law's most intricate. But here the normally difficult task of classifying union conduct is easy. As the Court of Appeals said, the "record amply justifies the conclusion that [Burns and the neutral subcontractors] were subjected to coercion in the form of threats or walkouts, or both." And, as the Board said, it is clear that this coercion was designed "to achieve the assignment of [the] disputed work" to operating engineers.

Local 825's coercive activity was aimed directly at Burns and the subcontractors that were not involved in the dispute. The union engaged in a strike against these neutral employers for the specific, overt purpose of forcing them to put pressure on White to assign the job of operating the welding machine to operating engineers. . . . It was . . . using a sort of pressure that was unmistakably and flagrantly secondary.

Local 825's . . . operating engineers sought to force Burns to bind all the subcontractors on the project to a particular form of job assignments. The clear implication of the demands was that Burns would be required either to force a change in White's policy or to terminate White's contract. The strikes shut down the whole project. If Burns was unable to obtain White's consent, Local 825 was apparently willing to continue disruptive conduct that would bring all the employers to their knees.

Certainly, the union would have preferred to have the employers capitulate to its demands; it wanted to take the job of operating the welding machines away from the ironworkers. It was willing, however, to try to obtain this capitulation by forcing neutrals to compel White to meet union demands. To hold that this flagrant secondary conduct with these most serious disruptive effects was not prohibited by §8(b)(4)(B) would be largely to ignore the original congressional concern. . . .

Since the Court of Appeals did not believe that §8(b)(4)(B) was applicable, it did not consider the propriety of the portion of the Board's order relating to that section. . . . [S]o we must remand these cases for the Court of Appeals to consider whether the order is necessary to further the goals of the Act.

Questions
1. What is a primary boycott by a union? What is a secondary boycott?
2. Why should secondary boycotts be illegal?

INFORMATIONAL PICKETING

NLRB v. Fruit Packers
377 U.S. 58 (1963)
Supreme Court of the United States

Justice Brennan

Under . . . the National Labor Relations Act, as amended, it is an unfair labor practice for a union . . . [to use secondary picketing] with the object of "forcing . . . any person to cease using, selling, handling, transporting, or otherwise dealing in products of any other producer. . . ." A proviso excepts, however, "publicity, *other than picketing,* for the purpose of truthfully advising the public . . . that a product or products are produced by an employer with whom the labor organization has a primary dispute and are distributed by another employer, as long as such publicity does not have an effect of inducing any individual employed by any person other than the primary employer in the course of his employment to refuse to pick up, deliver, or transport any goods, or not to perform any services, at the establishment of the employer engaged in such distribution." The question in this case is whether the respondent unions violated this section when they limited their secondary picketing of retail stores to an appeal to the customers of the stores not to buy the products of certain firms against which one of the respondents was on strike.

Respondent Local 760 called a strike against fruit packers and warehousemen doing business in Yakima, Washington. The struck firms sold Washington State apples to the Safeway chain of retail stores in and about Seattle, Washington. Local 760 . . . instituted a consumer boycott against the apples in support of the strike. They placed pickets who walked back and forth before the customers' entrances of 46 Safeway stores in Seattle. The pickets— two at each of 45 stores and three at the 46th store—wore placards and distributed handbills which appealed to Safeway customers, and to the public generally, to refrain from buying Washington State apples, which were only one of numerous food products sold in the stores. Before the pickets appeared at any store, a letter was delivered to the store manager informing him that the picketing was only an appeal to his customers not to buy Washington State apples, and that pickets were being expressly instructed "to patrol peacefully in front of the consumer entrances of the store, to stay away

from the delivery entrances and not to interfere with the work of your employees, or with deliveries to or pickups from your store." A copy of written instructions to the pickets— which included the explicit statement that "you are also forbidden to request that the customers not patronize the store"—was enclosed with the letter. Since it was desired to assure Safeway employees that they were not to cease work, and to avoid any interference with pickups or deliveries, the pickets appeared after the stores opened for business and departed before the stores closed. At all times during the picketing, the store employees continued to work, and no deliveries or pickups were obstructed. Washington State apples were handled in normal course by both Safeway employees and the employees of the other employers involved. Ingress and egress by customers and others was not interfered with in any manner.

A complaint issued on charges that this conduct violated §8(b)(4) as amended . . . that "by literal wording of the proviso (to Section 8(b)(4) as well as through the interpretive gloss placed thereon by its drafters, consumer picketing in front of a secondary establishment is prohibited."

The Board's reading of the statute—that the legislative history and the phrase "other than picketing" in the proviso reveal a congressional purpose to outlaw all picketing directed at customers at a secondary site—necessarily rested on the finding that Congress determined that such picketing always threatens, coerces or restrains the secondary employer. . . . [However], throughout the history of federal regulation of labor relations, Congress has consistently refused to prohibit peaceful picketing except where it is used as a means to achieve specific ends which experience has shown are undesirable. We have recognized this congressional practice . . . reflect[s] concern that a broad ban against peaceful picketing might collide with the guarantees of the First Amendment.

We have examined the legislative history

of the amendments to §8(b)(4), and conclude that it does not reflect with the requisite clarity a congressional plan to proscribe all peaceful consumer picketing at secondary sites, and, particularly, any concern with peaceful picketing when it is limited, as here, to persuading Safeway customers not to buy Washington State apples when they traded in the Safeway stores. All that the legislative history shows in the way of an "isolated evil" believed to require proscription of peaceful consumer picketing at secondary sites, was its use to persuade the customers of the secondary employer to cease trading with him in order to force him to cease dealing with, or to put pressure upon, the primary employer. This narrow focus reflects the difference between such conduct and peaceful picketing at the secondary site directed only at the struck product. In the latter case, the union's appeal to the public is confined to its dispute with the primary employer, since the public is not asked to withhold its patronage from the secondary employer, but only to boycott the primary employer's goods. On the other hand, a union appeal to the public at the secondary site not to trade at all with the secondary employer goes beyond the goods of the primary employer, and seeks the public's assistance in forcing the secondary employer to cooperate with the union in its primary dispute. This is not to say that this distinction was expressly alluded to in the debates. It is to say, however, that the consumer picketing carried on in this case is not attended by the abuses at which the statute was directed. . . .

Peaceful consumer picketing to shut off all trade with the secondary employer unless he aids the union in its dispute with the primary employer, is poles apart from such picketing which only persuades his customers not to buy the struck product. The proviso indicates no more than that the Senate conferees' constitutional doubts led Congress to authorize publicity other than picketing which persuades the customers of a secondary employer to stop all trading with him, but not such publicity which has the effect of cutting off his deliveries or inducing his employees to cease work. On the other hand, picketing which persuades the customers of a secondary employer to stop all trading with him was also to be barred.

In sum, the legislative history does not support the Board's finding that Congress meant to prohibit all consumer picketing at a secondary site, having determined that such picketing necessarily threatened, coerced, or restrained the secondary employer. Rather, the history shows that Congress was following its usual practice of legislating against peaceful picketing only to curb "isolated evils."

This distinction is opposed as "unrealistic" because, it is urged, all picketing automatically provokes the public to stay away from the picketed establishment. The public will, it is said, neither read the signs and handbills, nor note the explicit injunction that "This is not a strike against the store or market." Be that as it may, our holding today simply takes note of the fact that Congress has never adopted a broad condemnation of peaceful picketing, such as that urged upon us by petitioners and an intention to do so is not revealed with the "clearest indication in the legislative history," which we require.

Questions
1. What "evil" was Congress legislating against in Section 8(b)(4)?
2. Why did Congress feel the "proviso" was necessary in this legislation?
3. As a result of the decision in *Fruit Packers*, under what conditions is "secondary picketing" permitted?
4. Could a radio publicity compaign *without secondary picketing* be directed to

consumers requesting their *total* boycott of retailers selling goods of the primary employer?

5. Could publicity be directed to employees or deliverypersons of a secondary employer?

FEATHERBEDDING

NLRB v. Gamble Enterprises
345 U.S. 117 (1952)
Supreme Court of the United States

Justice Burton

The question here is whether a labor organization engages in an unfair labor practice, within the meaning of §8(b)(6) of the National Labor Relations Act, as amended by the Labor Management Relations Act, 1947, when it insists that the management of one of an interstate chain of theaters shall employ a local orchestra to play in connection with certain programs, although that management does not need or want to employ that orchestra. . . .

For generations professional musicians have faced a shortage in the local employment needed to yield them a livelihood. They have been confronted with the competition of military bands, traveling bands, foreign musicians on tour, local amateur organizations and, more recently, technological developments in reproduction and broadcasting. To help them conserve local sources of employment, they developed local protective societies. Since 1896, they also have organized and maintained on a national scale the American Federation of Musicians, affiliated with the American Federation of Labor. By 1943, practically all professional instrumental performers and conductors in the United States had joined the Federation. . . .

The Federation uses its nationwide control of professional talent to help individual members and local unions. It insists that traveling band contracts be subject to its rules, laws and regulations. Article 18, §4, of its By-Laws provides: "Traveling members cannot, without the consent of a Local, play any presentation performances in its jurisdiction unless a local house orchestra is also employed."

From this background we turn to the instant case. For more than 12 years the Palace Theater in Akron, Ohio, has been one of an interstate chain of theaters managed by respondent, Gamble Enterprises, Inc., which is a Washington corporation with its principal office in New York. Before the decline of vaudeville and until about 1940, respondent employed a local orchestra of nine union musicians to play for stage acts at that Theater. When a traveling band occupied the stage, the local orchestra played from the pit for the vaudeville acts and, at times, augmented the performance of the traveling band.

Since 1940, respondent has used the Palace for showing motion pictures with occasional appearance of traveling bands. Between 1940 and 1947, the local musicians, no longer employed on a regular basis, held periodic rehearsals at the theater and were available when required. When a traveling band appeared there, respondent paid the members of the local orchestra a sum equal to the minimum union wages for a similar engagement but they played no music.

The Taft–Hartley Act, containing §8(b)(6), was passed, over the President's veto, June 23, 1947, and took effect August 22. Between July 2 and November 12, seven performances of traveling bands were presented on the Palace stage. Local musicians were neither used nor paid on those occasions. They raised no objections and made no demands for "stand-by" payments. However, in October, 1947, the American Federation of Musicians, Local No. 24 of Akron, Ohio, here called the union, opened negotiations with respondent . . . for the latter's employment of a pit orchestra of local musicians whenever a traveling band performed on the stage. The pit orchestra was to play overtures, "intermissions" and "chasers" (the latter while patrons were leaving the theater). The union required acceptance of this proposal as a condition of its consent to local apearances of traveling bands. Respondent declined the offer and a traveling band scheduled to appear November 20 canceled its engagement on learning that the union had withheld its consent.

* * *

In 1949, respondent filed charges with the National Labor Relations Board asserting that the union was engaging in the unfair labor practice defined in §8(b)(6). . . .

We accept the finding of the Board, made upon the entire record, that the union was seeking actual employment for its members and not mere "stand-by" pay. The Board recognized that, formerly, before §8(b)(6) had taken effect, the union had received "stand-by" payments in connection with traveling band appearances. Since then, the union has requested no such payments and has received none. It has, however, requested and consistently negotiated for actual employment in connection with traveling band and vaudeville

appearances. It has suggested various ways in which a local orchestra could earn pay for performing competent work and, upon those terms, it has offered to consent to the appearance of traveling bands which are Federation-controlled. Respondent, with equal consistency, has declined these offers as it had a right to do.

Since we and the Board treat the union's proposals as in good faith contemplating the performance of actual services, we agree that the union has not, on this record, engaged in a practice proscribed by §8(b)(6). It has remained for respondent to accept or reject the union's offers on their merits in the light of all material circumstances. We do not find it necessary to determine also whether such offers were "in the nature of an exaction." We are not dealing here with offers of mere "token" or nominal services. The proposals before us were appropriately treated by the Board as offers in good faith of substantial performances by competent musicians. There is no reason to think that sham can be substituted for substance under §8(b)(6) any more than under any other statute. Payments for "standing by," or for the substantial equivalent of "standing-by," are not payments for services performed, but when an employer receives a bona fide offer of competent performance of relevant services, it remains for the employer, through free and fair negotiation, to determine whether such offer shall be accepted and what compensation shall be paid for the work done.

Questions
1. What is featherbedding? Had the local musicians in *Gamble Enterprises* ever engaged in featherbedding?
2. What is makework? Is it illegal? What about the offer to perform "token" services?

FEDERAL PREEMPTION

Through constitutional decisions the Supreme Court has allocated to Congress the power (1) to enact national labor legislation and (2) to forbid the application of state laws in labor relations. The Congress may choose not to exercise this power or to use only part. However, the actual enactment of federal legislation does not necessarily exclude the jurisdiction of state tribunals nor the application of state law. But the expansion of national power over industrial relations raised significant questions concerning the portion of government power shared between the states and the nation.

First, how far does actual federal regulation of labor relations extend? The National Labor Relations Act is the most significant labor legislation in the United States. In upholding the constitutionality of the NLRA, the Supreme Court assumed without so holding that the act asserted federal power to the outermost limits of the commerce power. But in fact, the National Labor Relations Board exercises more narrow jurisdiction. Congress has never appropriated sufficient funds to the board to fully cover the scope of the act. Therefore, through self-restraint imposed by limited funds and administrative discretion, several million employees and employers are left outside the board's jurisdiction. In the 1957 decision of *Guss* v. *Utah Labor Relations Board,* 353 U.S. 1, the Supreme Court held that state agencies could not take jurisdiction in areas over which the NLRB declined to exercise its statutory jurisdiction. The result was a "no man's land" in which the federal agency declined to act and the states were excluded by federal legislation. Finally, in 1959, the Congress allowed the state law to operate in the area over which the NLRB had declined to exercise jurisdiction. The same legislation prohibits the NLRB from any further contractions of its jurisdiction.

Second, how far does federal regulation of labor relations exclude the application of supplementary state law? The Court has determined that, with limited exceptions, the states have no authority over the aspects of labor relations under NLRB jurisdiction. A state may not decide questions of union representation, remedy employer unfair labor practices, or regulate the concerted activities (picketing and strikes) of employees when such activities are arguably within the jurisdiction of the NLRB. These activities lie within the protection of Section 7 or the prohibition of Section 8 of the NLRA. As such, they are areas that are exclusive to the NLRB and excluded from state courts. The principal judge-made exception is the power of state courts to enjoin or award damages resulting from conduct marked by violence or imminent threats to public order. Previously in *San Diego Building Trades Council* v. *Garman,* 359 U.S. 236 (1959), the Court had concluded that the states need not yield jurisdiction "where the activity regulated was a merely peripheral concern of the Labor Management Relations Act. . . . Or where the regulated conduct touched interests so deeply rooted in local feeling and responsibility that, in the absence of compelling congressional direction, we could not infer that Congress had deprived the States of the power to act." Consequently, states may legislate to supplement the federal law if such legislation does not concern an area of labor relations arguably within the area covered by federal legislation. The "peripheral" aspects of labor relations are within the reach of state legislation.

COURT ENFORCEMENT OF LABOR CONTRACTS

As previously indicated, the Norris–LaGuardia Act generally prohibits federal court injunctions in labor disputes. However, Section 301 of the Taft–Hartley Act provides that unions may sue and be sued as an entity. Suits for violation of labor contracts may be brought in any district court and money judgments against labor unions or the employer may be obtained. However, the language of the Taft–Hartley Act did not expressly overrule the Norris–LaGuardia anti-injunction provisions. Thereafter, the question naturally arose as to whether the courts could use an injunction against either party to a labor contract who refused to abide by the collective bargaining agreement.

INJUNCTIONS

In *Textile Workers Union v. Lincoln Mills*, 353 U.S. 448 (1957), the Supreme Court held that Section 301 of the Labor-Management Act authorizes federal courts to fashion a body of federal law for the enforcement of collective bargaining agreements and includes within that federal law specific performance of promises to arbitrate grievances under collective bargaining agreements. This construction of Section 301 means that the agreement to arbitrate grievance disputes, contained in a collective bargaining agreement, can be specifically enforced by court injunctions.

However, in 1962 the Supreme Court held in *Sinclair Refining Co. v. Atkinson*, 370 U.S. 195, that the anti-injunction provisions of the Norris–LaGuardia Act precluded a federal district court from enjoining a strike in breach of a no-strike obligation under a collective bargaining agreement, even though that agreement contained provisions, enforceable under Section 301(a) of the Labor-Management Relations Act for binding arbitration of the grievance dispute concerning which the strike was called. The Court reexamined its holding in *Sinclair* in the following case.

Boys Markets, Inc. v. Retail Clerks Local 770
398 U.S. 235 (1970)
Supreme Court of the United States

Justice Brennan

In February 1969, at the time of the incidents that produced this litigation, petitioner and respondent were parties to a collective bargaining agreement which provided that all controversies concerning its interpretation or application should be resolved by adjustment and arbitration procedures set forth therein

and that during the life of the contract, there should be "no cessation or stop-page of work, lock-out, picketing or boycotts. . . ." The dispute arose when petitioner's frozen foods supervisor and certain members of his crew who were not members of the bargaining unit began to rearrange merchandise in the frozen food cases of one of petitioner's supermarkets. A union representative insisted that the food cases be stripped of all merchandise and be restocked by union personnel. When petitioner did not accede to the union's demand, a strike was called and the union began to picket petitioner's establishment. Thereupon petitioner demanded that the union cease work stoppage and picketing and sought to invoke the grievance and arbitration procedures specified in the contract. . . .

The Norris–LaGuardia Act was responsive to a situation totally different from that which exists today. In the early part of this century, the federal courts generally were regarded as allies of management in its attempt to prevent the organization and strengthening of labor unions; and in this industrial struggle the injunction became a potent weapon which was wielded against the activities of labor groups. . . .

In 1932 Congress attempted to bring some order out of the industrial chaos that had developed and to correct the abuses which had resulted from the interjection of the federal judiciary into union-management disputes on the behalf of management. Congress, therefore, determined initially to limit severely the power of the federal courts to issue injunctions "in any case involving or growing out of any labor dispute. . . ." Even as initially enacted, however, the prohibition against federal injunctions was by no means absolute. Shortly thereafter Congress passed the Wagner Act, designed to curb various management activities which tended to discourage employee participation in collective action.

As labor organizations grew in strength and developed toward maturity, congressional emphasis shifted from protection of the nascent labor movement to the encouragement of collective bargaining and to administrative techniques for the peaceful resolution of industrial disputes. This shift in emphasis was accomplished, however, without extensive revision of many of the older enactments, including the anti-injunction section of the Norris–LaGuardia Act. Thus it became the task of the courts to accommodate, to reconcile the older statutes with the more recent ones.

* * *

The *Sinclair* decision, however, seriously undermined the effectiveness of the arbitration technique as a method peacefully to resolve industrial disputes without resort to strikes, lockouts, and similar devices. Clearly employers will be wary of assuming obligations to arbitrate specifically enforceable against them when no similar efficacious remedy is available to enforce the concomitant undertaking of the union to refrain from striking. On the other hand, the central purpose of the Norris–LaGuardia Act to foster the growth and viability of labor organizations is hardly retarded—if anything, this goal is advanced—by a remedial device which merely enforces the obligation that the union freely undertook under a specifically enforceable agreement to submit disputes to arbitration. We conclude, therefore, that the unavailability of equitable relief in the arbitration context presents a serious impediment to the congressional policy favoring the voluntary establishment of a mechanism for the peaceful resolution of labor disputes, that the core purpose of the Norris–LaGuardia Act is not sacrificed by the limited use of equitable remedies to further this important policy, and consequently that the Norris–LaGuardia Act does not bar the granting of injunctive relief in the circumstances of the instant case.

Questions

1. Why was the *Sinclair* decision considered wrongfully decided?
2. What reasons were cited by the Court for allowing court enforcement (injunctions) of no-strike provisions in collectively bargained contracts?

SUITS FOR DAMAGES

In a long line of decisions defining the conditions for federal court suits over violations of collective-bargaining agreements, the Supreme Court began with the decision in the early 1960s that individual union officials could not be held liable for damages caused by a strike in violation of a contract. Later, in 1979, the Court ruled that the union, itself, could not be sued for damages for a wildcat strike not sanctioned by the union. Finally, in 1981 the Court ruled that employers cannot sue their workers for damages caused by wildcat strikes. Instead, the Court said employers have alternative steps to handle wildcat strikes. Wildcat strikers can be fired or disciplined. Moreover, the employer can obtain an injunction to halt a wildcat walkout that could have been arbitrated as provided by the contract. Thus, Section 301 of the Taft–Hartley Act allows a damages remedy for breach of the no-strike provision of a collective-bargaining agreement only against *unions,* not *individuals,* and only when the unions participated in or authorized the strike.

ARBITRATION

Labor arbitration is the process in which a neutral third party, selected jointly by labor and management, decides a dispute that the parties have been unable to resolve. The arbitrator's decision is final and binding and enforceable through the courts. The Supreme Court has approved of labor arbitration in a series of cases in 1960. These cases establish arbitration as the preeminent process in deciding contract disputes. In one case, the company refused to arbitrate what the lower court called a frivolous and patently baseless claim by the union. Consequently, the lower court held the employer was not subject to arbitration under the labor contract. The Supreme Court reversed the lower court's determination and ordered arbitration. The Court identified the proper role of the lower courts in the following language:

The collective agreement calls for the submission of grievances in the categories which it describes, irrespective of whether a court may deem them to be meritorious. In our role of developing a meaningful body of law to govern the interpretation and enforcement of collective bargaining agreements, we think special heed should be given to the context in which collective bargaining agreements are negotiated and the purpose which they are intended to serve. . . . The function of the court is very limited when the parties have agreed to submit all questions of contract interpretation to the arbitrator. It is confined to ascertaining whether the party seeking arbitration is making a claim which on its face is governed by the contract. Whether the moving party is right or wrong is a question of contract interpretation for the arbitrator. In these circumstances the moving party should not be deprived of the arbitrator's judgment, when it was his judgment and all that it connotes that was bargained for.

The courts, therefore, have no business weighing the merits of the grievance, considering whether there is equity in a particular claim, or determining whether there is a particular language in the written instrument which will support the claim. The agreement is to submit all grievances to arbitration, not merely those which the court will deem meritorious. The processing of even frivolous claims may have therapeutic values of which those who are not a part of the plant environment may be quite unaware.

The union claimed in this case that the company had violated a specific provision of the contract. The company took the position that it had not violated that clause. There was, therefore, a dispute between the parties as to "the meaning, interpretation and application" of the collective bargaining agreement. Arbitration should have been ordered. When the judiciary undertakes to determine the merits of a grievance under the guise of interpreting the grievance procedure of collective bargaining agreements, it usurps a function which under that regime is entrusted to the arbitration tribunal. *United Steelworkers of Am. v. American Mfg. Co.*, 363 U.S. 564 (1960).

Questions
1. Are the courts to separate frivolous and meritorious claims before ordering arbitration?
2. What therapeutic value could result from processing even frivolous claims?

NATIONAL EMERGENCIES

The Taft–Hartley Act sets forth detailed procedures to govern strikes that are deemed to create a national emergency. The act provides that if the President believes a strike will imperil the national health or safety, he may impanel a board of inquiry. This board is directed to investigate the causes and circumstances of the labor controversy and report to the President. After reviewing the report, the President may direct the Attorney General to petition a federal district court for an injunction. If the district court finds that the continuation of the strike will imperil the national health and safety, the court has jurisdiction to enjoin the strike. Thereafter, bargaining between the parties is to continue under the aid of the Federal Mediation and Conciliation Service. After 60 days, the board of inquiry must submit another report detailing the current status of the dispute and the employer's last offer of settlement. Within the next 15 days, a vote is to be taken among the employees to determine whether they will agree to accept the last offer of the employer. If no settlement is reached, the injunction is dissolved at the end of 80 days.

The hope of the "80 days' cooling-off period" is that the parties will be able to reach an agreement. If no agreement is reached, the employees may strike again, and no further injunctions are provided by law. Accordingly, Congress must deal with the "national emergency" in some fashion. In 1963, the railroad unions threatened a strike because the railroad companies had proposed modifications of certain work rules. In an effort to avoid the strike, Congress enacted a law requiring compulsory arbitration over the two most controversial work rule changes (the retention of stokers on diesels and the size and complement of train crews). The arbitration panel satisfactorily settled the controversy and avoided the strike. Most elements in American industry and labor would reject the compulsory arbitration alternative as a solution to major labor disputes; nevertheless, compulsory arbitration has been utilized on one occasion, and thus the possibility of its subsequent employment cannot be ruled out. The fear by both labor and management of congressional action often helps formulate an agreement.

LABOR-MANAGEMENT REPORTING AND DISCLOSURE ACT

The Labor-Management Reporting and Disclosure Act of 1959 (Landrum–Griffin Act) regulates the internal affairs of unions. During the 1950s, congressional hearings produced evidence of misconduct by the officials of some unions. To cope with the abuses, such as embezzlement and "sweetheart" contracts with employers, Congress enacted a wide variety of provisions. Certain provisions, often referred to as a union member's "bill of rights," require elections to be held periodically for union officers and that union members be assured the right to vote, nominate candidates, run for office, or comment on qualifications of candidates for office. Moreover, union members were given the right to attend membership meetings and participate in the voting and deliberations of such meetings. Other provisions of the act require that filing of extensive information concerning the financial affairs of the union and its officials. The act outlaws the embezzlement of union funds and restricts the making of loans by the union to its officials in excess of a stipulated amount.

In *Hall v. Cole*, 83 LRPN 1390 (1973), a union member introduced a set of resolutions alleging undemocratic actions and misguided policies on the part of union officers in the Seafarers Union. When the resolutions were defeated by the union membership, the member was expelled from the union on the grounds that the resolutions violated a union rule prohibiting "deliberate and malicious vilification with regard to execution of the duties of any office." Finding no success with efforts to secure an intraunion remedy, the expelled member filed suit under the Labor-Management Reporting and Disclosure Act, claiming that his expulsion violated the union member's right of free speech. The courts regained union membership for the petitioner and awarded $5,500 in legal fees. The petitioner's vindication of free speech rights was conceived by the courts to have worked to the benefit of all members of the union and, hence, justified the union's bearing the expense of the petitioner's litigation.

When members of the unions feel their rights under the Labor-Management Reporting and Disclosure Act have been violated and internal union procedures are exhausted, the union member may complain to the Secretary of Labor, who, after investigation, may bring an action in court for the vindication of the union member's rights.

CONCLUSION

The essence of labor laws is the fostering of collective bargaining. The labor laws outline unfair labor practices that cannot be utilized by management or the union to modify the economic relationship of employer and employees. Having established the boundaries of unfair practices, the parties are left to their respective positions of economic power and political skill in negotiating a labor-management agreement. This collectively bargained contract becomes legally enforceable and establishes the rights and privileges enjoyed by both management and the union. Though not without critics, the labor laws appear to work reasonably well in reducing industrial strife.

DISCUSSION QUESTIONS

1. Within Easy-Heat, Inc., an "Employee's Council" was formed, composed only of employees. The firm's attorney spoke to the council to encourage the formation of an in-plant bargaining committee. The speech was made on company time. The company lawyer and facilities were made available for the council to discuss the transformation of the council into a more formally structured labor organization. Soon thereafter, a management employee questioned a worker about whether a friend of that worker might want to organize an in-plant group. All of this occurred following an outside union's unsuccessful organizing campaign. The outside union has filed a charge of an 8(a)(2) violation. Decide.

2. After the union lost the election for the formation of a union, it filed a complaint against Florida Steel for alleged unfair labor practices in connection with the election.

   While the charge was pending, Florida Steel distributed a letter to all employees, which read in part as follows:

   . . . If you should want some legal counsel or just help in handling any of the situations described above, all you need to do is let your supervisor know. He will put you in touch with someone who can help you.

   By distributing this letter, did Florida Steel violate Section 8(a)(1)?

3. One election for the formation of a union within Clapper's Manufacturing resulted in a loss for the union, a result openly sought by the company. On the eve of a second such election, the company president questioned an employee about how he thought the election was going to go and how several of his fellow employees planned to vote. On the day of the election, a company supervisor questioned another employee about how the election would go and asked this employee "who he should talk to." The supervisor told a third employee that he planned to question employees in all of the plants about their feelings toward the union. The union lost the second election and initiated charges against the company for violations of 8(a)(1).

   In the circumstances given, were the company's actions lawful?

4. The Retail Store Employees Union fired one of its employees, who then presented a wrongful discharge claim against the union to the NLRB. Anna P. was asked by the union president to testify at the resulting unfair labor

practice hearing, to substantiate improprieties allegedly committed by the discharged employee. Although pressured to testify by the president, who claimed she had knowledge of such misconduct, Anna P. refused and denied that she could substantiate the grounds for termination. Anna P. was not called as a witness, although she could have been subpoenaed.

Thereafter, Anna P. was fired by the president by means of a letter in which the president detailed his reasons for letting her go, including that she "conveniently forgot" facts about the discharged employee, that she was disloyal, and that she had released a union mailing list to a man running for union office.

Anna P. brought her own complaint to the NLRP, charging an unfair labor practice under 8(a)(4) LMRA, that the union fired her for her refusal to testify. Section 8(a)(4) prohibits discharge of or discrimination against an employee who has filed a charge or given testimony in an NLRB proceeding. What is the result?

5. A plant manager for V-Co, Inc. was informed by his corporate headquarters that two representatives of the Warehouse Employees Union would be at the plant on a certain day to organize the workers, and he was to treat them courteously. Supervisors were then instructed to assemble the employees by departments to meet with the union organizers. Employees were paid for time spent in the series of meetings, and foremen or supervisors also were present for some part of each meeting, but did not participate. By day's end the union had obtained authorization cards from 101 of the 125 employees attending these meetings. After it reviewed these cards, the company granted recognition of the union the same day.

Collective bargaining resulted shortly thereafter in an agreement between company and union.

Do you discern any legal problems with this organizing effort?

6. Unionized employees of Eastex requested permission from the company to distribute a newsletter to production employees in nonworking areas of the company plant during nonworking time. Of the four sections of the newsletter, first and fourth sections urged employees to support the union and generally extolled the benefits of union solidarity. The second section encouraged employees to write to their political representatives to oppose incorporation of the state right-to-work law in the state constitution. The third section noted that the President had vetoed an increase in the minimum wage, and admonished, "As working men and women, we must defeat our enemies and elect our friends. If you haven't registered to vote, please do so today."

When company permission was denied, the union filed a complaint with the NLRB that Eastex has violated Section 8(a)(1) of the LMRA by restraining employees' exercise of their right under Section 7 to engage in ". . . concerted activities for the purpose of collective bargaining or other mutual aid or protection." Eastex countered that sections two and three of the newsletter did not pertain to "aid or protection" for the employees in its plant, because they were not related to Eastex's association with the union, the state already had a right-to-work law, and all plant employees were already paid more than minimum wage. Further, the company felt that this communication could be distributed elsewhere and not on company property.

Does Section 7 protect activity for the "aid and protection" of employees other than those of the company, and does it protect the urging of political activity on matters not related to the immediate employer-employee relationship? Could the company prevent the distribution of this union literature on its property?

7. Union Local 810 was conducting a strike against Can Co. Advance Co. leased Can automobiles and drivers to transport nonstriking employees between Can's manufacturing plant and the railroad station. Local 810 then, through picketing, encouraged employees of Advance to stop work in connection with the contract with Can.

In response to an allegation that this is unlawful secondary activity, Local 810 asserts that by its contract with Can, Advance became an "ally" of Can and subject to primary strike measures. Should Advance's rendering of services cause it to be considered an ally of Can, so that the two could be identified together for purposes of the strike by manufacturing employees?

8. Immediately after midnight on the day when a union representation election was being held and again at 7:15 A.M. when the polls opened, the Steelworkers Union distributed leaflets urging an affirmative vote by the employees of General Knit, which read:

"Who is fooling who???
"General Knit can cry poor mouth if they want, but let's look at the facts.
"In 1976, General Knit had sales of $25 million.
"General Knit is owned by Itoh, who has a net worth in excess of $200 million.
"This company had an increase of 12.5% in sales for period ending March 31, 1977.
"During this period this company had a profit of $19.3 million.
"Don't be fooled by General Knit and their high-priced lawyers.
"Itoh, who owns General Knit, is making it big and can afford decent wages for its employees.
"Vote yes, today, and make the company share some of their high profits with you—the worker."

For the period ending March 31, 1977, General Knit sustained a loss exceeding $5 million, while Itoh had a profit of about $17.3 million. The company got out a response to the leaflet at about 10:15 A.M., after the first voting session was over.

General Knit petitioned the NLRB to set aside the election.

Is the leaflet untrue or misleading? What rule should be applied by the Board in deciding whether to set aside the election results?

9. ABC Company engaged primarily in the distribution of steel channels, metal lathes, and related products, and also manufactured some steel channels

on its own premises for two to three weeks per year. Its employees, 3 truck drivers and 10 warehousemen, were covered by a collectively bargained contract with the Teamsters Union.

The cutting of steel channels is a fully automated process, done by a machine operated by a warehouseman. ABC's policy had been to hire a lather from the Wood, Wire and Metal Lathers Union to be present during the cutting, but the lather performed no work.

A demand was made by Local 46 of the Wood, Wire and Metal Lathers Union that ABC hire a lather full time. When the ABC's president refused, saying he had no work for a lather, the union exerted pressure to change his mind. The president relented and hired a lather at $400 per week who, being barred from delivery and warehouse work by the Teamsters contract, did some office work, for which he was found unfit, addressed envelopes, which he eventually refused to do because it was "demeaning," and made various office deliveries.

During the time of his employment, the lather spent at most four hours per day doing the small tasks given him, and was idle for the remainder of his eight-hour day. When the president complained to the union that there was no work for which the lather was suited, the union suggested he be used to run errands.

ABC has charged the Lathers Local 46 with violation of the LMRA. What result?

10. The Wood, Wire and Metal Lathers Union Local 46 retaliated against ABC's refusal to hire and retain a lather by instructing its shop stewards on construction sites where Lathers Union members were employed by lathing contractors to require that union members refuse to accept or handle the materials from ABC Company. When these actions were carried out, materials were actually turned back from construction sites where lathing contractors had projects underway.

ABC charged this was an unfair labor practice. What result?

SUGGESTED READINGS

Blinzer, Alan, P., "The Complete Closing Doctrine and the Successorship Cases," *American Business Law Journal*, Vol. 17, No. 2, Summer 1979, pp. 155–174.

Castle, Robert C. and Lansing, Paul, "Arbitration of Labor Grievances Brought Under Contractual and Statutory Provisions: The Supreme Court Grows Less Deferential to the Arbitration Process," *American Business Law Journal*, Vol. 21, No. 1, Spring 1983, pp. 49–88.

DeLorme, Charles, D., Jr. and Wood, Norman J., "NLRB Voting on Important Unfair Labor Practices Decisions 1955–1975," *American Business Law Journal*, Vol. 16, No. 2, Fall 1978, pp. 223–229.

Henkel, Jan W., "Illegal Strikes By Public Employees—Fourteenth Amendment Does Not Prevent Discharge," *American Business Law Journal*, Vol. 15, No. 3, Winter 1978, pp. 375–378.

Naffziger, Fred J., "All Power to the Arbitrator: Aftermath of the Steelworkers Trilogy,

Collyer Wire and ENA," *American Business Law Journal,* Vol. 12, No. 3, Winter 1975, pp. 281–294.

Naffziger, Fred J., "Partial Business Close-Downs by an Employer and the Duty to Bargain Under the National Labor Relations Act," *American Business Law Journal,* Vol. 20, No. 2, Summer 1982, pp. 223–242.

Twomey, David, P., "NLRB v. Yeshiva University: Faculty as Managerial Employees Under the NLRA," *American Business Law Journal,* Vol. 19, No. 1, Spring 1981, pp. 63–72.

Zollers, Frances E., "From Gridiron to Courtroom to Bargaining Table: The New National Football League Agreement," *American Business Law Journal,* Vol. 17, No. 2, Summer 1979, pp. 133–154.

chapter 18

SAFE EMPLOYMENT REGULATIONS

Ignoring the issues of morality and equity, the ideal free market could handle the problem of harmful risk. For the market to work, the risk must be known to those in danger and the risk must be voluntarily accepted. The free market will then make adjustments in prices and quantities so that the right amounts of risk and risk prevention (safety) will be provided.

Workers are willing to accept risk when they are fully informed about the potential cost of the hazards and they are compensated for them with higher wages than those offered in safer occupations. In addition, the wage premium for risky work becomes an inducement for the employer to provide some job safety to lower the risk premium he must pay to attract workers. Consequently, the efficiency of the ideal market avoids too much risk (too little safety) or too much safety (too little risk).

However, "real" markets do not always adhere to the ideal market's requirements of full knowledge of risk and voluntary exposure to risk. The problem of informing workers of risk is enormous. Workers would have difficulty processing the information about complex technical matters. In addition, the employers have little incentive to make such information available to workers. Without full knowledge by workers, the market allocation of risk is faulty.

Moreover, the market system fails to deal with involuntary risk exposure (externalities). While some workers may be willing to expose themselves to risk in the course of employment, their exposure may cause others to be exposed to risk involuntarily. Also, the costs of these accidents or illnesses are not always limited to the worker voluntarily assuming the risk. The family of a worker killed on the job, for example, may qualify for survivor benefits under social security. His medical care expenses may be borne by the employer (society) or by taxpayers providing subsidies to the medical care system. In effect, the market system allows too much risk because transacting parties do not confront the full impact of their action.

Finally, some individuals may think that the free market's results are too risky in light of certain noneconomic value judgments. Some moralize that workers are entitled to a risk-free work environment. Others contend that the distribution of risk under the market system is tilted unfavorably against low-income people, who are forced to take the high-risk, high-paying jobs because of their frail financial circumstances. Consequently, considerable state and federal legislation has been enacted to protect the employee from physical injury on the job. The principal statutes covering these risks are workers' compensation laws and the Occupational Safety and Health Act of 1970.

WORKERS' COMPENSATION LAWS

Safety and health problems in the workplace have always existed. However, with the coming of industrialization and its combining of power machinery, chemicals, heat, and electricity with large numbers of minimally trained workers laboring long hours, the ever-enlarging number of work injuries were predictable. Nevertheless, little thought was given to safety improvement. The oversupply of labor made workers so cheap that investment in safety seemed unwarranted. Employees, so desperate for jobs, accepted the risk of injury as part of the job. These social beliefs toward workplace injuries were also evident in the law.

Under tort law, the courts generally held that employees accepted all the customary risks associated with an occupation when they took the job. If employees were injured on the job, they could sue their employer to collect damages only if they could prove the employer was negligently at fault. Moreover, if the employers could establish any of three possible defenses, they could avoid any liability to the injured worker. These defenses were (1) assumption of risk, (2) contributory negligence, and (3) the fellow servant rule. For example, if the employer knowingly supplied a hazardous working tool for employees, the employee injured in handling the equipment would not be entitled to recover damages because the employee had understood the hazards of the defective equipment and knowingly assumed the risk of this injury. In addition, the employee could not recover if he or she were in some way contributorily negligent in the manner in which the machine was handled. Finally, if a fellow servant was negligent and caused the injury to the employee, the employee was denied recovery under the fellow servant rule. Hence, at common law it was only in rare instances that an employee was able to gain a recovery against an employer because of an injury sustained at work. Even if an injured employee was fortunate enough to win, legal fees ate up a good portion of any award. Thus, the "fault system" of tort liability provided little protection for employees, wasted time and money in the legal process, and failed to stimulate any action toward accident prevention by employers.

The first effort to reform the laws to promote safety and health in the workplace began in the states in the form of workmen's (now workers') compensation laws. These laws require the employer to pay damages to employees injured on the job regardless of who was at fault. Since the negligence or fault of the employer or employees are not an issue, the law affords the employee an assured recovery. In turn, the law limits the dollar amount of damages the employer must pay to the injured employee. Sometimes, the employers pay monies to a state fund and an industrial commission decides which employees are entitled to recovery. Other states allow employers to be self-insured or to purchase insurance for the protection of the employees.

INJURED ON THE JOB?

Littlefield v. Pillsbury Co.
6 Ohio St. 3d _____. (1983).
Supreme Court of Ohio

[Littlefield was employed as a grain operator for The Pillsbury Company. No food was provided at the employer's plant and the employees were therefore required to leave the premises to obtain their lunch unless they elected to bring their lunch, which could be eaten in a room provided for that purpose. Littlefield obtained his lunch with his co-worker at the closest available luncheon facility. This was approximately one-eighth (1/8th) of a mile from the Pillsbury plant on River Road, a four-lane public highway.

Upon returning to the entrance of the Pillsbury plant, by the most necessary and direct possible route, the vehicle in which Littlefield was a passenger was required to wait before turning left due to ongoing heavy truck traffic as is customarily found on River Road. Immediately before the crash, Littlefield's vehicle was stopped, with its left turn signal on. Pillsbury's entrance, at which Littlefield was waiting on River Road, was the only means of ingress and egress to Pillsbury's plant. While so waiting, the car was struck from the rear by a grain truck causing multiple injuries including quadriplegia to Littlefield.

Littlefield was denied compensation from the Bureau of Workers' Compensation because Littlefield had ". . . failed to establish the necessary causal connection between his injuries and his employment."]

Our analysis begins with the fundamental requirement in R.C. 4123.01(C) that a compensable injury must occur in the "course of, and arising out of, the injured employee's employment." The statutory mandate has been clarified and defined over the years by the judiciary. This court set forth "[t]he test of the right to participate in the Workers' Compensation Fund is not whether there was any fault or neglect on the part of the employer or his employees, but whether a 'causal connection' existed between an employee's injury and his employment either through the activities, the conditions or the environment of the employment."

The determination of whether an injury has occurred in the "course of and arising out of employment" has been aided by the "going and coming" rule. "As a general rule where an employee, having a fixed and limited place of employment, sustains an injury while traveling to and from his place of employment, such injury does not evidence the required causal connection to the employment: it therefore does not arise out of and in the course of his employment and is not compensable."

The "special hazard or risk" exception is a means of avoiding the strict application of the general rule. Accordingly, an employee will be entitled to compensation, if the employment creates a special risk, for injuries sustained in the scope of that risk. A special risk may be on the employer's premises or involve the necessary means of access to the premises, even when the access is not under the employer's control or management. Thus, when the injury occurs on the only route or at least on the normal route, which the employees must use to reach the premises, the special hazards of that route may become hazards of the employment.

The exception has been applied by other jurisdictions in left-turn cases. For example, in *Pacific Indem N. Co.* v. *Indus. Acc. Comm.* (1946), 28 Cal. 2d 329, the employee's route to work required a left-turn across oncoming traffic to enter the company parking lot. The court found that the required left turn was a special risk of the employment and held that the injury occurred in the course of employment.

Although Ohio has not specifically enunciated the special hazards exception, we have said that a compensable injury need not occur on the premises. "Compensability, however, is not in every instance limited to injuries sustained on the employer's premises." *Bralley* v. *Daugherty* 61 Ohio St. 2d 302 (1980).

Ohio courts have also concluded that an employee is no longer subject to the strict application of the general rule excluding compensation for going and coming to work once the zone of employment is reached.

Young's treatise on Ohio workers' compensation law states that

the theme of the decisions which have considered the geography aspects of course of employment are uniform in noting that the environment of the em-

ployment may extend out beyond the premises of the employer and that the additional territory is described as being within the zone of employment. Environment means the capability of producing injury and it is usually described as the existence of hazards that are peculiar to the employment as contrasted with hazards that are likely to exist anywhere and bear no relationship to the employment.

Young notes that the control of the area or zone in which the injury occurred has been a significant factor in establishing the injury occurred in the course of the employment. However, a hazard may exist in an area beyond the control of the employer. In appropriate cases, a special hazard may "form a basis for causation to satisfy the requirement of the component, arising out of employment."

A special hazard peculiar to the employment was the basis for awarding compensation in an earlier Ohio case. In *Henry*, compensation was allowed when an employee sustained fatal injuries in crossing a railroad track which was immediately adjacent to the sole means of ingress and egress to this employer's plant.

Thus, this court has found exceptions to the strict application of the going and coming rule. Compensation has been allowed for injuries which have occurred off the premises when there has been a causal connection between the injuries and the employment.

Based upon the aforementioned cases, we join other jurisdictions in adopting a special hazard rule which allows compensation for injuries occurring off the work premises, before or after work, if the injury occurs because of the hazard created by the employment. This position is consistent with the test this court has used to determine the right to compensation, whether a causal connection exists between an employee's injuries and the activities, conditions or environment of the employment. We agree with the New York Court of Appeals that the mere fact that an accident took place on a public street does not *ipso facto* negate the right to compensation. Instead the totality of the circumstances should be considered when applying the causal connection test.

To aid in determining whether the special hazard rule should apply, we adopt the two-prong test devised by the California Supreme Court . . . (which) held that the rule will apply "(1) if 'but for' the employment, the employee would not have been at the location where the injury occurred and (2) if the 'risk is distinctive in nature or quantitatively greater than risks common to the public.'"

Applying these principles to this case, the facts are similar to those which constituted a special hazard in *Henry*. Littlefield and his co-worker chose the closest available lunch facility, approximately one-eighth of a mile from the plant. They returned by the necessary and most direct possible route. As they waited to make a left turn, with the left-turn signal on, into the only means of ingress and egress to the plant, the car was struck from the rear. Thus, in both cases the accident occurred immediately adjacent to the sole means of ingress and egress to the employer's plant.

Furthermore, applying the California test for a special hazard, the first prong of a test is met. It is clear that "but for" his employment, Littlefield would not have been making a left turn into the plant. The second prong of the test is also satisfied because, although the risk attendant to the busy road was common to the general public using it, Littlefield's risk was peculiar and to an abnormal degree. That is, his risk was "quantitatively greater" than that to which other motorists occasionally driving down the road are subjected. The regular exposure to the common risk plus the risk of making a left turn creates a greater degree of risk and sustains the causal relationship between the employment and the accident resulting from the risk.

This conclusion is buttressed by the fact that Littlefield had already reported for work and was merely on an overdue break compared to the claimants in other jurisdictions,

which apply the special hazard rule, who were going to work or leaving after the workday. Littlefield was scheduled to work a twelve-hour day, had been required to work through a fifteen minute paid morning break as well as an unpaid thirty minute lunch break. . . .

In comparison, the record in *Henry* indicates that the employee arrived for work about 2:00 A.M. After about an hour on the job, he left the premises for breakfast at a nearby restaurant and the accident occurred as he returned to work. The off-premises breakfast practice was acquiesced in by the employer as it contributed to the worker's efficiency. The court concluded that it was a custom incidental to the employment. Thus, compared to *Henry*, Littlefield had worked many more hours before taking an overdue break. Therefore, the break should have contributed more to his productivity than to the worker in *Henry* and could similarly be considered incidental to the employment.

We are mindful that R.C. 4123.95 requires that sections 4123.01 to 4123.94, inclusive, be liberally construed in favor of employees. Therefore, we agree with courts of other jurisdictions which have adopted the special hazard rule. That is, an employee will be entitled to workers' compensation benefits when the employment creates a special hazard and the injuries are sustained because of that hazard. When a special hazard causes an injury to an employee on his way to or from work, the injury is compensable as arising out of the employment.

The facts of this case satisfy the two-pronged test for applying the special hazard rule. Therefore, Littlefield should not be precluded from recovering compensation.

J. Locher, dissenting.

Today's decision will ruin the Workers' Compensation Fund in Ohio. The majority has elected to state a broad rule . . . which effectively insures all risks, coming and going, portal to portal and beyond.

In effect, the majority has legislated a universal super-insurance without actuarial basis via the Workers' Compensation Fund. Endless ramifications are certain to follow, because the majority position creates insurance without consideration of moral hazard. That is, an employee who is negligent on his way to or from work can now recover from his employer for his own damages.

All of this creates another uncontrollable cost of doing business elsewhere. For example, fixed-situs service employees typically encounter much less on-the-job risk than do industrial employees. Yet, the majority deems commuting to work to be an appropriate cost for all employers to bear. Just as the economies of Ohio and the entire country are adjusting away from industry toward more services, the majority creates a new burden on business for service employers.

Liability under the Workers' Compensation Fund will now also extend into employees' homes. We need only to examine the two-pronged standard . . . to understand why.

"But for" their jobs, many employees would not live in a certain "location" which may, for example, have convenient access to the employer's place of business. Furthermore, given the facts of this case, future claimants need not take the "distinctive in nature or quantitatively greater" risk standard seriously. That is, in today's Ohio there is nothing either distinctive or exceptionally risky about making a left-hand turn.

By comparison, therefore, employees who bathe at home before leaving for work each morning because they are expected to "look good on the job" will have viable workers' compensation claims should they slip in the bathtub. Their employment creates the "distinctive" risk of good hygiene, and recovery—under the majority view—naturally follows.

At the very least, the holding and facts of this case make compensable the injuries of an employee who negligently makes a left-hand turn from a public road anywhere along that employee's commute to or from work or during his lunch hour. It is difficult to comprehend why anyone should accept responsibility for insuring risks such as those, except the people best able to minimize them—the employees themselves.

I recognize that R.C. 4123.95 requires that we construe workers' compensation statutes liberally. Certainly, we should strive to ensure that injured workers recover for every compensable injury for which there is a legitimate, work related basis. Yet, the majority . . . opinion is so broad that this case will wreak havoc on the Workers' Compensation Fund and ultimately harm the workers whom the fund is intended to protect.

I must, therefore, dissent from both the result and the rationale of the majority.

Questions
1. What is the "going and coming" rule? What is the special "hazard and risk" exception?
2. What is the two-prong test, adopted by the court, to apply the special hazard rule? How were these tests met in Littlefield's situation?
3. According to the dissenting opinion, how is the majority opinion ruining the Workers' Compensation Fund?
4. Do you agree with the dissent's conclusion that employees who are injured while bathing at home in preparation for work will be able to obtain recovery from the Workers' Compensation Fund?

OCCUPATIONAL DISEASES

While all states provide coverage for occupational diseases, the award of compensation for this type of "injury" has lagged behind compensation for occupational accidents. In the following case the court was faced with the question of whether psychological problems arising from stressful employment are compensable as an occupational disease.

Transportation Insurance Co. v. Maksyn
567 S.W.2d. 845 (1978)
The Texas Court of Civil Appeals

[Maksyn sought to recover a workers' compensation award from Transportation Insurance on the basis of an occupational disease obtained in the course of his employment. He claimed that the pressures of his employment caused him to suffer from anxiety depression, which caused numbness of his hands and feet, high blood pressure, and vertigo. The jury found (1) that Maksyn had an occupational disease as a result of traumatic repetitious physical activities extending over a period of time; (2) that the occupational disease sustained by Maksyn arose out of and in the course of his employment; (3) that the occupational disease was a cause of his total incapacity; and (4) that the total incapacity was permanent. Maksyn was awarded weekly payments of $70 each. The employer, called plaintiff on this appeal, sought to set aside the award.]

Defendant, at time of suit, was 62 years old. He began working with the Express-News Publishing Company in 1932 when he was 17 years of age, as a copy boy. He was later promoted to assistant merchandise manager, to display advertising salesman, to production manager, to administrative executive, and finally to advertising service manager, a position that he held for approximately 28 years.

Defendant testified that he never worked less than 55 hours a week and frequently worked for 65 hours a week. His work schedule ran from Monday through Saturday and he generally worked some time on Sunday. He stated that at night he would receive phone calls from the office and many times had to return to work at night and that he frequently took work home.

Defendant testified that during the week before September 4, 1974, he worked 87½ hours, and that on the evening of September 4, 1974, he started feeling bad, that he felt pressure in his head and felt like he was going to black out. He then went home and went to bed and the next morning when he tried to get up, he felt weak and dizzy and later that day he went to his family physician. He thereafter returned to his office and advised his supervisors of his illness and requested that he be given vacation time, which was granted. He remained on vacation for three weeks. On the fourth week, he began working approximately three to four hours a day. The following week, he worked approximately four to five hours a day, and the following week approximately seven to eight hours a day. On October 28, 1974, he was retired by his employer. At that time, he was sixty years of age.

* * *

In 1971, the Texas Legislature amended the section of the Workmen's Compensation Act relating to the definition of "injury" and "occupational diseases," which new provision is as follows:

. . . Whenever the term "Occupational Disease" is used in the Workmen's Compensation Laws of this

State, such [term] shall be construed to mean any disease arising out of and in the course of employment which causes damage or harm to the physical structure of the body and such other diseases or infections as naturally result therefrom. An "Occupational Disease" shall also include damage or harm to the physical structure of the body occurring as the result of repetitious physical traumatic activities extending over a period of time and arising in the course of employment; provided, that the date of the cumulative injury shall be the date disability was caused thereby.

* * *

Plaintiff argues vigorously that it was not the intent of the Legislature to include mental traumatic activities and discusses in some detail the legislative background in connection with such amendment to [the Act], and points out that the House version of the amendment omitted the word "mental" from that of the Senate version. However, it is noteworthy that the amendment as adopted provides in Section 5, as follows:

It is the express intent of the Legislature in enacting this Act that nothing contained in this Act shall ever be deemed or considered to limit or expand recovery in cases of mental trauma accompanied by physical trauma.

* * *

We have found no Texas cases holding that recovery will never be permitted for mental injury or mental disease, and, as we construe the applicable cases, the court seems to be saying not that there can never be a recovery for a mental injury or mental illness, but that the claimant must produce sufficient probative evidence to convince the jury.

There is a conflict of authorities in out-of-state jurisdictions with some out-of-state jurisdictions holding that a disabling mental condition brought about by a gradual buildup of emotional stress over a period of time and not by one exceptional injury causing event, is not compensable unless accomplished by physical force of exertion.

* * *

Other out-of-state jurisdictions have reached a contrary result. . . .

* * *

Plaintiff argues that the disability here involved results purely from mentally traumatic activities and as such is not compensable under the Workmen's Compensation Act. The record here shows that the disability resulted from a combination of physical and mental activities including exceedingly long working hours, nerve racking working schedule, continuous pressure, strain, overwork, and physical exhaustion culminating in high blood pressure, numbness in some parts of the body, dizziness, vertigo and, ultimately, inability to work. There was ample evidence of a combination of physical and mental activities that produced the occupational disease here involved, and it is clear that the claimant has suffered damage or harm to the physical structure of his body.

Questions
1. Did this court recognize any difference in "mental" traumatic activities and "physical" traumatic activities? Did the Texas legislature mean for a difference to exist?
2. Should recovery for psychic injury be limited to a slow buildup of stressful activities or include a psychic injury that results from a single traumatic event?

OCCUPATIONAL SAFETY AND HEALTH ACT

Workers' compensation laws allow businesses to deal with their safety problems as they see fit. Businesses are free to adopt the strategy of reducing accidents and lowering their insurance premiums or operating costs. On the other hand, if actions to reduce accidents would be prohibitively costly, businesses are not forced to undertake them. Instead, businesses would merely be required to pay the cost of injuries in the workplace. Given these options available to employers, it is not surprising that workers' compensation laws did not make a significant impact on the safety and health problems in the workplace.

The Occupational Safety and Health Act of 1970 (OSHA) was the result of testimony and documentary evidence presented before Congress that pointed out that the American worksite was a place of peril. More than 14,500 workers were killed annually in connection with their jobs, a mortality rate two and one half times greater than that experienced by U.S. troops in Vietnam. More than 2,200,000 workers are disabled in America each year, and this represents a loss of about 250 million worker-days, which is in excess of lost work time due to strikes. Of course, these statistics do not measure the social and emotional cost to the individuals injured or to their families.

The purpose of the act was "to assure so far as possible every working man and woman in the nation safe and healthful working conditions to preserve our human resources." To accomplish this mandate, Congress outlined the following specific means.

1. Encourage employers and employees to reduce hazards in the workplace and to implement new or improved existing safety and health programs.
2. Establish "separate but dependant responsibilities and rights" for employers and employees for the achievement of better safety and health conditions.
3. Establish reporting and record-keeping procedures to monitor job-related injuries and illnesses.
4. Develop mandatory job safety and health standards and enforce them effectively.
5. Encourage the state to assume the fullest responsibility for establishing and administering their own occupational safety and health programs, which must be "at least as effective as" the federal program.

Three federal agencies were created to develop and enforce occupational safety and health standards. The Occupational Safety and Health Administration is a component part of the Department of Labor with authority to promulgate standards, make inspections, and enforce the act. The National Institute for Occupational Safety and Health (NIOSH) is a component part of the Department of Health and Human Resources. Its primary function is to conduct research on various safety and health problems and recommend standards for OSHA administrators to adopt. The Occupational Safety and Health Review

Commission is an independant agency whose primary functions are to handle all appeals from actions taken by OSHA administrators and to evaluate penalties recommended by OSHA administrators.

SAFE WORK ENVIRONMENT

OSHA requires business organizations to maintain a work environment free from recognized hazards. The duty placed on the employer is no more than the common law concept that a person must refrain from action that will cause harm to others. The following case illustrates a situation where the employer failed to remove the dangers of a recognized hazard and discusses whether OSHA administrators or the employer has the burden of proof that feasibility of compliance was nonexistent.

Ace Sheeting & Repair v. Occup. S. & H. Review Commission
555 F.2d 439 (1977)
U.S. Court of Appeals (5th Cir.)

The facts are undisputed. Petitioner Ace Sheeting and Repair Company is a roof repair company. In September 1973 J. C. Ledger, the owner of Ace, and employee Stroud were replacing corrugated metal panels on the roof of a warehouse in Houston. The roof was pitched rather steeply and contained 60 skylight openings arranged in two rows running the length of the building. The skylights were covered with a translucent plastic material called coralux. There was no guard rail or cover around or over any of these skylights. While walking to another section of the roof to obtain additional materials Stroud stepped in the middle of one of the coralux sheets. The sheet gave way beneath his 175-pound weight, and Stroud fell 25 feet to his death.

A few days after this fatality the Secretary of Labor inspected the job site. On the basis of this inspection, Ace was served with a citation for violation of § 1926.500(b)(4). That section provides:

Wherever there is danger of falling through a skylight opening, it shall be guarded by a fixed stan-

dard railing on all exposed sides or a cover capable of sustaining the weight of a 200-pound person.

This regulation was promulgated by the Secretary under the Act. Title 29 U.S.C.A § 654(a)(2) imposes on all employers covered by the Act the duty to comply with such regulations. The proposed penalty in the citation served on Ace was a $30 fine.

Ace challenged the citation, and a hearing was held before an administrative law judge. . . . The administrative law judge vacated the citation on the ground that the Secretary had failed to prove that compliance with the regulation was feasible under the circumstances. The Commission reversed by a two-to-one vote. Ace petitioned this Court for review of that decision. . . .

The outcome of this case turns on who has the burden of proof. Must the Secretary prove that compliance with the regulation is feasible, as thought by the administrative law judge; or is feasibility of compliance assumed unless the employer proves otherwise

Title 29 U.S.C.A. §654(a) creates two kinds

of obligations requiring employers to take steps for the occupational safety and health of their employees:

Each employer—
(1) shall furnish to each of his employees employment and a place of employment which are free from recognized hazards that are causing or are likely to cause death or serious physical harm to his employees;
(2) shall comply with occupational safety and health standards promulgated under this chapter.

Paragraph (1) has come to be called the "general duty clause," while paragraph (2) is referred to as the "specific duty clause." This case involves a safety standard promulgated under the specific duty clause. The Act itself gives no guidance as to who must bear the burden of proving the feasibility of eliminating a particular hazard under either clause.

Ace relies on *National Realty & Construction Co., Inc.* v. *OSHRC*, 489 F.2d 1257 (1973), to show that this burden is properly placed on the Secretary. But *National Realty* dealt with the general duty clause. No regulation or standard guided the employer as to the way to eliminate the hazard there involved. The D.C. Circuit for that reason placed the burden on the Secretary of demonstrating in what manner the Company's conduct fell short of the statutory mandate. The court reasoned that "the Secretary must be constrained to specify the particular steps a cited employer should have taken to avoid citation, and to demonstrate the feasibility and likely utility of those measures."

Two circuits have extended the *National Realty* principle to "specific duty clause" situations. . . .

In both [of those cases] . . . however, there was no specific direction as to what the employer should do. The regulations involved did nothing more than create, in effect, a general duty of the employer to meet a safety standard, without stating what specific employer conduct was required for compliance.

Here, the regulation stated specific ways for the employer to eliminate the hazard. If the employer put up guard rails or covered the skylights, the safety standard would have been met. If for any reason guard rails or covers are not feasible, the employer knows this better than anyone else, and it is reasonable to require him to come forward with the evidence to prove it.

Regulations are promulgated only after industry-wide comment during which time general feasibility considerations can be voiced. If a regulation contains a proposed method of abating a safety hazard which employers consider to be infeasible in the ordinary case, they can directly challenge the regulation as factually unsupported. Furthermore, a particular employer who finds that he cannot comply with the safety measures required by the regulations can request a variance. . . . When the citation stage is reached, it is eminently reasonable for courts to cast upon the employer the burden of proving impossibility of compliance.

The standard prescribed the precise conduct required of the employer. It may be easily complied with in many shops. Others may have difficulty, but where compliance with either of two specific alternatives, a guard rail or cover, would eliminate the hazard with which the deceased employee in this case was confronted, the employer should prove why he cannot meet either of those alternatives. We therefore hold that where a specific duty standard contains the method by which the work hazard is to be abated, the burden of proof is on the employer to demonstrate that the remedy contained in the regulation is infeasible under the particular circumstances.

To state this rule is to decide the present case. The factual decisions of the Commission are to be sustained if supported by substantial evidence on the record as a whole. Ace argues that even if it did have the burden of showing infeasibility, that burden was carried by the testimony of the Secretary's witnesses. Ace itself presented no evidence as to why it could not use skylight covers on this particular roof. Although the Secretary's witnesses did express some concern that skylight covers might slide off the pitched roof, the possibility of using "some type of abrasive surface on the bottom of a covering to . . . prevent the covering from sliding off the roof" was also discussed. In any event, on the state of the record, it was not the Secretary's job to describe precisely how covers or guard rails could be placed on Ace's premises. There is therefore sufficient evidence in the record to support the Commission's finding that "[i]mpossibility has not been established in this case." That being so, the citation for violation of 29 C.F.R. § 1926.500(b)(4) was proper, and the Commission's decision enforcing the $30 penalty is affirmed.

Questions

1. What is the employer's "general duty" under the act?
2. What is the employer's responsibility under the "specific duty clause"?
3. When must the Secretary of Labor prove that compliance with the regulations of OSHA is feasible in order to sustain its citations and penalties? When does the violating employer have the burden of proof that feasibility of compliance was nonexistent?

STANDARD SETTING

A safety or health standard is "a legally enforceable regulation governing conditions, practices, or operations to assure safe and healthful workplaces." These standards are published in the Federal Register.

To prod OSHA's inauguration, Congress ordered OSHA to adopt existing "national consensus standards." Within one month of its creation, OSHA adopted about 4400 consensus standards from previous federal regulations and from voluntary codes written by safety experts as voluntary industry guidelines. Unfortunately, many of these consensus standards were obsolete, irrelevant, and even trivial. For example, OSHA required toilet seats to be split and not round, and prohibited ice in drinking water because it might have been cut from polluted lakes.

These nitpicking regulations subjected OSHA to ridicule and criticisms. Finally, OSHA revoked over 900 of these early standards in 1978.

Two other criticisms of OSHA's early standards to some extent remain today. First, the standards were dominated by design standards rather than performance standards. Design standards are specification-oriented, as in requiring ladders to have rungs one inch thick. Performance standards would, in contrast, stipulate that the ladder must support some capacity of pounds. The disadvantage of design standards is their interference with safety innovations. Beginning with the Carter Administration, OSHA has attempted to convert many of its design standards into performance standards.

A second criticism of OSHA's early standards was their emphasis on safety, rather than health. Because of the complex nature of the hazards to health caused by dangerous chemicals, OSHA's initial efforts in this field were slow.

During OSHA's first five years, only three health-related standards were formulated. During OSHA's next five years, eight health-related standards were completed, but many were challenged in the courts.

Significant Risk

Industrial Union v. American Petrol. Inst.
448 US 607 (1980)
Supreme Court of the United States

Justice Stevens

The Occupational Safety and Health Act of 1970 was enacted for the purpose of ensuring safe and healthful working conditions for every working man and woman in the Nation. This litigation concerns a standard promulgated by the Secretary of Labor to regulate occupational exposure to benzene, a substance which has been shown to cause cancer at high exposure levels. The principal question is whether such a showing is a sufficient basis for a standard that places the most stringent limitation on exposure to benzene that is technologically and economically possible.

The Act delegates broad authority to the Secretary to promulgate different kinds of standards. The basic definition of an "occupational safety and health standard" is found in § 3(8), which provides:

The term 'occupational safety and health standard' means a standard which requires . . . the adoption or use of one or more practices . . . reasonably necessary or appropriate to provide safe or healthful employment. . . .

Where toxic materials or harmful physical agents are concerned, a standard must also comply with § 6(b)(5), which provides:

The Secretary, in promulgating standards dealing with toxic materials, shall set the standard which most adequately assures, to the extent feasible, on the basis of the best available evidence, that no employee will suffer material impairment of health or functional capacity even if such employee has regu-

lar exposure to the hazard dealt with by such standard for the period of his working life. . . .

Wherever the toxic material to be regulated is a carcinogen, the Secretary has taken the position that no safe exposure level can be determined and that §6(b)(5) requires him to set an exposure limit at the lowest technologically feasible level that will not impair the viability of the industries regulated. In this case, after having determined that there is a causal connection between benzene and leukemia (a cancer of the white blood cells), the Secretary set an exposure limit on airborne concentrations of benzene of one part benzene per million parts of air. . . .

*　*　*

Any discussion of the 1ppm exposure limit must, of course, begin with the Agency's rationale for imposing that limit. The written explanation of the standard fills 184 pages of the printed appendix. Much of it is devoted to a discussion of the voluminous evidence of the adverse effects of exposure to benzene at levels of concentration well above 10ppm. This discussion demonstrates that there is ample justification for regulating occupational exposure to benzene and that the prior limit of 10ppm . . . was reasonable. It does not, however, provide direct support for the Agency's conclusion that the limit should be reduced from 10ppm to 1ppm.

The evidence in the administrative record of adverse effects of benzene exposure at 10ppm is sketchy at best. OSHA noted that there was "no dispute" that certain nonmalignant blood disorders, evidenced by a reduction level of red or white cells or platelets in the blood, could result from exposures of 25–40 ppm. It then stated that several studies had indicated that relatively slight changes in normal blood values could result from exposures below 25ppm and perhaps below 10ppm. OSHA did not attempt to make any estimate based on these studies of how significant the risk of nonmalignant disease would be at exposures of 10ppm or less.

* * *

In the end OSHA's rationale for lowering the permissible exposure limit to 1ppm was based, not on any finding that leukemia has ever been caused by exposure to 10ppm of benzene and that it will *not* be caused by exposure to 1ppm, but rather on a series of assumptions indicating that some leukemias might result from exposure to 10ppm and that the number of cases might be reduced by reducing the exposure level to 1ppm. In reaching that result, the Agency first unequivocally concluded that benzene is a human carcinogen. Second, it concluded that industry has failed to prove that there is a safe threshold level of exposure to benzene below which no excess leukemia cases would occur. In reaching this conclusion OHSA rejected industry contentions that certain epidemiological studies indicating no excess risk of leukemia among workers exposed at levels below 10ppm were sufficient to establish that the threshold level of safe exposure was at or above 10ppm. . . .

[Instead] . . . the Agency applied its standard policy with respect to carcinogens, concluding that, in the absence of definitive proof of a safe level, it must be assumed that any level above zero presents some increased risk of cancer.

Under the Government's view, §3(8), if it has any substantive content at all, merely requires OSHA to issue standards that are reasonably calculated to produce a safer or more healthy work environment. Apart from this minimal requirement of rationality, the Government argues that § 3(8) imposes no limits on the Agency's power, and thus would not prevent it from requiring employers to do whatever would be "reasonably necessary" to eliminate all risks of any harm from their workplaces. With respect to toxic substances and harmful physical agents, the Government takes an even more extreme position. Relying on § 6(b)(5)'s direction to set a standard "which most adequately assures . . . that no employee will suffer material impairment of health or functional capacity," the Government contends that the Secretary is required to impose standards that either guarantee workplaces that are free from any risk of material health impairment, however small, or that come as close as possible to doing so without ruining entire industries.

If the purpose of the statute were to eliminate completely and with absolute certainty any risk of serious harm, we would agree that it would be proper for the Secretary to interpret §§3(8) and 6(b)(5) in this fashion. But we think it is clear that the statute was not designed to require employers to provide absolutely risk-free workplaces whenever it is technologically feasible to do so, so long as the cost is not great enough to destroy an entire industry. Rather, both the language and structure of the Act, as well as its legislative history, indicate that it was intended to require the elimination, as far as feasible, of significant risks of harm.

By empowering the Secretary to promulgate standards that are "reasonably necessary or appropriate to provide safe or healthful employment and places of employment," the Act implies that, before promulgating any standard, the Secretary must make a finding that the workplaces in question are not safe. But "safe" is not the equivalent of "risk-free." There are many activities that we engage in every day—such as driving a car or even breathing city air—that entail some risk of accident or material health impairment; nevertheless, few people would consider these activities "unsafe." Similarly, a workplace can hardly be considered "unsafe" unless it threatens the workers with a significant risk of harm.

Therefore, before he can promulgate any permanent health or safety standard, the Secretary is required to make a threshold finding that a place of employment is unsafe—in the sense that significant risks are present and can be eliminated or lessened by a change in practices. . . .

*   *   *

Contrary to the Government's contentions, imposing a burden on the Agency of demonstrating a significant risk of harm will not strip it of its ability to regulate carcinogens, nor will it require the Agency to wait for deaths to occur before taking any action. First, the requirement that a "significant" risk be identified is not a mathematical straitjacket. It is the Agency's responsibility to determine, in the first instance, what it considers to be a "significant" risk. Some risks are plainly acceptable and others are plainly unacceptable. If, for example, the odds are one in a billion that a person will die from cancer by taking a drink of chlorinated water, the risk clearly could not be considered significant. On the other hand, if the odds are one in a thousand that regular inhalation of gasoline vapors that are 2% benzene will be fatal, a reasonable person might well consider the risk significant and take appropriate steps to decrease or eliminate it. Although the Agency has no duty to calculate the exact probability of harm, it does have an obligation to find that a significant risk is present before it can characterize a place of employment as "unsafe."

Second, OSHA is not required to support its finding that a significant risk exists with anything approaching scientific certainty. Although the Agency's findings must be supported by substantial evidence, §6(b)(5) specifically allows the Secretary to regulate on the basis of the "best available evidence." As several Courts of Appeals have held, this provision requires a reviewing court to give OSHA some leeway where its findings must be made on the frontiers of scientific knowledge. Thus, so long as they are supported by a body of reputable scientific thought, the Agency is free to use conservative assumptions in interpreting the data with respect to carcinogens, risking error on the side of overprotection rather than underprotection.

Finally, the record in this case and OSHA's own rulings on other carcinogens indicate that there are a number of ways in which the Agency can make a rational judgment about the relative significance of the risks associated with exposure to a particular carcinogen.

It should also be noted that, in setting a permissible exposure level in reliance on less-than-perfect methods, OSHA would have the benefit of a backstop in the form of monitoring and medical testing. Thus, if OSHA properly determined that the permissible exposure limit should be set at 5ppm, it could still require monitoring and medical testing for employees exposed to lower levels. By doing so, it could keep a constant check on the validity of the assumptions made in developing the permissible exposure limit, giving it a sound evidentiary basis for decreasing the limit if it was initially set too high. Moreover, in this way it could ensure that workers who were unusually susceptible to benzene could be removed from exposure before they had suffered any permanent damage.

*   *   *

In this case the record makes it perfectly clear that the Secretary relied squarely on a special policy for carcinogens that imposed the burden on industry of proving the existence of a safe level of exposure, thereby avoiding the Secretary's threshold responsibility of establishing the need for more stringent standards. In so interpreting his statutory authority, the Secretary exceeded his power.

Questions

1. OSHA requires the Secretary of Labor to set standards "reasonably necessary" for healthful employment "to the extent feasible." Do these words simply imply a congressional intent to make the workplace "risk-free" or "safe"?
2. To promulgate a health standard, OSHA requires a finding that the work environment be "unsafe," justifying the new standard. Did the Secretary make such a finding in this instance?
3. Under OSHA's cancer policy, the Secretary required the industry to prove the existence of a safe level of exposure prior to OSHA's finding of an "unsafe environment." Is this procedure authorized under the act?

Cost-Benefit Analysis?

American Textile Mfrs. Inst. v. Donovan
452 US 490 (1981)
Supreme Court of the United States

Justice Brennan

In 1978, the Secretary, acting though the Occupational Safety and Health Administration (OSHA), promulgated a standard limiting occupational exposure to cotton dust, an airborne particle byproduct of the preparation and manufacture of cotton products, exposure to which induces a "constellation of respiratory effects" known as "byssinosis."

* * *

Byssinosis, known in its more severe manifestations as "brown lung" disease, is a serious and potentially disabling respiratory disease primarily caused by the inhalation of cotton dust. Byssinosis is a "continuum . . . disease," that has been categorized into four grades (Grade ½, Grade 1, Grade 2, Grade 3.)

* * *

While there is some uncertainty over the manner in which the disease progresses from its least serious to its disabling grades, it is likely that prolonged exposure contributes to the progression. It also appears that a worker may suddenly contract a severe grade without experiencing milder grades of the disease.

Estimates indicate that at least 35,000 employed and retired cotton mill workers, or 1 in 12 workers, suffer from the most disabling form of byssinosis. The Senate Report accompanying the Act cited estimates that 100,000 active and retired workers suffer from some grade of the disease.

* * *

In 1974, the Director of the National Institute for Occupational Safety and Health (NIOSH), pursuant to the Act, submitted to the Secretary of Labor a recommendation for a cotton dust standard with a permissible exposure limit (PEL) that "should be set at the lowest level feasible, but in no case at an environmental concentration as high as 200 $\mu g/m^3$ of lint-free respirable dust. Several months later, OSHA published an Advance Notice of Proposed Rulemaking, requesting comments from interested parties on the NIOSH recommendation and other related matters. Soon thereafter, the Textile Worker's Union of America, joined by the North Carolina Public Interest Research Group, petitioned the Secretary, urging a more stringent PEL of 100 $\mu g/m^3$.

On December 28, 1976, OSHA published a proposal on cotton dust with a new permanent standard. The proposed standard contained a PEL of 200 $\mu g/m^3$ . . . for all segments of the cotton industry. It also suggested an implementation strategy for achieving the PEL that relied on respirators for the short term and engineering controls for the long term. OSHA invited interested parties to submit written comments within a 90-day period.

Following the comment period, OSHA conducted three hearings in Washington, D.C., Greenville, Miss., and Lubbock, Tex., that lasted over 14 days. . . .

The Cotton Dust Standard promulgated by OSHA establishes mandatory PEL's over an 8-hour period of 200 $\mu g/m^3$ for yarn manufacturing, 750 $\mu g/m^3$ for slashing and weaving operations, and 500 $\mu g/m^3$ for all other processes in the cotton industry. These levels represent a relaxation of the proposed PEL of 200$\mu g/m^3$ for all segments of the cotton industry.

OSHA chose an implementation strategy for the Standard that depended primarily on a mix of engineering controls, such as installation of ventilation systems, and work practice controls, such as special floor-sweeping procedures. Full compliance with the PEL's is required within four years, except to the extent that employers can establish that the engineering and work practice controls are infeasible. During this compliance period, and at certain other times, the Standard requires employers to provide respirators to employees. Other requirements include monitoring of cotton dust exposure, medical surveillance of all employees, annual medical examinations, employee education and training programs, and the posting of warning signs.

On the basis of the evidence in the record as a whole, the Secretary determined that exposure to cotton dust represents a "significant health hazard to employees," and that "the prevalence of byssinosis should be significantly reduced" by the adoption of the Standard's PEL's. In assessing the health risks from cotton dust and the risk reduction obtained from lowered exposure, OSHA relied particularly on data showing a strong linear relationship between the prevalence of byssinosis and the concentration of lint-free respirable cotton dust. Even at the 200 $\mu g/m^3$ PEL, OSHA found that the prevalence of at least Grade ½ byssinosis would be 13% of all employees in the yarn manufacturing sector. In promulgating the Cotton Dust Standard, OSHA interpreted the Act to require adoption of the most stringent standard to protect against material health impairment, bounded only by technological and economic feasibility. OSHA therefore rejected the industry's alternative proposal for PEL of 500 $\mu g/m^3$ in yarn manufacturing, a proposal which would produce a 25% prevalence of at least Grade ½ byssinosis. The agency expressly found the Standard to be both technologically and economically feasible based on the evidence in the record as a whole. Although recognizing that permitted levels of exposure to cotton dust would still cause some byssinosis, OSHA nevertheless rejected the union proposal for a 100 $\mu g/m^3$ PEL because it was not within the "technological capabilities of the industry." Similarly, OSHA set PEL's for some segments of the cotton industry at 500 $\mu g/m^3$ in part because of limitations of technological feasibility. Finally, the Secretary found that "engineering dust controls in weaving may not be feasible even with massive expenditures by the industry," and for that and other reasons adopted a less stringent PEL of 750 $\mu g/m^3$ for weaving and slashing.

* * *

The principal question presented in these cases is whether the Occupational Safety and Health Act requires the Secretary, in promulgating a standard pursuant to §§6(b)(5) and 3(8) of the Act, to determine that the costs of the standard bear a reasonable relationship to its benefits. Relying on §§6(b)(5) and 3(8) of the Act, petitioners urge not only that OSHA must show that a standard addresses a significant risk of material health impairment, but also that OSHA must demonstrate that the reduction in risk of material health impairment is significant in light of the costs of attaining that reduction. Respondents on the other hand contend that the Act requires OSHA to promulgate standards that eliminate or reduce such risks "to the extent such protection is technologically and economically feasible." To resolve this debate, we must turn to the language, structure, and legislative history of the Act.

The starting point of our analysis is the language of the statute itself. Section §6(b)(5) of the Act, (emphasis added), provides:

The Secretary, in promulgating standards dealing with toxic materials or harmful physical agents under this subsection, shall set the standard which most adequately assures, *to the extent feasible,* on the best available evidence, that no employee will suffer material impairment of health or functional capacity even if such employee has regular exposure to the hazard dealt with by such standard for the period of his working life.

Although their interpretations differ, all parties agree that the phrase "to the extent feasible" contains the critical language in §6(b)(5) for purposes of these cases.

The plain meaning of the word "feasible" supports respondents' interpretation of the statute. According to *Webster's Third New International Dictionary of the English Language* 831 (1976), "feasible" means "capable of being done, executed, or effected." . . . Thus, §6(b)(5) directs the Secretary to issue the standard that "most adequately assures . . . that no employee will suffer material impairment of health," limited only by the extent to which this is "capable of being done." In effect then, as the Court of Appeals held, Congress itself defined the basic relationship between costs and

benefits, by placing the "benefit" of worker health above all other considerations save those making attainment of this "benefit" unachievable. Any standard based on a balancing of costs and benefits by the Secretary that strikes a different balance than that struck by Congress would be inconsistent with the command set forth in §6(b)(5). Thus, cost-benefit analysis by OSHA is not required by the statute because feasibility analysis is.

When Congress has intended that an agency engage in cost-benefit analysis, it has clearly indicated such intent on the face of the statute. . . . These . . . statutes demonstrate that Congress uses specific language when intending that an agency engage in cost-benefit analysis. Certainly in light of its ordinary meaning, the word "feasible" cannot be construed to articulate such congressional intent. We therefore reject the argument that Congress required cost-benefit analysis in §6(b)(5).

* * *

The legislative history of the Act, while concededly not crystal clear, provides general support for respondents' interpretation of the Act, The congressional Reports and debates certainly confirm that Congress meant "feasible" and nothing else in using that term. Congress was concerned that the Act might be thought to require achievement of absolute safety, an impossible standard, and therefore insisted that health and safety goals be capable of economic and technological accomplishment. Perhaps most telling is the absence of any indication whatsoever that Congress intended OSHA to conduct its own cost-benefit analysis before promulgating a toxic material or harmful physical agent standard. The legislative history demonstrates conclusively that Congress was fully aware that the Act would impose real and substantial costs of compliance on industry, and believed that such costs were part of the cost of doing business. . . .

Questions

1. What standard for cotton dust exposure was recommended by the National Institute for Occupational Safety and Health? What standard did the labor unions recommend? What standard did OSHA establish?
2. Did the evidence support the Secretary's determination that exposure to cotton dust represents a "significant health hazard"?
3. Did OSHA present evidence that this health hazard could be significantly reduced by the adoption of OSHA's standards?
4. Why did OSHA reject the union's proposal?
5. Did Congress intend for OSHA to engage in cost-benefit analysis prior to setting standards?
6. Explain the difference between a cost-benefit standard and a feasibility standard?

Variances

Variances from promulgated standards may be petitioned for and granted under certain circumstances. A *permanent* variance may be permitted if the Secretary of Labor decides that employers have demonstrated that they are using or will use safety measures that are at least as effective as the OSHA standards from which the variance is sought. A *temporary* variance will be granted only if the company can establish that it lacks the material, personnel, equipment, or some other item to comply with the standard and that it is taking all available steps to protect the employees against the hazard contemplated by the standard. Moreover, the company must demonstrate that it has an effective program to bring about compliance in the future. However, cost of compliance is not a valid factor to be considered in application for a variance.

OSHA ENFORCEMENT

Inspections

The act granted inspectors the right to have unannounced access to business establishments for inspection. This unannounced entry was challenged by an employer as a violation of the Fourth Amendment's protection against unreasonable searches of private property. The Supreme Court ruled that employers may bar OSHA inspectors who do not have search warrants and that the provision of OSHA's granting unannounced access to private property was unconstitutional. (See *Marshall* v. *Barlow's, Inc.* in Chapter 6.)

With employer consent or with a warrant, OSHA compliance officers may enter and inspect all facilities of any establishment covered by OSHA, which includes any business "affecting commerce." The employer or a designated representative participates in an opening conference with the compliance officer and then accompanies the officer during inspection of the facilities. The officer may confer with employees if no employee representative accompanies the officer during inspection. In any case, the officer may question any employee in private.

The OSHA representative must point out and discuss with the employees accompanying him or her any violation that the inspector discovers. However, the compliance officer does not suggest solutions or methods of correction for any violation discovered. After the inspection, the compliance officer confers with the employer and advises the employer concerning any conditions and practices that may constitute safety or health violations.

OSHA inspections are of four types.

1. *Accident investigations* are inspections following incidences involving fatalities and catastrophies. OSHA conducted 2304 such investigations in 1979.
2. *Employee complaints* can trigger an inspection. Over 20,000 investigations in 1979 resulted from employee complaints.
3. *Programmed inspections* are scheduled on the basis of sample selections where high-hazard industries are emphasized. In 1979, 23,763 programmed inspections were conducted. The Reagan Administration created an exemption for nearly three fourths of all U.S. manufacturing industries. Those firms that remain subject to routine safety inspection possess above-average injury incidences and account for 78 percent of the nation's annual serious manufacturing injuries.
4. *Follow-up inspections* occur in situations where citations have been issued. However, follow-up inspections for nonserious violations are rare. OSHA conducted 11,700 follow-up investigations in 1979.

Violations and Citations

When the inspector discovers an alleged violation, he or she issues the company a written citation, which describes the specific nature of that violation and the standard allegedly violated. The citation also fixes a time for abatement. All citations will be issued by the area director of OSHA and sent to the employer by certified mail. Thereafter, each citation must be prominently posted at or near the place where the violation occurred. There are four types of violations.

Imminent Danger. The act defines imminent danger as "any conditions or practices in any place of employment which are such that a danger exists which could reasonably be expected to cause death or serious physical harm immediately or before the imminence of such danger can be eliminated through the enforcement procedures otherwise provided by this Act." Consequently when an inspection officer determines that an imminent danger exists, he or she will try to have the danger corrected immediately through voluntary compliance. The employer will be advised that such a danger exists and, if it threatens any employees, they will also be informed of the imminent danger. Such violations, of course, carry a penalty.

Serious Violation.   A serious violation is defined under the act as one in which there is a "substantial probability" that the consequences of an accident would be death or serious physical harm unless the employer did not, and could not with the exercise of "reasonable diligence," know the hazard was present. In OSHA's initial enforcement, before a serious violation occurred, the inspector had to find "substantial probability" of both a violating condition *and* that death or serious harm would result. More recent OSHA policy states that there need only be exposure to a violating condition that *could* result in injury or illness *and* that it is "reasonably predictable" that the result would be death or serious physical harm. The consequence of this reinterpretation is that the OSHA inspector no longer needs to consider the degree of probability of whether an accident or illness will occur in classifying a violation as serious. If a serious violation is determined, a monetary penalty must be assessed.

Nonserious Violation.   A nonserious violation occurs when the likely consequence of the violation is something less than death or serious physical harm, or if the employer did not know of the hazard. For example, a violation of housekeeping standards may result in a tripping hazard that could be classified as nonserious. Nonserious violations may or may not carry a monetary penalty.

De Minimis Violation.   Instead of a citation, the officer will issue a notice for *de minimis* violations, which have no direct relation to safety or health. An example of a *de minimis* violation is a lack of partitions in toilet facilities.

Other types of violations include willful violations and repeated violations. A willful violation occurs when evidence shows either of the following.

1. The employer committed an intentional and knowing violation of the act.
2. Even though the employer did not consciously violate the act, he or she was aware that a hazardous condition existed and yet made no reasonable effort to eliminate it.

A repeated violation occurs when a second citation is issued for a violation. It differs from a failure to abate in that it is clear the employer has abated an earlier violation, but a second violation of the same standard has occurred.

Record-Keeping Requirements

Every employer with more than seven employees is covered by the act and is required to keep occupational injury and illness records for each employee. The employer must keep records for each employee at each building or plant at which the employee reports for work. Each record must be kept and updated for a continuous five-year period and made available for inspection at any time in that period.

To aid in the enforcement of the act, employers are required to make reports of work-related injuries and diseases to OSHA. The administrators of OSHA summarize the data and make periodic reports to the President and Congress on the progress of their administration. Moreover, OSHA utilizes the data received from industry to promulgate the rules of safety that must be followed by employers.

If an employee is killed in an industrial accident or if five or more employees are hospitalized by one accident, the Department of Labor must be notified within 48 hours. The company will be fined if OSHA is not so notified. Thereafter, a complete inspection of the premises on which the accident occurred is mandatory.

RESPONSIBILITIES AND RIGHTS

The following listing of employer and employee responsibilities and rights seems to reveal that the employer has more responsibilities than rights and that the employee has more rights than responsibilities. Parallel to that argument is the fact that employees cannot receive citations under the act. The employer has been held responsible for employee compliance with safety regulations. Refusal by employees to comply with safety rules is no defense for an employer. Employers must make clear to employees that compliance with safety standards is a condition of continuing employment.

Congress in enacting OSHA created certain employee rights. In addition to rights specifically enumerated, certain other rights exist by necessary implication, as is revealed in the *Whirlpool* v. *Marshall* case on page 425.

Employer Responsibilities

* Meet your general duty responsibility to provide a hazard-free workplace and comply with the occupational safety and health standards, rules, and regulations issued under the act.

* Be familiar with mandatory OSHA standards and make copies available to employees for review on request.

* Inform all employees about OSHA.

* Examine workplace conditions to make sure they conform to applicable safety and health standards.

* Remove or guard hazards.

* Make sure employees have and use safe tools and equipment (including personal protective equipment) and that such equipment is properly maintained.

* Use color codes, posters, labels, or signs to warn employees of potential hazards.

* Establish or update operating procedures and communicate them so that employees follow safety and health requirements for their own protection.

* Provide medical examinations when required by OSHA standards.

* Report to the nearest OSHA office, *within 48 hours,* the occurrence of any employment accident that is fatal to one or more employees or that results in the hospitalization of five or more employees.

* Keep OSHA-required records of work-related injuries and illnesses, and post the annual summary during the entire month of February each year. (This applies to employers with eight or more employees.)

* Post, at a prominent location within the workplace, the OSHA poster (OSHA 2203) informing employees of their rights and responsibilities. (In states operating OSHA-approved job safety and health programs, the state's equivalent poster and/or OSHA 2203 may be required.)

* Cooperate with the OSHA compliance officer by furnishing the names of authorized employee representatives who may be asked to accompany the compliance officer during the inspection. (If there are none, the compliance officer will consult with a reasonable number of employees concerning safety and health in the workplace.)

* Not discriminate against employees who properly exercise their rights under the act.

* Post OSHA citations of apparent violations of standards or of the general duty clause at or near the worksite involved. Each citation, or copy thereof, shall remain posted until the violation has been abated, or for three working days, whichever is longer.

* Abate cited violations within the prescribed period.

<u>Employer Rights</u>

* Seek advice and off-site consultation as needed by writing, calling, or visiting the nearest OSHA office. (OSHA will not inspect merely because an employer requests assistance.)

* Be active in your industry association's involvement in job safety and health.

* Request and require proper identification of the OSHA compliance officer prior to inspection of the workplace.

* Be advised by the compliance officer of the reason for an inspection.

* Have an opening and closing conference with the compliance officer.

* File a Notice of Contest with the nearest OSHA area director within 15 working days of receipt of a notice of citation and proposed penalty.

* Apply to OSHA for a temporary variance from a standard if unable to comply because of the unavailability of materials, equipment, or personnel to make necessary changes within the required time.

* Apply to OSHA for a permanent variance from a standard if you can furnish proof that your facilities or method of operation provide employee protection that is at least as effective as that required by the standard.

* Take an active role in developing job safety and health standards through participation in OSHA Standards Advisory Committees, through nationally recognized standards-setting organizations, and through evidence and views presented in writing or at hearing.

* Avail yourself, if you are a small business employer, of long-term loans through the Small Business Administration (SBA) to help bring your establishment into compliance, either before or after an OSHA inspection.

* Be assured of the confidentiality of any trade secrets observed by an OSHA compliance officer during an inspection.

Employee Responsibilities

* Read the OSHA post at the jobsite.
* Comply with all applicable OSHA standards.
* Follow all employer safety and health rules and regulations and wear or use prescribed protective equipment while engaged in work.
* Report hazardous conditions to the supervisor.
* Report any job-related injury or illness to the employer, and seek treatment promptly.
* Cooperate with the OSHA compliance officer conducting an inspection if he or she inquires about safety and health conditions in your workplace.
* Exercise your rights under the act in a responsible manner.

Employee Rights

* Review copies of any of the OSHA standards, rules, regulations, and requirements that the employer should have available at the workplace.
* Request information from your employer on safety and health hazards in the area, on precautions that may be taken, and on procedures to be followed if an employee is involved in an accident or exposed to toxic substances.
* Request (in writing) the OSHA area director to conduct an inspection if you believe hazardous conditions or violation of standards exist in your workplace.
* Have your name withheld from your employer, on request to OSHA, if you file a written and signed complaint.
* Be advised of OSHA actions regarding your complaint and have an informal review, if requested, of any decision not to make an inspection or not to issue a citation.
* File a complaint to OSHA within 30 days if you believe you have been discriminated against, discharged, demoted, or otherwise penalized because of asserting an employee right under the act, and be notified by OSHA of its determination within 90 days of filing.
* Have the authorized employee representative where you work accompany the OSHA compliance officer during the inspection tour.
* Respond to questions from the OSHA compliance officer, particularly if there is no authorized employee representative accompanying the compliance officer.
* Observe any monitoring or measuring of hazardous materials and have the right to access to records on those materials, as specified under the act.
* Request a closing discussion with the compliance officer following an inspection.
* Submit a written request to the National Institute for Occupational Safety and Health (NIOSH) for information on whether any substance in your workplace has potential toxic effects in the concentrations being used, and have your name withheld from your employer if you so request.
* Object to the abatement period set in the citation issued to your employer by writing to the OSHA area director within 15 working days of the issuance of the citation.
* Be notified by your employer if he or she applies for a variance from an OSHA standard, testify at a variance hearing, and appeal the final decision if you disagree with it.
* Submit information or comment to OSHA on the issuance, modification, or revocation of OSHA standards, and request a public hearing.

Source: OSHA 2056, April 1976 (revised), pp. 27–32.

Whirlpool v. Marshall
445 U.S. 1 (1980)
Supreme Court of the United States

Justice Stewart

The Occupational Safety and Health Act of 1970 (Act) prohibits an employer from discharging or discriminating against any employee who exercises "any right afforded by" the Act. The Secretary of Labor (Secretary) has promulgated a regulation providing that, among the rights that the Act so protects, is the right of an employee to choose not to perform his assigned task because of a reasonable apprehension of death or serious injury coupled with a reasonable belief that no less drastic alternative is available. The question presented in the case before us is whether this regulation is consistent with the Act.

The petitioner company maintains a manufacturing plant in Marion, Ohio, for the production of household appliances. Overhead conveyors transport appliance components throughout the plant. To protect employees from objects that occasionally fall from these conveyors, the petitioner has installed a horizontal wire mesh guard screen approximately 20 feet above the plant floor. This mesh screen is welded to angle-iron frames suspended from the building's structural steel skeleton.

Maintenance employees of the petitioner spend several hours each week removing objects from the screen, replacing paper spread on the screen to catch grease drippings from the material on the conveyors, and performing occasional maintenance work on the conveyors themselves. To perform these duties, maintenance employees usually are able to stand on the iron frames, but sometimes find it necessary to step onto the steel mesh screen itself.

In 1973 the company began to install heavier wire in the screen because its safety had been drawn into question. Several employees had fallen partly through the old screen, and on one occasion an employee had fallen completely through to the plant floor below but had survived. . . .

On June 28, 1974, a maintenance employee fell to his death through the guard screen in an area where the newer, stronger mesh had not yet been installed. Following this incident, the petitioner effectuated some repairs and issued an order strictly forbidding maintenance employees from stepping on either the screens or the angle-iron supporting structure. . . .

On July 7, 1974, two of the petitioner's maintenance employees . . . reported for the night shift at 10:45 P.M. Their foreman, after himself walking on some of the angle-iron frames, directed the two men to perform their usual maintenance duties on a section of the old screen. Claiming that the screen was unsafe, they refused to carry out this directive. The foreman then sent them to the personnel office, where they were ordered to punch out without working or being paid for the remaining six hours of the shift. The two men subsequently received written reprimands, which were placed in their employment files.

A little over a month later, the Secretary filed suit alleging that the petitioner's actions against [the employees] constituted discrimination in violation of Section 11(c)(1) of the Act. As relief, the complainant prayed that the petitioner be ordered to expunge from its personnel files all references to the reprimands issued to the two employees, and for a permanent injunction requiring the petitioner to compensate the two employees for the six hours of pay they had lost by reason of their disciplinary suspensions.

. . . The District Court . . . denied relief, holding that the Secretary's regulation was inconsistent with the Act and therefore invalid.

The Court of Appeals for the Sixth Circuit reversed the District Court's judgment. . . .

The Act itself creates an express mechanism for protecting workers from employment conditions believed to pose an emergent threat of death or serious injury. Upon recepit of an employee inspection request stating reasonable grounds to believe that an imminent danger is present in a workplace, OSHA must conduct an inspection. In the event this inspection reveals workplace conditions or practices that "could reasonably be expected to cause death or serious physical harm immediately or before the imminence of such danger can be eliminated through the enforcement procedures otherwise provided by" the Act, the OSHA inspector must inform the affected employees and the employer of the danger and notify them that he is recommending to the Secretary that injunctive relief be sought. At this juncture, the Secretary can petition a federal court to restrain the conditions or practices giving rise to the imminent danger. By means of a temporary restraining order or preliminary injunction, the court may then require the employer to avoid, correct, or remove the danger or to prohibit employees from working in the area.

To ensure that this process functions effectively, the Act expressly accords to every employee several rights, the exercise of which may not subject him to discharge or discrimination. An employee is given the right to inform OSHA of an imminently dangerous workplace condition or practice and request that OSHA inspect that condition or practice. He is given a limited right to assist the OSHA inspector in inspecting the workplace, and the right to aid a court in determining whether or not a risk or imminent danger in fact exists. Finally, an affected employee is given the right to bring an action to compel the Secretary to seek injunctive relief if he believes the Secretary has wrongfully declined to do so.

In the light of this detailed statutory scheme, the Secretary is obviously correct when he acknowledges in his regulation that, "as a general matter, there is no right afforded by the Act which would entitle employees to walk off the job because of potential unsafe conditions at the workplace." By providing for prompt notice to the employer of an inspector's intention to seek an injunction against an imminently dangerous condition, the legislation obviously contemplates that the employer will normally respond by voluntarily and speedily eliminating the danger. And in the few instances where this does not occur, the legislative provisions authorizing prompt judicial action are designed to give employees full protection in most situations from the risk of injury or death resulting from an imminently dangerous condition at the worksite.

As this case illustrates, however, circumstances may sometimes exist in which the employee justifiably believes that the express statutory arrangement does not sufficiently protect him from death or serious injury. Such circumstances will probably not often occur, but such a situation may arise when (1) the employee is ordered by his employer to work under conditions that the employee reasonably believes pose an imminent risk of death or serious bodily injury, and (2) the employee has reason to believe that there is not sufficient time or opportunity either to seek effective redress from his employer or to apprise OSHA of the danger.

Nothing in the Act suggests that those few employees who have to face this dilemma must rely exclusively on the remedies expressly set forth in the Act at the risk of their own safety. But nothing in the Act explicitly provides otherwise. Against this background of legislative silence the Secretary has exercised his rule-making power under [the law] and has determined that, when an employee in good faith finds himself in such a predicament, he may refuse to expose himself to the dangerous condition, without being subjected to "subsequent discrimination" by the employer.

* * *

The regulation clearly conforms to the fundamental objective of the Act—to prevent occupational deaths and serious injuries. . . .

To accomplish this basic purpose, the legislation's remedial orientation is prophylactic in nature. The Act does not wait for an employee to die or become injuried. It authorizes the promulgation of health and safety standards and the issuance of citations in the hope that these will act to prevent deaths or injuries from ever occurring. It would seem anomalous to construe an act so directed and constructed as prohibiting an employee, with no other reasonable alternative, the freedom to withdraw from a workplace environment that he reasonably believes is highly dangerous.

Moreover, the Secretary's regulation can be viewed as an appropriate aid to the full effectuation of the Act's "general duty" clause. That clause provides that "[e]ach employer . . . shall furnish to each of his employees employment and a place of employment which are free from recognized hazards that are causing or are likely to cause death or serious physical harm to his employees." As the legislative history of this provision reflects, it was intended itself to deter the occurrence of occupational deaths and serious injuries by placing on employers a mandatory obligation independent of the specific health and safety standards to be promulgated by the Secretary. Since OSHA inspectors cannot be present around the clock in every workplace, the Secretary's regulation ensured that employees will in all circumstances enjoy the rights afforded them by the "general duty" clause.

The regulation thus on its face appears to further the overriding purpose of the Act, and rationally to complement its remedial scheme. In the absence of some contrary indication in the legislative history, the Secretary's regulation must, therefore, be upheld, particularly when it is remembered that safety legislation is to be liberally construed to effectuate the congressional purpose.

Questions
1. What conditions must exist to justify the employee's refusal to work without reprimand?
2. Why did the Court feel the Secretary's regulation was lawful?

REFORM PROPOSALS

Critics have complained of the fact that OSHA is not required to conduct cost-benefit analyses prior to the issuance of regulations. In response to this complaint, the Reagan Administration is reviewing the standards-setting process of OSHA with a view to requiring cost-benefit analysis.

Other critics have pointed out that the worker's own behavior, not the work environment, is the major cause of accidents. Therefore, they maintain that OSHA's efforts to set standards related to work environment are misguided. Improved supervision and training would be more effective in reducing accidents than capital-equipment regulations. They call for more research to establish the true causes of most accidents so as to guide an effective program to reduce them.

Finally, an alternative approach to safety and health regulations has been suggested that uses incentives to encourage employers to improve their safety and health record. Instead of OSHA's setting and enforcing standards altering the physical conditions of the workplace, a performance-based approach utilizing an injury or exposure tax, for example, is a possibility. An injury tax could be based on industry-wide averages for accident frequency and severity rates. Employers that exceed the standard would be taxed a substantial amount of money. Efforts to avoid these taxes would provide an incentive to improve the company's record. If injury rates were not reduced, the higher taxes would increase the prices of the goods produced, thereby shifting demand away from goods that are produced under hazardous conditions. Employers would also be given the freedom to find the most efficient method of improving safety instead of automatically installing the system mandated by an OSHA regulation.

Despite the advantages alleged to be connected to performance-oriented approaches, labor unions are generally opposed to the adoption of economic incentives, particularly if such adoption is at the expense of the existing system of OSHA inspection and enforcement.

CONCLUSION

The Department of Labor's enforcement of OSHA has made it one of the most controversial of governmental agencies. While OSHA's goals are acceptable to everyone, its enforcement has been questioned. In the past OSHA's standards have been more "technologically" than "economically" feasible, thereby ignoring cost-effectiveness standards urged by industries. But recently, OSHA has announced that it would apply cost-effectiveness analysis rather than cost-benefit analysis to occupational health standards. The agency will consider four aspects for future standards: (1) demonstration of significant risk, (2) demonstration that the standard will actually protect workers, (3) the "economic feasibility" of a standard for an entire industry rather than for a single firm, and (4) the cost-effectiveness of the standard.

Enforcement of OSHA's standards has relied on inspections and citations. Responding to criticisms of this approach, OSHA administrators under the Reagan Administration have moderated their enforcement efforts. Consultation, education, and cooperation are the newest hallmarks of OSHA enforcement. For example, OSHA has proposed to restrict "surprise" workplace inspections only to those made in response to employee complaints. The agency has also proposed a year-long experimental program under which many companies may take over routine inspections through labor-management committees or through "management initiatives" in firms where advanced safety and health systems are already in place.

The Reagan Administration is also expected to ask Congress for changes in the law. Critics maintain that the basic role of OSHA should be changed from that of a legal adversary conducting inspections and insisting on compliance with detailed standards, to a safety leader expanding the techniques of safety engineering and disseminating information for safety improvement. Moreover, they insist that Congress should clarify OSHA's standards-setting process to be conducted on a cost-benefit basis.

DISCUSSION QUESTIONS

1. A police lieutenant was "on call" at all times. Consequently, he normally was armed with his revolver. On the day in question, he went home to change his uniform pursuant to a departmental requirement. At home, he accidentally discharged his revolver and injured his hand. Is the police lieutenant entitled to a workers' compensation award?

2. A worker in New York left the office to purchase a soda and sandwich "to go." While returning to his place of employment, he was robbed and shot. Is the worker entitled to a workers' compensation award?

3. An employee was injured on a public sidewalk. He slipped on some ice as he reached for the door handle of his place of work. Is this employee entitled to a workers' compensation award?

4. Mrs. Shimp, an employee who is allergic to cigarette smoke, sought an injunction to force the New Jersey Bell Telephone Company to prevent cigarette smoking in her work area. She contends that the "second hand" passive inhalation of smoke from burning tobacco is deleterious to her health. She maintains her employer, by permitting employees to smoke in the work area, is allowing an unsafe condition to exist. Is Mrs. Shimp entitled to the injunction under the Occupational Safety and Health Act?

5. A conveyor belt at an REA shipping terminal became inoperative when an electrical circuit shorted out. The REA manager called a licensed electrical contractor. When the electrician arrived, REA's maintenance supervisor was in the circuit breaker room attempting to soak up water on the floor with sawdust. While attempting to fix the short circuit, the electrician, standing on a wet floor, was electrocuted. The maintenance supervisor, who was standing on a wooden platform, was burned and knocked unconscious. When OSHA attempted to assess a fine against REA, the company defended itself by arguing the defense of contributory negligence or assumption of risk by the electrician. What result?

6. Vinyl chloride causes a fatal form of liver cancer. Therefore, in 1974 OSHA administrators proposed a standard to reduce the allowable level of vinyl chloride gas exposure from 500 parts per million parts of air to 1 part per million. Industry replied with studies that predicted that this strict standard would shut down all the polyvinyl chloride plants and severely cripple the entire plastics industry. The studies indicated that the probable costs to the economy would be between $65 billion and $90 billion in lost production. The studies also estimated that the standard would cause the elimination of between 1.7 million and 2.2 million jobs.

   Technological developments after the standard was set, however, "saved" the industry. The total costs of implementing the standard did not exceed $250 million, and few workers actually lost their jobs. Moreover, the price of the products produced through the use of vinyl chloride rose by only 6 percent. Would this history encourage OSHA administrators to adopt "technology-forcing" standards? While the industry's credibility was never questioned in this case, would their cost predictions in the future suffer credibility problems?

SUGGESTED READINGS

Cann, Wesley, A., Jr., "Cost-Benefit Analysis v. Feasibility Analysis: The Controversy Resolved in the Cotton Dust Case," *American Business Law Journal,* Vol. 20, No. 1, Spring 1982, pp. 1–36.

Reed, Lee and Davison, Art, "Employee Complaints and the Scope of OSHA Inspections: Heading for a Showdown?", *American Business Law Journal,* Vol. 19, No. 2, Summer 1981, pp. 186–196.

Rothstein, Mark A., "OSHA After Ten Years: A Review and Some Proposed Reforms," *Vanderbilt Law Review,* Vol. 34, January 1981, pp. 71–134

chapter 19

REGULATION OF EQUAL EMPLOYMENT OPPORTUNITIES

"Equality" has always been an important value in American society. However, specific practices of "equality" in America have been less than the ideal of equality suggests. The political freedom of slaves and the "liberation" of women and other minorities have evolved slowly. Economic "equality" in the marketplace has similarly developed at a slow pace. Laws requiring equal access to markets for housing, hotel accommodations, food service, consumer credit, and other goods and services have emerged only in recent decades. Laws protecting equality in labor markets are also recently new. The aim of these policies is to eliminate certain discriminatory practices that deny persons an *equal opportunity* regarding employment, wages, fringe benefits, promotions, and working conditions.

Economic data suggest the presence of substantial labor market discrimination against minorities and women. Even as recently as 1970, the average annual earnings of blacks and females were only 60 percent of that obtained by white males.[1] A portion of this discrepancy can be attributed to racial and sexual discrimination in labor markets. This and other invidious discrimination in employment opportunities misallocates labor resources. It depresses wage rates for the discriminated group and enlarges the number of unemployed among the discriminated group. Moreover, it misdirects skills and abilities into jobs that fail to utilize such talents. The resulting unemployed and underemployed laborers deprive society of the full productive capabilities of their labors. Hence, besides the moral arguments against "discrimination," it makes economic sense as well to avoid labor market discrimination.

ANTIDISCRIMINATION REGULATIONS

Labor market discrimination can involve three types: (1) wage rate differences among fellow employees, (2) employment bias in terms of hiring, firing, overtime, promotions, and the like, and (3) occupational discrimination, such as withholding certain jobs from the discriminated group. The laws aimed at labor market discrimination have attempted to prohibit all three types of discrimination.

EQUAL PAY ACT

The first statute aimed at labor market discrimination was the Equal Pay Act of 1963. Basically, the Equal Pay Act requires that men and women receive the same wage rate if they are employed in jobs that are substantially similar. However, the Equal Pay Act guarantees equal pay only to women who are employed on the same job as men. If does not outlaw discrimination on the basis of sex in hiring new employees or in granting promotions.

The determination of whether the Equal Pay Act is violated requires analysis of the content of the jobs held by the men and women. If the jobs are different, the Equal Pay act is not applicable. Moreover, the Equal Pay Act is not violated if the wage rate differential is based on any justifiable factor other than sex. For example, an employer may pay a higher rate to a male employee performing the same job as a female if the male has a longer term of service or "seniority." But insignificant differences in the contents of the job will not justify different wage rates. Consider the following case.

Wirtz, Secretary of Labor, v. Basic Inc.
256 F. Supp. 786 (1966)
U.S. District Court (Nev.)

. . . The case for the plaintiff was presented by a feminine attorney of the Department of Labor, resisted by a masculine attorney of the Nevada Bar, and considered by a Judge who, for the purposes of this case at least, must be sexless, a possibility not apparent when the oath of office was taken and one which may bespeak the appointment of older judges. . . .

The employees involved in the instant dispute are laboratory analysts Jo Ann Barredo, Ann Jones, and Byron O'Dell. Barredo was hired by Thompson, the then Chief Chemist, on September 1, 1959, and was trained under his supervision to perform the analytical tests required to determine the metallurgy of the various ores and compounds required to be analyzed. She had had no previous experience. Jones was hired by Thompson in 1953 and was trained by him. She had had no previous experience. O'Dell was hired by Thompson in

March, 1962. He was trained by Thompson, with the assistance of Barredo and Jones, in the particular analytical procedures used at Basic. In his early life, he had been employed as a miner and mill superintendent and from 1949 until 1962, was employed by Standard Slag Co. at Gabbs, Nevada, as a laboratory analyst, using similar analytical procedures to those at Basic to determine the metallurgy of similar ores and products. . . .

The primary work of all three laboratory analysts is the running of relatively simple, standardized chemical tests on various materials performed strictly in accordance with the company's testing mannual and directives. . . .

After the passage of the Equal Pay Act of 1963, the then Chief Chemist, Thompson, discussed with his superiors the necessity of either equalizing the pay of the laboratory analysts or setting up legal job classifications of jobs requiring different skill, effort, or responsibility or which were to be performed under different working conditions, but no final action was taken. Thompson resigned before September 1, 1964, and the present Chief Chemist, Lawson, succeeded him. . . .

The defendant's answer to the complaint, after denying any discrimination among employees on the basis of sex, affirmatively alleges:

Any lesser pay received by Jo Ann Barredo and Ann Jones results from the fact that their work requires less skill, effort, and/or responsibility than the work of higher paid employees who work under similar conditions. . . .

The burden of proof in this case is upon the Secretary to show that the jobs under consideration require equal work, equal skill, equal effort, and equal responsibility and are performed under similar working conditions. The defendant has invoked none of the statutory exceptions permitting payment differentials made pursuant to a seniority system, a merit system, a system which measures earnings by quantity or quality of production or a differential based on any other factor other than sex, which are affirmative defenses the burden of proof of which would be borne by the employer.

The Secretary has promulgated comprehensive regulations interpreting the equal pay provisions. Such regulations are generally valid and binding . . . and our perusal of them persuades us that the Secretary has produced a helpful and reasonable aid to a correct interpretation of the law.

Fundamental in the application of the law is the premise that it establishes an objective standard requiring that a judgment with respect to alleged discrimination between sexes be based upon the requirements of the particular jobs being compared, rather than a comparison of the skill of individual employees, the effort of individual employees, or their previous training and experience. "Application of the equal pay standard is not dependent on job classifications or titles but depends rather on actual job requirements and performance." Equal does not mean identical and insubstantial differences in the skill, effort, and responsibility requirements of particular jobs should be ignored. The job requirements should be viewed as a whole.

The preponderance of the evidence clearly shows that the work performed by O'Dell, Barredo, and Jones is substantially equal and that their jobs as laboratory analysts require substantially equal skill, effort, and responsibility. The only requirement, as we see it, as to which there is room for a reasonable difference of opinion concerns the existence of similar working conditions.

We have no doubt that this defendant may, as it apparently has attempted to do, establish a position for a male analyst designated "Shift Analysts," if you will, where the working conditions are different from other analysts' jobs, provided the classification is made in good faith and there is no unreasonable discrimination on the basis of sex. The Secretary agrees. "However, in situations where some employees performing work . . . have working conditions substantially different from those required for the performance of other jobs the equal pay principle would not apply." The evidence shows that O'Dell's swing shift work every two weeks is performed under substantially different working conditions; the supervising chemists are absent after 5 P.M., the other analysts are absent after 5 P.M., and part of the work is at night.

The difficulty here is that what the defendant company has done belies any announced intention to differentiate between a day shift and a swing shift analyst on the basis of dissimilar working conditions. The facts are: Between June 11, 1964, the effective date of the Equal Pay Act, and September 1, 1964, O'Dell, Barredo, and Jones all worked the day shift, performed the same work, and received different wages; since September 1, 1964, O'Dell has worked a swing shift every alternate two-week period and has received an additional five cents per hour for such work; during the alternate two-week periods that O'Dell works the day shift, his job requires substantially the same skill, effort, and responsibility as those performed by Barredo and Jones, yet he receives a higher hourly rate of compensation. We think these facts compel the conclusion that the job classification "Swing Analyst" is a paper classification unrelated to the true working conditions, and that the five-cent pay differential for swing shift work is intended to compensate for the different working conditions.

Section 800.145 of the Regulations states:

When applied without distinction to employees of both sexes, shift differentials, incentive payments, production bonuses, performance and longevity raises, and the like will not result in equal pay violations. For example, in an establishment where men and women are employed on a job, but only men work on the night shift for which a night shift differential is paid, such a differential would not be prohibited. However, the payment of a higher hourly rate to all men on that job for all hours worked because some of the men may occasionally work nights would result in a prohibited wage differential.

These provisions seem reasonable on their face and as applied to our situation. There could be no effective enforcement of the equal pay provisions if differentials between sexes were permitted for all hours worked because of the substantially different working conditions and responsibilities entailed in a specific part of the work performed at identifiable times and places. As a "Shift Analyst," O'Dell is entitled to a different rate of pay while he is working as a shift analyst, but not while working on the day shift. He and the company apparently have agreed that five cents per hour is a reasonable differential.

The Equal Pay Act of 1963, which, like other Congressional enactments concerning employment practices, was induced by social conditions and working conditions pertaining in metropolitan and industrial areas, presents unique headaches in application to an agrarian-mining-tourist economy such as Nevada's where employers of large numbers of employees are few and far between. Nevertheless, just as the interpretive opinions of the Act by industrially oriented courts in Michigan, New York, Ohio, California, and elsewhere will be persuasive authority for us in future cases, so should we interpret the law with deference to the expressed intention of Congress in the light of its nationwide application. Provincial differences in business practices and customs are not excepted by the law.

Anomalously, the compensation of two females, Barredo and Jones, will also be equalized by our decree. We see no escape from this result. The last proviso of 29 U.S.C. 206(d)(1) states:

That an employer who is paying a wage rate differential in violation of this subsection shall not, in order to comply with the provisions of this subsection, reduce the wage rate of any employee.

We cannot adjust O'Dell's wage rate downward, and inasmuch as Barredo and Jones are doing equal work, must increase the wage rate of both their jobs to equal O'Dell's.

Questions
1. Must jobs be identical in all respects to require equal pay?
2. What justifications are allowed for differences in wage rates?

CIVIL RIGHTS ACT

The policy of antidiscrimination in employment opportunities has been enunciated in a wide variety of federal laws and directives. The most prominent statute is Title VII of the Civil Rights Act of 1964, as amended in 1972. It prohibits discrimination in employment on the basis of race, sex, religion, color, or national origin, except in the relatively rare instances when a *bona fide* occupational qualification (*bfoq*) justifies the discriminatory practice. Nearly all public and private sector organizations, including labor unions and employment agencies, are covered under the act. The terms of employment covered under the act include hiring, training, paying, promoting, and firing workers.

Title VII of the Civil Rights Act makes it an unlawful employment practice for an employer "to discriminate against" any individual because of such individual's race, color, religion, sex, or national origin. However, the law does not define the word "discriminate." To discriminate means to distinguish, segregate, or classify. While the employer must "discriminate" between applicants for a job or a promotion, the law restricts the employer from using race, color, religion, sex, or national origin as the criteria for "discriminating" between applicants. Furthermore, the statute does not say that the employer must *intend* to discriminate in order for a violation to occur.

Disparate Treatment

Disparate treatment is the name given to the situation where the employer is making employment decisions solely on the basis of a prohibited criterion. For example, an advertisement for a job opening that states "no blacks need apply" would be a clear example of blatant, disparate treatment. While announced discriminatory policies have generally disappeared, more subtle types of disparate treatment may occur. For example, qualified white and black applicants may be permitted to interview for a job, but only whites are hired.

For a *prima facie* case of disparate treatment to be established, plaintiffs must prove (1) that they are members of a protected class (race, color religion, sex, or national origin), (2) that they applied to the job in which the employer was seeking applicants, (3) that they were qualified to perform the job, (4) that they were denied the job, and (5) that the job remained open and the employer continued to accept applications thereafter. Once the plaintiff has established the *prima facie* case, the defendant employer must prove a legitimate and non-discriminatory reason for rejecting the plaintiff's application. Employers usually attempt to substantiate their reason for denying the plaintiff's application by pointing out that the applicant's credentials are inadequate in comparison with those of the other applicants for the job or in relation to the job itself. Whether this is a credible "reason" or a mere pretext for discrimination is a question often to be resolved in litigation.

Disparate Impact

Given the fact that employers can normally defend a disparate treatment case by establishing that the applicant's credentials failed to meet the stated requirements of the job, the impact of Title VII would have been minimal if it had been confined to instances of intentional discrimination or disparate treatment. Hiring standards and employment practices that make no reference to race, color, religion, sex, or national origin can nevertheless reduce the possibility that a member of these protected classes will obtain employment. Consequently, the use of neutral employment policies, such as an achievement test or a requirement of a high school diploma, many cause a disparate impact on protected groups with low levels of achievement in education. When it was asserted that these employment practices had a disparate impact, the court was forced to determine whether this constituted unlawful "discrimination."

Griggs v. Duke Power Co.
401 U.S. 424 (1971)
Supreme Court of the United States

Chief Justice Burger

We granted the writ in this case to resolve the question whether an employer is prohibited by the Civil Rights Act of 1964, Title VII, from requiring a high school education or passing of a standardized general intelligence test as a condition of employment in or transfer of jobs when (a) neither standard is shown to be significantly related to successful job performance, (b) both requirements operate to disqualify Negroes at a substantially higher rate than white applicants, and (c) the jobs in question formerly had been filled only by white employees as part of a long-standing practice of giving preference to whites.

* * *

The Court of Appeals' opinion, and the partial dissent, agreed that, on the record in the present case, "whites fare far better on the Company's . . . requirements" than Negroes. This consequence would appear to be directly traceable to race. Basic intelligence must have the means of articulation to manifest itself fairly in a testing process. Because they are Negroes, petitioners have long received inferior education in segregated schools. . . . Congress did not intend by Title VII, however, to guarantee a job to every person regardless of qualifications. In short, the Act does not command that any person be hired simply because he was formerly the subject of discrimination, or because he is a member of a minority group. What is required by Congress is the removal of artificial, arbitrary, and unnecessary barriers to employment when the barriers operate invidiously to discriminate on the basis of racial or other impermissible classifications.

. . . The Act proscribes not only overt discrimination but also practices that are fair in form, but discriminatory in operation. The touchstone is business necessity. If an employment practice which operates to exclude Negroes cannot be shown to be related to job performance, the practice is prohibited.

On the record before us, neither the high school completion requirement nor the general intelligence test is shown to bear a demonstrable relationship to successful performance of the jobs for which it was used. Both were adopted, as the Court of Appeals noted, without meaningful study of their relationship to job-performance ability. Rather, a vice president of the Company testified, the requirements were instituted on the Company's judgment that they generally would improve the overall quality of the work force.

The evidence, however, shows that employees who have not completed high school or taken the tests have continued to perform satisfactorily and make progress in departments for which the high school and test criteria are now used. The promotion record of present employees who would not be able to meet the new criteria thus suggests the possibility that the requirements may not be needed even for the limited purpose of preserving the avowed policy of advancement within the Company. . . .

The Court of Appeals held that the Company had adopted the diploma and test requirements without any "intention to discriminate against Negro employees." We do not suggest that either the District Court or the Court of Appeals erred in examining the employer's intent; but good intent or absence of discriminatory intent does not redeem employment procedures or testing mechanisms that operate as "built-in headwinds" for minority groups and are unrelated to measuring job capability. . . .

The facts of this case demonstrate the inadequacy of broad and general testing devices as well as the infirmity of using diplomas or degrees as fixed measures of capability. History is filled with examples of men and women who rendered highly effective performance without the conventional badges of accomplishment in terms of certificates, diplomas, or degrees. Diplomas and tests are useful servants, but Congress has mandated the common-sense proposition that they are not to become masters of reality.

The Company contends that its general intelligence tests are specifically permitted by §703(h) of the Act. That section authorizes the use of "any professionally developed ability test" that is not "designed, intended, *or used* to discriminate because of race. . . ." (Emphasis added by Court).

The Equal Employment Opportunity Commission, having enforcement responsibility, has issued guidelines interpreting §703(h) to permit only the use of job-related tests. The administrative interpretation of the Act by the enforcing agency is entitled to great deference. Since the Act and its legislative history support the Commisssion's construction, this affords good reason to treat the guidelines as expressing the will of Congress. . . .

Nothing in the Act precludes the use of testing or measuring procedures; obviously they are useful. What Congress has forbidden is giving these devices and mechanisms controlling force unless they are demonstrably a reasonable measure of job performance. Congress has not commanded that the less qualified be preferred over the better qualified simply because of minority origins. Far from disparaging job qualifications as such, Congress has made such qualifications the controlling factor, so that race, religion, nationality, and sex become irrelevant. What Congress has commanded is that any tests used must measure the person for the job and not the person in the abstract.

Questions

1. Must the employer "intend" to discriminate before an employment practice is unlawfully discriminatory?
2. Why did the intelligence test used by the Duke Power Company fail to be an acceptable "exception" under Section 703(h)?
3. How did the Court define "equal opportunity" for jobs? Does the court's definition allow the employer to select the most qualified?

Relevant Pool

An adverse or disparate impact can be established only in relation to a relevant pool of available and qualified workers. By comparing the percentage of minorities or women employed in a company with some relevant worker pool, an adverse impact may be revealed if the percentage of minorities or women employed was less than the workforce percentage of qualified minorities or women. The EEOC has established a rule of thumb to determine a disparate impact. If the company's overall utilization of persons from protected classes is at least four fifths (80 percent) of the number that would have been predicted on the basis of the number of persons from that class in the relevant pool, no adverse impact is apparent. The EEOC has announced that it would not formally take action against the company that complied with the four-fifths rule.

Validation

According to the fundamental principle announced in *Griggs,* if an "adverse impact" on employment opportunities for any race, sex, or ethnic group is present, then selection devices (such as educational and experience requirements, interview results, or test scores) must be validated to determine whether they are accurate and reliable predictors of job performance and a "business necessity." The legal requirements of "job-relatedness" and "business necessity" have proven to be substantial barriers to the utilization of testing devices in hiring decisions.

Under the 1978 Uniform Guidelines on Employee Selection Procedures prepared by federal enforcement agencies, there are three methods of validating tests for "job-relatedness."

1. The "criterion-related validity" test allows a study to determine if those who do well on the test also do well on the job, and if those who do poorly on the test do poorly on the job.
2. A "content validity" test allows the testing of a representative sample of important or critical job behaviors, such as typing test used to hire a typist.
3. A "construct validity" test measures the degree to which candidates have identifiable characteristics that have been determined to be important for successful job performance, such as a test for emotional stability used to hire a security or police officer.

Each of these tests require professional development and review if they are to stand up to a challenge in the courts.

To satisfy the "business necessity" test of *Griggs,* companies are required to show that no other procedure or testing device could have been used that would have been just as effective in selecting suitable employees without having the "adverse impact" on minorities or women. In the field of personnel practices, this is known as a "cosmic search" for alternative selection procedures that have less adverse effect on minorities or women.

These standards developed by the EEOC and the courts are quite difficult to meet. Consequently, many companies have abandoned testing programs entirely. The EEOC has encouraged companies to form consortiums where they have similar job classifications and devise tests that could be used throughout the industry. To further reduce the burdens of "validation," the Uniform Guidelines have adopted the "bottom-line" concept. Under this concept, the firm is not required to individually validate each component of the selection process; only the end results of the selection process must be adequately predictive of future job performance. Consequently, an employer utilizing a minimum passing score on a written examination that is not job-related and has an adverse impact on minorities would not be in violation of the law if the composite selection procedures (the application form, interviews, and written test) do not cause the firm's overall selection rate to be less than the 80 percent of the nonminority selection rate. Hence, if the employer compensates for the negative effect of a single test by hiring a sufficient proportion of minorities who otherwise meet its standards, the "bottom-line" concept protects the employer's use of the written test that is not job-related and has an adverse impact on minorities.

Seniority Systems

In the *Griggs* decision, the seniority rights of the victims of discrimination were "to be considered on a plant-wide, rather than a departmental, basis." The Court added that "to apply a strict departmental seniority would result in the continuation of present effects of past discrimination." After the *Griggs* decision, most courts and employers operated on the principle that any seniority system that locked minorities or women into positions of previous discrimination was illegal. For example, one case dealing with seniority involved black truck drivers who were hired for city driving only and were kept there because of a discriminatory transfer policy that prevented them from transferring to over-the-road trucking. Finding that blacks had been denied over-the-road jobs because of this discriminatory policy, the Supreme Court held that granting retroactive seniority back to the date of application was an appropriate remedy.[2]

However, addressing the question in *U.S.* v. *Teamsters,* 431 U.S. 324 (1977), the Supreme Court said that a seniority system that perpetuated the effects of discrimination that took place before Title VII became law (July 1965) was legal. The court refused to bar a departmental seniority system that was part of a *bona fide* labor contract when it was neutral and equally applied. The company seniority system can perpetuate past discrimination, but only if it is part of a *bona fide* labor contract and the original discrimination took place before July 1965.

The Supreme Court dealt with this issue again in *United Arlines* v. *Evans,* 431 U.S. 553 (1977). In *Evans,* an employee who was discharged and later rehired sued to obtain seniority back to the date of her original employment despite the fact that the current seniority system of the company was based solely on current employment. She had been originally discharged because of the company's policy of not retaining stewardesses that got married. The company abandoned its policy later, enabling her to be reemployed. The Court, however, rules that the seniority system was *bona fide* and could not be attacked by the employee. The Court's rationale included the argument that the discriminatory act of the employer had not been challenged at the time of discharge. Hence, the failure to timely challenge the discriminatory act was the "equivalent of a discriminatory act which occurred before the statute was passed."

The Supreme Court dealt with the issue of seniority systems again in the following case.

American Tobacco Company v. Patterson

50 L.W. 4364 (1982)
Supreme Court of the United States

Justice White

Under *Griggs* v. *Duke Power Co.,* a *prima facie* violation of Title VII of the Civil Rights Act of 1964, "may be established by policies or practices that are neutral on their face and in intent but that nonetheless discriminate in effect against a particular group." A seniority system "would seem to fall under the *Griggs* rationale" if it were not for §703(h) of the Civil Rights Act. That section provides in pertinent part:

Notwithstanding any other provision of this subchapter, it shall not be an unlawful employment practice for an employer to apply different standards of compensation, or different terms, conditions, or privileges of employment pursuant to a *bona fide* seniority or merit system, . . . provided that such differences are not the result of an intention to discriminate because of race, color, religion, sex, or national origin, nor shall it be an unlawful employment practice for an employer to give and to act upon the results of any professionally developed ability test provided that such test, its administration or action upon the results is not designated, intended, or used to discriminate because of race, color, religion, sex, or national origin. . . .

Under §703(h) the fact that a seniority system has a discriminatory impact is not alone sufficient to invalidate the system; actual intent to discriminate must be proved. The Court of Appeals in this case, however, held that §703(h) does not apply to seniority systems adopted after the effective date of the Civil Rights Act. We granted the petition for *certiorari* to address the validity of this construction of the section.

Petitioners argue that the plain language of §703(h) applies to post-Act as well as pre-Act seniority systems. The respondent employees claim that the provision "provides a narrow exemption [from the ordinary discriminatory impact test] which was specifically designed to protect *bona fide* seniority systems which were in existence before the effective date of Title VII."

* * *

On its face §703(h) makes no distinction between pre- and post-Act seniority systems, just as it does not distinguish between pre- and post-Act merit systems or pre- and post-Act ability tests. . . .

* * *

Although the plain language of §703(h) makes no distinction between pre-Act and post-Act seniority systems, the court below found support for its distinction between the two in the legislative history. Such an interpretation misreads the legislative history.

We have not been informed of and have not found a single statement anywhere in the legislative history saying that §703(h) does not protect seniority systems adopted or modified after the effective date of Title VII. Nor does the legislative history reveal that Congress intended to distinguish between adoption and application of a *bona fide* seniority system. The most which can be said for the legislative history of §703(h) is that it is inconclusive with respect to the issue presented in the case.

*   *   *

Going behind the plain language of a statute in search of a possibly contrary Congressional intent is "a step to be taken cautiously" even under the best of circumstances. "[I]n light of its unusual legislative history and the absence of the usual legislative materials," we would in any event hesitate to give dispositive weight to the legislative history of §703(h). More importantly, however, the history of §703(h) does not support the far-reaching limitation on the terms of §703(h) announced by the court below and urged by respondents. The fragments of legislative history cited by respondent, regardless of how liberally they are construed, do not amount to a clearly expressed legislative intent contrary to the plain language of the statue.

*   *   *

Our prior decisions have emphasized that "seniority systems are afforded special treatment under Title VII itself," and have refused to narrow §703(h) by reading into it limitations not contained in the statutory language. In *Teamsters* v. *United States,* we held that §703(h) exempts from Title VII the disparate impact

of a *bona fide* seniority system even if the differential treatment is the result of pre-Act racially discriminatory employment practices. Similarly, by holding that "[a] discriminatory act which is not made the basis for a timely charge is the legal equivalent of a discriminatory act which occurred before the statute was passed," *United Air Lines, Inc. v. Evans,* 431 U.S. 553, 558 (1977), the Court interpreted §703(h) to immunize seniority systems which perpetuate post-Act discrimination. Thus taken together, *Teamsters* and *Evans* stand for the proposition stated in *Teamsters* that "[s]ection 703(h) on its face immunizes *all bona fide* seniority systems, and does not distinguish between the perpetuation of pre- and post-Act" discriminatory impact. Section 703(h) makes no distinction between seniority systems adopted before its effective date and those adopted after its effective date. Consistent with our prior decisions, we decline petitioners' invitation to read such a distinction into the statute.

Seniority provisions are of "overriding importance" in collective bargaining, and they "are universally included in these contracts." The collective bargaining process "lies at the core of our national labor policy. . . ." Congress was well aware in 1964 that the overall purpose of Title VII, to eliminate discrimination in employment, inevitably would, on occasion, conflict with the policy favoring minimal supervision by courts and other governmental agencies over the substantive terms of collective bargaining agreements. Section 703(h) represents the balance Congress struck between the two policies, and it is not this Court's function to upset that balance.

Because a construction of §703(h) limiting its application to seniority systems in place prior to the effective date of the statute would be contrary to its plain language, inconsistent with our prior cases, and would run counter to the national labor policy, we vacate the judgment below and remand for further proceedings consistent with this opinion.

Questions
1. Under the *Griggs* decision, a practice may be neutral on its face and in intent but cause a disproportionate negative impact on a particular group, and thereby become illegal unless required by "business necessity." A seniority system may have a disproportionate impact on a particular group and fall under the *Griggs* rationale (ignoring "intent") if not exempted by Section 703(h). From the language of Section 703(h), is a seniority system with a disproportionate impact exempt from a violation of Title VII?
2. The respondent employees claimed that Section 703(h) contains a narrow exemption from the discriminatory impact rationale to protect *bona fide* seniority systems that were in existence *before* the effective date of Title VII. How does the Supreme Court respond to this argument?
3. What other legislative enactment of Congress suggests a policy contrary to Title VII and consistent with Section 703(h)?
4. When can a seniority system be illegal because of racial discrimination?

During a recession, companies following a seniority system must utilize the principle of last in/first out (LIFO) in deciding which employees are to be laid off. Obviously, many of the gains that minorities and women may have obtained during prosperous times are wiped out by a declining economy. Since a *bona fide* seniority system is legitimate despite its discriminatory effect, no charge of illegality can be advanced against the company for following the LIFO principle in making layoffs. However, about three fourths of the nation's workforce is not covered by union contracts. Companies not bound to use seniority as a basis for layoffs may not follow a practice in layoffs that has a discriminatory effect. They would be open to a charge of discrimination.

Protected Classes

Race. It is clear that the principal purpose of the Civil Rights Act's prohibition against racial discrimination is the expansion of employment opportunities for blacks. American Indians and Orientals also are protected classes under Title VII. The protection against racial discrimination is even greater than that of the other listed protected groups. For example, employers can normally defend against a charge of discrimination by establishing a *bona fide* occupational qualification (bfoq) that is reasonably necessary to the operation of the business. However, the section authorizing bfoq's does not list race. Consequently, employers cannot assert that being white is a bfoq for a particular job.

Religion. Title VII does not define "religion." Therefore, the courts have usually applied the definitional test employed in constitutional cases. Religion can be other than one of the standard denominations. One need not acknowledge acceptance of a standard set of beliefs. Any sincere and meaningful belief that is important in the life of its possessor can be considered a "religion." Besides prohibiting discrimination against religious affiliation or beliefs, Title VII also outlaws discrimination against persons who lack religious beliefs.

Title VII permits religion to be a *bona fide* occupational qualifiaction. Religious institutions can require employees for certain jobs to be of their own religious persuasion. Moreover, a kosher butchery can require the butcher to be Jewish.

Employers often claim that employees have not been terminated from employment because of their religious beliefs, but because of religious practices that interfere with the normal operation of the business. Therefore, Congress amended Title VII in 1972 to permit an employer to discriminate if the employer "demonstrates that he is unable to reasonably accommodate an employee's or prospective employee's religious observance or practice without undue hardship on the conduct of the employer's business." Consider the person whose religion regarded Saturday as the Sabbath and forbade work on the Sabbath. The union refused to allow any violations in the seniority system, and the person had insufficient seniority to bid for a shift with Saturdays off. The company refused to permit the employee to work a four-day week or to replace the employee with another worker on the fifth day. When the employer dismissed the employee, the court held that the discharge did not violate the law because "accommodations" to the employee's beliefs would have caused an "undue hardship" on the employer.[3]

National Origin. "National origin" refers to the country in which the person is born or the country from which his or her ancestors came. National origin is not the same as citizenship. Employers may follow a policy of employing only citizens. However, a citizenship policy must not mask an intent to discriminate against some national origins. A policy of hiring only citizens of English ancestry would be illegal.

Employers often create rules that employees must be fluent in English. Such policies may have an adverse impact on certain groups, such as Mexican-Americans. For the employer to avoid a discriminatory charge of adverse impact, the employer must show that the requirement is dictated by business necessity. Courts have accepted this defense where employees must deal with customers and suppliers, or speak with fellow employees or supervisors. On the other hand, prohibiting the speaking of a language other than English while working may be difficult to justify as job-related.

Sex. Since the word "sex" was added to Title VII as a floor amendment without much debate, Congress's intent on this point is not clear. The courts have interpreted "sex" as prohibiting employers from discriminating against a person because that person is male or female. However, Title VII does not outlaw discrimination on the basis of marital status or sexual preference as long as the employer applies these rules equally to members of both sexes.

The Pregnancy Discrimination Act of 1978 amends Title VII and adds Section 701(k), which defines "sex" to include pregnancy and childbirth. Thus, disability arising from pregnancy or childbirth must be treated in the same manner as other disabilities affecting the employee's ability or inability to work. Consequently, an employer's medical, disability, and leave programs cannot exclude or especially treat pregnancy and maternity.

Initial cases of sexual discrimination involved disparate treatment, such as refusing to hire women as miners. Such policies were held illegal.

More recent cases of sex discrimination are based on claims of adverse impact; that is, that an employment rule neutral on its face operated to the disadvantage of women. For example, rules concerning height and weight minimums have an adverse impact on women. Of course, employers have the burden of proving that these requirements are "job-related" and a "business necessity." In most cases, the employer fails to establish either of these defenses.

Congress has authorized a bfoq exception for sex discrimination. Except in situations where a person *must* be a male of female because physical characteristics or abilities are involved, it is difficult to defend "sex" as a *bona fide* occupational qualification. Nonphysical characteristics possessed by one sex do not justify restricting employment to members of that sex.

In *Diaz* v. *Pan American World Airlines, Inc.*, 442 F. 2d 385 (5th Cir. 1971), Pan Am attempted to defend its policy that female flight attendants were superior to male flight attendants in the "nonmechanical" aspects of the job. Pan Am argued females were superior at "providing reassurance to anxious passengers, giving courteous personalized service," and "making flights as pleasurable as possible." The district court agreed with Pan Am that many women, but only a few men, possess these nonmechanical skills. Therefore, removing the sex requirement would force Pan Am to cease using the easiest way of screening out unsatisfactory applicants. The court of appeals reversed the district court's finding of a bfoq, saying the bfoq defense applies only where it is necessary, not merely convenient. Other cases have followed this narrow "necessity" approach to a bfoq for sex discrimination.

Advocates opposing sex discrimination against women are beginning to argue the theory of "comparable worth," which claims that jobs traditionally held predominantly by females have been systematically undervalued and underpaid in light of their intrinsic worth. Since the Equal Pay Act applies only to situations where men and women are employed on substantially similar work, comparable work claims are not covered. However, in 1981 the Supreme Court held that a claim of intentional sex-based wage discrimination could be brought under Title VII where men's and women's jobs are sufficiently dissimilar.[4] Just what constitutes "wage discrimination" and "intentional" wage discrimination is yet to be determined. Yet the economic repercussions of the "comparable worth" theory are enormous.

Another theory of sex discrimination is discussed in the following case.

Bundy v. Jackson
641 F. 2d 934 (1981)
U.S. Court of Appeals (D.C. Cir.)

In *Barnes* v. *Costle,* 561 F.2d 983 (D.C. Cir., 1977), we held an employer who abolished a female employee's job to retaliate against the employee's resistance of his sexual advances violated Title VII of the Civil Rights Act of 1964. The appellant in this case asks us to extend *Barnes* by holding that an employer violates Title VII merely by subjecting female employees to sexual harassment, even if the employee's resistance to that harrassment does not cause the employer to deprive her of any tangible job benefits.

The District Court in this case made an express finding of fact that in (defendant's office) . . . "the making of improper sexual advances to female employees [was] standard operating procedure, a fact of life, a normal condition of employment," and that the (defendant) . . . to whom she complained of the harrassment, failed to investigate her complaints or take them seriously. Nevertheless, the District Court refused to grant (plaintiff) any declaratory or injunctive relief, concluding that sexual harassment does not in itself represent discrimination "with respect to . . . terms, conditions, or privileges of employment" within the meaning of Title VII. . . .

* * *

We . . . made clear in *Barnes* that sex discrimination within the meaning of Title VII is not limited to disparate treatment founded solely or categorically on gender. Rather, discrimination is sex discrimination whenever sex is for no legitimate reason a substantial factor in the discrimination.

We thus have no difficulty inferring that [plaintiff] Bundy suffered discrimination on the basis of sex. Moreover, applying *Barnes*, we have no difficulty ascribing the harrassment— the "standard operating procedure"—to Bundy's employer. . . . Although Delbert Jackson himself appears not to have used his position as Director to harass Bundy, an employer is liable for discriminatory acts committed by supervisory personnel, and there is obviously no dispute that the men who harassed Bundy were her supervisors. *Barnes* did suggest that the employer might be relived of liability if the supervisor committing the harassment did so in contravention of the employer's policy and without the employer's knowledge, and if the

employer moved promptly and effectively to rectify the offense. Here, however, Delbert Jackson and other officials in the (office) who had some control over employment and promotion decisions had full notice of harassment committed by (office) supervisors and did virtually nothing to stop or even investigate the practice. And though there was ample evidence in this case that at least two other women in the (office) suffered from this harassment, *Barnes* makes clear that the employer could be held liable even if Bundy were the only victim, since Congress intended Title VII to protect *individuals* against class-based prejudice.

We thus readily conclude that Bundy's employer discriminated against her on the basis of sex. What remains is the novel question whether the sexual harassment of the sort Bundy suffered amounted by itself to sex discrimination with respect to the *"terms, conditions, or privileges of employment."* Though no court has as yet so held, we believe that an affirmative answer follows ineluctably from numerous cases finding Title VII violations where an employer created or condoned a substantially discriminatory work *environment,* regardless of whether the complaining employees lost any tangible job benefits as a result of the discrimination.

Bundy's claim on this score is essentially that "conditions of employment" include the psychological and emotional work environment—that the sexually stereotyped insults and demeaning propositions to which she was indisputably subjected and which caused her anxiety and debilitation, illegally poisoned that environment. This claim invokes the Title VII principle enunciated by Judge Goldberg in *Rogers* v. *Equal Employment Opportunity Com'n,* 454 F.2d 234 (5th Cir. 1971). . . . Granting that the express langauge of Title VII did not mention this situation, Judge Goldberg stated:

Congress chose neither to enumerate specific discriminatory practices, nor to elucidate *in extenso* the parameter of such nefarious activities. Rather, it pursued the path of wisdom by being unconstrictive, knowing that constant change is the order of our day and that the seemingly reasonable practices of the present can easily become the injustices of the morrow. . . .

The Fifth Circuit then concluded that the employer had indeed violated Title VII, Judge Goldberg explaining that "terms, conditions, or privileges of employment"

is an expansive concept which sweeps within its protective ambit the practice of creating a work environment heavily charged with ethnic or racial discrimination as to destroy completely the emotional and psychological stability of minority group workers. . . .

. . . Racial or ethnic discrimination against a company's minority clients may reflect no intent to discriminate directly against the company's minority employees, but in poisoning the atmosphere of employment it violates Title VII. Sexual stereotyping through discriminatory dress requirements may be benign in intent, and may offend women only in a general, atmospheric manner, yet it violates Title VII. Racial slurs, though intentional and directed at individuals, may still be just verbal insults, yet they too may create Title VII liability. How then can sexual harassment, which injects the most demeaning sexual stereotypes into the general work environment and which always represents an intentional assault on an individual's innermost privacy, not be illegal?

* * *

Thus, unless we extend the *Barnes* holding, an employer could sexually harass a female employee with impunity by carefully stopping short of firing the employee or taking any other tangible actions against her in response to her resistance, thereby creating the impression—the one received by the District Court in this case—that the employer did not take the ritual of harassment and resistance "seriously."

Indeed, so long as women remain inferiors in the employment hierarchy, they may have little recourse against harassment beyond the legal recourse Bundy seeks in this case. The law may allow a woman to prove that her resistance to the harassment cost her her job or some economic benefit, but this will do her no good if the employer never takes such tangible actions against her.

And this, in turn, means that so long as the sexual situation is constructed with enough coerciveness, subtlety, suddenness, or onesidedness to negate the effectiveness of the woman's refusal, or so long as her refusals are simply ignored while her job is formally undisturbed, she is not considered to have been sexually harassed.

It may even be pointless to require the employee to prove that she "resisted" the harassment at all. So long as the employer never literally forces sexual relations on the employee, "resistance" may be a meaningless alternative for her. If the employer demands no response to his verbal or physical gestures other than good-natured tolerance, the woman has no means of communicating her rejection. She neither accepts nor rejects the advances; she simply endures them. She might be able to contrive proof of rejection by objecting to the employer's advances in some very visible and dramatic way, but she would do so only at the risk of making her life on the job even more miserable. It hardly helps that the remote prospect of legal relief under *Barnes* remains available if she objects so powerfully that she provokes the employer into firing her.

The employer can thus implicitly and effectively make the employee's endurance of sexual intimidation a "condition" of her employment. The woman then faces a "cruel trilemma." She can endure the harassment. She can attempt to oppose it, with little hope of success, either legal or practical, but with every prospect of making the job even less tolerable for her. Or she can leave her job, with little hope of legal relief and the likely prospect of another job where she will face harassment anew.

Bundy proved that she was the victim of a practice of sexual harassment and a discriminatory work environment permitted by her employer. Her rights under Title VII were therefore violated. We thus reverse the District Court's holding on this issue and remand it to that court so it can fashion appropriate injunctive relief.

The Final Guidelines on Sexual Harassment in the Workplace (Guidelines) issued by the Equal Employment Opportunity Commission on November 10, 1980, offer a useful basis for injunctive relief in this case. . . . The general goal of these Guidelines is *preventive*. An employer . . . should fashion rules within its firm . . . to ensure that . . . corrective action never becomes necessary.

Applying these Guidelines to the present case, we believe that the (employer) . . . should be ordered to raise affirmatively the subject of sexual harassment with all his employees and inform all employees that sexual harassment violates Title VII of the Civil Rights Act of 1964. . . . The Director should also establish and publicize a scheme whereby harassed employees may complain to the Director immediately and confidentially. The Director should promptly take all necessary steps to investigate and correct any harassment, including warnings and appropriate discipline directed at the offending party, and should generally develop other means of preventing harassment. . . .

Perhaps the most important part of the preventive remedy will be a prompt and effective procedure for hearing, adjudicating, and remedying complaints of sexual harassment. . . .

Questions

1. How is "sexual harassment" considered to be sex discrimination in respect to "terms, conditions or privileges of employment"?
2. Can racial slurs by supervisors violate Title VII?
3. What policies should the employer adopt to avoid charges of sexual harassment on the job?
4. Bundy's claim for lost wages due to the denial of a promotion because of the sexual discrimination was remanded to the District Court with the following instructions:

    To establish a *prima facie* case of illegal denial of promotion in retaliation against the plaintiff's refusal of sexual advances by her supervisors, the plaintiff must show (1) that she was a victim of a pattern or practice of sexual harassment attributable to her employer (Bundy has, of course, already shown this); and (2) that she applied for and was denied a promotion for which she was technically eligible and of which she has a reasonable expectation. If the *prima facie* case is made out, the employer then must bear the burden of showing, by clear and convincing evidence, that he had legitimate nondiscriminatory reasons for denying the claimant promotion. . . . [If] the employer successfully rebuts the *prima facie* case, the claimant should still have the opportunity to prove that the employer's purported reasons were mere pretexts.

    If Bundy was eligible for promotion and had reasonable expectation of the promotion, how could the employer show a "legitimate and nondiscrimatory" reason for denying the promotion?

Older Workers. The Age Discrimination in Employment Act (ADEA) of 1967 prohibits discriminatory hiring and firing practices against individuals between the ages of 40 and 70. In 1979, 3097 complaints of age discrimination were filed with the EEOC. In 1980 the EEOC received 8779 such complaints. Sixty days after registering their complaints with the EEOC, individuals may file suits on their own. Most experts agree that the explosive growth of these actions will continue, fueled by periodic weakening of the economy with its ensuing layoffs, by an aging workforce, and by the increasing propensity of employees to fight back when their companies fire them.

The emphasis of ADEA is placed on evaluating the working ability of employees in the protected age group, rather than gearing employment decisions solely to age without regard to physical and mental capabilities. As a means of attaining this objective, the ADEA exempts employers in cases where the discrimination against persons in that age bracket is based on "reasonable factors other than age." Physical fitness requirements geared directly to the job would be an acceptable exemption, expecially if physical inability or health pose a significant threat to production or safety. The burden of proof is on the employer to justify discriminatory treatment. The jobs involving public safety appear to impose a less stringent demand on employers to legitimize discrimination. For example, bus line officials were not required to individually evaluate each driver applicant over age 40 to determine whether he or she could safely operate a bus.[5] Since the court recognized that medical examinations could not always detect problems in older drivers, it allowed a blanket prohibition of hiring drivers over 40. Apparently, similar exemptions would be permitted for aircraft pilots, fire fighters, police officers, and others serving the public when safety is a consideration.

The 1978 amendments to the ADEA created another exemption. Forced retirement of employees between the ages of 65 and 70 is permitted if an employee has been working as an executive in a high policy-making position for at least two years and is entitled to receive employer-financed pension benefits of at least $27,000 annually.

Coates v. National Cash Register Co.
433 F. Supp. 655 (1977)
U.S. District Court (WD. VA.)

Section 623(a)(1) of the Age Discrimination in Employment Act . . . states that it is unlawful for an employer to discharge or to discriminate against any individual "because of such individual's age." The phrase "because of such individual's age" is used several times throughout the prohibitory sections of ADEA and constitutes the standard by which to judge employment decisions. The problem with this standard for courts has been to interpret how much weight age must be given in the employment decision before the Act is violated. . . .

The court in *Laugesen* v. *Anaconda Co.,* 510 F.2d 307 (6th Cir. 1976) adopted a "determining factor" test and explained how the jury should judge the legality of the employment decision:

[W]e believe that it was essential for the jury to understand from the instructions that there could be more than one factor in the decision to discharge him and that he was nevertheless entitled to recover if one such factor was his age and if in fact it made a difference in determining whether he was retained or discharged. This is so even though the need to reduce the employee force generally was also a strong, and perhaps even more compelling reason. . . .

NCR has several reasons for its reduction of the Danville field engineers staff, including deteriorating economic conditions in mid-1975. While the company can discharge its employees, it cannot base the decision about which employee to discharge on age or on factors created by age discrimination.

NCR's decision to discharge plaintiffs was not directly based on age, but it was based on the training of plaintiffs. The evidence clearly established that the relative training levels of NCR employees was directly related to the age of the employees. So by using the training level as the basis of the discharge decision, NCR indirectly discharged plaintiffs because of their age. Therefore this court holds that the training or lack of training, which ostensibly is an objective and valid criterion for employment decisions cannot form the basis of an employment decision when that lack of training is created by age discrimination. The age discrimination which invalidates an employment decision need not be direct or intentional. This court further holds that both plaintiffs were discharged "because of" their "age."

Damages

Besides asking for reinstatement, plaintiffs requested back wages from May 2, 1975, until reinstatement, liquidated damages and attorney's fees and costs. . . .

To summarize the measure of back pay, it is still the difference between the salary an employee would have received but for the violation of the Act and the salary actually received from other employment. The period of back pay is measured from the time of the loss of employment as a result of the violation to the time when the employee accepts or declines reinstatement at his former position or at a position of comparable status, salary, benefits, and potential for advancement. The back pay amount computed in this way must be reduced by severance pay received, unemployment compensation collected, and any amounts earnable with reasonable diligence. Finally, the back pay amount should be increased by the value of any pension benefits, health insurance, seniority, leave-time, or other fringe benefits which the employee would have accrued during the back pay period but for the violation of the Act.

* * *

Both plaintiffs also prayed for liquidated damages and attorney's fees and costs. Liquidated damages are only available for "willful violations" of ADEA.

In this case, the advisory jury was instructed that they should find that the discharges were willful violations of ADEA only if the acts were "done voluntarily and intentionally, and with the specific intent to do something which is forbidden by law." This court finds that neither discharge was a willful violation of the law; therefore, no liquidated damages are available to plaintiffs.

Finally, it is well settled that plaintiffs who are victims of age discrimination are entitled to reasonable attorney's fees and costs.

Questions
1. In what fashion did NCR discriminate on the basis of age?
2. Besides gaining reinstatement, what damages were ordered to paid to the plaintiffs?

Handicapped Workers. Section 503 of the Vocational Rehabilitation Act of 1973 requires that all contractors and subcontractors holding federal contracts in excess of $2500 hire the physically and mentally handicapped on an affirmative basis. Section 504 requires nondiscriminatory rather than affirmative hiring of the handicapped by employers receiving federal financial assistance. The act's definition of "handicapped individual" includes "any person who (1) has a physical or mental impairment which substantially limits one or more of such person's major life activities, (2) has a record of such impairment, or (3) is regarded as having such an impairment." This definition not only protects persons with the obvious types of handicaps such amputated limbs, impaired vision or hearing, and the like, but also cancer victims, diabetics, and those with a history of heart disease. In 1978, however, Congress amended the act to exclude from the definition of a handicapped person alcoholics and those addicted to drugs.

While discrimination against handicapped individuals is forbidden and affirmative action may be required, there is no obligation to hire persons who are unable to perform or who are less skilled than others. The act protects only "qualified handicapped individuals" who are capable of performing a particular job with "reasonable accommodation" to his or her handicap. An employer must make reasonable accommodation to the physical and mental limitations of qualified employees possessing requisite skills unless such accommodation would impose an undue hardship on the employer. The employer's accommodation obligations are not clear, but financial cost and business necessity are among factors to be considered.

Employers may not use tests or other selection standards that may screen out handicapped persons unless the tests are job-related and alternative unbiased job-related measures are not available. The use of physical examinations or health-related inquiries in hiring or promotion decisions must be limited to an applicant's ability to perform job-related functions.

ENFORCEMENT PROCESSES

EQUAL EMPLOYMENT OPPORTUNITIES COMMISSION

The Civil Rights Act of 1964 created the Equal Employment Opportunity Commission (EEOC), which is granted the authority to investigate, conciliate, and litigate grievances under the act. (See Figure 19-1.) Prior to 1972, the EEOC only had authority to investigate complaints filed by individuals and attempt to settle them by conciliation. The EEOC had to convince the Justice Department that a case was worth prosecuting in the court before litigation would ensue. Consequently, not many cases were pursued through litigation. The Equal Employment Opportunity Act of 1972 amended Title VII, broadening its coverage and giving the EEOC power to bring enforcement action in the courts. Part of the enforcement authority of the EEOC is to require and preserve records that must be filed by employers. Requiring employers and unions to file detailed reports of their hiring and training programs forces the companies to consider corrective action to avoid any problems with the EEOC.

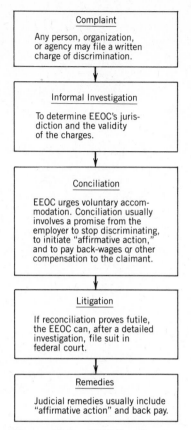

Figure 19-1.   EEOC enforcement processes.

Complaints

Most cases begin with an individual filing a complaint with EEOC against his or her employer. The aggrieved individual has 180 days after the alleged discrimination occurs to file a charge with the EEOC. If a state or local fair employment agency is involved, the EEOC must refrain from taking action for 60 days. If those agencies fail to resolve the controversy to the EEOC's satisfaction, the EEOC may act.

The EEOC must first attempt to settle the case by conciliation. If conciliation results are unsatisfactory, the EEOC may file suit against the employer in a federal district court. If the EEOC declines to file suit, the complainant is then permitted to file suit on his or her own behalf. If the individual suit is filed, the EEOC may intervene in the suit if the case is "of general public importance."

Pattern or Practice Suits

Sometimes, the EEOC's investigation of an individual's complaint may reveal a widespread practice of discrimination. Other times, the EEOC may initiate investigations of its own to determine whether a "pattern or practice" of discrimination exists. Section 707 of Title VII allows the EEOC to take direct action against an employer who is allegedly engaging in a "pattern or practice" of discrimination. This authority has been a powerful weapon in the EEOC's arsenal attacking prohibited discrimination.

The most famous case dealing with a pattern or practice of discrimination involved American Telephone and Telegraph (AT&T). The EEOC accused AT&T of systematic job discrimination of blacks, Spanish-Americans, and women. While AT&T denied the charges, it agreed to two consent decrees in 1973 and 1974. Back pay and salary adjustments for thousands of employees cost AT&T over $68 million. AT&T also agreed to establish percentage goals to put women and minorities into higher craft jobs and managerial positions. These decrees involved a controversial override provision to allow preferential treatment of women and minorities by overriding the seniority provisions of the union contract. After a supplemental order further prodded AT&T management, AT&T was found to be in substantial compliance with the original decrees by January 1979.

Other such pattern and practice agreements have been reached with a major steel company and General Electric Company. A complaint against Sears, Roebuck and Co. is currently being prosecuted. This process of attacking systematic discrimination is likely to be a more efficient use of taxpayers' monies and of greater benefit to the discriminated groups than the traditional suit to vindicate a single victim of discrimination.

The EEOC, through the issuance of standards, has put employers on notice about personnel policies that could lead to a charge of "pattern or practice" discrimination. The outlined six standards are as follows.

1. Employers who follow policies and practices that result in "low utilization" of available minorities and women despite the law's requirement that they recruit, hire, and promote such persons.
2. Employers who pay minorities and women less than other employers who use such workers for comparable work.
3. Companies that pay minorities and women less than other workers in comparable job categories.
4. Employers who follow personnel policies that have an "adverse impact" on those protected by federal antidiscrimination laws when such policies cannot be justified by "business necessity."
5. Employers whose discriminatory practices are likely to be emulated by other employers because of the company's size, influence in the community, or competitive position in the industry.
6. Employers who have an opportunity to hire and promote more minorities and women because of expansion or high turnover rates but neglect such workers in filling those positions.

Affirmative Action

The literal wording of Title VII seems to rule out any form of preferential treatment. The act ignores the moral issue of whether groups that had been discriminated against in the past were owed something more than simply an equal chance to compete with those who had benefited from the discrimination. Additionally, the act ignores the practical questions of how discriminated groups were supposed to obtain the education (training) and experience necessary to qualify themselves for jobs without some kind of preferential treatment that would overcome deficiencies in education and experience that were the result of discrimination. Instead, the act merely requires equal employment opportunity. Each person is to get an equal chance at a job or promotion.

Initial enforcement of Title VII followed this passive approach to implementing the concept of equal opportunity. It was soon recognized, however, that the mere prohibition of discrimination was insufficient. What was needed was some kind of "affirmative action" program where positive steps would be taken to hire some minorities and women and promote them into higher paying positions.

Eventually, the courts came to accept civil rights legislation as requiring some preferential procedures to implement the intent of Congress. Besides being ordered into an affirmative action program, some firms voluntarily elected to adopt affirmative action programs to demonstrate the firm's "good faith" effort to comply with equal rights legislation and avoid EEOC challenge. Consequently, the use of goals (or quota systems) became the preferred means of correcting known deficiencies in workforce composition.

Affirmative action implies a set of specific results-oriented procedures designed to achieve employment opportunity at a pace beyond that which would normally occur. Affirmative action programs establish specific goals (quotas) and reasonable timetables designed to obtain an employee workforce that reflects the makeup of the relevant external labor market.

The widespread use of goals and quotas in affirmative action programs inevitably gave rise to charges of reverse discrimination. Reverse discrimination involves a situation where minorities or women who are equally qualified, or perhaps less qualified, than white male applicants for the same position are given preference over the latter for jobs or promotions. The following case deals with the charge of reverse discrimination by an employer that had reserved half of the positions in a company training program for minorities.

United Steelworkers v. Weber
443 U.S. 193 (1979)
Supreme Court of the United States

Justice Brennan

In 1974 petitioner United Steelworkers of America (USWA) and petitioner Kaiser Aluminum & Chemical Corporation (Kaiser) entered into a master collective-bargaining agreement covering terms and conditions of employment at 15 Kaiser plants. The agreement contained an affirmative action plan designed to eliminate conspicuous racial imbalances in Kaiser's then almost exclusively white craft work forces. Black craft hiring goals were set for each Kaiser plant equal to the percentage of blacks in the respective local labor forces. To enable plants to meet these goals, on-the-job training programs were established to teach unskilled production workers—black and white—the skills necessary to become craft workers. The plan reserved for black employees 50% of the openings in these newly created in-plant training programs.

This case arose from the operation of the plan at Kaiser's plant in Gramercy, La. Until 1974 Kaiser hired as craft workers for that plant only persons who had had prior craft experiece. Because blacks had long been excluded from craft unions, few were able to present such credentials. As a consequence, prior to 1974 only 1.83% (five of 273) of the skilled craft workers at the Gramercy plant were black, even though the work force in the Gramercy area was approximately 39% black.

Pursuant to the national agreement Kaiser altered its craft hiring practice in the Gramercy plant. Rather than hiring already trained outsiders, Kaiser established a training program to train its production workers to fill craft openings. Selection of craft trainees was made on the basis of seniority, with the proviso that at least 50% of the new trainees were to be black until the percentage of black skilled craft workers in the Gramercy plant approximated the percentage of blacks in the local labor force.

During 1974, the first year of the operation of the Kaiser-USWA affirmative action plan, 13 craft trainees were selected from Gramercy's production work force. Of these, 7 were black and 6 white. The most junior black selected into the program had less seniority than several white production workers whose bids for admission were rejected. Thereafter one of those white production workers, respondent Brian Weber, instituted this class action in the United States District Court for the Eastern District of Louisiana.

The complaint alleged that the filling of craft trainee positions at the Gramercy plant pursuant to the affirmative action program had resulted in junior black employees receiving training in preference to more senior white employees, thus discriminating against respondent and other similarly situated white employees in violation of §§703(a) and (d) of Title VII. . . .

We emphasize at the outset the narrowness of our inquiry. Since the Kaiser-USWA plan does not involve state action, this case does not present an alleged violation of the Equal Protection Clause of the Constitution. Further, since the Kaiser-USWA plan was adopted voluntarily, we are not concerned with what Title VII requires or with what a court might order to remedy a past proven violation of the Act. The only question before us is the narrow statutory issue of whether Title VII *forbids* private plans that accord racial preferences in the manner and for the purpose provided in the Kaiser-USWA plan. . . .

Respondent argues that Congress intended in Title VII to prohibit all race-conscious affirmative action plans. Respondent's argument rests upon a literal interpretation of §§703(a) and (d) of the Act. Those sections make it unlawful to "discriminate . . . because of . . . race" in hiring and in the selection of apprentices for training programs. Since, the argument runs, . . . the Kaiser-USWA affirmative action plan operates to discriminate against white employees solely because they are white, it follows that the Kaiser-USWA plan violates Title VII.

Respondent's argument is not without force. But it overlooks the significance of the fact that the Kaiser-USWA plan is an affirmative action plan voluntarily adopted by private parties to eliminate traditional patterns of racial segregation. In this context respondent's reliance upon a literal construction of §703 (a) and (d) . . . is misplaced. It is a "familiar rule, that a thing may be within the letter of the statute and yet not within the statute, because not within its spirit, nor within the intention of its makers." The prohibition against racial discrimination in §703 (a) and (d) of Title VII must therefore be read against the background of the legislative history of Title VII and the historical context from which the act arose. . . .

Congress' primary concern in enacting the prohibition against racial discrimination in Title VII of the Civil Rights Act of 1964 was with "the plight of the Negro in our economy." Before 1964, blacks were largely relegated to "unskilled and semi-skilled jobs." As a consequence "the relative position of the Negro worker [was] steadily worsening. . . ."

Congress feared that the goals of the Civil Rights Act—the integration of blacks into the mainstream of American society—could not be achieved unless this trend were reversed. And Congress recognized that that would not be possible unless blacks were able to secure jobs "which have a future." . . . Accordingly, it was clear to Congress that "the crux of the problem [was] to open employment opportunities for Negroes in occupations which have been traditionally closed to them," and it was to this problem that Title VII's prohibition against racial discrimination in employment was primarily addressed.

It plainly appears from the House Report accompanying the Civil Rights Act that Congress did not intend wholly to prohibit private and voluntary affirmative action efforts as one method of solving this problem. The Report provides:

No bill can or should lay claim to eliminating all the causes and consequences of racial and other types of discrimination against minorities. There is reason to believe, however, that national leadership provided by the enactment of Federal legislation dealing with the most troublesome problems *will create an atmosphere conductive to voluntary or local resolution of other forms of discrimination.* H. R. Rep. No. 914, 88th Cong., 1st Sess. (1963), at 18. (Emphasis supplied.)

Given this legislative history, we cannot agree with respondent that Congress intended to prohibit the private sector from taking effective steps to accomplish the goal that Congress designed Title VII to achieve. The very statutory words intended as a spur or catalyst to cause "employers and unions to self-examine and to self-evaluate their employment practices and to endeavor to eliminate, so far as possible, the last vestiges of an unfortunate and ignominious page in this country's history," cannot be interpreted as an absolute prohibition against all private, voluntary, race-conscious affirmative action efforts to hasten the elimination of such vestiges. It would be ironic indeed if a law triggered by a Nation's concern over centuries of racial injustice and intended to improve the lot of those who had "been excluded from the American dream for so long," constituted the first legislative prohibition of all voluntary, private, race-conscious efforts to abolish traditional patterns of racial segregation and hierarchy.

Our conclusion is further reinforced by examination of the language and legislative history of §703(j) of Title VII. Had Congress meant to prohibit all race-conscious affirmative action, as respondent urges, it easily could have provid[ed] that Title VII would not require or *permit* racially preferential integration efforts. But Congress did not choose such a course. Rather Congress added Section 703(j) which . . . provides that nothing contained in Title VII "shall be interpreted to *require* any employer . . . to grant preferential treatment . . . to any group because of the race . . . of such . . . group on account of" a *de facto* racial imbalance in the employer's work force. The section does *not* state that "nothing in Title VII shall be interpreted to *permit*" voluntary affirmative efforts to correct racial imbalances. The natural inference is that Congress chose not to forbid all voluntary race-conscious affirmative action.

. . . In view of this legislative history and in view of Congress' desire to avoid undue federal regulation of private businesses, use of the word "require" rather than the phrase "require or permit" in Section 703(j) fortifies the conclusion Congress did not intend to limit traditional business freedom to such a degree as to prohibit all voluntary, race-conscious affirmative action.

We therefore hold that Title VII's prohibition in Sections 703(a) and (d) against racial discrimination does not condemn all private, voluntary, race-conscious affirmative action plans. . . .

We conclude, therefore, that the adoption of the Kaiser-USWA plan for the Gramercy plant falls within the area of discretion left by Title VII to the private sector voluntarily to adopt affirmative action plans designed to eliminate conspicuous racial imbalance in traditionally segregated job categories. . . .

Questions

1. Why was the charge of "reverse discrimination" not within the purpose of Title VII?
2. Did Congress intend to prohibit all race-conscious affirmative action? What language could Congress have used if it intended to accomplish that goal?

OFFICE OF FEDERAL CONTRACT COMPLIANCE PROGRAMS

The OFCCP is located in the labor department and responsible for the administration of Executive Orders 11246 and 11375. These executive orders forbid employment discrimination on the basis of race, color, religion, sex, or national origin by prime contractors and subcontractors who have federal government contracts in excess of $10,000. Such federal contractors are required to develop affirmative action plans in "good faith" for the hiring and training of minorities. Employers with contracts of over $50,000 and with 50 or more employees were initially required to develop written affirmative action programs that identify minority and female underutilization and establish goals and timetables to correct existing deficiencies in the employment of minorities and women. Failure to meet these provisions satisfactorily could lead to cancellation of a contract or to being barred from future government contracts.

In 1980, Firestone Tire and Rubber Company was removed from the roster of possible government contractors. Because of the dispute over Firestone's affirmative action program at one of its Texas plants, the Office of Federal Contract Compliance banned Firestone from selling goods and services to the federal government. The potential cost to Firestone is about $40 million annually. This made Firestone the largest of the 27 companies to be denied future federal contracts because of violation of executive orders requiring antibias hiring.

The specifics of the affirmative action requirements under the executive orders were relaxed by the Reagan Administration in 1981. For example, contractors with fewer than 250 employees and contract business of less than $1 million were made exempt from preparing the *written* affirmative action plans. Still, the standards exceed those of EEOC under Title VII. Moreover, these regulations cover 30 million workers in about 200,000 firms with federal contracts.

CONCLUSION

The precise impact of equal employment opportunity policies is impossible to measure. Individual cases can be cited that reveal progress. On the other hand, some individual situations suggest perverse effects, as in the location of new plants in largely white communities to avoid minority group applicants. Aggregate data suffer from the same problems of revealing both progress and continued discrepancies. No doubt the debate over policies of affirmative action will continue. But business managers should clearly recognize that the basic public policies of Title VII are not likely to be changed in the near future. While the Reagan Administration has largely abandoned the pursuit of quotas, any further retreat from affirmative action will fuel the arguments of the proponents of equal opportunity. Consequently, professional business managers must adopt Title VII's purposes of using job-related criteria for employment and promotion decisions. Initially, because of the costs and imprecision in validating job-related criteria, employers may have been justified in adopting the approach of improving their "statistics" in new hiring and promotions to avoid a "disparate impact." However, this approach does not fulfill Title VII's purpose of neutral job criteria and breeds perceptions of "reverse discrimination." To avoid compliance policies of the statistic-oriented nature, management must eschew the "easy road" and instead develop the appropriate job-related criteria that are mandated by the law and suggested by professional business practices.

DISCUSSION QUESTIONS

1. In Scott Co. both blacks and whites worked in "production" jobs and in the more skilled "maintenance" jobs. Within each department, however, blacks were channeled into the lower paying, physically demanding jobs.

   In order to remedy this acknowledged discrimination, Scott Co. announced that no job would be barred to any employee because of race. However, Scott felt that it was a business necessity that the production job holders have a high school diploma as well as a passing score on an aptitude test. A large number of black employees could not meet these requirements.

   Under what conditions would Scott prevail on a discrimination claim under the Civil Rights Act of 1964?

2. Collectively bargained union contracts established and perpetuated over a period of time separate job classifications for airline stewardesses (all

female) and airline pursers (all male). Persons in each of these positions served as cabin attendants. Separate seniority lists were maintained for each classification pursuant to the union contracts and, also pursuant to contract, the purser wage scale ranged from 20 to 55 percent higher than salaries paid to stewardesses of equivalent seniority. Women were dominant in the stewardesses' union.

A female cabin attendant filed a claim under the Equal Pay Act. Is the women-dominated union contract with the company a bar to the claim?

3. S, a black male employee of seven years, is accused of starting a fist fight with his supervisor, a man he knew to be suffering from a hernia, pulmonary embolism, and poor clotting of the blood, over the signing of a leave slip for early departure from work. After investigation, a superior recommends termination, stating that "In this instance an employee of greater strength struck a recently hospitalized supervisor when the issue was one hour of annual leave," and that the employee threatened to finish the fight "outside after work."

Two years earlier an unrelated fight had occurred between a white employee and his black supervisor, where the employee had struck his supervisor after being provoked. It was found that the supervisor exercised "exceedingly poor supervisory judgement" and "in large measure precipitated the fracas." That white employee received an official reprimand and a transfer.

A year before the incident involving S, two black female employees receive reprimands for fighting with each other.

S claims that he is a victim of discrimination on the basis of race and sex.

What justification might the employer argue to explain the disparate treatment in the disciplinary actions? Has there been a violation of law?

4. Cariddi, a school principal's assistant, worked a summer job supervising ticket takers for the Kansas City Chiefs. Cariddi and 1 other of the 6 supervisors were Italian-Americans, and on Cariddi's recommendation, 18 Italian-Americans were hired by the stadium director as ticket takers. Cariddi's wife and daughter were also employed by the Kansas City Chiefs. The stadium director referred to Cariddi and other Italian-American employees as "dagoes" or "the Mafia."

Cariddi was fired, and after he sued for discrimination on the basis of national origin, the trial court found that the firing was for insubordination and failure to comply with club policy with respect to the use of the press box on game days.

What is your opinion of the discrimination in employment claim?

5. When Rodney was first hired as a millwright, his supervisor praised his work and treated him as a friend, but after Rodney mentioned that he believed in Judaism, his supervisor, named Evans, changed his attitude and referred to Rodney as "the Jew-boy," "the kike," "the Christ-killer," "the damn Jew," and "the goddamn Jew." Any employee with the misfortune to be Rodney's work partner feared constant harrassment, incident reports on minor mis-

takes, and snide responses from Evans to work-related questions. Rodney's work was given intense scrutiny. Eventually Rodney was one of several employees discharged for failing to comply with "reporting-off" rules of the company, an allegation Rodney could not contest.

Rodney sued under the Civil Rights Act for discrimination in his discharge. As a manager for the company, what would you want to point out to the company lawyer? What type of remedy might Rodney be entitled to if the court accepts his discrimination argument?

6. A savings and loan association enforced a dress code for its employees, under which female office employees wore a uniform consisting of slacks or a choice of three skirt styles, and a jacket or tunic or vest, and male office employees were to wear business suits or business-type sport jackets and pants and ties, or a leisure suit with suitable shirt and tie. The uniforms were all of one color, were provided by the employer savings association, but the value of the uniform was included in their income for tax purposes. On the last Tuesday of each month the women were permitted to wear clothing of their own choosing while the uniforms were being cleaned, and the uniform requirement was suspended during the week between Christmas and New Year's.

A female employee sued the savings association, claiming a violation of the Civil Rights Act by reason of the fact that female office employees were required to wear uniforms while comparable male office employees were not. The association believed that the uniform requirement was necessary to preserve a business atmosphere, because dress competition exists among women and current fashion might not promote a business atmosphere. Some women favored the uniform. Was the Civil Rights Act violated?

7. H. B. has been an account manager for Sim Co. since 1959. From 1959 through 1969 he was assigned to the Chicago area, and in each of those years he met or exceeded his sales quota. His sales volume each year placed him in the top rankings (often top 4 percent) for all account managers, and in his worst year he was in the top 37 percent. In 1970 H. B. requested and received a transfer to Wisconsin where, from 1970 through 1972, H. B. continued to maintain his sales rankings and to receive letters of commendation. H. B.'s base salary was $13,000 plus a sales commission on assigned accounts. His sales in 1972 totalled $392,954.

In a November 1972 meeting with his Wisconsin supervisor, Nolan, and Nolan's superior, Senneke, H. B.'s performance was criticized, and he was informed that his four major accounts were being reassigned to Nolan. When H. B. objected, Nolan commented, "Hell, you've only got four more years to go." H. B. was then 61 years old. After this meeting H. B.'s relationships with Nolan and Senneke were strained. H. B. took as "good natured ribbing" comments reminding him of other retiring employees, and made known that he had no intention to retire early.

In September 1973 Nolan wrote to his superiors and recommended that H. B. be retired at age 62 on the basis that customers were complaining of H. B.'s "lack of performance." At another meetings with Nolan and Senneke in October 1973, H. B. learned that 14 of his accounts were being assigned to Vander, a 22-year-old Sim Co. engineer. H. B. was given the option of staying on as account manager in Wisconsin, taking early retirement, or transferring to another territory if one was available. In November 1973 H.B. looked into early retirement with the personnel director. When forms for retirement were prepared and sent to him on January 10, 1974, H.B. returned them, saying there was an error and he did not want early retirement. Later that month all of H.B.'s accounts were assigned to Vander, and on February 1, 1974, H.B. was informed that no territory was available for him and since he would not retire he was terminated as of March 1, 1974, at age 62. A follow-up letter gave as reasons for his firing "adverse customer reaction, ineffective job servicing, and a lack of technical understanding." No specific customer complaint was ever brought to H.B.'s attention, no written records of them were found, and H.B. did not lose customers except by reassignment.

After the reassignments, Vander's sales record was inferior to H.B.'s, but Vander was retained by Sim Co.

H.B. sued Sim Co., claiming age discrimination.

8. Lumber Supply Co. had a rule prohibiting employees from speaking Spanish on the job unless they were communicating with Spanish-speaking customers. Lumber Supply adopted the rule because (1) English-speaking customers objected to communications between employees that they could not understand; (2) pamphlets and trade literature were in English and not available in Spanish, and therefore employees had to be fluent in English apart from dealing with customers; (3) employees who spoke Spanish off the job would improve their English if they were required to use English at all times on the job; and (4) supervisors who did not speak Spanish could better oversee the work of subordinates if they conversed in English. The rule did not apply to lumberyard employees, nor did it apply to private conversation during work breaks.

Mr. Garcia, a 24-year-old native citizen of the United States, was raised in a household where only Spanish was spoken, but he speaks English as well, having completed 9½ years in Texas public schools. Garcia worked for Lumber Supply as a salesman with the responsibility for assisting other salespersons and selling lumber, hardware, and supplies. Eight such salesmen were employed, and seven were Hispanic. Thirty-one of Lumber Supply's 39 employees were Hispanic. Most of the employees were bilingual; those who were not worked in the lumberyard.

Garcia was asked a question by another bilingual employee about an item requested by a customer, and he responded in Spanish that it was not available. An officer of the company overheard this, and since Garcia had been repeatedly warned, he was discharged. Garcia admitted that he had violated the English-only rule repeatedly since his hiring but claims that he is more comfortable in Spanish, his primary language. As Garcia is of Mexican extraction, the Spanish language is central in his ethnic background.

Garcia claims that Lumber Supply's enforcement of its English-only rule constitutes discrimination on the basis of national origin.

Consider whether Gracia was discriminated against on the basis of national origin and whether he suffered discrimination in the "terms and conditions of employment" because he was not permitted to use the language he felt most comfortable with while other employees whose primary language was English were permitted to use their most comfortable language.

9. Williams, age 52, applied to Montgomery Ward for a job as a seller of heavy household appliances. Six years earlier, Williams had had a heart attack that left him with continuing angina. After a physical examination by a Montgomery Ward physician, Williams was refused employment because of the heart condition, and because of a possibility, perceived by the employer, that Williams could become incapacitated in the future, thus affecting the employer's interest in continuity of job performance.

Was Ward's failure to hire Williams an illegal discrimination against the handicapped?

10. An employee of a life insurance company had maintained a good work record for several years. In April he admitted himself into a hospital for treatment of a "drinking problem," and he remained there for one month, after which time he returned to work. The reason for his hospital stay was known to his employer. When he returned to work, he was assigned a special project to coordinate, and the project was on schedule when the employee left for his vacation on June 27. While he was gone, the project fell behind schedule, and overtime hours were required to complete it. On July 10 the employee was told he was being put on "demand performance" by the company, signifying dissatisfaction with his work. On July 31 he was fired.

The employee complained that he had been discriminated against because of a handicap, his "drinking problem." Under the applicable state law, a "handicap" is a disability that makes achievement unusually difficult.

Should the employee's current alcholic problem be considered a handicap, protected from discrimination?

11. Martin Marietta (MM) refused to hire women with preschool-age children. MM argued this hiring practice did not discriminate against women, because approximately 70 percent of the job applicants were women and approximately 80 percent of those hired were women. Hence, there was no bias against women as such. Has this practice violated Title VII?

12. Several white employees were fired for misappropriating their employer's property. However, one of their accomplices, a black employee, was not dismissed. Is this illegal race discrimination?

13. Fernandez was employed by the Wynn Oil Company. During her employment, she held various positions, the last being that of administrative

assistant to the vice president of Wynn's International Operations Division. When Wynn failed to promote her to the Director of International Operations, she sued Wynn alleging sex discrimination. Wynn defended on the ground that male sex is a *bona fide* occupational qualification for a job performed in foreign countries where women are barred from business. Evaluate Wynn's defense.

14. Plaintiff, a black female employed by Bank of America, alleges that she was discharged because she refused her supervisor's demands for sexual favors. Prior to her discharge plaintiff's job performance had been rated "superior." Plaintiff has sued the Bank claiming that they are responsible for the discriminating practices of their supervisors. The Bank in defense claims that they have an established internal policy to guard against discrimination of this type. The Bank further claims that plaintiff's refusal to utilize internal company proceedings as a means of redress against the supervisor voids any claim by plaintiff that the Bank should be held responsible.

    In light of the Bank's internal procedures to guard against discrimination, does plaintiff have a valid Title VII action?

15. Sharon M. Powell, also known as Michael D. Powell, was legally a male who was living as a woman as a prerequisite to having a sex change operation. Sharon a/k/a Michael was hired as a waitress at a department store. The first day at work a patron at the restaurant recognized Powell and informed the restaurant supervisor that his waitress was in fact a male. Powell was immediately fired. Does Powell have a claim against the department store under Title VII of the Civil Rights Act?

SUGGESTED READINGS

Bowers, L. Thomas, "Daniel Thrown to the Lions: An Analysis of International Bhd. of Teamsters v. Daniel," *American Business Law Journal,* Vol. 18, No. 1, Spring 1980, pp. 39–58.

Phillips, Michael J., "Reverse Racial Preferences Under the Equal Protection Clause: Round II. Fullilove v. Klutznick," *American Business Law Journal,* Vol. 19, No. 2, Summer 1981, pp. 197–213.

Phillips, Michael J., "'Voluntary' Racial Employment Preferences Under Title VII. United Steel Workers of America v. Weber," *American Business Law Journal,* Vol. 18, No. 1, Spring 1980, pp. 94–106.

Stone, R. Thomas, Jr., "Sex Discrimination in Reverse—Kahn v. Shevin," *American Business Law Journal,* Vol. 13, No. 3, Winter 1976, pp. 388–391.

Wines, William A., "Seniority, Recession, and Affirmative Action: The Challenge for Collective Bargaining," *American Business Law Journal,* Vol. 20, No. 1, Spring 1982, pp. 37–58.

ENDNOTES

1. Bradley, R. Shiller, *The Economics of Poverty and Discrimination* (Englewood Cliffs, N.J.: Prentice-Hall, 1973), pp. 125–26.

2. *Franks* v. *Bowman Transportation Co.*, 419 U.S. 1050 (1976).

3. *Trans World Airlines, Inc.* v. *Hardison*, 432 U.S. 73 (1977).

4. *County of Washington* v. *Gunther*, 452 U.S. 161 (1981).

5. *U.S. Dept. of Labor* v. *Greyhound Lines, Inc.* (CA-7, 1974), 7 EPD ¶ 9286; and *Usery* v. *Tamiami Trial Tours*, 531 F 2d 224 (CA-4, 1976), 11 EPD ¶ 10,916.

chapter 20

SECURITIES REGULATION

Although securities and the trading of securities have deep historical roots, laws regulating the securities trading process are of more recent origin. The speculative pricing of securities in unchartered stock companies of England caused Parliament to pass the South Sea Bubble Act of 1720, which substantially prohibited the formation of unchartered corporations and outlawed the dishonest issuance of securities of unchartered companies. In the United States, however, the laws dealing with transactions in securities were not passed until states authorized general incorporation statutes during the industrialization process following the Civil War.

HISTORICAL BACKGROUND

BLUE-SKY LAWS

Nearly every state in the country has laws regulating the issuance of securities to its residents. The purpose of such laws is to prevent abuses by promoters of speculative ventures. To avoid fraudulent sales of securities, states passed "blue-sky" laws, so named became a judge once referred to a fraudulent security as having no more value "than so many feet of blue sky."

The blue-sky laws differ from state to state. Most states have a *fraud-type* law that imposes penalties if evidence indicates the fraudulent sale of securities. A securities violation can result in criminal prosecution and injunctions barring future utilization of such practices. Other states require *registration of brokers and dealers* who sell securities. Such laws were enacted in an effort to regulate the persons who sell securities in those states. Still other states utilize *registration of information* about the issuer with some state official. The laws of these states empower state officials to determine whether the securities themselves are "fair" deals for the buying public. For example, in California, a security offering must meet a "fair, just, and equitable" standard before the security can be registered for distribution.

NEED FOR FEDERAL LEGISLATION

The absence of blue-sky laws in some states and the inadequacy of such laws in other states allowed fraudulent and deceptive sales of securities to continue in spite of the laws of some states. The most widely used method of evading state blue-sky laws was to operate across state lines.

The speculative securities market of the 1920s afforded numerous opportunities for abuses in the trading of securities. One practice involved price manipulation through "wash sales" or "matched orders." Through successive buy and sell orders brokers created a false impression of market activity and of higher prices. Brokers using these devices reaped profits before the price collapsed to true market levels. Another practice involved issuing false and misleading statements in order to profit at the expense of unwary investors. Finally, the misuse of corporate information by "inside" corporate officials allowed them to trade with misinformed stockholders and investors before important inside information became public.

Before the "market crash" in the autumn of 1929, the New York Stock Exchange (NYSE) had an aggregate value of about $89 billion. However, in 1932 the aggregate value of NYSE stocks was only about $15 billion. This traumatic drop in stock value, which probably could not have been prevented by legislation, nevertheless caused a social awakening to the need for federal legislation to deal with abusive practices in securities transactions.

FEDERAL SCHEME OF REGULATION

When Congress determined to regulate securities, it had the advantage of surveying the various state efforts at security regulation before determining the federal approach to this problem. Congress rejected the notion that a federal bureaucracy should make a judgment concerning the worth or fairness of securities offered to the public. Instead, Congress utilized concepts embodied in blue-sky laws that include the designation of fraudulent activities, the registration of dealers in securities, and the registration of information about the issuers of securities to be offered to the public. The essence of the federal approach is disclosure. The drafters of the federal laws viewed the responsibility of the federal government as being one primarily to assure investors of access to enough information to enable them to arrive at rational decisions. The fundamental purpose of securities law is to substitute the philosophy of full disclosure for the philosophy of *caveat emptor* and thus achieve a higher standard of business ethics in the securities industry.

SECURITIES AND EXCHANGE COMMISSION

The Securities and Exchange Commission (SEC) was created by the Securities Exchange Act of 1934. As an independent, bipartisan agency, it administers laws that seek to protect investors and the general public in securities transactions. Laws administered by the SEC are briefly explained in Table 20-1. The commission also advises federal courts in corporate reorganization proceedings under Chapter 11 of the National Bankruptcy Act. It studies any proposed reorganization plan and issues a report on whether the proposal is fair, feasible, and equitable.

The commission is composed of five members who are appointed by the President, with the advice and consent of the Senate. The commissioners hold five-year terms, which are staggered so that one expires on June 5 of each year. The chairman of the commission is designated by the President, and no more than three members of the commission may be from the same political party.

Table 20-1
LAWS ADMINISTERED BY THE SEC

Securities Act of 1933	Previously administered by the Federal Trade Commission, this law is now under the jurisdiction of the SEC. It provides that securities offered to the public must be registered with the SEC unless there is a specific exemption for the transaction. Assuming no exemption, the registration statement containing a prospectus must be filed giving specified information, and the SEC will judge the completeness and accuracy of the filing. The prospectus then must be delivered to potential buyers as a means of disclosing critical information about the company. There are specific penalties for material misstatement in registration.
Securities Exchange Act of 1934	This act created the SEC and is concerned with the trading of securities. The companies listed on stock exchanges or having more than 500 shareholders must file certain regular reports with the SEC, including a Form 10-K annually, and Form 10-Q quarterly, annual proxy statements, and a Form 8-K for special events. The 1934 Act also contains a general fraud provision applicable to all securities sold in interstate commerce, even though they are exempt from registration.
Public Utility Holding Company Act of 1935	This act was enacted to correct abuses in the financing and operation of electric and gas public-utilities holding-company systems. Such systems had been complicated by the formation of large holding companies on top of the operating companies and a substantial amount of pyramiding.

(*continued*)

Table 20-1—*Continued*

Trust Indenture Act of 1939	This act requires that publicly held debt be issued, pursuant to contract, an indenture, which must contain specific provisions to protect the public. For each debt issued, there must be a trustee who is obligated in the event of default to protect the public debt holder as if the trustee were acting prudently on his or her own behalf.
Investment Company Act of 1940	This act subjects investment holding companies (mutual funds) to certain statutory prohibitions and to commission regulation deemed necessary to protect the interest of investors and the public. The commission does not supervise the investment activities of these companies, but the law requires disclosure of their financial condition and investment policies to afford investors full and complete information about their activities.
Investment Advisers Act of 1940	This act establishes a pattern of regulation of investment advisers. It requires that persons or firms who engage for compensation in the business of advising others about their securities transactions must register with the commission and conform their activities to statutory standards designed to protect the interests of investors.
Securities Investor Protection Act of 1970	This act created the Securities Investor Protector Corporation (SIPC), a nonprofit organization whose membership comprises the brokers and dealers registered under the 1934 Act and members of the national securities exchanges. The SIPC creates a fund by collecting fees from the membership, which is used for the protection of investors to a limit of $500,000 for each customer and a maximum of $100,000 for cash claims from each customer. The SEC has regulatory authority over the SIPC.
Foreign Corrupt Practices Act of 1977	This act makes it a criminal offense for any United States business enterprise to offer a bribe to a foreign official for the purpose of obtaining or directing business to any person. It also amends the 1934 Act to require registrants to maintain reasonably complete and accurate records and to devise sufficient systems of internal accounting controls.

ISSUANCE OF SECURITIES

The financial community that deals in securities may be divided into two activities: the initial *distribution* (issuance) of securities and the *trading* of securities. The *issuance* involves the raising of capital for corporations and government entities through the new issuance of securities. The distribution function is often called underwriting, and this activity is principally regulated by the Securities

Act of 1933. On the other hand, the *trading* of securities involves transactions whereby outstanding securities are traded or bought and sold among members of the public. Transactions are often executed through professional financial houses, through the exchanges, or through the over-the-counter market. These secondary transactions are regulated primarily by the Securities Exchange Act of 1934.

SECURITIES ACT OF 1933

The Work of the SEC
(Published by the SEC, October 1980)

SECURITIES ACT OF 1933

This "truth in securities" law has two basic objectives: (a) to provide investors with material financial and other information concerning securities offered for public sale; and (b) to prohibit misrepresentation, deceit and other fraudulent acts and practices in the sale of securities generally (whether or not required to be registered).

Registration of Securities

The first objective applies to securities offered for public sale by an issuing company or any person in a control relationship to such company. Before the public offering of such securities, a registration statement must be filed with the commission by the issuer, setting forth the required information. When the statement has become effective, the securities may be sold. The purpose of registration is to provide disclosure of financial and other information on the basis of which investors may appraise the merits of the securities. To that end, investors must be furnished with a prospectus (selling circular) containing the salient data set forth in the registration statement to enable them to evaluate the securities and make informed and discriminating investment decisions.

The Registration Process

To facilitate the registration of securities by different types of issuing companies, the Commission has prepared special registration forms which vary in their disclosure requirements to provide disclosure of the essential facts pertinent in a given type of offering while at the same time minimizing the burden and expense of compliance with the law. In general, the registration forms call for disclosure of information such as (1) a description of the registrant's properties and business, (2) a description of the significant provisions of the security to be offered for sale and its relationship to the registrant's other capital securities, (3) information about the management of the registrant, and (4) financial statements certified by independent public accountants.

The registration statement and prospectus become public immediately on filing with the Commission; but it is unlawful to sell the securities until the effective date. After the filing of the registration statement, the securities may be offered orally or by certain summaries of the information in the registration statement as permitted by rules of the Commission. The Act provides that registration statements shall become effective on the 20th day after filing (or on the 20th day after the filing of the last amendment thereto); but the Commission, in its discretion, may advance the effective date if . . . such action is deemed appropriate.

Registration statements are examined by the Division of Corporation Finance for compliance with the disclosure requirements. If a statement appears to be materially incomplete or inaccurate, the registrant usually is informed by letter and given an opportunity to file correcting or clarifying amendments. The Commission, however, has authority to refuse or suspend the effectiveness of any registration statement if it finds, after hearing, that material representations are misleading, inaccurate, or incomplete. Accordingly, if material deficiencies in a registration statement appear to stem from a deliberate attempt to conceal and mislead, or if the deficiencies otherwise are of such nature as not to lend themselves readily to correction through the informal letter process, the Commission may conclude that it is in the public interest to resort to a hearing to develop the facts by evidence and to determine on the evidence whether a stop order should issue refusing or suspending effectiveness of the statement.

A stop order is not a permanent bar to the effectiveness of the registration statement or sale of the securities, for the order must be lifted and the statement declared effective if amendments are filed correcting the statement in accordance with the stop order decision. The Commission may issue stop orders after the sale of securities has been commenced or completed. Although losses which may have been suffered in the purchase of securities are not restored to investors by the stop order, the Commission's decision and the evidence on which it is based may serve to put investors on notice of their rights and aid in their own recovery suits.

This examination process naturally contributes to the general reliability of the registration disclosures—but it does not give positive assurance of the accuracy of the facts reported. Even if such a verification of the facts were possible, the task, if not actually prohibitive, would involve such a tremendous undertaking (both in time and money) as to seriously impede the financing of business ventures through the public sale of securities.

PENDING REGISTRATION

Section 5 of the 1933 Act contains a double prohibition. First, it is unlawful for any person to *offer to sell* a security unless a registration statement has been *filed* with the SEC. Second, it is unlawful to *sell* a security unless a registration statement is *effective*. These prohibitions, in effect, mean that only when a preliminary prospectus has been filed is it permissible for the securities to be offered to the public, but no sales can take place until the prospectus has become effective. The preliminary prospectus contains wording in red ink declaring that the instrument is subject to amendment and that the securities described in the prospectus may not be sold prior to the time the registration statement becomes effective. Because of the red ink utilized in the preliminary prospectus, it is often referred to as a "red herring."

The period of time between the preliminary filing and the effective date is known as the waiting period, during which the public may become familiar with the new proposed offering. The management of the offering company must be careful during this period to avoid publicity that "puffs" the value of the company securities. The SEC's Release 5180 urges companies to respond factually to unsolicited inquiries from securities analysts during this period, but companies often limit communication while "in registration." Companies desire to avoid inadvertently violating the 1933 Act by releasing a statement that could be perceived by the SEC as initiating the type of publicity that would subject the company's new offer to an SEC stop order. A stop order can have disastrous consequences because the timing of the offering of securities is critical in ever-changing financial markets.

SECTION 2: A "SECURITY"

Section 2 of the 1933 Act defines a "security." The section includes any note, stock, treasury stock, investment contract, guarantee, warrant, and any interest or instrument commonly known as a security. However, there are many cases in which various obscure financial instruments are determined to be securities, as the following case illustrates.

SEC v. Glenn W. Turner Enterprises, Inc.
474 F. 2d 476 (1973)
U.S. Court of Appeals (9th Cir.)

This is an appeal from an order granting the SEC a preliminary injunction. The injunction prohibits offering and selling by defendants of certain of their "Adventures" and "Plans." . . . Dare To Be Great, Inc. (Dare), a Florida corporation is a wholly owned subsidiary of Glenn W. Turner Enterprises, Inc. The individual defendants are, or were, officers, directors, or employees of the defendant corporations.

The trial court's findings, which are fully supported by the record, demonstrate that defendant's scheme is a gigantic successful fraud. The question presented is whether the "Adventure" or "Plan" enjoined are "securities" within the meaning of the federal securities laws. . . .

The five courses offered by Dare ostensibly involve two elements. In return for his money, the purchaser is privileged to attend seminar sessions and receives tapes, records, and other material, all aimed at improving self-motivation and sales ability. He also receives, if he purchases either Adventure III or IV or the $1,000 Plan, the opportunity to help to sell the courses to others; if successful he receives part of the purchase price as his commission. There

is no doubt that this latter aspect of the purchase is in all respects the significant one. . . .

It it apparent from the record that what is sold is not of the usual "business motivation" type of courses. Rather, the purchaser is really buying the possibility of deriving money from the sale of the plans by Dare to individuals whom the purchaser has brought to Dare. The promitional aspects of the plan, such as seminars, films, and records, are aimed at interesting others in the Plans. Their value for any other purpose, is, to put it mildly, minimal.

. . . (Adventure) meetings are like an old time revival meeting, but directed toward the joys of making easy money rather than salvation. Their purpose is to convince prospective purchasers, or "prospects," that Dare is a sure route to great riches. . . .

. . . [T]he task of the purchaser is to find prospects and induce them to attend Adventure Meetings. He is not to tell them that Dare to Be Great, Inc. is involved. Rather, he catches their interest by intimating that the result of attendance will be significant wealth for the prospect. It is at the meetings that the sales effort takes place. The "salesman" is told that to maximize his chances of success he should impart an aura of affluence, whether spurious or not—to pretend that through his association with Dare he has obtained wealth of no small proportions. The training that he has received at Dare is educating him on this point. He is told to "fake it 'til you make it," or to give the impression of wealth even if it has not been attained. He is urged to go into debt if necessary to purchase a new and expensive automobile and flashy clothes, and to carry with him large sums of money, borrowing if necessary, so that it can be ostentatiously displayed. The purpose of all this is to put the prospect in a more receptive state of mind with respect to the inducements that he will be subject to at the meetings. . . .

The 1933 and 1934 Acts are remedial legislation, among the central purposes of which is full and fair disclosure relative to the issuance of securities. It is a familiar canon of legislative construction that remedial legislation should be construed broadly. The Acts were designed to protect the American public from speculative or fraudulent schemes of promoters. For that reason Congress defined the term "security" broadly, and the Supreme Court in turn has construed the definition liberally. . . . In *SEC* v. *W. J. Howey Co.* the Court stated that the definition of a security "embodies a flexible rather than a static principle, one that is capable of adaptation to meet the countless and variable schemes devised by those who seek the use of the money of others on the promise of profits." . . .

In *SEC* v. *W. J. Howey Co.* the Supreme Court set out its by now familiar definition of an investment contract:

The test is whether the scheme involves an investment of money in a common enterprise with profits to come solely from the efforts of others.

In *Howey* the Court held that a land sales contract for units of a citrus grove, together with a service contract for cultivating and marketing the crops, was an investment contract

and hence a security. The Court held that what was in essence being offered was "an opportunity to contribute money and to share in the profits of a large citrus fruit enterprise managed and partly owned by respondents." The purchasers had no intention themselves of either occupying the land or developing it; they were attracted only "by the prospects of a return on their investment." It was clear that the profits were to come "solely" from the efforts of others.

For purposes of the present case, the sticking point in the *Howey* definition is the word "solely," a qualification which of course exactly fitted the circumstances in *Howey*. All the other elements of the *Howey* test have been met here. There is an investment of money, a common enterprise, and the expectation of profits to come from the efforts of others. Here, however, the investor, or purchaser, must himself exert some efforts if he is to realize a return on his initial cash outlay. He must find prospects and persuade them to attend Dare Adventure Meetings, and at least some of them must then purchase a plan if he is to realize that return. Thus it can be said that the returns or profits are not coming "solely" from the efforts of others.

We hold, however, that in light of the remedial nature of the legislation, the statutory policy of affording broad protection to the public and the Supreme Court's admonitions that the definition of securities should be a flexible one, the word "solely" should not be read as a strict or literal limitation on the definition of an investment contract, but rather must be construed realistically, so as to include within the definition those schemes which involve in substance, if not form, securities. . . .

Strict interpretation of the requirement that profits to be earned must come "solely" from the efforts of others has been subject to criticism. Adherence to such an interpretation could result in a mechanical, unduly restrictive view of what is and what is not an investment contract. It would be easy to evade by adding a requirement that the buyer contribute a modicum of effort. Thus the fact that the investors here were required to exert some efforts if a return were to be achieved should not automatically preclude a finding that the Plan or Adventure is an investment contract. To do so would not serve the purpose of the legislation. Rather we adopt a more realistic test, whether the efforts made by those other than the investor are the undeniably significant ones, those essential managerial efforts which affect the failure or success of the enterprise.

In this case, Dare's source of income is from selling the Adventures and the Plan. The purchaser is sold the idea that he will get a fixed part of the proceeds of the sales. In essence, to get that share, he invests three things: his money, his efforts to find prospects and bring them to the meetings and whatever it costs him to create an illusion of his own affluence. He invests them in Dare's get-rich-scheme. What he buys is a share of the proceeds of the selling efforts of Dare. Those efforts are the . . . [basis] of the scheme; those

efforts are what keeps it going; those efforts are what produces the money which is to make him rich. In essence, it is the right that he buys. In our view, the scheme is no less an investment contract merely because he contributes some effort as well as money to get into it.

Let us assume that in *Howey* the sales and service agreements had provided that the buyer was to buy and plant the citrus trees. Unless he did so, there would be no crop to cultivate, harvest and sell, no moneys in which he could share. The essential nature of the scheme, however, would be the same. He would still be buying, in exchange for money, trees and planting, a share in what he hoped would be the company's success in cultivating the trees and harvesting and marketing the crop. We cannot believe that the Court would not have held such a scheme to be an investment contract. So here. Regardless of the fact that the purchaser here must contribute something besides his money, the essential managerial efforts which affect the failure or success of the enterprise are those of Dare, not his own. . . .

Questions
1. What is the definition of a security? What are the elements of the *Howey* test?
2. To create a security, must the profit to be realized from the investment of money be gained "solely" from the efforts and management of others?
3. What is "remedial" legislation? How does it influence judicial interpretation of the legislation?

EXEMPTIONS

Because the definition of security under Section 2 is so broad and all-encompassing, Section 5 appears to prohibit the sale of any security without an effective registration statement. However, Section 3 of the 1933 Act exempts certain securities, and Section 4 exempts certain transactions from the registration requirements. Section 3 exempts commercial paper, securities of government, banks, charitable organizations, savings and loan associations, common carriers, insurance policies, annuity contracts, and securities issued in bankruptcy reorganizations. In addition, "intrastate offerings" are exempt. However, to qualify as an "intrastate offering" certain elements must be established. The following case illustrates the difficulties of complying with the "intrastate offering" exemption.

Intrastate Offering

SEC v. McDonald Investment Co.
343 F. Supp. 343 (1972)
U.S. District Court, Minnesota

The question presented to the court is whether the sale exclusively to Minnesota residents of securities, consisting of unsecured installment promissory notes of the defendants, a Minnesota corporation, whose only business office is situate(d) in Minnesota, is exempt from the filing of a registration statement under § 3(a)(11) of the 1933 Securities Act, when the proceeds from the sale of such notes are to be used principally, if not entirely, to make loans to land developers outside of Minnesota. . . .

Plaintiff, the Securities and Exchange Commission, instituted this lawsuit. . . . The defendants are McDonald Investment Company, a Minnesota corporation, and H. J. McDonald, the company's president, treasurer, and owner of all the company's outstanding common stock. Plaintiff requests that the defendants be permanently enjoined from offering for sale and selling securities without having complied with the registration requirements of Section 5 of the Act. . . .

Section 3(a)(11) of the Act, however, sometimes called the intrastate exemption, exempts from registration:

(11) Any security which is a part of an issue offered and sold only to persons resident within a single State or Territory, where the issuer of such security is a person resident and doing business within or, if a corporation, incorporated by and doing business within, such state or Territory. . . .

The Plaintiff predicates its claim for a permanent injunction on the ground that the defendants will be engaged in a business where the income producing operations are located outside the state in which the securities are to be offered and sold and therefore not available for the 3(a)(11) exemption. . . .

In *Truckee* v. *Showboat* the exemption was not allowed because the proceeds of the offering were to be used primarily for the purpose of a new unrelated business in another state, i.e., a California corporation acquiring and refurbishing a hotel in Las Vegas, Nevada. Likewise, in *Chapman* v. *Dunn* the 3(a)(11) exemption was unavailable to an offering by a company in one state, Michigan, of undivided fractional oil and gas interests located in another state, Ohio. The *Dunn* court specifically stated at page 159:

. . . in order to qualify for the exemption of § 3(a)(11), the issuer must offer and sell his securities only to persons resident within a single State and the issuer must be a resident of that same State. *In addition to this, the issuer must conduct a predominant amount of his business within his same State.* This business which the issuer must conduct within the same State refers to the income producing operations of the business in which the issuer is selling the securities. . . . [Emphasis added]

This language would seem to fit the instant case where the income producing operations of the defendant, after completion of the offering, are to consist entirely of earning interest on its loans and receivables invested outside the state of Minnesota. While the defendant will not participate in any of the land developer's operations, nor will it own or control any of the operations, the fact is that the strength of the installment notes depends perhaps not legally, but practically, to a large degree on the success or failure of land developments located outside Minnesota, such land not being subject to the jurisdiction of the Minnesota court. The investor obtains no direct interest in any business activity outside of Minnesota, but legally holds only an interest as a creditor of a Minnesota corporation, which of course would be a prior claim on the defendant's assets over the shareholder's equity. . . .

This case does not evidence the deliberate attempt to evade the Act as in the example posed by plaintiff of a national organization or syndicate which incorporates in several or many states, opens an office in each and sells securities only to residents of the particular state, intending nevertheless to use all the proceeds whenever realized in a venture beyond the boundaries of all, or at best all but one of the states. Defendant corporation on the contrary has been in business in Minnesota for some period of time, is not a "Johnny come lately" and is not part of any syndicate or similar enterprise; yet to relieve it of the federal registration requirements where none or very little of the money realized is to be invested in Minnesota, would seem to violate the spirit if not the letter of the Act. . . .

Exemptions under the Act are strictly construed, with the burden of proof on the one seeking to establish the same.

Defendant notes that agreements with land developers will by their terms be construed under Minnesota law; that the income producing activities will be the earnings of interest which occurs in Minnesota; that the Minnesota registration provides at close proximity all the information and protection that any investor might desire; that whether or not registered with the Securities and Exchange Commission, a securities purchaser has the protection of 15 U.S.C. § 77e which attaches liability to the issuer whether or not registration of the securities are exempted for fraudulent or untrue statements in a prospectus or made by oral communications; that plaintiff blurs the distinction between sale of securities across state lines and the operation of an intrastate business; and that if injunction issues in this case it could issue in any case where a local corporations owns an investment out of the particular state in which it has its principal offices and does business such as accounts receivable from its customers out of state. While these arguments are worthy . . . on balance and in carrying out the spirit and intent of the Securities Act of 1933, plaintiff's request for a permanent injunction should be granted.

Questions
1. Must the revenue from the security sales be applied or invested in the state itself to come within the "intrastate offering" exemption?
2. Should the intrastate offering exemption be narrowly or broadly interpreted?
3. Does the reasoning of the *McDonald Investment Co.* decision make it difficult to comply with the intrastate offering exemption?

To avoid confusion concerning the scope of the intrastate offering exemption, the SEC has adopted Rule 147, which outlines a series of guidelines to determine the applicability of a Section 3 exemption. Under Rule 147, a firm incorporated and doing 80 percent of its business within a state may sell its securities without registering them if at least 80 percent of the proceeds of the offering are used within the state and all offerees are residents of that state. In addition, resales of the stock for nine months must be limited to state residents, and the stock certificates must bear a legend indicating these restrictions. As one can imagine, the limitations of Rule 147 are too severe for it to be widely utilized. Therefore, businesses with a substantial volume of interstate sales or interstate purchases of the stock would be denied an intrastate offering exemption.

Private Placements

Section 4 provides that the registration requirements shall be inapplicable to "transactions by an issuer not involving any public offering." The courts have struggled to come up with a useful definition of a "nonpublic offer," which is often referred to as a private placement.

The relationship between the offerees and the issuer is most significant. If the offerees know the issuer and have special knowledge as to its business affairs, such as knowledge high executive officers of the issuer would possess, then the offering is apt to be private. The Supreme Court laid special stress on this consideration in *Ralston Purina* by stating that "[t]he focus of the inquiry should be on the need of the offerees for the protections afforded by registration. The employees here were not shown to have access to the kind of information which registration would disclose." Also to be considered is the relationship between the offerees and their knowledge of each other. For example, if the offering is being made to a diverse and unrelated group, i.e. lawyers, grocers, plumbers, etc., then the offering would have the appearance of being public; but an offering to a select group of high executive officers of the issuer who know each other and of course have similar interests and knowledge of the offering would more likely be characterized as a private offering.

Other factors to be considered include the size and the manner of the offering. The smaller the size of the offering, the more probability it is private. A private offering is more likely to arise when the offer is made directly to the offerees rather than through the facilities of public distribution such as investment bankers or the securities exchanges. In addition, public advertising is incompatible with the claim of private offering.

Hill York Corp. v. American International Franchises, Inc.

488 F. 2d 680 (1971)
U.S. Court of Appeals (5th Cir.)

It is conceded that no registration statement had been filed with the SEC in connection with this offering of securities. The defendants contend, however, that the transactions come within the exemptions to registration found in . . . Section 4(2). Specifically, they contend that the offering of securities was not a public offering. . . .

"The design of the statute is to protect investors by promoting full disclosure of information thought necessary to informed investment decisions." Thus the ultimate test is whether "'the particular class of persons affected need the protection of the Act.'" . . .

The defendants rely most strongly on the fact that the offering was made only to sophisticated businessmen and lawyers and not the average man in the street. Although this evidence is certainly favorable to the defendants, the level of sophistication will not carry the point. In this context, the relationship between the promoters and the purchasers and the "access to the kind of information which registration would disclose" become highly relevant factors. . . . Obviously if the plaintiffs did not possess the information requisite for a registration statement, they could not bring their sophisticated knowledge of business affairs to bear in deciding whether or not to invest in this franchise sales center. There is abundant evidence to support the conclusion that the plaintiffs did not in fact possess the requisite information. The plaintiffs were given: 1. a brochure representing that the defendants had just left the very successful firm of Nationwide, but without disclosing the fact that Nationwide was then under investigation by the SEC; 2, a brochure representing Browne as an expert in capitalization consulting, when in fact he had no expertise in such consulting; 3, a brochure stating that the franchise fee would be 25,000 dollars, when in fact the franchise fee turned out to be 25,000 dollars plus a 1,000 dollar per month royalty; 4. a brochure representing that the existing sales centers were successfully operating, without disclosure of the fact that most of them were under investigation by various state securities commissions. No reasonable mind could conclude that the plaintiffs had access to accurate information on the foregoing points since the only persons who reasonably could have relieved their ignorance were the ones that told them the untruths in the first instance. This proof . . . inexorably leads to the conclusion that even the most sanguine of the purchasers would have entertained serious, if not fatal, doubts about investing in this scheme if completely accurate information had been furnished.

. . . (Furthermore) the record contains no evidence as to the number of offerees. The fact that there were only thirteen actual purchasers is of course irrelevant. We do know that the purchasers were a diverse and unrelated group, or at least this was so at the time the offering occurred. Furthermore, the defendants admit that the plaintiffs had never met or in any way communicated with them prior to purchasing their stock. . . .

. . . Faced with the state of evidentiary development when the parties rested, the court below could probably reach the same conclusion as the court in *Repass* v. *Rees*, 174 F. Supp. 898, 904 (D. Colo. 1959):

> . . . there is no evidence as to the experience of the buyers other than the plaintiffs. And there is no evidence as to how many offers were made to other persons, or the experience of those persons. The defendants did not testify that they had made no other offers. Without such evidence in the record the Court cannot determine whether the class needed protection. It was incumbent on the defendants to submit this evidence. Since they did not, they must suffer the consequences.

Questions
1. What is the "ultimate test" identified by the court to be considered in determining whether the offer is "public"?
2. If the securities are offered to "sophisticated businessmen and lawyers," will this entitle the offering to be designated as private?
3. On what other issues was evidence lacking that would be necessary to establish the nature of a private offering?

In 1974 the SEC adopted Rule 146, which defines criteria to establish the clearly legal "private placement." However, if one is not able to fully comply with all the criteria of Rule 146, the offering may be held nevertheless to be a private offering under case law. Consequently, lawyers in the securities field try to comply with Rule 146 as much as possible in an effort to satisfy the court of the private nature of the offering. The provisions of Rule 146 require that there be a limitation of offerees to around 35 persons, that no solicitation or general advertising be undertaken, that the offerees or their representative be sophisticated investors with access to or disclosure of company information (by employment or economic bargaining power), and that the purchasers buy the securities for their own account without intent to resell.

After having acquired securities in a private placement, the investor is prohibited from reselling the securities unless he or she complies with the provisions of Rule 144. Following Rule 144 is the only way for persons who have purchased securities under a private placement to resell their securities without being designated "underwriters" who are selling securities without registration. Rule 144 requires that the securities be held for two years from the date of the purchase and that the amount of distribution be limited to less than 1 percent of the average market trading volume within a four-week period. In addition, information must be delivered to the public prior to such distributions. This requirement means the company must have "gone public" (through registration) so that the general public will have information with which to evaluate whether to purchase stock. If the company has not gone public, the seller should follow Rule 237, which requires a holding period of five years and a sale within a one-year period of no more than $50,000 worth of securities or 1 percent of the securities outstanding in a particular class, whichever is the lesser.

Small Issue Exemptions

In an effort to aid small businesses in their attempts to raise risk capital, the SEC has an exemption from the registration requirements for issues smaller than $1.5 million. The commission's promulgated Regulation A covers these situations. Under a "Reg. A" procedure, the offeror prepares a short form of registration to be filed with the nearest SEC regional office.

A second exemption for small offerings is provided by SEC Rule 240. To qualify, the issuer cannot sell more than $100,000 of securities within any 12-month period. Sales to full-time employees of the issuer are excluded from the $100,000 figure, regardless of their degree of sophistication. However, there can be no more than 100 holders of the securities issued by the corporation, and no general solicitation of the public is permitted. A simplified report of the security sales is filed with the SEC regional office.

Finally, Rule 242 enlarges the small offering exemption to $2 million in securities within any six-month period if sales are made to an unlimited number of "accredited persons." Accredited persons include institutional investors, purchasers of at least $100,000 in securities, and the issuer's executive officers and directors. A corporation may also sell to as many as 35 nonaccredited investors.

However, if nonaccredited persons are avoided, the corporation need not furnish the accredited persons with any prospectus-type information. The inclusion of nonaccredited persons in the sale requires the company to furnish a simplified prospectus to all purchasers.

ANTIFRAUD PROVISION

The 1933 Act contains a general antifraud provision in Section 17(a). This provision outlaws fraudulent transactions in securities whether or not the security is entitled to an exemption from registration. The following case illustrates the utilization of this antifraud provision.

SEC v. Manor Nursing Centers, Inc.

458 F. 2d 1082 (1972)
U.S. Court of Appeals (2d Cir.)

The conduct of appellants in connection with the public offering of Manor shares, upon analysis, demonstrates beyond a peradventure of a doubt that they violated the antifraud provisions of the federal securities laws— § 17(a) of the 1933 Act and § 10(b) of the 1934 Act.

The gravamen of this case is that each of the appellants participated in a continuing course of conduct whereby public investors were fraudulently induced to part with their money in the expectation that Manor and the selling stockholders would return the money if all Manor shares were not sold and all the proceeds from the sale were not received by March 8, 1970. It is undisputed that, as of March 8, Manor and the selling stockholders had not sold all the 450,000 shares and that all the proceeds expected from the sale had not been received. Moreover, it is clear that all appellants knew, or should have known, that the preconditions for their retaining the proceeds of the offering had not been satisfied. Nevertheless, rather than complying with the terms of the offering by returning the funds of public investors, appellants retained these funds for their own financial benefit. This misappropriation of the proceeds of the Manor offering constituted a fraud on public investors and violated the anti-fraud provisions of the federal securities laws. . . .

It also is clear that appellants violated the antifraud provisions of the federal securities laws by offering Manor shares when they knew, or should have known, that the Manor prospectus was misleading in several material respects. After the registration statement became effective on December 8, 1969, at least four developments occurred which made the prospectus misleading: the public's funds were not returned even though the issue was not fully subscribed; an escrow account for the proceeds of the offering was not established; shares were issued for consideration other than cash; and certain individuals received extra compensation for agreeing to participate in the offering. These developments were not disclosed to the public investors. That these developments occurred after the effective date of the registration statement did not provide a license to appellants to ignore them. Post-effective developments which materially alter the picture presented in the registration statement must be brought to the attention of public investors. "The effect of the antifraud provisions of the Securities Act is to require the prospectus to reflect any post-effective changes necessary to keep the prospectus from being misleading in any material respect."

Having concluded that appellants had violated the federal securities laws, the district court permanently enjoined all appellants . . . from further violations of the antifraud provisions of the 1933 and 1934 Acts. . . .

In addition to granting the SEC's request for injunctive relief, the district court ordered appellants to disgorge all the proceeds . . . received in connection with the public offering of Manor stock; appointed a trustee to receive such funds, to distribute them to defrauded public investors and to report to the court on the true state of affairs; and, to prevent a wasting of assets, ordered a temporary freeze on appellants' assets pending transfer of the funds to the trustee.

Questions
1. Identify the fraudulent activities of the defendants in *Manor Nursing Center*.
2. Must a prospectus be "up-dated" by subsequent developments that would be materially important to public investors?
3. What actions did the court take to protect public investors?

LIABILITIES FOR ILLEGAL SALES AND REGISTRATION

The SEC can enjoin the illegal distribution of securities without a registration statement and obtain a $5,000 fine or up to five years imprisonment for violation of the 1933 Act. Private parties also have the right to litigate securities violations under the 1933 Act.

Under Section 12(1), purchasers of securities may directly sue for rescission or damages any person who violated Section 5 by selling the securities to them without the required registration. Section 12(2) imposes liability for material misstatements or omissions in the distribution of securities. Since Section 12 contains a requirement of "privity," purchasers may sue only their immediate sellers and not the issuer. Consequently, Section 12 is drafted to impose potential liability on *broker-dealers* who violate the act in the merchandising of securities.

Section 11 of the 1933 Act contains potential liability for the *issuer* of a security should a registration statement be filed that contains material misstatements or omissions. Section 11 entitles any person acquiring a security not knowing of the misstatement or omission to sue every person who has signed the registration statement, including the issuer. All directors who have signed the registration statement and the underwriters who have also signed are subject to suit. Even a director who has not signed the registration statement may not be relieved of potential liability. However, Section 11 also provides that no person, other than the issuer, shall be liable if the person can establish his or her "due diligence" defense. The following case illustrates the efforts of the defendants to establish their due diligence defense.

Escott v. BarChris Construction Corp.
283 F. Supp. 643 (1968)
U.S. District Court (S.D.N.Y.)

The action is brought under Section 11 of the Securities Act of 1933. Plaintiffs allege that the registration statement with respect to these debentures filed with the Securities and Exchange Commission, which became effective on May 16, 1961, contained false statements and material omissions. . . .

. . . [T]here is not doubt that many of the misstatements and omissions in this prospectus were material. This is true of all of them which relate to the state of affairs in 1961, i.e., the overstatement of sales and gross profit for the first quarter, the understatement of contingent liabilities as of April 30, the overstatement of orders on hand and the failure to disclose the true facts with respect to officers' loans, customers' delinquencies, application of proceeds and the prospective operation of several alleys. . . .

The "Due Diligence" Defenses

Every defendant . . . has pleaded these affirmative defenses. Each claims that . . . he made a reasonable investigation, as a result of which he had reasonable ground to believe and did believe that the registration statement was true and that no material fact was omitted. . . .

Russo

Russo was, to all intents and purposes, the chief executive officer of Bar-Chris. He was a member of the executive committee. He was familiar with all aspects of the business. He was personally in charge of dealings with the factors. He talked with customers about their delinquencies. . . .

In short, Russo knew all the relevant facts. He could not have believed that there were no untrue statements or material omissions in the prospectus. Russo has no due diligence defenses.

* * *

Kircher

Kircher was treasurer of BarChris and its chief financial officer. He is a certified public accountant and an intelligent man. He was thoroughly familiar with BarChris's financial affairs. . . . He knew of the customers' delinquency problem. . . .

Moreover, as a member of the executive committee, Kircher was kept informed as to those branches of the business of which he did not have direct charge. . . .

Kircher worked on the preparation of the registration statement. . . . He supplied information . . . about the company's business. He read the prospectus and understood it. He knew what it said and what it did not say.

Kircher's contention is that he had never before dealt with a registration statement, that he did not know what it should contain, and that he relied wholly on [the attorneys] and Peat, Marwick to guide him. . . .

There is an issue of credibility here. In fact, Kircher was not frank in dealing with [the attorneys]. He withheld information from them. But even if he had told them all the facts, this would not have constituted the due diligence contemplated by the statute. Knowing the facts . . . he did not have a resonable ground to believe it to be true. On the contrary, he must have known that in part it was untrue. Under these circumstances, he was not entitled to sit back and place the blame on the lawyers for not advising him about it.

Kircher has not proved his due diligence defenses. . . .

* * *

Auslander

Auslander was an "outside" director, i.e., one who was not an officer of BarChris. He was chairman of the board of Valley Stream National Bank in Valley Stream, Long Island.

In February 1961 Vitolo asked him to become a director of BarChris. Vitolo gave him an enthusiastic account of BarChris's progress and prospects. As an inducement, Vitolo said that when BarChris received the proceeds of a forthcoming issue of securities, it would deposit $1,000,000 in Auslander's bank. . . .

Auslander was elected a director on April 17, 1961. The registration statement in its original form had already been filed, of course without his signature. On May 10, 1961, he signed a signature page for the first amendment to the registration statement which was filed on May 11, 1961. This was a separate sheet without any document attached. Auslander did not know that it was a signature page for a registration statement. He vaguely understood that it was something "for the SEC."

Auslander attended a meeting of BarChris's directors on May 15, 1961. At that meeting he, along with the other directors, signed the signature sheet for the second amendment which constituted the registration statement in its final form. Again, this was only a separate sheet without any document attached. Auslander never saw a copy of the registration statement in its final form.

At the May 15 directors' meeting, however, Auslander did realize that what he was signing was a signature sheet to a registration statement. This was the first time that he had appreciated that fact. A copy of the registration statement in its earlier form as amended on May 11, 1961, was passed around at the meeting. Auslander glanced at it briefly. He did not read it thoroughly.

At the May 15 meeting, Russo and Vitolo stated that everything was in order and that the prospectus was correct. Auslander believed this statement.

Section 11 imposes liability in the first instance upon a director, no matter how new he is. He is presumed to know his responsibility when he becomes a director. He can escape liability only by using that reasonable care to investigate the facts which a prudent man would employ in the management of his own property. In my opinion, a prudent man would not act in an important matter without any knowledge of the relevant facts, in sole reliance upon representations of persons who are comparative strangers and upon general information which does not purport to cover the particular case.

To say that such minimal conduct measures up to the statutory standard would, to all intents and purposes absolve new directors from responsibility merely because they are new. This is not a sensible construction of Section 11, when one bears in mind its fundamental purpose of requiring full and truthful disclosure for the protection of investors.

I find and conclude that Auslander has not established his due diligence defense. . . .

Grant

Grant became a director of BarChris in October 1960. His law firm was counsel to BarChris in matters pertaining to the registration of securities. . . .

Grant is sued as a director and as a signer of the registration statement. This is not an action against him for malpractice in his capacity as a lawyer. Nevertheless, in considering Grant's due diligence defenses, the unique position which he occupied cannot be disregarded. As the director most directly concerned with writing the registration statement and assuring its accuracy, more was required of him in the way of reasonable investigation than could fairly be expected of a director who had no connection with this work. . . .

I find that Grant honestly believed that the registration statement was true and that no material facts had been omitted from it.

In this belief he was mistaken, and the fact is that for all his work, he never discovered any of the errors or omissions. . . .

It is claimed that a lawyer is entitled to rely on the statements of his client and that to require him to verify their accuracy would set an unreasonably high standard. This is too broad a generalization. It is all a matter of degree. To require an audit would obviously be unreasonable. On the other hand, to require a check of matters easily verifiable is not unreasonable. Even honest clients can make mistakes. The statute imposes liability for untrue statements regardless of whether they are intentionally untrue. The way to prevent mistakes is to test oral information by examining the original written record. . . .

Grant was entitled to rely on Peat, Marwick for the 1960 figures. He had no reasonable ground to believe them to be inaccurate. But of the matters which were not within the expertised portion of the prospectus, . . . Grant was obliged to make a reasonable investigation. I am forced to find that he did not make one. . . . In my opinion, this finding on the evidence in this case does not establish an unreasonably high standard in other cases for company counsel who are also directors. Each case must rest on its own facts. I conclude that Grant has not established his due diligence defenses except as to the audited 1960 figures.

The Underwriters

The underwriters other than Drexel made no investigation of the accuracy of the prospectus. They all relied upon Drexel as the "lead" underwriter.

Drexel did make an investigation. . . . Drexel's attorneys acted as attorneys for the entire group of underwriters. . . .

On the evidence in this case, I find that the underwriters' counsel did not make a reasonable investigation of the truth of those portions of the prospectus which were not made on the authority of Peat, Marwick as an expert. Drexel is bound by their failure. It is not a matter of relying upon counsel for legal advice. Here the attorneys were dealing with matters of fact. Drexel delegated to them, as its agent, the business of examining the corporate minutes and contracts. It must bear the consequences of their failure to make an adequate examination.

The other underwriters, who did nothing and relied solely on Drexel and the lawyers, are also bound by it. It follows that although Drexel and the other underwriters believed that those portions of the prospectus were true, they had no reasonable ground for that belief, within the meaning of the statute. Hence, they have not established their due diligence defenses, except as to the 1960 audited figures.

Peat, Marwick

Section 11(b) . . . defines the due diligence defense for an expert. Peat, Marwick has pleaded it.

The part of the registration statement purporting to be made upon the authority of Peat, Marwick as an expert was the 1960 figures. . . . [The] question is whether at that time Peat, Marwick, after reasonable investigation, had reasonable ground to believe and did believe that the 1960 figures were true and that no material fact had been omitted from the registration statement which should have been included in order to make the 1960 figures not misleading. In deciding this issue, the court must consider not only what Peat, Marwick did in its 1960 audit, but also what it did in its subsequent "S-1 review." . . .

Most of the actual work was performed by a senior accountant, Berardi. . . .

It is unnecessary to recount everything that Berardi did in the course of the audit. We are concerned only with the evidence relating to what Berardi did or did not do with respect to those items which I have found to have been incorrectly reported in the 1960 figures in the prospectus. . . .

First and foremost is Berardi's failure to discover that [a subsidiary] . . . had not been sold. This error affected both the sales figure and the liability side of the balance sheet.

As to factors' reserves, it is hard to understand how Berardi could have treated this item as entirely a current asset when it was obvious that most of the reserves would not be released within one year. If Berardi was unaware of that fact, he should have been aware of it.

Berardi erred in computing the contingent liability on Type B leaseback transactions at 25 percent. Berardi did not examine the documents which are in evidence which established that BarChris's contingent liability on this type of transaction was in fact 100 percent. Berardi did not make a reasonable investigation in this instance.

The purpose of reviewing events subsequent to the date of a certified balance sheet (referred to as an S-1 review when made with reference to a registration statement) is to ascertain whether any material change has occurred in the company's financial position which should be disclosed in order to prevent the balance sheet figures from being misleading. The scope of such a review, under generally accepted auditing standards, is limited. It does not amount to a complete audit.

Peat, Marwick prepared a written program for such a review. I find that this program conformed to generally accepted auditing standards. . . .

Berardi made the S-1 review in May 1961. He devoted a little over two days to it, a total of 20½ hours. He did not discover any of the errors or omissions pertaining to the state of affairs in 1961. . . .

What Berardi did was to look at a consolidating trial balance as of March 31, 1961, which had been prepared by BarChris, compare it with the audited December 31, 1960, figures, discuss . . . certain unfavorable developments which the comparison disclosed, and read certain minutes. He did not examine any "important financial records" other than the trial balance. . . .

Since he never read the prospectus, he was not even aware that there had ever been any problem about loans from officers.

There had been a material change for the worse in BarChris's financial position. That change was sufficiently serious so that the failure to disclose it made the 1960 figures misleading. Berardi did not discover it. As far as results were concerned, his S-1 review was useless.

Accountants should not be held to a standard higher than that recognized in their profession. I do not do so here. Berardi's review did not come up to that standard. He did not take some of the steps which Peat, Marwick's written program prescribed. He did not spend an adequate amount of time on a task of this magnitude. Most important of all, he was too easily satisfied with glib answers to his inquiries.

This is not to say that he should have made a complete audit. But there were enough danger signals in the materials which he did examine to require some further investigation on his part. Generally accepted accounting standards required such further invesitgation under these circumstances. It is not always sufficient merely to ask questions.

Here again, the burden of proof is on Peat, Marwick. I find that the burden has not been satisfied. I conclude that Peat, Marwick has not established its due diligence defense.

Questions

1. As to the nonexpert portion of the registration statement, what must a director do to establish a "due diligence" defense?
2. Identify some of the things that the "insiders" failed to do to establish their reasonable investigations and reasonable beliefs in the accuracy of the registration statement.

3. What did the underwriters fail to do to establish their due diligence defense?
4. What did the expert accountants have to do to establish their due diligence defense? What did they fail to do to establish the defense?

THE TRADING OF SECURITIES

After the original issuance of securities from the corporation to the public, such securities are traded among members of the public. To improve the fairness of the trading process, Congress passed the Securities and Exchange Act of 1934, which extended the "disclosure" doctrine of investor protection to the securities listed and registered for public trading on national securities exchanges. And in 1964 the Securities Acts Amendment applied the disclosure and reporting provisions to equity securities of hundreds of companies traded over the counter (if their assets exceed $1 million and their shareholders number 500 or more). The requirements of the 1934 Act as amended impose new responsibilities on corporations and individuals, as explained in the following excerpt from an SEC publication.

SECURITIES AND EXCHANGE ACT OF 1934

The Work of the SEC
(SEC, 1980)

Corporate Reporting
Companies which seek to have their securities listed and registered for public trading on . . . an exchange must file a registration application with the exchange and the Commission. A similar registration form must be filed by companies whose equity securities are traded over-the-counter if they meet the size test. . . . The Commission's rules prescribed the nature and content of these registration statements, including certified financial statements. Their data are generally comparable to, but less extensive than, the disclosures required in Securities Act registration statements. Following the registration of their securities, such companies must file annual and other periodic reports to keep current the information contained in the original filing. Copies of any of the reported data may be obtained from the Commission at nominal cost. . . .

The law prescribes penalties for filing false statements and reports with the Commission, as well as provision for recovery by investors who suffer losses in the purchase or sale of registered securities in reliance thereon.

Proxy Solicitations
Another provision of this law governs the solicitation of proxies (votes) from holders of registered securities (both listed and over-the-counter), whether for the election of directors or for approval of other corporate action. In any such solicitation, whether by the management or minority groups, disclosure must be made of all material facts con-

cerning the matters on which such holders are asked to vote; and they must be afforded an opportunity to vote "Yes" or "No" on each matter. Where a contest for control of the management of a corporation is involved, the rules require disclosure of the names and interests of all "participants" in the proxy contest. Holders of such securities thus are enabled to vote intelligently on corporate actions requiring their approval. The Commission's rules require that proposed proxy material be filed in advance for examination by the Commission for compliance with the disclosure requirements.

Tender Offer Soliciations
In 1968, Congress amended the Exchange Act to extend its reporting and disclosure provisions to situations where control of a company is sought through a tender offer or other planned stock acquisition of over 10 percent of a company's equity securities. The amount was reduced to 5 percent by an amendment in 1970. These amendments and Commission rules thereunder require disclosure of pertinent information by the person seeking to acquire over 5 percent of the company's securities by direct purchase or by tender offer, as well as by any persons soliciting shareholders to accept or reject a tender offer. Thus, as with the proxy rules, public investors who hold stock in the subject corporation may now make informed decisions on take-over bids.

* * *

Margin Trading
The statute also contains provisions governing margin trading in securities. It authorizes the Board of Governors of the Federal Reserve System to set limitations on the amount of credit which may be extended for the purpose of purchasing or carrying securities. The objective is to restrict the excessive use of the nation's credit in the securities markets. While the credit restrictions are set by the Board, investigation and enforcement is the responsibility of the Commission.

Market Surveillance
The Securities Exchange Act also provides a system for regulating securities trading practices in both the exchange and the over-the-counter markets. In general, transactions in securities which are effected otherwise than on national securities exchanges are said to take place "over the counter." Designed to protect the interests of investors and the public, these provisions seek to curb misrepresentations and deceit, market manipulation and other fraudulent acts and practices and to establish and maintain just and equitable principles of trade conducive to the maintenance of open, fair and orderly markets.

While these provisions of the law establish the general regulatory pattern, the Commission is responsible for promulgating rules and regulations for their implementation. Thus, the Commission has adopted regulations which, among other things, (1) define acts or practices which constitute a "manipulative or deceptive device or contrivance" prohibited by the statute, (2) regulate short selling, stabilizing transactions and similar matters, (3) regulate the hypothecation of customers' securities and (4) provide safeguards with respect to the financial responsibility of brokers and dealers.

Registration of Exchanges and Others
In addition, the law as amended requires registration with the Commission of (1) "national securities exchanges" (those having a substantial securities trading volume); (2) brokers and dealers who conduct securities business in interstate commerce; (3) transfer agents; (4) clearing agencies; (5) municipal brokers and dealers; and (6) securities information processors.

To obtain registration, exchanges must show that they are so organized as to be able to comply with the provisions of the statute and the rules and regulations of the Commission and that their rules contain provisions which are just and adequate to insure fair dealing and to protect investors.

Each exchange is a self-regulatory organization, and its rules, among other things, must provide for the expulsion, suspension or other disciplining of member broker-dealers for conduct inconsistent with just and equitable principles of trade. While the law contemplates that exchanges shall have full opportunity to establish self-regulatory measures insuring fair dealing and the protection of investors, it empowers the Commission by order, rule or regulation to amend the rules of exchanges with respect to various phases of their activities and trading practices if necessary to effectuate the statutory objective. For the most part, exchange rules and revisions thereof suggested by exchanges or by the Commission reach their final form after discussion between representatives of the exchange and the Commission without resort to formal proceedings.

By an amendment to the law enacted in 1938, Congress also provided for creation of a self-regulatory organization to prevent fraudulent and manipulative acts and practices, to promote just and equitable principles of trade among over-the-counter brokers and dealers. One such association, the National Association of Securities Dealers, Inc., is registered with the Commission under this provision of the law. The establishment, maintenance and enforcement of a voluntary code of business ethics is one of the principal features of this provision of the law.

Not all broker-dealer firms are members of the NASD; thus, some are not subject to supervision and control by the agency. To equalize the regulatory pattern, Congress provided in the 1964 Amendments that the Commission should undertake to establish investor safeguards applicable to non-NASD firms comparable to those applicable to NASD members. Among the controls adopted by the Commission is a requirement that persons associated with non-NASD firms meet certain qualification standards similar to those applied by the NASD to its members.

Broker-Dealer Registration

Applications for registration as broker-dealers and amendments thereto are examined by the Office of Reports and Information Services with the assistance of the Division of Market Regulation. The registration of brokers and dealers engaged in an interstate over-the-counter securities business also is an important phase of the regulatory plan of the Act. They must conform their business practices to the standards prescribed in the law and the Commission's regulations for the protection of investors (as well as to the fair trade practice rules of their association); in addition, . . . they may violate these regulations only at the risk of possible loss of registration with the Commission and the right to continue to conduct an interstate securities business, or of suspension or expulsion from the association and loss of the benefits of such membership.

Investigation and Enforcement

It is the duty of the Commission under the laws it administers to investigate complaints or other indications of possible law violations in securities transactions, most of which arise under the Securities Act of 1933 and the Securities Exchange Act of 1934. Investigation and enforcement work is conducted both by the Commission's Regional Offices and the Division of Enforcement.

Most of the Commission's investigations are conducted privately, the facts being developed to the fullest extent possible through informal inquiry, interviewing of witnesses, examination of brokerage records and other documents, reviewing and trading data and similar means. The Commission, however, is empowered to issue subpoenas requiring sworn testimony and the production of books, records and other documents pertinent to the subject matter under investigation; in the event of refusal to respond to a subpoena, the Commission may apply to a Federal court for an order compelling obedience thereto.

Inquiries and complaints of investors and the general public provide one of the primary sources of leads for detection of law violations in securities transactions. Another is the surprise inspections by Regional Offices of the books and records of brokers and dealers to determine whether their business practices conform to the prescribed rules. Still another is the conduct of inquiries into market fluctuations in particular stocks which appear not to be the result of known developments affecting the issuing company or of general market trends.

The more general types of investigations concern the sale without registration of securities subject to the registration requirement of the Securities Act, and misrepresentation or omission of material facts concerning securities offered for sale (whether or not registration is required). The anti-fraud provisions of the law also apply equally to the *purchase* of securities, whether involving outright misrepresentations or the withholding or omission of pertinent facts to which the seller was entitled. For example, it is unlawful in certain situations to purchase securities from another person while withholding material information which would indicate that the securities have a value substantially greater than that at which they are being acquired. Such provisions of the law apply not only to transactions between brokers and dealers and their customers but also to the reacquisition of securities by an issuing company or its "insiders."

Other types of inquiries relate to the manipulation of the market prices of securities; the misappropriation or unlawful hypothecation of customers' funds or securities; the conduct of a securities business while insolvent; the purchase or sale of securities by a broker-dealer, from or to his customers, at prices not reasonably related to the current market prices therefore; and violation by the broker-dealer of his responsibility to treat his customers fairly.

The most common of the latter type of violation involves the broker-dealer who, on gaining the trust and confidence of a customer and thereby establishing an agency relationship demanding the highest degree of fiduciary duty and care, takes secret profits in his securities transactions with or for the customer over and above the agreed brokerage (agency) commission. For example, the broker-dealer may have purchased securities from customers at prices far below, or sold securities to customers at prices far above, their current market prices. In most such cases, the broker-dealer subjects himself to no risk of loss, since his purchases from customers are made only if he can make simultaneous sales of the securities at prices substantially in excess of those paid to the customer, and his sales to customers are made only if he can make simultaneous purchases of the securities at prices substantially lower than those charged the customer. Or the firm may engage in large-scale in-and-out transactions for the customer's account ("churning") to generate increased commissions, usually without regard to any resulting benefit to the customer.

There is a fundamental distinction between a broker and a dealer; and it is important that investors should understand the difference. The *broker* serves as the customer's *agent* in buying or selling securities *for* his customer. As such, he owes the customer the highest fiduciary responsibility and care and may charge only such agency commission as has been agreed to by the customer. On the other hand, a *dealer* acts as a principal and buys securities *from* or sells securities *to* his customers. In such transactions, the dealer's profit is measured by the difference between the prices at which he buys and sells securities. Since the dealer is operating for his own account, he normally may not charge the customer a fee or commission for services rendered. Even in the case of such dealer transactions, however, the Commission and the courts have held that the conduct of a securities business carries with it the implied representation that customers will be dealt with fairly and that dealers may not enter into transactions with customers at prices not reasonably related to the prevailing market. The law requires that there be delivered to the customer a written "confirmation" of each transaction disclosing whether the securities firm is acting as a principal for its own account or as an agent for the customer (and, if the latter, the broker's compensation from all sources.)

Statutory Sanctions

It should be understood that Commission investigations (which for the most part are conducted in private) are essentially fact-finding inquiries. The facts so developed by the staff are considered by the Commission only in determining whether there is *prima facie* evidence of a law violation and whether an action should be commenced to determine whether, in fact, a violation actually occurred and, if so, whether some sanction should be imposed.

Assuming that the facts show possible fraud or other law violation, the laws provide several courses of action or remedies which the Commission may pursue:

  a. *Civil injunction.* The Commission may apply to an appropriate United States District Court for an order enjoining those acts or practices alleged to violate the law or Commission rules.
  b. *Criminal prosecution.* If fraud or other willful law violation is indicated, the Commission may refer the facts to the Department of Justice with a recommendation for criminal prosecution of the offending persons. The Department, through its local United States Attorneys (who frequently are assisted by Commission attorneys), may present the evidence to a Federal grand jury and seek an indictment.
  c. *Administrative remedy.* The Commission may, after hearing, issue orders suspending or expelling members from exchanges or the over-the-counter dealers association; denying, suspending or revoking the registrations of broker-dealers; or censuring individuals for misconduct or barring them (temporarily or permanently) from employment with a registered firm.

Broker-Dealer Revocations

All of these sanctions may be applied to any person who engages in securities transactions violative of the law, whether or not he is engaged in the securities business. However, the administrative remedy is generally only invoked in the case of exchange or association members, registered brokers or dealers, or individuals who may associate with any such firm. In any such administrative proceeding, the Commission issues an order specifying the acts or practices alleged to have been committed in violation of law and directing that a hearing be held for the purpose of taking evidence thereon. At the hearing, counsel for the Division of Enforcement (often a Regional Office attorney) undertakes to establish for the record those facts which support the charge of law violation, and the respondents have full opportunity to cross-examine witnesses and to present evidence in defense. The procedure followed in the conduct of such proceedings . . . [conform to the Administrative Procedure Act]. If the Commission in its ultimate decision of the case finds that the respondents violated the law, it may take remedial action as indicated above. Such action may effectively bar a firm from the conduct of a securities business in interstate commerce or on exchanges or an individual from association with a registered firm—subject to the respondent's right to seek judicial review of the decision by the appropriate United States Court of Appeals.

* * *

SHORT-SWING PROFITS

Section 16 of the 1934 Act attempts to prohibit the use of inside information by insiders to reap profits on short-swing transactions in securities markets. Section 16(a) requires that all directors, officers, and beneficial owners of at least 10 percent of the stock file a form with the SEC disclosing the amount of securities of the issuer they hold. Subsequently, a report must be filed whenever a change in beneficial ownership occurs during any calendar month. These reports are public information and are scrutinized by individuals who may be interested in instituting lawsuits against the insiders. Section 16(b) allows recovery of short-swing profits realized by a director, officer, or 10 percent beneficial stockowner resulting from any sale or purchase, or purchase and sale, of any equity security of the company within a period of less than six months. The suit may be instituted by the company or by any owner of stock of the company, if the company refuses to bring suit within 60 days after request by the complaining stockholder. It is possible for an individual to purchase one share of the company stock and bring suit in the name of the company to recover short-swing profits. The person's motivation for bringing the suit is often explained by the right of the person's attorney to claim an attorney's fee out of the short-swing profits recovered by the suit. In this manner, private litigants serve as "enforcers" of Section 16.

A person may be held to be a "beneficial" owner of securities that are legally owned by a spouse, minor children, or any relative who resides in his or her home. Moreover, securities owned by a trustee who is under the direction of an insider also are considered to be beneficially owned by the insider.

In determining whether a short-swing profit has been secured, the courts arbitrarily match purchases and sales during any six-month period. For example, consider the following transactions:

Day 1—a purchase of 100 shares @ $10 per share.
Day 2—a sale of 100 shares @ $8 per share.
Day 3—a purchase of 100 shares @ $5 per share.
Day 4—a sale of 100 shares @ $3 per share.

It would appear that in this declining price market the insider has suffered losses. However, the court would compare the purchase at $5 per share with the sale at $8 per share and determine a short-swing profit has been obtained. In addition, the courts have held that any losses incurred during the six-month period (the purchase at $10 per share and the sale at $3 per share) could not be used as a set-off against the profits obtained during the same period. Consequently, the insider would be obligated to pay the short-swing profit to the corporation.

INSIDER TRADING

Rule 10b-5 provides:

It shall be unlawful for any person, directly or indirectly, by the use of any means or instrumentality of interstate commerce, or of the mails, or of any facility of any national securities exchange

(1) to employ any device, scheme, or artifice to defraud,
(2) to make any untrue statement of a material fact or to omit to state a material fact necessary in order to make the statements made, in the light of the circumstances under which they were made, not misleading, or
(3) to engage in any act, practice, or course of business which operates or would operate as a fraud or deceit upon any person,

in connection with the purchase or sale of any security.

Rule 10b-5 was promulgated pursuant to the grant of authority given to the SEC by Congress in Section 10(b) of the Securities Exchange Act of 1934. By that Act Congress purposed to prevent inequitable and unfair practices and to ensure fairness in securities transactions generally, whether conducted face-to-face, over the counter, or on exchanges. The rule is based on the policy that all investors trading on impersonal exchanges should have relatively equal access to material information. The essence of the Rule is that anyone who has access, directly or indirectly, to information intended to be available only for corporate purpose and not for the personal benefit of anyone may not take advantage of such information knowing it is unavailable to those with whom he is dealing, i.e., the investing public. Insiders, as directors or management officers are, of course, by this Rule, precluded from so unfairly dealing, but the Rule is also applicable to one possessing the information who may not be strictly termed an "insider" within the meaning of Sec. 16(b) of the Act. Thus, the SEC has contended that anyone in possession of material inside information must either disclose it to the investing public, or, if he is disabled from disclosing it in order to protect a corporate confidence, or he chooses not to do so, must abstain from trading in or recommending the securities concerned while such inside information remains undisclosed.

Trying to stop insiders from using "inside information" illegally to make money in the stock market is difficult. A study by an investment banking concern shows a clear pattern of preannounced buying in stocks of companies that have become targets of tender offers or are involved in merger negotiations. The study examined the premiums above market prices offered for target companies' shares. The study calculated the premium's percentage above market values one month before the initial takeover announcement and one day before the announcement. In a sample of 24 unopposed cash offers in the first three quarters of 1980, it was revealed that the average premium shrank to 60 percent the day before the announcement from 82 percent the month before. Although some of the premium shrinkage can be attribute to the acquiring companies' acquisition of shares in the open market to gain a "toehold," a large portion of the premium shrinkage results from leaks, rumors, and more buying prior to the announcement.

SEC officials investigate suspicious stock-price movements. They often have to sift through mounds of data to connect buyers with the sellers and piece together a relationship between the trader and those who have inside information. Despite the difficulty, in the late 1970s the commission increased its efforts to obtain prosecution against violators of the insider trading rules.

In the last few years the SEC has brought several civil suits charging investors with trading on the basis of nonpublic information. For example, the SEC obtained a consent order against a stockbroker and his father for trading on confidential takeover information leaked by a paralegal employee of a law firm. The stockbroker was fired by his employer and his personal transactions based on inside information were canceled. In addition, the New York Stock Exchange barred the stockbroker from employment in any capacity with any member firm for four years. The stockbroker's father, who obtained the inside information from his son, agreed to give up the almost $100,000 in profit he netted while trading on the confidential tip. In most civil suits of this type the violators settled the charges of the SEC by negotiating a consent order in which they neither admit nor deny guilt but agree to relinquish their alleged insider trading profits.

Although the SEC has been successful in many civil cases, the Supreme Court overturned the insider-trading criminal conviction of an employee of a financial printing company. The employee had deduced the identities of take-over targets from legal documents he had helped print. His transactions based on this information resulted in handsome profits which, in settlement of the civil charges with the SEC, he agreed to return to the sellers of the shares. His criminal conviction was appealed to the Supreme Court for determination of the legal effect of the petitioner's silence. The District Court had permitted the jury to convict the petitioner if it found that he willfully failed to inform sellers of target company securities that he knew of a forthcoming takeover bid that would make their shares more valuable. In *Chiarella* v. *U.S.*, 445 U.S. 292 (1980), the Court admitted that:

[A]dministrative and judicial interpretations have established that silence with the purchase or sale of securities may operate as a fraud actionable under Sec. 10(b) despite the absence of statutory language or legislative history specifically addressing the legality of nondisclosure. But such liability is premised upon a duty to disclose arising from a relationship of trust and confidence between parties to a transaction. Application of a duty to disclose prior to trading guarantees that corporate insiders, who have an obligation to place the shareholder's welfare before their own, will not benefit personally through fraudulent use of material nonpublic information.

In this case, the petitioner was convicted of violating Sec. 10(b) although he was not a corporate insider and he received no confidential information from the target company. . . . Petitioner's use of that information was not a fraud under Sec. 10(b) unless he was subject to an affirmative duty to disclose it before trading. . . .

* * *

[However] . . . , the element required to make silence fraudulent—a duty to disclose—is absent in this case. No duty could arise from petitioner's relationship with the sellers of the target company's securities, for petitioner had no prior dealings with them. He was not their agent, he was not a fiduciary, he was not a person in whom the sellers had placed their trust and confidence. He was, in fact, a complete stranger who dealt with the sellers only through impersonal market transactions.

* * *

. . . When an allegation of fraud is based upon nondisclosure, there can be no fraud absent a duty to speak. We hold that a duty to disclose under Sec. 10(b) does not arise from the mere possession of nonpublic market information.

The Supreme Court had an opportunity to further clarify inside-trading rules in the following case.

Dirks v. Securities and Exchange Commission
51 LW 5123 (1983)
Supreme Court of the United States

Justice Powell

In 1973, Dirks was an officer of a New York broker-dealer firm who specialized in providing investment analysis of insurance company securities to institutional investors. On March 6, Dirks received information from Ronald Secrist, a former officer of Equity Funding of America. Secrist alleged that the assets of Equity Funding, a diversified corporation primarily engaged in selling life insurance and mutual funds, were vastly overstated as the result of fraudulent corporate practices. Secrist also stated that various regulatory agencies had failed to act on similar charges made by Equity Funding employees. He urged Dirks to verify the fraud and disclose it publicly.

* * *

During the two-week period in which Dirks pursued his investigation and spread word of Secrist's charges, the price of Equity Funding stock fell from $26 per share to less than $15 per share. This led the New York Stock Exchange to halt trading on March 27.

Shortly thereafter California insurance authorities impounded Equity Funding's records and uncovered evidence of the fraud. . . .

The SEC began an investigation into Dirks' role in the exposure of the fraud. After a hearing by an administrative law judge, the SEC found that Dirks had aided and abetted violations of . . . SEC Rule 10b-5, by repeating the allegations of fraud to members of the investment community who later sold their Equity Funding stock. The SEC concluded: "Where 'tippees'—regardless of their motivation or occupation—come into possession of material 'information that they know is confidential and know or should know came from a corporate insider,' they must either publicly disclose that information or refrain from trading." Recognizing, however, that Dirks "played an important role in bringing [Equity Funding's] massive fraud to light," the SEC only censured him.

* * *

In the seminal case of *In re Cady, Roberts & Co.*, (1961), the SEC recognized that the common law in some jurisdictions imposes on "corporate 'insiders,' particularly officers, directors, or controlling stockholders" an "affirmative duty of disclosure . . . when dealing in securities." The SEC found that not only did breach of this common-law duty also establish the elements of a Rule 10b-5 violation, but that individuals other than corporate insiders could be obligated either to disclose material nonpublic information before trading or to abstain from trading altogether. In *Chiarella*, we accepted the two elements set out in *Cady Roberts* for establishing a Rule 10b-5 violation: "(i) the existence of a relationship affording access to inside information intended to be available only for a corporate purpose, and (ii) the unfairness of allowing a corporate insider to take advantage of that information by trading without disclosure." In examining whether Chiarella had an obligation to disclose or abstain, the Court found that there is no general duty to disclose before trading on material nonpublic information, and held that "a duty to disclose under 10(b) does not arise from the mere possession of nonpublic market information." Such a duty arises rather from the existence of a fiduciary relationship.

Not "all breaches of fiduciary duty in connection with a securities transaction," however, come within the ambit of Rule 10b-5. There must also be "manipulation or deception." In an inside-trading case this fraud derives from the "inherent unfairness involved where one takes advantage" of "information intended to be available only for a corporate purpose and not for the personal benefit of anyone." Thus, an insider will be liable under Rule 10b-5 for inside trading only where he fails to disclose material nonpublic information before trading on it and thus makes "secret profits."

We were explicit in *Chiarella* in saying that there can be no duty to disclose where the person who has traded on inside information "was not [the corporation's] agent, . . . was not a fiduciary, [or] was not a person in whom the sellers [of the securities] had placed their trust

and confidence." Not to require such a fiduciary relationship, we recognized, would "depar[t] radically from the established doctrine that duty arises from a specific relationship between two parties" and would amount to "recognizing a general duty between all participants in market transactions to forgo actions based on material, nonpublic information." This requirement of a specific relationship between the shareholders and the individual trading on inside information has created analytical difficulties for the SEC and courts in policing tippees who trade on inside information. Unlike insiders who have independent fiduciary duties to both the corporation and its shareholders, the typical tippee has no such relationships. In view of this absence, it has been unclear how a tippee acquires the *Cady, Roberts* duty to refrain from trading on inside information.

The SEC's position, as stated in its opinion in this case, is that a tippee "inherits" the *Cady, Roberts* obligtaion to shareholders whenever he receives inside information from an insider.

* * *

This view differs little from the view that we rejected as inconsistent with congressional intent in *Chiarella*. In that case, the Court of Appeals agreed with the SEC and affirmed Chiarella's conviction, holding that "'[a]nyone—corporate insider or not—who regularly receives material nonpublic information may not use that information to trade in securities without incurring an affirmative duty to disclose.'" Here, the SEC maintains that anyone who knowingly receives nonpublic material information from an insider has a fiduciary duty to disclose before trading.

In effect, the SEC's theory of tippee liability in both cases appears rooted in the idea that the antifraud provisions require equal information among all traders. This conflicts with the principle set forth in *Chiarella* that only some persons, under some circumstances, will be barred from trading while in possession of material nonpublic information. Judge

Wright correctly read our opinion in *Chiarella* as repudiating any notion that all traders must enjoy equal information before trading: "[T]he 'information' theory is rejected. Because the disclose-or-refrain duty is extraordinary, it attaches only when a party has legal obligations other than a mere duty to comply with the general antifraud proscriptions in the federal securities laws." We reaffirm today that "[a] duty [to disclose] arises from the relationship between parties . . . and not merely from one's ability to acquire information because of his position in the market."

Imposing a duty to disclose or abstain solely because a person knowingly receives material nonpublic information from an insider and trades on it could have an inhibiting influence on the role of market analysts, which the SEC itself recognizes is necessary to the preservation of a healthy market. It is common-place for analysts to "ferret out and analyze information," and this often is done by meeting with and questioning corporate officers and others who are insiders. And information that the analysts obtain normally may be the basis for judgments as to the market worth of a corporation's securities. The analyst's judgment in this respect is made available in market letters or otherwise to clients of the firm. It is the nature of this type of information, and indeed of the markets themselves, that such information cannot be made simultaneously available to all of the corporation's stockholders or the public generally. The conclusion that recipients of inside information do not invariably acquire a duty to disclose or abstain does not mean that such tippees always are free to trade on the information. The need for a ban on some tippee trading is clear. Not only are insiders forbidden by their fiduciary relationship from personally using undisclosed corporate information to their advantage, but they may not give such information to an outsider for the same improper purpose of exploiting the information for their personal gain. Similarly, the transactions of those who knowingly participate with the fiduciary in such a breach are

"as forbidden" as transactions "on behalf of the trustee himself." Thus, the tippee's duty to disclose or abstain is derivative from that of the insider's duty. As we noted in *Chiarella*, "[t]he tippee's obligation has been viewed as arising from his role as a participant after the fact in the insider's breach of a fiduciary duty."

Thus, some tippees must assume an insider's duty to the shareholders not because they receive inside information, but rather because it has been made available to them improperly. And for Rule 10b-5 purposes, the insider's disclosure is improper only where it would violate his *Cady, Roberts* duty. Thus, a tippee assumes a fiduciary duty to the shareholders of a corporation not to trade on material nonpublic information only when the insider has breached his fiduciary duty to the shareholders by disclosing the information to the tippee and the tippee knows or should know that there has been a breach. . . . Tipping thus properly is viewed only as a means of indirectly violating the *Cady, Roberts* disclose-or-abstain rule.

In determining whether a tippee is under an obligation to disclose or abstain, it thus is necessary to determine whether the insider's "tip" constituted a breach of the insider's fiduciary duty. All disclosures of confidential corporate information are not inconsistent with the duty insiders owe to shareholders. In contrast to the extraordinary facts of this case, the more typical situation in which there will be a question whether disclosure violates the insider's *Cady, Roberts* duty is when insiders disclose information to analysts. In some situations, the insiders will act consistently with his fiduciary duty to shareholders, and yet release of the information may affect the market. For example, it may not be clear—either to the corporate insider or to the recipient analyst—whether the information will be viewed as material nonpublic information. Corporate officials may mistakenly think the information already has been disclosed or that it is not material enough to affect the market. Whether disclosure is a breach of duty therefore depends in large part on the purpose of the disclosure. This standard was identified by the SEC itself in *Cady, Roberts*: a purpose of the securities laws was to eliminate "use of inside information for personal advantage." Thus, the test is whether the insider personally will benefit, directly or indirectly, from his disclosure. Absent some personal gain, there has been no breach of duty to stockholders. And absent a breach by the insider, there is no derivative breach. As Commissioner Smith stated in *Investors Management Co.*: "It is important in this type of case to focus on policing insiders and what they do . . . rather than on policing information *per se* and its possession. . . ."

The SEC argues that, if inside-trading liability does not exist when the information is transmitted for a proper purpose but is used for trading, it would be a rare situation when the parties could not fabricate some ostensibly legitimate business justification for transmitting the information. We think the SEC is unduly concerned. In determining whether the insider's purpose in making a particular disclosure is fraudulent, the SEC and the courts are not required to read the parties' minds. Scienter in some cases is relevant in determining whether the tipper has violated his *Cady, Roberts* duty. But to determine whether the disclosure itself "deceive[s], manipulate[s], or defraud[s]" shareholders, the initial inquiry is whether there has been a breach of duty by the insider. This requires courts to focus on objective criteria, i.e., whether the insider receives a direct or indirect personal benefit from the disclosure, such as a pecuniary gain or a reputational benefit that will translate into future earnings. ("The theory . . . is that the insider, by giving the information out selectively, is in effect selling the information to its recipient for cash, reciprocal information, or other things of value for himself. . . .") There are objective facts and circumstances that often justify such an inference. For example, there may be a relationship between the insider and the recipient that suggests a *quid pro quo* from the latter, or an intention to benefit the particular recipient. The elements of fiduciary duty and exploita-

tion of nonpublic information also exist when an insider makes a gift of confidential information to a trading relative or friend. The tip and trade resemble trading by the insider himself followed by a gift of the profits to the recipient.

Determining whether an insider personally benefits from a particular disclosure, a question of fact, will not always be easy for courts. But it is essential, we think, to have a guiding principle for those whose daily activities must be limited and instructed by the SEC's inside-trading rules, and we believe that there must be a breach of the insider's fiduciary duty before the tippee inherits the duty to disclose or abstain. In contrast, the rule adopted by the SEC in this case would have no limiting principle.

Under the inside-trading and tipping rules set forth above, we find that there was no actionable violation by Dirks. It is undisputed that Dirks himself was a stranger to Equity Funding, with no pre-existing fiduciary duty to its shareholders. He took no action, directly or indirectly, that induced the shareholders or officers of Equity Funding to repose trust or confidence in him. There was no expectation by Dirks' sources that he would keep their information in confidence. Nor did Dirks misappropriate or illegally obtain the information about Equity Funding. Unless the insiders breached their *Cady, Roberts* duty to shareholders in disclosing the nonpublic information to Dirks, he breached no duty when he passed it on to investors. . . .

It is clear that neither Secrist nor the other Equity Funding employees violated their *Cady, Roberts* duty to the corporation's shareholders by providing information to Dirks. The tippers received no monetary or personal benefit for revealing Equity Funding's secrets, nor was their purpose to make a gift of valuable information to Dirks. As the facts of this case clearly indicate, the tippers were motivated by a desire to expose the fraud. In the absence of a breach of duty to shareholders by the insiders, there was no derivative breach by Dirks. Dirks therefore could not have been a "participant after the fact in [an] insider's breach of a fiduciary duty."

We conclude that Dirks, in the circumstances of this case, had no duty to abstain from use of the inside information that he obtained.

Justice Blackmun, with whom Justice Brennan and Justice Marshall join, dissenting.

The court today takes still another step to limit the protections provided investors by § 10(b) of the Securities Exchange Act of 1934. The device employed in this case engrafts a special motivational requirement on the fiduciary duty doctrine. This innovation excuses a knowing and intentional violation of an insider's duty to shareholders if the insider does not act from a motive of personal gain. Even on the extraordinary facts of this case, such an innovation is not justified.

As the Court recognizes, the facts here are unusual. After a meeting with Ronald Secrist, a former Equity Funding employee, on March 7, 1973, petitioner Raymond Dirks found himself in possession of material nonpublic information of massive fraud within the company. In the Court's words, "[h]e uncovered . . . startling information that required no analysis or exercise of judgment as to its market relevance." In disclosing that information to Dirks, Secrist intended that Dirks would disseminate the information to his clients, those clients would unload their Equity Funding securities on the market, and the price would fall precipitously, thereby triggering a reaction from the authorities.

Dirks complied with his informant's wishes. Instead of reporting that information to the Securities and Exchange Commission or to other regulatory agencies, Dirks began to disseminate the information to his clients and undertook his own investigation. One of his first steps was to direct his associates at Delafield Childs to draw up a list of Delafield clients holding Equity Funding securities. On March 12, eight days before Dirks flew to Los Angeles

to investigate Secrist's story, he reported the full allegations to Boston Company Institutional Investors, Inc., which on March 15 and 16 sold approximately $1.2 million of Equity securities. As he gathered more information, he selectively disclosed it to his clients. To those holding Equity Funding securities he gave the "hard" story—all the allegations; others received the "soft" story—a recitation of vague factors that might reflect adversely on Equity Funding's management.

Dirks' attempts to disseminate the information to nonclients were feeble, at best. On March 12, he left a message for Herbert Lawson, the San Francisco bureau chief of *The Wall Street Journal*. Not until March 19 and 20 did he call Lawson again, and outline the situation. William Blundell, a *Journal* investigative reporter based in Los Angeles, got in touch with Dirks about his March 20 telephone call. On March 21, Dirks met with Blundell in Los Angeles. Blundell began his own investigation, relying in part on Dirks' contacts, and on March 23 telephoned Stanley Sporkin, the SEC's Deputy Director of Enforcement. On March 26, the next business day, Sporkin and his staff interviewed Blundell and asked to see Dirks the following morning. Trading was halted by the New York Stock Exchange at about the same time Dirks was talking to Los Angeles SEC personnel. The next day, March 28, the SEC suspended trading in Equity Funding securities. By that time, Dirks' clients had unloaded close to $15 million of Equity Funding stock and the price had plummeted from $26 to $15. The effect of Dirks' selective dissemination of Secrist's information was that Dirks' clients were able to shift the losses that were inevitable due to the Equity Funding fraud from themselves to uninformed market participants.

No one questions that Secrist himself could not trade on his inside information to the disadvantage of uninformed shareholders and purchasers of Equity Funding securities. Unlike the printer in *Chiarella*, Secrist stood in a fiduciary relationship with these shareholders.

As the Court states, corporate insiders have an affirmative duty of disclosure when trading with shareholders of the corporation. This duty extends as well to purchasers of the corporation's securities.

The Court also acknowledges that Secrist could not do by proxy what he was prohibited from doing personally. But this is precisely what Secrist did. Secrist used Dirks to disseminate information to Dirks' clients, who in turn dumped stock on unknowing purchasers. Secrist thus intended Dirks to injure the purchasers of Equity Funding securities to whom Secrist had a duty to disclose. Accepting the Court's view of tippee liability, it appears that Dirks' knowledge of this breach makes him liable as a participant in the breach after the fact.

The Court holds, however, that Dirks is not liable because Secrist did not violate his duty; according to the Court, this is so because Secrist did not have the improper purpose of personal gain. In so doing, the Court imposes a new, subjective limitation on the scope of the duty owed by insiders to shareholders. The novelty of this limitation is reflected in the Court's lack of support for it.

The insider's duty is owed directly to the corporation's shareholders. As *Chiarella* recognized, it is based on the relationship of trust and confidence between the insider and the shareholder. That relationship assures the shareholder that the insider may not take actions that will harm him unfairly. The affirmative duty of disclosure protects against this injury.

The fact that the insider himself does not benefit from the breach does not eradicate the shareholder's injury. It makes no difference to the shareholder whether the corporate insider gained or intended to gain personally from the transaction; the shareholder still has lost because of the insider's misuse of nonpublic information. The duty is addressed not to the insider's motives, but to his actions and their consequences on the shareholder. Personal gain is not an element of the breach of this duty.

* * *

The improper purpose requirement not only has no basis in law, but it rests implicitly on a policy that I cannot accept. The Court justifies Secrist's and Dirks' action because the general benefit derived from the violation of Secrist's duty to shareholders outweighed the harm caused to those shareholders, in other words, because the end justified the means. Under this view, the benefit conferred on society by Secrist's and Dirks' activities may be paid for with the losses caused to shareholders trading with Dirks' clients.

Although Secrist's general motive to expose the Equity Funding fraud was laudable, the means he chose were not. Moreover, even assuming that Dirks played a substantial role in exposing the fraud, he and his clients should not profit from the information they obtained from Secrist. Misprision of a felony long has been against public policy. A person cannot condition his transmission of information of a crime on a financial award. As a citizen, Dirks had at least an ethical obligation to report the information to the proper authorities. The Court's holding is deficient in policy terms not because it fails to create a legal norm out of that ethical norm, but because it actually rewards Dirks for his aiding and abetting.

Dirks and Secrist were under a duty to disclose the information or to refrain from trading on it. I agree that disclosure in this case would have been difficult. I also recognize that the SEC seemingly has been less than helpful in its view of the nature of disclosure necessary to satisfy the disclose-or-refrain duty. The Commission tells persons with inside information that they cannot trade on that information unless they disclose; it refuses, however, to tell them how to disclose it. This seems to be a less than sensible policy, which it is incumbent on the Commission to correct. The Court, however, has no authority to remedy the problem by opening a hole in the congressionally mandated prohibition on insider trading, thus rewarding such trading.

In my view, Secrist violated his duty to Equity Funding shareholders by transmitting material nonpublic information to Dirks with the intention that Dirks would cause his clients to trade on that information. Dirks, therefore, was under a duty to make the information publicly available or to refrain from actions that he knew would lead to trading. Because Dirks caused his clients to trade, he violated § 10(b) and Rule 10b-5. Any other result is a disservice to this country's attempt to provide fair and efficient capital markets. I dissent.

Questions
1. According to the Court, what two elements must be established for a Rule 10b-5 violation?
2. What was the SEC's theory of tippee liability?
3. According to the Supreme Court, when is a tippee obligated to disclose or abstain from trading?
4. In fairness, who should absorb the loss resulting from the fraud perpetrated by Equity Funding's management? Does the Supreme Court's ruling impose the loss on the correct party?
5. Should the securities laws attempt to police insiders or the possession of inside information?
6. When Dirks received this inside information, what was his ethical obligation? Does the law assist him in fulfilling his ethical obligation?

Currently, the SEC has two weapons when faced with an insider trading violation. The Commission can seek repayment of the trader's illegal profit in a civil lawsuit and refer the case for criminal prosecution to the Justice Department. To enhance its continuing enforcement against insider trading, the SEC has proposed a bill before Congress that would set a maximum civil penalty for the insider trading offense of three times a trader's profit. The idea of increasing the civil penalty for insider trading seems to have broad support in Congress.

Two objections to the bill came from the brokerage-houses, which complained that the measure could subject their salesmen to the penalty if they executed trades for customers with inside information or make the companies liable for the penalty if their employees violated the law. To forestall the derailment of the bill by these objections, the SEC agreed to limit the bill's scope. To satisfy the brokerage industry, the bill was rewritten to exempt from the new penalty anyone who assists an illegal insider trade, unless the person was the trader's source of inside information. It also exempts firms (persons) that employ or "control" an inside trader. These exemptions, however, merely insulate a person against the civil penalty proposal in the bill. They do not prevent the SEC from seeking the existing penalties under the law.

ACCOUNTANTS AND RULE 10b-5

If accountants (or attorneys and underwriters) were to participate intentionally in a fraudulent or misleading scheme, they would clearly be violating Rule 10b-5.

However, it is a more difficult question to determine if the accountant should be liable to third parties for *negligent* failure to expose a client corporation's fraud. The following case examines this specific question.

Ernst & Ernst v. Hochfelder
425 U.S. 185 (1976)
Supreme Court of the United States

Justice Powell

Petitioner, Ernst & Ernst, is an accounting firm. From 1946 through 1967 it was retained by First Securities Company of Chicago (First Securities), a small brokerage firm and member of the Midwest Stock Exchange and of the National Association of Securities Dealers, to perform periodic audits of the firm's books and records. In connection with these audits Ernst & Ernst prepared for filing with the Securities and Exchange Commission (the Commission) the annual reports required of First Securities under § 17(a) of the 1934 Act. . . .

Respondents were customers of First Securities who invested in a fraudulent securities scheme perpetrated by Leston B. Nay, president of the firm and owner of 92 percent of its stock. Nay induced the respondents to invest funds in "escrow" accounts that he represented would yield a high rate of return. Respondents did so from 1942 through 1966, with the majority of the transactions occurring in the 1950's. In fact, there were no escrow accounts as Nay converted respondents' funds to his own use immediately upon receipt. These transactions were not in the customary form of dealings between First Securities and its customers. The respondents drew their personal checks payable to Nay or a designated bank for his account. No such escrow accounts were reflected on the books and records of First Securities, and none was shown on its periodic accounting to respondents in connection with their own investments. Nor were they included in First Securities' filings with the Commission. . . .

This fraud came to light in 1968 when Nay committed suicide, leaving a note that described First Securities as bankrupt and the es-crow accounts as "spurious." Respondents subsequently filed this action for damages against Ernst & Ernst. . . . The complaint charged that Nay's escrow scheme violated § 10(b) and Commission Rule 10b-5, and that Ernst & Ernst had "aided and abetted" Nay's violations by its "failure" to conduct proper audits of First Securities. As revealed through discovery, respondents' cause of action rested on a theory of negligent nonfeasance. The premise was that Enrst & Ernst had failed to utilize "appropriate auditing procedures" in its audits of First Securities, thereby failing to discover internal practices of the firm said to prevent an effective audit. The practice principally relied on was Nay's rule that only he could open mail addressed to him at First Securities or addressed to First Securities to his attention, even if it arrived in his absence. Respondents contended that if Ernst & Ernst had conducted a proper audit, it would have discovered this "mail rule." The existence of the rule then would have been disclosed in reports to the Exchange and to the Commission by Ernst & Ernst as an irregular procedure that prevented an effective audit. This would have revealed the fraudulent scheme. Respondents specifically disclaimed the existence of fraud or intentional misconduct on the part of Ernst & Ernst. . . .

We granted *certiorari* to resolve the question whether a private cause of action for damages will lie under § 10(b) and Rule 10b-5 in the absence of any allegation of "scienter"—intent to deceive, manipulate, or defraud. . . .

Section 10(b) makes unlawful the use or employment of "any manipulative or deceptive device or contrivance" in contravention of Commission rules. The words "manipulative or deceptive" used in conjunction with "device or contrivance" strongly suggests that § 10(b) was intended to proscribe knowing or intentional misconduct. . . .

. . . The Commission contends, however, that subsections (2) and (3) of Rule 10b-5 are cast in language which—if standing alone—could encompass both intentional and negligent behavior. These subsections respectively provide that it is unlawful "[t]o make any untrue statement of a material fact or to omit to state a material fact necessary in order to make the statements made, in light of the circumstances under which they were made, not misleading . . ." and "to engage in any act, practice, or course of business which operates or would operate as a fraud or deceit upon any person. . . ." Viewed in isolation the language of subsection (2), and arguably that of subsection (3), could be read as proscribing, respectively, any type of material misstatement or omission, and any course of conduct, that has the effect of defrauding investors, whether the wrongdoing was intentional or not.

We note first that such a reading cannot be harmonized with the administrative history of the rule, a history making clear that when the Commission adopted the rule it was intended to apply only to activities that involved scienter. More importantly, Rule 10b-5 was adopted pursuant to authority granted the Commission under § 10(b). The rulemaking power granted to an administrative agency charged with the administration of a federal statute is not the power to make law. Rather, it is "'the power to adopt regulations to carry into effect the will of Congress as expressed by the statute.'" . . . Thus, despite the broad view of the Rule advanced by the Commission in this case, its scope cannot exceed the power granted the Commission by Congress under § 10(b). For the reasons stated above, we think the Commission's original interpretation of Rule 10b-5 was compelled by the language and history of § 10(b) and related section of the Acts. . . . When a statute speaks so specifically in terms of manipulation and deception, and of implementing devices and contrivances—the commonly understood terminology of intentional wrongdoing—and when its history reflects no more expansive intent, we are quite unwilling to extend the scope of the statute to negligent conduct. . . .

Questions
1. What do the respondents contend was the "error" of Ernst & Ernst in auditing First Securities? Was the error intentional (fraudulent)? Did the error in auditing cause a negligent misrepresentation to investors? Did the Court decide whether Ernst & Ernst was negligent?
2. Should the language "manipulative or deceptive device or contrivance" limit the use of Rule 10b-5 to "intentional" practices?

FOREIGN CORRUPT PRACTICES ACT

The scandal of illegal corporate payments in the 1970s was largely uncovered by the SEC. The staff of the SEC heard testimony in the Senate Watergate Hearings that the Republican Party regularly received secret donations from corporations in violation of the maximum amount that corporations are legally permitted to contribute to political parties. Thereafter, the SEC brought suits against a few corporations, alleging such secret payments were improperly withheld from the disclosure documents that the corporations were required to file with the commission. However, since corporate disclosure regulation pursuant to the Securities Acts is limited to *material* information, corporate officials often asserted that the SEC cannot require the disclosure of most secret corporate payments for political or foreign bribes, because the amounts were usually small compared to sales or earnings of the company. The SEC argued, nevertheless, that information that reflects the integrity of management, or the integrity of the company's books and records, is material even if the dollar amount is very small. Since secret corporate payments often involve mislabeling of accounts in the books and records, the SEC contended that the transactions are generally material and required disclosure.

The SEC argued further that books and records must be accurately maintained for the company's financial statements to be relied on by stockholders. Congressional agreement with the SEC's position was subsequently evidenced in the Foreign Corrupt Practices Act (FCPA) of 1977, which amended the 1934 Securities Act in prohibiting the making of false entries in books and records of publicly traded companies. The act requires that the company's books, records, and accounts accurately and fairly reflect, in reasonable detail, the transactions and dispositions of the company's assets. Since the reliability of the company's books and records depends on the effectiveness of the company's system of internal accounting controls, the act also requires that each company devise and maintain a system of internal accounting controls sufficient to provide reasonable assurances that accurate records are being kept. Companies found to have willfully violated the accounting standards provisions of the FCPA are subject to fines of not more than $10,000 or imprisonment of not more than five years or both. The possibility also exists that a violating company may be subject to civil litigation brought by third parties.

The sections of the act that deal with "foreign corrupt practices" are quite limited in scope, but can involve a fine of up to $1 million for a violation. There are five separate parts that make up a violation: (1) the use of an instrumentality of interstate commerce (such as the telephone or mails) in furtherance of (2) a payment, or even an offer to pay, "anything of value," directly or indirectly, (3) to any foreign official with discretionary authority or to any foreign political party or foreign political candidate, (4) if the purpose of the payment is the "corrupt" one of getting the recipient to act (or refrain from acting) (5) in such a way as to assist the company in obtaining or retaining business for or with or directing business to any person.

The act provides that a foreign official does not include any government employee whose duties are "essentially ministerial or clerical." Consequently, there is no prohibition against paying substantial sums to minor officials, so long as their duties are ministerial or clerical. Such payments are frequently called "grease" or "facilitating" payments to minor foreign officials to get them to perform customary services that they might refuse to perform, or perform only slowly, in the absence of such payments.

For the payments to be illegal under the act, the word "corruptly" is used to make clear that the offer, payment, promise, or gift must be intended to induce the recipient to misuse his or her official position to wrongfully direct business to the payor or the client, or to obtain preferential legislation or regulation. The word "corruptly" connotes an evil motive or purpose, but there is no require-ment that the payment violate the law of the host country for it to be labeled "corrupt."

Though not in the act itself, Congress made clear in its hearings that it did not attempt to outlaw an extortion payment. However, no precise guidance is provided in this area except that Congress expects the U.S. diplomatic service to render aid to American businesses abroad who are threatened by extortion.

Numerous bills to clarify the FCPA have been introduced before Congress. It seems likely that some modifications in the law will be enacted.

CORPORATE GOVERNANCE

The SEC has often settled suits of alleged wrongdoing by corporate officials by requiring the defending companies to appoint "independent" persons to investi-gate the full extent of wrongdoing. In-house investigators were either outside directors of the company or specially hired lawyers and accountants who were to report to a committee of the board of directors, such as an audit committee. This technique became the basis of the SEC's handling of the "Corporate Payment Scandal." The SEC requested companies to participate in a "voluntary disclosure program." Almost 400 companies agreed to conduct independent internal inves-tigations and make the findings available to the SEC. A summary of the internal investigation was reported to investors. The SEC also required the participating companies to develop corporate codes of conduct that prohibit illegal payments, require proper record keeping, and prohibit other types of unethical conduct. The codes also established compliance and monitoring procedures so that, in effect, the codes became in-house extensions of the securities laws.

As a "voluntary disclosure program" indicates, corporate disclosure regula-tion appears to be expanding from merely providing information to investors. Instead, disclosure rules are becoming instruments for social regulation. Critics of the "corporate system" have asserted that companies are "undemocratic" because management controls the nomination procedures for the board of di-rectors. Opposing shareholders must bear an expensive proxy fight to nominate any other person for a directorship. As a response to these criticisms, Congress and the SEC held public hearings on corporate governance in 1977. Most re-form proposals have involved the corporate disclosure machinery as a means for shareholders to gain greater control over boards of directors. Such reforms attempt to make companies more responsible, accountable, and democratic.

Although it already requires many shareholder social accountability pro-posals to be included in management's proxy materials, the SEC appears to believe that an increase in federal intervention into corporate control is un-justified by past corporate transgressions. The SEC is satisfied with the disclosure program and has been successful in convincing Congress not to further interfere with corporate decision making.

CRITICISMS AND REFORM PROPOSALS

New academic theories and congressional criticism have raised fundamental questions about the federal disclosure system of security regulation. These questions will undoubtly affect the future course of innovation in this field. One fundamental issue is whether disclosure is an effective remedy to deal with the ills that affect the securities markets. For example, the federal securities laws were passed in part as a reaction to the 1929 stockmarket crash. However, the federal securities laws have not prevented continuing gyration in securities markets. The goal of stability in the financial markets has not been achieved. In theory, full information revealed by the disclosure system should result in more stable prices. However, conclusions on this matter are difficult to determine since the instability of markets may result more from uncertainty and imperfection of financial and economic predictions and forecasts, rather than from the failure of securities laws to make adequate disclosures of historical facts.

Connected with this criticism is the debate about historical cost financial statements. Such statements do not reflect current market values or provide information of future projection, which are more valuable to the professional or average investor. In addition, the overly permissible treatment of accounting standards tends to destroy the comparability of financial information published through the registration process. Historically, the SEC has essentially delegated the regulation of accounting principles to the accounting profession. In January of 1977, however, a Senate subcommittee led by Senator Lee Metcalf lambasted the SEC and the accounting profession. Senator Metcalf reported:

Corporations presently have substantial discretion in choosing among alternative accounting standards to report similar business transactions. As a result, the amounts of earnings or losses reported to the public can vary drastically depending on which accounting alternatives are chosen. . . . In particular, I am disturbed by two . . . findings. The first is the extraordinary manner in which the SEC has insisted upon delegating its public authority and responsibilities on accounting matters to private groups with obvious self-interests in the resolution of such matters. The second is the alarming lack of independence and the lack of dedication to public protection shown by the large accounting firms.

As a consequence of the Metcalf report, the SEC is likely to place increasing pressure on the accountants' Financial Accounting Standards Board to set more specific accounting standards to allow for comparability of financial statements. The flexibility of accounting standards will probably be reduced and the relationship of the SEC to the accounting profession will continue to be a source of controversy for years to come.

Another criticism of the present disclosure system is that the disclosed data are beyond the skills and background of the average investor to understand. The system attempts to protect relatively unsophisticated individuals who are presently inundated with overly complex material. It will be a continuing problem of the SEC to develop simpler documents and otherwise provide a more meaningful disclosure to the average investor.

Companies and critics have complained also of the extensive paperwork that must be filed with the commission. The Advisory Committee on Corporate Disclosure has recommended that the SEC create one "continuous disclosure report" which could be used for all 1933 and 1934 Act filings. Further, the American Law Institute has proposed a bill to Congress that combines the 1933 and 1934 Acts. The new act would deemphasize the company's public offerings of securities and make the company's annual report the "key-disclosure document."

Finally, some have argued that the disclosures mandated by the securities laws have not been effective in preventing fraud. They maintain that scandals such as BarChris, Manor Nursing Centers, and Equity Funding were not prevented by the securities law. However, it is impossible to know what frauds would have been perpetrated had the securities laws not been enacted. The incidence of fraud and manipulation may well have been reduced by virtue of disclosure requirements. The fact that some frauds are perpetrated does not preclude the possible conclusion that other frauds have been prevented by the securities laws. Moreover, many have argued that the requirement of full disclosure not only results in the prevention of fraud but also reduces shareholder-management conflicts of interest and deters other questionable practices.

CONCLUSION

The Securities Act of 1933 is basically a registration of information law designed to give the prospective investor more information about the management and finances of corporations seeking to sell their securities to the public. The Securities and Exchange Act of 1934 as amended is designed to promote investor confidence in American capital markets by the extension of the "disclosure" doctrine to securities traded on the national exchange and over-the-counter markets. Some opponents of the disclosure doctrine argue that its costly operation imposes artificial barriers on entry that inefficiently allocate capital. On the other hand, supporters of the disclosure system maintain that it is necessary to protect the "purity" of the securities distribution system and the confidence of the investors, which are essential to the process of raising capital investments. Only a few would contend that the economic and social benefits accruing from the laws enhancing the capital-raising system are less than the costs associated with securities regulations.

DISCUSSION QUESTIONS

1. A pension plan entered into under a collective-bargaining agreement between a local labor union and employer trucking firms required all employees to participate in a pension plan but not to pay anything into it. All

contributions to the plan were to be made by employers at a specified amount per week for each worker. To be eligible for a pension, an employee was required to have 20 years of continued service. Petitioner employee, who had over 20 years' service, was denied a pension on retirement because of a break in service. He then brought suit in Federal District Court, alleging that the union and the trustee of the pension funds had misrepresented and omitted a statement of material facts with respect to the value of a covered employee's interest in the pension plan, and that such misstatements and omissions constituted a fraud in connection with the sale of a security in violation of Section 10(b) of the Securities Exchange Act of 1934 and Rule 10b-5. As a prerequisite matter, the district court held that petitioner's interest in the pension fund constituted a "security" within the meaning of the Securities Act because the plan created an "investment contract." Do you agree?

2. Defendant engaged in a fraudulent "short selling" scheme by placing orders with brokers to sell certain shares of stock which he believed had peaked in price and which he falsely represented that he owned. Gambling that the price would decline substantially before he was required to deliver the securities, he planned to take offsetting purchases through other brokers at lower prices. But the market price rose sharply before the delivery date so that defendant was unable to make covering purchases and never delivered the securities. Consequently, the brokers were unable to deliver the securities to the investor-purchasers and were forced to borrow stock to make the delivery. In order to return the borrowed stock the brokers had to purchase replacement shares on the open market at the now higher prices, a process known as "buying in." The investors were thereby shielded from direct injury, but the brokers suffered substantial financial losses. The district court found defendant guilty of employing "a scheme and artifice to defraud" in the sale of securities in violation of Section 17(a)(1) of the Securities Act of 1933, which makes it unlawful "for any person in the offer or sale of any securities . . . directly or indirectly . . . to employ any device, scheme, or artifice to defraud." The court of appeals, though finding the evidence sufficient to establish that defendant had committed fraud, vacated the conviction on the ground that the purpose of the Securities Act was to protect investors from fraudulent practices in the sale of securities and that since defendant's fraud injured only brokers and not investors, defendant did not violate Section 17(a)(1). Is the court of appeals correct?

3. A limited partnership agreement divided partners into "participants" whose capital contributions were to be applied first to defray intangible expenses incurred in the partnership's oil drilling venture, and "special participants" whose capital was to be used for tangible drilling expenses. One of the two original special participants, PMC and ITR Corp., located four participants to join the partnership. PMC attracted only Doran, who became a special participant. Doran was the fourth person contacted by PMC in regard to joining in the venture.

    A broker had linked PMC and Doran. PMC sent Doran some drilling logs and technical maps and informed him that two of the four wells planned had been completed. Doran contributed $25,000 down and assumed liability on a $113,643 note owed by PMC to an outsider. Doran's share of production payments was to be used to make payments on the note, and Doran's name was added to the note as obligor directly to the outsider. He contracted to hold PMC harmless on the liability.

Because of a state law violation in the operation of the wells, the wells were sealed by a state authority for 388 days. The note went into default; the outsider took judgment against Doran and PMC. Doran seeks federal court relief voiding his agreements with PMC and the limited partnership because he was sold a security that was not registered.

What defense might PMC offer for not registering?

4. Bangor Corporation in its registration statement listed its 98.7 percent holding in Bangor and Aroostook Railroad (BAR) at $18.4 million. The Bangor Corporation failed to disclose that it had negotiated for a sale of the BAR at a price substantially below $18.4 million. The board had authorized Hutchins to enter into a deal to sell the BAR to Amos on whatever terms he decided were best. The agreement that was entered into resulted in Bangor's sustaining a $13.8 million book loss and a reduction in retained earnings from $37.9 million to $20.5 million.

First Boston was the underwriter reviewing the registration statement and had ready access to the books and records of Bangor. It examined the minutes of the Bangor board meeting and questioned Bangor's management regarding the BAR. It was informed that there were no plans at that time to dispose of the railroad. First Boston did not seek verification of the official answer that a sale was not anticipated at that time, nor did it talk to officials at Amos after it discovered from the minutes that Amos was the likely buyer.

Is First Boston's action sufficient to support a due diligence defense when charged as a participant in the registration of a misleading registration statement?

5. The petitioner was a managerial employee at E. L. Aaron & Co. (the firm), a registered broker-dealer with its principal office in New York City. Among other responsibilities at the firm, the petitioner was charged with supervising the sales made by its registered representatives and maintaining the so-called due diligence files for these securities in which the firm served as a market maker. One such security was the common stock of Lawn-A-Mat Chemical & Equipment Corp. (Lawn-A-Mat), a company engaged in the business of selling lawn care franchises and supplying its franchisees with products and equipment.

Between November 1974 and September 1975, two registered representatives of the firm conducted a sales campaign in which they repeatedly made false and misleading statements in an effort to solicit orders for the purchase of Lawn-A-Mat common stock. During the course of this promotion, they informed prospective investors that Lawn-A-Mat was planning or in the process of manufacturing a new type of small car, and that the car would be marketed within six weeks; Lawn-A-Mat, however, had no such plans. The two registered representatives also made projections of substantial increases in the price of Lawn-A-Mat common stock and optimistic statements concerning the company's financial condition. These projections and statements were without basis in fact, since Lawn-A-Mat was losing money during the relevant period.

On receiving several complaints from prospective investors, an officer of Lawn-A-Mat informed the representatives that their statements were false and misleading and requested them to cease making such statements. This request went unheeded.

Thereafter, an attorney representing Lawn-A-Mat communicated with the petitioner twice by telephone. In these conversations, he informed the petitioner that the representatives were making false and misleading statements and described the substance of what they were saying. The petitioner, in addition to being so informed, had reason to know that the statements were false, since he knew that the reports in Lawn-A-Mat's due diligence file indicated a deteriorating financial condition and revealed no plans for manufacturing a new car. The petitioner took no affirmative steps to prevent the recurrence of the misrepresentations. The petitioner's only response to the telephone calls was to inform the representatives of the complaints. Otherwise, the petitioner did nothing to prevent the two registered representatives under his direct supervision from continuing to make false and misleading statements in promoting Lawn-A-Mat common stock.

In February 1976, the commission filed a complaint in the district court against the petitioner in connection with the offer and sale of Lawn-A-Mat common stock. In seeking preliminary and final injunctive relief, the commission alleged that the petitioner had violated and aided and abetted violations of Section 10(b) of the 1934 Act and Rule 10b-5. The gravamen of the charges against the petitioner was that he knew or had reason to know that the employees under his supervision were engaged in fraudulent practices but failed to take adequate steps to prevent those practices from continuing.

Following a trial, the district court found that the petitioner had violated and aided and abetted violation of Section 10(b) and Rule 10b-5 during the Lawn-A-Mat sales campaign and enjoined him from future violations of these provisions. The district court's finding of violations was based on its factual finding that the petitioner had intentionally failed to discharge his supervisory responsibility to stop his employees from making statements to prospective investors that the petitioner knew to be false and misleading. The district court concluded that the fact that the petitioner "intentionally failed to terminate the false and misleading statements made by his employees, knowing them to be fraudulent, is sufficient to establish his scienter under the securities laws."

The Court of Appeals for the Second Circuit declined to decide the question whether the petitioner's conduct would support a finding of scienter. It held, instead, that when the commission is seeking injunctive relief, "proof of negligence alone will suffice" to establish a violation of Section 10(b) and Rule 10b-5. Will the court of appeal's conclusion be upheld on appeal?

6. An independent public accountant, M, audited Yale Company's financial statements for inclusion in its 19XX annual report to stockholders and certified the figures contained in the statements. This annual report was prepared in April of the following year, 19YY. The accountant was then engaged by Yale to conduct some special studies relating to its internal functioning. In the process, M discovered that the figures in the annual report for 19XX were substantially false and misleading. In June 19YY, Yale filed its form 10-K Report with the SEC, containing the same financial statement as the annual report.

   M is sued by members of the trading public who relied on the published financial statements. Do they have a cause of action against M?

7. A customer of a brokerage firm charged the firm with churning his account, a deceptive device under Section 10(b), Securities Exchange Act. The investor, Buckley, was interested in speculation and was "intensely interested" in his account. At the end of a four-year period with the firm, the account had a deficit of $332,000, and Buckley owed the firm $75,000 in commissions. The account had been very active, and even though 80 or 90 percent of the transactions resulted from the firm's suggestions, Buckley did often reject the firm's recommendations and sometimes initiated transactions himself. Buckley was a Cornell University graduate in economics and international marketing and subscribed to various financial journals.

   Each year, total purchases on the account averaged approximately seven times the sum invested by Buckley.

   Evaluate Buckley's claim.

8. In a meeting between a financial analyst and the chief financial adviser for Liggett and Myers, Inc., the analyst asked whether earnings for the second quarter would be down and received an affirmative answer. He inquired whether this was a "good possibility," and the answer again was yes, but the financial adviser then asked the analyst to keep this information confidential. The analyst relayed this information to a stockbroker friend who, that same day, sold 1800 shares of Liggett and Myers stock for his customers. The following day Liggett and Myers released a preliminary earning report showing the decline in second-quarter earnings. The report was published in the *Wall Street Journal* the day after it was released.

   Has Liggett and Myers, Inc., violated Rule 10b-5?

9. Livingston was employed by Merrill Lynch as a securities salesman with the title of "Account Executive." In January 1972, Merrill Lynch began an "Account Executive Recognition Program" for its career Account Executives to reward outstanding sales records. As part of the program, Merrill Lynch awarded Livingston and 47 other Account Executives the title "Vice

President." Livingston had exactly the same duties after he was awarded the title as he did before the recognition. Livingston never attended, nor was he invited or permitted to attend, meetings of the Board of Directors or the Executive Committee. He acquired no executive or policy-making duties. Executive and managerial functions were performed by approximately 350 "Executive Vice Presidents."

Livingston received the same kind of information about the company as an Account Executive both before and after he acquired his honorary title. As an Account Executive, he did obtain some information that was not generally available to the investing public, such as the growth production rankings on the various Merrill Lynch retail offices. Information of this kind was regularly distributed to other salesmen for Merrill Lynch.

In November and December, 1972, Livingston sold a total of 1000 shares of Merrill Lynch stock. He repurchased 1000 shares of Merrill Lynch stock in March 1973, realizing a profit. Merrill Lynch sued Livingston seeking $14,836.37, which represented the profit he made on the short-swing transaction. What decision?

10. George Bunker, President and Chief Executive of Martin Marietta Corporation, served as a member of the Sperry Rand Corporation Board of Directors. During Bunker's tenure on the board of directors at Sperry, Martin Marietta purchased stock of Sperry Rand. Less than six months after the purchase of stock, Martin Marietta sold its Sperry stock at a profit. This sale occurred four days after Bunker resigned as a member of the Sperry Board of Directors. A stockholder of Sperry commenced an action pursuant to Section 16(b) of the Securities Exchange Act alleging that Martin Marietta had received short swing insider profits. Is Martin Marietta liable?

11. If you were a United States attorney in the Justice Department, what would you do with the following situations:
    (a) A U.S. manufacturer gives an automobile to an African official to obtain a contract.
    (b) A U.S. tobacco producer gives several million dollars in "donations" to a charitable organization in a South American country. The organization is headed by the wife of the country's President.
    (c) A U.S. company that arranges hunting trips gives guns and travel to officials of an African country's wildlife agency that issues licenses to hunt game.

SUGGESTED READINGS

Basi, Bart A., "The Responsibility of the Broker-Dealer to the Investing Public," *American Business Law Journal*, Vol. 13, No. 3, Winter 1976, pp. 371–384.

Bowers, L. Thomas, "Cash Tender Offers and Mandated Disclosure," *American Business Law Journal*, Vol. 20, No. 1, Spring 1982, pp. 59–74.

Davies, Jonathon A., "The Changing Legal Environment of Public Accounting: Lower

Court Applications of the *Hochfelder* Decision," *American Business Law Journal*, Vol. 15, No. 3, Winter 1978, pp. 394–401.

Davis, Jonathon A. and Mason, John O., Jr., "The Civil Liability of Accountants Engaged in Audits of Computer Based Information Systems: Adams v. Standard Knitting Mills," *American Business Law Journal*, Vol. 14, No. 1, Spring 1976, pp. 424–430.

Ferrera, Gerald R., "Corporate Board Responsibility Under the Foreign Corrupt Practices Act of 1977," *American Business Law Journal*, Vol. 18, No. 4, Winter 1981, pp. 259–268.

Hull, J. K., "Insider Trading: An End to the Debate in Britain," *American Business Law Journal*, Vol. 17, No. 1, Spring 1979, pp. 85–98.

Mahaney, Mary Claire, "The Foreign Corrupt Practices Act: Curse or Cure," *American Business Law Journal*, Vol. 19, No. 1, Spring 1981, pp. 73–86.

Siedel, George H., "Internal Accounting Controls Under the Foreign Corrupt Practices Act: A Federal Law of Corporations?", *American Business Law Journal*, Vol. 18, No. 4, Winter 1981, pp. 443–476.

Wiesen, Jeremy, "U. S. Securities and Exchange Commission: A Forty-Five Year Perspective," *American Business Law Journal*, Vol. 17, No. 1, Spring 1979, pp. 129–130.

chapter 21

CONSUMER PROTECTION REGULATIONS: RIGHTS TO CHOOSE AND TO BE INFORMED

Classical economists have advanced the theory of consumer sovereignty as an essential ingredient of free competitive markets. Informed consumers with equal bargaining power were to interact with sellers in the marketplace to establish mutually satisfactory bargains. Government protection of either consumers or producers was considered unnecessary. *Caveat emptor*—let the buyer beware— was acceptable public policy because the seller and the buyer generally had equal knowledge of the simple goods that revealed their quality through inspection. In effect, consumers could protect themselves. The consumer could avoid unsafe products because most goods did not contain hidden defects or dangerous tendencies. The nontechnical wares allowed consumers to protect themselves concerning the attributes of the product. In addition, the large number of sellers in the competitive market provided the consumer with the right to choose among producers and, thereby, forced producers to supply satisfactory quality and service at a fair price. And because the buyer and seller often dealt face to face, the consumers' complaints fell upon the sympathetic ears of producers who in their desire to make sales, responded to the consumer's voice.

During the final years of the nineteenth century, however, the marketplace began to change. New technology developed more sophisticated products, and producers began to organize into larger and fewer economic units. The "sovereignty" of consumers waned. The sophistication of technology incorporated into new products widened the gap between the knowledge of sellers and the ignorance of consumers. Moreover, the opportunity for sellers to misrepresent their wares has increased. The buyer's ignorance and the seller's deception of buyers cause serious economic problems. First, buyer ignorance can stifle price and quality competition among sellers. Second, it can encourage wasteful forms of competition, such as noninformative and excessive advertising. Finally, but not least, the consumer may suffer economic loss causing economic waste.

Laws of consumer protection were among the first economic regulations passed by the federal government. Outcries of consumers brought about congressional regulation of monopolistic practices of railroads and the passage of the antitrust laws. Subsequent legislation included the Federal Food and Drug Act in 1906 and the Federal Trade Commission Act in 1914. More recent consumer legislation includes the creation of the National Highway Traffic and Safety Administration and The Consumer Product Safety Commission. While the development of consumer protection laws continues to be sporadic, President Kennedy's address concerning consumer protection in 1962 brought clarity and definition to the problems of consumers. The President asserted four basic rights of the consumer.

1. The right to choose (variety in product sources).
2. The right to be informed (avoid ignorance and deceptions).
3. The right to safety (avoid hazardous goods).
4. The right to be heard (to assert consumer interests in the formulation of governmental policy).

These rights as enunciated by the President have given direction to the "consumer movement" throughout the sixties and seventies. They also provide some insights concerning probable future trends and legislation. For example, recent consumer advocates have advanced the notion that consumers should also have the right to recover. The right of recovery is considered an essential consumer right. However, consumer rights as advocated have not been completely fulfilled in law. Consequently, the debate over the content and passage of consumer protection laws is continuous.

The purpose of this chapter is to review policy solutions that have been fashioned to protect the consumer's right (1) to choose and (2) to be informed. The next chapter continues the exposition of laws designed to protect consumers; specifically the consumer's right (3) to safety and (4) to be heard.

CONSUMER'S RIGHT TO CHOOSE

The consumer's right to choose involves the assurance, whenever possible, of access to a variety of products and services at competitive prices. In effect, the consumer's right to choose is primarily protected by the market system itself.

Competitive vendors provide a variety of goods from which the consumer may exercise independent choice for products and prices that suite the consumer's taste. However, when vendors cooperate with one another in contravention to the competitive process, consumer's choices for products or competitive prices are likely reduced. The response of the political process to such industry cooperation has been the enactment of antitrust laws to protect the competitive process. The theory, substance, and process of the antitrust laws has been fully explained in prior chapters. Suffice it to say at this point that both private and public remedies are provided by the antitrust statutes in an effort to protect the consumer's right to choose. To the extent that antitrust laws are ineffective in eliminating industry collusion or concentration, which reduce the competitive process, the consumer's right to choose will likely be impaired. Consequently, consumer groups continue to support efforts to improve antitrust laws and resist efforts of other groups that seek relaxation of antitrust rules.

CONSUMER'S RIGHT TO BE INFORMED

DECEPTIVE AND UNFAIR PRACTICES

In 1942 the Supreme Court in *Valentine v. Chrestensen*, 316 U.S. 52, held that "commercial advertising" was not protected by the First Amendment right of "free speech." In effect, the First Amendment imposed no restraints on governmental regulation of commercial advertising. The fact that advertising was a form of speech, a means of communicating ideas or information, and literally within the First Amendment's language was ignored by the Court. Consequently, the government and, in particular, the Federal Trade Commission had authority to regulate advertising without such governmental action being construed as an infringement on the advertiser's right to free speech.

Then, in 1976 the Court held that even if the advertiser's interest is "a purely economic one," it "hardly disqualifies him for protection under the First Amendment."[1] The Court added:

It is a matter of public interest that (private economic) decisions in the aggregate, be intelligent and well-informed. To this end, the free flow of commercial information is indispensable. . . . (E)ven if the First Amendment were thought to be primarily an instrument to enlighten public decision making in a democracy, we could not say that free flow of (commerical) information does not serve that goal.

However, the Court emphasized that its decision that "commercial speech, like other varieties, is protected" does not mean "it can never be regulated in any way." The Court acknowledged that reasonable "time, place, and manner" restrictions on speech are valid. The Court added:

[U]ntruthful speech, commercial or otherwise, has never been protected for its own sake. . . . Obviously, much commercial speech is not provably false, or even wholly false, but only deceptive or misleading. We foresee no obstacle to a state's dealing effectively with this problem.

The Court also recognized in a footnote, that because advertisements are calculated and supported by large financing, it is "less necessary to tolerate inaccurate statements for fear of silencing the speaker." These attributes "may also make it appropriate to require that a commercial message appear in such a form, or include such additional information, warnings, and disclaimers, as are necessary to prevent its being deceptive." Finally, the Court advised that the nature of commercial advertising "may also make inapplicable the prohibition against prior restraints."

The Court's language quickly aborts any foolish notion that the Court was attempting to repeal the Federal Trade Commission Act or any other laws prohibiting false and deceptive advertising. The Court wanted to make sure that its decision was not misconstrued as giving commercial speech the same degree of constitutional protection as political and literary speech. Advertising is to become constitutionally protected speech, but advertisers do not need or deserve as much protection as politicians and editorial writers.

The law of advertising regulation will inevitably be affected by the introduction of the First Amendment as a relevant and important factor. While deceptive advertising will remain constitutionally unprotected, regulators will find it necessary to articulate more carefully the necessity and justification for governmental control of particular advertising. The method of regulation or restriction imposed on the advertiser also must be the least restrictive alternative available.

Deceptive Advertising

At common law, the consumer's legal action for misrepresentations (deceptions) by the seller was difficult to prove. The consumer had to prove in court that:

1. The seller misrepresented a product claim as a fact (not as mere puffery or opinion).
2. The seller knowingly intended (scienter) to deceive the buyer.
3. The buyer was justified (not just stupid) in relying on the claim.
4. The buyer suffered financial injury by relying on the claim.

The success of consumer plaintiffs at common law was rare. These burdens of proving actual deception in the mind of the buyer and deliberate intent in the mind of the seller were often insurmountable.

The Federal Trade Commission Act of 1914 did not greatly improve the opportunity for consumers to recover from the deceptive seller, but did authorize the FTC, under lesser burdens of proof, to prohibit the continuing use of the deceptive selling claim. The FTC Act authorizes the commissioners to prohibit "unfair or deceptive acts or practices" under Section 5. Under Section 5, the commission is not required to make a finding of intent to deceive by the seller.

Instead, the commission looks at the ad for claims that are likely to deceive, not at the advertiser's intent. Moreover, proof of actual deception is not required.[2] The commissioners may use their own expertise to determine whether the ad has a potential for deception, rather than requiring consumers to testify of actual deception. Despite this statutorial authority for commissioner-determined deception, the FTC has in recent years begun to rely more on the views of outside experts and consumers for advice concerning the "representation" made by the advertisement.

The strategy of the FTC Act is one of prevention, rather than punishment and remedy. Consequently, except in instances where the misrepresentation could cause the consumer's physical well-being to be threatened, reprimands for selling deceptions usually involve no more than a "cease and desist" order.

What is "Deception"?   The law aims at the prevention of *deception* of potential buyers. Consequently, that which is deceptive is illegal. However, it should be noted that falsity and deception are not necessarily the same. While most falsehoods are deceptive, a claim may be false but not deceptive. And conversely, while most true claims are not deceptive, some true claims may be deceptive. Truth and falsity are determined by the literal content of the message sent. On the other hand, deception depends on the impression on the potential buyer receiving the message.

For example, an oil company promised to put a "tiger in your tank" and a soap company gave assurance that its cleanser has the power of a "white tornado." Both are patently false. There is no tiger, nor a white tornado to enhance the product's power. Yet no one is deceived by the claims, and FTC has taken no action. Such expressions are considered "puffery," similar to expressions of subjective opinions, and not generally subject to FTC challenge.[3]

On the other hand, the examples of literal truth that actually deceive are numerous. Old Gold cigarettes once proclaimed that they were found to have the lowest throat-irritating tars in a research study published in *Reader's Digest.* The claim that Old Gold was lowest of the brands tested was true, but the *Reader's Digest* article revealed, "the difference between brands are, practically speaking, small, and no single brand is superior to its competitors as to justify its selection on the ground that it is less harmful." The FTC found deception in Old Gold's claim. The court in upholding the FTC said "To tell less than the whole truth is a well known method of deception; and he who deceives by resorting to such method cannot excuse the deception by relying upon the truthfulness per se of the partial truth."[4]

Since deception is in the mind of the observer rather than in the content of the advertisement, one may well wonder if the advertisement would be illegal if one gullible person was misled. While no direct answer is available to this question, the courts have adopted the approach that the act protects "the public—the vast multitude which includes the ignorant, the unthinking and the credulous."[5] However, an advertiser will not be liable for "every conceivable misconception, however outlandish, to which his representation might be subject among the foolish or feebleminded."[6] Consequently, commissioners are free to determine an advertisement to be deceptive if the ignorant, the unthinking, and the trusting would be misled by the ad. Moreover, advertisements directed at special audience groups will be interpreted on the basis of their meaning to that group. Children may be more easily misled.

Examples of Deception.   FTC enforcement over the years has revealed a wide variety of illegal deceptions. A few broad categories of deception would include the following.

Deceptive Claims of Composition.   False claims of composition are illegal. For example, Algoma Lumber Company was prevented from selling yellow pine as "California white pine."[7] Also, Winsted Hosiery Company was prohibited from labeling some underwear manufactured partly from wool ingredients as "wool."[8] Indeed, a host of packaging and labeling acts of Congress empower the FTC to regulate the ingredient claims of many products. Under the authority of these enactments, the FTC has explicitly defined particular products so as to avoid false claims. For example, "down" is defined as including feathers of any aquatic bird, but not chicken feathers. Likewise, "vanilla" is described as only that which can be obtained from the vanilla bean.

Deceptive Claims of Business or Trade Status.   The FTC has successfully prosecuted claims misrepresenting business or trade status. For example, when a seller performs a retailing function, it has been held deceptive to represent itself as a "mill," "manufactuer," or "wholesaler."[9] Also, numerous FTC orders have been issued and upheld by the courts prohibiting the use of the word "college" or "university" when the defendant is not in fact an institution of higher education.[10]

Deceptive Use of Trademarks and Tradenames.   The deceptive use of trademarks or tradenames is also outlawed. For example, Carter Products Inc., was forced to excise "liver" from its trademark when it was demonstrated that the drug had no effect on the liver.[11]

Deceptive Claims of Function.   In the late sixties, Firestone advertised that its "Super Sport Wide Oval" tires were,

". . . build lower, wider. Nearly two inches wider than regular tires. To corner better, run cooler, stop 25% quicker."

When challenged by the FTC, Firestone produced evidence that cars with these tires traveling at speeds of 15 miles per hour were able to stop 25 percent faster than those with ordinary width tires. Moreover, these tests were conducted on a low-friction surface, approximately equivalent to a waxed linoleum floor. The FTC had no trouble deciding that these slipper surfaces and slow speeds were not typical of United States driving conditions and that the advertisements were deceptive.[12]

Deceptive Claims of Efficacy.   Also in the sixties, Wonder Bread ran a commercial showing bread-eating children growing dramatically before the viewers' eyes while the narrator boasted that Wonder Bread was "enriched," and "helps build strong bodies twelve ways." The FTC held that the ads deceptively represented Wonder Bread as an "extraordinary food for producing dramatic growth in children."[13]

Deceptive Endorsements. Many movie and athletic stars have endorsed products in advertisements over the years. The FTC has recently determined that such endorsers must be "bona fide" users of the product (unless it is clearly inappropriate, as with Joe Namath's pantyhose commercial). Moreover, any association of professional athletes that "selects" (or designates as "offical") any particular brand of food or beverage is regarded by the FTC as holding itself out as an expert in the field of nutrition. The FTC argues that consumers would expect the association to select only nutritious foods as part of its business needs. Consequently, the association's endorsement must be based on an expert evaluation of the nutritional value of the endorsed product. Also, the advertisement would be deceptive unless the association has in fact performed comparisons among competing brands. Such comparisons must reveal the net impression created by the advertisement.

Deceptive Price Claims. Advertisements that offer goods and services at deceptive prices are illegal under Section 5, also.[14] When an advertiser is willing to sell "two for the price of one," such ads are deceptive if the merchant marks up the price of the one unit that must be purchased. The one unit must be sold at the advertiser's regular price in that geographical or trade area prior to the advertisement. Moreover, when an advertiser claims prices have been reduced, they must have been reduced from the former regular prices.

Deceptive Mock-ups.

FTC v. Colgate-Palmolive Co.

380 U.S. 374 (1964)
Supreme Court of the United States

Chief Justice Warren

The basic question before us is whether it is a deceptive trade practice to represent falsely that a televised test, experiment, or demonstration provides a viewer with visual proof of a product claim, regardless of whether the product claim is itself true.

The case arises out of an attempt by defendant Colgate-Palmolive Company to prove to the television public that its shaving cream, "Rapid Shave," . . . could soften even the toughness of sandpaper. Each of the commercials contained the same "sandpaper test." The announcer informed the audience that, "To prove RAPID SHAVE'S super-moisturizing power, we put it right from the can onto this tough, dry sandpaper. It was apply . . . soak . . . and off in a stroke." While the announcer was speaking. Rapid Shave was applied to a substance that appeared to be sand-

paper, and immediately thereafter a razor was shown shaving the substance clean. The Federal Trade Commission issued a complaint against respondent Colgate . . . charging that the commercials were false and deceptive. The evidence before the . . . Administrative Law Judge (ALJ) disclosed that . . . the substance resembling sandpaper was in fact a simulated prop, or "mock-up," made of plexiglass to which sand had been applied. . . .

The Commission . . . found that the undisclosed use of a plexiglass substitute for sandpaper was . . . a material misrepresentation that was a deceptive act. . . . [T]he Commission found that viewers had been misled into believing they had seen it done with their own eyes. As a result of these findings the Commission entered a cease-and-desist order against the [defendant]. . . .

We accept the Commission's determination that the commercials involved in this case contained [the] representation . . . that the viewer was seeing this experiment for himself . . . which was clearly false. The parties agree that Section 5 prohibits the intentional misrepresentation of any fact which would constitute a material factor in a purchaser's decision whether to buy. They differ, however, in their conception of what "facts" constitute a "material factor" in a purchaser's decision to buy. [Defendant] submits, in effect, that the only material facts are those which deal with the substantive qualities of a product. The Commission, on the other hand, submits that the misrepresentation of *any* fact so long as it materially induces a purchaser's decision to buy is a deception prohibited by §5.

* * *

. . . We find an especially strong similarity between the present case and those cases in which a seller induces the public to purchase an arguably good product by misrepresenting his line of business, by concealing the fact that the product is reprocessed, or by misappropriating another's trademark. In each the seller had used a misrepresentation to break down what he regards to be an annoying or irrational habit of the buying public—the preference for particular manufacturers or known brands regardless of a product's actual qualities, the prejudice against reprocessed goods, and the desire for verification of a product claim. In each case the seller reasons that when the habit is broken the buyer will be satisfied with the performance of the product he receives. . . . It is generally accepted that it is a deceptive practice to state falsely that a product has received a testimonial from a respected source. In addition, the Commission has consistently acted to prevent sellers from falsely stating that their product claims have been "certified." We find these situations to be indistinguishable from the present case. We can assume that in each the underlying product claim is true and in each the seller actually conducted an experiment sufficient to prove to himself the truth of the claim. But in each the

seller has told the public that it could rely on something other than his word concerning both the truth of the claim and the validity of his experiment. We find it an immaterial difference that in one case the viewer is told to rely on the word of a celebrity or authority he respects, in another on the word of a testing agency, and in the present case on his own perception of an undisclosed simulation. . . .

We agree with the Commission, therefore, that the undisclosed use of plexiglass in the present commercials was a material deceptive practice. . . . Nor was it necessary for the Commission to conduct a survey of the viewing public before it could determine that the commercials had a tendency to mislead, for when the Commission finds deception it is also authorized, within the bounds of reason, to infer that the deception will constitute a material factor in a purchaser's decision to buy. . . .

We turn our attention now to the order issued by the Commission. . . .

The Court of Appeals has criticized the reference in the Commission's order to "test, experiment or demonstrate" as not capable of practical interpretation. It could find no difference between the Rapid Shave commercial and a commercial which extolled the goodness of ice cream while giving viewers a picture of a scoop of mashed potatoes appearing to be ice cream. We do not understand this difficulty. In the ice cream case the mashed potato prop is not being used for additional proof of the product claim, while the purpose of the Rapid Shave commercial is to give the viewer objective proof of the claims made. If in the ice cream hypothetical the focus of the commercial becomes the undisclosed potato prop and the viewer is invited, explicitly or by implication, to see for himself the truth of the claims about the ice cream's rich texture and full color, and perhaps compare it to a "rival product," then the commercial has become similar to the one now before us. Clearly, however, a commercial which depicts happy actors delightedly eating ice cream that is in fact mashed potatoes or drinking a product appearing to be coffee but which is in fact some other substance is not covered by the present order.

* * *

In commericals where the emphasis is on the seller's word, and not on the viewer's own perception, the defendants need not fear that an undisclosed use of props is prohibited by the present order. On the other hand, when the commercial not only makes a claim, but also invites the viewer to rely on his own perception for demonstrative proof of the claim, the defendants will be aware that the use of undisclosed props in strategic places might be a material deception. We believe that defendants will have no difficulty applying the Commission's order to the vast majority of their contemplated future commercials.

Questions

1. For an advertising misrepresentation to be illegal, must it relate false information about the substantive qualities of the product or misrepresent any fact that may induce a purchaser to buy the product?
2. Should misrepresenting mock-ups be allowed on television if the substantive facts behind the mock-up are true?
3. An advertisement showing a family enjoying ice cream uses mashed potatoes for ice cream because of the hot lights in filming. Is this an illegal mock-up?
4. Must the Commission conduct a survey of the viewing public to determine if a commercial has a tendency to mislead? Must the Commission put some individual on the stand who will admit to being deceived?

"Unfair" Practices

Besides FTC enforcement actions against "deceptive" product claims, various "unfair" product claims may be held to be illegal, also. For example, the FTC has argued that advertising product claims for which the advertiser possesses no substantiation is both deceptive and "unfair."[15] The substantiation requirement developed from the FTC's conclusion that the poliferation of highly technical products places the consumer in a distinct disadvantage in knowledge and ability to evaluate product claims. Consequently, the FTC feels that if it can prove the advertiser lacked a "reasonable basis" for its claim, the advertiser's claim is deceptive because the advertiser has impliedly claimed to have such "reasonable basis." In addition, the Commission argues that unsubstantiated claims are "unfair" to consumers even if the claim, in fact, is true.

One type of unsubstantiated and, therefore, "unfair" claim is an improper "uniqueness" claim. For example, it was held that ITT Continental Baking Company's claim that its "enriched" bread contained some unique feature (nutritional) when it merely contained ingredients that are in all manufacturers' bread was "unfair."[16] Likewise, Firestone's "Safe" tire was held to be an unfair uniqueness claim.[17] Its tire, like Continental Baking's bread, possessed no uniqueness in comparison with competing brands, and the assertion of uniqueness in the ads was "unfair" to consumers.

Certain techniques of advertising and selling have been outlawed as "unfair." For example, the "bait and switch" advertising and selling technique consists of an attractive but insincere advertisement offering to sell a product or service that the seller in truth does not intend or desire to sell. Instead, the advertiser is merely using its "baiting" ad as a technique to attract customers to the store. When the customers arrive, they are told the advertiser has sold out. The advertiser then attempts to make the consumer "switch" to another product.

A second and similar unfair selling technique is known as "disparagement." Again a very attractively priced item is advertised, but disparaged or "knocked" when members of the public make inquiries. The firm then attempts to sell another item which is more expensive, but now seems to be a bargain in comparison to the disparaged advertised product. While these advertisements contain no content falsehoods, they are used unfairly to lure customers to the store in order to sell them the nonadvertised products. Similarly, an "undisclosed condition" that must be met prior to selling the advertised product is considered an unfair "tie-in" selling technique.

Perhaps no case has done more to delineate the parameters of the Commission's power to regulate "unfair" practices than the 1972 case of *FTC* v. *Sperry & Hutchinson Co.,* 405 U.S. 233. In that case the Supreme Court concluded:

> . . . [L]egislative and judicial authorities alike convince us that the Federal Trade Commission does not arrogate excessive power to itself if, in measuring a practice against the elusive, but congressionally mandated standard of fairness, it . . . considers public values beyond simply those enshrined in the letter of the law or encompassed in the spirit of the antitrust laws.

The Court even offered some guidelines in a footnote for determining the existence of "unfairness." The Court cited a previous FTC suggestion that a three-factor test could be employed. The factors include (1) whether the practice offends public policy as it has been established by statutes, the common law, or otherwise; (2) whether it is immoral, unethical, oppressive, or unscrupulous; and (3) whether it causes substantial injury to consumers or competitors.

Thereafter, the Commission proposed standards for determining "unfairness" that balanced consumer injury against commercial necessity. The difficulty with the standards announced by the Commission is that consumer injury is not always quantifiable (i.e., damage from emotional distress or effect on future employment). Therefore, the balancing process is not predictable if the weights of the various factors involved are not precise. Consequently, many have argued that the "balancing test" needs considerable clarification before it can become an effective tool in the regulation of "unfair" practices.

When Congress renewed the FTC's rulemaking powers in 1975, the FTC announced its intention to promulgate rules under the "unfairness" doctrine. Without any congressional disapproval, the FTC proposed rules that probably would have banned all children's advertising under the "unfairness" notion that even if such ads were truthful, they were unfair when aimed at a particularly vulnerable audience. The FTC also initiated proceedings for possible "unfair" regulations in the funeral industry. However, by 1980 congressional approval had disappeared. The FTC Improvements Act of 1980 terminated the rulemaking proceedings on children's advertising. Moreover, the act stated that "unfairness" cannot be used as a basis for a trade regulation rule concerning advertisements aimed at children. The 1980 Act also forbade the FTC from using any funds for the years 1980–1982 to initiate rulemaking proceedings that involve *unfair* acts or practices. While the FTC is again empowered to issue industry-wide rules that are based on unfairness, the new Reagan-appointed officials at the FTC are not likely to pursue any new rulemaking initiatives under the "unfairness" doctrine.

Remedies for Deceptive and Unfair Practices

The FTC may prosecute "deceptive" or "unfair" practices (1) on a case-by-case approach or (2) by the issuance of trade regulation rules. The former approach involves enforcement of a complaint issued to the defendant. The defendant may oppose the complaint at a hearing before an administrative law judge and on through the judicial system. Such case-by-case proceedings are piecemeal, in that only the "losing" defendant is bound by the provisions of the order.

A more sweeping coverage against deception and unfair practices may be obtained by the issuance of guides and rules. Guides summarize and clarify case law for the benefit of advertisers. However, the guides are not law. In contrast, trade regulation rules embody the full force of law. Individuals may be prosecuted for violating rules. Rules ease the burden of proof imposed on the FTC because the practices covered by the rule have already been established through the rulemaking hearings before the commission as being deceptive or unfair. Therefore, if the rule is violated, the only defense available for the violator is that the rule did not apply in his or her case.

Cease and Desist Orders. The traditional remedy imposed by the FTC is an order to "cease and desist," which prohibits the defendant from engaging further in the unlawful practice. Normally no other penalties are levied. If the defendant fails to obey the cease and desist order, the commission may request a federal court to impose civil penalties of up to $10,000 per day of violation. Since penalties are not issued for the original violation, it has often been argued that advertisers are not significantly deterred from developing another deceptive advertising campaign. For example, Firestone had three violations in a 15-year period. In an effort to avoid such recidivism, the FTC publishes its guides and rules.

Affirmative Disclosure. The affirmative disclosure remedy is normally issued in two types of deception, (1) misrepresentation by silence and (2) exaggerated claims of brand uniqueness. An affirmative disclosure order prohibits the advertiser from making certain claims unless the advertiser discloses simultaneously the other facts necessary to negate deceptive inferences induced by the silence. For example, when a correspondence school chose to continue to advertise its law courses, it was required to affirmatively disclose that those individuals who completed its law courses by correspondence would not be qualified to sit for any bar examination (to obtain the privileges of practicing law) in any of the 50 states.[18] Moreover, the FTC required affirmative disclosures by cigarette advertisers concerning the dangers inherent in smoking. Likewise Geritol, in advertising that its product has a cure for tiredness, was required to disclose that the vast majority of people who are tired are not tired because of iron deficiency and that there is little connection between tiredness and iron deficiency.[19] Hence, these firms, if they chose to advertise, had to make simultaneous disclosures to avoid deception.

Corrective Advertising. While the affirmative disclosure remedy prevents the advertiser from the continuance of misleading claims in future advertisements if the advertiser chooses to advertise, the corrective advertising remedy seeks to eliminate any lingering effects of deception created in prior ads. Deceptive advertising may continue to generate sales even after it has been discontinued. More truthful competitors will thereby suffer at a disadvantage. Consumers may also suffer because they may continue to believe the deceptive claim and fail to switch to an alternate, more effective product.

The remedy of "corrective advertising" requires the advertiser to run advertising disclosures that it previously created a false impression in prior advertisements. There have been *consent* orders in which companies have agreed to advertising disclosures that correct previous false impressions created by advertising. However, the companies did not admit to any wrongdoing or to the FTC's authority to order such corrective advertising. For example, ITT Continental Baking Corp., agreed to a twelve-month advertising disclosure that Profile Bread was not a dietary product.[20] Ocean Spray Cranberries, Inc., likewise, admitted in corrective ads that cranberry juice had more "energy" only because it contained more calories.[21] However, in the following case the FTC "ordered" the corrective advertising and the defendant, Warner-Lambert, challenged the authority of the Commission to issue such an order.

Warner-Lambert Co. v. FTC
   562 F. 2d 749 (1977)
   U.S. Court of Appeals (D.C. Cir.)

The Warner-Lambert Company petitions for review of an order of the Federal Trade Commission requiring it to cease and desist from advertising that its product, Listerine antiseptic mouthwash, prevents, cures, or alleviates the common cold. The FTC order futher requires Warner-Lambert to disclose in future Listerine advertisements that: ". . . Listerine will not help prevent colds or sore throats or lessen their severity." . . .

Listerine has been on the market since 1879. Its formula has never changed. Ever since its introduction it has been represented as being beneficial in certain respects for colds, cold symptoms, and sore throats. Direct advertising to the consumer, including the cold claims as well as others, began in 1921. . . .

Petitioner contends that even if its advertising claims in the past were false, the portion of the Commission's order requiring "corrective advertising" exceeds the Commission's statutory power. The argument is based upon a literal reading of Section 5 of the Federal Trade Commission Act, which authorizes the Commission to issue "cease and desist" orders against violators and does not expressly mention any other remedies. The Commission's position, on the other hand, is that the affirmative disclosure that Listerine will not prevent colds or lessen their severity is absolutely necessary to give effect to the prospective cease and desist order; a hundred years of false cold claims have built up a large reservoir of erroneous consumer belief which would persist unless corrected, long after petitioner ceased making the claims.

Petitioner's narrow reading of Section 5 was at one time shared by the Supreme Court. . . .

But the modern view is very different. In 1963 the Court ruled that the Civil Aeronautics Board has authority to order divestiture in addition to ordering cessation of unfair methods of competition by air carriers. *Pan American World Airways, Inc.* v. *United States*, 371 U.S. 296 (1963). The CAB statute, like Section 5, spoke only of the authority to issue cease and desist orders, but the Court said, "[W]here the problem lies within the purview of the Board, . . . Congress must have intended to give it authority that was ample to deal with the evil at hand. . . . [The] power to order divestiture need not be explicitly included in the powers of an administrative agency to be part of its arsenal of authority. . . ."

Later, in *FTC* v. *Dean Foods Co.*, the Court applied *Pan American* to the Federal Trade Commission. In upholding the Commission's power to seek a preliminary injunction against a proposed merger, the Court held that it was not necessary to find express statutory authority for the power. "Such ancillary powers have always been treated as essential to the effective discharge of the Commission's responsibilities."

Thus it is clear that the Commission has the power to shape remedies which go beyond the simple cease and desist order. Our next inquiry must be whether a corrective advertising order is for any reason outside the range of permissible remedies. . . .

According to petitioner, "The first reference to corrective advertising in Commission decisions occurred in 1970, nearly fifty years and untold numbers of false advertising cases after passage of the Act." In petitioner's view, the late emergence of this "newly discovered" remedy is itself evidence that it is beyond the Commission's authority. This argument fails on two counts. First the fact that an agency has not asserted a power over a period of years is not proof that the agency lacks such power. Second, and more importantly, we are not convinced that the corrective advertising remedy is really such an innovation. The label may be newly coined, but the concept is well established. It is simply that under certain circumstances an advertiser may be required to make affirmative disclosure of unfavorable facts.

One such circumstance is when an advertisement that did not contain the disclosure would be misleading. For example, the Commission has ordered the sellers of treatments for baldness to disclose that the vast majority of cases of thinning hair and baldness are attributable to heredity, age, and endocrine balance (so-called "male pattern baldness") and that their treatment would have no effect whatever on this type of baldness. It has ordered the promoters of a device for stopping bedwetting to disclose that the device would not be of value in cases caused by organic defects or diseases. And it has ordered the makers of Geritol, an iron supplement, to disclose that Geritol will relieve symptoms of tiredness only in persons who suffer from iron deficiency anemia, and that the vast majority of people who experience such symptoms do not have such a deficiency.

Each of these orders was approved on appeal over objections that it exceeded the Commission's statutory authority. . . .

Affirmative disclosure has also been required when an advertisement, although not misleading if taken alone, becomes misleading considered in light of past advertisements. For example, for 60 years Royal Baking Powder Company has stressed in its advertising that its product was superior because it was made with cream of tartar, not phosphate. But, faced with rising costs of cream of tartar, the time came when it changed its ingredients and became a phosphate baking powder. It carefully removed from all labels and advertisements any reference to cream of tartar and corrected the list of ingredients. But the new labels used the familiar arrangement of lettering, coloration, and design, so that they looked exactly like the old ones. A new advertising campaign stressed the new low cost of the product and dropped all reference to cream of tartar. But the advertisements were also silent on the subject of phosphate and did not disclose the change in the product.

The Commission held, the Second Circuit agreed, that the new advertisements were deceptive, since they did not advise consumers that their reasons for buying the powder in the past no longer applied. The court held that it was proper to rquire the company to take affirmative steps to advise the public. To continue to sell the new product on the strength of the reputation attained through 60 years of its manufacture and sale and wide advertising of its superior powder, under an impression induced by its advertisements that the product purchased was the same in kind and as superior as that which had been so long manufactured by it, was unfair alike to the public and to the competitors in the baking powder business.

It appears to us that the order in *Royal* . . . [was] the same kind of remedy the Commission has ordered here. Like Royal . . . , Listerine has built up over a period of many years a widespread reputation. When it was ascertained that that reputation no longer applied to the product, it was necessary to take action to correct it. Here, as in *Royal*, it is the accumulated impact of *past* advertising that necessitates disclosure in *future* advertising. To allow consumers to continue to buy the product on the

strength of the impression built up by prior advertising—an impression which is now known to be false—would be unfair and deceptive.

Having established that the Commission does have the power to order corrective advertising in appropriate cases, it remains to consider whether use of the remedy against Listerine is warranted and equitable. . . .

The Commission has adopted . . . [a] standard for the imposition of corrective advertising . . . [which] dictates two factual inquiries: (1) did Listerine's advertisements play a substantial role in creating or reinforcing in the public's mind a false belief about the product? and (2) would this belief linger on after the false advertising ceases? It strikes us that if the answer to both questions is not yes, companies everywhere may be wasting their massive advertising budgets. Indeed, it is more than a little peculiar to hear petitioner assert that its commercials really have no effect on consumer belief.

. . . [In any case] the Commission adduced survey evidence to support both propositions. We find that . . . survey data and the expert testimony interpreting them constitute substantial evidence in support of the need for corrective advertising in this case.

Finally, petitioner challenges the duration of the disclosure requirement. By its terms it continues until respondent has expended on Listerine advertising a sum equal to the average annual Listerine advertising budget for the period April 1962 to March 1972. That is approximately ten million dollars. Thus if petitioner continues to advertise normally the corrective advertising will be required for about one year. We cannot say that is an unreasonably long time in which to correct a hundred years of cold claims. But, to petitioner's distress, the requirement will not expire by mere passage of time. If petitioner cuts back its Listerine advertising, or ceases it altogether, it can only postpone the duty to disclose. The Commission concluded that correction was required and that a duration of a fixed period of time might not accomplish that task, since petitioner could evade the order by choosing not to advertise at all. The formula settled upon by the Commission is reasonably related to the violation it found.

Questions
1. The FTC Act authorizes the commission to issue cease and desist orders. It does not expressly mention other remedies, such as corrective advertising. Does this mean that the FTC does not possess the authority to order corrective advertising?
2. What particular precedents did the court of appeals cite as containing essentially the same kind of remedy that the commission ordered against Warner-Lambert?
3. When does the commission feel corrective advertising is an appropriate remedy? What factual inquiries are necessary to impose corrective advertising?
4. A mail survey study was conducted before and during the corrective ad campaign. The results showed that the number of people who considered a mouthwash's ability to prevent colds or sore throats dropped from 31% before the corrective campaign to 25% when it was over. The study found that while the usage of Listerine for clean breath remained the same, there was about a 40% drop in the amount of the mouthwash used for colds and sore throats. In contrast, 42% of the respondents still believe colds and sore throats effectiveness was the principal Listerine advertising theme and 39% of Listerine users reported they still use mouthwash to relieve or prevent a cold or sore throat. A second study concluded that viewers apparently understood the commercial's primary purpose as not being the communication of the correction, but to promote the product. What is your opinion of the effectiveness of the corrective advertising remedy?

PRODUCT STANDARDIZATION AND INFORMATION DISCLOSURE

Besides prohibiting unfair and deceptive practices, consumer protection laws also use product standardization and disclosure of information as techniques to enhance the consumer's right to be informed.[22] With expanded and helpful (standardized) information, consumers' purchasing decisions should be more economically efficient, promote price competition among producers, and discourage excessive, noninformative advertising.

Because of consumer ignorance or seller deception, consumers often rely on trademarks to guide their purchasing decisions. Trademarks often help to identify quality in products. However, too heavy a reliance on trademarks may contribute to erroneous purchasing decisions. Owners of prominent trademarks, of course, favor consumer purchasing based on trademarks. They gain at the expense of buyers. However, with an alternate quality identification system, consumers need not rely on trademarks alone. Consequently, laws requiring product standardization and quality disclosures attempt to formulate alternate quality identification systems to the advantage of consumers and the operation of the economic system itself.

Standardization policies promote either simplification or uniformity of product offerings. Tire manufacturers could match each other's product offerings and achieve *uniformity*. They could *simplify* the variety of tires to 20 basic types. The uniformity of tires would facilitate the comparison of different manufacturers' tires. Simplification would help reduce the buyer's burden of decision making.

In contrast, quality disclosures enhance the buyer's awareness of "better" or "worse." For example, even if tire manufacturers uniformly produce 20 types of tires, this would say nothing about the range of quality therein. Sometimes, disclosure of ingredients would be helpful to consumers, but in the case of tires, grade ratings would be more helpful. Thus, policies revealing ingredients and establishing grades may be viewed as quality disclosure systems.

Standardization to Ease Price Comparisons

Advocates in the consumer movement have long complained of the variety of content measures used in selling goods. Grocery shoppers have faced weight and fluid volumes for the same products and meaningless adjectives, such as "jumbo" and "large servings." Such circumstances led to the enactment of the Fair Packaging and Labeling Act (FPLA) in 1966.

The FPLA directs the Federal Trade Commission (in the case of many commodities) to promulgate labeling requirements that pertain:

1. To the identification of the commodity's manufacturer, packer, or distributor.
2. To the location and legibility of a statement of net quantity of the contents.
3. To any description in terms of weight, volume, or size.

The act authorizes the issuance of labeling regulations to determine what size packages may be represented by words such as "small," "medium," and "large." It also regulates the use of "cents-off" or "economy" sizes for packaging and prohibits "nonfunctional slack fill" or "packaged air."

The FPLA's requirement standardizing "net quantity" and eliminating some abuse of size characterizations is of some help to consumers. However, price comparisons would be even easier for consumers if sellers adhered to a few common sizes of packaging. Nevertheless, the effort to "standardize" packaging sizes was defeated in Congress. Instead, nonmandatory standards for package sizes were suggested by the Act.

In contrast, several states have standardized the packaging of some basic commodities, like bread, butter, flour, cornmeal, and milk. And European countries and Canada have mandated extensive standardization of package sizes.[23]

Price standardization is perhaps the best approach for helping consumers. In the United States, price standardization exists in two major forms—unit pricing and Truth-in-Lending regulations.

Unit pricing restates all package prices into a price per standard weight or measure, such as 50.2 cents per pound, or 49.3 cents per hundred count. While studies have revealed that unit pricing reduces price comparison errors and shopping time, national regulations of this type are found only in Germany and Switzerland.[24] In the United States, only a few states have adopted unit-pricing regulations.[25] Also, many grocery stores have voluntarily adopted unit pricing. Of course, consumer advocates have called for federal legislation requiring nationwide unit pricing.

The purpose of the Truth-in-Lending (TIL) Act of 1969 is to inform consumers of the price of consumer credit and allow for price comparisons. To achieve these goals, the law mandates disclosure of (1) the finance charge (the amount of money paid to obtain the credit) and (2) the annual percentage rate, or APR (standard calculation for simple comparison of credit prices). After the enactment of the TIL Act, numerous studies have revealed increased debtor awareness of credit costs.

The TIL Act authorized the Federal Reserve Board to prescribe regulations to effectuate the purposes of the act and prevent circumvention or evasion thereof. Regulation Z attempts to let consumers (borrowers) know the cost of credit so they can compare costs between various credit sources. Regulation Z also regulates the issuance of credit cards, sets maximum liability ($50.00) for the unauthorized use of credit cards, and provides a procedure for resolving billing errors that occur in open-end credit accounts. It applies to credit card issuers and any individual or organization that extends or arranges consumer credit for which a finance charge is or may be payable or which is repayable by agreement in more than four installments. The law obviously applies to all financial institutions and may also apply to department stores, automotive, furniture, and appliance dealers, craftsmen such as plumbers and electricians, and professional people.

Failure to make disclosures as required under the TIL Act subjects the violator to suit for actual damages by consumers plus twice the amount of the finance charge in the case of a credit transaction, as well as court costs and attorney fees. Willfully or knowingly violating the act or Regulation Z can result in criminal action and fines up to $5,000 or imprisonment for up to one year, or both. In addition, failure to comply with the fair credit billing provisions can result in a forfeiture penalty of up to $50. The disclosure requirements are not lax, as the following case reveals.

General Finance Corp. v. Garner
556 F. 2d 772 (1977)
U.S. Court of Appeals (5th Cir.)

In 1974, Ernest Garner purchased a car from Cantrell's Auto Sales in Columbus, Georgia. Garner signed a conditional sales contract granting the seller a security interest in the car. The contract required Garner to make 30 monthly payments of $86.19 each for a total of

$2,585.70. In the same document, Cantrell's Auto Sales assigned the contract to General Finance Corp.

The record indicates that Garner made 11 monthly payments on the car. On February 11, 1975, after Garner made the payment that was due for that month, he filed . . . a petition for relief under Chapter XIII of the Bankruptcy Act. Garner proposed to pay his creditors all that he owed them through the extension mechanism provided by Chapter XIII. Garner's plan called for a monthly payment to General Finance in the amount of $47.88.

General Finance rejected the plan. It filed a reclamation petition seeking possession of the car. Garner answered the petition alleging that the conditional sales contract violated the federal Truth-in-Lending Act. The bankruptcy judge agreed with Garner that the contract violated the Truth-in-Lending Act. The Court concluded that Garner was entitled to a statutory penalty of $1,000.00 and to an attorney's fee of $150.00. The Court, however, did not order General Finance to pay the penalty directly:

The proof of claim filed by General Finance Corporation is in the amount of $1,637.61. We shall apply the $1,000.00 to this claim and allow the claim in the amount of $637.61. This would appear preferable to requiring General Finance Corporation to pay the sum of $1,000.00 to the debtor and increasing the payments under the plan to General Finance Corp. to $86.19 per month. The Chapter XII Trustee should be instructed to pay to General Finance Corp. the sum of $47.88 per month as proposed in the original plan until General Finance Corporation has received the total of $637.61. . . .

The district court approved the bankruptcy judge's conclusion that the conditional sales contract violated the disclosure provisions of the Truth-in-Lending Act and the Federal Reserve Board's regulations thereunder (Regulation Z), because the disclosure statement on the contract did not call attention to a provision in small type on the reverse side of the

document dealing with a security interest in future indebtedness. . . .

The Truth-In-Lending Act requires the creditor in the kind of transaction involved here to disclose

[a] description of any security interest held or to be retained or acquired by the creditor in connection with the extension of credit, and a clear identification of the property to which the security interest relates.

The Federal Reserve Board's regulations require

If after-acquired property will be subject to the security interest, or if other or future indebtedness is or may be secured by any such property, this fact shall be clearly set forth in conjunction with the description or identification of the type of security interest held, retained or acquired.

The future indebtedness term on the reverse side of the conditional sales contract here seems clearly to fall within the language both of the Act and of Regulation Z. . . .

. . . General Finance contends that the spirit of the Truth-in-Lending Act will be served if disclosure is made at the time of any future advances, the theory being that Garner could then choose to go elsewhere for credit. This notion has been rejected by the Federal Reserve Board. Section 226.8(b)(5) . . . provides in part that

[i]f after-acquired property will be subject to the security interest, or *if other or future indebtedness* is or may be secured by any such property, *this fact shall be clearly set forth* in conjunction with the description or identification of the type of security interest held, retained or acquired.

While this language is not without ambiguity . . . it is at least clear that the creditor may not wait until the future transaction to tell the debtor about the future indebtedness provision. . . .

The implication of General Finance's argument is that it should be of no moment to the potential borrower that he is binding the collateral to cover any future debts owed to the creditor. We think, on the contrary, that Congress meant for the potential debtor to have such information when deciding whether he ought to deal with a particular lender. . . .

Questions

1. What did General Finance Company fail to disclose in its credit terms with Garner that violated the Truth-in-Lending Act? What did this failure cost General Finance?
2. Do you agree that the consumer has the right to be informed of "credit terms" and of the various "security interests" retained by the creditor?

Federal Warranty Standardization

Historically, consumers perceived warranties as added assurance of quantity and value. They assumed that product performance was guaranteed if a written warranty accompanied its purchase. They viewed warranty provisions as a means of consumer redress for defective products. On the other hand, marketers often regarded warranties as promotional devices, rather than additional benefits for the consumer. They also viewed warranties as legal instruments that limited their obligations to consumers. The result of these opposing viewpoints was consumer confusion in comprehending warranty messages. The "legalese" language employed in warranties impeded the message to the consumers that the sellers intended to limit their responsibilites in relation to the products sold. Consumer dissatisfaction with warranties as an assurance of quality and consumer frustration with attempts to gain "satisfaction" through complex warranty provisions caused Congress to respond with the Magnuson-Moss Warranty Act, which became law in 1975. The act provides only an outline of principles that were to be further defined and implemented through rules promulgated by the Federal Trade Commission.

The Warranty Act has five primary purposes.

1. To improve the adequacy of warranty information available to consumers.
2. To prevent deception with respect to warranties.
3. To improve competition in warranties in the marketing of consumer products.
4. To improve incentives for product reliability.
5. To encourage warrantors to establish informal dispute settlement mechanisms.

'though the act imposes no requirement that a consumer product be expressly warranted or any requirement regarding the duration of expressed warranties, it does impose certain disclosure requirements and standards on warrantors who choose to give written warranties. Failure to comply with the act's standards for warranties will subject the warrantor to action by the FTC or to action by a consumer class-action suit, if consumers have been damaged by the warrantor's failure to comply. The act authorizes the courts to award the consumer his or her legal expenses, including attorney's fees, as part of a judgment in favor of the consumer.

The act applies when a written warranty is given in connection with the sale of consumer products—"any tangible personal property which is distributed in commerce and which is normally used for personal, family or household purposes." A warranty that is unambiguous and applies solely to services or workmanship is not covered by the act. However, should the written warranty affirm both product performance and workmanship, such as basement waterproofing, it will be interpreted as a warranty subject to the terms of the act. A service contract may not be a warranty, but the act nevertheless stipulates that the terms of the service contract must be fully, clearly, and conspicuously disclosed in simple and readily understood language.

When a written warranty is given on a consumer product that costs the consumer more than $10, the warranty must be clearly and conspicuously designated a "full warranty" or a "limited warranty." If a warranty is designated a full warranty, it must meet the act's minimum standards for warranty.

1. There must be no charge for repairing the product if there is a defect within the warranty period.
2. There must be no limitation on the duration of implied warranties.
3. Any exclusion or limitation of consequential damages for breach of express or implied warranty must appear clearly and conspicuously on the face of the warranty.
4. If the product cannot be repaired after a reasonable number of attempts, the consumer is permitted to elect either a replacement without charge or a refund.

The consumer's choice of refund or replacement is often referred to as a "lemon-aid" provision because it aids a consumer who purchased a "lemon." Unfortunately, most consumers are not aware that "lemon-aid" is served only to those who purchase products under a "full warranty."

Two additional requirements for full warranties under the act are as follows.

1. Warranty terms cannot be limited to the original purchaser only, but must extend to each purchaser who is a consumer of the product within the warranty period.
2. The warrantor may not impose any unreasonable duties on consumers as a condition of securing performance under the warranty.

Although the act did not establish any criteria for determining what is a "reasonable" duty to impose on a consumer, the FTC is authorized to develop rules to define such duties in detail. Any warranty that does not meet the minimum standards for a full warranty must be designated as a "limited warranty."

Under the FTC Warranty Rule 702, sellers have the affirmative duty to make the text of the written warranties available for the buyer's review prior to sale. A variety of techniques are allowed by the FTC to accomplish this purpose. Rule 701 establishes the requirements for disclosures of warranty terms. It requires that the terms of the warranty clearly and conspicuously disclose the following.

1. The identity of the party to whom the warranty is extended.
2. A clear identification of products, parts, or characteristics covered and excluded by the warranty.
3. A statement of what the warrantor will do in the event of a defect or failure of the product to perform.
4. The point in time in which the warranty becomes effective if different from the purchase date.
5. A step-by-step explanation of the procedure that the consumer should follow to obtain performance under the warranty.
6. Information respecting any informal dispute settlement mechanism adopted by the warrantor.
7. Certain mandatory statements if limitations are imposed on duration of implied warranties or consequential damages.
8. A statement that the warranty confers specific legal rights.

The act allows warrantors an option to establish an informal dispute settlement procedure for resolving consumer complaints arising out of warranty obligations. Rule 703 defines the duties of the warrantor and the minimum requirements that must be met if the warrantor elects to implement such an informal procedure. The informal procedure must be disclosed in the written warranty and the warrantor must fund and operate the mechanism so that it is provided free of charge to consumers. If the warrantor provides such a mechanism, consumers may not bring civil suits under the act until the dispute has been submitted to the informal proceedings. Although the decision of the informal proceedings is not binding on the parties, it is admissible as evidence in subsequent civil suits relating to the matter decided.

Studies of the impact of the warranty law reveal that it has not been particularly successful in translating written warranties into "simple and readily understood language."[26] However, warranty coverage in terms of duration, scope, and remedies seems to have improved.[27]

Questions
1. How is warranty standardization an aid to consumers?
2. What are the rights of the consumer under a "full warranty"?
3. Are services covered by the Warranty Act?
4. How has the Warranty Act expanded the consumer's right to be informed?

Quality Disclosures

Standardization policies help consumers make price comparisons more easily. However, they do not allow for any quality differences in the competing products. Quality disclosure policies attempt to help consumers identify quality differences.

Disclosure of Ingredients.   Various labeling acts call for the disclosure of ingredients. The Wool Products Labeling Act of 1939, the Fur Products Labeling Act of 1951, and the Textile Fiber Products Identification Act of 1958 are all enforced by the Federal Trade Commission. Under the Wool Products Act, wool products must have labels showing the percentage of the total fiberweight that is composed of "virgin", reprocessed, or reused wool. Inclusion of any other fiber must be identified by generic name if it exceeds 5 percent of the total.

The Fur Act requires labels for fur products. The labels must disclose the true English name of the animal that grew the fur. If the fur is imported, the label must designate the animal's home country. Furthermore, the label must indicate whether the fur has been bleached, dyed, or otherwise artificially colored. Also, the lable is to indicate the part of the animal from which the fur was taken.

The proliferation of man-made chemical fibers and the variety of tradenames has created confusion among consumers. The Textile Act requires labels revealing the *generic* names and percentages of all fibers that go into a fabric, except those that represent less than 5 percent of the fabric. The FTC has specified 17 generic families. This law would be helpful to those consumers that have familiarized themselves with the washing, drying, pressing, or wearing properties of these generic fabrics.

About 1972, the Food and Drug Administration expanded the labeling requirements for most processed food products. Detailed disclosures of composition are now required. The disclosures include information concerning nutrition and artificial ingredients. In addition, special information is required on foods directed to infants, nursing mothers, or diabetics. Information to protect the allergic and the obese is also included.

Sometimes, there is a problem with the creation of ingredient standards. Either the producers or consumers or both may be disappointed with the established standards. Consider the dispute in the following case.

Federation of Homemakers v. Hardin
328 F. Supp. 181 (1971)
U.S. District Court (D.C.)

[T]he Federation of Homemakers, a consumer organization dedicated to protecting the integrity of food products, challenges the use of "All Meat" labels on frankfurters when such products actually contain up to 15 percent of non-meat ingredients. . . .

The underlying statute in this case is the Wholesome Meat Act, enacted to protect the health and welfare of consumers by ensuring that they have access to wholesome and properly marked meats. . . .

The sections of the Wholesome Meat Act relating to misleading labeling, prohibit any meat product from being sold under a label which is misleading and provides a procedure whereby the Secretary [of Agriculture] may enforce the prohibition. . . .

In reviewing the adoption of a regulation by an agency under its rule-making procedures, the Court is limited to considering whether the administrative action was "arbitrary, capricious, an abuse of discretion, or otherwise not in accordance with law." In this matter, the Secretary's determination that "All Meat" labels were authorized for frankfurters which contained up to 15 percent of non-meat ingredients represented a codification of a term in common use in the meat industry. However, there is nothing in the record to suggest that this "term of art" is understood by the general public.

The primary purpose of the Wholesome Meat Act is to benefit the consumer and to enable him to have a correct understanding of and confidence in meat products purchased. Prohibitions against mislabeling are an integral part of this purpose. Clearly, any rule-making procedure conducted under this Act which fails to primarily emphasize the understanding of the consumer is a procedure not conducted "in accordance with [the applicable] law" (the Act).

The leading case in this jurisdiction on the problem of mislabeling is *Armour and Company v. Freeman.* . . . The Court stated:

To measure whether a label employing ordinary words of common usage is false or not, the words must be taken in their ordinary meaning. . . .

This Court finds the *Armour* case controlling. In applying the "ordinary meaning" test to the word "all," it is clear when that adjective is used on a label with the word "meat," the common understanding is that it describes a substance that is *totally and entirely* meat. The application of the "All Meat" label to frankfurters that are 15 percent nonmeat is a contradiction in terms and is misleading within the meaning of . . . [the Act]. The use of the term "All Meat" or "All (*species*)" as applied to frankfurters is invalid, and the defendants should be enjoined from permitting any frankfurter product to be so labeled.

Questions

1. Why did the Secretary of Agriculture adopt a rule for labeling frankfurters "all meat" when they may contain up to 15 percent nonmeat ingredients?
2. What was the reasoning of the court in rejecting the secretary's rule?

Disclosure of Freshness.   Another measure of quality is freshness. It is obviously important in the sale of perishable food products. For many years food manufacturers have coded their freshness dates on merchandise. "Open" dating is simply mandating the disclosure of dates. While federal law has not required open dating of grocery products, almost half the states have enacted some form of mandatory open dating. In addition, many grocery chains have voluntarily adopted the practice.

The Federal Government has enacted the Motor Vehicle Information and Cost Savings Act. It follows the lead of over 30 states that have prohibited odometer tampering. This federal law mandates a written, true-mileage disclosure statement at the time of sale of all motor vehicles. In effect, this law attempts to ensure that the odometer reading properly measures the auto's "freshness."

Disclosure of Performance.   The Federal Energy Act of 1975 requires disclosures concerning fuel efficiency on all new cars sold in the United States. Labels disclose the estimated number of miles per gallon of gas for the auto and an estimate of what yearly fuel costs would be if 15,000 miles were traveled per year. These disclosures aid the consumer in making efficiency comparisons. The

Federal Energy Act also requires the efficiency ratings to appear on major home appliances like refrigerators, freezers, and hot water heaters.

Another type of performance disclosure is gasoline octane posting, sporadically enforced by the FTC. Since octane merely indicates the anti-knock properties of gasoline and does not produce greater power, the FTC has argued that many motorists waste money purchasing gasoline with higher octane than they really need.

Grade Rating.   Grade rating is a means of simplifying complex quality information into a grade format, such as grades A, B, and C. The U.S. Department of Agriculture grades meat, eggs, butter, poultry, grain, fruits, and vegetables. However, the grades for beef into "prime," "choice," and "good" is not compulsory. Large brand-name meatpackers prefer to promote the sale of beef on a brand basis. They have successfully opposed any effort to make the grading for beef compulsory.

Historically, the biggest problem with USDA grade ratings was their lack of standardization across product groups. For example, rop-rated apples are No. 1, but for peaches it is Extra No. 1. Moreover, the top-graded chickens are Fancy and the top grades for other foods are often referred to as Grade A. For still other product groups, these designations could indicate a lower grade. The U.S. Department of Agriculture has promised to improve its grade designations in the near future.

In 1966 Congress recognized that there was great consumer confusion as to quality of tires offered for sale to the public and as to the meaning of the variety of trade terminology used in marketing new passenger car tires. This conclusion led to a provision in the National Traffic and Motor Vehicle Safety Act of 1966 that a system be established to assist the consumer in making an informed choice in purchasing new tires. The Department of Transportation (DOT) Act required the Secretary of Transportation to develop a "uniform quality grading system for motor vehicle tires." However, because of the failure of the tire industry to initially provide test and cost information requested by DOT and because of the technical difficulties in developing acceptable tire testing procedures, the tire-grading system was not implemented until 1979.

Tires were to be rated on three characteristics.

1. Treadwear, to be indicated by a numeral, with higher numerals indicating higher mileage.
2. Traction, where A, B, and C respectively represent good, fair, and poor traction on wet roads.
3. Temperature, where A indicates the coolest running tire and B and C rank higher temperatures.

Tire manufacturers do their own testing and interpretation, which led to different grades for very similar test results and different grades for very similarly priced tires. Continuing charges by the tire industry that the "treadwear" grade was particularly confusing and misleading to consumers led the Department of Transportation in February 1983 to suspend the grading of treadwear.

CONCLUSION

Under the Reagan Administration, the FTC will likely restrict its prosecution efforts to outright deception. However, some writers have suggested that marketing and psychological research is likely to influence advertising regulation in the future.[28] Marketing research already discusses the effect of incomplete comparisons, hedge words, and puffery on the consumers' cognitive processing of information. Such research may well influence future FTC prosecuting decision making concerning deception to include "tricks of phrasing" that deliberately mislead consumers.

Psychological research also reveals that "emotional" advertising that associates the product with the "good life" influences consumer behavior. While consumers deny they believe such associations implied by the ads, research suggests the subconscious that is conditioned by the ad often directs irrational consumer behavior. Since proof of deception requires evidence that the ad has the capacity to create misleading *beliefs,* the deception doctrine may offer little protection for consumers from emotional claims, which consumers stress they do not believe. Hence, if such "emotional" commercials are to be regulated, the "unfairness" doctrine may need to be expanded.

Some conservative economists contend that consumers are rational decisionmakers when they choose to purchase heavily advertised products, because such advertisers with large advertising outlays possess great incentives to ensure the quality of their brands. However, their theoretical assertion is not convincingly supported by empirical research and ignores the ethical question of whether the consumers would even buy such items in the absence of massive or "emotional" advertisements. Consequently, the results of research on the emotional decision making of consumers will likely challenge the FTC of the future in developing appropriate policy positions concerning "deceptive" and "unfair" advertising.

Moreover, the utilization of standardization and information disclosure is far from complete. With continually rising levels of consumer education, one would expect that consumers could properly utilize any further information disclosed by sellers. The expansion of these policies seems inevitable. However, recent events would seem to imply that little improvement in informational disclosure will occur soon. For example, in 1980, Congress enacted the FTC Improvements Act, which allows the lawmakers to pass a legislative veto, within a 90-day period, on any rules issued by the commission. In 1982, both houses of Congress rejected a modified rule requiring used car dealers to disclose known defects in the cars they sell. The veto by Congress of this proposed FTC regulation may set a precedent for congressional review of all independent regulatory agency rules. But also, it sets a tone of congressional concern favoring deregulation and ignoring consumer needs for truthful disclosure of information.

Classical economists assumed the free and full flow of information as a precondition to the obtainment of the classical welfare conclusions of "pure competiton." Correctly informed consumers are a prerequisite to the efficient operation of the marketplace. Advertising regulation, whether from self-regulation or government regulation, is designed to ensure the effective functioning of the competitive system. Just as antitrust law attempts to ensure the continuation of alternatives for consumer choice, advertising regulation attempts to ensure the flow of honest and helpful information to consumers to enable them to make rational choices among competing products. Dysfunctional advertising information misallocates society's scarce resources. Consequently, business firms interested in the economy's efficient operation and in the reduction of the burdens of advertising regulation can adopt, and urge other firms to adopt, an advertising policy of supplying consumers only with relevant, accurate, and complete information.

DISCUSSION QUESTIONS

1. Several bakers who are engaged only in the sale of bakery products at wholesale prices are charged with conspiring to fix and maintain *retail* prices. Wholesale prices are fixed at 80 percent of retail, and the bakers stamp retail prices on product wrappers. Is this pricing method lawful?

2. A floor wax manufacturer markets a product under the name "Continental Six Month Floor Wax" for general home use. Some of the manufacturer's tests showed that following wear simulating six months of home traffic some of the wax "would be left sticking to a floor." The FTC contends that this name constitutes deceptive advertising, and has ordered that the words "Six Month" be deleted from the name. Would you consider the name to be deceptive?

3. S. Inc., a catalog house, issued a catalog offering a "dollar sale," i.e. on the purchase of one bedspread, blanket, quilt, sheet, etc., the consumer could purchase a second item of the same product for one additional dollar. The items were pictured and prices were stated as "only $9.98 each or any two for $10.98" and then "save $8.98 when you buy any two spreads." No price was specifically designated as a "regular" price, but this "amazing offer" of "special purchase" items "now sale priced" was termed a "sale" and was to end at a specified time.

   The items pictured had not, during the last three years, ever been sold or offered by S for sale as single units on a regular basis for a substantial period of time. Other bedspreads, sheets, etc. were regularly sold by S at various prices.

   Under FTC Act Section 5, the Commission claims S is guilty of a deceptive price advertising. What result?

4. Litton Industries Inc. has advertised that its microwave ovens are superior to others and that independent technicians prefer Litton ovens over competing products. The survey to substantiate the ad only surveyed Litton service agencies. The technicians interviewed, who "chose" Litton ovens over other products, were not always experienced in servicing all the brands they compared. Is this "substantiation" sufficient to support the ads against an FTC charge of deceptive advertising?

5. The manufacturer of "Snail Jail," a garden pesticide, makes advertising claims that its product is "Completely safe for children and pets." The package label warning mandated by the Environmental Protection Agency states in part: "This Pesticide may be fatal to children and dogs or other pets if eaten." The plastic housing covering the pesticide is thin and could be torn open by pets, especially dogs. Is this advertising lawful?

6. Universal Bodybuilding sells "courses" consisting of booklets describing an exercise program designed to build muscles. The bodybuilding products included protein supplements and weightlifting belts. Universal advertises in comic books that buyers of its programs will quickly improve their physical appearance, add muscles, and lose fat. The ad's pictures of muscular men made such claims as, "Double or triple your strength in record time!" and "Fat? Fat will disappear—replaced by muscles." The FTC charged that these ads were deceptive because the company did not have proof of them and because young people could not ordinarily achieve the promised results. Decide.

7. General Motors Acceptance Corp. is the credit subsidiary of General Motors Corp. GMAC often conducted sales of repossessed motor vehicles without informing defaulting cusomters of their right to any surplus receipts over the amount of debt owed. Is this practice in violation of the FTC Act?

8. CDC advertises that a college education or other post-high-school training is not an advantage for obtaining a job in the computer field. Instead, the purchasers of CDC's computer courses could rely entirely on the job-placement services offered by the company. Moreover, the sales representatives of the company were referred to as "vocational counselors." Are such marketing practices lawful?

9. Charles of the Ritz Rejuvenescence Cream was advertised as containing a "vital organic ingredient" and "essences and compounds" that bring to one's skin quickly "the clear radiance . . . the petal-like quality and texture of youth" and it "restores natural moisture necessary for a live, healthy skin "so that one's "face need know no drought years," but have "a bloom that is wonderfully rejuvenating" and is "constantly active in keeping your skin clear, radiant and young looking." The FTC sought to prohibit the advertisement as deceptive. Charles of the Ritz contended that a consumer would not be deceived by such an ad, in that "no straight-thinking person could believe that its cream would actually rejuvenate." Must the FTC produce a person who will admit to being "deceived" by these ads?

10. A trade association called the National Commission on Egg Nutrition (NCEN) was formed by egg producers to counteract anticholesterol attacks on eggs, which had resulted in reduced egg consumption. NCEN advertised to promote consumption of eggs, announcing that they are harmless, are needed in human nutrition, and that there is no scientific evidence that eating eggs increases the risk of . . . heart (and circulatory) disease. . . ." The FTC sought to enjoin these advertisements as false and misleading.

    NCEN presented evidence that some scientists and doctors are not persuaded by studies showing a correlation between the ingestion of high-cholesterol foods and the presence of a high level of cholesterol in the blood stream, and between the presence of cholesterol in the blood and the incidence of heart disease. NCEN presented experts in whose opinion these studies are not "evidence" and would not convince anyone that the number of eggs consumed increases the risk of heart disease. NCEN did not dispute, however, that these studies do exist, and that egg yolks contain more cholesterol than any other commonly eaten food, and that many other medical and science experts hold opinions opposite to those of NCEN's experts. Was NCEN's advertising false and misleading?

11. The Pratts purchased a motor home from the Norris Agency, a Winnebago dealership outside of Cleveland, Ohio, after test driving it. A Norris employee delivered the vehicle to the Pratts' home in Erie, Pennsylvania. Four days after delivery, the Pratts tried to use the motor home two or three times and compiled a list of complaints ranging from a transmission that would only allow operation in reverse to a chipped signal light. GM, which manufactured the chassis, arranged for the replacement of the transmission at a GM agency in Erie, as well as for adjustments to the brakes, which Mr. Pratts claimed were "spongy" with excessive pedal travel. During the four weeks it took to make these repairs, the Pratts were provided with another vehicle by Winnebago. Also during this time, the Pratts decided that they no longer wanted the vehicle, and asked Norris to replace the vehicle or return their money.

    The Pratts' complaints included a leaking roof in kitchen area, oil leaks from the lighting system support generator, faulty generator operation, failure of driver's seat to lock into driving position, faulty cab air conditioner, fluid leaks from power steering hoses, loose wiring on furnace gas valve controls, damaged trim panel on the dashboard, windshield wipers making an incomplete stroke, loosely fastened clearance light by radio antenna, plus various others. The GM and Winnebago warranties required the Platts to return the motor home to the Norris Agency or some other authorized dealer for repairs. The distance involved was over 100 miles, and the Platts refused to transport the vehicle to Ohio because they claimed the brakes were unsafe, it would cost $300 for a tow to Norris Agency, and the 30-day temporary license supplied by the dealer had expired, and they would have to pay $1200 tax to register the vehicle in Pennsylvania when they no longer wished to keep the motor home.

Pratts sued for a refund under the Magnuson Moss Act, which provides that a warranter of a consumer product must permit a refund or replacement without charge if the product contains defects after a reasonable number of attempts by the warranter to remedy the defects. The Pratts felt that they need only notify Norris of the defects and cannot be required to return the home from a distance of over 100 miles for repairs. If the vehicle were returned, GM and Winnebago could remedy the defects at a cost to them of about $500, within two or three days.

What would be Winnebago and GM's responsibilities under the Magnuson Moss Act?

12. In December 1973, the Public Service Commission of New York ordered electric utilities in New York State to cease all advertising that promotes the use of electricity because the intraconnected utility system in New York did not have a sufficient supply to furnish all customers' demands for the 1973–74 winter. After the fuel shortage had ceased in 1977, the prohibiton was extended for "promotional" advertising (that intended to stimulate the purchase of electrical services) as being contrary to the national policy of conserving energy.

Con Edison contends that this prohibition of promotional advertising is a violation of its First Amendment rights of free speech in that the "prohibition" is more extensive than necessary to serve the state's interest in conserving energy. Decide.

SUGGESTED READINGS

Reed, O. Lee, "The Psychological Impact of TV Advertising and the Need for FTC Regulation," *American Business Law Journal*, Vol. 13, No. 2, Fall 1975, pp. 171–185.

Reed, O. Lee, "The FTC and Corrective Advertising: Act One," *American Business Law Journal*, Vol. 17, No. 2, Summer 1979, pp. 246–256.

Whitman, Douglas, "Parens Patriae: An Effective Consumer Remedy in Antitrust," *American Business Law Journal*, Vol. 16, No. 3, Winter 1979, pp. 249–276.

ENDNOTES

1. *Virginia State Board* v. *Virginia Citizens Consumer Council,* 425 U.S. 748 (1976).
2. *FTC* v. *Algoma Lumber Co.,* 291 U.S. 67 (1934), and *Charles of the Ritz Distrib. Co.* v. *FTC,* 143 F. 2d 676 (2d Cir. 1944).
3. *Pfizer, Inc.,* 3 Trade Reg. Rep. ¶ 20,056 at 22,034 (FTC 1972).
4. *P. Lorillard Co.* v. *FTC,* 186 F. 2d 52 (4th Cir. 1950).
5. *FTC* v. *Standard Educ. Society,* 302 U.S. 113, 116 (1937).
6. *Heinz W. Kirchner,* Trade Reg. Rep. ¶ 16,664 at 21,539–40 (FTC 1963).
7. *FTC* v. *Algoma Lumber Co.,* 291 U.S. 67 (1934).
8. *FTC* v. *Winsted Hosiery Co.,* 258 U.S. 483 (1922).
9. *FTC* v. *Royal Milling Co.,* 288 U.S. 590 (1933).
10. *Branch* v. *FTC,* 141 F. 2d 31 (7th Cir. 1941).

11. *Carter Products Inc.* v. *FTC,* 268 F. 2d 461 (9th Cir. 1959).
12. *Firestone Tire and Rubber Co.,* 81 FTC 398 (1972).
13. *ITT Continental Baking Co.,* 83 FTC 865 (1973).
14. *Diener's Inc.,* v. *FTC,* 1974 Trade Cases ¶74,977 (D.C. Cir. 1974).
15. *Pfizer, Inc.,* 3 Trade Reg. Rep. ¶20,056 (FTC 1972).
16. *ITT Continental Baking Co.,* 3 Trade Reg. Rep. ¶20,464 (FTC 1973).
17. *Firestone Tire and Rubber Co.* v. *FTC,* 481 F 2d. 246 (6th Cir. 1973).
18. *La Salle Extension University,* 3 Trade Reg. Rep. ¶19,691 (FTC 1971).
19. *J. B. Williams Co., Inc.* v. *FTC,* 381 F 2d. 884 (1976).
20. *ITT Continental Baking Co.,* Trade Reg. Rep. ¶19,780 (FTC 1971).
21. *Ocean Spray Cranberries, Inc.,* Trade Reg. Rep. ¶19,981 (FTC 1972).
22. Scheme for organization of this material is derived from David Hemenway, *Industrywide Voluntary Products Standards* (Cambridge, Mass.: Ballinger Publishing Co., 1975).
23. Committee on Consumer Policy, *Package Standardization, Unit Pricing, Deceptive Packaging* (Paris: Organization for Economic Co-operation and Development, 1975).
24. General Accounting Office, *Report to the Congress on Food Labeling: Goals, Shortcomings, and Proposed Changes* (# MWD-75-19) Januray 1975.
25. *State Consumer Action: Summary '74,* Office of Consumer Affairs, Dept. of Health, Education, and Welfare [Pub. No. (05) 75-116], pp. ix–x.
26. F. Kelly Shuptrine and Ellen M. Moore, "Even After the Magnuson-Moss Act of 1975, Warranties Are Not Easy to Understand," *Journal of Consumer Affairs* (Winter 1980), pp. 394–404.
27. T. Schmitt, L. Kauter, and R. Miller, *Impact Report on the Magnuson-Moss Warranty Act* (Washington, D.C.: Federal Trade Commission, 1980).
28. O. Lee Reed, "The Next 25 Years of Advertising Regulation," *The Collegiate Forum* (Princeton N.J.: Dow Jones & Co., Inc. Fall 1981), p. 7.

chapter 22

CONSUMER PROTECTION REGULATIONS: RIGHTS TO SAFETY AND TO BE HEARD

CONSUMER'S RIGHT TO SAFETY

The consumer's right to safety involves protection against the marketing of goods that are hazardous to health, life, or economic well-being. The consumer's right to safety found initial expression in the judicial doctrines that began the erosion of the concept of *caveat emptor*. Judges developed rules expressing the notion that consumers are entitled to some reasonable quality of goods to avoid personal harm.

PRODUCT LIABILITY

Product liability refers to those cases involving the liability of the seller, manufacturer, processor, or supplier for injuries caused to the person or property of the buyer or user because of a defect in the product sold. This area of the law has changed rapidly, producing pronounced effects on sellers of products. The result has been substantially to increase the liability of the seller, manufacturer, processor, and supplier of goods and the classes of injured parties who may seek recovery in such cases.

Initially, product liability was restricted in application to the sale of foodstuffs for human consumption. It has since been expanded to include almost any product that causes injuries to the person or property of the buyer. The seller can be held liable on the basis of negligence, breach of implied warranty, or strict liability.

Negligence

Some jurisdictions adhere to the use of negligence as the theory of recovery in products liability cases. This theory requires that the plaintiff trace the defective condition of the product to a fault (negligence) in manufacturing. A manufacturer must exercise due care to make the product safe for the purpose for which it is intended. This requires the exercise of care in the design of the product, in the selection of materials and component parts, in inspection and testing, and in giving adequate warnings of any danger in the use of the product that an ordinary person might not be able to detect.

The development of manufacturer liability for negligent production of defective products was initially blocked by the doctrine of "privity." An English case in 1843 held that the breach of a contract to keep a passenger coach in good repair after sale provided no legal remedy to a passenger in the coach who was injured when it collapsed.[1] The court reasoned that the passenger, who was not a party to the contract involving the maintenance of the coach, was not in "privity of contract." To allow the passenger to recover, the judges argued, would lead to "the most absurd and outrageous consequences" with no limit to liability, unless the court confined liability to the contracting parties. This ruling later developed into a general rule that the original seller of goods was not liable for damages caused by defects in the goods to anyone except the immediate buyer; that is, the one in privity with the seller.

Later, both British and U.S. courts began to reject the strict privity requirement when dealing with goods that were considered inherently dangerous. In the case of *MacPherson* v. *Buick Motor Company*,[2] the manufacturer of an automobile with a defective wheel was held liable to the ultimate purchaser of the automobile, who was injured when the defective wheel collapsed. The court held the manufacturer liable for its negligence—despite the absence of privity of contract between the manufacturer and MacPherson, the ultimate consumer who purchased through a retail distributor. Judge Cardozo wrote the following.

If the nature of a thing is such that it is reasonably certain to place life and limb in peril when negligently made, it is then a thing of danger. Its nature gives warning of the consequences to be expected. If to the element of danger there is added knowledge that the thing will be used by persons other than the purchaser and used without new tests, then irrespective of the contract, the manufacturer of this thing of danger is under a duty to make it carefully.

Cardozo's interpretation of "inherently dangerous" became the touchstone for the expansion of products liability cases. One writer has commented that inherent danger was extended beyond Cardozo's interpretation to include physical harm to property, and even to negligence to the sale of goods, such as animal food, which involves no recognizable risk of personal injury, and are foreseeably dangerous only to property.[3]

Despite the breach in the wall of privity, it is still very difficult for an injured consumer to successfully pursue a products liability case on the basis of negligance. This is true because the plaintiff must prove a duty owed by the manufacturer or seller; the existence of a breach of that duty must be demonstrated; and a proximate causal connection between the plaintiff's injury and the defendant's breach of duty must be shown. Besides these difficult burdens of proof on the plaintiff-consumer, the defendant-manufacturer may also have a complete defense to negligence by proving the contributory negligence of the plaintiff or the assumption of risk of injury by the plaintiff.

The present state of the law of negligence by a manufacturer is best expressed in the *Restatement of the Law of Torts, Second*, Section 395, which provides the following.

A manufacturer who fails to exercise reasonable care in the manufacture of a chattel, which, unless carefully made, he should recognize as involving an unreasonable risk of causing substantial bodily harm to those who lawfully use it for a purpose for which it is manufactured and those whom the supplier should expect to be in the vicinity of its probable use, is subject to liability for bodily harm caused to them by its lawful use in a manner and for a purpose for which it is manufactured.

The liability for negligence of a seller other than the manufacturer (retailers and wholesalers) is set forth in Section 401. It provides the following.

A seller of a chattel manufactured by a third person who knows or has reason to know that the chattel is, or is likely to be, dangerous when used by a person to whom it is delivered or for whose use it is supplied, or to others whom the seller should expect to share in or be endangered by its use, is subject to liability for bodily harm caused thereby to them if he fails to exercise reasonable care to inform them of the danger or otherwise to protect them against it.

This liability is imposed on the seller (retailer or wholesaler) based on his or her "reason to know" the dangerous character of the product. The retailer's duty is to exercise reasonable care to inform the purchaser or user of this danger in order to protect the consumer from it. Section 402 excuses from liability the seller of goods manufactured by a third person if the seller does not know or have reason to know of the dangerous character of the goods. Moreover, Section 402 indicates that the retailer or wholesaler will not be liable for failure to inspect or test the goods before selling them. This Section, therefore, protects the retailer who sells goods that are prepackaged or placed in sealed containers by a manufacturer. The seller-retailer would not be liable for negligence on the basis of the theory of failure to inspect. However, in those states utilizing an alternative theory of liability, the retailer may be liable even if not negligent.

LaRue v. National Union Electric Corp.

571 F. 2d 51 (1978)

U.S. Court of Appeals (5th Cir.)

Conrad LaRue brought this . . . action in January 1972, on behalf of his minor son Michael, for injuries suffered by Michael. The complaint charged National Union Electric Corp. with negligent design and manufacture of a vacuum cleaner. National Union denied all liability and alleged contributory negligence on the part of Michael. After a trial in March 1977 . . . the jury . . . [found] for Michael on the negligence count. The jury determined that $125,000 would fully compensate Michael but that his own comparative negligence required reduction of the award to $93,750. National Union and LaRue both appealed, the former . . . attacking the verdict as contrary to law . . . and the latter arguing the issue of comparative negligence should not have been submitted to the jury.

On January 25, 1971, Michael LaRue, then 11 years old, was playing with his parents' canister-type vacuum cleaner, a Eureka Model 842A. He and his sister were home because they had missed the bus for school; his father was at work and his mother in school. The previous evening his mother had taken out the two filters that rested above the fan housing and motor in order to clean them. The morning of the accident, the vacuum cleaner was left out in a hallway, plugged in, with the filters not yet replaced and the hood that covered its top half left open. . . .

According to Michael's testimony, he was sitting on the yellow plastic filter support, which in turn rested on the metal casing that covered the fan and engine, riding the vacuum cleaner as if it were a toy car. He was dressed in pajamas. His older sister was in another room watching television. At some point in his play the motor was turned on. Michael continued to ride the vacuum cleaner until his penis slipped through openings in the filter support and casing into the fan. He immediately suffered an amputation of the head of his penis and part of the shaft. He rushed outside to seek help, was taken to the hospital, and underwent the first of a number of complicated operations to repair the damage to his penis. . . .

The principal issue at trial was the adequacy of safety features in the Eureka vacuum cleaner in light of foreseeable risks of injury resulting from household use. The LaRues contended National Union had failed to take sufficient precautions both by not installing a shield over the opening in the engine and fan casing to prevent insertion of stray parts of the human body and by not using an "interlock" switch that would prevent the motor from turning on while the hood was up. The strongest evidence in support of these contentions was the testimony of plaintiff's expert, Dr. Paul, a design engineer on the MIT faculty. Dr. Paul . . . explained that the rotation of the fan at 15,000 rpm left it invisible. Someone fiddling around with the interior of the machine, and especially a child, would have no warning of the danger created by the sharp, quickly moving fan blades. Some amount of exposure to the risk was inherent in the design, as the filters that covered the fan casing periodically had to be removed. Dr. Paul testified that suction created by the fan was sufficient to pull in stray items through the overlarge openings. He asserted that the safety devices that could eliminate this risk—a shield or an interlock switch—were feasible and, at least with regard to the switch, inexpensive.

To demonstrate the reasonableness of installing a protective shield over the fan housing, plaintiff produced a Eureka 4001 vacuum cleaner, manufactured during the same period as the 842A model and marketed overseas. The 4001 was in all material respects identical to the 842A, except that it was wired to take the higher voltages used in Europe and contained a shield over the fan housing such as would have prevented Michael's accident. The shield was required by Swedish safety regulations. . . .

National Union . . . argues that regardless of the nature of the hazard presented by the vacuum cleaner, this accident resulted from unforeseeable misuse of the product for which the manufacturer cannot be charged with liability. That question was submitted to the jury as part of the issue of negligence. National Union . . . argues that as a matter of law this use and the ensuing accident were simply not foreseeable. . . .

In the analogous situation of a store-owner's duty of care to child invitees on the premises, the Supreme Judical Court of Maine has ruled that the critical factor is

the *reasonableness*, or the *unreasonableness*, of the risks of harm engendered by the premises, facilities, instrumentalities, or combinations thereof, in the light of the *totality of the circumstances*, as the ordinarily prudent storekeeper would apprehend the circumstances and foresee the dangers of harm generated by them—including the reasonably recognizable dangers resulting from the reasonably foreseeable *misuse* of the premises by children in the light of their known, or reasonably recognizable, propensities. *Orr v. First National Stores, Inc.*, 280 A.2d 785, 792 (Me. 1971) [Emphasis in original.]

In determining what kind of reasonable for-seeable misuse might arise from the play of children, the court recognized

that children as old as thirteen years of age are likely to act dangerously to themselves even though, upon reflection, they know better. *Id.* at 790.

It also observed:

It should be emphasized that it is unessential that the *precise* manner in which injuries might have occurred, or were sustained, be foreseeable, or foreseen. It is sufficient that there is a reasonable generalized gamut of greater than ordinary dangers of

injury and that the sustaining of injury was within this range. . . .

It was undisputed that National Union realized that the Eureka 842A vacuum cleaner would be used in households where children would be present and appreciated the risks of children playing with the insides of the machine. Based on all the evidence presented at trial, there was a sufficient basis for holding that the vacuum cleaner presented an unreasonable risk of harm to children who might reasonably be foreseen to explore and fiddle with the device. The inadvertent intrusion of Michael's penis into the fan, perhaps the product of the machine's suction, fell within this class of dangers, even though the precise circumstances of the accident might have been improbable. Under the principles expressed in *Orr*, the district court had a sufficient basis for refusing to rule that as a matter of law the injury to Michael was so unforeseeable as to be outside the scope of National Union's duty to consumers of its product.

By the same token, we reject plaintiff's argument that the evidence concerning the hidden danger presented by the vacuum cleaner was so unequivocal as to bar the district court from letting the issue of Michael's own negligence go to the jury. Plaintiff exaggerates the strength of his own case. Evidence was presented suggesting that the vacuum cleaner motor was switched on as long as two minutes before the accident; during that time Michael continued to ride the machine. Perhaps, as plaintiff's expert contended, the fan blades rotated at too great a speed to be visible, but the jury well might have believed that the sound of the motor alone should have been enough to warn Michael that some danger existed. There was evidence that Michael was familiar with the operation of the machinery in general and engines in particular. The district court properly submitted the issue of comparative negligence to the jury.

Questions

1. Was the use of the machine as a toy car by a child "reasonably foreseeable" by the manufacturer?
2. What is "comparative negligence"? Was it properly applied in *LaRue*?

Safety Labeling.   Numerous federal statutes have been designed to provide the consumer with precise warnings as to any dangers in the use of the product. The Cigarette Labeling and Advertising Act and the Federal Hazardous Substances Labeling Act are two examples. Failure to comply with these statutes not only can subject the firm to some agency's administrative penalties but can also provide injured plaintiffs with evidence of negligence by the manufacturer. The following case is illustrative.

Murray v. Wilson Oak Flooring Co., Inc.
475 F. 2d 129 (1973)
United States Court of Appeals (7th Cir.)

The plaintiff was the owner of a small brick residential property located in Chicago. On the evening of October 3, 1969, Murray was preparing to install a parquet-wood flooring on a portion of the second floor of this building, pursuant to a plan for overall remodeling. He planned to use Latex "45" Adhesive to hold the flooring in place. . . .

Affixed to the five-gallon can of Latex "45" Adhesive were two labels, one of which, bright red and diamond shaped, set forth its message in boldface black letters having the following content. . . "Keep Away From Fire, Heat and Open Flame Lights. . . ." Another label was affixed to the opposite side of the can. White with red lettering, it set forth, in part, this message; "Caution: Inflammable Mixture, Do Not Use Near Fire or Flame. . . Use in Well Ventilated Area, Do Not Smoke— Extinguish flame—including pilot lights. . . " Prior to spreading any of the mastic, Murray thoroughly familiarized himself with the contents of these labels. . . .

. . . While on his knees near the bathroom floor, facing the front of the building and nearly finished with applying mastic, Murray heard an explosive noise, later described by him as a "whompf." This was accompanied by

a bright orange flame. . . . In an ensuring fire, Murray sustained burns which resulted in his permanent injury.

This suit for damages followed. Evidence produced at trial established that the warnings placed on the can of Latex "45" Adhesive were not in conformance with either the Federal Hazardous Substances Labeling Act or the Illinois Hazardous Substances Labeling Act. To comply with those Acts, a product having the combustibility of Latex "45"—equivalent to that of gasoline—would have required labeling which read "danger" rather than "caution" and "extremely flammable" rather than "inflammable."

The evidence also established that the fire was caused when combustible vapors from the adhesive came in contact with one of the lit pilot lights, the most likely candidate being the pilot light of the water heater in the storage-utility room. . . .

After hearing all of the evidence, the jury in the cause returned a verdict in favor of Murray, and assessed damages against Wilson in the sum of $20,429.00. Wilson then filed a motion for a judgment in its favor *non obstante veredicto* (i.e. not withstanding the verdict) which was granted by the district judge. He based his decision of the following facts:

[T]he plaintiff Frederick H. Murray admitted on the trial that at the time of the occurrence there were burners blazing and that he knew they were there. The product was plainly marked as inflammable. Said plaintiff's action was clearly a contributing cause of the explosion and fire that occurred, and he was therefore guilty of contributory negligence herein.

By "blazing burners" we take the judge to have meant the various pilot lights adjacent to the applied mastic.

We have carefully considered the evidence in this case, and conclude that the trial judge erred in entering a judgment *non obstante veredicto* for Wilson. Perhaps the most crucial fact relevant to our decision is the presence of the word "near" the primary warning on Wilson's adhesive can, a term which we think must be taken to modify subordinate warnings on the same level. The most important of these is the recitation: "Do Not Smoke—Extinguish flame—*including pilot lights*." (emphasis added). Reexamining the floor plan introduced as evidence in this case, and taking the evidence at its worst for Murray, it would appear that he spread mastic to within four or five feet of the water heater pilot and within seven to eight horizontal feet of the stove pilot lights. . . .

We cannot say as a matter of law that the term "near" was sufficient to inform Murray that his spreading of adhesive within four feet of a pilot light *located behind a closed door* and within eight feet of stove pilot lights three feet off the floor exposed him to the risk of an explosion and attendant fire damage. All of the evidence, when viewed in its aspect most favorable to Murray, fails to "so overwhelmingly [favor] movant [Wilson] that no contrary verdict based on that evidence could ever stand." Nearness is a matter of degree. To the president of Wilson, "near" included the entire house in which an application of Latex "45" was taking place. The reasonable man, we think, would disagree. Thus, whether "near" fairly encompassed the door and distances of this case was a question for the jury. . . .

Lastly, we note . . . (the) evidence . . . establish(ed) (1) a case of *prima facie* negligence on the part of the defendant by failure to comply with industry-wide standards of warning, and (2) Murray was not an experienced carpenter with extensive practice in using the material causing the accident complained of.

Questions
1. How were the defendant's labels not in conformance with the Federal Hazardous Substance Labeling Act?
2. Why did the trial judge grant a judgment for the defendant *non obstante veredicto*?
3. Why did the Court of Appeals feel the judgment *non obstante veredicto* was inappropriate in this case?

Breach of Warranty

A second type of theory of recovery against the seller of a defective product is called breach of warranty. A warranty under the law of sales in Article 2 of the Uniform Commercial Code (UCC) is an obligation imposed by law on the seller with respect to the goods. Such warranties can arise from (1) the mere fact of the transaction of sale (a warranty of title) or (2) by affirmations of fact or promise by the seller to the buyer (warranties of quality). The latter warranties are referred to as express warranties, which are explicit undertakings by the seller with respect to quality, description, or performability of the goods. For example, in *Baxter* v. *Ford Motor Company*,[4] the court held that the manufacturer's advertisement of a "shatter-proof" windshield made the defendant liable, when the windshield subsequently shattered and caused injuries to the plaintiff. These expressed warranties constitute a portion of the bargain between the parties. Accordingly, if the seller chooses not to give any expressed warranties, he or she is free to avoid this potential liability by refusing to affirm the quality or nature of the goods. Of course, the buyer is thereby put on notice and perhaps less likely to make the purchase.

In addition, the merchant-seller who deals in goods of a certain kind impliedly warrants the "merchantability" of those goods. This warranty is implied by law into the bargain without any express bargaining on the matter by the parties. To be merchantable, the goods must be of such quality as to pass in the market without objection and to be honestly resalable by the buyer in the normal course of business. The implied warranty of merchantability is an obligation on the merchant-seller that the goods are reasonably fit for the general purpose for which they are manufactured and sold and, also, that they are of fair, average, and merchantable quality. When goods are sold to a consumer, merchantability generally means reasonably fit for consumption.

The second implied warranty is the warranty of "fitness for *particular* purpose," which arises when a seller has reason to know the particular purpose of the buyer and the buyer is relying on the seller's skill and judgment in selecting goods to fit that particular purpose. Fitness for the buyer's particular purpose may be the same as merchantability. A restauranteur impliedly warrants that the meals are fit for the *particular* purpose and *ordinary* purpose for which goods are sold—human consumption.

The implied warranties are imposed on the seller by law, not by the bargaining of the parties. The UCC makes clear that the seller may modify or exclude these implied warranties with the buyer's consent; however, the disclaimers must be positive, explicit, unequivocal, and conspicuous, so that the buyer's acknowledgment of the change in implied warranties is clear. In addition, since the Code requires that notice of any breach of warranty be given to the seller in a reasonable time after the defect has occurred, the buyer's failure to notify the seller may result in his being barred from any remedy.

Many states require that since the warranty extends with the contract of sale of the goods, the absence of a contractual relationship (privity) with the seller would preclude recovery by a victim that was not the buyer of the goods from the defendant-seller. However, many courts have abolished the requirement of privity. The Code itself has relaxed the requirement of privity of contract. It permits recovery for breach of warranty that causes injury to members of the family or the household of the buyer or guests to his or her home even though such persons are without privity of contract.

The contributory negligence of the buyer is no defense to an action for a breach of warranty. However, the buyer's discovery of a defect would preclude recovery against the seller for injuries caused by the known defect (voluntary assumption of risk).

Warranties are limited to sales of goods. No warranty attaches to the performance of a service. If the service is performed negligently, the cause of action accruing is for that negligence. In contrast, the case of a sale of goods gives rise to a breach of warranty action without proof of fault by the seller. Consequently, victims prefer a breach of warranty action over an action for negligence. Therefore, problems often arise over the determination of whether the transaction was a service or a sale. In one case, it was held that injuries to scalp and hair from the application of a product in a beauty treatment was not a sale and, consequently, no breach of warranty action could be maintained. The victim was left with only a negligence action in which she had to prove that the beauty operator failed to exercise reasonable care. Contrast this result with the following case.

Newmark v. Gimbel's Inc.
246 A. 2d 11 (1968)
Supreme Court, Appellate Division of New Jersey

Mrs. Newmark sued for injury to her skin and loss of hair following a permanent wave treatment at defendant's beauty parlor. . . . She was waited on by one Valente, a beauty technician, who told her that her fine hair was not right for the special permanent and that she needed a "good" permanent wave. She agreed to this. . . .

Valente admitted that the permanent wave procedure followed was at his suggestion. It is conceded that the permanent wave solution he used was "Candle Glow," a product of Helene Curtis. Valente testified that the processing products he used were applied as they were taken from the original packages or containers, and that it was common for a customer to feel a burning or tingling sensation when the waving lotion was applied. He stated that persons were affected "in varying degrees" by the treatment. When he began the treatment there was "nothing wrong" with her hair or scalp. . . .

The core question here presented is whether warranty principles permit a recovery against a beauty parlor operator for injuries sustained by a customer as a result of use on the customer of a product which was selected and furnished by the beauty parlor operator. . . .

. . . In ruling that warranty did not apply here the trial judge reasoned that the transaction between the parties amounted to the rendition of services rather than the sale of a product, hence defendant could be held liable only for negligence in the performance of such services. Our consideration of the question convinces us that his ruling was a mistaken one.

It would appear clear that the instances in which implied warranties may be imposed are not limited to "sales" that come strictly within the meaning of Article 2 of the Uniform Commercial Code. . . .

In *Cintrone* v. *Hertz Truck Leasing*, 45 N.J. 434, 446 (1965), the court said:

There is no good reason for restricting such warranties to sales. Warranties of fitness are regarded by law as an incident of a transaction because one party to the relationship is in a better position than the other to know and control the condition of the chattel transferred and to distribute the losses which may occur because of a dangerous condition the chattel possesses. These factors make it likely that the party acquiring possession of the article will assume it is in a safe condition for use and therefore refrain from taking precautionary measures himself. . . .

The policy reasons applicable in the case of sales would likewise justify the extension of liability for breach of warranty to any commercial transaction where one person supplies a product to another, whether or not the transaction be technically considered as a sale. . . . The rationale underlying the liability of a retailer for defects in a product obtained from a reputable supplier and sold to a customer, has been explained as follows:

. . . If reliance upon the seller is needed, it may be found in the customer's reliance on the retailer's skill and judgment in selecting his sources of supply. Broader considerations are also urged. The retailer should bear this as one of the risks of his enterprise. He profits from the transaction and is in a fairly strategic position to promote safety through pressure on his supplier. Also, he is known to his customers and subject to their suits, while the maker is often unknown and may well be beyond the process of any court convenient to the customer. Moreover, the retailer is in a good position to pass the loss back to his supplier, either through negotiations or through legal proceedings. 2 Harper and James, *Torts*, §28.30, p. 1600 (1956).

Weighing the foregoing policy considerations, we are satisfied and hold that, stripped of its nonessentials the transaction here in question, consisting of the supplying of a product for use in the administration of a permanent wave to plaintiff, carried with it an implied warranty that the product used was reasonably fit for the purpose for which it was to be used.

Mrs. Newmark was a regular customer of defendant and had a weekly appointment to have her hair washed and set. On the day in question she received something in addition—a permanent wave. In essence, it involved application of a permanent wave lotion or solution and thereafter a neutralizer. The lotion was selected by one of defendant's operators who was familiar with her scalp and hair from current examination and prior visits. The product was secured from sources known to defendant and only defendant knew of any special instructions concerning its use. The risk from use of the lotion was incident to the operation of defendant's business, a business which yielded it a profit and placed it in a position to promote safety through pressure on suppliers. It was in a position to protect itself by making inquiry or tests to determine the susceptibility of customers to the use of the product, or by using another lotion which did not present the possibility of an adverse effect. It could secure indemnity from its suppliers through legal proceedings or otherwise. The fact that there was no separate charge for the product did not preclude its being considered as having been supplied to the customer in a sense justifying the imposition of an implied warranty against injurious defects therein. . . .

While the statement of facts presently before us leaves something to be desired, we are satisfied that the jury could have found from the evidence that the product was defective within the intent of the statute. In the first place the record does not show that plaintiff's dermatitis was the result of an allergic attack peculiar to her own sensitivities. Neither medical witness so testified. Second, the product was accompanied by an instruction in the form of a warning from which it could be inferred that its use, in the absence of certain precautions, could adversely affect an appreciable number of persons. Some support for such an inference is found in Valente's testimony that a burning or tingling sensation is fairly common (in such cases) and that each person was affected "in varying degrees." It is conceded that plaintiff testified that she had received permanent wave treatments prior to and for two years subsequent to the incident in question with no adverse effects to her hair or scalp.

It follows that the issue of defendant's liability for breach of implied warranties of fitness for purpose and merchantability should have been submitted to the jury.

Questions

1. Why did the trial judge decide there was no cause of action for breach of warranty?
2. What "policy reasons" justify the "extension of liability for breach of warranty to any commercial transaction where one person supplies a product to another, whether or not the transaction be technically considered as a sale"?
3. Forty-one states have enacted statutes that expressly provide that a blood transfusion is a service and not a sale, or alternatively state that the hospital is not liable in blood transfusions except for negligence or willful misconduct. Such statutes protect the hospital in the sale of blood that may contain a hepatitis virus, because such viruses cannot be detected and excluded from blood components. Is this reason sufficient to override the policy reasons for imposing liability for defective goods in a "sale"?

Hunt v. Ferguson-Paulus Enterprises
415 P. 2d 13 (1966)
Supreme Court of Oregon

The plaintiff bought a cherry pie from the defendant through a vending machine owned and maintained by the defendant. On biting into the pie one of plaintiff's teeth was broken when it encountered a cherry pit. He brought this action to recover damages for the injury, alleging breach of warranty of fitness of the pie for human consumption. In a trial to the court without a jury the court found for the defendant and plaintiff has appealed.

Under . . . [the law] if the cherry pie purchased by the plaintiff from the defendant was not reasonably fit for human consumption because of the presence of the cherry pit there was a breach of warranty and plaintiff was entitled to recover his damages thereby caused.

In the consideration of similar cases some of the courts have drawn a distinction between injury caused by spoiled, impure, or contaminated food or food containing a foreign substance, and injury caused by a substance natural to the product sold. In the latter class of cases, these courts hold there is no liability on the part of the dispenser of the food.. Thus in the leading case of *Mix* v. *Ingersoll Candy Co.*, 59 P. 2d 144, the court held that a patron of a restaurant who ordered and paid for chicken pie, which contained a sharp sliver or fragment of chicken bone, and was injured as a result of swallowing the bone, had no cause of action against the restauranteur either for breach of warranty or negligence. Referring to cases in which recovery had been allowed the court said:

All of the cases are instances in which the food was found not to be reasonably fit for human consumption, either by reason of the presence of a foreign substance, or an impure and noxious condition of the food itself, such as for example glass, stones, wires, or nails in the food served, or tainted, decayed, diseased, or infected meats or vegetables.

The court went on to say that:

. . . despite the fact that a chicken bone may occasionally be encountered in a chicken pie, such chicken pie, in the absence of some further defect, is reasonably fit for human consumption. Bones which are natural to the type of meat served cannot legitimately be called a foreign substance, and a consumer who eats meat dishes ought to anticipate and be on his guard against the presence of such bones.

Further the court said:

Certainly no liability would attach to a restaurant keeper for the serving of a T-bone steak, or a beef stew which contained a bone natural to the type of meat served, or if a fish dish should contain a fish bone, or if a cherry pie should contain a cherry stone—although it be admitted that an ideal cherry pie would be stoneless. 59 P.2d at 148.

The so-called "foreign-natural" test of the *Mix* case has been applied in the following cases: *Silva* v. *F. W. Woolworth Co.,* 83 P.2d 76 (turkey bone in "special plate" of roast turkey); *Musso* v. *Picadilly Cafeterias,* 178 So. 2d 421 (cherry pit in a cherry pie); *Courter* v. *Dilbert Bros.,* 186 N.Y.S. 2d 334 (prune pit in prune butter); *Adams* v. *Great Atlantic & Pacific Tea Co.,* 112 S.E. 2d 92 (crystalized grain of corn in cornflakes); *Webster* v. *Blue Ship Tea Room Inc.,* 198 N.E. 2d 309 (fish bone in a fish chowder).

Other courts have rejected the so-called foreign-natural test in favor of what is known as the "reasonable expectation" test, among them the Supreme Court of Wisconsin, which, in *Betehia* v. *Cape Cod Corp.,* 103 N.W. 2d 64, held that a person who was injured by a chicken bone in a chicken sandwich served to him in a restaurant, could recover for his injury either for breach of an implied warranty or for negligence. "There is a distinction," the court said, "between what a consumer expects to find in a fish stick and in a baked or fried fish, or in a

chicken sandwich made from sliced white meat and in roast chicken. The test should be what is reasonably expected by the consumer in the food as served, not what might be natural to the ingredients of that food prior to preparation. What is to be reasonably expected by the consumer is a jury question in most cases; at least, we cannot say as a matter of law that a patron of a restaurant must expect a bone in a chicken sandwich either because chicken bones are occasionally found there or are natural to chicken."

Among other decisions adopting the reasonable expectation test are: *Bonenberger* v. *Pittsburgh Mercantile Co.,* 28 A. 2d 913 (oyster shell in canned oysters used in making oyster stew); *Bryer* v. *Rath Packing Co.,* 156 A. 2d 442 (chicken bone in chow mein); *Varone* v. *Calaro,* 199 N.Y.S. 2d 755 (struvite in canned tuna).

In view of the judgment for the defendant, we are not required in this case to make a choice between the two rules. Under the foreign-natural test the plaintiff would be barred from recovery as a matter of law. The reasonable expectation test calls for determination of a question of fact. . . .

The court has found the fact in favor of the defendant and this court has no power to disturb the finding.

Questions

1. What is the foreign-natural test? How would it be applied in this instance to determine if a breach of the warranty of merchantability occurred?
2. What is the "reasonable expectation" test? According to this test, was there a breach of the warranty of merchantability?

Strict Liability

The most recent and far-reaching development in the field of products liability is that of strict liability in tort. The theory of strict liability, for those states that are adopting this approach, is best expressed in Section 402A of the *Restatement of Torts, Second,* which provides the following.

(1) One who sells any product in a defective condition unreasonably dangerous to the user or consumer or to his property is subject to liability for physical harm thereby caused to the ultimate user or consumer, or to his property, if

(a) the seller is engaged in the business of selling such a product (no distinction between a manufacturer or retailer), and

(b) it is expected to and does reach the user or consumer without substantial change in the condition in which it is sold.

(2) The rule stated in Subsection (1) applies although

(a) the seller has exercised all possible care in the preparation and sale of his product, and

(b) the user or consumer has not bought the product from or entered into any contractual relation with the seller.

It is to be emphasized that Subsection (2)(a) makes clear that negligence is not the basis of this liability. The seller may still be liable in spite of the fact that he or she "has exercised all possible care in the preparation and sale of his product." In addition, (2)(b) indicates that a "contractual relation" or privity is not required in order to establish manufacturer liability. The elements of this action were summarized by the Supreme Court of Wisconsin in *Dippel* v. *Sciano,* 155 N.W. 2d 55 (1967), as follows.

From a reading of the plain language of the rule, the plaintiff must prove (1) that the product was in defective condition when it left the possession or control of the seller, (2) that it was unreasonably dangerous to the user or consumer, (3) that the defect was a cause (a substantial factor) of the plaintiff's injuries or damages, (4) that the seller engaged in the business of selling such product or, put negatively, that this is not an isolated or infrequent transaction not related to the principal business of the seller, and (5) that the product was one which the seller expected to and did reach the user or consumer without substantial change in the condition it was when he sold it.

This liability is imposed by law as a matter of public policy. It arises out of common law in tort and does not require any contract; therefore, it is not subject to any disclaimer or modification by contractual agreement. The expanding scope of this liability is being developed by the courts in various states.

At common law, contributory negligence of the plaintiff is a bar to his or her recovery on any action based on negligence of the defendant. However, under strict liability (or negligence) in a products liability case, the plaintiff's failure to discover the defect or to guard against the probability of its existence (contributory negligence) is no defense for the seller of a defective product. Nevertheless, the maker or seller of a product is entitled to assume that the product he or she sells will be put to its normal use. The plaintiff's use of the product in some unintended, unusual, or unforeseeable manner will prevent recovery from the defendant on the ground of assumption of risk. Moreover, the plaintiff who used a product with a known defect would be precluded from recovery of injury resulting from the defect.

EMBS v. Pepsi-Cola Bottling Co. of Lexington, Kentucky, Inc.

528 S.W. 2d 703 (1975)
Court of Appeals of Kentucky

On the afternoon of July 25, 1970, plaintiff entered the self-service retail store operated by the defendant, Stamper's Cash Market, Inc., for the purpose of "buying soft drinks for the kids." She went to an upright soft drink cooler, removed five bottles and placed them in a carton. Unnoticed by her, a carton of Seven-Up was sitting on the floor at the edge of the produce counter about one foot from where she was standing. As she turned away from the cooler she heard an explosion that sounded "like a shotgun." When she looked down she saw a gash in her leg, pop on her leg, green pieces of bottle on the floor and the Seven-Up carton in the midst of the debris. She did not kick or otherwise come into contact with the carton of Seven-Up prior to the explosion. Her son, who was with her, recognized the green pieces of glass as part of a Seven-Up bottle.

She was immediately taken to the hospital by Mrs. Stamper, a managing agent of the store. Mrs. Stamper told her that a Seven-Up bottle had exploded and that several bottles had exploded that week. Apparently, all of the physical evidence went out with the trash. The location of the Seven-Up carton immediately before the explosion was not a place where such items were ordinarily kept.

The defendant, Arnold Lee Vice, was the distributor of Seven-Up in the Clark County area. . . .

The defendant, Pepsi-Cola Bottling Co. of Lexington, Kentucky, Inc., was the bottler who produced and supplied Vice with his entire stock of Seven-Up. . . .

In *Dealers Transport Co.* v. *Battery Distributing Co.*, 402 S.W. 2d 441 (1966), we adopted the view of strict liability in tort expressed in Section 402A of the American Law Institute's *Restatement, Second, Torts.* . . .

Our expressed public policy will be furthered if we minimize the risk of injury and property damage by charging the costs of injuries against the manufacturer who can procure liability insurance and distribute its expense among the public as a cost of doing business; and since the risk of harm from defective products exists for mere bystanders and passerby as well as for the purchaser or user, there is no substantial reason for protecting one class of persons and not the other. The same policy requires us to maximize protection for the injured third party and promote the public interest in discouraging the marketing of products having defects that are a menace to the public by imposing strict liability upon retailers and wholesalers in the distributive chain responsible for marketing the defective product which injures the bystander. The imposition of strict liability places no unreasonable burden upon sellers because they can adjust the cost of insurance protection among themselves in the course of their continuing business relationship.

We must not shirk from extending the rule to the manufacturer for fear that the retailer or middleman will be impaled on the sword of liability without regard to fault. Their liability was already established under Section 402A of the *Restatement of Torts 2d.* As a matter of public policy the retailer or middleman as well as the manufacturer should be liable since the loss for injuries resulting from defective products should be placed on those members of the marketing chain best able to pay the loss, who can then distribute such risk among themselves by means of insurance and indemnity agreements. . . .

The result which we reach does not give the bystanders a "free ride." When products and consumers are considered in the aggregate, bystanders, as a class, purchase most of the same products to which they are exposed as bystanders. Thus, as a class, they indirectly subsidize the liability of the manufacturer, middleman and retailer and in this sense do pay for the insurance policy tied to the product.

Public policy is adequately served if parameters are placed upon the extension of the rule so that it is limited to bystanders whose injury from the defect is reasonably foreseeable.

For the sake of clarity we restate the extension of the rule. The protections of Section 402A of the Restatement, Second, Torts extend to bystanders whose injury from the defective product is reasonably foreseeable. . . .

It matters not that the evidence be circumstantial for as Thoreau put it "Some circumstantial evidence is very strong, as when you find a trout in the milk." There are some accidents, as where a beverage bottle explodes in the course of normal handling, as to which there is common experience that they do not ordinarily occur without a defect: and this permits the inference of a defect. This is particularly true when there is evidence in the case of the antecedent explosion of other bottles of the same product.

In cases involving multiple defendants the better reasoned view places the onus of tracing the defect on the shoulders of the dealers and the manufacturer as a policy matter, seeking to compensate the plaintiff and to require the defendants to fight out the question of responsibility among themselves.

Questions
1. How is public policy best served by imposing strict liability on sellers, distributors, and manufacturers for defective products?
2. What is the limit of "strick liability"? Is the seller liable for all possible damages following from a defective product?

In many states, implied warranty of merchantability is more akin to the concept of strict liability in tort than it is to a warranty attached to a contract of sale. The courts' desire to impose strict liability on the seller is merely camouflaged in contractual terms of warranty. Confusion in legal terminology results, but the effect of increasing liability on sellers is the same. In those states adopting a strict liability theory in products liability, whether under Section 402A of the Restatement of Torts or under a strict liability theory of implied warranty, the courts are increasingly inclined to expand the concept of liability beyond the mere sale of goods. The following case is illustrative of the expanding concepts of strict liability in areas outside of the sale of tangible personal property.

Humber v. Morton
426 S.W. 2d 554 (1968)
Supreme Court of Texas

The widow Humber brought suit against Claude Morton, alleging that Morton was in the business of building and selling new houses; that she purchased a house from him which was not suitable for human habitation in that the fireplace and chimney were not properly constructed and because of such defect, the house caught fire and partially burned the first time a fire was lighted in the fireplace. Morton defended upon (the) . . . ground . . . that the doctrine of "*caveat emptor*" applied to all sales of real estate. . . .   .

According to Morton, the only warranty contained in the deed was the warranty of title . . . and that he made no other warranty written or oral, in connection with the sale. While it is unusual for one to sell a house without saying something good about it . . . we shall assume that such conversation as may have taken place did not involve anything more than mere sales talk or puffing, and that no express warranties, either oral or written, were involved. However, it is undisputed that Morton built the house and then sold it as a new house. Did he thereby impliedly warrant that such house was constructed in a good workmanlike manner and was suitable for human habitation? We hold that he did. Under such circumstances, the law raises an implied warranty. . . .

It might further be pointed out that generally in Texas, the notion of implied warranty arising from sales is considered to be a tort rather than a contract concept. . . .

We return to the crucial issue in the case— Does the doctrine of *caveat emptor* apply to the sale of a new house by a builder-vendor?

In 1964, the Colorado Supreme Court in *Carpenter* v. *Donohoe*, 388 P. 2d 399, extended the implied warranty rule . . . to cover sales of a new house by a builder-vendor. The court said:

We hold that the implied warranty doctrine is extended to include agreements between builder-vendor and purchasers for the sale of newly constructed buildings, completed at the time of contracting. There is an implied warranty that builders-vendors have complied with the building code of the area in which the structure is located. Where, as here, a home is the subject of sale, there are implied warranties that the home was built in work-manlike manner and is suitable for habitation.

. . . [In] the case of *Schipper* v. *Levitt & Sons*, 207 A. 2d 314 (1965) . . . (t)he Supreme Court of New Jersey recognized "the need for imposing on builder-vendors an implied obligation of reasonable workmanship and habitability which survives delivery of the deed." This was a case in which a person other than a purchaser had been injured by a defective water heater which had been installed in a new house by Levitt, the builder-vendor. The opinion cited and quotes from *Carpenter* v. *Donohoe* but proceeded upon the theory of strict liability in tort. The court placed emphasis upon the close analogy between a defect in a new house and a manufactured chattel. The opinion states:

The law should be based on current concepts of what is right and just and the judiciary should be alert to the never ending need for keeping its common law principles abreast of the times. Ancient distinctions which make no sense in today's society and tend to discredit the law should be readily rejected. . . .

When a vendee buys a development house from an advertised model . . . he clearly relies on the skill of the developer and on its implied representation that the house will be erected in reasonably workmanlike manner and will be reasonably fit for habitation. He has no architect or other professional adviser of his own, he has no real competency to inspect on his own, his actual examination is, in the nature of things, largely superficial, and his opportunity for obtaining meaningful protective changes in the conveyancing documents prepared by the builder vendor is negligible. If there is improper construction such as a defective heating system or a defective ceiling, stairway and the like, the well-being of the vendee and others is seriously endangered and serious injury is forseeable. The public interest dictates that if such injury does result from the defective construction, its costs should be borne by the responsible developer who created the danger and who is in the better economic position to bear the loss rather than by the injured party who justifiably relied on the developer's skill and implied representation.

If at one time in Texas the rule of *caveat emptor* had application to the sale of a new house by a vendor-builder, that time is now past. . . .

Obviously, the ordinary purchaser is not in a position to ascertain when there is a defect in a chimney flue, or vent of a heating apparatus, or whether the plumbing work covered by a concrete slab foundation is faulty. . . .

The *caveat emptor* rule as applied to new houses is an anachronism patently out of harmony with modern home buying practices. It does a disservice not only to the ordinary prudent purchaser but to the industry itself by lending encouragement to the unscrupulous, fly-by-night operator and purveyor of shoddy work. . . .

Questions
1. What policy reasons are advanced by the court to expand the doctrine of implied warranty to the sale of a newly constructed building?
2. Should the doctrine of implied warranty or strict liability be extended to the sale of used goods? A used house?

Insurance Crisis

The sharp increase in product liability awards for injured victims has escalated insurance premiums for product liability coverage. Often, smaller firms cannot afford to obtain liability coverage. However, the premiums are higher than required by the risk. One reason is the failure of insurance companies to segregate actuarial data for proper assessment of a firm's liability loss experience. Another problem is the wide variance in state laws, which increases the range of probability of loss.

One suggestion for dealing with the product liability insurance crisis is the Model Uniform Product Liability Act (UPLA). If the UPLA is voluntarily adopted by the states, more uniformity and predictability of product liability awards will likely stabilize insurance premiums. The UPLA adopts a strict liability standard for production defects and for disconformity with express warranties. In contrast, it utilizes a negligent standard for products with a defective design or inadequate warning labels. The contrasting legal theories of liability are based on the belief that the manufacturer should be better able to avoid production defects and unconforming warranties because these are violations of his own selected standards of performance. On the other hand, the failure to adequately design or label is a violation of outside standards based on the existing "state of the art" knowledge. The UPLA grants the manufacturer the usual affirmative defenses, including contributory negligence, assumption of risk, and misuse or alteration of the product. However, it suggests a comparative responsibility approach in which the defenses do not fully bar recovery. Instead, the monetary award is reduced by an amount approximating the plaintiff's contribution to the injury. The UPLA also attempts to discourage frivolous consumer claims. Any consumer who sues without a legal or factual basis becomes liable for the defendant's reasonable attorney fees and the costs of the litigation. Because of the magnitude of the product liability awards and the corresponding insurance premiums, it seems likely that the UPLA or other acts incorporating its concepts will be enacted by the various states.

CONSUMER PROTECTION LEGISLATION

The judicial approach for dealing with sellers of defective goods is one of compensating the consumer for injuries sustained from the defective product. The tort system is founded on the belief that the cost of the award to the injured consumer will motivate the manufacturer to improve production processes to avoid such costs arising from defective goods. However, society felt other *preventive* measures were necessary; consequently, legislation attempting to prevent the marketing of unsafe products was created.

National product safety legislation consists of a series of isolated statutes designed to remedy specific hazards existing in a narrow range of product categories. The following enactments are illustrative of this product-oriented approach. The Federal Food and Drug Administration (FDA) was made responsible for the safety of drugs and medical devices and the purity of foods. The Flammable Fabrics Act of 1953 was passed after serious injuries and deaths resulted from the ignition of clothes made from synthetic fibers. The Federal Hazardous Substances Labeling Act of 1960 mandated warnings on labels of potentially hazardous substances such as cleaning agents and paint removers. The Child Protection Act of 1966 outlawed the marketing of potentially harmful toys and other articles intended for children. The National Traffic and Motor Vehicle Safety Act of 1966 was related specifically to motor vehicles. Continual passage of legislation designed to protect consumers included the Public Health Smoking Act and the Poison Prevention Packaging Act in 1970 and in the following year the Lead-Based Paint Elimination Act.

Finally, Congress determined that the fragmentation of legislation over different consumer items was an insufficient process that left other products involving hazards to the consumer without any controls. Consequently, Congress passed the Consumer Product Safety Act of 1972 with broad powers to cover a host of consumer products.

Food and Drug Administration

Legislation enforced by the FDA dates back to 1906 with major modifications being added over the years. The agency's authority covers foods, drugs, cosmetics, and medical devices. Depending on the product covered, the FDA sets standards to achieve safety, purity, production cleanliness, and product efficacy.

Safety. The FDA's standards for safety of drugs and medical devices weighs risk against benefits. For example, a drug that kills 1 out of every 10 patients who take it may nevertheless be approved for sale if it is fairly successful in curing cancer malignancies that are otherwise incurable. Drawing the line in benefit-risk tradeoffs for drugs is a difficult task.

Safety standards for foods and cosmetics involve less balancing of benefits and risks. The 1958 Delaney Amendment to the Food, Drug and Cosmetic Act states that "no additive shall be deemed to be safe . . . if it is found, after tests which are appropriate for the evaluation of the safety of food additives, to induce cancer in man or animal." This amendment expresses the congressional decision that no risk is warranted for carcinogenic food additives. This law required the FDA to ban the use of cyclamate and saccharin as artificial sweeteners, since both were found carcinogenic in laboratory animals. Later, Congress granted an exception for saccharin if accompanied by a warning label.

When a food ingredient is not an additive or when the risk involved is not cancer, the standards are more lenient. For example, mercury pollution often is absorbed by fish. The mercury attacks the human nervous system in individuals eating such fish. Also, peanuts naturally contain a known carcinogen. But because the carcinogen in the peanuts is not an additive and because mercury does not cause cancer, permitted levels of these substances are judged "safe enough" to avoid a ban.

If a cosmetic is not hazardous under normal use, it is considered "safe." Hence, a nail polish is considered "safe" even if it would be fatal if swallowed. Even though a cosmetic may be slightly hazardous in normal use, it will be permitted if it bears a warning of its danger. Consequently, hair dyes, with proper warnings, may be marketed despite their slightly hazardous condition.

Purity. Purity standards are designed to prevent contamination or dilution. The FDA has developed fairly absolute standards of purity for foods and drugs.

FDA's contamination standards prohibit any variations from "absolute cleanliness or soundness in foods." Nevertheless, foreign matter is permitted "below the irreducible minimum after all precautions humanly possible have been taken to prevent contamination."

The standards prohibiting dilution require, for example, that a five-grain tablet of aspirin contain five grains of "aspirin," within a tolerance of plus-or-minus 5 percent. Likewise, food standards are developed to prohibit "watering down" of products, such as milk or tomato paste.

Production Cleanliness. The FDA has made it clear that the mere processing of food under unsanitary conditions contaminates the food under the law. The FDA has written:

The maintenance of sanitary conditions requires extermination and exclusion of rodents, inspection and sorting of raw materials to eliminate the insect-infested and decomposed portions, fumigation, quick handling and proper storage to prevent insect development or contamination, the use of clean equipment, control of possible sources or sewage pollution, and supervision of personnel who prepare food so that the acts of misconduct may not defile the product they handle.[5]

The FDA publishes *Current Good Manufacturing Practice Regulations,* which are designed to enhance cleanliness. The FDA has promulgated similar standards for drugs, cosmetics, and medical devices.

Efficacy. Since all drugs are dangerous to some degree, an ineffective drug would pose a risk without any corresponding benefit. Moreover, the ineffective drug would supplant the use of effective treatment. Therefore, the FDA is enpowered to develop standards of efficacy.

A drug may be banned if "there is a lack of substantial evidence that the drug will have the effect it proports or is represented to have under the condition of use prescribed, recommended or suggested. . . "[6] The power to judge efficacy was given to the FDA in 1962. Drugs on the market prior to 1962 had to be reviewed for efficacy. The FDA's effectiveness review caused more than 6000 drug products to be removed from the market during the sixties and seventies.[7] The FDA's judgment of ineffectiveness of laetrile also caused its ban.

The social costs of the FDA's review for safety and efficacy are the lives lost and the suffering endured as the result of delays in marketing new drugs. This "social cost" is the price paid for the benefits of increased certainty about the drugs that are marketed. The FDA has come under strong criticism for unreasonably delaying the introduction of new drugs. Proposed amendments in Congress for reform are suggesting the FDA alter its present approach of intensive premarket research coupled with little postmarket surveillance to a new system of reduced premarket research coupled with greatly expanded postmarket surveillance.

FDA Enforcement.   One technique of FDA enforcment is certification permitting sale of the product. For drugs, premarket clearance or certification is based on research data supplied by the drug companies. Medical devices are subject to premarket clearance for safety and efficacy also.

"New" food additives, defined as those brought into use after the 1958 amendment, also must be certified for safety prior to use. "Old" food additives are generally recognized as safe and are not required to be certified. In cosmetics, prior FDA approval is not required.

The FDA is also involved in (1) inspecting warehouses and production plants and (2) testing samples of drugs, foods, medical devices, and cosmetics. Samples of animal drugs and feed are tested also. The FDA conducts wharf inspections and analyzes samples of imported products, too.

Serious violations of FDA regulations usually result in recall. For example, Procter and Gamble Company, under pressure from the FDA, withdrew its "Rely" tampons from the market after they became associated with "toxic shock." The company's aftertax loss was reported to be $75 million.[8] The FDA may also being criminal actions against violators, as the following case reveals.

U.S. v. Park
   721 U.S. 658 (1975)
   Supreme Court of the United States

[Acme Markets, Inc. is a national retail food chain with over 800 retail outlets and 12 warehouses. Acme Markets, Inc. and its chief executive officer, Park, were charged with criminal violations of the Federal Food, Drug, and Cosmetic Act. It was alleged that Acme Markets, Inc. held food in a building accessible and exposed to contamination by rodents. In April 1970, the FDA advised Park by letter of the unsanitary conditions in Acme's warehouse. A second inspection by the FDA in March 1972 revealed continued evidence of rodent activity in the building. While Acme pleaded guilty, Park pleaded not guilty. Park moved for a judgment of acquittal on the grounds that the evidence did not show that he was personally concerned in this violation. He maintains that he directed a divisional vice president to investigate the situation and take corrective action. Park stated that he did not believe there was anyting else he could have done more constructively than what he had done. Park was found guilty by a jury and sentenced to pay a fine of $50 on each of five counts. The Court of Appeals reversed.]

Chief Justice Burger

The rule that corporate employees who have "a responsible share in the furtherance of the transaction which the statute outlaws" are subject to the criminal provision of the Act was not formulated in a vacuum. Cases under the Federal Food and Drugs Act of 1906 reflected the view both that knowledge or intent were not required to be proved in prosecutions under its criminal provision, and that responsible corporate agents could be subjected to the liability thereby imposed. Moreover, the principle had been recognized that a corporate agent, through whose act, default, or omission the corporation committed a crime, was himself guilty individually of that crime. The principle had been applied whether or not the crime required "consciousness of wrongdoing," and it has been applied not only to those corporate agents who themselves committed the criminal act, but also to those who by virtue of their managerial positions or other similar relations to the act could be deemed responsible for its commission.

In the latter class of cases, the liability of managerial officers did not depend on their knowledge of, or personal participation in, the act made criminal by the statute. Rather, where the statute under which they were prosecuted dispenses with "consciousness of wrongdoing," an omission or failure to act was deemed a sufficient basis for a responsible corporate agent's liability. It was enough in such cases that, by virtue of the relationship he bore to the corporation, the agent had the power to have prevented the act complained of. . . .

. . . [T]he Court has reaffirmed the proposition that "the public interest in the purity of its food is so great as to warrant the imposition of the highest standard of care on distributors." In order to make "distributors of food the strictest censors of their merchandise," the Act punishes "neglect where the law requires care, or inaction where it imposes a duty." "The accused, if he does not will the violation, usually is in a position to prevent it with no more care than society might reasonably expect and no more exertion than it might reasonably exact from one who assumed his responsibilities." Similarly, . . . the court of appeals have recognized that those corporate

agents vested with the responsibility, and power commensurate with that responsibility, to devise whatever measures are necessary to ensure compliance with the Act bear a "responsible relationship" to, or have a "responsible share" in, violations.

Thus . . . the cases . . . reveal that in providing sanctions which reach and touch the individuals who execute the corporate mission—and this is by no means necessarily confined to a single corporate agent or employee—the Act imposes not only a positive duty to seek out and remedy violations when they occur but also and primarily a duty to implement measures that will insure that violations will not occur. The requirements of foresight and vigilance imposed on responsible corporate agents are beyond question demanding, and perhaps onerous, but they are no more stringent than the public has a right to expect of those who voluntarily assume positions of authority in business enterprises whose services and products affect the health and well-being of the public that supports them. . . .

The Act does not . . . make criminal liability turn on "awareness of some wrongdoing" or "conscious fraud." The duty imposed by Congress on responsible corporate agents is, we emphasize, one that requires the highest standard of foresight and vigilance, but the Act, in its criminal aspect, does not require that which is objectively impossible. The theory upon which responsible corporate agents are held criminally accountable for "causing" violations of the Act permits a claim that a defendant was "powerless" to prevent or correct the violation to "be raised defensively at a trial on the merits." If such a claim is made, the defendant has the burden of coming forward with evidence, but this does not alter the Government's ultimate burden of proving beyond a reasonable doubt the defendant's guilt, including his power, in light of the duty imposed by the Act, to prevent or correct the prohibited condition. Congress has seen fit to enforce the accountability of responsible corporate agents dealing with products which may affect the health of consumers by penal sanctions cast in rigorous terms, and the obligation of the courts is to give them effect so long as they do not violate the Constitution.

Questions

1. Do managerial officers have to know of or personally participate in the activity before they can be convicted of a crime?
2. Just what was the criminal behavior of Parks? Was he "powerless" to prevent the violation?
3. A previous court decision dealing with the same problem recognized that the act dispenses with the need to prove "consciousness of wrongdoing." As such, it may result in a hardship as applied to those who share "responsibility in the business process." But, the Court added, "In such matters the good sense of prosecutors, the wise guidance of trial judges, and the ultimate judgment of juries must be trusted." Are these sufficient protections against a "hardship" prosecution?

National Highway Traffic Safety Administration

Congress created the National Highway Traffic and Safety Administration (NHTSA) in 1966 to devise and enforce specific standards in furtherance of "motor vehicle safety." The NHTSA has issued specific equipment standards that have been classified into three major groups.

The "precrash standards" attempt to improve the capacity of drivers to *avoid* crashes and reduce the capacity of cars to *cause* crashes. Examples include standards requiring controls to be well-illuminated and within the reach of a driver restrained by safety belts. Also, tires must meet minimum standards of quality, endurance, and high-speed performance.

The "crash standards" attempt to protect auto occupants and pedestrains during a crash. Examples include head restraints to prevent "whiplash" and padded dashboards to soften the blows.

The "postcrash standards" attempt to keep injuries to a minimum in the period *after* the crash has occurred. Examples include specifying flame resistant materials in auto interiors and requiring special design of fuel tanks and fuel tank connections. Besides equipment standards, the NHTSA also requires product identification and recordkeeping to facilitate recalls and notification of vehicle owners of possible equipment failures.

Manufacturers are responsible for testing equipment for compliance with NHTSA standards. Manufacturers then certify to NHTSA that their products meet the standards. The NHTSA selects various motor vehicles for tests to determine compliance with standards.

The agency also maintains a free Auto Safety Hot Line, which allows consumers to complain to NHTSA directly about safety-related vehicle problems. Manufacturers also must notify the agency of any hazards of which they become aware. These sources of information may cause the NHTSA to launch a "defects investigation." Such an investigation may lead to recall, some as dramatic as

Firestone's recall of its "500" steel-belted radial tires that had apparently caused 41 fatalities. Approximately 7.5 million of these tires were recalled, costing Firestone $155 million.

Consumer Product Safety Commission

The Consumer Product Safety Act created the five-member Consumer Products Safety Commission (CPSC), whose major goal is to substantially reduce injuries associated with consumer products in or around the home, schools, and recreational areas. Congress directed the Commission to protect the public against unreasonable risk of injury associated with consumer products; to develop uniform safety standards for consumer products so as to minimize conflicting state and local regulations; and to promote research and investigation into the causes and prevention of product-related deaths, illnesses, and injuries. The Commission sets and enforces mandatory safety standards for consumer products and in certain instances bans hazardous products. The Commission deals with over 10,000 consumer products—from architectual glass, stairs, and power tools to stoves, ladders, and lawnmowers.

The Consumer Product Safety Act also transferred the authority for enforcing the Federal Hazardous Substances Act, Flammable Fabrics Act, Poison Prevention Packaging Act, and the Refrigerator Safety Act to the Consumer Product Safety Commission.

A major function of the Commission is to gather and dissimulate information related to product injuries. The Commission can require manufacturers and distributors to establish and maintain books and records and make available such information as the Commission deems necessary. The law holds the manufacturer accountable for knowing all safety criteria applicable to the product, for testing programs to ensure that their products conform to established safety standards, and for maintaining technical data relating to the performance and safety of the product. This information may have to be given to the consumer when purchasing the product. The Commission can require the use of specific labels that set forth the results of product testing. The Commission also operates the National Electronic Injury Surveillance System, which monitors over 100 hospital emergency rooms nationwide for injuries associated with consumer products.

The CPSC relies mainly on "voluntary standards" developed by industry groups acting under the guidance and prodding of the CPSC. Sometimes the CPSC has developed mandatory standards. Difficulties of standard formulation of enforcement are illustrated in the following case.

D. D. Bean & Sons v. Consumer Products Safety Commission
574 F. 2d 643 (1978)
U.S. Court of Appeals (1st Cir.)

Petitioner D. D. Bean & Sons Co. (Bean), a manufacturer of paper bookmatches . . . , seeks review of the Consumer Product Safety Commission's matchbook safety regulations. . . . The Commission stated that the proposed regulation was "designed to reduce or eliminate . . . [e]ye injuries sustained by persons who use bookmatches that fragment and cause particles from such matches to lodge in a person's eye. . . ."

The Commission's final rule contained the following design or "general" requirements. . . .

No matchhead in the matchbook shall be split, chipped, cracked, or crumbled.

The rule also listed the following "performance requirement" with which matchbooks must comply:

A matchbook is defective . . . if it has, when tested. . . .
    (b) A splint that separates into two or more pieces.
    (c) A matchhead that produces fragments. . . .

The Commission will test for violations in accordance with detailed testing procedures that are set out at length in the Rule. The testing procedures call for a visual, post-manufacture inspection of matchbooks to insure compliance with the "general" requirements governing such matters as . . . splitting . . . of match-heads, etc. "Performance" defects are to be minimized by more elaborate testing. Samples from a lot are to be . . . tested under laboratory conditions for the incidence of fragmentation. . . .

In ascertaining the sufficiency of the basis for the Commission's Rule we shall first inquire whether there is substantial evidence for its findings that . . . the listed hazard is in fact such. If it is, we shall next inquire whether the requirements addressed to . . . [the] hazard have been shown to be likely to reduce or eliminate it at a reasonable cost. Only after the existence of [the] hazard and the likelihood of its reduction at a reasonable cost have been established by the Commission may it be said that the requirements are "reasonably necessary."

The Commission's performance standards are fashioned to reduce the occurrence of matchhead fragmentation. and heads breaking off matches. . . . The data from the Commission's survey of hospital emergency rooms and other studies indicate that roughly one-third of reported match-related injuries consist of fragments lodging in the eye. There are also some reported cases where a flaming fragment ignited a victim's clothing. One study indicated that entire matchheads occasionally fly off upon ignition, lodging in the eye or on clothing. We think therefore that there is sufficient evidence in the record to support the Commission's finding that a substantial hazard exists from matchhead fragmentation. We also think that the Commission was entitled to adopt the "general" requirements addressed to the fragmentation hazard. These call essentially for assurance that the matchbooks and matches do not contain obvious defects such as broken splints and matchheads and projecting staples which could lead to particles flying off when a match is struck. Compliance with these requirements may be insured by visual testing, a procedure which is presently the industry norm. . . . And the design requirements themselves merely amount to insisting that the manufacturer produce matchbooks and matches that, on their face, do not contain obvious defects that seem logically to relate to a fragmentation risk. Since the cost of testing to ensure compliance with the general requirements geared to meeting the fragmentation hazard will therefore be slight, and the object of the requirement—ensuring a properly functioning product—seems only reasonable, we think that these requirements can be said to be "reasonably necessary" to reduce the risk from fragmentation.

However, we are not satisfied that the Commission has carried its burden of showing that the "performance" requirements geared to fragmentation are "reasonably necessary to eliminate or reduce" the risk to any significant degree. Performance requirements, unlike design requirements, cannot be tested for visually. The Commission itself concedes "that the principal cost effects on producers will arise from implementation of testing programs." Hence the effectiveness of these performance requirements in reducing risk is a matter of considerable importance.

There is a complete absence from the record of evidence tending to show the causes of fragmentation. The Commission has evidently proceeded on the assumption that the fragmentation results from defective manufacturing procedures and will show up upon testing at the plant. However, manufacturers, in submissions to the Commission, asserted that experience showed that post-manufacturer factors such as high humidity, perspiration, or misuse by consumers were principally responsible for fragmentation.

In view of the lack of evidence establishing the causes of fragmentation, and of the manu-facturers' submissions claiming that post-manufacture handling causes most fragmentation, it is a large assumption that fragmentation is almost wholly attributable to the manufacturing process. Even then, the Commission's position on fragmentation establishes only that, at most "gross manufacturing errors" will be detected. But there is no evidence in the record from which the Commission could have determined that "gross errors," much less occasional defects occur with any frequency. It is just as possible to hypothesize that post-manufacture handling is the principal cause of fragmentation. We therefore think it speculative for the Commission to find, on the present record, that the proposed fragmentation performance requirements will result in a significant decrease on the fragmentation risk. In view of this, the substantial, added cost of testing to insure compliance with the performance requirements cannot be justified. . . .

Questions

1. What is the difference between a "design" or "general" requirement and a "performance" requirement? How was the manufacturer to ensure compliance with the design requirements? With the performance requirements?
2. What was the consumer hazard in *Bean*? Were the requirements to reduce the hazard obtainable "at reasonable cost" to the manufacturer in relation to the likely benefits of reducing the consumer hazard?

Because of judicial setbacks as illustrated in *Bean,* the Commission began to weigh its standards by benefit-cost criteria to establish the "reasonably necessary" requirement for the standards promulgated. For example, the CPSC defended its power mower regulations by asserting that they would save consumers over $211 million in avoiding injury expenses while costing $190 million in implementation.[9] However, in late 1981, the agency voted to accept less stringent standards governing safety features of power lawnmowers sold after June 1982. Moreover, Congress in 1982 directed the commission to rely more heavily, when possible, on voluntary, industry-developed safety standards and to conduct forms of cost-benefit analysis in its standard-setting process. Finally, CPSC safety standards were made subject to congressional veto.

In late 1978, CPSC released its interpretative statement of the reporting requirements under the Consumer Product Safety Act. The CPSC allows five days for "reportable knowledge" to travel from "an official or employee who may reasonably be expected to be capable of appreciating the significance of the information" to the company's chief executive officer (CEO). Unless a written delegation of authority has been filed with CPSC, the CEO must notify the Commission within 24 hours of receiving reportable information. Reporting may be delayed an additional 10 days if the firm feels an investigation is needed to determine reportability. The Commission will usually require a much more detailed "full report" at a later date. A "knowing" failure to report can result in civil penalty (fine); and a "knowing and willful" failure can result in a criminal penalty. It should be noted that the original equipment manufacturer and the component manufacturer are equally liable under the reporting requirements.

Under the new CPSC reporting policy, efficient internal procedures are essential to ensure that product safety information reaches the reporting officer. Internal controls are important to monitor the system to be sure that all the information is being transmitted quickly and accurately. People should be designated within the company (more than one if possible, to ensure cross-checking) to bear responsibility for reporting to top officials even the slightest chance that a defect may be occurring. Employees should be notified in writing that they are expected to report possible product defects, and all parts suppliers should likewise be notified that the company expects immediate reporting of any possible defects that may cause a safety hazard. Once the reporting system is set up and a specific routine becomes mandatory, it should be regularly reviewed for effectiveness.

The firm will be required to submit a corrective action plan indicating the steps it intends to take to remedy any product hazard. The commission may accept the plan or enter into a consent order agreement. If the corrective action plan is unacceptable, the commission can initiate formal enforcement proceedings seeking notice to known customers or recall of the hazardous product. If recall procedures are selected, the consumer may not be charged any costs. However, any refund of monies to consumers may be reduced by a reasonable deduction for consumer use.

Finally, an individual who has been injured as a result of a knowing or willful violation of a consumer product safety rule may seek damages in a federal district court (if the damages exceed the $10,000 jurisdictional requirement). The aggrieved consumer may also recover the cost of the suit and reasonable attorney fees at the discretion of the court.

Knowing violation of consumer product safety rules will subject the violater to a civil penalty of $2000 for each offense or the maximum penalty of $500,000 for any related series of violations. Criminal penalties of $50,000, a year in jail, or both, can result when the act is knowingly and willfully violated after the company has received notice of noncompliance. Consciousness of the wrongdoing is not required, as was illustrated in the *Park* case. In addition, the commission can bring action to restrain the distribution of any consumer products that do not comply with its safety rules.

CONSUMER'S RIGHT TO BE HEARD

The consumer's right to be heard includes the right to receive full consideration of the consumer's interests in the formulation of governmental policy. Increasingly, this right includes the right to fair and active participation by consumer advocates in hearings that formulate governmental policy.

As mentioned in Chapter 6, the imbalance of consumer advocacy in administrative hearings has been increasingly recognized in judicial decisions. In *United Church of Christ* v. *FCC,* 359 F. 2d 994 (D.C. Cir. 1966), the court of appeals ordered some "audience participation" in proceedings before the FCC. The court determined that unless consumers could be heard, there might be no one bringing the consumers' views to the attention of the administrative body in an effective manner. As this case indicates, there is a growing body of case law in which the courts are requiring federal agencies to take into account the consumer groups that are being affected by the agency's decisions.

Consumers have also sought legislation that improves the consumers' voice. For example, many states have enacted an "office of consumers' council" to represent utility customers in utility regulation hearings. Also, the federal Public Utility Regulatory Policies Act (PURPA) of 1978 grants the consumer the right to intervene in state public utility regulation hearings.

There has also been a consumer movement to establish a federal consumer protection agency to represent the consumer interest in other federal agencies. In 1971, the House of Representatives passed a consumer protection agency bill by a vote of 344 to 44. However, the Senate did not pass a similar version, and by 1975, the vote in the House on the proposed agency was only 208 to 199. In February of 1978 the House scuttled the consumer protection agency bill by a 227 to 198 vote. The proponents of consumer advocacy have since proposed acts that would authorize federal agencies to pay the fees of lawyers and expert witnesses who participate in agency proceedings. When individuals and organizations that represent a consumer or public interest viewpoint would be foreclosed from participation because the cost of representation would be prohibitive or the financial interest of the consumer groups would be too small in relation to the cost of representation, such participants would be eligible for payment from the agency. The consumer proponents feel that such "participation acts" do not have the same effect as the creation of an office of consumer representation. They feel the participation approach carries less of the "big government" connotation that was utilized to defect the consumer protection agency bill. Those consumer groups "representing" the consumers are likely to continue to pursue efforts to improve their voice before governmental bodies.

CONCLUSION

It seems clear that the consumer's rights are not being automatically protected by the marketplace. The market has to be augmented by laws to protect the rights of consumers, particularly the right to safety.

Initially, consumer protection laws sought to provide consumers with better market information. These laws were aimed at making the market better. Consumers were to be fully informed of the potential risk, and allowed to make their own choices. However, consumers may not be able or willing to make effective use of the information made available. Many consumers purchase habitually or routinely on the basis of brand loyalties. Some consumers make choices based on emotion. Others are not willing to take the time in gathering and using information. Furthermore, in one view the consumer is helplessly subject to manipulation by large oligopolistic organizations that control not only output and prices (supply) but also consumer demand. In this view, consumers are judged not to be capable of protecting themselves. Instead, laws are needed to protect the consumer from unsafe products and set minimum standards of quality or performance for products. These laws provide protection for all consumers regardless of their access to relevant information about particular products or their ability or willingness to use that information. If dangerous products are kept off the market, society does not need to worry about the thoroughness or rationality of consumer decision making. However, these latter policies are intrusive into the free market system and place restrictions on freedom of choice by both businesses and consumers. There is the danger that law enforcers will force protection in areas valued little by society or not valued at all.

A more recent approach asserts that regardless of how many standards are developed and enforced or how much information is made available, some consumers will continue to have their rights violated. Hence, this approach opts for the development of easier means for consumers to obtain compensation for losses suffered. They call for legislation designed to make it easier and less costly for consumers to take action on their own initiative for losses and grievances. An obvious disadvantage to this approach is evident in a situation where a consumer is killed by a defective or unsafe product. Compensation is obviously an inadequate remedy. In addition, people must be made aware of the ability to obtain redress for their grievances. And better means for the resolution of grievances are needed also.

A mixture of consumer philosophies has been adopted in consumer protection laws. The consumer helplessness approach has emphasized the necessity of product bans and product safety standards. The recognition of consumer ignorance has initiated laws of disclosure and warnings. The consumer remedy approach has emphasized the consumer's right to recovery as is evident in product liability laws. It seems reasonable to expect all three approaches to continue to fashion the laws of the future.

DISCUSSION QUESTIONS

1. Graham was a diesel mechanic employed by Kinnie Co., which leased and serviced trucks. Kinnie sent Graham to replace a flat tire on a truck at a Kinnie customer's garage. So that he could fit the jack under the truck, Graham attempted to raise the truck about ⅜″ by inflating the flat tire. As he

did so, the side ring, a portion of the multi-piece wheel assembly manufactured by Firestone Tire and Rubber Co., explosively disengaged from the rim base and struck Graham, causing severe injuries to his arms and legs.

Graham sued Kinnie's customer for failing to warn him that the truck had been run with a flat. However, a Kinnie employee had directed the truck driver to drive the truck with its flat to the garage. What result?

2. Graham also sued Firestone for failing to warn of the hazards of the wheel and for negligence in the design of the wheel assembly.

Graham was considered an "expert" in changing truck tires because of his experience, and it is a common practice of diesel mechanics to inflate tires to elevate a vehicle. Although running on a flat tire can damage the wheel or ring, Graham observed no obvious deformity or defect. Forty previous blowouts similar to Graham's had been reported to Firestone. What result?

3. A four-year-old child clothed in cotton "flannelette" pajamas suffered burns over 20 percent of her body when the garment ignited as she reached across the top of an electric range to turn off a kitchen timer. The material was not treated with flame retardant chemicals. Such chemicals were available and could have increased the garment's resistance to fire.

According to the garment manufacturer, the cotton flannelette was not unreasonably dangerous because it contained only normal and obvious hazards, and that the only flame retardant chemicals available at the time of manufacture would make the fabric unsaleable because of their effect on texture. As sold, the product was lightweight, warm, absorbent, and soft to the touch. Moreover, the manufacturer asserted that the garment complied with tests suggested in the Flammable Fabrics Act of 1953. Congressional intent in passing this act was to identify (through tests) highly flammable *synthetic* products and not all unreasonably dangerous clothing. The manufacturer knew the test used in this instance was a poor indicator of safety. The test would approve of a dry newspaper with a 48 percent margin of safety.

Suit was commenced under Minnesota law in state court. What is your analysis of the manufacturer's responsibilities?

4. As an amenity to its passengers, KLM Air supplies slippers for their comfort in-flight in the first-class compartment. A passenger who had received such slippers during a flight from Amsterdam to New York, later gave the slippers to his mother, who suffered injuries when she slipped and fell while wearing the slippers.

Give your assessment of KLM Air's legal liability.

5. Property Protection Co. did not manufacture but did supply and install for B. L. a burglar alarm system with a stand-by battery source of power in case the home's electrical system failed. Installation of the system carried a 90-day express warranty, which also purported to limit the liability of the installer to repair or replace the alarm. The Uniform Commercial Code

allows the contractual limitation or exclusion of consequential damages unless the limitation or exclusion is unconscionable.

Within 90 days of installation, burglars destroyed B. L.'s electric meter, entered the home, and took $35,815 worth of jewelry. The alarm failed to function because Property Protection had installed dead batteries. B. L. now claims that the limitation on liability contained in Property Protection's express warranty is unconscionable and, therefore, invalid under the Uniform Commercial Code. Hence, B. L. argues that Property Protection should be strictly liable under the common law of product liability for the harm to (theft of) her property caused by the defective product.

Property Protection relies on the validity of the contractual limitation saying it is not unconscionable and that it should not be made an insurer of B. L.'s possessions. Second, Property Protection argues that strict liability should not apply where a defect in the product did not directly *cause* B. L.'s property loss.

Did Property Protection's defective product "cause" B. L.'s loss?

Is the limitation of liability conscionable?

6. The Consumer Product Safety Commission issued a notice of inspection to the State Fair of Texas, seeking access to a "Swiss skyride" and to all relevant records regarding the skyride. Commission action was prompted by the second of two accidents involving such rides, in which passengers are carried in open gondolas along a single cable high above the fairground. Four gondolas had collided and fallen to the ground, killing one passenger. The State Fair refuses to permit inspection by the commission of the device itself and of its records, because it claims that the ride is not a "consumer product" and therefore not subject to the jurisdiction of the commission. The skyride is owned by the State Fair of Texas, is operated by an independant lessee, and was manufactured in Switzerland by a Swiss company.

Section 3 of the CPSA defines a "consumer product" as "any article, or component part thereof, produced or distributed

(i) for sale to a consumer for use in or around a permanent or temporary household or residence, a school, in recreation, or otherwise, or (ii) for the personal use, consumption, or enjoyment of a consumer in or around a permanent or temporary household or residence, a school, in recreation, or otherwise. . . .

The State Fair contends the ride is not a consumer "article" because it is too large to be exchanged between consumers, and it is not "distributed" because it is not sold directly to consumers or directly controlled by them.

What result?

7. No more than about 12 percent of all auto travelers use safety belts, which are called "active restraints" because people must consciously buckle up. If lap and shoulder belts received 100 percent usage, an estimated 16,300 lives would be saved each year. Compulsory inclusion of automatic belts or automatically inflating air cushions in all new cars (i.e., passive restraints) would

save approximately 10,000 lives annually. The estimated costs of automatic belts would raise the cost of the auto by $75 to $100 and air bags would add $300 to $1100. If you were the administrator of NHTSA, would you adopt a passive restraint standard?

SUGGESTED READINGS

Bohlman, H. M., "Product Liability: Present and Past," *American Business Law Journal*, Vol. 17, No. 1, Spring 1979, pp. 115–116.

Dworkin, Terry Morehead and Zollers, Frances E., "Market Share Liability—Porposals for Application," *American Business Law Journal*, Vol. 19, No. 4, Winter 1981, pp. 523–538.

Elfin, Rodman, M., "Products Liability Developments and Tactics," *American Business Law Journal*, Vol. 16, No. 3, Winter 1979, pp. 315–328.

Elfin, Rodman M., "The Changing Philosophy of Products Liability and the Proposed Model Uniform Product Liability Act," *American Business Law Journal*, Vol. 19, No. 3, Fall 1981, pp. 267–294.

Henszey, Benjamin N., "Caveat Emptor in Full Retreat—Application of Implied Warranty to the Sale of Used Housing," *American Business Law Journal*, Vol. 15, No. 3, pp. Winter 1978, 351–363.

Leibman, Jordan H., "Strict Tort Liability for Unfinished Products," *American Business Law Journal*, Vol. 19, No. 4, Winter 1981, pp. 407–440.

Mallor, Jane P., "Extension of the Implied Warranty of Habitability to Purchasers of Used Homes," *American Business Law Journal*, Vol. 20, No. 3, Fall 1982, pp. 361–390.

Metzger, Michael B., "Consumer Suits Against Manufacturers and the Code's Statute of Limitations: Her Majesty's Edict," *American Business Law Journal*, Vol. 17, No. 2, Summer 1979, pp. 221–229.

ENDNOTES

1. *Winterbottom* v. *Wright*, 10 M. & W. 109, 152 Eng. Rep. 402 (1842).
2. *MacPherson* v. *Buick Motor Co.*, 217 N.Y. 382, 111 N.E. 1050 (1916).
3. Prosser, *Law of Torts*, 4th ed. (Minneapolis, Minn.: West Pub. Co., 1971), p. 643.
4. *Baxter* v. *Ford Motor Company*, 166 Wash. 453, 12 R. 2d 409, affirmed on rehearing (1932).
5. Food and Drug Administration, *Requirements of the United States Food, Drug and Cosmetic Act* (1972), p. 5.
6. Federal Food, Drug and Cosmetic Act, Section 505(d).
7. *FDA Annual Report 1975*, p. 36; 1976, p. 33.
8. *Wall Street Journal*, February 26, 1981, pp. 1, 19; June 26, 1981, pp. 1, 25.
9. Douglas F. Greer, *Business, Government, and Society* (New York: MacMillan Publishing Co., Inc., 1983), p. 442.

chapter 23

ENVIROMENTAL PROTECTION REGULATIONS

The pollution problem is largely a consequence of population. It did not much matter how a lonely American frontiersman disposed of his waste. But as population became denser, the natural chemical and biological recycling processes became overloaded, calling for redefinition of legal rights. Since it is practically impossible to spell out all the conditions under which it is safe to permit some burning or some discharge into the environment, by law we have delegated the detail to bureaus. Our experience has indicated that "temperance in pollution" can best be accomplished through the mediation of administrative law.

The laws and administrative regulations for environmental quality have imposed extensive requirements and cost on society. In 1979, for example, it is estimated that public and private enterprises spent over $55 billion on the purchase, operation, and maintenance of pollution control equipment. It is also estimated that over 75 percent of the money spent by business in complying with all government regulations is spent on meeting environmental regulations. While some believe that these costs are too high, others think the cost is simply necessary to prevent the continuing deterioration of our natural resources.

INITIAL POLLUTION REGULATIONS

THE COMMON LAW

Most societies at some time in their development have expressed concern over the pollution of their natural environment. The task of defining what constitutes pollution is dependent on society's choice in the use of its environment and resources. It is society's concept of "public interest," therefore, that becomes the controlling factor in defining pollution.

Under the common law, the environment was thought to be able to "cleanse itself." The discharge of waste into the environment became "unreasonable" when the environment's cleansing ability was exceeded. Consequently, business firms were allowed to discharge "reasonable" amounts of waste into the environment without legal liabilities. However, when discharges became unreasonable interferences with the use and enjoyment of a neighbor's land, the court labeled such activity a "nuisance," entitling the adjoining land owner to compensation for the harm caused to his or her property. If it could be shown that polluted air, for example, was injuring his or her house or crops, the plaintiff could secure judicial aid to prevent the injury and obtain compensation from the polluter. However, if the plaintiff could not establish that he or she sustained specific harm that was distinct from the harm that all members of the public at large sustained, the plaintiff could be denied standing to object to the polluter's behavior. Moreover, the crowding conditions of industrial and urban society had made it more difficult for the plaintiff to establish which polluter was the single cause of the harm. Without proof of causation, the plaintiff was not entitled to legal relief. Finally, the court would balance harm caused by the pollution against the benefits of the polluting activity to the community. If the court considered the "social value" of the business and its payroll (employment) to exceed the harm caused by the pollution, the pollution was considered reasonable, denying the plaintiff any right to relief. As a result, the tort system was not effective in eliminating the growing levels of pollution in industrial and urban society.

STATUTORY REGULATION

The growing crisis of environmental degradation caused society to redefine pollution. The federal environmental quality laws, therefore, have defined pollution in terms of its effects on the public health and welfare. However, efforts to clean the environment often come in conflict with the other goals of society. It is the task of the legislature to establish basic priorities and strategies in dealing with environmental pollution. The implementation and enforcement of environmental improvement laws lie with the decisional process of administrative agencies and the courts.

Initially, Congress believed that pollution control was the responsibility of state and local governments. Accordingly, congressional enactments during the fifties and sixties were largely aimed at directing attention to problems of pollution and providing states with economic and technical assistance.

It became apparent in the late sixties that state environmental pollution programs were insufficient. Congress responded in the early seventies by enacting several laws that were designed to increase the federal authority and responsibility in combating pollution. One of the first acts of Congress was, so to speak, to get its "own house in order" through the enactment of the National Environmental Policy Act.

NATIONAL ENVIRONMENTAL POLICY ACT

BASICS PROVISIONS

Declaration of National Policy

The National Environmental Policy Act (NEPA) was enacted in 1970 as the culmination of efforts by the Congress to recognize the need for establishing a federal policy on the environment. Various federal acts preceding NEPA had dealt with narrow, specific problems. The enactment of NEPA, however, represented the first federal government statement of its basic policy on environmental quality. The purposes of the act are as follows.

. . . To declare a national policy which will encourage productive and enjoyable harmony between man and his environment; to promote efforts which will prevent or eliminate damage to the environment and biosphere and stimulate the health and welfare of man; to enrich the understanding of the ecological system and natural resources important to the Nation. . . . (NEPA Sec. 2)

Council on Environmental Quality

Besides broadly declaring the national policy toward the environment, NEPA requires appropriate action to achieve that policy, and establishes the Council on Environmental Quality. The Council, composed of "three members who shall be appointed by the President to serve at his pleasure," advises the President of growing environmental problems, and aids the President in formulating his administration's environmental policies. The Reagan Administration indicated in early 1981 that it would seek to abolish the Council. Instead, the Administration reduced its budget by half in 1981 to $3 million and projected to further reduce the budget to $1 million annually in 1982 and 1983.

Substantive Provisions

NEPA requires all federal agencies to consider values of environmental preservation in their spheres of activity. Section 101 of NEPA sets forth the act's basic substantive policy: that the federal government "use all practicable means and measures" to protect environmental values. Congress did not establish environmental protection as an exclusive goal; rather, it desired a reordering of priorities, so that environmental costs and benefits will assume their proper place along with other considerations. In Section 101(b), imposing an explicit duty on federal officials, the act provides that "it is the continuing responsibility of the

Federal Government to use all practicable means, consistent with other essential considerations of national policy," to avoid environmental degradation, preserve "histroic, cultural, and natural" resources, and promote "the widest range of beneficial uses of the environment without . . . undesirable and unintended consequences." Thus the general substantive policy of the act is a flexible one. It leaves room for a responsible exercise of discretion and may not require particular substantive results in particular problematic instances.

Procedural Provisions

NEPA also contains very important "procedural" provisions—provisions designed to see that all federal agencies do in fact exercise the substantive discretion given them. These provisions are not highly flexible. Indeed, they establish a strict standard of compliance.

Section 102(2)(A) and (B) requires all agencies to use a "systematic, interdisciplinary approach" to environmental planning and evaluation "in decisionmaking which may have an impact on man's environment." In order to include all possible environmental factors in the decisional equation, agencies must "identify and develop methods and procedures . . . which will insure that presently unquantified environmental amenities and values may be given appropriate consideration in decisionmaking along with economic and technical considerations." "Environmental amenities" will often be in conflict with "economic and technical consideration." To "consider" the former "along with" the latter must involve a balancing process. In some instances environmental cost may outweigh economic and technical benefits and in other instances they may not. But NEPA mandates a rather finely tuned and "systematic" balancing analysis in each instance.

To ensure that the balancing analysis is carried out and given full effect, Section 102(2)(C) requires that responsible officials of all agencies prepare a "detailed statement" covering the impact of particular actions on the environment, the environmental costs that might be avoided, and alternative measures that might alter the cost-benefit equation. The apparent purpose of the "detailed statement," (or as it has come to be known, the environmental impact statement, EIS) is to aid in the agencies' own decision-making process and to advise other interested agencies and the public of the environmental consequences of planned federal action. Beyond the "detailed statement," Section 102(2)(D) requires all agencies specifically to "study, develop and describe appropriate alternatives to recommended courses of action in any proposal which involves unresolved conflicts concerning alternative uses of available resources." This requirement, like the "detailed statement" requirement, seeks to ensure that each agency decision maker has before him and takes into proper account all possible approaches to a particular project (including total abandonment of the project) that would alter the environmental impact and the cost-benefit balance. Only in that fashion is it likely that the most intelligent, optimally beneficial decision will ultimately be made. Moreover, by compelling a formal "detailed statement" and a description of alternatives, NEPA provides evidence that the mandated decision-making process has in fact taken place and, most importantly, allows those removed from the initial process to evaluate and balance the factors on their own.

Of course, all of these Section 102 duties are qualified by the phrase "to the fullest extent possible." However, this language does not provide an escape hatch for foot-dragging agencies. Instead, the requirement of environmental consideration "to the fullest extent possible" sets a high standard for the agencies, a standard rigorously enforced by the reviewing courts.

The reviewing courts probably will not reverse a substantive decision on its merits, unless it can be shown that the actual balance of costs and benefits struck was arbitrary or clearly gave insufficient weight to environmental values. But if the decision was reached procedurally without individualized consideration and balancing of environmental factors—conducted fully and in good faith—it is the responsibility of the courts to reverse.

Questions
1. Must federal officials take environmental values into account in federal decision making?
2. What "approach" to environmental planning and evaluation is mandated by NEPA Section 102(A) and (B)?
3. According to Section 102(2)(C), what must the "detailed statement" include? What does 102(2)(D) add as a requirement?
4. What is the true value of EIS preparation? Does the review of environmental alternatives under the NEPA require that the least damaging alternative always be used? Or does the agency in fact have discretion in choosing an alternative?
5. When is a reviewing court to reverse the substantive environmental decision of an agency?

ENFORCEMENT

While all federal agencies are required to comply with NEPA requirements and complete an EIS when their actions significantly affect the natural environment, enforcement of NEPA comes almost exclusively from the private sector. In most cases, the plaintiff in the NEPA case is a private citizen or conservation organization that has some interest in the environment about to be affected by the agency action. However, not just anyone who objects to a proposed agency action can bring suit under NEPA. The concept of "standing to use" requires the persons bringing suit to allege that the challenged agency action has caused them "injury in fact" or they are about to be injured in fact. The "standing" limitation on plaintiffs seeks to ensure that only those persons with a legitimate interest in the litigable issues be permitted to represent the alleged injured parties and present their best arguments in court.

The primary remedy sought by private litigants is an injunction, which prevents continuation of the project or activity until the agency complies with NEPA. Once the agency has met NEPA requirements and considered the environmental alternatives, it is free to exercise its discretion to choose the most appropriate alternative. Only where the agency has clearly abused its discretion, exceeded its statutory authority, or made its decision in disregard of the facts can it be prevented from going forward with its decision.

ENVIRONMENTAL PROTECTION AGENCY

Many argued that the initial inadequacy of federal pollution controls resulted from the dispersal of power among too many federal agencies. A more centralized government agency was believed to be an improvement. Consequently, 15 pollution-control administrative functions from five different agencies were combined and merged with the creation of the Environmental Protection Agency (EPA). The EPA is responsible for the regulation of four basic types of environmental pollutants that are emitted by industry into the external environment. It is to control air pollution through the Clean Air Act, water pollution through the Clean Water Act, various kinds of land pollution through the Resource Conservation and Recovery Act, and pollutants derived from the use of products by consumers through a variety of acts (see Figure 23-1).

AIR POLLUTION REGULATION

The involvement of the federal government in air pollution regulation developed slowly. The Air Pollution Control Act of 1955 empowered the Surgeon General to study the problem of air pollution and its control. The original Clean Air Act (CAA) of 1963 was administered by the Department of Health, Education, and Welfare (HEW) and contained such a cumbersome enforcement process that it was only used once. The Air Quality Act of 1967 amended the Clean Air Act and strengthened the federal role in air pollution control by authorizing HEW to oversee the establishment of state ambient air quality standards and state implementation plans. Despite the increased federal role, the states retained such wide latitude in air quality standards and in time periods for compliance that by the beginning of 1970, no states had adopted complete standards or an implementation plan.

The Clean Air Act amendments of 1970 sharply expanded federal authority. It instructed the newly formed EPA to establish nationally uniform primary and secondary ambient air quality standards for air pollutants. The EPA was given nine months to establish these standards, and each state was required to create an implementation plan to meet the federal standards within the state. The state implementation plan (SIP) had to be submitted to the EPA for approval, and deadlines were specified in the act.

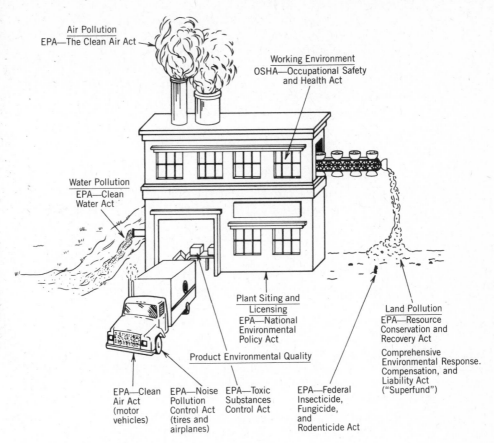

Figure 23-1. Environmental pollution regulations.

The Clean Air Act required the EPA administrator to publish National Ambient Air Quality Standards (NAAQS) for six major pollutants: sulfur dioxides, particulates, carbon monoxide, photochemical oxidants, hydrocarbons, and nitrogen oxides. Later, the EPA administrator added standards for the pollutant lead. The *primary* standards prescribed the maximum concentration that an air pollutant is not to exceed in order to protect the public against adverse health effects. These standards were set with an "adequate margin of safety" to protect against a potential hazard not yet identified. The *secondary* standards are more restrictive than the primary standards and attempt to protect the environment, vegetation, visibility, climate, property, and personal comfort and well-being. Economic and technological feasibility were not to be considered by the EPA in the development of national ambient air quality standards. According to the act, the standards were to be developed solely on the basis of the adverse effects of the pollutant on the public health and welfare.

Mobile sources of pollution run by internal combustion engines account for most of the unnatural carbon monoxide in the atmosphere and for about half of the hydrocarbons and nitrogen oxides. Mobile sources also are responsible for most airborne lead pollution and photochemical oxidants (smog). *Stationary sources,* which include electric utilities and industrial plants, generate most of the sulfur dioxide and particulates and account for about half of the nitrogen dioxide pollution in the atmosphere. The EPA directly regulates the producers of internal combustion engines for compliance with national ambient air quality standards, and state governments are primarily responsible for achievement of federal ambient quality standards for stationary sources.

State Implementation Plans

The first step in developing the state implementation plans is the measurement of pollution actually existing in the air. Some numerical "average of air quality" for each pollutant is established. Then, the degree to which the current levels exceed the permitted levels under the national standards (NAAQS) is determined. Finally, each state must decide how the burden of reducing emissions is to be allocated among its industrial sources. A least-cost abatement approach would allocate the degree of pollution reduction to those firms with the lowest cost of pollution reduction. However, businesses with lower costs of pollution reduction have opposed this approach as being unfair to them. Consequently, most states have adopted an equal percentage reduction for all industrial sources. Nevertheless, particular businesses may argue with the state that economic and technological infeasibility prohibit their compliance. In effect, they would prefer to have their "emission limitations" raised under the state plan. If the state is to concede to any industry's request for lower "emission limitations," it must require other polluters to further reduce their pollution levels so that the state can comply with national ambient air quality standards. Once the SIP has been adopted by the state and approved by the EPA, all industry sources have been assigned "emission limitations" to which they must comply. Failure to comply can result in the plants being shut down. Only good faith efforts at compliance and the presentation of a tight compliance schedule to accomplish its assigned emission limitations would protect a firm from being shut down if it did not comply within the appropriate time frame.

SIPs must require businesses to use "continuous emission controls" that either prevent pollutants from being generated or remove them from "waste air" on a continuous basis. "Dispersion" techniques (high smokestacks) are permitted only if the state has already adopted regulations that require the maximum degree of continuous emission controls achievable.

The EPA has the power to accept or reject the SIP. If a plan was not submitted and accepted, or if an accepted plan is not being properly enforced by the state, the EPA is empowered to step in and assume the full burden of enforcement. Further, under certain conditions, a state's failure to develop or enforce its SIP could result in a complete halt to construction of major sources of pollution.

Thirty states received extensions until December 1987 to meet the national ambient air quality standards for ozone and carbon monoxide and were to submit SIPs by July 1, 1982. Of the plans submitted, the EPA has proposed to disapprove 17 plans, threatening to ban construction in nonattainment counties.

Union Electric Co. v. Environmental Protection Agency

427 U.S. 246 (1976)
Supreme Court of the United States

Justice Marshall

* * *

Petitioner is an electric utility company servicing the St. Louis metropolitan area, large portions of Missouri, and parts of Illinois and Iowa. Its three coal-fired generating plants in the metropolitan St. Louis area are subject to the sulfur dioxide restrictions in the Missouri implementation plan. Petitioner did not seek review of the [EPA] Administrator's approval of the plan within 30 days, as it was entitled to do under §307(b)(1) of the Act, but rather applied to the appropriate state and county agencies for variances from the emission limitations affectings its three plants. Petitioner received one-year variances, which could be extended upon reapplication. The variances on two of petitioner's three plants had expired and petitioner was applying for extensions when, on May 31, 1974, the Administrator notified the petitioner that sulfur dioxide emissions from its plants violated the emission limitations contained in the Missouri plan. Shortly thereafter, petitioner filed a petition in the Court of Appeals for the Eighth Circuit for review of the Administrator's 1972 approval of the Missouri implementation plan.

Section 307(b)(1) allows petitions for review to be filed in an appropriate court of appeals more than 30 days after the Administrator's approval of an implementation plan only if the petition is "based solely on grounds arising after such 30th day." Petitioner claimed to meet this requirement by asserting, that various economic and technological difficulties had arisen more than 30 days after the Administrator's approval and that these difficulties made compliance with the emission limitations impossible.

* * *

Since a reviewing court—regardless of when the petition for review is filed—may consider claims of economic and technological infeasibility only if the Administrator may consider such claims in approving or rejecting a state implementation plan, we must address ourselves to the scope of the Administrator's responsibility. . . . After surveying the relevant provisions of the Clean Air Amendments of 1970 and their legislative history, we [hold] that Congress intended claims of economic and technological infeasiblity to be wholly foreign to the Administrator's consideration of a state implementation plan.

* * *

The Amendments place the primary responsibility for formulating pollution control strategies on the States, but nonetheless subject the States to strict minimum compliance requirements. These requirements are of a "technology-forcing character," and are expressly designed to force regulated sources to develop pollution control devices that might at the time appear to be economically or technologically infeasible.

* * *

Section 110(a)(2)(A)'s three-year deadline for achieving primary air quality standards is central to the Amendments' regulatory scheme and, as both the language and the legislative history of the requirement make clear, it leaves no room for claims of technological or economic infeasibility.

Accordingly, a court of appeals reviewing an approved plan under Section 307(b)(1) cannot set it aside on those grounds, no matter when they are raised.

* * *

Perhaps the most important forum for consideration of claims of economic and technological infeasibility is before the state agency formulating the implementation plan. So long as the national standards are met, the State may select whatever mix of control devices it desires, and industries with particular economic or technological problems may seek special treatment in the plan itself.

Even if the State does not intervene on behalf of an emission source, technological and economic factors may be considered in at least one other circumstance. When a source is found to be in violation of the state implementation plan, the Administrator may, after a conference with the operator, issue a compliance order rather than seek civil or criminal enforcement. Such an order must specify a "reasonable" time for compliance with the relevant standard, taking into account the se-

riousness of the violation and "any good faith efforts to comply with applicable requirements." Claims of technological or economic infeasibility, the Administrator agrees, are relevant to fashioning an appropriate compliance order. . . .

In short, the Amendments offer ample opportunity for consideration of claims of technological and economic infeasibility. Always, however, care is taken that consideration of such claims will not interfere substantially with the primary goal of prompt attainment of the national standards. . . . Technology forcing is a concept somewhat new to our national experience and it necessarily entails certain risks. But Congress considered those risks in passing the 1970 Amendments and decided that the dangers posed by uncontrolled air pollution made them worth taking.

Questions
1. Who made the policy decision to remove economic and technological factors from consideration in setting deadlines for compliance with the Clean Air Act's "primary" standards?
2. What costs or benefits do you see from the "technological forcing" concept embodied in the Clean Air Act?
3. What procedures exist in the act for consideration of economic and technological aspects in its enforcement?

Business Growth?

The Clean Air Act required the EPA and the states to reduce air pollution to the national levels as quickly as possible. Those states in which the air was dirtier than the national standards could not permit new air-polluting businesses to be built. Also, those states in which the air was cleaner than national standards were required under the act to "protect and enhance" the existing quality of air. If a strict interpretation of the act were followed, new construction of any air pollution business would be prohibited everywhere.

To avoid the no-growth consequence, the EPA developed different policies for "dirty" and "clean" air regions. For dirty air areas, called "nonattainment" areas, the EPA adopted the Emissions Offset Policy. For clean air areas, or attainment areas, it adopted regulations to "prevent significant deterioration" of air quality.

Dirty Air Areas.   The Emissions Offset Policy for "nonattainment" areas delineates preconstruction requirements on major new or modified plants. First, the new plant has to install the greatest pollution control technology possible. Second, the plant owner has to certify that any other plants it owns are in compliance with any applicable state implementation plan (emission limitations) requirements. Third, new emissions from the proposed plant have to be offset by emission reductions of the same pollutant from other existing plants in the nonattainment area. The reductions in pollutants could be achieved by utilizing pollution control devices on other plants of the owner or by purchasing pollution control devices for other firms, if that is a less costly selection of the proposed plant owner. Finally, the emission offsets achieved have to be sufficient to create a "net air quality benefit" so as to ensure that the area would be making "reasonable further progress" toward obtaining the national ambient air quality standards.

The 1977 amendments to the Clean Air Act approved of the EPA's Emissions Offset Policy and required each state to submit to the EPA a list identifying its nonattainment areas. The 1977 amendments also defined a "major emitting facility" as one that emits 100 tons of pollutants per year. Such a facility must obtain a permit before it can undertake construction or modification. The permit system contains the same basic requirements as that adopted by the EPA in its "emissions offset policy" and requires that the states' implementation plans be designed to achieve the national ambient air quality standards by the end of 1982.

Beginning in 1981 the EPA approved of the "bubble concept." The bubble concept treats all the buildings and facilities of a firm's industrial complex as a single pollution source to be evaluated in the aggregate. The complex is considered under an imaginary bubble with a single stack emitting pollutants from the top of the bubble. Increases in emission from modifications or additions to the complex can occur as long as decreases in emissions from other components of the complex more than offset the new increase. The net effect of such changes would be a decrease in emissions from the imaginary smoke stack on the top of the bubble.

The bubble concept grants discretion to the owners of industrial complexes to apply whatever control measures they select for major emitting facilities. Owners can develop a mix of controls at the lowest possible costs.

From an economic point of view, both the Offset Policy and the "bubble concept" produce a more efficient allocation of resources. The EPA's adoption of the Offset Policy was a retreat from the strict regulatory scheme of the 1970 Act and allowed owners to find the least expensive offsets available. However, the bubble concept is even more efficient because it allows owners to avoid the application of the expensive "lowest achievable emissions rate" technology requirement imposed by the Offset Policy.

States have been urged to revise their State Implementation Plans to allow existing industrial complexes to use the bubble concept. However, in 1982, the D.C. Court of Appeals held that the EPA's use of the "bubble concept" in nonattainment areas was impermissible under current law.[1]

Clean Air Areas. Initially the EPA imposed no requirement to control new sources of pollution in clean air areas. Hence, new plants were free to pollute in those areas up to the national ambient air quality standards. The Sierra Club sued the EPA, arguing that the Clean Air Act demanded the EPA to "protect and enhance" the air quality in clean air areas. Thus, the Sierra Club maintained, the EPA's approval of state implementation plans that did not attempt to prevent "significant deterioration" of the air was in violation of the act. The Supreme Court upheld the trial court's decision to enjoin the EPA from approving any SIP that did not set regulations to prevent significant deterioration in clean air areas.[2]

As a result of the Court's decision in *Sierra Club,* clean air areas were to be protected from "significant deterioration" even though the areas were already below the national ambient air quality standards. Therefore, the EPA developed regulations to prevent "significant deterioration" but also to allow for economic growth.

The "prevention of significant deterioration" (PSD) regulations divided clean air areas into three classes. Class I includes the cleanest areas, including wilderness areas and national parks. Class II and Class III areas are progressively less clean. Increased air pollution in each class is allowed, but limited to a *maximum allowable increase.* Maximum allowable increases vary in size with each class. Class I has the smallest maximum allowable increase and Class II and III are allowed progressively larger increases. Hence, new plants that emitted pollution up to the maximum allowable increase could be constructed. Beyond that point, plant construction would be prohibited.

The EPA created these classes and maximum allowable increases for two air pollutants: sulfur dioxide and particulate matter. The EPA contended that monitoring techniques were not adequate to measure significant deterioration from other pollutants. Only the largest facilities from a list of industries were required to obtain preconstruction review by the EPA. Owners of such new facilities had to use the best available control technology for minimizing particulate matter and sulfur dioxide and show that the proposed plant's emissions would not cause the maximum allowable increase in the area to be exceeded. Smaller plants and those not on the list of industries were not subject to the preconstruction review by the EPA.

Congress approved of the EPA's PSD regulations in 1977 amendments to the Clean Air Act, but reduced the maximum allowable increase in Class III areas. The maximum allowable increase in Class III areas now approximately equals one half of the national secondary standards. Congress also prohibited the EPA from reclassifying Class I areas.

Finally, the 1977 amendments defined new plants subject to the preconstruction permit process as any "major emitting facility" (emission of 100 tons of pollutants per year), if it is on the especially designated industries list. All stationary sources not on the designated industries list must also go through the preconstruction permit process if the source emits 250 tons per year of any air pollutant. Consequently, owners of these proposed facilities meeting these size requirements in clean air areas must install the best available control technology and show that their operation will not cause the "maximum allowable increase" to be exceeded.

Kennecott Corp. v. Environmental Protection Agency

684 F.2d 1007 (1982)

U.S. Court of Appeals (D.C. Cir. 1982)

Kennecott Corporation (and five other firms operating nonferrous smelters) seek review of the final regulation of the Environmental Protection Agency (EPA) promulgated under Section 119 of the Clean Air Act (Act) as amended and governing issuance of primary nonferrous smelter orders (NSO's).

The nonferrous smelting process produces waste gas streams, denoted "weak streams" and "strong streams," which contain quantities of SO_2. Constant control technology, typically a sulfuric acid plant, has been used to remove SO_2 from strong streams but has been considered ineffective in removing SO_2 from weak streams. Smelters have therefore relied primarily upon dispersion techniques, in conjunction with acid plants, to meet EPA standards.

In 1977 amendments to the Act provide . . . that only constant control technology could be relied upon to meet ambient air quality standards. Congress created an exception, however, for nonferrous smelters, giving them additional time to develop their emission limitations solely through constant controls.

Before enactment of the 1977 amendments, EPA had concluded that constant control technology was reasonable for most smelters only to control "strong streams" and that constant control of "weak streams" was in cases "economically unreasonable and could in some cases result in shutdown." EPA had therefore allowed smelters to use dispersion techniques in conjunction with acid plants to meet ambient standards. In enacting §119, Congress

"confirmed the authority of EPA to pursue the Agency's present smelter policy."

Section 119 authorized EPA or the States to issue up to two NSO's permitting a smelter to continue reliance for a limited time on dispersion techniques, where constant controls sufficient to meet the emission limitations for SO_2 were not "adequately demonstrated to be reasonably available." During an NSO term, the smelter is required, however, to use constant control equipment in addition to dispersion techniques in attaining the ambient standards, unless such equipment "would be so costly as to necessitate permanent, or prolonged temporary cessation of operations." . . . Finally, smelters receiving NSO's must commit reasonable resources to research and development of appropriate emission control technology.

EPA published proposed regulations implementing § 119 on January 31, 1979. The proposed regulations set forth . . . a financial test for NSO eligibility *i.e.,* whether additional constant controls are "adequately demonstrated to be reasonably available" to the smelter. . . .

Under EPA's financial test, a smelter is eligible for NSO if it cannot install the required constant control equipment "without reducing the present value of [its] net income and terminal value below [its] current salvage value." The test thus compares the new revenues a smelter would receive from its operations after installing constant controls with salvage value upon closure. Constant control are deemed "reasonably available" if the smelter, on being required to install them immediately, would elect to continue operation, rather than close down. Hence the parties' appellation, "closure," to EPA's test. Revenue and cost forecasts for use in making that determination are based upon EPA estimates of metals prices, labor and energy costs, inflation rates, and the cost of capital.

* * *

Under § 119(b)(3), a smelter is eligible for an NSO if the constant controls required to meet the ambient standards for SO_2 have not been "adequately demonstrated to be reasonably available" to the smelter, "as determined by the Administrator, taking into account the cost of compliance, non-air quality health and environmental impact, and energy consideration."

Petitioners say that EPA's "closure," *i.e.*, shut down of all operations, test is inconsistent with § 119(b)(3); that the legislative history of § 119 makes clear that "reasonably available" is a less strict standard than closure and was intended to measure whether a smelter would experience a significant decrease in profitability if constant controls were required.

In response, EPA says: That § 119(b)(3) gives the agency broad discretion in formulating an eligibility test, leaving to the agency the precise means and criteria for assessing the significance of the costs of compliance; that had Congress intended application of a specific test, such as that focusing on profitability as suggested by petitioners, it would have expressly so provided; that Congress in § 119(b)(3) adopted EPA's pre-1977 practice of authorizing the use of dispersion techniques when the only alternatives are permanent production curtailment, shutdown or delays in attainment of the national standards. . . .

In reviewing substantive challenges, a court may reverse only those EPA actions found "arbitrary, capricious, an abuse of discretion or otherwise not in accordance with law. . . ."

We look first to the statutue before us, for agency action contrary thereto is necessarily

"not in accordance with law." Section 119(b)(3) requires that EPA determine whether controls are "reasonably available." In making its determination, EPA's application of a closure standard is, in our view, inconsistent with that statuory mandate. To employ EPA's "if" approach, had Congress intended that a closure standard be applied, it could have chosen language similar to that of § 119(d)(2), wherein it required NSO applicants to demonstrate that interim use of constant controls would cause a "cessation of operations." Indeed, Congress' election to employ "cessation" in § 119(d)(2) and to employ that distinctly different standard "reasonably available" in § 119(d)(3), is strong evidence that Congress intended application of something less that a "closure" test in determining eligibility for an NSO under § 119(b)(3).

In the 1977 amendments, as EPA correctly states, Congress clearly intended to adopt the substance of EPA's then existing smelter policy. The legislative history of those amendments, however, establishes that Congress viewed that policy as mandating a standard short of "closure" or smelter shutdown. The House Report indicates that Congress viewed that policy as allowing use of dispersion techniques if constant controls were "economically unreasonable."

* * *

Moreover, the report noted that § 119 is necessary because of "technological and economic problems confronting existing primary nonferrous smelters." Quoting from EPA's new sources performance standards for primary nonferrous smelters, the report described the difficulties involved in installing constant controls as producing "a significant decrease in profitability, a significant loss in sales, or a closing of some mines and a decrease in mining activity." Contrary to EPA's contentions, Congress did not, therefore, endorse a test based solely on preventing smelters from closing. As the legislative history makes clear, it sought to provide relief to the nonferrous smelter industry from a number of adverse economic consequences short of actual shutdown.

*   *   *

Because EPA's regulations establishing a closure standard are based on misinterpretation of the phrase "reasonably available" in § 119(b)(3), they are without support in the statute and are contrary to the intent gleanable from the statute's legislative history. They are therefore not in accordance with law and cannot stand.

Questions

1. What was the EPA's "closure" test? What did failure to pass this test mean for a smelter?
2. What test was suggested by the petitioners?
3. Was the EPA's or the petitioner's test more consistent with the intent of Congress?

Hazardous Air Pollutants

A hazardous air pollutant is defined under the Clean Air Act as an "air pollutant which may result in an increase in mortality or in a very serious illness." The EPA is required under the act to determine which air pollutants are hazardous and to develop appropriate emission standards to protect public health. Any plant emitting hazardous air pollutants must use the best available technology to reduce such emissions to the appropriate standards, or plant closure may result.

The EPA has issued emissions standards for four hazardous pollutants: asbestos, beryllium, mercury, and vinyl chloride. Pressure from environmental groups is likely to induce the EPA to identify other hazardous air pollutants and establish appropriate emission standards in the future.

Enforcement

A summary of air pollution regulations is provided in Figure 23-2. The CAA provides for enforcement by empowering the states, the federal government, and the private citizen to seek compliance by bringing action against violators.

The states, through their state implementation plans, have the primary responsibility for the day-to-day enforcement of their respective SIPs. The states may also be delegated certain federal enforcement powers on meeting prescribed conditions.

A private citizen may bring a lawsuit on his or her own behalf against (1) anyone who is believed to be violating the emission standards of the CAA, (2) the administrator of the EPA if the administrator fails to act within the law in cases where he or she has no discretion, and (3) any person who violates clean air standards or standards restricting increases in emissions in nonattainment areas. The chief remedy sought by private citizens is an injunction, and as an incentive when it is in the "public interest" the CAA provides for payment of the costs of

---

EPA—National Ambient Air Quality Standards (NAAQS)
  1. Primary Standards—maximum concentration allowed; set with adequate margin of safety to protect against adverse health effects.
  2. Secondary Standards—more restrictive concentration standards to protect property and personal comfort.
  3. Standards are set for the following pollutants: (1) sulfur dioxide, (2) particulates, (3) ozone, (4) carbon monoxide, (5) hydrocarbons, (6) nitrogen dioxide, and (7) lead.

State Implementation Plans
  1. Assigns "emission limitations" to all industry sources of pollutants so that EPA's National Standards (NAAQS) are obtained.
  2. Identifies state's attainment and nonattainment regions and imposes appropriate regulations.

"Dirty Air" Regions	"Clean Air" Regions
(Nonattainment areas—pollution above national standards)	(Attainment areas—pollution below national standards)
Regulations: "emission offset policy."	*Regulations:* "prevention of significant deterioration" (PSD) Divide area into three classes and permit "maximum allowable increases" in sulfur dioxide and particulate matter for each class.
Preconstruction requirements of "major emitting facility": 1. Use of best control technology possible—"lowest achievable emission rate" technology. 2. Certification that *all* other plants are in compliance with "emission limitations" of SIP. 3. New emissions being more than offset by emission reductions elsewhere in area. (Bubble concept—finds the least expensive offsets under "bubble" rather than force the utilization of expensive best technology.)	*Preconstruction requirements* of "major emitting facilities" from a list of industries: 1. Use of best control technology. 2. "Maximum allowable increase" not to be exceeded.

Hazardous Air Pollutants: (1) asbestos, (2) beryllium, (3) mercury, and (4) vinyl chloride.

Figure 23-2. Summary of air pollution regulations.

litigation, including attorney fees, by the polluter. However, if the citizen's action is obviously frivolous or harassing, the court may assess litigation costs to the citizen.

In passing the Clean Air Act, Congress made its intent clear that the CAA was to have its desired effect. Congress presented the EPA and the states in some instances with strong enforcement tools, designed to encourage compliance and to soundly penalize noncompliance. It then becomes the responsibility of the EPA and the states to utilize these tools to enforce the Clean Air Act.

WATER POLLUTION REGULATION

Origin of Water Regulations

The role of the federal government in water quality regulations has developed through a series of federal legislative enactments. The Rivers and Harbors Appropriation Act of 1899 imposed regulation of specific source discharge into navigable waters, primarily seeking to avoid the blockage of navigation. The Water Pollution Control Act of 1958 authorized the surgeon general to investigate the nature of industrial and municipal waste and, therefore, to inform and encourage the states to develop water pollution abatement programs. The Water Pollution Control Act amendments of 1956 provided grants for municipal sewage plants and created a cumbersome "enforcement conference" to prohibit water pollution in one state from endangering the health and welfare of the citizens of another state. The Water Quality Act of 1965 created the Federal Water Pollution Control Administration, later merged into the EPA, and required the states to establish water quality standards for waterways which had to be first "zoned" as to use. Thereafter, the states were to test water quality according to its "zoned" standards and, if it was poor, develop an implementation plan. However, barely over half of the states had developed standards by 1970.

In light of the poor performance of the states, Congress enacted the Federal Water Pollution Control Act of 1972, which established a comprehensive program for making waters safe for fishing and swimming by 1983 and eliminating pollutants from navigable waters by 1985. The act authorized the EPA to specify industrial and municipal effluent emission standards. The EPA was also authorized to specify the pollution control technology that was to be applied to each pollutant source. The act was amended in 1977, and its name was changed to the Clean Water Act (CWA).

National Uniform Effluent Standards

Since water pollution comes from such a wide variety of sources, creating an impossible regulatory task to control all sources, the EPA concentrates on "point sources" which involve all industrial and municipal sources that discharge liquid waste. Agricultural and urban runoff (nonpoint sources) have to be ignored by the EPA for the present.

As to industrial sources, the EPA establishes national uniform effluent limitations on an industry-by-industry basis. Consequently, the pollution control standards for each industry are technology-based. Every firm in the industry utilizes the same technology to meet its effluent limitations. The 1972 Act required industries to comply with EPA standards by July 1, 1977. The technology adopted by the EPA was the "best practicable control technology currently available."

The 1972 Act contained a second phase, in which new standards incorporating the top-of-the-line water pollution control technology were to be instituted by July 1, 1983. However, the 1977 Clean Water Act amendments extended the deadline to 1984 and divided water pollutants into three types, with separate deadlines and control provisions.

Conventional (nontoxic) pollutants are to be controlled by the "best conventional pollutant control technology" by July 1, 1984. The EPA, in determining the appropriate technology, is required to consider the "reasonableness of the relationship between the costs of attaining a reduction in effluents and the effluent reduction benefits derived." New control technologies for conventional pollutants were not to be adopted unless justified by cost-benefit.

The EPA is also required to develop effluent standards to control *toxic* pollutants with the "best available control technology economically achievable" by July 1, 1984. More than 65 toxic pollutants must be controlled, but information on control strategies for toxic pollutants is sorely lacking. Development of toxic standards and control technology will be difficult and costly.

Nonconventional pollutants, such as thermal pollution, are to be controlled by the "best available control technology economically achievable" within three years after the EPA has designated the pollutant and the technology.

The Clean Water Act also requires the EPA to set "new source" effluent standards for 27 major water-polluting industries. Although the goal is no discharge of pollutants, the EPA is required to consider the costs in setting standards for the greatest degree of effluent reduction achievable.

Permit System

The Clean Water Act provides that "the discharge of any pollutant is illegal" without a discharge permit. The EPA applies the uniform effluent standards to each permit application, and thereby defines the obligations of the applicant business. The permit spells out the water pollution control technology that must be utilized, the date of compliance, and the actual limits of pollution that the source may legally discharge. Also, the EPA may reserve the right to modify the permit should new information of toxic pollutants become available. The Clean Water Act requires the permit system to be designed so that states, if they choose, may insert stricter standards than those imposed by the federal standards. For heavily polluted waterways, the federal standards alone are probably insufficient.

Variances

Businesses that are unable to comply with water pollution control specified by the EPA are forced to close down. However, the act provides for two exceptions. First, a business discharging nonconventional pollutants may seek a variance if adoption of the phase II compliance technology would be a significant economic hardship on a firm already implementing pollution control to its financial limits. Second, owners may apply for variance from state water quality limitations on thermal wastewaters. If other businesses along the waterway can absorb additional requirements and the variance would not interfere with public water supplies, the variance from the state water quality limitations may be granted.

Finally, if a business within an industry utilizes different methods of productions for which the standard's technology is inappropriate for their wastewater characteristics, the EPA will develop an alternative set of limitations specifically for that business.

Penalties for Violations

The enforcement provisions of the Clean Water Act are similar to those discussed under the Clean Air Act. The act authorizes the state authority or the EPA to bring civil actions against business violators to obtain compliance. When the EPA determines that a business is violating a law, it must first notify the appropriate state authority about the violation. Thirty days thereafter the EPA may bring action on its own to obtain compliance if the state has taken no action.

The CWA can be enforced through an administrative compliance order, civil action including injunction and civil penalties up to $10,000 per day of violation, or criminal penalties of between $2500 and $25,000 for each day of violation or imprisonment up to one year, or both. Additionally, knowingly making false statements in any required reports or knowingly tampering with monitoring devices carries fines of up to $10,000 or imprisonment of up to six months, or both. It should be noted that the criminal penalties of imprisonment apply only to natural persons and include "responsible corporate officers" when corporations are involved.

Prior to the mid-1970s, the chief emphasis of enforcement of federal water pollution legislation was a combination of negotiation, public opinion, voluntary compliance, and appropriate civil action. The late 1970s witnessed a departure from that emphasis. The EPA began using the criminal sanctions provided in the CWA.

SOLID WASTE REGULATION

The first major attempt to regulate solid waste, the Solid Waste Disposal Act, was passed by Congress in 1965. This act encouraged states to make efficient and safe disposal of solid waste by providing federal assistance to state and local governments in developing solid waste disposal systems.

In 1976, Congress acted to strengthen federal authority in the solid waste disposal area. With air and water pollution laws being given new "teeth" by the amendments of the mid-1970s, it was only appropriate that Congress act in the same manner in the area of solid waste. Accordingly, the Resource Conservation and Recovery Act (RCRA) became the primary solid waste regulatory statute. It absorbed the Solid Waste Disposal Act and placed primary federal authority within the EPA. The act is patterned after the Clean Air and Clean Water Acts, giving the EPA overall national regulatory authority while placing the primary authority for day-to-day enforcement for nonhazardous solid waste disposal on the states.

The EPA's primary responsibility is to identify and issue national guidelines for *hazardous* solid waste. After identifying hazardous wastes, the RCRA authorizes the EPA to provide "cradle-to-grave" control over hazardous waste by utilizing two major control methods. First, the owner of a hazardous waste disposal site must obtain a permit from the EPA and comply with EPA performance standards in order to be considered an approved hazardous waste disposal facility.

The second control mechanism is the "manifest system," which records the movement of hazardous waste from the generator's premises to an approved disposal facility. Generators of hazardous wastes must properly package and label the substances and prepare a document, the "manifest," indicating the name of the generator, the name of the transporter, the name and address of the approved facility to which the wastes are being transported, a description of the waste, and the quantity. The generator must give copies of the manifest to the transporter who obtains the signature of the owner of the approved hazardous waste facility after delivery. The transporter must notify the EPA of any spill in transport and clean up the spill. The owner of the approved disposal facility must send a signed copy of the manifest to the generator so that the generator knows that the quantity of waste shipped was actually received.

The RCRA provides for both civil and criminal penalties. A civil fine of $25,000 per day of violation can be imposed through judicial action. Criminal violations of the act can result in fines up to $25,000 per day of violation or up to one year in prison, or both, for individuals found guilty. If an individual, which is defined to include business organizations and responsible natural persons, knowingly engages in the transportation, treatment, storing, or disposal of solid wastes without a permit, conviction can result in fines up to $50,000 per day of violation or up to two years in prison, or both. Cognizant of the potential for serious health problems developing from improper solid waste disposal, Congress provided for more severe criminal penalties under certain circumstances. If it is shown that there is a knowing violation of any part of the act, that the violator has knowledge that his or her acts place another person in imminent danger of death or serious injury, and that the action demonstrates an unjustified and inexcusable disregard for human life, the violator can be fined up to $250,000 or imprisoned for up to two years, or both. If, however, the violator manifests an extreme indifference for human life rather than an unjustified and inexcusable disregard to human life, then the violator can be fined up to $250,000 or imprisoned for up to five years, or both. Finally, if an organization is found guilty of such violations, it can be fined up to $1 million. Since the RCRA did not deal with problems of cleaning up inactive dump sites or with the cleanup of hazardous waste spills, Congress enacted the Comprehensive Environmental Response, Compensation, and Liability Act in 1980. This act created the "Superfund," which is supported mostly by a system of taxes levied on the production of 42 hazardous chemicals and petroleum products. The act does not apply to oil spills, but it does provide the President with funds to clean up abandoned hazardous sites and to provide assistance in the case of a hazardous spill. However, the President's actions are limited to the expenditure of $1 million. The taxes to support the Superfund are set to terminate at the end of September 1985.

Owners of polluting facilities, whether production or disposal, are liable for all costs of remedial action. The owner's liability may be limited if he or she cooperates in the cleanup efforts and if the release of the pollutant was not from "willful negligence or misconduct." The act also requires businesses to obtain insurance to help pay for damages from the release of hazardous waste.

Private citizens injured by the release of a hazardous substance must litigate their claims in state courts. However, if the injury to the citizen is caused by waste at a dump site in which the owner is unknown, the injured party may make limited claims against the Superfund.

Finally, the act creates a special $200 million Post-Closure Tax and Trust Fund. This is supported by a tax on hazardous waste delivered to a disposal facility and it is to be used to pay for the monitoring and maintenance cost for "closed" hazardous waste sites that have been previously issued permits under RCRA.

ENVIRONMENTALLY HARMFUL PRODUCTS REGULATION

The EPA also enforces laws regulating the production of products that could have adverse affects on the environment. For example, the Clean Air Act requires the EPA to regulate pollution emissions from automobiles, the greatest contributor to the nation's air pollution. The EPA prescribes emission standards for motor vehicles, regulates fuel and fuel additives, and requires the industries to test and document the control devices developed to meet EPA's standards.

The Noise Control Act of 1972 empowers the EPA to develop noise emission standards "to protect the public health and welfare, taking into account the magnitude and conditions of the use of the product, the degree of noise reduction achievable through the use of the best available technology, and the cost of compliance." The EPA has issued noise emission standards for a variety of construction equipment, most transportation equipment, and some electric equipment, such as air conditioners and compressors. A manufacturer found selling a product not in compliance with the noise emission standards is subject to fines up to $25,000 per day, a jail term of not more than one year, or both.

The Federal Insecticide, Fungicide, and Rodenticide Act and the Federal Environmental Pesticide Control Act provide that pesticides must be registered with the EPA before they can be sold to consumers. Only pesticides that will not cause "unreasonable adverse affects in the environment" may be registered.

In 1976, Congress took steps to control the introduction of new chemical substances into the environment that are threatening to the environment and to human health. Under the Toxic Substances Control Act (TOSCA), the EPA is empowered to identify and regulate the use of new toxic substances or new uses of old toxic substances. TOSCA requires the testing of substances that may present "an unreasonable risk of injury to health or environment" so that the dangers of products can be known and prevented prior to the products' distribution.

TOSCA prohibits the manufacture of new substances or new uses of old substances unless the manufacturer or user files a notice with the EPA (together with the results of prescribed tests, a description of quality controls, the disposal characteristics, and other information) 90 days prior to the initiation of use of the substance. If the EPA determines that the proposed substance poses a danger to the environment or to human health, the administrator may issue a proposed order regulating or prohibiting manufacture or use of the substance. The proposed order is challengeable through the administrative process.

As might be imagined, utilization of this process can be long and drawn out. In order to give the administrator additional powers to act quickly where it is deemed necessary, TOSCA empowers the administrator to obtain federal court permission to seize the hazardous substance or to obtain an injunction, or both. Finally, TOSCA empowers the EPA to impose fines up to $25,000 for each violation of the law by way of administrative judicial proceeding. If TOSCA is knowingly or willfully violated, criminal penalties in the form of fines up to $25,000 for each day of violation or imprisonment up to one year, or both, are provided.

OTHER ENVIRONMENTAL REGULATIONS

WILDLIFE PROTECTION REGULATION

Another example of federal regulation of the environment is the Endangered Species Act of 1966 as amended in 1973. This act was designed to identify and protect forms of life in danger of extinction.

The legislative proceedings in 1973 contain numerous expressions of concern over the risk that might lie in the loss of *any* endangered species. Typifying these sentiments is the following statement:

From the most narrow possible point of view, *it is in the best interests of mankind to minimize the losses of genetic variations.* The reason is simple: they are potential resources. They are keys to puzzles which we cannot solve, and may provide answers to questions which we have not yet learned to ask.

To take a homely, but apt, example: one of the critical chemicals in the regulation of ovulations in humans was found in a common plant. Once discovered, and analyzed, humans could duplicate it synthetically, but had it never existed—or had it been driven out of existence before we knew its potentialities—we would never have tried to synthesize it in the first place.

Who knows, or can say, what potential cures for cancer or other sourges, present or future, may lie locked up in the structures of plants which may yet be undiscovered, much less analyzed? . . . Sheer self-interest impels us to be cautious.

The institutionalization of that caution lies at the heart of . . . [the Endangered Species Act].[3]

Application of the act can best be exemplified by the now famous "snail darter" case, *Tennessee Valley Authority* v. *Hill* (1978).[4] In that case, the Tellico

Dam project was halted because it was determined that completion of the project would jeopardize the existence of the snail darter, a small fish on the endangered species list. After the United States Supreme Court had upheld the injunction prohibiting completion of the dam, Congress in 1979 passed legislation specifically exempting the Tellico Dam project from the Endangered Species Act. Congress weighed the social value of the dam (its electrical power while saving consumption of oil) over the value of the snail darter. Congress also noted that over 700 snail darters have been transplanted from the Little Tennessee to the Hiwassee River and seem to be thriving.

STATE REGULATION OF THE ENVIRONMENT

It should not be forgotten that state governments, in addition to participating in the federal scheme of environmental regulation, have the power of environmental regulation within their boundaries. In exercising their "police power," the states have long legislated in the areas of zoning, environmental planning, and regulation of specific uses of land. Recently, for example, all states, and over 500 municipalities, have enacted landmark preservation laws designed to preserve historic landmarks from destruction. In *Penn Central Transportation Co.* v. *City of New York,* 98 S.Ct. 2646 (1978), the U.S. Supreme Court upheld the validity of such laws as long as they did not unreasonably interfere with the reasonable use of such property. If unreasonable interference with the use of the property is embodied within the law, then such legislation is, in effect, held to be an exercise of the "eminent domain" power rather than the police power. Of course, the exercise of eminent domain requires the legislation to compensate the property owner for the state's unreasonable interference with the property.

The steps taken by local governments to improve the environment almost always involve increasing economic costs for private or public enterprises. To minimize pollution abatement costs, the polluters have tried many arguments to avoid the local laws. One argument often advanced is the notion that the Commerce Clause of U.S. Constitution requires uniformity of regulation which is not achieved by state and local ordinances of pollution control and, consequently, the local ordinances are said to be in violation of the U.S. Constitution. The court in the following case had to deal with this argument in relation to Oregon's new "bottle bill."

Bottle Bill

American Can Co. v. Oregon Liquor Control Commission
517 P. 2d 691 (1974)
Court of Appeals of Oregon

This is an appeal from a circuit court decree declaring that Oregon's so-called bottle bill, is valid and denying plaintiffs' . . . application for injunctive relief against the enforcement of the law. Plaintiffs are (a) manufacturers of cans . . . (b) brewers in California and

Arizona . . . (c) out-of-state soft drink canners . . . (d) soft drink companies . . . and (e) the Oregon Soft Drink Association. . . .

The primary legislative purpose of the bottle bill is to cause bottlers of carbonated soft drinks and brewers to package their products for distribution in Oregon in returnable, multiple-use deposit bottles toward the goals of reducing litter and solid waste in Oregon and reducing the injuries to people and animals due to discarded "pull tops." . . .

Plaintiffs' most substantial challenge to the bottle bill is under the Commerce Clause of the United States Constitution.

The development of the one-way container provided a great technological opportunity for the beverage industry to turn logistical advantages into economic advantages. By obviating the expensive necessity of reshipping empty bottles back to the plant for refilling, the new containers enabled manufacturers to produce in a few centralized plants to serve more distant markets. The industry organized its manufacturing and distribution systems to capitalize maximally on the new technology.

The Oregon legislature was persuaded that the economic benefit to the beverage industry brought with it deleterious consequences to the environment and additional cost to the public. The aggravation of the problems of litter in public places and solid waste disposal and the attendant economic and esthetic burden to the public outweighed the narrower economic benefit to the industry. Thus the legislature enacted the bottle bill over the articulate opposition of the industries represented by plaintiffs.

As with every change of circumstance in the market place, there are gainers and there are losers. Just as there were gainers and losers, with plaintiffs apparently among the gainers, when the industry adapted to the development of nonreturnable containers, there will be new gainers and losers as they adapt to the ban. The economic losses complained of by plaintiffs in this case are essentially the consequences of readjustment of the beverage manufacturing and distribution systems to the older technology in order to compete in the Oregon market.

The purpose of the Commerce Clause . . . was to assure to the commercial enterprises in every state substantial equality of access to a free national market. It was not meant to usurp the police power of the states which was reserved under the Tenth Amendment. Therefore, although most exercises of the police power affect interstate commerce to some degree, not every such exercise is invalid under the Commerce Clause.

Plaintiffs acknowledge the authority of the state to act, but assert that the state exercise of its police power must yield to federal authority over interstate commerce because, they claim, the impact on interstate commerce in this case outweighs the putative benefit to the state and because alternative methods exist to achieve the state goal with a less deleterious impact on interstate commerce. . . .

Specifically upholding the authority of the states to enact environmental legislation affecting interstate commerce, the court held in *Huron Cement Co.* v. *Detroit*, 362 U.S. 440 (1960):

. . . Legislation designed to free from pollution the very air that people breathe clearly falls within the exercise of even the most traditional concept of what is compendiously known as the police power. In the exercise of that power, the states and their instrumentalities may act, in many areas of interstate commerce and maritime activities, concurrently with the federal government.

The United States Supreme Court has also made clear that it will not only recognize the authority of the state to exercise the police power, but also its right to do so in such manner as it deems most appropriate to local conditions, free from the homogenizing constraints of federal dictation. . . .

The Oregon legislature is thus constitutionally authorized to enact laws which address the economic, esthetic and environmental consequences of the problems of litter in public places and solid waste disposal which suit the particular conditions of Oregon even though it may, in doing so, affect interstate commerce.

The enactment of the bottle bill is clearly a legislative act in harmony with federal law. Congress has directed that the states take primary responsibility for action in this field. By enacting the Federal Solid Waste Disposal Act (1970), Congress specifically recognized that the proliferation of new packages for consumer products has severely taxed our disposal resources and blighted our landscapes. It disclaimed federal preemption and assigned to local government the task of coping with the problem with limited federal fiscal assistance. . . .

While it is clear that the Oregon legislature was authorized to act in this area, plaintiffs assert that the means incorporated in the bottle bill are not effective to accomplish its intended purpose and that alternative means are available which will have a lesser impact upon interstate commerce. Particularly, they offered evidence to show: (1) that the deposit system is inadequate to motivate the consuming public to return containers, (2) that mechanical means are being developed for improved collection of highway litter; and (3) that public education, such as the "Pitch In To Clean Up America" campaign, is a desirable means of dealing with container litter.

Selection of a reasonable means to accomplish a state purpose is clearly a legislative, not a judicial, function. . . . In particular, the courts may not invalidate legislation upon the speculation that machines may be developed or because additional and complementary means of accomplishing the same goal may also exist. The legislature may look to its imagination rather than to traditional methods such as those which plaintiffs suggest, to develop suitable means of dealing with state problems, even though their methods may be unique. Each state is a laboratory for innovation and experimentation in a healthy federal system. What fails may be abandoned and what succeeds may be emulated by other states. The bottle bill is now unique; it may later be regarded as seminal.

We conclude, therefore, that the bottle bill was properly enacted within the police power of the state of Oregon and that it is imaginatively, but reasonably, calculated to cope with problems of legitimate state concern.

Questions
1. What scheme of regulation was developed by Oregon to reduce litter and solid waste?
2. Does the commerce clause of the U.S. Constitution usurp the police power of the state?
3. Does the state's police power include aesthetic values that may be protected by government?
4. Have federal laws indicated the proper role for states to take in dealing with environmental pollution?

CONCLUSION

Congress, in passing the recent pollution laws, clearly intended to achieve an improved natural environment. Although there has been a significant improvement in reducing environmental pollution, particularly in water, the continuation of improvements remains in doubt.

The laws themselves and their interpretation by the courts have not yet been fully clarified. And in some instances, control technologies have yet to be developed. Congress, the EPA, and industry, each for its own reasons, continue to grapple with the pollution control laws. Even now there have been proposals for the relaxation of pollution laws, particularly the Clean Air Act, in Congress. Industry is bringing many cases to court seeking interpretation of many sections of the statutes. And the EPA itself, under the Reagan Administration, is reconsidering its enforcement policies in several areas. It is unclear what future environmental policies will develop from these political adjustments.

DISCUSSION QUESTIONS

1. Plaintiffs filed a "citizens suit" under Section 304 of the Clean Air Act requesting the court to declare the defendant, Potomac Electric Power Company (PEPCO), in violation of regulations establishing emissions standards and limitations promulgated under the act and to enjoin PEPCO to comply with all regulations under the act. The coal-fire stoker boilers at defendant's facility emit smoke with visible emissions. Clean Air Act regulations prohibit any visible emissions. However, PEPCO asserts that the technological and economic infeasibility of the absolute prohibition on visible emissions constitutes a defense. The plaintiff argues that the act is meant to be "technology-forcing" and that the public health should be given absolute priority over continued operations by noncomplying polluters.

   What is the decision?

2. Georgia's state implementation plan (SIP) for achieving compliance with the National Ambient Air Quality Standards (NAAQS) of the Clean Air Act allows Georgia's power plants to construct tall smokestakes to disperse harmful pollutants over a wider area, thereby reducing the ground level concentration of pollutants in the immediate vicinity of the facility in order to comply with NAAQS. The Natural Resources Defense Council (NRDC) challenged the EPA approval of Georgia's SIP, arguing that the Clean Air Act's policy of "nondegradation" prohibits areas of clean air from being degraded, even though the degradation in issue will not reduce the quality of the air below the level specified by the NAAQS. NRDC argued that the use of dispersion techniques is at odds with the nondegradation policy. The only techniques fully capable of guaranteeing nondegradation are "emission limitation" controls.

   Under what circumstances could Georgia adopt the "tall stack" strategy?

3. Widget Company desires to build a new plant that will emit 150 tons per year of sulfur dioxide. The area selected for the plant site is classified as a "non-attainment" area. What requirements does the Clean Air Act place on Widget Company before it can begin building the plant?

4. Kopy, Inc., discharges pollutants into the local river, which is heavily polluted. The EPA permit requests Kopy to install pollution-control equipment to clean the discharged waters beyond the national standards. The state had requested the tougher standards, and the EPA complied. Kopy seeks a court order to prohibit the EPA from imposing the tougher state standards.

What is the result?

5. Private plaintiffs filed a petition seeking an injunction against the McKeesport Coal and Coke Company, an operator of a large coal mine. In the process of mining, certain impurities are found in coal veins, which are known to the industry as glob. It is the general practice in the industry to dispose of as much of the glob as possible in the underground workings of the mine and to bring the remainder to the surface.

On November 3, 1933, the McKeesport glob pile caught fire through spontaneous combustion, so the defendant started a new glob pile. There is no feasible method of operating a coal mine without a glob pile on the surface, and sooner or later these piles all ignite. Practically every large mine in western Pennsylvania has a burning glob pile.

The plaintiffs ask an injunction against the defendant from depositing glob on the new pile or any place near it, claiming that such an act constitutes a nuisance under the law. Plaintiffs are subjected to annoyance, personal inconvenience, and esthetic damage by the burning of the glob pile. Plaintiffs also testified to complaints of irritated throats, hay fever, asthma, coughs, headaches, and eye and nose irritations, all caused by the noxious effects of smoke, dust, and odors emanating from the glob pile. An equal number of witnesses called by the defendant testified that they lived close to or adjacent to the glob fire, yet they suffered no injurious effects because of that proximity.

Four hundred thirteen men are employed at the mine, and the defendant has never paid a dividend because no year's operation has shown a profit. A decree ordering the plaintiff to buy additional land and deposit the glob elsewhere would be equivalent to ordering the closing down of the mine because defendant cannot afford it.

Applying the common law of torts, how did the court decide in 1935?

6. Defendant, Atlantic Cement Company, operates a large cement plant near Albany, New York. Neighboring land owners alleged the operation of the plant constituted a legal nuisance that creates injury to property from dirt, smoke, and vibration emanating from the plant. Atlantic has an investment in the plant in excess of $45 million and employs over 300 people.

The court held the nuisance existed and that the plaintiffs were entitled to damages for various amounts up to the time of the trial. The court denied the injunction, which left the plaintiff with the opportunity to maintain successive actions for damages thereafter as further damages were incurred.

On appeal, the plaintiffs seek an injunction against the defendant in either of two alternative forms. One alternative is to grant the injunction but postpone its effect to a specified future date so as to give opportunity for technical advances that will permit defendant to eliminate the nuisance. The second alternative is to grant the injunction conditioned on the payment of permanent damages to plaintiffs, which would compensate them for the total economic loss to the property, present and future, caused by defendant's operations.

Should the appellate court approve the trial court's refusal on an injunction (successive damage claims) or adopt one of the plaintiffs' alternatives?

7. ABC Company and XYZ Company both produce products in State W. The companies are the major emittors of particulates in the state. State W must lower its particulates pollution by 20 percent to comply with EPA national standards. ABC is located in an urban city. XYZ is located in a rural area.

What schemes could State W use to allocate the particulates reduction requirement between ABC and XYZ?

8. SAI, Inc. desires to build a new plant in a clean air area. SAI is not in one of the industries listed by the EPA as automatically requiring a preconstruction permit. The new plant will emit 300 tons of pollutants per year. What requirements are imposed on SAI by the Clean Air Act?

9. Tom Herbert owned a truck and was an adventurous man who would "do about anything for a buck." Hot Chemical Co. asked Tom to deliver some hazardous chemical wastes to a dump site. Does Tom have any special legal duties besides being careful?

10. In 1974 the Secretary of Defense announced the closure of the Lexington-Bluegrass Army Depot, which eliminated 18 military jobs and 2630 civilian jobs in the Lexington area. The army prepared an environmental assessment, which concluded that there would be no sufficient effect on the human environment, so no formal environmental impact statement was prepared. The greater Lexington Chamber of Commerce and other plaintiffs sued for an injunction against the Army, saying NEPA extended to the closing of a military base because it had a significant effect on the "human environment." What results?

SUGGESTED READINGS

Jensen, Walter, Jr., Stern, Duke Nordlinger and Mazze, Edward M., "New Efforts Toward a Quieter Environment: The Noise Control Act of 1972," *American Business Law Journal,* Vol. 13, No. 1, Spring 1975, pp. 45–64.

Karp, James P., "Substantive Rights Under the National Environmental Policy Act," *American Business Law Journal,* Vol. 13, No. 3, Winter 1976, pp. 289–314.

Karp, James P., "Judicial Review of Environmental Impact Statement Contents," *American Business Law Journal,* Vol. 16, No. 2, Fall 1978, pp. 127–156.

Karp, James P., "The NEPA Regulations," *American Business Law Journal,* Vol. 19, No. 3, Fall 1981, pp. 295–318.

Roberts, Paul E., "Benefit-Cost Analysis: Its Use (Misuse) in Evaluating Water Resource Projects," *American Business Law Journal,* Vol. 14, No. 1, Spring 1976, pp. 73–84.

Samuels, Linda B., "Surface Mining: Will Supreme Court Precedent Be Reclaimed," *American Business Law Journal*, Vol. 19, No. 1, Spring 1981, pp. 47–62.

ENDNOTES

1. *Natural Resources Defense Council, Inc.* v. *Gorsuch,* 685 F. 2d 752 (1982).
2. *Sierra Club* v. *Ruckelshaus,* 412 U.S. 41 (1973).
3. *Tennessee Valley Authority* v. *Hill,* 98 S. Ct. 2279 (1978).
4. *Ibid.*

part V
MANAGERIAL RESPONSE PROCESS

As large corporations have grown in economic and social power during the twentieth century, more of their activities have become regulated by a number of laws designed to control their activities. Many corporate practices formerly considered simply unethical have now become illegal. The social costs of violating these laws run into billions of dollars. Besides the usual financial losses, these costs include injuries and health hazards to workers and consumers. They also involve the damages done to the physical environment. But perhaps the greatest social cost is the erosion of public confidence in the moral base of our business institutions and of the free capitalistic system. Corporate crime is clearly a subject area in need of research on which better public policies and control techniques can be fashioned. Chapter 24 explores some research on corporate crime and contains an article about a new approach by the law to improve corporate behavior.

It is also true that many individuals argue that business violates ethical obligations today, most of them closely linked to corporate crime: misrepresentation in advertising; deceptive packaging; the sale of harmful and unsafe products; the sale of virtually worthless products; the restricting of product development and the building in of obsolescence; the pollution of the environment, kickbacks and payoffs; improper influences on government; unreasonable competitive practices; personal gain for management; the improper treatment of workers; and the victimization of local communities where plants are located for the benefit of the corporation. However, businesses, and particularly large corporations, commonly complain that most government regulations are largely unnecessary. One could agree readily with this complaint if assurances could be believed that strong ethical practices guided the conduct of corporate business. Chapter 25 contains discussions of basic ethical theories and reveals a Model Code of Business Responsibility. These materials provide a basis for moral inquiry and, hopefully, the development of ethical business conduct.

The final chapter contains discussions of the management of business-government relations. This topic is a vital responsibility of the expanding professional obligations of management.

chapter 24
THE LIMITS OF LAW

The corporate form of organization has allowed business to accumulate large amounts of capital. The capital resources, in turn, enable corporations to develop and adopt technology on a massive scale. The result has been that large numbers of the American population have become relieved of the pressures of physical want. The corporate form has served a useful social purpose.

Yet, there is considerable evidence from opinion surveys that corporate executives believe that unethical and illegal practices are common among corporations. The social-cultural environment within many modern American corporations actually encourages unethical or criminal behavior. Lawbreaking can become a normative pattern within certain corporations. The goals of the corporation often take precedence over the personal ethics of corporate executives. To avoid these results, corporate crime should be studied and public strategies for corporate reform must be developed.

ILLEGAL CORPORATE BEHAVIOR

The following is an excerpt from a report on a study of corporate crime. It was conducted under the auspices and funding of the National Institute of Justice, part of the Law Enforcement Assistance Administration of the U.S. Department of Justice.[1] Besides providing important data concerning illegal corporate behavior, the report discusses some limitations of law in dealing with corporate misconduct. The report also suggests a variety of public strategies for dealing with corporate crime in the future.

Illegal Corporate Behavior

Marshall B. Clinard, Project Director, and Peter C. Yeager, Jeanne Brissette, David Petrashek, Elizabeth Harries (October 1979)

This research represents the first large-scale comprehensive investigation of corporate violations of law. The only previous study of a somewhat similar nature was Edwin H. Sutherland's famed *White Collar Crime,* which was the study of the violations of law by 70 of the 200 largest U.S. non-financial corporations. Corporate crime is, of course, white collar crime, but it is white collar crime of a particular type. Actually, it is organizational crime that occurs in the context of extremely complex and varied sets of structured relationships and inter-relationships between boards of directors, executives, and managers on the one hand and parent corporation, corporate divisions and subsidiaries on the other.

* * *

The Research Study of Corporate Violations

This study has investigated the extent and nature of corporate illegal activities, the data being examined in terms of the corporate structure and the economic setting in which the violations occur. It has concentrated on an empirical investigation of the 582 largest publicly owned corporations in the United States in these areas: 477 manufacturing, 18 wholesale, 66 retail, and 21 service. The major focus has been on manufacturing enterprises, corporations in banking, insurance, transportation, communication, and utilities being excluded. . . . Data cover all enforcement actions obtainable, actions initiated or imposed by 24 federal agencies during 1975 and 1976. This reveals for the first time the wide range of the types of corporate violations, as well as actions initiated and imposed by government agencies. Predictions of violations were attempted through analyses of data in terms of corporate structure and finance that were then used to compare with firm and industry-level data.

Enforcement Actions Initiated

The world of the giant corporations does not necessarily require illegal behavior in order to compete successfully. The fact that 40 percent of the corporations in this study did not have a legal action instituted against them during a two-year period by 24 federal agencies attests to this conclusion. On the other hand, more than 60 percent had at least one enforcement action initiated against them in the period. An average of 4.8 actions were taken against the 300 parent *manufacturing* corporations that violated the law at least once. Moreover, a single instance of illegal corporate behavior, unlike "garden variety" crime, often involves millions of dollars and can affect the lives of thousands of citizens. This study found that almost one-half of the parent manufacturing corporations had one or more serious or moderate violations; and these firms had an average of 3.1 such violations.

The study found that more than 40 percent of the manufacturing corporations engaged in repeated violations. About one-fourth had two or more serious or moderate violations. Further, 83 firms (17.4 percent) had 5 or more violations; 32 corporations (6.7 percent) had 5 or more serious or moderate violations. One parent corporation had 62 actions initiated against it.

Over three-fourths of all actions were in the manufacturing, environmental and labor areas of violation. About one-fourth of the corporations violated these regulations at least once. Illegal corporate behavior was found less often in the financial and trade areas, but even here 5 to 10 percent of the corporations did violate.

Large corporations had a greater proportion of the violations than their share in the sample would indicate. Over 70 percent of the actions were against them but they made up less than one-half of all corporations; and they had more than two-thirds of all serious or moderate violations. Each large parent manufacturing corporation averaged 5.1 violations and 3.0 serious or moderate violations. They most often violate enviornmental and manufacturing related regulations.

The motor vehicle, drug and oil refining industries accounted for almost one-half of all violations, and 4 out of every 10 serious or moderate violations. About 90 percent of the firms in these industries violated the law at least once, and 80 percent had one or more serious or moderate violation.

* * *

Enforcement Actions Completed.

Over 60 percent of the corporations in this study had at least one enforcement action completed against them in 1975 and 1976. The average for those with one or more was 4.2 actions. There were twice as many warnings used as compared to any other sanction type, with an average of 3.6 warnings for those corporations with at least one. Monetary penalties and orders were used many times more often than injunctions and, generally, corporations were not subjected to the full force of the legally possible sanctions when they violated the law. Corporate actions that directly harm the economy were more likely to receive the greater penalties, while those affecting consumer product quality were responded to with the least severe sanctions. Although over 85 percent of all sanctions were administrative in nature, those harming the economy were most likely to receive criminal penalties.

Large corporations received more sanctions than their proportion in the sample would indicate. They had about 70 percent of all sanctions, and tended to be assessed a monetary penalty. Small and medium firms tended to more often receive warnings and orders.

The oil refinining, motor vehicle and drug industries accounted for approximately 4 out of every 10 sanctions for all cases and for serious and moderate cases. They had 3 times more actions than their size in the sample indicates, and they had 2.7 times more actions for serious and moderate cases.

* * *

The average time to complete a case was 6.7 months. Civil cases took the longest (two and one-half years) and administrative cases took about 4 months. Serious cases took approximately 1 year and minor cases about 1 month.

Monetary penalties, although at times extremely large, tend to be in the $1000 range. Less than 1 percent were over $1 million, while over 80 percent were for $5000 or less. When those for $5000 or less were removed from consideration, there were still only about one-fifth that were over $100,000. Because of the fact that large corporations are more often assessed a monetary penalty for their minor violations, there is a general negative relationship between corporate size and amount of monetary penalty.

Corporations were most likely to consent to a future effect court order and to a retroactive administrative order. Consent agreements were more likely than unilateral orders to have a retroactive effect. . . .

Corporate Executives

* * *

Legal difficulties are encountered in the criminal prosecution of executives. First of all, it is not easy to specify legal responsibility due to the division of tasks within a corporation and criminal liability cannot be determined without solid proof of actual knowledge of the violation. Second, corporate violations are usually far more complex than conventional crimes. Antitrust violations, for example, generally necessitate high-order economic statistical data, as well as proof of a written or unwritten conspiracy among individuals. Third, the effects of the violation are extremely diffuse in nature, such as antitrust conspiracies, pollution and substandard foods or drugs.

The government's response to corporate violations cannot be compared to its response to ordinary crime. Generally penalties imposed on top corporate management are quite lenient, particularly if one looks at them in relation to the gravity of the offenses committed, as compared to the penalties imposed on ordinary offenders. Few members of corporate management ever go to prison even if convicted; generally, they are placed on probation. If they do go to prison, it is almost always for a very short period of time. In this study, for example, of the 56 federally convicted executives of all 582 corporations, 62.5 percent received probation, 21.4 percent had their sentences suspended and 28.6 percent were incarcerated. Almost all (96.4 percent) had a criminal fine imposed. Those convicted of price conspiracies and income tax violations were most frequently given more severe sentences. . . .

A total of 16 officers of 582 corporations were sentenced to a total of 597 days imprisonment (not suspended sentences); 360 days (60.6 percent) were accounted for by two officers who received six months each in one case. Of the remaining 234 days, one officer received a 60 day sentence, another was sentenced to 45 days, and another received 30 days. The average for all imprisoned executives was 37.1 days; excluding the two six-month sentences the remaining 14 averaged 16.7 days; and excluding the 60, 45 and 30 day sentences the remaining eleven averaged 9.0 days. The 14 executives who received 60 days or less were all involved in the folding carton price-fixing conspiracy. The other case involved tax fraud. The sentences were often suspended after some parts of them were served.

Problems of modest sentence following criminal conviction of corporate executives may lie with the statutes and the judges, but there are other difficulties in securing a prison sentence. Businessmen may have sought legal advice as to how to circumvent the law even before they committed the offense, and this advice may be cited as evidence of good faith in avoiding any violation of law. Businessmen defendants in criminal cases also hire lawyers known for their skills in defending their clients, presenting arguments about the health problem of the client, his previous clear record, and the unlikely event of his becoming a recidivist, all of which should warrant a light sentence. These legal experts are able to cite many precedents where a businessman charged with similar behavior had not been punished for it. Skilled corporate counsel seek, furthermore, to restrict the evidence presented in court in an attempt to conceal other offenses; plea bargaining by a corporation in a violation may, in fact be used to avoid naming individual members of corporate management so that they will not even be tried. Due to the problems entailed in the imposition of a prison sentence on prestigious corporate executives, some judges have restored to imposing sentences of the performance by them of socially useful activities, a privilege rarely extended to ordinary offenders.

No pattern seems to have evolved from what happens to corporate executives after they have been charged with serious law violations or have been convicted of them. In general, however, most of them are allowed to retain lucrative retirement benefits, while others may have their salaries reduced temporarily. Some are kept in the firm for some time, or at least until the case is finally resolved, largely for public relations purposes. An ordinary criminal offender is almost never retained in his position after he has been found guilty or even charged with an offense. One year after twenty-one corporate executives were fined or sent to prison for making illegal campaign contributions in 1973–1974, for example, twelve still remained in their pre-conviction corporate positions, five had resigned or retired, two were serving as consultants, and two had been discharged.

Predicting Corporate Violations

The various analyses of financial and economic factors produced mixed findings in terms of the original hypotheses. While the financial results have produced some contradictions, financial strain leading to increased violations receives general—if not complete—support, especially for the measures of five-year trends in performance. The measures of firm and industry structure variously act as predicted for some violation types, contradict the hypotheses for others, and prove irrelevant to violations in many cases. . . .

The results indicate that, except for manufacturing violations, the measures of firm and industry characteristics were not strong predictors of corporate violations. This was not an unexpected result. Clearly something else has to be added. A more satisfactory hypothesis is that economic factors operate largely in a "corporate environment" that is conducive to unethical and illegal practices.

Questions

1. What is corporate crime?
2. During the relevant two-year period, did the majority of major corporations avoid violations of law?
3. Since the number of violations per major corporation is small, does this mean the issue of illegal corporate behavior is overdone?
4. Which industries account for most of the violations of law?
5. Did large or small corporations have the greater proportion of violations? Which received more sanctions?
6. On the average, how much time in jail was spent by corporate executives as a result of corporate violations? Why is the figure rather small?
7. What happens to corporate criminals? Do they have difficulty in seeking employment?
8. Are there any variables that are good predictors of corporate crime? What is a "corporate environment" that is conducive to unethical or illegal practices?

CONTROLLING CORPORATE CRIME

The previous study also suggested three broad approaches for controlling corporate crimes: (1) self-developed attitudes and programs of reform, (2) government intervention, or (3) market-consumer pressures. While advocates of free market forces would prefer the latter alternative, it is important to note that it was precisely because of social perceptions of market failures that social pressures developed for government intervention. While the cooperative consumer movement, in theory, offers an alternative method of controlling corporate crime, there are weaknesses to this approach. In the first place, it assumes that persons who will withdraw patronage *know* that a corporation has been engaging in either irresponsible or illegal activities. The identification of social irresponsibility and illegality to a corporation is complicated by the existence of multiple component firms. Secondly, when cognizant of the reputation of the corporation and constantly pressured by favorable corporation advertising to purchase a product, the consumer is not likely to relate the personal failure to purchase a product to the possible control of the corporation. In short, consumer control is lacking and the organization of consumer groups to countervail large corporate sellers has not been widespread, and does not appear to be growing substantially.

Government intervention, in substance and in technique, has been the subject of this book. Parts III and IV have included extensive discussions of the approaches of antitrust and administrative regulations. A few alternate techniques of government intervention should be mentioned here and, then, the prospect of business developing new attitudes and programs of self-reform will be explored in the following chapter.

CORPORATE CHARTERING

Another technique of government intervention is the requirement that all large corporations be federally chartered and consequently subject to the control provisions of such a charter. At present, corporations are chartered under the laws of the various states, not under federal law. Over the years most large corporations have been incorporated in the state of Delaware, where the corporation laws were very permissive. Delaware lacked strong enforcement resources as well as the will to use them. Since the states cannot effectively accomplish regulation against the large corporations, one alternative is for the federal government to take over the chartering.

Advocates maintain that federal chartering would result in greater social responsibility, increased accountability, and wider disclosure of corporate activities. It would also make possible more effective regulation of corporations by various federal agencies, both in prevention and enforcement. Opponents of federal chartering feel the proposal would ultimately destroy the *private* enterprise system.

PUBLICITY AS A SANCTION

Media publicity can be either informal or formal. Informal publicity is that ordinarily carried in the media as news items. Formal publicity is the requirement that the corporation, as part of an enforcement action, give the media some statement of acknowledgement of a violation and the corrective measures being taken. However, studies have indicated that a relatively small number of violations, as well as enforcement actions that involve corporations, are publicized in the general media.

Publicity can also be a sanction in itself and become an effective and practical means of deterrence. Formal publicity methods could include mass media advertisements (e.g., corrective advertising) setting out the details of a corporation's illegal conduct, compulsory notification to the stockholders and to others by means of an annual report, or even a temporary ban on corporate advertising. The proposed new Federal Criminal Code (Section 2005) states that a court may order a convicted corporation to "give notice and explanation of such corrections, in such form as the court may approve to the class of persons or to the section of the public affected or financially interested in the subject matter of the offense, by mail, by advertising in designated areas or through designated media or by other appropriate means."

PUBLIC OWNERSHIP

Public ownership, or nationalization, is one alternative means of socially controlling certain large corporations, possibly the means of last resort. It has been suggested that public ownership should be considered only for those large industries that have become oligopolies with little or no competition and socially irresponsible both to national interests and those of the consumer. Moreover, public ownership could be limited to one firm which, through its competition, could improve the behavior of the remaining firms in the industry.

REGULATING MANAGEMENT STRUCTURE AND DECISION MAKING

In Chapter 3, it was expressed that some people believe the inadaquacy of present regulatory techniques preclude their adoption as the primary means of achieving responsible corporate behavior. They argue that laws and government regulations are generally ineffective in dealing with institutions like business corporations. They point out that the lawmaking process itself suffers from a time lag problem in identifying behavior that should be outlawed. The legal process also operates under an information gap because the government seldom knows as much about business as corporate officials. Finally, they maintain that the legal forums are generally unsuitable to the resolution of complex business-social issues. Christopher Stone argues "that trust in the legal machinery as a means of keeping corporations in bound is misplaced—and that, therefore, something more is needed."[2] And the "something more," according to Stone, is voluntary moral judgments by responsible business people. The role of the law should be limited. Stone's reliance on voluntary moral judgment of businessmen is not novel, but his proposed role for law is an important departure from traditional regulatory techniques.

Controlling Corporate Misconduct[3]
Christopher D. Stone

The control of corporate misconduct has become one of the most significant challenges the society faces. . . . More and more, it is they who invest, produce, distribute, and farm. As a result, a large measure of wrongdoing is inevitably corporate.

* * *

This preeminence of corporations in social activity is a state of affairs that the law inherited, but unfortunately did not plan for. When much of the law and political theory was taking shape, there were indentifiable humans, operating independently of complex institutional frameworks, who did the things that it is the job of the law to prevent. The law responded with rules and concepts concerning what motivated people, and what was possible, just, and appropriate toward them. There were, of course, all manner of corporations—churches, municipalities, guilds, universities—during the years the law was forming. But the courts were rarely pressed to consider whether the rules they were developing might be inappropriate or ineffective to deal with this new breed of social actor. . . .

The industrial revolution gave corporations a prominence, size, and complexity that made further disregard impossible. But only in a few ways did the law account for the corporation as a special sort of actor demanding the attention of specially adapted laws. The exceptions were almost entirely in shareholder-management relations, where the problems that arose were unique to corporations and where there were thus no preexisting rules to accommodate each emerging situation: How many directors did a corporation need? On what grounds could dividends be compelled? To deal with such questions, the law, unfettered by precedent, often ventured directly inside the organization itself, laying down express requirements on the structure of management and the decision process. The directors could vest some of their power in a management committee, but certain decisions (the declaration of dividends, for example) could not be delegated; the corporate officers could make day-to-day decisions (such as how many units to produce), but major organic changes (the sale of assets, or a merger) had to be submitted to the shareholders for two-thirds approval.

But such meddlings with the corporations' internal governance were almost always designed to protect and define in advance the increasingly complex interests of the investor—not those of the corporation's customers, its neighbors, or its fellow citizens. Where the corporation was performing acts that, in theory, the ordinary person could perform—polluting the environment, producing harmful goods, committing crimes (in other words, where it was dealing with the "outside world" rather than with its shareholders)—there already existed a network of rules addressed to "persons." The most economical solution was simply to fit the corporation into this preexisting body of law. . . .

Applying existing law to corporations without distinction was the simplest but not necessarily the best course of action. Had the law considered the problem afresh, it might better have taken into account the special institutional features that render corporations, as a concern of the law, distinct from individuals. Instead, we found ourselves confronting corporations with two basic strategies that had evolved in dealing with ordinary people.

Counterorganizational Measures
Since the corporation itself cannot be imprisoned, the primary counterorganizational measure is simply to confront it, as we do the man in the.street, with a negative profit

contingency (a civil judgment, a criminal fine), if it should wander outside the law—in other words, to threaten its pocketbook. The punishment must "fit the crime," so that a good bookkeeper would recognize that, when the likely gains are balanced against the likely losses, the organization will find the prohibited activity a "bad bargain."

The likelihood that this sort of threat will succeed obviously depends on a corporation's sensitivity to profits, the subject of a debate that has suffered some unfortunate exaggerations on both sides. For example, the supposition that corporations seek to maximize profits is not undermined merely because other goals seem to attract them as well—prestige, expansion, etc. As Alfred D. Chandler has observed, "these other goals also take money . . . profits provide it." The more precise question is whether the pursuit of profit is ever subordinated to the realization of other aims; I think the answer to this is: Yes—but not ordinarily, and not in large measure. Thus, at least as far as the profit-making organizations are concerned, it makes sense to use profit threats as the foundation of our corporate-control strategies. The government communicates to the firms—through law—the price tag for failing to meet society's standards, and then allows each company to make the necessary changes to avoid the penalty in whatever way it can most economically and fittingly devise. This doesn't work badly in the typical situations. Indeed, the law is often less successful in controlling the not-for-profit corporations, such as municipalities and hospitals, whose motives are less easy to identify and grasp.

The problem is that the law must deal with the aberrant as well as the average; thus I think we should be cautious before presuming that the modern business corporation presents nothing more complex than Economic Man writ large. To begin with, the individual actors at each level of corporate activity (shareholders, directors, middle management, workers) are subject to constraints that are often incongruent with the profit of "the corporation" as a whole. In fact, the absence of identity between the shareholders' interests and those of "the corporation" is the very idea behind two of the most basic notions of corporate and commercial activity: limited liability and bankruptcy. The shareholders of a tanker company, for example, are not indifferent if one of its ships runs aground. But if there is a wreck, the shareholders know that, except in rare cases, they cannot be sued as individuals by the injured parties to recover any damages the corporation cannot satisfy. What this means (assuming perfect economic rationality) is that in deciding such matters as routes and how much money to spend on hulls and safety devices (and, indeed, how much money to put into the company), the investors' calculations are skewed toward letting the company impose high risks on society. If no accident results, the shareholders will reap the profits of skimping on safety measures. If a ship runs aground, they will be shielded from full responsibility for the harm they have helped to cause.

Incongruities of this sort are no less troublesome when we turn to the giant "public" corporations that are effectively under the direction of hired managers rather than shareholders. Threats to the corporate treasury do not necessarily intimidate the top executives, whose tenure and salary almost inevitably survive lawsuits untouched; the burden falls on the shareholders. (In fact, an ironic twist of this reasoning has led some courts to treat corporate wrong-doers less severely than individuals, lest the "innocent shareholders"—or, in the case of municipalities, "innocent taxpayers"—suffer). And the vast majority of workers are even more insulated. The farther down the operational ladder, the more the "profit goal" of the total organization (so far as there is one) takes the form of targets and objectives for the shop, the department, and the plant; these "immediate" subgoals and objectives determine the horizons and interests of the employees. The potential for future corporate penalties—the possibility that the controller of the corporation someday might have to write a check in payment of a penalty (perhaps five or six years in the future, given the delays of litigation)—is at most a distant and abstract part of the subgroup's reality.

And to the extent that the individual managers or the organization as a whole are not "rational"—to the extent they do subordinate profit to prestige, or to the excitement of carrying out technology to its logical and dramatic limits—the money threats of the law are oblique, at best.

None of this means that the law's counterorganizational threats are fundamentally misplaced. My concern is rather that there can exist—even within business corporations and more commonly in other organizations—pockets of activity (in the boardroom, or in the plant) that are relatively impervious, for certain periods of time, to the law. However atypical and however limited these pockets may be, we should be concerned that they may exist often enough, and may be of significant enough magnitude, to warrant adopting alternative measures.

Counterpersonnel Measures

The classic alternative—the second basic approach—has been for the law to hold employees individually liable through fines, damages, and even imprisonment. These counterpersonnel measures are undeniably a valuable supplement. But they are less effective than one might suppose, and in some ways may even do more harm than good.

I know this sounds odd, especially to followers of the business press, who are regularly forewarned of the increased vulnerability—if not the imminent imprisonment—of the managerial class. Still, the real risk of personal liability ought to be put in perspective. For willful, self-serving wrongdoing, such as stock swindling (which can be identified with a particular hand and mind), the threat of personal legal liability is certainly real. But for other kinds of corporate misbehavior—e.g., when the employee and his company are unleashing a toxic substance into the community, or allowing distribution of a faulty product—the law's bite is not half as bad as its bark.

Why should this be so? To begin with, when an employee injures others by acting on his own account (as, for example, in many self-benefiting securities violations), he will be the sole target of legal action. But in the more ordinary cases, where an employee is acting on his company's behalf, the corporation, as his principal, will be liable as well. The practical effect is that in most situations a plaintiff proceeds against the corporation, rather than troubling to identify and collect from a particular employee.

Moreover, even when someone—a diligent prosecutor, for example—tries to pursue some accountable flesh, it is not easy to do so. If there really was someone clearly responsible, the organizational underbrush may be too thick to find him. (Did the malfeasance occur during the morning shift, or at night?) More frustrating, the division of tasks may be so extensive that responsibility is impossible to assign, even using the term in its ordinary, moral sense; settling *legal* responsibility is all the more difficult, especially in criminal actions, since the law is reluctant to impose liability without proof of actual knowledge, and the burden of proof favors the defense.

These considerations make it particularly hard for the law to pressure top-level corporate managers, who wield the most power to keep the corporation steered within the law, but who can also claim with considerable justification that they "didn't know" what was going on in the bowels of their organizations, where so much of the trouble is brewing. It is also fairly common that in prosecuting corporate employees (particularly those at the top of their organizations) the law runs into a series of socially ordained hurdles; the prosecution finds itself trying to convict well-spoken, well-dressed, church-going, white community leaders—persons not likely to be judged harshly. Prison sentences are rare, reserved for the headline-grabbing crimes only.

Fines and civil judgments are invoked against corporate employees more liberally than imprisonment. But one should not assume that the individual executive really bears the final brunt. Under the corporation codes of the major states, when an employee suffers a judgment or fine for actions undertaken on behalf of the corporation, he can often get reimbursement (indemnification) from corporate funds; the arrow of whatever law he has broken is obligingly deflected to the corporation itself, and passed through it to the shareholders, and perhaps the consumers and creditors. In other cases, the director or officer may be protected by liability insurance, a coverage provided by perhaps 85 per cent of major American corporations. And even in cases of conduct so willful and unlawful that neither indemnification nor insurance is available, it is almost impossible to prevent a corporation from reimbursing its errant officer (or "good soldier") in other ways—by "bonuses," a delayed raise, or a sweet "consulting" contract.

Some General Problems

There are additional difficulties rooted in the complexity of modern commerce and technology—the sort of society corporations make possible. The legal system evolved around, and responds to, a simpler set of difficulties than the most critical problems we now face.

Consider, for example, the law of negligence, which is at the heart of private legal "repair." A model negligence case is one in which Smith, who is walking across the street, is accidentally but negligently hit by Jones' carriage. Note that 1) Smith knows *that* he has been injured; 2) Smith knows *who* has caused the injury; 3) it is possible to assess fairly well the *nature and extent* of his injuries; and 4) the *technical inquiry* involved in analyzing what happened is not too complex—i.e., simple laws of physics are involved, within common-sense experience. (The model also assumes that if the legal damages can be lain at the feet of the responsible actor, he is likely to change his behavior in the future; as we have already seen, this assumption is problematic when a corporation is involved.)

But contrast this model case with the situations that are increasingly of concern in society today. The food we will eat tonight (grown, handled, packaged, and distributed by various corporations) may contain chemicals that are slowly killing us. But while we may have misgivings in principle, we cannot know with certainty *that* we are being injured by any particular product, or *who* might be injuring us. We would also have a difficult time proving the *nature and extent* of our injuries (even more so proving the extent attributable to any particular source). Finally, the evidence to be evaluated is far more complex and technical than in the model case—perhaps so much so that the courts or even agencies cannot realistically be expected to unravel it, especially after the fact. Worst of all, by the time we discover what is happening—for example, that teenage girls are developing vaginal cancer because of medication their mothers took before they were born—it is often too late.

Moreover, at some point the costs associated with the law's traditional approaches transcend the benefits. Some rules are clear enough, and command enough respect, that they are ordinarily self-enforced. But the less the sense that the law is right, the greater the costs of policing. Some of the costs are obvious: administering and staffing court systems and administrative agencies. There are costs of carefulness: Keeping harmful drugs off the market is a valuable goal, but the result may be a delay in getting valuable medicine to patients who need it. There is overkill: injunctions that shut down factories to obviate what would have been a lesser harm to the community. There are the costs of outright error: We command less flammability in children's sleepware, only to discover later that the "remedy"—a flame retardant—is carcinogenic. And there are the subtle costs of delay: By the time we comprehend the dangers posed by polyvinyl chloride and asbestos, huge investments and even patterns of life have built up around them, making changes "unrealistic."

Invading the Corporate Structure

It is against these drawbacks that we should evaluate the emergence of a new approach to the control of corporate misconduct. The harbingers are so unheralded, and on such scattered frontiers, that few people have yet recognized it as a distinct new legal genus, and one of considerable significance.

Traditionally, the legal efforts to control corporate misconduct have taken two tacks. The first has been to allow a firm a great deal of autonomy in its planning and implementation, but to subject it to penalties if its choices turn out badly. If a manufacturer's product is substandard and causes injury, the company (under the counter-organizational strategies) or sometimes select employees (under the counterpersonnel strategies) may be held answerable. The second approach (which can be viewed as evolving from perceived short-comings in the first approach), has been to displace the judgment of the firms with the judgment of public agencies regarding certain product, service, or more recently, work-place qualities. Department of Transportation regulations, for example, require that autos include seatbelts; the Occupational Safety and Health Administration (OSHA) requires that certain guard rails be 42 inches high.

By contrast, in the developing style of corporate control, the law neither stands aside until harm has been done, nor does it impose inflexible standards. The idea, instead, is to decrease the likelihood of harmful behavior through direct legal requirements regarding corporate *management structure* and *decision processes*. This is not a wholly new approach, but it has been used in the past only sparingly and, as I observed earlier, ordinarily in the interests of the investor. As a condition of enjoying corporate privileges, a business must establish a board of directors (usually with at least three members), a president, and (varying from state to state) perhaps a secretary and a treasurer. But traditional law has not gone beyond that to insist upon designated medium-level and lower-level management positions. We allow a company handling explosives to decide, wholly on its own, whether to have an executive in charge of safety, and if so, to determine his powers and level in the management structure.

In the past few years, however, there have been indications that this historical reluctance to invade the corporate management structure is fading. In 1973, a consent decree settling numerous charges of discrimination against women and racial minorities directed the Bell companies to establish compliance officers whose duties—mostly monitoring of hiring, firing, and advancement—were spelled out in detail. The current regulations of the Food and Drug Administration (FDA) require the drug companies to establish quality-control units, many of whose powers and obligations are prescribed by the government—i.e., withdrawn from the sole discretion of the companies. In 1974, in settling a civil fraud action against Mattel, Inc. (growing out of improper financial reporting), the Securities and Exchange Commission (SEC) forced the giant toy manufacturer to establish two special committees of the board—one on financial control and audit, the other on litigations and claims. The functions of the committees are not left for the corporation to establish—as is traditional—but are spelled out in the order of the court.

Such recent "invasions" of organizational autonomy have not been limited to establishing new posts and committees. In several areas, the "outside world" has begun to prescribe criteria concerning who may hold, and who may be disqualified from holding, certain corporate jobs. Requirements have been imposed on corporate internal information systems, with provisions that data of a specified sort must be gathered by firms, and considered by designated officers for action. The recent FDA regulations, for example, require that responsible corporate officials be notified in writing of possible drug-products defects, so they will not be able to claim later that they "knew nothing about it."

In other areas, the managerial level at which decisions of a certain kind must be made is no longer solely a matter of company discretion: The Federal Communications Commission allows radio broadcasters the final say on playing records that glorify illegal drugs, but insists that "someone in a responsible position [i.e., "a management-level executive at the station"] know the content of the lyrics." Internal lines of authority have been specified; by law, those who audit a quality-assurance program at a nuclear plant must be independent of the areas being audited.

Perhaps most intrusively of all, the "outside world" is increasingly taking a hand in the selection process by which key corporate slots are filled: Directors and special counsels have been "negotiated" into corporations, with court, agency, and/or plaintiff-shareholder approval. Such actions are appearing mostly in response to securities-law violations. But at least one federal judge has warned a recidivist corporate polluter that if it did not mend its ways, the court would send its own designate into the company—as a sort of in-house "probation officer"—to take over the pollution-control activities of corporate officers who might be interfering with the process of rehabilitation.

It is not just the profit-making corporations that have been subject to these developments. Within the past few years mental hospitals, prison systems, and school systems have been placed in "receivership," as it were, by federal and state judges, with the courts appointing trustees or their equivalents and occasionally ordering some restructuring of internal organization and procedures. Recent reports on the CIA and FBI have urged bureaucratic restructuring as a means toward tighter control. And the National Institute of Mental Health is laying down guidelines for genetic research (primarily in universities and research institutions) that detail critical features of internal management.

Organizational-Adjustment Measures

All these forms of control can be classified as what I call "organizational-adjustment measures." Unlike the traditional approaches, their focus is not so much on what the organizations *do,* but on the ways that the organizations *decide.* In general, the strengths of these new approaches are almost point for point the drawbacks of the traditional measures. The traditional measures are oriented remedially. The organizational-adjustment measures focus on prevention. The traditional measures undeniably have a prospective element insofar as they raise threats of future liability. But as we saw, there are reasons to doubt that threats to organizations or their employees will induce the most appropriate changes in information systems, role definitions, authority structures, technical programs, etc. By contrast, the new measures prescribe the presumably appropriate changes directly.

The traditional approaches, insofar as they are based on administrative or legislative rule-making, have an even more fundamental drawback: the inevitable lag between the identification of a problem and the institution of a rule to cover it. Are employees who work with asbestos being subjected to high risks of cancer? What psychological and physical dangers lurk in various forms of manufacturing processes? What are the dangers of various forms of pesticides to field workers, consumers, and the environment? Tragically, these are all problems that corporations were anticipating (or could have anticipated, given adequate adjustments) long before the lawmakers got wind of them. It is the company doctors who first treat the injuries, company chemists who live with and first test the new compounds, and company health records in which data gathers. One of the virtues of the organizational-adjustment measures is that by requiring corporations to pinpoint areas in which rule-making may be needed, organizations are, in effect, brought into the law-making process.

Now, of course, nothing the law does is ever so one-sidedly good, and I cannot deny that these organizational-adjustment measures, like much else that emanates from our vast governmental bureaucracy, will have their own costs and complications. Requiring special personnel and tasks imposes expenses that can, from case to case, exceed the most optimistically anticipated benefits. Other measures risk politicizing corporate policies and personnel selection, with unforeseeable but troublesome implications. And there is a toll these measures could exact in organizational innovation and efficiency. Universities aim to educate; armies, to fight; hospitals, to treat and cure. These goals provide a context in which commands are interpreted and actions synchronized. The more the intrusions reinforce aims that seem inconsistent or discordant—or are just plain stupid—the more energy will be wasted, in resistance and bad feelings.

The True Costs

All these costs concern me, but I think they must be kept in perspective. Sometimes the true costs seem rather low on any scale of measurement. Consider the Nuclear Regulatory Commission's decision that a licensee establish a security organization and "maintain and follow written procedures which document its structure and . . . detail the duties of . . . individuals responsible for security." Such an approach, which leaves it up to the licensee to supply the details of organizational responsibility, can hardly be faulted as either expensive or stultifying. Yet it has the virtue of forcing the company to think through problems and relationships that it might not otherwise come to grips with, and to clarify what is expected of each individual. From the point of view of costs, one wonders what real objections there can be, other than that it increases the accountability of persons who would rather remain anonymous.

We should also keep in mind that in many situations the organizational-adjustment measures may prove a lot less costly and less stultifying than the most likely alternatives— such as an outright injunction against production, or a product recall, or increased government authority over the most minute details of operation. In one of the first occasions when the courts and the SEC became involved in the appointment of a special outside director, the idea came not from the government but from one of the corporation's own defense lawyers—the alternative would have been to plunge the company into receivership. Similarly, although Mattel had to spend many thousands of dollars to implement the settlement mentioned above, the arrangement may have been a relatively inexpensive way to restore consumer, creditor, and investor confidence in a scandal rocked company. Indeed, Mattel has not split apart—as some might have predicted—from the divergent forces of all those special directors, committees, and counsel, but has recently turned a profit.

Sometimes, it is true, the costs of internal invasions will prove large and nagging— such as with the extensive pre-market testing required under the new Toxic Substance Control Act. But even then, who can say that the benefits may not be greater still? Two chemical spills alone—of kepone into the James River and PCB into the Hudson—have caused losses running perhaps into the hundreds of millions of dollars, and considerable human suffering. The long-range effects of aerosols on the atmosphere are still unknown, but potentially beyond measure.

I do not mean to suggest that the organizational-adjustment measures are foolproof or that—had they been in operation—they would have nipped all these problems in the bud. But in so many of the commercial tragedies of recent years, it is striking how many clues of danger there were, which were not acted upon because of institutional weaknesses.

Some General Guidelines

I draw several conclusions from all this. Society will, and in my view should, increasingly explore organizational-adjustment measures as a means of preventing corporate misconduct. Such measures are, however, fraught with risks; before we see their wholesale employment, considerable thought must be given to the sorts of situations that might initially warrant their employment on an experimental basis, as we try to learn more about their strengths and weaknesses.

It is probably easiest to justify the use of the measures when the agency or group desiring the internal adjustments has access simply to bargain for the changes. . . . Traditional union demands have involved fixed targets (wages, hours) rather than an ongoing involvement in the decision process. But at some point, the employees' marginal welfare will dictate a shift in focus. For example, the Oil, Chemical, and Atomic Workers have increasingly sought representation on the company committees that establish health and safety standards. Rather than to discourage such demands or rule them out of order as "invasions of management prerogative," such practices should be encouraged, to see if they might be molded into practical alternatives to some of the externally imposed mechanisms of, e.g., OSHA, which are less subject to cost-benefit constraints.

* * *

There are other situations in which several companies in an industry—ordinarily the more responsible and financially stable—will favor a particular measure (an extra degree of pre-market testing, say), but will be reluctant to adopt it unilaterally, fearing a competitive disadvantage. In this case, a government-"mandated" organizational change is nothing more than a way of implementing broadly accepted minimum standards. As a result, resistance is likely to be minimal, and success high. Such changes do have one interesting drawback (in common with a good deal of legislation): Since the costs are more readily borne by the larger companies, the extra protection of the organizational-adjustment measures may clash with some of the values that underlie the antitrust laws—such as preserving competition.

Beyond these areas in which the organizational adjustments are negotiated or generally acceptable, justification becomes more difficult. The strongest argument for intercession is that an organization has already broken the law or caused serious injury, and the internal adjustments are demanded as a condition of probation. Corporate probation is a notion that has received surprisingly scant attention, especially considering the unavailability of other remedies used in dealing with individuals—e.g., imprisonment, or psycho-therapy as a condition of release. Under a model corporate rehabilitation bill that I have drafted, when a company has been convicted of a criminal offense or subjected to a civil judgment in an amount greater than $250,000, the court may hold a hearing to determine whether the conduct giving rise to the judgment arose from an uncorrected pattern of company policies, practices, or procedures, and whether the company might reasonably be demanded to make changes in them after considering costs and benefits.

If the court so found, it could order the company to report in a "proposed rehabilitation agenda" why, in its opinion, the wrongful conduct had occurred, what measures it proposed to prevent a recurrence, and which officers would be responsible for carrying out the agenda. (If the company believed that no special rehabilitative measures were necessary or feasible in the circumstances, it would so state and explain.) When an agenda acceptable to the court and interested parties was arrived at, its terms would be, in effect, a probation order. I doubt that there would be widespread need for the courts to exercise such powers, but they would be important to have on hand, especially to deal with corporate recidivists—the chronic price-fixers, polluters, etc.

*   *   *

Finally, there is a range of situations—unfortunately, the broadest—that possesses none of the simplifying features of the cases discussed above. Where our concern is with staving off damage from toxic substances or dangerous drugs, for example, the interests involved cannot as satisfactorily be brought into negotiation, the risks of allowing "one bite of the apple" may seem too large, and some of the measures the society might propose (e.g., intensive pre-market testing) may lie well beyond the minimum standards the organizations will accept as appropriate. Each case will have to be judged on its own merits, and one can only hope that some sense of proportion will be maintained. How serious, in terms of magnitude and irreversibility, is the harm we are trying to prevent? Are the existing measures for coping with the problem really inadequate, and are there alternative methods available? What costs will the contemplated organizational-adjustment measures impose? And if they are implemented, what is the likelihood that they will succeed? Are there procedural "ground rules" we can establish to allay the conflicts and confusions?

Restoring Cooperation

How well organizational-adjustment measures will work, I cannot say; the answers will obviously vary from case to case. But in spite of my own reservations, I think that in many areas such measures are going to spread—and spread successfully—precisely because the corporations will come to recognize that, as a way of dealing with a significant range of problems, the idea has something in it for them, as well as for the public.

This may sound odd. But what is most evidently missing in our corporate/social relations today, and needs to be restored, is a measure of mutual trust and respect. As things stand, we are settling into a self-defeating cycle in which the anti-corporate sentiment is increasingly shrill and ill-informed, and the corporate response is too often self-defensive, unheeding, and unconstructive. When the evidence suggests a possible problem—like work-related cancer—governmental agencies, distrustful of what is going on within the corporation's walls, will be inclined to slap together a battery of regulations without adequate information, if only to protect themselves from criticism.

In such circumstances, some systematic integration of the "inside" with the "outside" could lead—and may be the only way to lead—to new, more productive patterns of cooperation. From the point of view of corporate management, it seems no great hardship to provide assurances that internal regulations (for example, quality control) are being carried out effectively and in good faith—and to identify those now-anonymous employees who will be accountable if they are not.

In any event, such an arrangement is a lot less intrusive than having Washington take over a growing number of decisions on the most minute details of operations, or being forced to collect and hand over ream upon ream of undigested raw data. From the point of view of the regulator, there are also several advantages. It is far less costly for the government to send a single inspector to certify a quality-control system, than to try to oversee each and every detail of operation. Similarly, to contain bribery, it makes sense to conscript the firms themselves into enforcement service, by requiring them to institute appropriate internal accounting procedures—if only because there are simply not enough federal auditors, thank goodness, to go around. To regulate behavior in this fashion, with some degree of irreducible "self-policing," involves a larger measure of trust than the most outspoken corporate critics may be prepared to allow. But they should realize that when the law tries to overextend its reach, there is inevitably a tendency for the organizations increasingly to wink at violations that are not likely to be detected, and to comply only begrudgingly, when it is prudent to do so. (Resistance to law need not always take the form of foot-dragging or fudging data; one of the most effective ways for a corporation to keep "those idiots" off its back is to answer their requests with truckloads of data.)

All these measures will undeniably bring along their own red tape. My hope is that as a sort of historical quid pro quo, there will be a reduction elsewhere in the inevitable and unnecessary paperwork that results when the government has to second-guess the corporations from a distance, or fire shotguns—when a less suspicious and more cooperative effort might do every bit as well.

Questions
1. What reasons brought the law to treat corporations as individuals? What result has this approach had on the internal governance of the corporation?
2. What is the primary counterorganizational measure in dealing with corporate crime? What reasons exist for the poor success of this strategy?
3. What is the major counterpersonnel measure for dealing with corporate crime? What reasons exist for the poor success of this strategy?
4. Why are not consumer suits sufficient to bring about reformed corporate behavior?
5. Identify the two approaches that laws have taken to control corporate misconduct.
6. What is the newly developing style of corporate control called "organizational-adjustment measures"?
7. What are the "costs" of adopting organizational-adjustment measures? What are the benefits?
8. How might the organizational-adjustment measures clash with the purpose of antitrust laws?
9. How might the organizational-adjustment measures instill societal confidence in business institutions? Identify specific organizational-adjustment measures that may be adopted to improve corporate social behavior.

CONCLUSION

The effectiveness of law in controlling corporate misconduct is limited. In light of this fact, Stone argues the role of the law *should* be limited. The role of the law in corporate affairs should be analogous to the law's use of a jury: where the court doesn't second-guess the jury, but merely determines the information the jury receives and ensures that the jury is composed of a representative cross-section of the citizenry. Similarly, the law could mandate "impact studies" or otherwise ensure that corporate decision makers are fully informed, and, second, impose some requirements to make the corporate decision makers more representative of society. In this manner, Stone proposed legislation that regulates the decision-making process, but not the decision itself. Instead, he is willing to rely on the moral judgments of a representative cross-section of corporate directors in the same way that society relies on jury members to render competent decisions in trials.

DISCUSSION QUESTIONS

1. In 1972 Ford Motor Company was fined $7 million for violation of the Environmental Protection Act. Yet, according to *Business Week's* Executive Compensation Survey, the second and third highest paid executives in the U.S. were Ford Chairman, Henry Ford II ($887,795) and Ford President, Lee Iacocca ($873,852). Neither gentlemen received a pay cut in 1973; in fact each received pay increases. Do these facts suggest any problems in dealing with corporate crime?

2. The behavior of most individuals is socially responsible, not because of the threat of the law, but because of the mechanisms of guilt, shame, anxiety, or conscience. These have been internalized in such individuals through the forces of family, school, church, or peer groups. Hence, most potential antisocial activity is repressed by self-induced moral argument and the law is only a last resort. Does the corporation possess such mechanisms? Or must the law carry a greater burden of creating socially acceptable behavior by organizations?

3. The major sanctions of the law to control human beings are punishment, rehabilitation, or removal from society. Which of these has been utilized by society in dealing with corporate crime? Do these sanctions suggest any new approaches?

4. Fines are aimed at the corporation's profits. Is the strategy effective against corporations with multiple goals—expansion, prestige, or innovation?

5. Executives in business often indicate that production of an item that will not sell, or deterioration of market shares, are failures that they are supposed to avoid. But being sued by the antitrust division or being a defendent in a product liability suit are situations characterized by people in business as a "mess" which "could happen to anyone." Do they perceive these failures as attributable to other causes for which there is no "loss of face"?

6. An automobile company has retooled to produce a new model car. A test driver tells his supervisor that the car turns over too easily. The supervisor knows that this information is not going to be welcomed "upstairs." Is it a natural tendency for "bad news" not to rise to the top?

7. R-M is a pharmaceutical company that is developing a drug called MER/29, which it believes has a high promise of repressing cholesterol. When the

company filed a new drug application with the FDA seeking permission to place MER/29 on the market, the application contained false statements about the number of rats that had developed eye problems. The true results of the study were withheld from the FDA.

After the drug was marketed, approximately 500 individuals who took the drug developed cataracts. One individual who sued for damages was awarded $18,000 in compensation and $100,000 in punitive damages on the ground that responsible corporate officials had knowledge of the test results of MER/29 and joined in a policy of nondisclosure of information to the FDA.

On appeal, the justices observed that the possibilities of multiple punitive awards by hundreds of plaintiffs are "staggering," and if the company did not have sufficient insurance, innocent stockholders would suffer extinction of their investments for a "single management sin." Consequently, they reversed the punitive damage award. What is your opinion of the law's success in this case?

8. The insurance subsidiary of Equity Funding created $20 billion worth of bogus insurance. Corporate employees wrote policies for nonexisting human beings and "re-sold" these policies to other insurance companies. The mechanics of covering up this fraud were talked about in the offices and in company corridors. Teams of employees worked after hours forging policy files that auditors had specifically requested. Why is the threat of law enforcement not sufficient to eliminate these kinds of practices?

9. Reserve Mining Company mined iron ore on the shore of Lake Superior and disposed of waste by dumping it into the lake. The waste was supposed to fall to the bottom of the lake without mixing with the water. Reserve Mining was extremely profitable, having earned 90% on owner's equity in 1973–74.

In 1971 the Environmental Protection Agency determined that the discharged waste contained asbestos fibers that infiltrated the drinking water supply of Duluth, Minnesota. A trial was held to determine whether the threat to health was sufficient to shut down Reserve. During that trial, representatives of Reserve argued that they could modify their lake discharge method to avoid the problem, even though their own studies indicated that this was not feasible. Why would a corporation adopt a policy of "lying" to the court? What kind of organizational adjustments might be made by the law to avoid this kind of illegal corporate behavior?

10. Ford Motor Company produced the Pinto with the gas tank located behind the rear axle and only 3¼ inches behind the differential housing. In rear-end collisions, the tank would be pushed into the differential housing, which would work like a can opener on the tank, spewing contents into the passenger's compartment. Ford had films of this happening in 20 m.p.h. collisions. Ford carefully calculated whether the savings from failure to redesign would exceed the cost of possible lawsuit from the defective design. Ford

opted for the method of lowest cost, which was not to redesign safer tanks that would cost $10 to $15 per car. Is Ford's calculation economically justified? Socially justified? Is this an example of corporate crime?

11. Some authors have suggested that a role bias may cause a "systematic perceptual discrepancy" that occurs between the uninvolved observers of events and the actors as participants in those events. There is a general tendency for actors to explain their actions as a product of "situational" determinants, whereas observers tend to explain the same actions as a consequence of the actor's personal "dispositions." The bias is produced by the different availability and salience of relevant information to each party. For example, the party observing an individual trip on the sidewalk will conclude the person tripped due to clumsiness, whereas the person who tripped will tend to blame the paving of the sidewalk. The actor has more complete biographical knowledge and can recognize his or her own inconsistent behavior. The observer is better informed about the way other people respond to the same external events.

When executives from large companies that were convicted of price fixing were interviewed as to the cause of this illegality, senior corporate executives consistently identified *dispositional* factors of the individuals directly involved as the cause of the conspiracy. They viewed their company's involvement as the consequence of uncontrollable variations in human morals, obedience, and intelligence. Senior corporate executives saw violators as criminals to be punished for their wrongdoings as a deterrence from other such temptation. They look to tools such as employee selection surveillance, rewards tightening, and policy clarification to help improve legal compliance.

On the other hand, divisional executives, who were more involved in the conspiracy, had more sympathy for *situational* explanations of causality. They complained of nebulous conflicting company goals in the face of declining demand for their products and the external tightening of antitrust enforcement. The convictions, to this group, were not an example of unethical conduct; instead they represented the difficult business conditions and lack of political clout in the industry. Rather than tightening company disciplinary policies and formal controls, the divisional executives felt that the companies needed to make changes in their business strategy to gain more control over the market, and hence be less susceptible to external pressures.

May resentment of further discipline cause divisional executives to feel justified in devising means of avoiding detection rather than eliminating price fixing activity? Does the law have a role to play in developing an effective integration of the environmental perceptions of these two levels of management?

SUGGESTED READINGS

Brennan, Bartley A., "A Legal-Economic Dichotomy: Contributions to Failure in Regulatory Policy," *American Business Law Journal*, Vol. 14, No. 1, Spring 1976, pp. 53–72.

Ermann, M. David and Lundman, Richard J., *Corporate and Governmental Deviance* (New York: Oxford University Press, Inc., 1978).

Ermann, M. David and Lundman, Richard J., *Corporate Deviance* (New York: CBS College Publishing, 1982).

Herman, Edward S., *Corporate Control, Corporate Power* (Cambridge: Cambridge University Press, 1981).

Miller, Arthur Selwyn, *The Modern Corporate State* (Westport, Conn., Greenwood Press, Inc., 1976).

Millstein, Ira M. and Katsh, Salem M., *The Limits of Corporate Power* (New York: Macmillan Publishing Co., Inc., 1981).

Spiro, George W., "A Taxonomy for Comparative Research into Non-State Legal Systems in Economic Organizations," *American Business Law Journal,* Vol. 15, No. 2, Fall 1977, pp. 211–224.

Stone, Christopher D., "Corporate Vices and Corporate Virtues: Do Public-Private Distinctions Matter (Symposium: The Public-Private Distinction)," *University of Pennsylvania Law Review,* Vol. 130, June 1982, pp. 1441–1509.

ENDNOTES

1. The National Institute of Justice and the Project Director, Dr. Marshall B. Clinard, have granted permission to reprint this excerpt from the study. The opinions expressed in the study are those of its authors and do not necessarily represent the official positions of the U.S. Department of Justice. The study was supported by a grant of $247,839 from the National Institution of Justice for a period of 22 months. Previously, two pilot research grants were given by the University of Wisconsin Research Committee. Professor Clinard and Peter Yeager later published a more comprehensive book, *Corporate Crime,* in 1980 through the Free Press, Macmillan Publishing Co.

2. Christopher D. Stone, *Where the Law Ends: The Social Control of Corporate Behavior* (New York: Harper Colophon Books, 1975).

3. Reprinted with permission of the author from *The Public Interest,* No. 48, Summer 1977, pp. 55–71. © 1977 by National Affairs, Inc.

chapter 25
MANAGERIAL ETHICS

As was indicated in Chapter 3, professional managerial philosophy accepts the idea that the legitimacy of business is primarily based on economic and legal criteria. Consequently, business behavior must be responsive to market forces and legal directives. These social obligations imposed by the marketplace and by the law are proscriptive of business behavior. Management discharge of its economic and legal obligations begins with a thorough knowledge of the purposes and particulars of those obligations. Therefore, management devotes considerable time and energies to the research and investigation of present market conditions and anticipated trends. Similarly, management must understand the legal constraints on its decision making.

Preceding materials in this book have clearly demonstrated that business managers are increasingly encountered with rules and regulations of a variety of governmental regulatory bodies. The laws, in effect, have often emerged as basic determinants of business activities. Thus, fundamental regulatory schemes and institutional arrangements of the legal process become part of the necessary base of knowledge of every professional manager who wishes to understand the environment within which business operates.

In addition, Chapter 3 pointed out that society also expects business firms to be socially responsible. This implies that business behavior should be "congruent with prevailing social norms, values, and expectations."[1] In contrast to the proscriptive nature of business's economic and legal obligations, the social responsibilities are prescriptive in nature, involving the exercise of ethical analysis and discretionary judgment. Developing business decision-making systems to integrate social values and formulate decisions consistent with social expectations is an enlarged management challenge.

Despite the large body of literature dealing with the social responsibilities of business and the expansive rhetoric and expenditures of business in attempting to comply with its social responsibilities, it is very doubtful that anything like a truly socially responsible business firm will ever evolve. Business firms are limited in their ability to respond to social problems. They cannot sufficiently divorce themselves from their major function as an economic unit. Moreover, a firm cannot unilaterally engage in a social action that increases its cost and prices without suffering a competitive disadvantage with other firms that do not undertake social action. Moreover, the American competitive market system and the laws of antitrust preclude competitors from agreeing to pursue common policies dealing with social problems. Consequently, the only way that concerted action can be directed at social problems is when the government through laws makes all competitors engage in the same activity. Hence, socially acceptable business performance is less the function of self-initiated actions than it is the result of compulsive laws.

Neil Chamberlain, in *The Limits of Corporate Responsibility,* has noted:

. . . [E]very business . . . is, in effect, 'trapped' in the business system that it has helped create. It is incapable, as an individual unit, of transcending that system. . . . [T]he dream of the socially responsible corporation that, replicated over and over again, can transform our society is illusory. . . . Because their aggregate power is not unified, not truly collective, not organized, [business firms] have no way, even if they wished, of redirecting that power to meet the most pressing needs of society. . . . Such redirection could only occur through the intermediate agency of government rewriting the rules under which all corporations operate.[2]

Thus, it appears, the "social responsibilities" doctrine as a method for improved business behavior is limited.

However, as the previous chapter pointed out, there are limitations in the legal process as well. The weaknesses of the legal process preclude the obtainment of lawful business conduct, much less obtain social (ethical) goals that exceed the legal requirements. It was these "limits of law" that led Stone to propose a new legal approach to business-social problems. At least, Stone's ideas seem to deserve experimental use. But in the meantime, the weaknesses of the legal-regulatory system require the expansion of any alternate system that holds promise for improved social performance by business.

The growing societal expectations concerning business responsibilities places increased pressure on business to review the ethical conduct of its decisions and practices. Management must show more concern with the issue of ethical standards of business conduct. The inculcation of ethical principles forms the very basis of all crime prevention and control, whether ordinary, white collar, or corporate crime. The development of stronger business ethics must come first from the individual business firm and second from business ethical codes recognized and supported by the business community. The study of ethical theories seems warranted as a logical starting point for the development of ethical corporate conduct.

ETHICAL THEORIES

Moral theories may be initially divided into two basic groups: those that rely on consequences of an action in determining its morality, and those that rely on factors other than consequences.

CONSEQUENTIAL THEORIES

Many theorists argue that the moral rightness of an action is to be determined by looking at its consequences. Such consequentialists determine what is right by considering the ratio of good to evil that the action produces. One consequentialist, an egoist, contends that an act is moral when it promotes the individual's best long-term interests. While the Greek philosopher, Epicurus, is a famous egoist who expressed the view that only pleasure is good in itself and worth seeking, other ethical egoists identify alternate theories of what is good (knowledge or power) and what is bad for the individual. Nevertheless, the judgments of ethical egoists will always be colored by their own self-interests.

Another consequential theory, utilitarianism, emphasizes the best interest of everyone, rather than the individual alone. Utilitarianism asserts that the individual should always act so as to produce the greatest ratio of good to evil for everyone. Some utilitarians apply the principle of utility—that is, the greatest good for the greatest number—to the act itself, and are referred to as act utilitarians. Other utilitarians would not consider the consequences of a particular action, but rather would develop rules by applying the greatest good for the greatest number principle. Then, if an action is generally unethical as determined by the rule, it would remain unethical unless the particular effect of obeying the rule would produce a "net" evil over good. For example, if commercial bribery is determined to be unethical as a rule, it should not be allowed in most instances. However, if a bribe produces some good economic consequences (employment and profits) that exceed its evil, the rule may be broken.

In ethics, the term *ends* refers to the consequences or results of an action, whereas *means* refers to the action itself, its nature and characteristics. For all consequentialists (egoists or utilitarians), the end justifies the means. No action is in itself objectionable. It is only objectionable insofar as it is contrary to the long-run best interests of the individual (in egoism) or leads to a lesser ratio of good to evil for everyone (in utilitarianism). Consequentialists, therefore, ignore actions that appear to some as being wrong in and of themselves, saying such actions could be moral, depending on the "net" consequences of the action.

NONCONSEQUENTIAL THEORIES

Nonconsequential theories contend that other factors should be considered in evaluating the morality of an action. One single-rule nonconsequential theory is the golden rule; that is, "do unto others as you would have them do unto you." It commands us to treat others the way we would want to be treated. The essence of the golden rule is impartiality; never make an exception of yourself. Do not do to others what you are unwilling to have them do to you. This principle has played a prominent role in America's ethical philosophy, but suffers from the weakness that we cannot always know how others actually feel and think. This informational gap is further compounded by the multitude of others who are to be considered in the formulation of ethical decisions.

Another single-rule nonconsequential theory has been prepared by Immanuel Kant (1724–1804).[3] He attempted to exclude any consideration of consequences in moral decision making. Kant believed that nothing was good in itself, except a "good will"; that is, the uniquely human capacity to intentionally act according to principles (duties). Only when one acts from duty do one's actions have moral worth. Kant believed that through reason alone one could develop a moral law (absolute moral truth) that is free of contradiction. Kant formulated one universal command or catagorical imperative, which says one should act in such a way that one could wish the principle of one's actions to become a universal law. If the subjective principle of an action that someone formulates to guide conduct involves a logical contradiction (the principle of promise breaking contradicts the very nature of a promise), it is an immoral principle unworthy of universal adoption. On the other hand, if you could wish the (noncontradicting) principle of your action to become a universal law, and you act out of duty in obedience to the rule, your action is moral, regardless of the consequences.

Kant's categorical imperative takes the guesswork out of some moral decision making. No matter what the consequences may be, some actions are always wrong. For example, lying is wrong; no matter how much good may come from misrepresenting a product, such deliberate misrepresentation is always wrong. However, Kant's theories provide no clear way to resolve conflicts of duties. Also, there may be no compelling reason that Kant's principles, which prohibit certain actions, should hold without exception. A qualified rule produced by a utilitarian that prohibits lying except when more harm than good would result from telling the truth may be just as good as Kant's unqualified rule.

A MIX OF THEORIES

Ross's Prima Facie Duties

William David Ross has attempted to join certain aspects of utiliarianism with those of Kantianism.[4] Ross rejects both the utilitarian belief that consequences make an act right and Kant's absolute rules. In contrast to Kant, Ross believes consequences must be introduced into moral decision making, though not as a final judge of the morality of an action.

Ross argues that a *prima facie* duty imposes, at first sight, a moral obligation when other moral duties are not considered. Ross identifies six *prima facie* duties.

1. Duties of fidelity (based on prior acts of our own).
2. Duties of gratitude (based on acts of other people towards us).

3. Duties of justice (distributed based on merit).
4. Duties of beneficence (based on improving others).
5. Duties of self-improvement (based on improving self virtue, intelligence, or happiness).
6. Duties of noninjury (not to injure others).

In situations where conflicting *prima facie* duties arise, Ross tells us to follow the more obligatory duty. Hence, our actual duty is what we should do after considering and weighing all *prima facie* duties involved. While Ross's ethical system can expand the individual's consciousness of duties and of consequences of actions, it suffers from the probability that individuals will disagree about the merits of the moral principles and their relative weights in choosing the more obligatory duty.

Garrett's Principle of Proportionality

Moral decisions involve three elements: intention, means, and end. Consequentialists are primarily concerned with the *end* of an action. Nonconsequentialists generally put more emphasis on the *intention or means* employed. Proportionality theorists attempt to synthesize traditional moral theories and place emphasis on all three elements in moral decision making.

Thomas Garrett has prepared a synthesis and stated it in his Principle of Proportionality as follows:

"I am responsible for whatever I will as a means or an end. If both the means and the end I am willing are good in and of themselves, I may ethically permit or risk the foreseen but unwilled side effects if, and only if, I have a proportionate reason for doing so."[5]

Stated conversely, "I am not responsible for unwilled side effects if I have a sufficient reason for risking or permitting them, granted always that what I do will as a means or an end is good."

Garrett maintains that it is unethical to will a "major evil" (destruction of a "good" necessary for the individual, institution, or society to function and survive) as either a means or an end. Also, it is unethical to risk (foresee) or permit (allow to happen) a major evil without a "proportionate reason." A proportionate reason exists when the intended good result of an action is equal to or greater than the evil involved. Consequently, it is not morally irresponsible to risk or allow unwilled side effects, providing significant reason exists for risking or allowing them. In addition, a "minor evil" (harm to purely physical goods that are useful but not necessary for the individual and society) may be willed, permitted, or risked if there is a proportionate reason. Hence, risking "major evils" or even willing "minor evils" depends on a "proportionate reason." Willing "major evils" as a means or end is prohibited.

To apply these synthesized ethical principles, Garrett provides a three-step method. First, determine what is willed as a means or an end, and if what is willed involves a major evil, the proposed action is wrong. Second, determine the foreseen but unwilled side effects, and if there is no "proportionate" reason for risking or allowing the major or minor evil, or for willing the minor evil, then the action is wrong. The third step involves a consideration of alternatives. If there is an equally good method of obtaining good with less evil or risk of evil, that alternative must be pursued.

While the principle of proportionality only vaguely defines major and minor evils and provides little guidance in defining "proportionate reasons," Garrett's synthesis of moral theories has provided a helpful process of inquiry into moral decision making.

Questions

1. Explain the difference between a consequential and a nonconsequential ethical theory.
2. Name and explain two types of consequential ethical theories.
3. Identify two *single-rule* nonconsequential theories. Explain Kantianism.
4. What is the essence of Ross's *Prima Facie* Duties?
5. Explain the essence of Garrett's Principle of Proportionality.
6. Many large corporate enterprises engaged in bribery. Analyze this practice according to:
   (a) Egoism.
   (b) Utilitarianism.
   (c) The golden rule.
   (d) Kantianism.
   (e) Ross's *prima facie* duties.
   (f) Garrett's Principle of Proportionality.
7. Which moral theory is usually utilized by business decision makers?

MANAGERIAL CODE OF ETHICS

The preceeding review of a variety of ethical theories reveals that the fundamental value of studying ethical thought is not the obtainment of definitive guides to moral conduct, but rather the obtainment of an awareness of the process of moral inquiry and of moral options. Hence, the challenge to would-be moral decision makers is to utilize ethical theories as aids in the process of moral inquiry and to apply a reputable ethical standard in the process.

To assist the business decision maker facing moral questions, a variety of aids could be developed. First, an "angel's advocate" within the firm could be created. Certain corporate officers or directors could be appointed to review the extensive literature of ethics as applied to business. They could identify generic questions of an ethical nature that should be asked routinely in the formulation of business decisions. The main function of the individuals who compose such an ethics committee would be to ask questions rather than to pose answers. They would force the company into moral inquiry. The committee could also assist in the development of an ethical code for their company.

Corporate leaders and independent spokesmen have emphasized the importance of adopting written policy statements designed to curb unethical practices. The promulgation of corporate codes of ethics has proliferated, and the demand for their adoption by all public companies is likely to increase.

The model business code of ethics set forth below is patterned after the lawyer's Code of Professional Responsibility, which has three separate but interrelated parts: Canons, Ethical Principles, and Rules of Conduct. The Canons are affirmative, general statements of broad ethical goals. The Ethical Principles expand on the general statements found in the Canons. The Rules of Conduct are essentially regulatory, detailed standards setting forth the *minimum* conduct permissable in certain specified situations covered by the Canons.

A multiple-level code has a number of advantages. A general "creed" of business morality is provided by the affirmative Canons, which are simple and asspirational in nature. The "creed" enhances a feeling of professionalism by emphasizing broad ethical concepts. The Principles provide more specific guidance to business managers. The Rules of Conduct allow the code to include more detailed regulation on conduct and disclosure in a specific context related to the Canons or Principles.

Because the number of rules desired in a company code of ethics will vary from company to company and from industry to industry, the model code set forth below is not complete. Rather, the model offers a cross-section of the rules that may be most useful to a wide variety of businesses.

The model business code presented was prepared by attorney Charles E. Harris of The Florida Bar. The code was published as part of an article in the *University of Florida Law Review*.[6] To conserve space and more particularly focus on ethical responsibilities, the Rules of Conduct have been omitted.

Code of Business Responsibility

Canon 1. A Professional Manager Should Assist in Maintaining the Integrity and Competence of the Business Community.

ETHICAL PRINCIPLES

EP 1.1. The public and shareholders of this Company have a right to expect that the business of this Company will be efficiently and competently performed by our officers and employees. A professional manager should strive for excellence in performing his or her duties.

EP 1.2. A professional manager should maintain a high level of integrity in business conduct and should encourage other managers to do likewise. A manager should refrain from all illegal conduct, in personal and business affairs. In doing so, the manager should support and obey both the language and the spirit of the law, avoiding efforts to circumvent the law by devious means or questionable interpretations. A professional manager should be able to rely upon the opinions of lawyers, accountants, and other outside experts, but should not shirk the final responsibility of making the business decisions associated with those opinions.

EP 1.3. A professional manager should disclose, as may be necessary and appropriate, any illegal or unethical business activities by any director, officer, or employee that are likely to have an adverse effect upon the business reputation or affairs of the Company. Although the manager should respect the Company's organizational structure if possible, the integrity and interests of the Company, its shareholders, and our business community may dictate that the manager report such illegal or unethical activity directly to the Company's audit committee, board of directors or legal counsel, or, as a last resort, to appropriate governmental authorities.

Canon 2. A Professional Manager Should Preserve the Confidential Nature of Business and Customer Information

ETHICAL PRINCIPLES

EP 2.1. A professional manager should ensure that all confidential and proprietary information relating to the Company, its shareholders, and its existing and prospective customers and suppliers, acquired in the course of duty, is used solely for Company purposes and is not provided to unauthorized persons or used for the purpose of furthering a private interest or making a personal profit.

EP 2.2 A professional manager should ensure that all material non-public information concerning the securities, financial condition, earnings, and other performance of the Company remains confidential, unless and until it is fully and properly disseminated to the public.

EP 2.3. The obligation of a professional manager to preserve the confidential nature of business and customer information continues after termination of the manager's employment with the Company.

Canon 3. A Professional Manager Should Place the Interests of the Company Ahead of Any Private Interests and Should Disclose the Facts in any Situation Where a Conflict of Interests May Appear.

ETHICAL PRINCIPLES

EP 3.1. A professional manager should ensure that none of his or her outside personal, business, or investment activities unreasonably conflict with the interests of the Company. In all situations where an actual or potential conflict of interests exists or may appear to others to exist, the manager should disclose all details of the activity and conflict.

EP 3.2. A professional manager should not use his or her position with the Company for personal gain. Likewise, a professional manager should seperate personal interests and considerations from activities and decisions relating to the Company and its affairs.

EP 3.3. Except where expressly authorized by the terms of the manager's employment agreement or compensation arrangements with the Company, a professional manager should not directly or indirectly solicit or accept any fee, commission, entertainment, gift, gratuity, property, discount, or loan for himself or herself or his or her affiliates or immediate family as compensation for performing duties with the Company or for making, or causing the Company to make, any business decision.

EP 3.4. Except where expressly authorized by the Rules of Conduct, a professional manager should not directly or indirectly solicit or accept any fee, commission, entertainment, gift, gratuity, property, discount, or loan for himself or herself or his or her affiliates or immediate family from any existing or potential customer, competitor, or supplier of the Company.

EP 3.5. Except where expressly authorized by the Rules of Conduct, neither a professional manager nor his or her affiliates or immediate family should directly or indirectly solicit or receive any bequest or legacy from any customer, competitor, or supplier of the Company, or serve as executor, personal representative, trustee, or guardian of an estate, trust, or guardianship established by a customer, competitor, or supplier of the Company.

Canon 4. A Professional Manager Should Avoid Even the Appearance of Impropriety in Business Matters.

ETHICAL PRINCIPLES

EP 4.1. Continuation of the American free-enterprise system requires that the public have confidence in this system and, particularly, in the ethical conduct of its business leaders. Consequently, a professional manager should strive to promote public confidence in our business system by avoiding not only ethical impropriety but also the appearance of ethical impropriety in business matters.

EP 4.2. A professional manager should exercise prudence and restraint in personal financial affairs, including speculative investments and margin accounts, in order to avoid debts or other financial obligations that are, or might appear to be, significantly out of proportion to the manager's financial statement and personal or family financial condition.

EP 4.3. Although a professional manager should be encouraged to participate freely and actively in the political process, the manager should ensure that such activities are separated from those of the Company. Except where expressly permitted by the Rules of Conduct, no Company assets, funds, or loans should be used for political purposes. All contributions for political purposes should be made pursuant to law and accurately reflected in the Company's books.

EP 4.4. Except for campaign contributions and lobbying expenditures designated as such and authorized or permitted by applicable law in the jurisdiction for which the election is held, no fee, commission, property, bribe, or any other compensation should be offered or paid directly or indirectly by a professional manager to, for, or on behalf of, any elected, appointed, or ruling government official or head of state, in the United States or abroad, for the purpose of influencing in any way any decision by or within the influence of such official or head of state.

EP 4.5. If a professional manager has previously performed government or public service, or is presently performing such service, the manager should not perform activities for the Company in connection with any specific matter for which the manager had or has substantive responsibility as a government or public servant.

Canon 5. A Professional Manager Should be Honest in Dealing with the Public and with the Company's Officers, Directors, Employees, Experts, and Customers.

ETHICAL PRINCIPLES

EP 5.1. A professional manager should be open and honest in his business relationships with other officers and employees of the Company, the board of directors of the Company, and the lawyers, accountants, and other professionals retained by the Company. In this regard, honesty requires the furnishing of all information that the manager has that would be material to a given decision. The failure to furnish information that is known or thought to be necessary, or the provision of information that is known or thought to be inaccurate, misleading, or incomplete, is unacceptable.

EP 5.2. In order to preserve confidence in the information and advertising disseminated by our nation's businesses, a professional manager should strive to ensure that all information, advertising, and other statements released to the public by the Company are not misleading and do not omit to state any material fact necessary to make the information, advertising, or statements not misleading under the particular circumstances involved.

Questions
1. Identify the five Canons of the Code of Business Responsibility.
2. What processes of disclosure are provided in the code in the situation of irregular activities by a superior? How would an individual disclose this to the company?
3. What are the ethical obligations imposed by the code on the firm's advertising policy?
4. What kind of regular disclosure reports should be required by the code? Why should a professional manager's income tax return be subject to inspection by his employer?
5. Should the code be one of disclosure or of regulation?
6. Give examples of how the code is aspirational.
7. Do you observe any interrelationships between the law and the obligations of the code? Should the adoption of the Model Code of Business Responsibility serve to justify the refusal to disclose information to the public?

AN ISSUE IN MANAGERIAL ETHICS

The common law developed the concept of "employment at will," which maintains that "when the employment is not for a definite term and there is no contractual or statutory restrictions upon the right of discharge, an employer may lawfully discharge an employee whenever and for whatever cause he chooses, without incurring liability."[7] This concept secures employer discretion over discharge decisions. It also affords the employees protection from employer abuse by permitting the worker to terminate his employment; a right not available during medieval times.

As industrialization grew, the employer's economic power increased while the individual employee's power shrank. The formation of labor unions sought to restore the balance of bargaining power between the employer and the employee. Such unions negotiate labor contracts with employers and obtain provisions protecting the union member from termination without "just cause." However, without a union or some statute (such as the Civil Rights Act) employees are subject to termination at the will of the employer. The following case deals with this concept and its appropriateness to the economy of the twentieth century.

Geary v. United States Steel Corporation
319 A.2d 474 (1974)
Supreme Court of Pennsylvania

The complaint avers that plaintiff, George R. Geary, was continuously employed by defendant, United States Steel Corporation (hereinafter "company"), from 1953 until July 13, 1967, when he was dismissed from his position. Geary's duties involved the sale of tubular products to the oil and gas industry. His employment was at will. The dismissal is said to have stemmed from a disagreement concerning one of the company's new products, a tubular casing designed for use under high pressure. Geary alleges that he believed the product had not been adequately tested and constituted a serious danger to anyone who used it; that he voiced his misgivings to his superiors and was ordered to "follow directions," which he agreed to do; that he nevertheless contained to express his reservations, taking his case to a vice-president in charge of sale of the product; that as a result of his efforts the product was reevaluated and withdrawn from the market; that he at all times performed his duties to the best of his ability and always acted with the best interests of the company and the general public in mind; and that because of these events he was summarily discharged without notice. Geary asserts that the company's conduct in so acting was "wrongful, malicious and abusive," resulting in injury to his reputation in the industry, mental anguish, and direct financial harm, for which he seeks both punitive and compensatory damages.

* * *

The Pennsylvania law is in accordance with the weight of authority elsewhere. Absent a statutory or contractual provision to the contrary, the law has taken for granted the power of either party to terminate an employment relationship for any or no reason. . . .

We recognize that economic conditions have changed radically. . . . The huge corporate enterprises which have emerged in this century wield an awesome power over their employees. It has been aptly remarked that

We have become a nation of employees. We are dependent upon others for our means of livelihood, and most of our people have become completely dependent upon wages. If they lose their jobs they lose every resource, except for the relief supplied by the various forms of social security. Such dependence of the mass of the people upon others for all of their income is something new in the world. For our generation, the substance of life is in another man's hands. (F. Tannenbaum, *A Philosophy of Labor*, 1951, p. 9).

Against the background of these changes, the broad question to which plaintiff invites our attention is whether the time has come to impose judicial restrictions on an employer's power of discharge.

* * *

Plaintiff's . . . argument is an appeal to considerations of public policy. Geary asserts in his complaint that he was acting in the best interests of the general public as well as of his employer in opposing the marketing of a product which he believed to be defective. Certainly, the potential for abuse of an employer's power of dismissal is particularly serious where an employee must exercise independent, expert judgment in matters of product safety, but Geary does not hold himself out as this sort of employee. So far as the complaint shows, he was involved only in the sale of company products. There is no suggestion that he possessed any expert qualifications, or that his duties extended to making judgments in matters of product safety. In essence, Geary argues that his conduct should be protected because his intentions were good. No doubt most employees who are dismissed from their posts can make the same claim. We doubt that establishing a right to litigate every such case as it arises would operate either in the best interest of the parties or of the public.

* * *

The problem extends beyond the question of individual competence, for even an unusually gifted person may be of no use to his employer if he cannot work effectively with fellow employees. Here, for example, Geary's complaint shows that he by-passed his immediate superiors and pressed his views on higher officers, utilizing his close contacts with a company vice president.

The praiseworthiness of Geary's motives does not detract from the company's legitimate interest in preserving its normal operational procedures from disruption. In sum, while we agree that employees should be encouraged to express their educated views on the quality of their employer's products, we are not persuaded that creating a new non-statutory cause of action of the sort proposed by (Geary) is the best way to achieve this result. On balance, whatever public policy imperatives can be discerning here seem to militate against such a course.

We hold . . . that where the complaint itself discloses a plausible and legitimate reason for terminating an at-will employment relationship and no clear mandate of public policy is violated thereby, an employee at will has no right of action against his employer for wrongful discharge.

Justice Roberts, dissenting.

I cannot accept the view implicit in the majority's decision that today's jurisprudence is so lacking in awareness and vitality that our judicial process is incapable of affording relief to a responsible employee for an arbitrary and retaliatory discharge from employment. . . . I am unable to agree that this case presents only "a plausible and legitimate reason for terminating" Geary's employment or that "no clear mandate of public policy" has been violated.

As a salesman, Geary was required to know intimately the products he was selling. He represented United States Steel and it was expected that he would be alert to protect his employer's reputation. Likewise, it was natural that he would seek to shield himself and his employer from the consequences of a dangerous product. When he correctly recognized that the defective steel pipe had strong potential for causing injury and damage, he immediately notified his superiors. His reward for loyalty was dismissal. Of course, had Geary not informed his superiors of the defective product, he may well have been discharged for his failure to do so.

Geary's assessment of the danger of the steel pipe was correct, since after his notification, the corporation removed the steel pipe from the market. On these pleadings, it is manifestly clear that the employer realized Geary was right and that its interest lay in withdrawing from the market the dangerous product. Despite Geary's candor in seeking within the corporate family to advance the corporation's best interest, his employer fired him.

There is no doubt that strong public policies of this Commonwealth have been offended by Geary's discharge. First, the product asserted by plaintiff to be defective was, after plaintiff notified his superiors, withdrawn from the market. The manufacture and distribution of defective and potentially dangerous products does not serve either the public's or the employer's interest. Our courts have granted relief to those injured by defective merchandise. The majority, however, fails to perceive that the prevention of injury is a fundamental and highly desirable objective of our society.

Second, plaintiff as an employee was "subject to a duty to use reasonable efforts to give his (employer) information which is relevant to affairs entrusted to him. . . . Had Geary refrained from notifying his superiors of the defective product, he could have been discharged for violating this duty to come forward with information. No responsible policy is served which permits an employee to be discharged solely for obeying his legal duty to communicate information to his superiors. Indeed, the policy underlying this duty to communicate is frustrated by denying Geary the opportunity to present his case to the court.

. . . Unlike the majority, I believe the time has surely come to afford unorganized employees an opportunity to prove in court a claim for arbitrary and retaliatory discharge.

* * *

The Supreme Court of Indiana has recently provided a discharged employee an opportunity to prove a claim for wrongful and retaliatory discharge. There, the plaintiff was dismissed after she filed a claim for workmen's compensation. The Indiana court observed that "(i)f employers are permitted to penalize employees for filing workmen's compensation claims, a most important public policy will be undermined." A California court similarly recognized a cause of action for wrongful discharge where the employee had been dismissed after he refused to commit perjury.

The principle underlying these decisions should apply to the present case. Contrary to the majority's assertion, society's interest in protecting itself from dangerous products manifestly presents a mandate to the court to recognize a cause of action for wrongful discharge. That a loyal and responsible employee should be summarily and without cause or notice discharged for complying with his duty to communicate relevant information to his superiors provides further justification for affording plaintiff an opportunity to present his claim. That plaintiff was discharged without cause for doing that which, had he failed to do, he would have been subject to dismissal with cause amply demonstrates the illogic of the majority's refusal to recognize in these circumstances a cause of action for wrongful discharge.

Questions
1. What two basic reasons are given by the court to refuse Geary's action?
2. On what basis does the dissenting justice contend the majority's opinion is incorrect?
3. Do you agree with the court's opinion or the dissenting justice?
4. Had Geary been a safety engineer, rather than a salesman, would the court have decided differently?
5. Were Geary's actions ethical? Does the court's decision encourage ethical behavior?

CONCLUSION

Each business organization has its own personality, which can be reflected in its company code of ethics. Then, when people are faced with ethical decisions, codes of ethics can help them know what is considered right in their organization. There is also some research evidence that clearly stated codes tend to deter unethical behavior.[8] These results probably flow from the code's clear definition of organizational purpose, its establishment of an ethical climate within the organization, and its provision of guides for consistent decision making. However, if corporate members lack sufficient information of the code and its worth or assume the code is a public relations tool, its adoption will be futile. Instead, ideal situations would involve employee participation in developing the code in order to build more understanding and commitment to it. Equally important is the necessity for higher managers to support the code by example. Surveys have consistently shown that managers normally adapt their behavior to that revealed in the actions of their superiors.[9]

DISCUSSION QUESTIONS

1. Black worked for Widget Company and obtained information about the successful design of widgets during his employment. Black worked for Widget Company for six years before he decided to form his own company. Black's new Widgette Company became a competitor of Widget Company, and Black utilized information such as customer lists and principles of widget design in his new business. Has Black violated any ethical standards of the Model Code?

2. Kopy was employed by ABC Company. He would often be entertained on business trips at the expense of XYZ Company. He received meals and "entertainment tours" of the surrounding area. What additional information would you want to know of this situation in order to determine if it violates any ethical standards of the Model Code?

3. Mr. Smith was vice president of ABC Company in charge of marketing activities. Mr. Smith has recently purchased a 20 percent stock interest in Ace Company, which is a competitor of ABC Company. Is Mr. Smith's stock purchase in violation of any ethical standard imposed by the Model Code?

4. Mr. Jones is a director of Employee Relations for F & F Company. The union of F & F Company periodically sponsors a business trip to cabins in the Canadian north woods for the purpose of "getting to know" business personalities on a closer basis. Mr. Jones desires to join this trip but wants to comply with his ethical obligations. What must Mr. Jones do to comply with the Model Code?

5. Mr. Doe is a purchasing agent for Black Lumber Company. Mr. Doe is building a small cabin on a nearby lake and is seeking to purchase his lumber from a company that often supplies raw lumber to the Black Lumber Company. What ethical obligations are imposed on Mr. Doe by the Model Code in this situation?

6. Mr. Harper for the last four years has been employed in government service. The agency he has worked for has had numerous confrontations with Hooper Company. Hooper has offered Mr. Harper double his present government salary to become Hooper's officer in charge of government relations. What ethical obligations are imposed on Mr. Harper by the Model Code?

7. Mr. Dawson is a chief executive officier of Micro-Units, Inc. Mr. Dawson often is transported by the company jet. When leaving Washington during the upcoming Thanksgiving break, Mr. Dawson offers the local congressional representative a ride home. Are there any ethical problems with this practice as discussed by the Model Code?

8. Mr. Davis is the director of safety for Business Products, Inc. Because of his expertise in the field of safety, Mr. Davis also lectures and consults with many other companies. These outside activities are increasingly absorbing Mr. Davis' time, yet the renumeration is substantial. What ethical obligations are imposed on Mr. Davis by the Model Code in this situation?

9. Mr. Mansfield worked for Brakes, Inc. as an engineer. The chief engineer has designed a new brake system for government aircraft, and Brakes Inc. has obtained a government contract to supply these new brakes on this aircraft. During the testing of the brake models, substantial difficulties were detected in the design. The chief engineer refused to recognize the existence of any design difficulties, yet Mr. Mansfield felt the brakes, if installed, would not stop the plane. Mr. Mansfield has complained to the chief engineer of the necessity to redesign the brakes. The chief engineer is beginning to question the competency of Mr. Mansfield. What should Mr. Mansfield do, given the ethical obligations by the Model Code?

10. R-M is a pharmaceutical company that was testing a drug to be taken by expectant mothers. Top executives of the company were enthusiastic about the profit capabilities of the drug and began to prepare for a major marketing campaign. However, one laboratory test of small rats revealed that high doses of the drug caused death within six weeks. Subsequent tests on rats with a lower dosage revealed they suffered abnormal blood changes. Monkeys suffered blood changes and weight loss. A lower-level executive ordered the lab technician to "falsify" a chart of this test by recording false body weights for the monkeys and by adding data for an imaginary monkey that had never been in the test group. When the technician protested to her superior, she was told, "Do as you're told and be quiet."

    What ethical obligations are imposed on the lab technician by the Model Code?

11. A potent chemical increases the maturity of chickens, increasing productivity and reducing the consumer's cost of fryers by $500 million per year. "Statistically" or "randomly," 10 people will die from the chemical each year. If those deaths are "valued" at, say, $1 million each, their value of $10 million does not outweigh the $500 million value to society in lower priced chickens. Is this chemical additive ethical? Which ethical standard do you utilize to make the decision?

SUGGESTED READINGS

Barnett, Helaine Meresman, "Legal Ethics: Commentary," *Brooklyn Law Review,* Vol. 48, Summer 1982, pp. 1149–1168.

Blackburn, John D., "Restricted Employer Discharge Rights: A Changing Concept of Employment at Will," *American Business Law Journal*, Vol. 17, No. 4, Winter 1980, pp. 467–492,

Heyne, Paul T., *Private Keepers of the Public Interest* (New York: McGraw-Hill Book Company, 1968).

LaCroix, W. L., *Principles for Ethics in Business* (Washington University Press of America, Inc., 1979).

Lansing, Paul and Pegnetter, Richard, "Fair Dismissal Procedures for Non-Union Employees," *American Business Law Journal*, Vol. 20, No. 1, Spring 1982, pp. 75–91.

McElhaney, James W., "The Credibility of the Lawyer (Trial Notebook)," *Litigation 53*, Vol. 6, No. 5, Spring 1980.

Petit, Thomas A., *The Moral Crisis In Management* (New York: McGraw-Hill Book Company, 1967).

Stevens, George E., "The Legality of Discharging Employees for Insubordination," *American Business Law Journal*, Vol. 18, No. 3, Fall 1980, pp. 371–390.

ENDNOTES

1. S. Prakash Sethi, "Dimensions of Corporation Social Performance: An Analytical Framework," *California Management Review*, Spring 1975, pp. 58–64.

2. Neil W. Chamberlain, *The Limits of Corporate Responsibility* (New York: Basic Books, 1973), pp. 4, 6.

3. Sir David Ross, *Kant's Ethical Theory, A Commentary on the Grundlegung zur Metaphysik der Sitten* (London: Oxford University Press, 1965), pp. 43–48.

4. William David Ross, *The Right and the Good* (Oxford: Clarendon Press, 1930).

5. Thomas Garrett, *Business Ethics* (Englewood Cliffs, N.J.: Prentice-Hall, 1966), p. 8.

6. Charles F. Harris, "Structuring a Workable Business Code of Ethics," *Univ. of Florida Law Review* Vol. 30, 1978, p. 310–382. Reprinted with the permission of the University of Florida Law Review. Copyright 1978.

7. 53 Am. Jur. 2d *Master and Servant*, Section 43 (1969).

8. "The Chicken or the Egg: Which Comes First in Ethics?" *Management Review*, December 1977, p. 56, based on research of Henry P. Sims and W. Harvey Hogarty.

9. Steven N. Brenner and Earl A. Molander, "Is the Ethics of Business Changing?" *Harvard Business Review*, January–February 1977, p. 66.

chapter 26

MANAGEMENT OF BUSINESS-GOVERNMENT RELATIONS

For many years, the critical importance of a company's relations with the federal government has been a debatable topic. However, the tremendous increase in government legislation and regulation that directly affects business operations has brought about an evolution in business attitude concerning the business-government relationship. The traditional attitude of negativism toward government regulation is increasingly being replaced by an activist stand on the part of the business community. In short, defensive postures are giving way to aggressive strategies. The adversary relationship is being replaced by a policy of accommodation.

PUBLIC ISSUES MANAGEMENT

The demand for legal recognition often comes from a small group of individuals who undertake to mold public opinion into a demand for change that the government cannot ignore. For example, Karl Polanyi has pointed out that the English middle class forced its way to power in 1832 and abolished the Speenhamland Act of 1795.[1] The Speenhamland Act had been adopted as a humanitarian enactment to offset the ill effects of the Industrial Revolution. It subsidized the income of the poor and had the effect, as Polanyi argues, of eliminating the labor market in England. Once the middle class of England perceived the workings of the Speenhamland Act as an obstacle to their efforts to achieve an effective free market economy, they sought to gain political power to remove this governmental restraint. The resulting abolishment of the Speenhamland Act created a governmental policy favoring a free labor market.

All this is expressed to emphasize Polyani's main point: that the market economy in England did not just "happen" or arise (naturally) from men's "propensity to truck, barter, and exchange," as Adam Smith had argued. Instead, the market economic system was established by political action that legislatively modified the existing institutional structure into new arrangements that were compatible with the growing ideological beliefs in favor of a free market system. The government's action undoubtedly imposed hardships on those who had hitherto been protected by the previously existing and governmentally favored institutional structure. However, the changes in the balance of power in the political system allowed the government to judge that the social benefits of free markets justified the individual hardships created by the new legislation.

Just as legislation may be created to free the market from government restraints, the legislative process is available for the creation of renewed restraints on the marketplace when another social era finds it appropriate. Roosevelt's New Deal regulations are an obvious example of an era when society sought legislative solutions for an ill, but previously free, economy.

Part I of this book has emphasized that the political and economic systems of the business environment are contrived, not "naturally" formed or ordained, and evolutionary, not static. Hence, the process of social change in the political and economic systems has been generally described in terms of social events and ideology. However, a more particular clarification of the life cycle of social issues will be valuable for effective participation by business persons in the process of social change.

PUBLIC ISSUE LIFE CYCLE

Professor James Post has observed that social issues seem to evolve through a series of phases that may be treated as a life cycle.[2] He has identified four distinct stages in the life cycle of a public or social issue (see Figure 26-1).

The beginning of a public issue occurs when some segment of the public finds that its expectations of business performance are not met. Such disappointed individuals perceive a gap between their expectations of business performance and the actual performance of business firms. Often, organized groups are formed to generate media events or confrontations to increase public pressure against the firm's "social failings."

The second phase in the life cycle occurs when the social issue becomes successfully politicized. Political aspirants for elected offices adopt the issue for political discussion. They commit themselves to some governmental response to the social issue; normally by suggesting an appropriate legislative response. Lobbying and publicity are important activities in this prelegislation phase.

The third phase of the life cycle pertains to the legislative process. This involves legislative proposals, hearings, debates, and final adoption of legislation, which publicly legitimizes new social expectations of business performance.

It sets priorities and selects public strategies for closing the "gap" between social expectations and corporate performance.

The fourth phase of the public issue life cycle is an enforcement-litigation phase. This involves administrative interpretation of the legislative goals. Government agencies must articulate enforcement standards and establish timetables for compliance. Business often objects to the compliance standards or time schedules promulgated by the agencies. Predictably, litigation results.

The phases of the public issue life cycle can be illustrated by the civil rights movement, which began in the fifties and became a presidential campaign issue in 1960. The Civil Rights Act was passed in 1964, and administrative enforcement-litigation mushroomed in the 1970s. The environmental and consumer movements followed similar phases: development of the issue in the early sixties; political controversy in the late sixties; the Environmental Protection Act of 1970 and the Consumer Product Safety Act of 1972; and the Environmental Protectional Agency and the Consumer Product Safety Commission enforcement thereafter.

	Phase I	II	III	IV
	Changing Public Expectations	→ Political Controversy	→ Development of Legislation →	Goverment Litigation
EXAMPLES				
Civil Rights	1954–60	1960 (presidential campaign issue)	1964 (Civil Rights Act)	1970's (EEOC litigation backlog)
Environmental Protection	1963 (Rachel Carson *Silent Spring*)	1967 (campaign issue; political "sides" developing)	1970 (EPA established)	1970's (Tighter standards; negotiated or court-ordered settlements; nearly 300 cases in Federal courts)
Consumer Protection	1964 (Ralph Nader, *Unsafe at Any Speed*)	1968 (Presidential Consumer Affairs Advisor; proposed legislation)	1972 (Consumer Product Safety Act)	

Figure 26-1. Public issues life cycle. (*Source*: Reprinted with permission of Reston Publishing Co., Inc.)

CORPORATE RESPONSE PROCESS

Most researchers and practitioners agree that the process of the corporate response involves three basic steps.[3] First, the corporation becomes aware of the issue, by pickets at the plant gate (pressure) or by managerial foresight (anticipation). Second, the corporation becomes committed to developing some response, and finally, it selects and implements a response (see Figure 26-2.)

The action selected by the company may be either to modify organizational performance to meet new societal expectations or to change the public expectations, or some combination of both. These responses are typically referred to as *adaptive* (internal organizational change), *proactive* (organizational efforts to change the environment), or *interactive* (simultaneous change in both).[4]

The historical failure of corporations to recognize the need for a new perception of its social role has increased the degree of incompatibility between corporate behavior and societal expectations. Corporations did not feel the need to develop new strategies for dealing with emerging outside pressure. Instead, corporations usually ignored matters of public discontent until they reached crisis proportions. And then, when crisis blocked the avenues of escape, the resulting trauma and urgency would cause the development of makeshift solutions not likely to endure or please anybody.

Corporate responses to social pressures can be grouped into three broad categories.[5]

The Public Relations Response

This response often involves the self-imposed corporate duty to inform or "educate" the population about the vital role played by large corporations in provid-

---

STAGE 1 AWARENESS OR COGNIZANCE OF PUBLIC ISSUE
This can be accomplished through external public pressure and legal change or through management scanning for new public issues.

STAGE 2 COMMITMENT TO ACTION
Organizational commitment may develop from either "bottom up" pressures for policy endorsement of coping practices, or, from "top down" policy commitment of senior management.

STAGE 3 SELECTION AND IMPLEMENTATION OF RESPONSE
Organization must determine appropriate action response (including subsystem bargaining) and assign management responsibility for implementation of the chosen action.

Figure 26-2. The corporate response process. (*Source*: Reprinted with permission of Reston Publishing Co., Inc.)

ing material abundance. This response implies that the contributions of business to the American way of life have not been properly understood and appreciated by society. However, in 1950, William H. Whyte, Jr., noted that the billion-dollar attempt by business in the two earlier decades to "sell business to America" was an utter failure.

The free enterprise campaign is psychologically unsound, it is defensive, and it is negative. Most important in a great many of its aspects, it represents a shocking lack of faith in the American people, and in some cases downright contempt.[6]

Others have argued that "these public relations efforts have brought business neither more respectibility nor greater credibility."[7] Yet many corporate leaders are still trying to sell the free enterprise theme. Paradoxically, emphasis on the positive may provide a negative reaction. What business lists as achievements, others may label as devastation of natural resources for private gain. This "gospel" of business virtue usually wins little converts.

The Legal Response

Corporations frequently utilize arguments of their legal rights in responding to social-ethical issues raised by environmentalists, minority groups, or consumer advocates. Such legalistic responses question the legitimacy of others' claims and become, in the eyes of the critics, another form of evasive tactics. The assertion of legal rights often sidesteps the real issue and probably ensures a more hostile criticism in the future.

The Bargaining Response

The bargaining process is often employed in public news media or in direct confrontation with some interest group. Some concession is normally granted by business to the opposing party, but business expects some *quid pro quo,* usually some temporary social peace. However, such bargaining rarely deals with the basic causes of discontent, and usually treats only the symptoms. Not surprisingly, new demands soon follow.

These usual corporate responses to outside social pressures are often at odds with one another. For example, the legal approach emphasizes the lack of any company legal duty, while the bargainers agree to some constraints anyway. At the same time, the public relations office emphasizes that the outside groups lack appreciation of the corporation's contributions to the community. All three forms of response have met with a high instance of failure in the past, and are irrelevant and harmful to business interests today.

ANTICIPATORY MANAGEMENT

To survive as a private institution, corporations must adjust to the restless nature of the social system. Corporations must adopt new values and goals developed by society. This requires more effective "issues management" at the early stages of the public issue life cycle. Business cannot afford to follow old traditional responses or delay involvement in public issue formation until the "litigation stage."

Business must develop anticipatory management. Too much managerial discretion is lost when business fails to respond before legislation is enacted. Legislation and its evolving regulations tie a web of rules around managerial response, which limits the firm's opportunities for imaginative and innovative solutions. The challenge of corporate responsiveness is the development of tools of anticipatory management, not reactive.

A corporation must develop skills and programs to participate in "societal change" through effective *proactive* strategies. It must also learn to change its own performance through well-conceived *adaptive* strategies. Finally, business must manage its *interaction* as a subsystem of business with other social subsystems of society. These activities require imagination and leadership in corporate planning and in the management of external affairs. These are clearly the most challenging frontiers of professional management today.

Ackerman and Bauer have warned, however, that anticipatory managerial action in dealing with public issues is laden with uncertainties.[8] First, the urgency and durability of the issue is unknown. Predicting the implications of social trends in their early formulation phases is difficult. Second, defining the acceptable standards of business response is not easy. Third, the techniques for responding to public issues are probably unknown when the issue first arises. Consequently, management must decide whether to commit the firm's money and energy to the task of predicting which issues are significant and lasting, which performance standards are acceptable, and which techniques for business response are capable of development and acceptable to society. Management must weigh the cost of these uncertainties against the benefits expected from an early response by business to a public issue in its first phases of the life cycle. Anticipatory management action obviously hopes the benefits of a proactive strategy will ultimately outweigh any "early action" penalties imposed from errors in judging the probable outcomes of these issues (see Figure 26-3).

	Risks	
Proactive Managerial Action		Reactive Managerial Action
1. Issue dies		1. Loss of managerial discretion as to
2. Standard of compliance is unacceptable		(a) standards
		(b) timetables
3. Technique developed is unacceptable		2. Forced adoption of *more* expensive compliance programs

Figure 26.3 Risks of proactive or reactive managerial action.

Nevertheless, the concept of a public issue life cycle is important for anticipatory management because it emphasizes that different business strategies are required at different stages of the cycle. The options available to business are different at each stage. Therefore, it is necessary to "fit" the response of the corporation to the life cycle stage. This development of an appropriate business strategy to "fit" particular public issues is the purpose of public issues management.

Public Issues Management

Public issues management involves a series of steps or stages.[9] Figure 26-4 displays the various stages of a typical system of issues management.

The first stage involves identification of issues of interest to the business firm. Some forecasting system is utilized to discover and monitor trends and public expectations that are likely to affect business. The idea of environmental forecasting is to identify issues as early in their life cycle as possible.

After issues have been identified, their probable impact on business must be evaluated. Since the firm cannot respond to every public issue, priorities must be established among issues. Then, basic analysis and research on issues of highest priority must be conducted. Besides more analysis of the potential impact of the issue on the business firm, the research also seeks to analyze the different positions and strategies that can be adopted by management on the issues.

Ultimately, a strategy must be selected to close the gap between public expectations and business performance. Efforts could be directed to influence the environment by changing public expectations or the legislative response. Alternatively, a strategic choice could be made to close the gap by improving business performance. Other decisions involve whether the company wants to adopt a high or low profile on the issue and whether the company can afford to lag behind public expectations. Finally, the strategic option chosen must be integrated with the overall economic strategy of the business firm.

Specific tactics for changing business behavior or for influencing social expectations must be implemented. The tactics may include the development of alliances with other groups or the activation of lobbying efforts.

The evaluation stage requires the monitoring of tactics to determine their effects. Such evaluation may call for a modification in tactics or strategies or additional research for further evaluation.

Business has a great deal of technical and managerial expertise to bring to the public issues management program. However, issues management should not seek to manipulate government for strictly business purposes, but rather to cooperate with government in solving social problems. Frank Steckmest, a public affairs consultant for Shell Oil Company, argues that the "public policy corporate executive" must possess knowledge, skills, experience, and attitudes to oper-

Figure 26-4. Flowchart of public issues management. (*Source*: Rogene A. Buchholz, *Business Environment and Public Policy: Implications for Management*, © 1982, p. 472. Reprinted by permission of Prentice-Hall, Inc., Englewood Cliffs, N.J.)

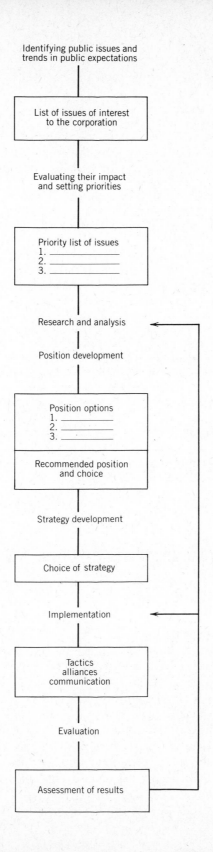

Identifying public issues and
trends in public expectations

List of issues of interest
to the corporation

Evaluating their impact
and setting priorities

Priority list of issues
1. _____
2. _____
3. _____

Research and analysis

Position development

Position options
1. _____
2. _____
3. _____

Recommended position
and choice

Strategy development

Choice of strategy

Implementation

Tactics
alliances
communication

Evaluation

Assessment of results

ate effectively in the public policy arena. Steckmest describes the qualifications as follows.

Knowledge: A basic understanding of the U.S. social, economic, and political systems, including history, structure, institutions, and processes; an understanding of current and emerging social, economic, and political issues impacting corporations and society; familiarity with the principles and techniques for public policy analysis; and an understanding of basic attitudes and viewpoints of the leadership of significant institutions and interest groups.

Skill: Ability to apply the foregoing knowledge in planning, day-to-day decision making and particularly in communicating effectively under the varying circumstances required in the public policy process; e.g., person-to-person, small meetings, speeches, legislative testimony, and press, television, and radio interviews.

Experience: Participation in the public policy process; e.g., analysis of public policy issues and formulation of corporate positions; explaining public issues and positions by speeches, legislative testimony and TV/radio appearances; and interaction with counterparts in government, the media, academia, unions, and public interest groups. Participation in the political process; e.g., activity on behalf of a political party or advocacy group; election campaign work, or service as an elected or appointed official.

Attitude: Personal commitment to sustain and improve the U.S. system of political democracy and capitalist economy. Also, as William S. Sneath, Chairman of the Union Carbide Corporation advises: "Corporate participation in the public policy process requires conduct which engenders credibility and trust; recognition that there is no perfect public policy; and understanding that the process works by balancing interests and the corporate goal must be to strengthen—not dominate—the system."[10]

These attributes are new to the business executive, but essential for effective management of the social and political role of the business firm.

REGULATIONS OF BUSINESS POLITICAL ACTIVITIES

LOBBYING

The First Amendment to the U.S. Constitution guarantees the right to petition the government for redress of grievances. Consequently, activities designed to influence governmental action are protected by the First Amendment. As was illustrated in the *Noers* case (see Chapter 15), even an agreement by competitors to associate together in an attempt to persuade the legislature or the executive to take particular action with respect to a law that would produce a restraint or a monopoly would be protected by the First Amendment. Consequently, lobbying cannot be outlawed, but lobbyists can be forced to register.

The Federal Regulation of Lobbying Act specifically defines lobbyists as those who, for pay, attempt to influence the passage or defeat of proposed legislation before Congress. Those who are uncompensated for their lobbying activities, lobby on their own behalf, or who restrict their lobbying activities to testimony before Congress are not covered by the act.

Those lobbyists required to register must supply information regarding their address, employer, compensation, expense account, and employment duration. Thereafter, quarterly reports are required detailing monies received and expended during the preceding quarter and the purposes of those payments.

Persons or organizations soliciting contributions to support or oppose legislation pending before Congress also are required to file detailed reports. These quarterly reports must include the name and address of each person making a contribution of $500 or more, the total amount of contributions received for the year, the name and address of each person receiving $10 or more during the year, and the amount of all expenditures for the year.

The Foreign Agents Registration Act of 1938 requires representatives of foreign governments to register also.

The purpose of the registration of lobbyists is disclosure, so that legislators and society at large may understand what financial interests are supporting the lobbyists. Nevertheless, significant ambiguities in the registration act have severely crippled its effectiveness. For example, organizations that are not principally involved in lobbying are not required to register. Hence, a citizen's lobbying group, Common Cause, advocates that the law be amended to require registration by anyone spending over $100 per quarter attempting to influence congressional representatives.

Finally, it should be noted that the Federal Criminal Code prohibits the giving of money or anything else of value to government employees as a bribe or to speed up the governmental process. Despite this clear directive of illegality, its enforcement is minimal (despite Abscam successes) because of the difficulties of proof and the ease of avoidance of illegality. For example, payments for "speeches" are not covered. However, Congress has sought to impose financial maximums on the amounts that can be accepted for such honorariums.

POLITICAL CONTRIBUTIONS

The Federal Corrupt Practices Act prohibits *corporate* contributions to candidates for federal office on the theory that a corporation should not be permitted to spend its shareholders' assets on political matters in which the shareholders' opinions are likely to be divergent. That theory was further solidified in the Federal Election Campaign Act of 1971, which prohibits federal election campaign contributions by federally chartered corporations, labor unions, and businesses that enter into or negotiate contracts with the federal government. All other persons and businesses are limited in the amount of contributions they can make. Individual contributions may not exceed $1000 to any one candidate and $25,000 in total during any calendar year.

The 1974 amendments to the Federal Election Campaign Act attempted to prohibit individuals from spending on their own, as opposed to contributing, more than specified amounts on political campaigns during the calendar quarter. However, the Supreme Court declared this provision unconstitutional in that it did not significantly deter corrupt election practices, but did severely limit individual freedom of expression.[11]

Moreover, the 1974 amendments legalized political action committees (PACs). Thus, any organization is free to create a PAC, including business organizations. Corporate PACs may solicit shareholders, executives, and other managerial employees for funds that must be kept segregated from corporate funds and administered separately. An individual may contribute up to $5000 per year to a PAC and a PAC may contribute $5000 per election to any one candidate.

The growth in PAC contributions has been phenomenal. PAC contributions have been large enough and growing to such an extent that the reform-minded argue that PACs constitute "interested money" that distorts the public policy process. They call for total public financing of congressional races. However, with the present administration there is not likely to be any dramatic shift in the existing framework of laws governing federal elections. Professor Edwin Epstein has warned:

If there is a public perception that too much money is coming into the election process from PAC's; or that funds are being raised by other than a voluntary manner—whether from union members or corporate employees; or that there has been a ganging up against particular candidates by political action committees identified with certain interests; or that PAC's are playing too much of a role so far as electoral politics is concerned; or if there is a major scandal as with the post-1972 revelations, it is not inconceivable that Congress will be forced to legislate new regulations. Congress will be obliged to act not because it *wants* to and, indeed, would do so much against its better judgments and preferences. Congress would have preferred to do nothing, but public outcry, sentiment, and pressure can propel Congress along ways that it would just as soon not go. This could happen again in the electoral area if PAC's are perceived by the public to be too dominant a force in the political process.[12]

ADVOCACY ADVERTISING

Advocacy advertising is an advertising message that supports a particular position in regard to a controversial public issue. Often, government agencies have sought to regulate such advertising but have run into problems with the First Amendment.

The First Amendment of the U.S. Constitution provides that "Congress shall make no law . . . abridging the freedom of speech. . . ." The First Amendment prohibits any federal government encroachment on freedom of speech. Moreover, the Supreme Court has ruled that the First Amendment freedoms are among those fundamental rights and liberties protected by the due process clause of the Fourteenth Amendment as well. In effect, the Court has absorbed the First Amendment freedoms into the Fourteenth Amendment's due process clause as a limitation on *state* action also.

The Supreme Court has never considered the First Amendment guarantee of freedom of speech to be absolute. The Court has recognized that "free speech will not protect a man in falsely shouting fire in a theatre and causing panic." Consequently, the Court has had to define which speech is protected and which speech is subject to governmental regulations.

First National Bank of Boston v. Bellotti

435 U.S. 765 (1978)
Supreme Court of the United States

Justice Powell

In sustaining a state criminal statute that forbids certain expenditures by banks and business corporations for the purpose of influencing the vote on referendum proposals, the Massachusett's Supreme Judicial Court held that the First Amendment rights of a corporation are limited to issues that materially affect its business, property, or assets.

The statute at issue, Mass. Gen. Laws Ann., Ch. 55, Section 8, prohibits . . . business corporations, from making contributions or expenditures "for the purpose of . . . influencing or affecting the vote on any question submitted to the voters, other than one materially affecting any of the property, business, or assets of the corporation." The statute further specifies that "[n]o question submitted to the voters solely concerning the taxation of the income, property or transactions of individuals shall be deemed materially to affect the property, business, or assets of the corporation."

[Plaintiffs] wanted to spend money to publicize their views on a proposed constitutional amendment that was to be submitted to the voters as a ballot question at a general election on November 2, 1976. The amendment would have permitted the legislature to impose a graduated tax on the income of individuals. After [defendant], the Attorney General of Massachusetts, informed [plaintiffs] that he intended to enforce Section 8 against them, they brought this action seeking to have the statute declared unconstitutional.

* * *

[Plaintiffs] argued that Section 8 violated the First Amendment, [and] the Due Process of the Fourteenth Amendment. . . . They prayed that the statute be declared unconstitutional on its face and as it would be applied to their proposed expenditures. . . .

The court below framed the principal question in this case as wehther and to what extent corporations have First Amendment rights. We believe that the court posed the wrong question. The Constitution often protects interests broader than those of the party seeking their vindication. The First Amendment, in particular, serves significant societal interests. The proper question, therefore, is not whether corporations "have" First Amendment rights and, if so, whether they are coextensive with those of natural persons. Instead, the question must be whether Section 8 abridges expression that the First Amendment was meant to protect.

The speech proposed by [plaintiffs] is at the heart of the First Amendment's protection.

The freedom of speech and of the press guaranteed by the Constitution embraces at the least the liberty to discuss publicly and truthfully all matters of public concern without previous restraint or fear of subsequent punishment. . . . Freedom of discussion, if it would fulfill its historic function in this nation, must embrace all issues about which information is needed or appropriate to enable the members of society to cope with the exigencies of their period. *Thornhill* v. *Alabama*, 310 U.S. 88, 101–102 (1940).

The referendum issue that [plaintiffs] wish to address falls squarely within this description. . . . The question in this case, simply put, is whether the corporate identity of the speaker deprives this proposed speech of what otherwise would be its clear entitlement to protection. We turn now to that question.

* * *

Freedom of speech and the other freedoms encompassed by the First Amendment always have been viewed as fundamental components of the liberty safeguarded by the Due Process Clause, and the Court has not identified a separate source for the right when it has been asserted by corporations. . . . [T]he Court's decisions involving corporations in the business of communication or entertainment are based not only on the role of the First Amendment in fostering individual self-expression but also on its role in affording the public access to discussion, debate, and the dissemination of information and ideas. Even decisions seemingly based exclusively on the individual's right to express himself acknowledge that the expression may contribute to society's edification.

* * *

We thus find no support in the First or Fourteenth Amendment, or in the decisions of this Court, for the proposition that speech that otherwise would be within the protection of the First Amendment loses that protection simply because its source is a corporation that cannot prove, to the satisfaction of a court, a material effect on its business or property. The "materially affecting" requirement is not an identification of the boundaries of corporate speech etched by the Constitution itself. Rather, it amounts to an impermissible legislative prohibition of speech based on the identity of the interests that spokesmen may represent and a requirement that the speaker have a sufficiently great interest in the subject to justify communication.

In the realm of protected speech, the legislature is constitutionally disqualified from dictating the subjects about which persons may speak and the speakers who may address a public issue. If a legislature may direct business corporations to "stick to business," it also may limit other corporations—religious, charitable, or civic—to their respective "business" when addressing the public. Such power in government to channel the expression of views is unacceptable under the First Amendment. Especially where, as here, the legislature's suppression of speech suggests an attempt to give one side of a debatable public question an advantage in expressing its views to the people, the First Amendment is plainly offended. Yet the State contends that its action is necessitated by governmental interests of the highest order. We next consider these asserted interests. The constitutionality of Section 8's prohibition of the "exposition of ideas" by corporations turns on whether it can survive the exacting scrutiny necessitated by a state-imposed restriction of freedom of speech. Especially where, as here, a prohibition is directed at speech itself, and the speech is intimately related to the process of governing, "The State may prevail only upon showing a subordinating interest which is compelling," "and the burden is on the Government to show the existence of such an interest." Even then, the State must employ means "closely drawn to avoid unnecessary abridgment. . . ."

Preserving the integrity of the electoral process, preventing corruption, and "sustain[ing] the active, alert responsibility of the individual citizen in a democracy for the wise conduct of the government" are interests of the highest importance. Preservation of the individual citizen's confidence in government is equally important.

[Defendant] advances a number of arguments in support of his view that these interests are endangered by corporate participation in discussion of a referendum issue. They hinge upon the assumption that such participants would exert an undue influence on the outcome of a referendum vote, and—in the end—destroy the confidence of the people in the democratic process and the integrity of government. According to [defendant], corporations are wealthy and powerful and their views may drown out other points of view. If [defendant's] arguments were supported by record or legislative findings that corporate advocacy threatened imminently to undermine democratic processes, thereby denigrating rather than serving First Amendment interests, these arguments would merit our consideration. But there has been no showing that the relative voice of corporations has been overwhelming or even significant in influencing referenda in Massachusetts, or that there has been any threat to the confidence of the citizenry in government. Nor are [defendant's] arguments inherently persuasive or supported by the precedents of this Court. Referenda are held on issues, not candidates for public office. The risk of corruption perceived in cases involving candidate elections, simply is not present in a popular vote on a public issue. To be sure, corporate advertising may influence the outcome of the vote; this would be its purpose. But the fact that advocacy may persuade the electorate is hardly a reason to suppress it: The Constitution "protects expression which is eloquent no less than that which is unconvincing."

We noted only recently that "the concept that government may restrict the speech of some elements of our society in order to enhance the relative voice of others is wholly foreign to the First Amendment. . . ." Moreover, the people in our democracy are entrusted with the responsibility for judging and evaluating the relative merits of conflicting arguments. They may consider, in making their judgment, the source and credibility of the advocate. But if there be any danger that the people cannot evaluate the information and arguments advanced by [plaintiffs], it is a danger contemplated by the Framers of the First Amendment. In sum, "[a] restriction so destructive of the right of public discussion [as Section 8], without greater or more imminent danger to the public interest than existed in this case, is incompatible with the freedom secured by the First Amendment.

* * *

Because that portion of Section 8 challenged by [plaintiffs] prohibits protected speech in a manner unjustified by a compelling state interest, it must be invalidated.

Questions

1. Is the free speech privilege solely designed to protect the speaker? Or is society's interest in hearing the speaker also protected by the First Amendment?
2. Is the question in *Bellotti* whether the corporation has First Amendment rights equal to those of natural persons? Or whether the state can abridge expression, which the First Amendment protects?
3. Does the fact that the speaker is a corporation deprive the "speech" of its First Amendment protection?
4. The state may prohibit speech when that speech interferes with some "compelling" state interest. Identify some "compelling state interests." Did plaintiff's speech threaten these state interests?
5. Could corporate views be regulated if their views eclipsed other points of view and undermined the democratic process?

Consolidated Edison Co. v. Public Service Commission of New York
447 U.S. 530 (1980)
Supreme Court of the United States

Justice Powell[1]

The Consolidated Edison Company of New York placed written material entitled "Independence Is Still a Goal, and Nuclear Power Is Needed to Win the Battle" in its January 1976 billing envelope. The bill insert stated Consolidated Edison's views on "the benefits of nuclear power," saying that they "far outweigh any potential risk" and that nuclear power plants are safe, economical, and clean. . . . The utility also contended that increased use of nuclear energy would further this country's independence from foreign energy sources.

In March 1976, the Natural Resources Defense Council, Inc. (NRDC) requested Consolidated Edison to enclose a rebuttal prepared by NRDC in its next billing envelope. . . . When Consolidated Edison refused, NRDC asked the Public Service Commission of the State of New York to open Consolidated Edison's billing envelopes to contrasting views on controversial issues of public importance. . . .

On February 17, 1977, the Commission denied NRDC's request, but prohibited "utilities from using bill inserts to discuss political matters, including the desirability of future development of nuclear power." . . . The Commission explained its decision in a Statement of Policy on Advertising and Promotion Practices of Public Utilities issued on February 25, 1977. The Commission concluded that Consolidated Edison customers who receive bills containing inserts are a captive audience of diverse views who should not be subjected to the utility's beliefs. Accordingly, the Commission barred utility companies from including bill inserts that express "their opinions or viewpoints on controversial issues of public policy." . . . The Commission did not, however, bar utilities from sending bill inserts discussing topics that are not "controversial issues of public policy." . . .

. . . The restriction on bill inserts cannot be upheld on the ground that Consolidated Edison is not entitled to freedom of speech. In *First National Bank of Boston* v. *Bellotti*, . . . we rejected the contention that a State may confine corporate speech to specified issues. . . .

. . . In the mailing that triggered the regulation at issue, Consolidated Edison advocated the use of nuclear power. The Commission has limited the means by which Consolidated Edison may participate in the public debate on this question and other controversial issues of national interest and importance. Thus, the Commission's prohibition of discussion of controversial issues strikes at the heart of the freedom to speak.

. . . The Commission's ban on bill inserts is not, of course, invalid merely because it imposes a limitation upon speech. . . . We must consider whether the State can demonstrate that its regulation is constitutionally permissible. The Commission's arguments require us to consider three theories that might justify the state action. We must determine whether the prohibition is (i) a reasonable time, place, or manner restriction, (ii) a permissible subject-matter regulation, or (iii) a narrowly tailored means of serving a compelling state interest.

. . . This Court has recognized the validity of reasonable time, place, or manner regulations that serve a significant governmental interest and leave ample alternative channels for communication. . . . But when regulation is based on the content of speech, governmental action must be scrutinized more carefully to ensure that communication has not been prohibited "merely because public officials disapprove the speaker's views."

. . . As a consequence, we have emphasized that time, place, and manner regulations must be "applicable to all speech irrespective of content."

. . . Therefore, a constitutionally permissible time, place, or manner restriction may not be based upon either the content or subject matter of speech.

. . . The Commission does not pretend that its action is unrelated to the content or subject matter of bill inserts. Indeed, it has undertaken to suppress certain bill inserts precisely because they address controversial issues of public policy. The Commission allows inserts that present information to consumers on certain subjects, such as energy conservation measures, but it forbids the use of inserts that discuss public controversies. The Commission, with commendable candor, justifies its ban on the ground that consumers will benefit from receiving "useful" information, but not from the prohibited information. . . . The Commission's own rationale demonstrates that its action cannot be upheld as a content-neutral time, place, or manner regulation.

The Commission next argues that its order is acceptable because it applies to all discussion of nuclear power, whether pro or con, in bill inserts. The prohibition, the Commission contends, is related to subject matter rather than to the views of a particular speaker. Because the regulation does not favor either side of a political controversy, the Commission asserts that it does not unconstitutionally suppress freedom of speech.

. . . The First Amendment's hostility to content-based regulation extends not only to restrictions on particular viewpoints, but also to prohibition of public discussion of an entire topic. As a general matter, "the First Amendment means that the government has no power to restrict expression because of its message, its ideas, its subject matter, or its content." . . .

. . . Where a government restricts the speech of a private person, the state action may be sustained only if the government can show that the regulation is a precisely drawn means of serving a compelling state interest. . . .

The Commission argues finally that its prohibition is necessary (i) to avoid forcing Consolidated Edison's views as a captive audience, (ii) to allocate limited resources in the public interest, and (iii) to ensure that ratepayers do not subsidize the cost of the bill inserts.

. . . The State Court of Appeals largely based its approval of the prohibition upon its conclusion that the bill inserts intruded upon individual privacy. The court stated that the Commission could act to protect the privacy of the utility's customers because they have no choice whether to receive the insert and the views expressed in the insert may inflame their sensibilities. . . . But the Court of Appeals erred in its assessment of the seriousness of the intrusion.

. . . Even if a short exposure to Consolidated Edison's views may offend the sensibilities of some consumers, the ability of government "to shut off discourse solely to protect others from hearing it (is) dependent upon a showing that substantial privacy interests are being invaded in an essentially intolerable manner." . . . A less stringent analysis would permit a government to slight the First Amendment's role "in affording the public access to discussion, debate and the dissemination of information and ideas." . . . Where a single speaker communicates to many listeners, the First Amendment does not permit the government to prohibit speech as intrusive unless the "captive" audience cannot avoid objectional speech.

. . . Passengers on public transportation . . . or residents of a neighborhood disturbed by the raucous broadcasts from a passing soundtruck . . . may well be unable to escape an unwanted message. But customers who encounter an objectionable billing insert may "effectively avoid further bombardment of their sensibilities simply by averting their eyes." . . .

. . . Finally, the Commission urges that its prohibition would prevent ratepayers from subsidizing the costs of policy-oriented bill inserts. But the Commission did not base its order on an inability to allocate costs between the shareholders of Consolidated Edison and the ratepayers. . . . Accordingly, there is no basis on this record to assume that the Commission could not exclude the cost of these bill inserts from the utility's rate base. Mere speculation of harm does not constitute a compelling state interest. . . .

The Commission's suppression of bill in-serts that discuss controversial issues of public policy directly infringes the freedom of speech protected by the First and Fourteenth Amendments. The state action is neither a valid time, place, or manner restriction, nor a permissible subject-matter regulation, nor a narrowly drawn prohibition justified by a compelling state interest. Accordingly, the regulation is invalid. . . .

Questions

1. When is governmental regulation of speech constitutionally justified?
2. What were the arguments advanced by the commission to justify its speech regulation? Why were each of the arguments considered without sufficient merit?

CONCLUSION

A 1979 Conference Board survey of 389 government relations executives showed an increase in government relations activity over the previous three years.[13] Ninety-two percent of those executives said they believed that government relations activity would continue to increase over the next three years also. The strongest factor prodding this growth was the impact of government regulations on their business. Other factors include changes in top management and a reassessment of corporate policy. The Conference Board study reached the following conclusion.

Government relations is gaining greater status within the organization, as government relations executives report direct involvement in the decision-making process of their companies. More and more chief executives are emphasizing the importance of this function and are taking a more direct, personal role in it. So, too, are other senior executives, and those in charge of technical areas, R and D, personnel, finance, and so on throughout the management team.[14]

The expansion of business interest in government relations is consistent with the argument of many that there is a societal movement toward a more coordinated, planned-development system, characteristic of a post-industrial society.[15] This movement suggests more centralization and politicization of economic as well as social decision making. The governmental process will coordinate the making of fundamental decisions affecting economic institutions. If business is to have an impact on this centralized decision making, business leaders of today and tomorrow must work within the political system. Our constitutional system provides an open atmosphere for the presentation of ideas. Increasingly, business is taking the opportunity to express its views and participate in the formulation of public policy.

DISCUSSION QUESTIONS

1. Is the free market a natural or politically contrived system?

2. Identify the stages of the public issue life cycle and give an example. Can you identify any new emerging issues still in their early stages of the life cycle?

3. What is your opinion of the appropriateness of business efforts to "educate" the public on the virtues of the free enterprise system?

4. Is it a wise decision for business to defned itself against social groups by indicating that the firm is complying with the law?

5. As a top executive of a firm, how would you respond to an organization demanding more jobs for their members based on the fact that they purchase a substantial volume of your firm's sales?

6. What risks do firms face when they seek to anticipate social expectations and design programs to meet those social expectations? What risks do firms face from inaction?

7. Identify and explain the basic steps in a public issue management system.

8. What is the purpose of laws requiring lobbyists to register? How effective are those laws?

9. A federal food inspector is required to "smell" the fish on the boat before they are allowed to be processed for canning. Your propose to offer the inspector a case of canned fish if he will inspect your boat next. Is this gratuity to "grease" or speed the inspection process lawful?

10. PACs contributed something over 20 percent of the monies raised for the last congressional election. The biggest PACs were not sponsored by business or labor unions, but single-issue or ideological groups. What is the likely impact of these PACs on political party loyalty? Will PACs cause politics to become more fragmented, frustrating the ability to obtain a consensus for national planning?

SUGGESTED READINGS

Buchsbaum, Andrew P., "Campaign Finance Re-Reform: The Regulation of Independent Political Committees," *California Law Review,* Vol. 71, March 1983, pp. 673–702.

Kottman, E. John, "The National Advertiser and the First Amendment," *American Business Law Journal,* Vol. 16, No. 3, Winter 1979, pp. 295–314.

Post, James E., *Corporate Behavior and Social Change* (Reston, Va: Reston Publishing Company, Inc., 1978).

Preston, Lee E and Post, James E., *Private Management and Public Policy: The Principle of Public Responsibility* (Englewood Cliffs, N.J.: Prentice-Hall Inc., 1975).

Richards, Eric L., "In Search of Consensus on the Future of Campaign Finance Laws: California Medical Association v. Federal Election Commission," *American Business Law Journal*, Vol. 20, No. 2, Summer 1982, pp. 243–266.

Richards, Eric L., "The Rise and Fall of the Contribution-Expenditure Distinction: Redefining the Acceptable Range of Campaign Finance Reform," *New England Law Review*, Vol. 18, Spring 1983, pp. 367–394.

Stokey, Edith and Zeckhauser, Richard, *A Primer for Policy Analysis* (New York: W. W. Norton & Company, Inc., 1978).

ENDNOTES

1. Karl Polanyi, *The Great Transformation: The Political and Economic Origins of Our Time* (New York: Rinehart and Co., Inc., 1944), pp. 77–85.
2. James E. Post, *Corporate Behavior and Social Change* (Reston, Va: Reston Publishing Co., 1978), pp. 22–24.
3. Robert Ackerman and Raymond Bauer, *Corporate Social Responsiveness: The Modern Dilemma* (Reston, Va: Reston Publishing Company, 1976); K. Davis and R. Blomstron, *Business and Society: Environment and Responsibility* (New York: McGraw-Hill, Inc., 1975); Preston and Post, *Private Management and Public Policy* (Englewood Cliffs, NJ: Prentice-Hall, Inc., 1975); G. Steiner, *Business and Society* (New York: Random House, Inc., 1975); and D. Votaw and S. P. Sethi, *The Corporate Dilemma* (Englewood Cliffs, N.J.: Prentice-Hall Inc., 1974).
4. Post, *op. cit.*, p. 39.
5. S. Prakash Sethi and Don Votaw, "Do We Need a New Corporate Response to a Changing Social Environment? *California Management Review*, Fall, 1969.
6. William H. Whyte, Jr., *"Is Anybody Listening?"* (New York: Simon and Schuster, 1950).
7. Votaw and Sethi, *The Corporate Dilemma, op. cit.*, p. 199.
8. Ackerman and Bauer, *op. cit.*, pp. 38–40.
9. Rogene A. Buchholz, *Business Environment and Public Policy* (Englewood Cliffs, N.J.: Prentice Hall, Inc., 1982), pp. 468–471.
10. Frank W. Steckmest, "Career Development of the 'Public Policy Corporate Executive,'" *Public Affairs Review*, 1981, p. 75. Quoted with permission.
11. *Buckley* v. *Valeo*, 424 U.S. 1 (1976).
12. Edwin Epstein, "Business and Electoral Politics," *Business Environment/Public Policy: The Field and Its Future,* 1981 Conference Papers (St. Louis, MO: American Assembly of Collegiate Schools of Business, 1982), p. 80. Copyright © 1982: American Assembly of Collegiate Schools of Business. Reprinted with permission.
13. Phyllis McGrath, *Redefining Corporate-Federal Relations* (New York: The Conference Board, 1979).
14. *Ibid.*, pp. 2–3.
15. Gerald R. Proust, "The Corporate Social Strategy in a Post-Industrial World," *The Conference Board Record*, Vol. XII, No. 9, September 1975, pp. 32–36.

glossary

Abate. To reduce or put a stop to a nuisance; to reduce or decrease a legacy because the estate is insufficient.

Ab initio. From the beginning. An agreement is said to be "void ab initio" if it at no time had any legal validity.

Abrogate. To annul, repeal.

Accessory after the fact. One who, after a felony has been committed, knowingly assists the felon.

Accessory before the fact. One who was not present at the commission of a crime but nevertheless had some part in its commission.

Acknowledgment. The act by which a party who has executed an instrument goes before a competent officer or court and affirms that its execution was a genuine and voluntary act on the party's part; certification by an authorized person on the face of an instrument that it has been acknowledged.

Action. A suit brought to enforce a right.

Act of God. Any injury or damage that happens by the direct and exclusive operation of natural forces, without human intervention, and that could not have been prevented or escaped from by any reasonable degree of care or diligence.

Adjudication. The giving or pronouncing of a judgment in a case; also the judgment given.

Ad litem. While an action is pending.

Advisory opinion. A nonbinding opinion of the Federal Trade Commission issued to businesses seeking the FTC's advice on whether a particular business practice is unfair competition.

Affiant. One who makes or attests to an affidavit.

Affidavit. A written declaration made voluntarily and confirmed by the oath of the party making it, taken before a person having authority to administer such an oath.

Affirmative defense. A matter which, assuming the complaint to be true, constitutes a defense to it.

A fortiori. By a stronger reason.

Agency. A relationship created by an express or implied contract or by law whereby one party (the principal) delegates the transaction of some business to another person (the agent), who undertakes a commercial transaction for him or her.

Agent. One who represents and acts for another under an agency relationship.

Allegation. The statement of a party to an action, made in a pleading, setting forth the charges he or she expects to prove.

Allege. To state or charge, to make an allegation.

Amicus curiae. A friend of the court, a person appointed by the court to assist in litigation by offering his or her opinion on some important matter of law.

Amortize. To provide for the paying of a debt in installments.

Ancillary. Auxiliary.

Answer. In a pleading, the written statement made by the defendant setting forth his or her defense.

Appeal. The removal of an adjudicated case from a trial court to a court of appellate jurisdiction for the purpose of obtaining a review or retrial.

Appearance. A coming into court as plaintiff or as defendant.

Appellant. A party who takes an appeal from one court to another.

Appellate jurisdiction. The power of a court to hear cases on appeal from another court or an administrative agency.

Appellee. The party in a legal action against whom an appeal is taken.

Arbitration. An agreement to submit a matter in dispute to selected persons and to accept their decision or award as a substitute for the decision of a court.

Arguendo. By way of argument.

Arrest of judgment. The act of staying a judgment or refusing to render judgment in an action at law after the verdict has been given, for some matter appearing on the face of the record that would render the judgment, if given, reversible.

Assault. A threat of an "offensive or injurious touch" to a person made by another person who is able to carry out the threat.

Assignment. The transfer of property or contract rights.

Assumption of risk. A negligence defense also applicable in some strict liability cases where the plaintiff knowingly accepts a certain risk of his or her own free will.

Attachment. Seizure of the property of a debtor by the service of process upon a third person who is in possession of the property.

Attest. To act as a witness to.

Attestation clause. A clause at the end of an instrument stating that the document has been properly witnessed as to its execution.

Attorney general. Society's attorney, or government attorney.

"Attractive nuisance." The courts hold a landowner liable for injuries sustained by small children while they were playing on his or her land if they were reasonably attracted there by something on the property.

Averment. A positive statement of fact.

Bad faith. The intent to mislead, deceive, or take unfair advantage of another.

Bailment. The giving up of the possession of personal property to another for some purpose, upon the accomplishment of which the goods are to be re-delivered to the owner.

Battery. An unlawful beating, wrongful physical violence, or "offensive touch" inflicted on another without his or her consent.

Beneficiary. A person for whose benefit property is held by a trustee, administrator, or executor.

Bill. A formal, written declaration, complaint, or statement of fact.

Bill of attainder. A legislative act which inflicts punishment without a judicial trial.

Bill of particulars. A written statement giving the details of the demand for which an action is brought, or of a defendant's counterclaim against such a demand, furnished by one of the parties to the other, either voluntarily or in compliance with a court order.

Bill of sale. Written evidence of the completion of a sale.

Blue-Sky laws. State laws regulating the sale of stocks and bonds to the general public.

Bona fide. In good faith.

Brief. A written statement of a party's case.

Burden of proof. The necessity of proving the facts at issue in court.

Case. A dispute to be resolved in a court of law or equity.

Case law. Legal principles evolved from case decisions.

Cause of action. Perhaps best defined as the fact or facts which give rise to a right of action; in other words, give to a person a right to judicial relief.

Caveat emptor. Let the buyer beware.

Caveat venditor. Let the seller beware.

Cestui que trust. A person who is the beneficial owner, or beneficiary, of property held in trust.

Charter. A grant of authority to exist as a corporation, issued by a state.

Chattel. An article of personal property.

Chattel mortgage. An instrument of sale of personalty that conveys the title of the property to the mortgagee and specifies the terms of defeasance.

Circumstantial evidence. Evidence relating to the circumstances of a case from which the jury may deduce what actually happened.

Civil rights. Private rights, protected by law, or members of society.

Class action. A legal action brought by a limited number of persons on behalf of a larger number of persons similarly situated.

Cognovit. Admission by the defendant of the legitimacy of the plaintiff's claim.

Closed shop. Such shop exists where the worker must be a member of the union as condition precedent to employment.

Collusion. An agreement between two or more persons to defraud, or a conspiracy for some other illegal purpose.

Common law. A body of unwritten law based on the customs, habits, and usages of society which is evidenced by the decisions of courts.

Comparative negligence. Provides for a comparison of the negligence of the plaintiff with the negligence of the defendant to determine a percentage of fault and degree of damages recovery, if any.

Complainant. The plaintiff in a legal or an equitable pleading.

Complaint. The first pleading on the part of the plaintiff in a civil action (corresponding to a declaration in common law). Also, a charge, preferred before a court in order to begin prosecution, that the person named (or a certain person whose name is unknown) has committed a certain offense, together with an offer to prove the facts alleged.

Compos mentis. Of sound mind.

Compounding a felony. The offense committed by a person who, after having been directly injured by a felony, makes an agreement with the felon that he or she will not prosecute the felon, on the condition that the latter will make reparation or will tender the person a bribe.

Concealment. The failure to volunteer relevant facts not apparent to the other party.

Confession of judgment. The act by which a debtor permits a judgment to be entered against him or her by his or her creditor without any legal proceedings having taken place.

Connivance. Secret or indirect consent to, or permission for, the commission of an unlawful act.

Consent order. A judicial decree rendered with the consent of the parties to an action which, in the absence of any fraud, binds the parties to the settlement.

Conservator. The court-appointed guardian of someone's property.

Consignee. One to whom a consignment is made; the person to whom goods are shipped for sale.

Consignment. Legal arrangement where seller of goods keeps title (ownership) but transfers possession to distributor who agrees to resell them.

Consignor. One who sends or makes a consignment; a shipper of goods.

Conspiracy. An agreement between two or more persons to work together to commit an act; perhaps a criminal act.

Constructive. Inferred, legally interpreted to be so; construed by the courts to have a particular character or meaning other than or beyond what is actually expressed.

Contempt. Conduct that is disruptive of a legislative or judicial proceeding or disobedience of a lawful order of a legislative or judicial body.

Contribution. The sharing of a loss or a payment among several individuals; also reimbursement of a surety who has paid the entire debt by his or her cosureties.

Contributory negligence. Negligence on the part of the plaintiff that contributes to his or her injury. At common law a person guilty of such negligence cannot recover damages.

Conversion. The unauthorized assumption of ownerhship of goods belonging to another.

Copyright. A grant to an author or publisher of an exclusive right to publish and sell literary work for a period of years, renewable for a second period.

Corporation. An artificial legal person, created by the state, which for some purposes may act as a natural person and be treated as such.

Corporeal property. Property that is discernible by the senses and may be seen and handled (as opposed to incorporeal property, which cannot be seen or handled and exists only in contemplation).

Corpus delicti. The body of the offense; evidence that a crime has been committed.

Costs. An allowance made to a successful party for his or her court costs in prosecuting or defending a suit. Costs rarely include attorney's fees.

Count. A division of a complaint, declaration, bill of petition wherein a separate cause of action is stated.

Counterclaim. A claim made by the defendant against the plaintiff; a cross-complaint.

"Court above"—"Court below." The "court above" is the court to which a case is removed for review; the "court below" is the court from which the case is removed.

Court of record. A court in which a permanent record is kept of proceedings.

Covenant. An agreement or promise of two or more parties, given in a written, signed delivered deed, by which one party promises the other that something either is done or shall be done, or by which one party stipulates the truth of certain facts. Also, a promise contained in such an agreement.

Covert. Covered, protected, sheltered, hidden, or secret.

Coverture. The condition or state of a married woman; her legal status.

Crime. A violation of the law punishable as an offense against the state.

Cross-complaint. A counterclaim made by the defendant against the plaintiff.

Cross-examination. The examination of a party's witness by the attorney for the other party.

Culpable. Evil or criminal.

Damage. Loss or injury to one's person or property caused by the negligence or intentional actions of another.

Damages. Compensation claimed or awarded in a suit for damage suffered.

Deceit. A fraudulent misrepresentation made to one or more persons who are ignorant of the true facts, to their injury.

Declaration. The initial pleading filed by the plaintiff on beginning an action, also called the complaint or petition.

De facto. In fact; actually.

Defalcation. Embezzlement.

Default. Failure to perform.

Defendant. The person against whom a declaration or complaint is filed and who is named therein.

Deficiency judgment. A judgment against a debtor for the amount that still remains due after a mortgage foreclosure that did not discharge the full amount of the debt.

De jure. Of right; legitimate, lawful.

Delictum. A tort, crime, or wrong.

De minimus. Smallest, being of the smallest size.

Demonstrative evidence. Evidence that consists of physical objects.

Demurrer. A plea by the defendant that concedes the truth of the facts in the case but alleges that the plaintiff does not have a cause of action.

De novo. Anew, over again.

Deponent. One who takes an oath in writing that certain facts are true.

Deposition. The testimony of a witness in response to questioning not given in court, but taken for use in court.

Derivative action. Action brought by shareholders to enforce a corporate cause of action.

Dictum. A statement of law by a judge in an opinion that is not essential to the determination of that controversy.

Directed verdict. An instrument by the trial judge to the jury to return a verdict in favor of one of the parties to an action. The party requests the instruction.

Disparagement. The unscrupulous sales tactic of enticing a customer to purchase a more expensive item by degrading the quality or value of the item originally sought.

Domestic corporation. A corporation chartered by the state in which it is doing business.

Duces tecum. Literally, to bring (the documents) with you.

Due care. The degree of care that a reasonable person can be expected to exercise in order to prevent harm that, under given circumstances, is reasonably foreseeable should such care not be taken.

Duress. A use of force or threat of force that deprives the victim of free will.

Easement. A right to use the land of another for a special purpose.

Ejectment. An action to determine the title to certain land.

Embezzlement. The fraudulent appropriation to one's own use or benefit of property or money entrusted to the appropriator by another.

Eminent domain. The right of the government to take private property for public use in the name of the people.

Equitable. Just, fair, or right; existing in equity.

Equity. A field of jurisdiction different in its origin, theory, and methodology from the common law.

Error. A mistaken judgment or incorrect belief of a trial court as to the existence or effect of matters of fact, or a false or mistaken conception or application of the law. (1) *Assignment of errors.* A statement of the errors upon which an appellant will reply, submitted to assist an appellate court in its examination of the transcript of a case under appeal. (2) *Harmless error.* An error committed during the progress of a trial that was not prejudicial to the rights of the party assigning it and for which therefore, an appellate court will not reverse a judgment. (3) *Reversible error.* An error in original proceedings for which an appellate court will reverse the judgment under review.

Estoppel. A rule of law designed to prevent a person from denying a fact that his or her conduct influenced others to believe was true.

Eviction. The act of depriving a person of the possession of lands held by him or her, pursuant to a court order.

Evidence. Any type of proof legally presented at a trial through witnesses, records, documents, or physical objects, for the purpose of inducing belief in the mind of the court or the jury as to the truth or falsity of the facts at issue.

Exception. A formal objection to the action of the court raised during a trial, implying that the objecting party does not agree with the decision of the court and will seek a reversal of the judgment handed down.

Ex contractu. From or out of a contract. The term is usually used to refer to a cause of action arising from a contract.

Exculpatory. Tending or serving to exculpate or clear from alleged fault or guilt.

Ex delicto. From a tort or crime.

Executor. A person appointed by a testator to carry out the directions and requests in his or her will and to dispose of the testator's property according to the testamentary provisions of the will.

Executory. Something that is yet to be executed or performed; that which is incomplete or dependent on a future performance or event.

Exemplary damages. Damages in excess of the amount needed to compensate the plaintiff for his or her injury, awarded to punish the defendant for malicious or willful conduct.

Exemption. A privilege allowed by law to a debtor by which he or she may hold a certain amount of property or certain classes of property free from all liability—free from seizure and sale by court order or from attachment by creditors.

Ex parte. On one side only; by one party; done for, or on behalf of, one party only.

Ex post facto law. A law which, in its operation, makes that criminal which was not so at the time of the act, or which increases the punishment, or, in short, which, in relation to the offense or its consequences, alters the situation of a party to his or her disadvantage.

Express. Set forth in direct and appropriate language (as opposed to that which is implied from conduct).

Ex rel (Ex relatione). On the relation or information.

Extant. Currently or actually existing.

Featherbedding. The requiring of an employer, usually under a union rule or safety statute, to pay more employees than are needed or to require payment without performing work.

Felony. An offense punishable by confinement in prison or by death, or an offense that statute has expressly deemed a felony.

Fiction. An assumption of the law.

Finis opus coronat. A finish, a fine, the end work, labor, benefit.

Fisc. Fiscal, belonging to the public treasury or revenue.

Foreign corporation. A corporation created by, or organized under, the laws of another state government.

Franchise. Any special privilege conferred by a governmental body on an individual or a corporation.

Fraud. A knowing and intentional misinterpretation of a material fact made in order to deprive another of his or her rights or to induce him or her to enter into a contract.

Fungible goods. Goods of a class in which any unit is the equivalent of any other unit.

Garnishment. See **Attachment.**

General creditor. A creditor who has an unsecured claim against a debtor.

General verdict. The ordinary form of verdict, either for the plaintiff or for the defendant, without answering special submitted questions.

Good faith. Honest intentions.

Gravamen. The material part or gist of a charge.

Guaranty. A promise to be responsible for the performance of another.

Habeas corpus. A writ obtained to test whether a prisoner is being lawfully held.

Hearsay. Evidence attested by a witness that is derived not from personal knowledge but from what others have told the witness.

Hung jury. A jury that is unable to agree on a verdict.

Hypothecation. Deposit of stocks, bonds, or negotiable instruments with another to secure the repayment of a loan, and with the power to sell the same in case the debt is not paid to reimburse the person with the proceeds.

Immunity. Freedom from legal duties and obligations.

Impanel. To make a list of those who have been selected for a jury.

Implied. Found from the circumstances of the case.

In camera. In chambers; secretly.

Inchoate. Not perfect, nor perfected.

Inculpatory. Incriminating.

Indemnify. To make good another's loss caused by a specified act or omission.

Indemnity. That which is given or granted to a person to prevent his or her suffering damage.

Indicia. A sign or indication.

Indictment. The formal written accusation of a crime, presented by a grand jury.

Infant. A person under lawful age; a minor.

Information. In criminal law, an accusation by a public officer (as distinguished from a finding by a grand jury) that is made the basis of a prosecution of a crime.

Injunction. An order issued by a court of equity directing a person or a group to do, or to refrain from doing, a specified act.

Injury. Any wrong or damage to the person, rights, reputation, or property of another.

In pari delicto. In equal fault; equally guilty.

In personam. Against a specific person (as opposed to *In rem*).

In re. In the matter.

In rem. Against a thing; directed at specific property or at a specific right or status.

Insolvency. A state in which debts and liabilities exceed assets.

Interbrand competition. Competition between sellers of different brands (Ford and Chevrolet) of the same type product (autos).

Interlocutory appeal. Incidence to a suit still pending; as an order or decree, made during the progress of a case, which does not amount to a final decision.

Interpleader. A form of action by which a third person who holds property or monies to which he or she has no claim and against whom conflicting claims are made may bring the complaining parties into court to settle their claims.

Inter alia. Among other things or matters.

Inter se. Between or among themselves.

Inter vivos. Any transaction that takes place among living persons.

Intrabrand competition. Competition between sellers of the same brand (Ford dealers).

Ipso facto. By the fact itself.

Jointly. Acting together. When persons are jointly liable, they all must be sued or none can be sued.

Jointly and severally. Acting together and separately. Anyone so liable can sue (or be sued) with or without the others joining (or being joined) in the action.

Judgment. The final order of a court, entered upon the completion of an action.

Judgment n.o.v. See *Non obstante veredicto.*

Judgment on the pleadings. A judgment entered on the request of either party to an action after the pleadings have been filed, when it is apparent from the content of the pleadings that one party is entitled to a decision in his or her favor without proceeding further.

Jurisdiction. The power and authority conferred on a court, either constitutionally or by statute.

Justiciable. Liable to trial in a court of justice.

"Last clear chance." In accident cases, the courts hold that if the defendant had the last clear chance to avoid an accident, he or she is liable even though the plaintiff may have been guilty of contributory negligence.

Leading question. A question that suggests to the witness what the response should be.

Legal tender. A medium of exchange that the law compels a creditor to accept in payment of a debt when it is legally offered to the creditor by the debtor.

Levy. To exact, collect, gather, seize.

Lex loci. The law of the place where an accident occurred.

Lex loci contractus. The law of the place where a contract was made.

Lex loci fori. The law of the place where an action was brought.

License. A personal privilege on authority to do something which would otherwise be inoperative.

Lien. A claim against, or a right to, property.

Liquidated. Determined, clarified, fixed.

Liquidated damages. A sum stipulated and agreed upon by the parties, at the time of entering into a contract, as being payable as compensation for loss suffered in the event of a breach.

Lis pendens. A suit pending; the filing of legal notice that there is a dispute about the title to property.

Malfeasance. The performance of an unlawful act.

Malum in se. An act that is wrong in itself.

Malum prohibitum. An act that is prohibited by law but not malum in se.

Mandamus. A court order compelling an individual to fulfill an official duty.

Mens rea. The state of mind of the actor.

Merchantable. Of good quality; salable in the regular course of business or intended purpose.

Merger. A joining of two corporations whereby one company retains its original identity.

Mesne. Intermediate, intervening.

Minor. A person who is under the age of legal competence specified by statute; usually, a person under 18 years of age.

Misdemeanor. A crime that is neither a felony nor treason.

Misfeasance. The performing of a lawful act in an improper manner.

Misprision. Maladministration, concealing, embezzlement.

Misrepresentation. An intentionally false statement of fact.

Mitigation of damages. The duty of the plaintiff to avoid increasing his or her damages and to limit them where possible.

Monopsony. Monopolistic buying power.

Moot case. A hypothetical or nonexisting controversy.

Motion to dismiss. To dismiss the defendant from the suit for lack of good cause shown to retain.

Motion to quash. See *motion to dismiss*; usually only consider questions of law as apparent on the face of the record.

Negative covenant. An agreement in a deed to refrain from doing something.

Negliglence. The failure to do something that a reasonable person would do or the commission of an act that a reasonable person would not commit, that results, in an ordinary and natural sequence, in damage to another.

Nisi prius. A trial court (as distinguished from an appellate court).

Nolo contendere. Not contesting the charge, it has the effect of a guilty plea in a criminal action.

Nominal damages. A token sum awarded to the plaintiff when he or she has suffered no actual damage.

No-fault laws. Laws barring tort actions by injured persons against third-party tortfeasors and requiring such persons to obtain recovery from their own insurers.

Non compos mentis. Not sound of mind; insane.

Nonfeasance. The neglect or failure to do something that one ought to do.

Non obstante veredicto. A judgment given that is contrary to the verdict of the jury.

Nonsuit. An abandonment of suit by the plaintiff.

Notary public. A public officer authorized to administer oaths and certify certain documents.

Nuisance. Improper personal conduct, or the unreasonable use by a person of his or her own property, that obstructs the rights of others or of the public and produces material inconvenience or hardship.

Oligopoly. Control of a commodity or service in a given market by a small number of companies or suppliers so that the sellers feel interdependent.

Operation of law. The automatic attaching of certain legal consequences to certain facts.

Opinion evidence. The conclusions that a witness draws from what he or she has observed (as opposed to the observation itself).

Ordinance. A statutory enactment of the legislative branch of a municipal government.

Ostensible agency. An implied agency that exists when a supposed principal by his or her conduct induces another to believe that a third person is the principal's agent, although the principal never actually employed him or her.

Parens patriae. The "father of the country" constituted in law by the state; in the capacity of legal guardian of persons not sui juris.

Patent. The giving of a privilege or property by a government to one or more individuals. (1) The conveyance by which a government grants lands in the public domain to an individual. (2) The privilege given to an inventor allowing him or her the exclusive right to make and sell the invention for a definite period of time.

Per curiam opinion. A written decision by the court which is not signed by the authoring judge or justice.

Perjury. The giving of false testimony under oath.

Per se. By itself; standing alone; not related to other matters.

Personal jurisdiction. Court power to deal with the person by reason of proper service of process (summons).

Petition. The first pleading by the plaintiff in a civil case, also called the complaint.

Petty jury, petit jury. The jury in a trial court.

Plaintiff. One who brings an action.

Plaintiff in error. A party who bases an appeal on an error in a judgment rendered by a trial court.

Plead. To make, deliver, or file a pleading.

Pleadings. The papers filed by the parties in an action.

Police power. The power of the state to enact laws for the protection of the public health, safety, welfare, and morals.

Polling the jury. Asking each member of the jury in open court how he or she voted on the verdict.

Presumption. An inference of the truth or falsehood of a proposition or a fact, in the absence of actual certainty as to its truth or falsehood, by a process of probable reasoning.

Prima facie. At first sight, on first appearance; presumably.

Privity. An immediate relationship. A party to a contract is said to have "privity" with regard to the making of the contract.

Process. A court order informing the defendant that he or she is required to appear in court.

Proffered evidence. Testimony or documentation presented to the trial court which is ruled inadmissible but is entered into the record for consideration on appeal.

Promoters. The organizers of a corporation.

Prosecute. To bring suit and carry on an action against a person in court.

Pro tanto. For so much; as far as it goes.

Proximate cause. That act which is the effective cause of an injury; an act from which the injury could reasonably be expected to result.

Proximate damage. Damage that is a reasonably foreseeable result of an action.

Puffing. Seller's talk that is legally only opinions and not facts; therefore these remarks may not be the basis for a lawsuit based on fraud.

Punitive damages. Damages over and above the amount necessary to compensate an injured party. They are imposed to punish a wrongdoer.

Quasi. As if it were; having the characteristics of.

Quo warranto. An action compelling someone (usually a corporation) to show by whose authority he or she is transacting business.

Remand. To send a case back to a trial court for a new trial in accordance with the decision of an appellate court.

Remedial. Pertaining to a legal remedy, or to the form of procedural details of such a remedy, that is to be taken after a legal or an equitable wrong has been committed.

Remedy. The means by which the violation of a right is prevented or compensated for.

Respondent superior. A legal maxim that a master is liable in certain cases for the wrongful acts of his servant, and a principal for those of his or her agent.

Respondent. One who makes an answer to or argues against an appeal.

Reversal. The decision of an appellate court to annul or vacate a judgment or decree of a trial court.

"Right to work." Section 14(b) of the National Labor Relations Act leaves to the various states the power to enact laws limiting or prohibiting labor agreements which make union membership a condition of employment. Such state laws simply declare unlawful any agreement which conflicts with the policy that individuals have the right to work without abridgement on account of nonmembership in any labor organization. A state statute outlaws a union shop contract—one by which an employer agrees to require membership in the union sometime after an employee has been hired as a condition of continued employment.

Scienter. Knowingly.

Scintilla. A spark, a remaining particle; hence, the least evidence.

Secondary boycott. Conspiracy or combination to cause the customers or suppliers of a secondary employer to cease doing business with the primary employer with which the union has its labor dispute.

Set-off. A counterclaim, a cross-demand.

Short sale. A sale of stock which the seller does not possess at the time, but which he or she expects to acquire subsequently for delivery under his or her contract.

(sic). So, thus, simply, in this manner. (Confirms a word that might be questioned.)

Slander. Oral defamation of character.

Slander per se. Words slanderous in themselves whether or not damage can be proven to result from them. To have a case, it is necessary merely to allege that they have been published.

Special appearance. A person's appearance in court for a specific purpose, without his or her submitting to the jurisdiction of the court.

Special damages. Damages that are the actual and natural, although not the necessary, result of the proximate cause of an injury. They must be proven according to the special circumstances of a particular case.

Specific performance. An equitable remedy by which a contracting party is compelled to perform obligations under the terms of the contract.

Standing to sue. The assertion of a bona fide claim in a court of proper jurisdiction.

Stare decisis. To stand by that which has been decided. A case decision serves as a legal precedent in the deciding of subsequent similar cases.

State of the forum. The state in which the court sits or has its hearing or forum.

Statute of limitations. A statute that limits the period of time in which an enforceable cause of action may be brought.

Stipulation. An agreement between opposing counsel that they will accept certain things in evidence without the necessity of proof.

Sua sponte. On its own responsibility or motion, as an order "sua sponte" made by a court without prior motion by either party.

Subrogation. The substitution of one thing for another, or of one person in place of another, with respect to rights, claims, or securities.

Substantive law. That part of the law that creates, defines, and regulates rights (as opposed to procedural law, which prescribes methods enforcing rights or obtaining remedies for this invasion).

Sui generis. Of its own kind of class.

Sui juris. Of his own right; having legal capacity to manage his own affairs.

Summary judgment. A judgment entered by a court when no substantial dispute of fact exists; consequently, there is no need for a trial.

Summary proceeding. A brief proceeding, usually conducted with less formality than a normal court proceeding.

Summons. A writ served on a person to secure his or her appearance in court.

Supra. Noted above or previously.

Surety. A person who makes himself or herself liable for the obligation of another.

Sweetheart Contract. Contract by union with management that neglects the interests of the workers, but serves the interests of the union leaders and management.

Tender. An unconditional offer by a party who is able to complete an obligation.

Tenor. The true meaning or effect of an instrument.

Toll the statute. To stop the operation of the time period specified by the statute of limitations.

Tort. A wrong committed upon the person or property of another; an invasion of a private right.

Tort feasor. One who commits a tort.

Tortious. Wrongful.

Transcript. A copy of a writing; a court record.

Transitory action. An action brought against a defendant in any county where service of process may be obtained.

Trespass. (1) An injury to the person, property, or rights of another. (2) A common-law action for money damages for injury to one's person, property, or rights.

Trier of fact. Usually a jury.

Trust. An equitable right to land or other property, held for a beneficiary by another person, in whom the legal title rests.

Trustee. One appointed to execute a trust; a person in whom an estate interest, or power is vested under an agreement that he or she shall administer or exercise it for the benefit or use of another.

Ultra vires. Beyond the powers conferred on a corporation by its charter.

Union shop. Such shop exists where the employer is permitted to employ a nonunion worker but such worker is required to join the union as a requisite to continuing employment.

Undue influence. Dominance of one person in a fiduciary relationship over another, sufficient to inhibit or destroy the weaker party's free will.

Vacation of judgment. The setting aside of a judgment by a court.

Valid. Legally sufficient.

Vendee. A purchaser, a buyer.

Vendor. A seller.

Venire. To appear in court. A writ of venire is used to summon a jury.

Veracity. Truthfulness.

Verdict. The decision of a jury.

Vested. Accrued, settled, absolute; not contingent upon anything; having an immediate right to the enjoyment of property.

Void. Having no legal effect; not binding.

Voidable. Subject to being declared ineffectual. A contract is voidable when one party has grounds for refusing to perform his or her obligations.

Voir dire examination. An examination to determine the qualifications of a juror or witness.

Voluntary nonsuit. A means available to the plaintiff for stopping a trial in a civil suit without prejudice to bring the suit again.

Waiver. The giving up of a legal right.

Ward. A person under the care of court.

Warrant. A guaranty that certain facts are true as represented.

Warranty of authority. An implied warranty that an agent possesses the authority that he or she represents himself or herself as possessing.

Writ of certiorari. An order from an appellate court to a lower court requesting the record of a case that is to be reviewed by the appellate court.

Writ of error. The order of an appellate court authorizing a lower court to remit to it the official record of the proceedings in a case in which an error sufficient to invalidate the verdict is claimed.

index

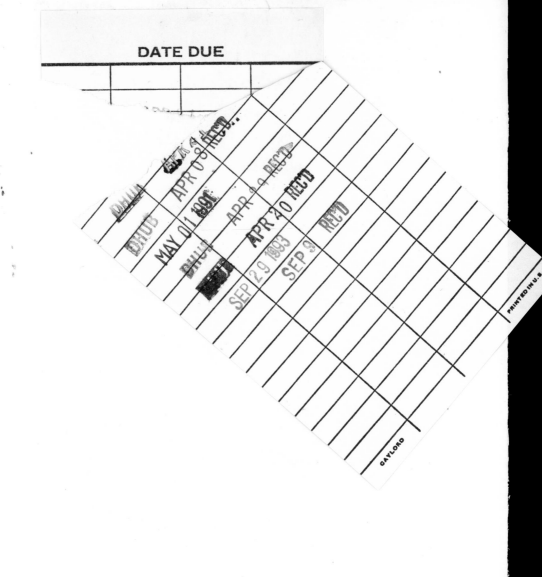